D1223764

Pictorial Guide to Christmas Ornaments & Collectibles

IDENTIFICATION AND VALUES

George Johnson

COLLECTOR BOOKS
A Division of Schroeder Publishing Co., Inc.

On the cover:

Front:

Santa Candy Containier, p. 372
Royalite Snowman Plastic Light-up, p. 390
Wire-wrapped Dirigible, p. 157
Dresden Angel, p. 196
Scrap Santa with a Cotton Skirt, p. 244
Lithographed Tin Stable Candle Chimes, p. 386
Santa on a Wooden Sled, p. 374
Santa Figural Light, p. 345
Lithographrd Angel with a Cornucopia, p. 218

Back:

Nuremberg Angel TreeTop, p. 360
Lithographed Angel with a Lily, p. 218
Santa Candy Container with Compostion Legs, p. 372
Pear Figural Light, p. 331
Royalite Santa with Bubble Light, p. 389
Santa's Candy Workshop, p. 392

Cover design:
Beth Summers

Book design:
Allan Ramsey

COLLECTOR BOOKS
P.O. Box 3009
Paducah, Kentucky 42002-3009
www.collectorbooks.com

The current values in this book should be used only as a guide. They are not intended to set prices, which vary from one section of the country to another. Auction prices as well as dealer prices vary greatly and are affected by condition as well as demand. Neither the author nor the publisher assumes responsibility for any losses that might be incurred as a result of consulting this guide.

Searching for a Publisher?

We are always looking for people knowledgeable within their fields. If you feel that there is a real need for a book on your collectible subject and have a large comprehensive collection, contact Collector Books.

Contents

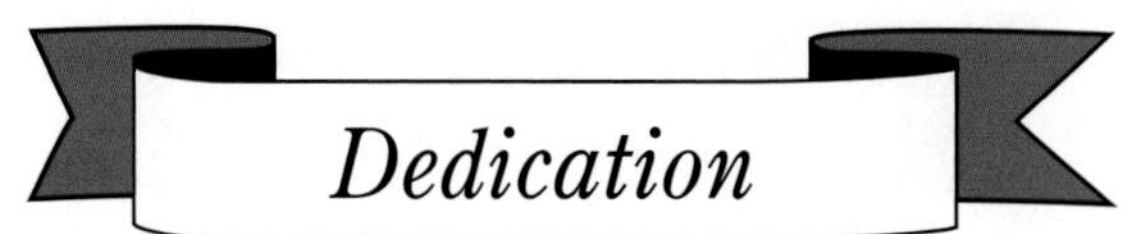

To Melissa, George C., Bryan, Mark, Brandon, and the child within us all.
May all your Christmases be bright.

Books of this magnitude are only possible with the support and assistance of many collectors. I would like to thank the following individuals and families, who not only gave their time and knowledge, but also shared their collections with you, the reader:

Contributors

Jerry and Darla Arnold
D. Blumchen and Co.
Evelynn Bowman
George and Beatrice Boyce
Diane Boyce
Peter Boyden
Lester Breininger
Marie and Richard Brosig
Scott and Cynthia Bulock
Fred Cannon
Diane and Don Carey
David K. Chenault
Cindy and Ken Chipps
Richard Christen
The Credmore Collection
Bill Cummins
George Davignon
Defina Auctions
John Dillon
Mary Ann and Bill Dunbar
Dave Eppleheimer
Bob and Sandy Fellows
Mary Flegle
Tom Fox
Pan and Norm Framberg
Antialee M. Garletts
Lorna Gorsuch
Charles and Grace Gottshall
Cynthia O'Grady
John Grossman
Dorothy Guirney
Dave Harms
Harold and Doris Hensley
George and Jean Hohman
Patrick Hubert
Bob Iwamasa
C. Roger Johnson
George and Jeanne Johnson
George and Martha Johnson
Mollie Johnson
Ron Kilfoil
Kim Knight
Barbara and Daryl Koppes
Bob and Diane Kubicki
Siegfried and Pat Kurtz
Ron and Sandy Lemilin
Jay Lewis
Jerry & LaRue Lewis
Bob Merck
Marie Miller
Jim Morrison
Leonard Mostek
Howard Myers
Ron Pavone
Ed and Bettie Petzoldt
Leonard Potkym
Emory and Jerry Prior
Christopher Radko
Jane Rayden
Malcolm Rogers
Tim Rose
Ruth Ruege
Melicent Sammis
Paul and Janet Schofield
Joe and Odine Sieter
Madeline Smith
Nancy Smith
Valeria Smith
Bobby Sollenberger
St. James Antiques
Roberta Taylor
John Wells Family
Daryl White
John and Evelyn Yoder
Doris Jean Yost
Alexander Zielinski
and several anonymous collectors

In a multitude of varying ways the following people were instrumental in the completion of this book. The holidays would be a little less bright without them.

Beatrice Boyce
Cindy Chipps
George Davignon
Dave Eppleheimer
George and Jean Hohman
George and Martha Johnson
Rudolf Leipold-Buttner
Ron Lemelin
Ron Pavone
Christopher Radko
Malcolm Rogers
Joe Sieter
John & Evelyn Yoder

Preface

The book you hold is the result of many years of work, picture taking from coast to coast, two trips to Europe, and the cooperation of many collectors who graciously shared their knowledge and their collections with you. As with *Christmas Ornaments, Lights, and Decorations, Volumes I, II,* and *III,* this is truly a book by collectors and for collectors. With the advice of fellow collectors and the cooperation of the editors of Collector Books behind me, I hope that you will find this new book both visually pleasing and informative. For those of you who kept anxiously asking when the next book was coming out, thank you for your confidence and patience.

About this Book

Photographs are a necessity in a catalog of this type. There are several things that the reader needs to keep in mind while enjoying them.

Although I have endeavored to photograph the best examples possible, the pieces shown do not always represent ornaments in good or fine condition. Because of this, they are not meant to be any type of standard for pricing.

Because there are no absolutes in the way an ornament was painted or decorated, those portrayed in the pictures are only typical examples.

Whenever possible, pre-war ornaments have been used in the photographs. However, believing the old adage that "a picture is worth a thousand words," I have occasionally used post-war pieces. Having been blown in the old molds, these will be exactly like their antique counterparts unless noted otherwise in the text.

You will find a one-inch scale for judging the relative size of the piece included in the photographs.

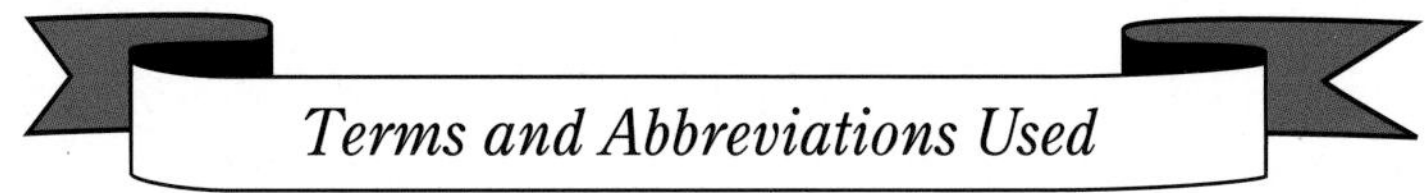

Terms and Abbreviations Used

In the catalog of ornaments, the reader will find these terms and abbreviations commonly used to help describe the pieces:

SG	Spun Glass — has added parts made from thin glass fiber, e.g., bird tails and angel wings.
Approx. 3"	Approximately 3" — size of the ornament measuring only the glass, not clip-ons or hangers. All sizes given are approximate, because the pike or stem left on the ornament could vary up to ½" in length. H, W, and L stand for height, width, and length. European ornaments were made and marketed in the metric measurements of millimeters and centimeters. Most sizes have ¼" variances.
2", 3", and 4"	Indicates that the ornament had separate moldings in these sizes.
German, Czech, Japanese, American, etc.	Indicates the country in which the ornament was made. No listing indicates that the author is not positive of the country of origin.
Standard Form	Form or molding most commonly found.
Scrap	Chromolithographed picture often added to an ornament; also called glanzbilder.
Dresden	Piece made of embossed and detailed cardboard usually colored gold or silver. Such pieces were often made in Dresden, Germany, hence their sobriquet.
Annealed	A piece made from two separate pieces of glass that have been melted or fused together, as opposed to a piece created from just one gather of glass.
TYPE I, II, III, etc.	The type number or order in which they are listed has nothing to do with rarity, desirability, or price.
Embossed	Indicates that the design described is molded into the shape or raised in bas relief.
OP	Old Production — the ornament was produced before 1940; any mold usage since then is unknown.
NP	New Production — ornament mold was made and used since 1940; no known old ones exist.

OP-NP(1985)	The mold is old, but it has also been reused since 1940; i.e., new ornaments from it can be found. The data in parantheses indicate dates of reissue.
Circa 1955	Approximate age of the piece.

Rarity Rating System

1. Very Rare, 2. Rare, 3. Scarce, 4. Uncommon, 5. Common

This will give the collector some idea as to how often they might expect to see a given ornament. The system is based on collectors, their collections, and how often the given item has been seen for sale. This seemingly haphazard way of determining rarity is the only option the collector has, because we have no records of how many ornaments were blown in a given mold or of how many of these have survived. Rarity does not always affect the value of a given ornament, nor does it reflect its beauty or desirability.

Abbreviations Used in Electric Lights

C6, C7, C9	Sizes of the screw in base as designated by the lighting industry.

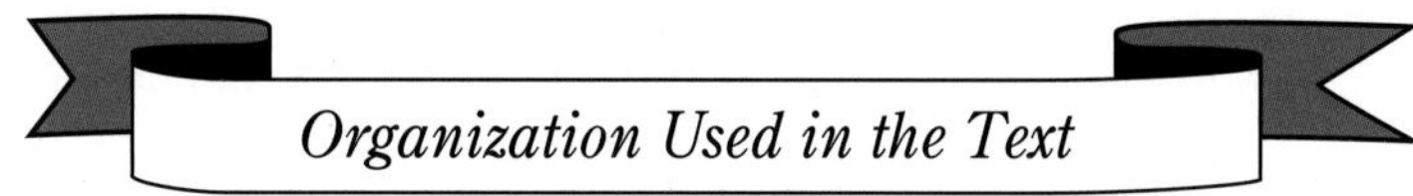

Organization Used in the Text

Cataloging invariably means grouping and subcategorizing. This is quite often a subjective decision, and not everyone would group items the same way. I have grouped them in a way that seemed most logical to me and tried to keep the same format throughout all the chapters. The first chapter had several categories, so a predominantly alphabetical listing was used.

Although the categories within this first chapter are listed alphabetically, it was not always feasible to list each item in a given category in the same manner. Also, whenever possible, I tried to make sure that all items in a picture were grouped according to the chapter in which they would be located. This was not always possible, and on occasion the reader may have to look for pictures that were placed in different sections or chapters.

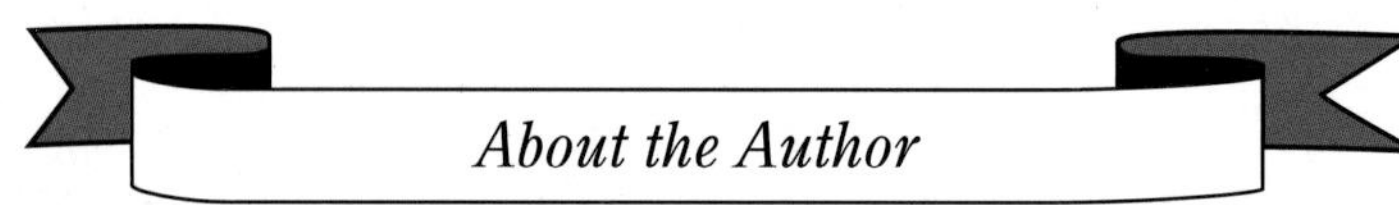

About the Author

George W. Johnson, Author.

George W. Johnson has been collecting antique Christmas decorations for over thirty years and is a member of the Golden Glow of Christmas Past, a club for enthusiasts of antique Christmas memorabilia.

He started collecting while trying to find some bubble lights and decorations that had been on his childhood tree.

George, his wife Jeanne, and their four children — Melissa, George, Bryan, and Mark — are residents of Logan, Ohio. George is an elementary and middle school teacher who specializes in working with talented and gifted students in Southern Local Schools.

Glass Ornaments

Glass Christmas ornaments, as we know them, have only been produced for a little more than 150 years, and it has not been until the last 75 years that they were the major type of decoration on the tree. For most Americans, however, the glass decoration, whether made in a mold or free blown, has come to symbolize *the* Christmas ornament.

Until 1940, the glass ornament capital of the world was the small German town of Lauscha. In its day, this village and its surrounding area produced upwards of 95% of the ornaments decorating American Christmas trees.

The early history of the glass ornament is lost in a certain amount of obscurity and confusion. Production of glass ornaments was considered only a secondary occupation to the glassblower's main business of making and selling scientific and pharmaceutical equipment, glass fruit, beads for the millinery trade, and glass toys such as marbles and glass eyes for dolls.

The products that eventually led to the development of Christmas ornaments were the small glass tubes and silvered beads that were used in the clothing and fashion industry in the eighteenth century. By the early years of the nineteenth century, the art of silvered decoration set the stage for the development of the silvered glass ornament.

By the early 1800s, the decorated tree had become an established and fast-growing custom; early decorations were cookies, cakes, candies, fruit, nuts, paper, and Christmas gifts themselves. Very few of these decorations were designed to be reused year after year. At this time, Lauschan glassmakers were making large glass balls, or kugels, as window decorations, "witches balls," or "garden panorama" balls. Someone decided that these reflective balls looked great on a candlelit tree. By 1848, the first recorded order of Lauschan silvered kugels for use as Christmas ornaments was placed.

These early pieces were made of thick-walled glass and do not resemble the ornaments known today. In 1870, Louis Greiner-Scholotfeger made the first thin-walled, silver-nitrate-finished ornament that was mold blown. The general sequence of events in the development of ornaments was certainly overlapping. First came the heavy glass kugels — some silvered with lead or zinc and coated with wax while others were unsilvered. Some were made of colored glass and some painted with lacquer. Then came the thick-walled kugels, such as grapes, that were made in molds. Next came the thin-walled ornaments with silver nitrate silvering; and finally, the paper-thin mold-blown ornament. Even after the development of molds for making fancy forms, the vast majority of ornaments continued to be free blown, i.e., made without the use of a mold.

The single most influential figure in the marketing of glass ornaments was F.W. Woolworth of five-and-dime fame. Woolworth was America's largest importer, bringing in hundreds of thousands of ornaments a year. He made a substantial fortune (estimated at $25 million) in glass Christmas ornaments; most of these were sold one at a time.

Other countries entered the glass ornament production market in the last decade of the nineteenth century. Goblanz, Czechoslovakia began to turn its famous bead business into a Christmas business. During the mid-1920s, the Japanese entered the Christmas decoration market. Their glass items were heavier and more crudely made than the European pieces. However, the prices of these ornaments were much cheaper. When World War I consumed much of Europe and the United States, the European ornament industry produced less, and embargoes prevented the pieces from being imported into the U.S. This allowed some U.S. glass ornament production to begin. American glassblowers did not have the detailed molds or the same high quality paints and lacquers used by the Germans. Most pieces were balls or free-blown shapes. After World War I, European glass ornaments came back stronger than ever. During the 1930s, American glassmakers began to establish themselves once more, and one Max Echardt would eventually dominate the business.

Echardt established the Shiney Brite Company, laying the groundwork for a new American ornament business. In 1939, he was able to make use of the Corning Glass Company's ribbon glassblowing machine to make round Christmas ornaments. With the help of a huge order from Woolworth's, Corning made its first ornaments in 1939. With the advent of World War II during that same year, Germany's world dominance of the ornament business died. During the war, Shiney-Brite continued to provide America with glass ornaments, but war needs finally took their toll. By 1944, ornaments were unsilvered and the cap and hanger were made of paper as both the silver and the steel in the cap went into the war effort. Eventually, the clear glass balls had only small stripes of paint for their decoration.

For post-war productions, many of the old German ornament molds were used, and some new ones were developed. During the late 1940s and 1950s, West Germany made an unsuccessful attempt to recapture the world ornament business, but by now, Americans were accustomed to buying the round, American-made ornaments an entire box at a time. Since the 1950s were a time of American-made-type patriotism, and these ornaments were less susceptible to breakage, most foreign products were considered junk. The fashionable practice in the 1960s of using an aluminum tree did not help the German ornament trade. Not until the 1980s and 1990s, with the nostalgic desire of many to have decorations like "grandmother's ornaments," was there a resurgence in collecting that helped the German ornament business. Today collectors, people looking for decorations like grandmother had, and those just looking for unique pieces can once again find German-molded ornaments in fairly large quantities. Many countries are now producing glass Christmas ornaments. Among them are Germany (including the village of Lauscha), Poland, Italy, the Czech Republic, Slovakia, Russia, Austria, Mexico, Columbia, India, China, Romania, and the United States. Those ornaments made in China and Poland have captured a considerable slice of the current market. Presently, a whole new generation of ornament lovers has the unique opportunity to find a wide selection of those beautiful pieces that were the fame and the glory of the European glassblowers.

Manufacture of Glass Ornaments

Glass Christmas ornaments were created in a unique manner. The individual cottage worker gathered the supplies necessary for his trade from a variety of sources. The Lauscha glasshouse or factory made the thin-walled glass tubes necessary for blowing the ornament. Lacquers, paints, silvering solution, metal caps and clip-ons, crinkle wire for wrapping, and scraps were among the other items bought by the cottage worker. The majority of glassblowers were laborers working out of their home workshops, with their family providing the labor to run the tiny factory.

To begin the process, long glass tubes were separated into smaller pieces by heating the glass to a certain point and pulling the two pieces apart. This separating process left a long thin spear or pike with a small opening. One end of this hollow tube was then melted shut. After preparing a large quantity of the small tubes, the glassblower was ready to make his ornaments.

Free-blown and ball shapes were made by heating the glass tube to a molten state. Then, by blowing through the spear or pike, the hot glass was expanded to a sphere. These spheres were blown into reasonably standard shapes, because the glassblower used a cardboard or wooden U-shaped gauge to judge the size during the blowing process. Indented reflectors started in the same manner, but a wooden or plaster plug, embossed with a desired design, was then pressed into the hot glass. Fancier free-blown shapes required simple tools such as a gloved hand, flat paddles, or sticks to help form their intricate shapes. For many of these shapes, it was not only the tools themselves, but also the way in which the glass was blown or the position of the glassblower's head or body that helped form the design. Pieces such as point tree tops, trumpets, lyres, anchors, pipes, teapots, and many animals were formed in a free-blown fashion. Often the free-blown piece was more time consuming than a molded one, and it took a true master craftsman with years of practice to produce many of these marvelous one-of-a-kind items.

Molded ornament formation began in the same general way. While the glass was still molten, it was quickly placed in the mold. The two halves of the mold were attached to either side of a foot-operated clamp that was closed around the hot glass. The glassmaker then blew downward into the pike, which extended from one end of the mold. This expanded the hot glass, causing it to fill the mold and thus pick up all of its embossed impressions.

The father and older sons of the family usually did the glassblowing. Then the ornaments were passed to the mother and oldest daughters, who did the silvering. In the next step, the ornaments were given a base coat of paint by dipping them into an aniline dye. They were then placed on nail-studded boards so that any excess solution would run down the pike. The boards were then placed in the rafters or over the oven so the ornaments would dry. The next day, the ornaments were lacquered and painted by the family. Other pieces were dipped into clear gelatin, which acted as an adhesive, and rolled in tiny glass balls to give them a "Venetian dew" finish. After more drying, the spears or spikes were scored and snapped off by one of the younger children, who used a grit-covered knife. Grandmothers added wire wrappings, fabric flowers or leaves, spun glass, tucksheer, tinsel, chenille, thread, and scraps as finishing touches. Then the youngest children added the metal caps and put the ornaments into boxes of a dozen each. After being shipped to distributors, the glass ornaments were sold individually in stores like Woolworth's or in sets from mail order companies like Sears and Roebuck.

A wide variety of Christmas ornaments have been made over the last two hundred years. Ironically, the most fragile was also the most enduring form of ornament. Metal, wax, fabric, paper, and cardboard have all come and gone. The glass ornament has survived the test of time and today remains the most popular of all Christmas decorations.

Animals

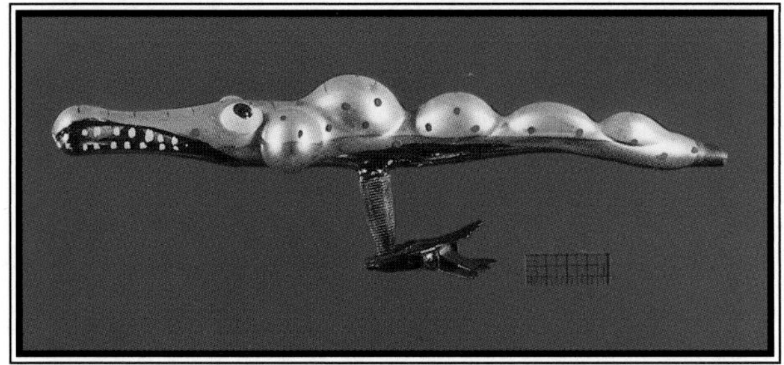

Free-blown Czech Alligator, approx. 6" – 8"; size may vary because it is free blown [Czech, OP-NP (Radko, 1993), R2]. 6" – 7", **$250.00–275.00.** 7" – 8", **$300.00–325.00.**

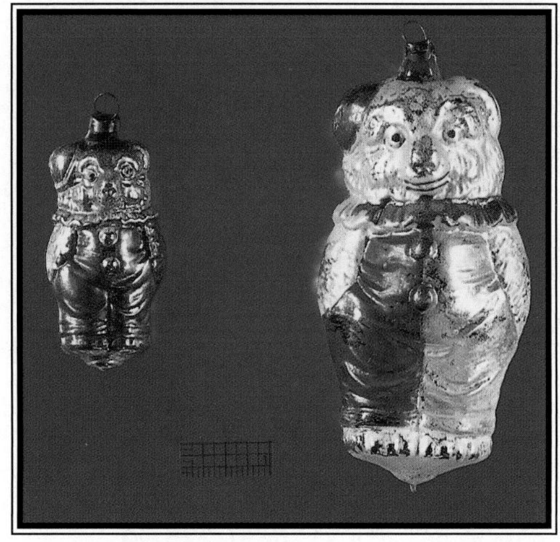

Bear in a Clown Suit, approx. 2½" (shown), 3¼", 4" (shown), and 4½" [German, OP, R3]. Small, **$50.00–75.00.** Medium, **$125.00–150.00.** Large, **$200.00–250.00.**

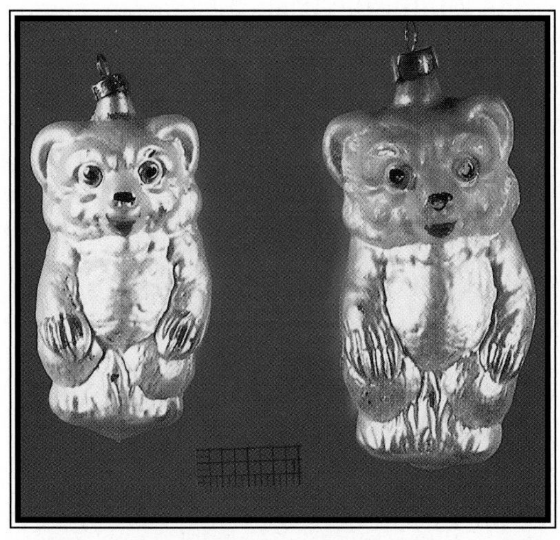

Standing Bear [OP, R2-3]. Small, 3", **$100.00–125.00.** Medium (3½"), **$150.00–200.00.** Large (4"), **$200.00-275.00.**

A. Bear Holding a Heart, approx. 3" (shown) & 3¾" [German, OP-NP (1985, small only), R2]. Small, **$125.00–150.00.** Large, **$175.00–200.00.** B. Rabbit in an Egg, approx. 3" & 3½" (shown) [OP, R1]. Small, **$175.00–200.00.** Large, **$250.00–300.00.** C. Bear in a Clown Suit, approx. 2½", 3⅕", 4" (shown), and 4½" [German, OP, R3]. Small, **$50.00–75.00.** Medium, **$125.00–150.00.** Large, **$200.00–250.00.**

A. Begging Bear, 3" [OP, R2]. **$175.00–200.00.** B. Elephant Standing on a Ball, approx. 2¾" & 3" (shown) [Austrian, OP, R2]. **$90.00–110.00.** C. Dancing Bear, 3⅛" [German, OP-NP (1950s & 1994), R3]. Old, **$150.00–175.00.** 1950s (shown), **$50.00–60.00.**

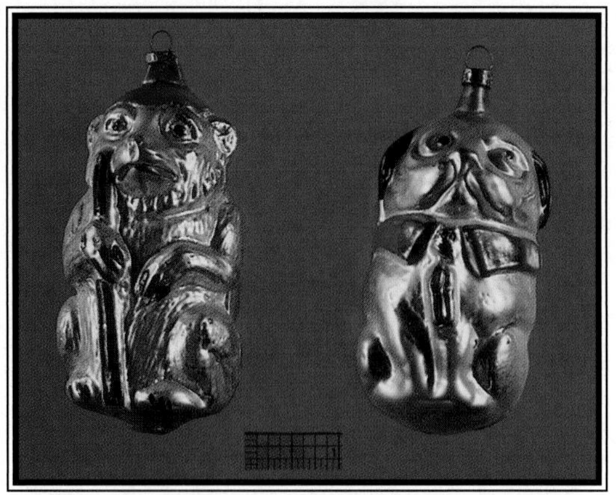

A. Bear Carrying a Stick, approx. 2", 2½", & 4" (shown) [German, OP, R2-3]. Small, **$75.00-100.00.** Medium, **$90.00-100.00.** Large, **$200.00-250.00.** B. Dog in a Collar and Necktie, approx. 4" [OP, R2]. **$175.00-225.00.**

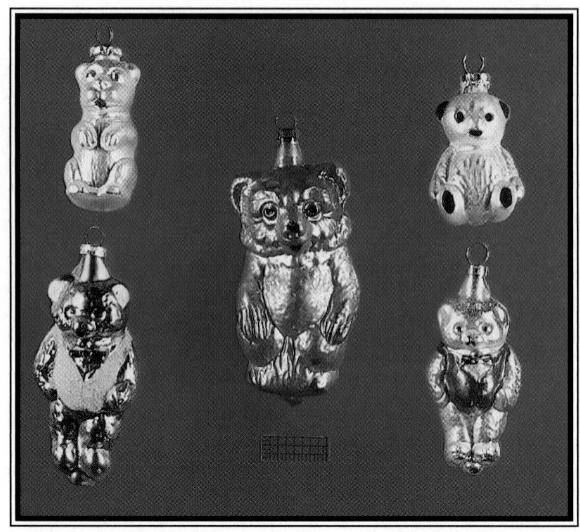

A. Begging Terrier, approx. 2¼" [Austrian, OP-NP (1970), R2-3]. **$30.00-40.00.** 1970s version (shown), **$15.00-20.00.** B. Sitting Teddy Bear, approx. 2" [German, OP-NP (1970s & 1990s), R1-2]. **$50.00-75.00.** 1970s version (shown), **$12.00-15.00.** C. Standing Bear, approx. 3", 3½", & 4" (shown) [OP, R2-3]. Small, **$100.00-125.00.** Medium, **$150.00-200.00.** Large, **$200.00-275.00.** D & E. Bear in a Vest and Bow Tie, approx. 2½" (shown), 3" (shown), & 4¾" [German, OP-NP (1980s & 1990s), R2]. Small, **$70.00-80.00.** Medium, **$80.00-90.00.** Large, **$125.00-150.00.** 1980s version (shown), **$10.00-15.00.**

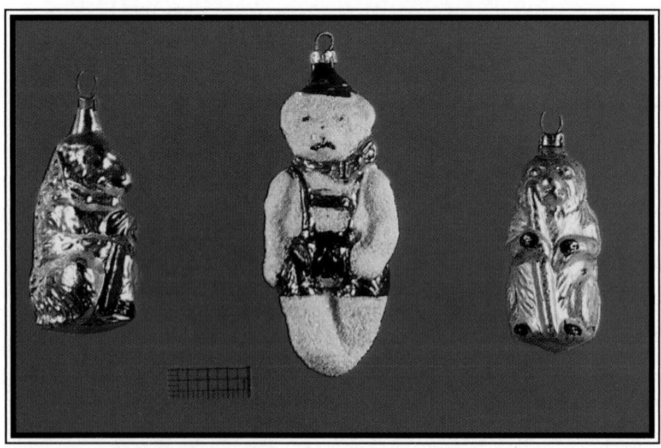

A. Bear with a Club, approx. 2½" [German, OP, R3]. **$75.00-100.00.** B. Bear in Leather Shorts and Suspenders, approx. 3½" [German, OP-NP (1950s & 1980s), R3]. **$45.00-55.00.** C. Bear Carrying a Stick, approx. 2" (shown), 2½", & 4" [German, OP, R3]. Small, **$75.00-100.00.** Medium, **$90.00-110.00.** Large, **$200.00-250.00.**

A. Bear Head, approx. 2½" [OP, R1]. **$300.00-350.00.** B. Builder Pig, approx. 3¼" & 3½" (shown), one of the Three Little Pigs [OP, R2]. Both sizes **$225.00-275.00.**

A. Bear with Chenille Arms & Legs, approx. 3" & 3½" (shown) [German, OP-NP (1993, glass body only), R1+]. **$400.00-500.00.** B. Bear with a Muff, approx. 3½" [OP, R2-3]. **$90.00-110.00.**

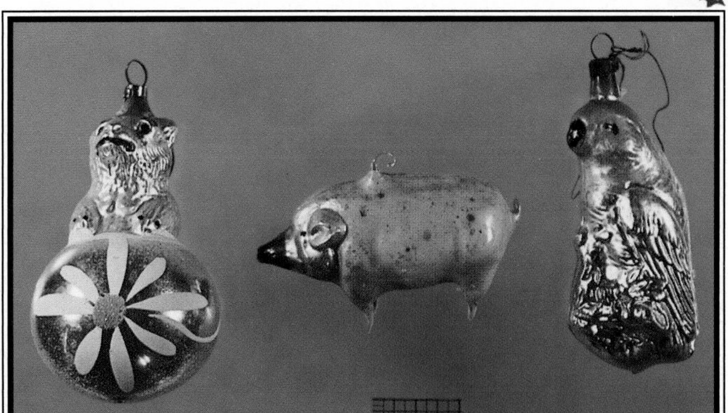

A. Begging Bear in a Ball, 3" [OP, R2]. **$150.00–175.00.** B. Pig with Annealed Legs, large, 3" [OP, R1]. **$300.00–350.00.** C. Eagle on a Branch, 3" [OP, R2-3]. **$150.00–175.00.**

A. Bear with Annealed Legs, 4" [OP, R1]. **$550.00–650.00.** B. Pig with Annealed Legs, 2¼" [OP, R1]. **$300.00–350.00.**

A. Bird and Gnome on a Tree Trunk, approx. 3" [German, OP-NP (Radko, 1990s), R2]. **$130.00–160.00.** B. Birdbath with Water, approx. 2". A glass ball in the center is filled with water and reflects off the sides of the ornament, making it appear that it is full of water [OP, R1]. **$100.00–125.00.** C. Birdbath, approx. 3"H x 4"W, 2" molded bird [OP, R1]. **$150.00–175.00.**

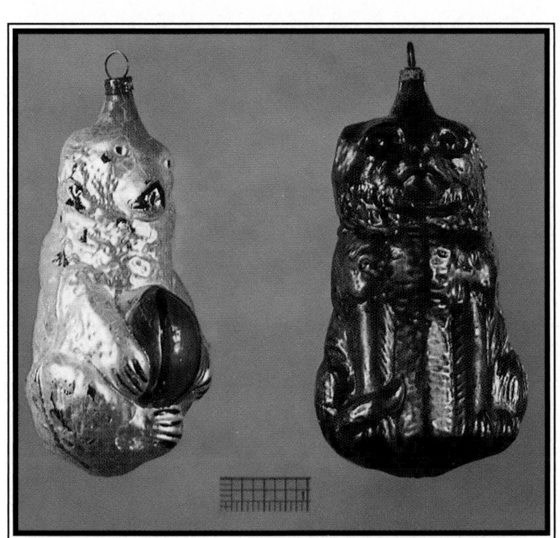

A. Bear with a Ball, approx. 3¾" (shown) & 4" [German, OP-NP (1993), R2]. Both sizes **$225.00–275.00.** B. Sitting Cat (Type I), approx. 3¾" (shown) & 4" [German, OP, R2]. Small, **$175.00–225.00.** Large, **$350.00–450.00.**

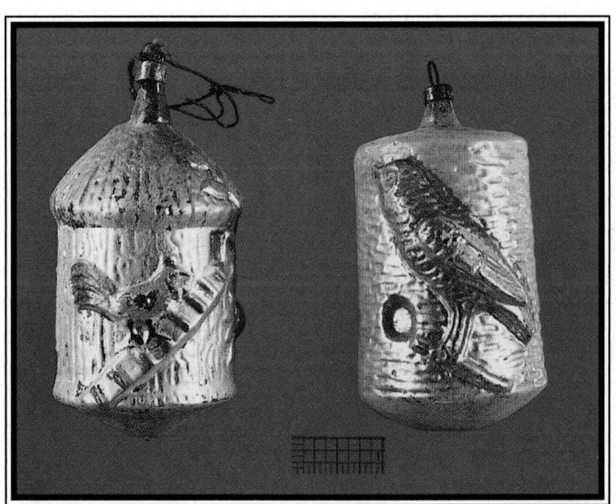

A. Rooster on a Chicken Coop, approx. 2¾" & 3" (shown). Small, **$35.00–50.00.** Large, **$50.00–75.00.** B. Birdhouse, approx. 1½", 2", 2¾", 3", & 3½" (shown) [German, OP-NP (1950s & 1980s), R4]. Small, **$30.00–40.00.** Medium, **$50.00–75.00.** Large, **$75.00–100.00.**

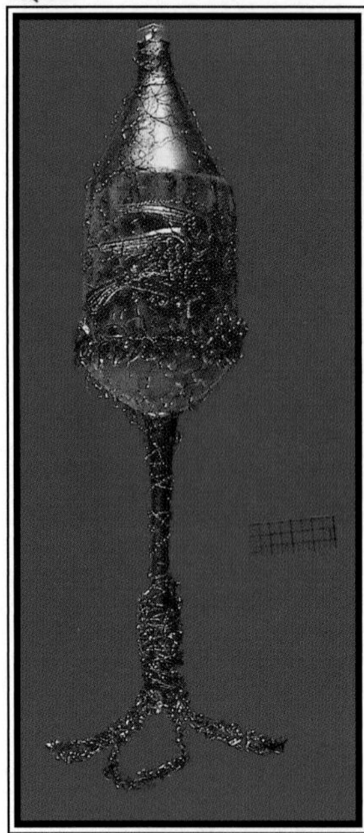

Victorian Birdcage, pedestal type with a Dresden bird, approx. 7½" [German, OP, R2]. **$175.00–225.00.**

A. Birdcage, square, art glass, 3¼" [OP-NP (1999), R2]. **$75.00–85.00.** B. Birdcage, round, art glass, 3" [OP, R2]. **$70.00–80.00.**

Mouse in a Cage, art glass (damaged), 2¾" [German, OP, R1]. **$75.00–100.00.** B. Square Birdcage of Art Glass, large, 5" [German, OP, R1-2]. **$125.00–150.00.**

A. Hummingbird with SG Wings, miniature, 1½" [OP, R1-2]. **$30.00–40.00.** B. Hollow Birdcage, 3" [OP, R1-2]. **$65.00–85.00.**

Bird at a Nest with Eggs, 4" [OP, R1]. **$125.00–175.00.**

Bird with Berries and Flowers, 4½" [OP, R2]. **$75.00–100.00.**

A. Chenille Bird on a Nest, approx. 2¾" [OP, R2]. **$50.00–75.00.** B. Bird on a Nest, standard form, approx. 4½". The bird and the indented ball (nest) are two separate pieces held together with wire tinsel [German, Czech, Austrian; OP-NP, R3-4]. **$50.00–75.00.** C. Bird on a Nest, 1980s version, approx. 3". **$10.00–20.00.**

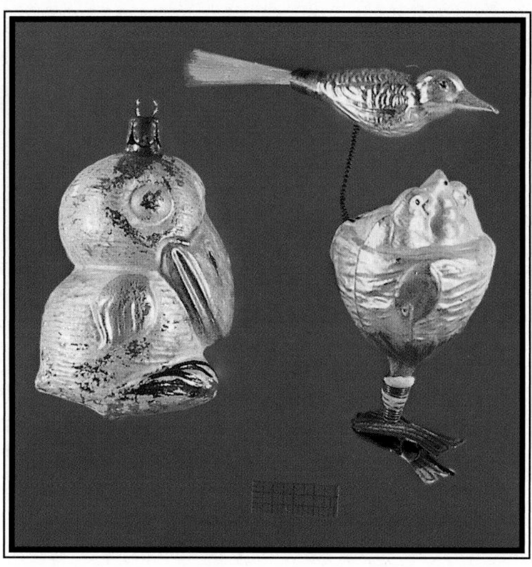

A. Pelican, approx. 3" [German, OP, R2]. **$150.00–175.00.** B. Mother Bird with Baby Birds in a Nest (Type II), approx. 3¼" [German, OP-NP (2002), R2]. The nest has molded leaves. **$200.00–250.00.**

A. Mother & Father Birds with Baby Birds in a Nest (Type I), approx. 3¼" [German, OP, R1-2]. **$250.00–275.00.** B. Woodpecker on a Tree Trunk, approx. 4" [German, OP, R1]. **$275.00–325.00.**

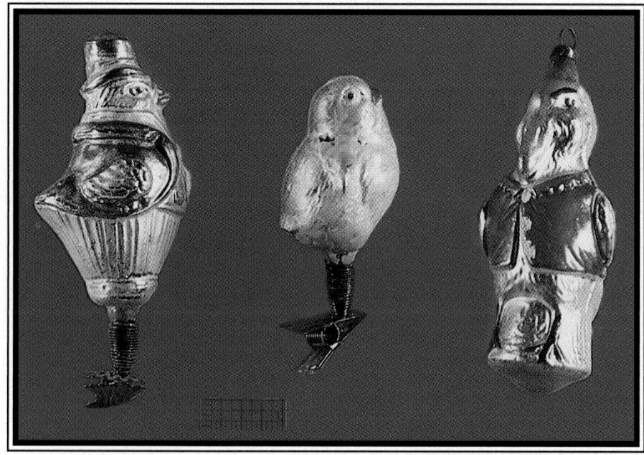

A. Cock Robin, also called Weather Bird, approx. 3", 3¼" (shown), & 3¾" [German, OP-NP (1980s – 1990s), R2-3]. Small, **$100.00–125.00.** Medium, **$125.00–150.00.** Large, **$200.00 – 250.00.** B. Chick, approx. 2" [German, OP, R2]. **$150.00–175.00.** C. Duck in a Vest, approx. 3¾" [OP, R1-2]. **$225.00–250.00.**

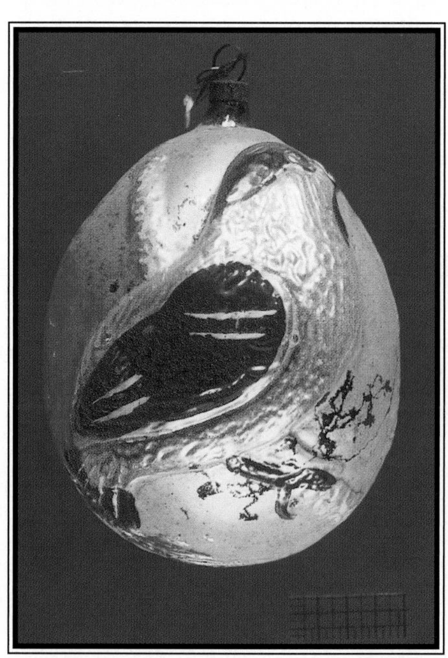

Bird Embossed on an Egg, large, 3½" [OP, R2]. **$50.00–75.00.**

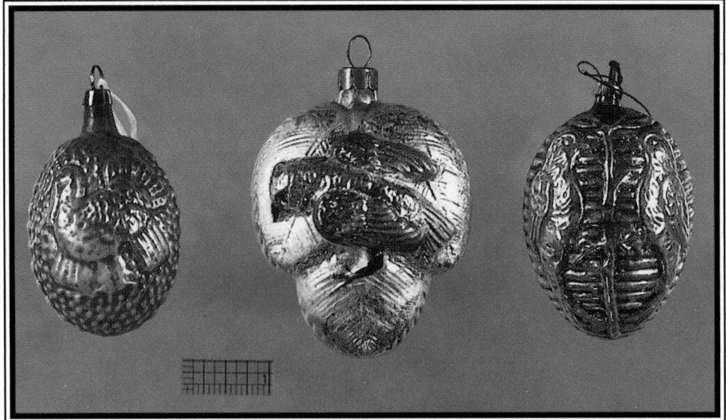

A. Turkey Embossed on an Oval, 2¼" [OP, R2-3]. **$15.00–25.00.** B. Bird on Three Pine Cones, embossed, approx. 2¼" & 2¾" (shown) [OP, R2-3]. Small, **$15.00–25.00.** Large, **$30.00–40.00.** C. Birds on Ribbed Egg, 2½" [OP, R2]. **$20.00–25.00.**

A. Cock Robin or Weather Bird, approx. 3", 3¼", & 3¾" (shown) [German, OP-NP (1980s & 1990s), R2-3]. Small, **$100.00–125.00.** Medium, **$125.00–150.00.** Large, **$200.00–250.00.** B. Birds and Berries, 6" [OP, R2]. **$125.00–150.00.**

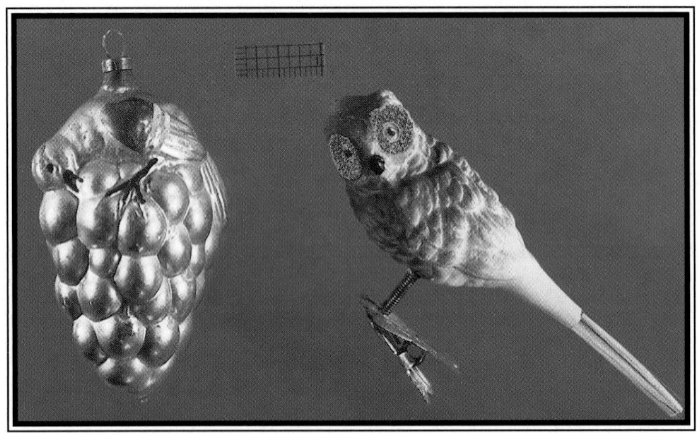

A. Birds Embossed on Berries, double sided, 3½" [OP, R1]. **$100.00–150.00.** B. Owl with Glass Eyes & SG tail (Type II), 3¾" [OP, R1]. **$75.00–100.00.**

A. Chick in an Eggshell, large, 3¾" [OP, R1]. **$300.00–350.00.** B. Rainbow Trout, large, 5½" [OP-NP (1992), R1-2]. Old, **$60.00–75.00.** New, **$10.00–15.00.**

A. Bird on a House, approx. 2¾" (shown) and 3¼" [German, NP (1950s), R2-3]. **$100.00–125.00.** B. Duck on a Disk, 2½" [NP (1950s), R2-3]. **$40.00–50.00.** C. Songbird with SG Wings, 3¾" [OP-NP (1980s), R3]. **$70.00–90.00.**

A. Duck, 2¾" [West German, OP-NP (1950s & 1970s), R3]. Old, **$25.00–35.00.** 1950s – 1970s, **$15.00–20.00.** B. Stork on a House, 4" [German, OP-NP (1950s), R2-3]. **$125.00–150.00.** C. Mother and Baby Bear on a Motorcycle, 2¾" [West German, NP (1950s), R1-2]. **$125.00–150.00.**

Cockatiel with SG Wings, 3¼" glass, 5" wing span, unusual green spun glass wings [OP, R2]. **$125.00–150.00.**

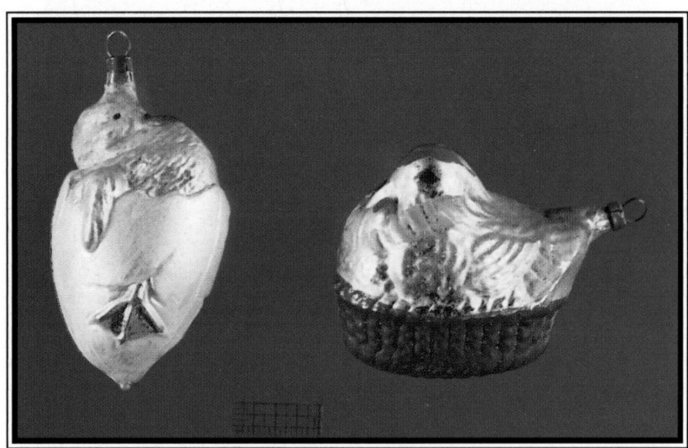

A. Duck in an Egg, approx. 3¼" [German, OP, R1]. **$250.00–275.00.** B. Hen on a Basket, approx. 3" [OP, R1-2]. **$175.00–200.00.**

A. Duck in a Bonnet, "Baby Huey," 4½" [German, OP, R2]. **$425.00–500.00.** B. Mouse or Rat, 3" [OP, R1]. **$350.00–400.00.**

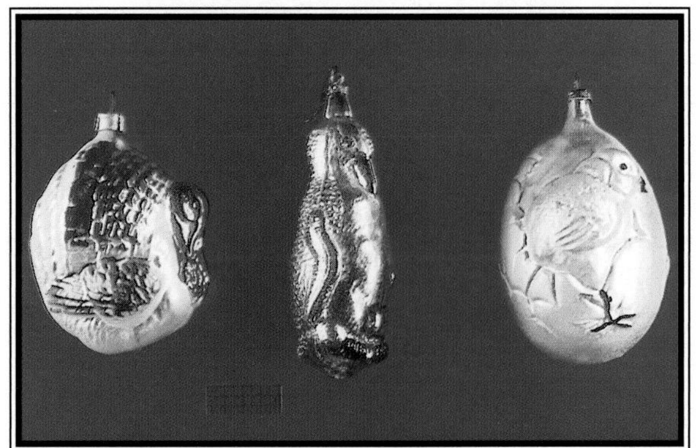

A. Turkey (Type I), approx. 3¼" [German, OP-NP (1970s), R2]. **$100.00–150.00.** 1970s version (shown), **$15.00–25.00.** B. Penguin (Type I), approx. 4" & 4½" (shown) [German, OP, R1-2]. **$150.00–175.00.** C. Chick on an Egg, approx. 3½" [German, OP-NP (1980s), R1]. **$200.00–250.00.**

A. Duck/Goose, art glass, 3¾" [German, OP, R2]. **$30.00–35.00.** B. Swan, art glass, 2½" [German, OP, R3]. **$30.00–40.00.**

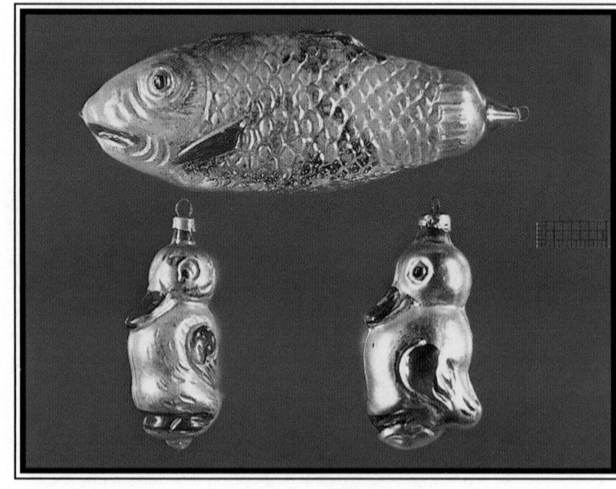

A. Fish, standard form, large, 5½" [OP-NP, R3-4]. **$40.00–50.00.** B. Two Versions of a Molded Duck, both 3" [OP-NP (1950s & 1970s), R3]. Old, **$25.00–35.00.** 1950s & 1970s, **$15.00–20.00.**

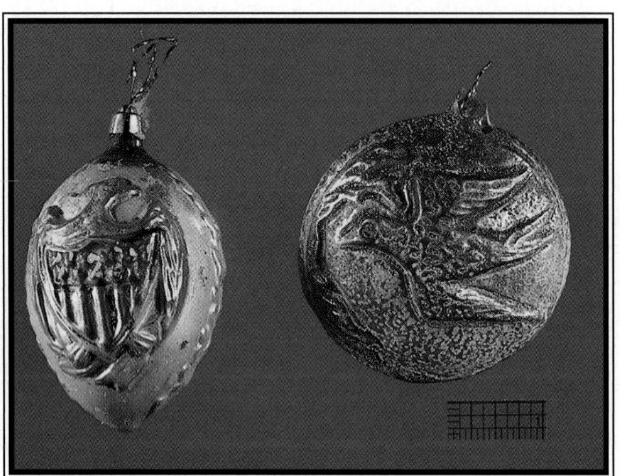

A. Eagle and Liberty Shield, egg shaped, approx. 3½", same design on both sides [OP, R1]. **$300.00–350.00.** B. Bird Embossed on a Disk, approx. 3¼" [OP, R2]. **$25.00–30.00.**

American Eagle with Liberty Shield on its Chest (Type I), approx. 4" [German, OP, R1+]. **$500.00–600.00.** Other Patriotic ornaments can be found on page 88.

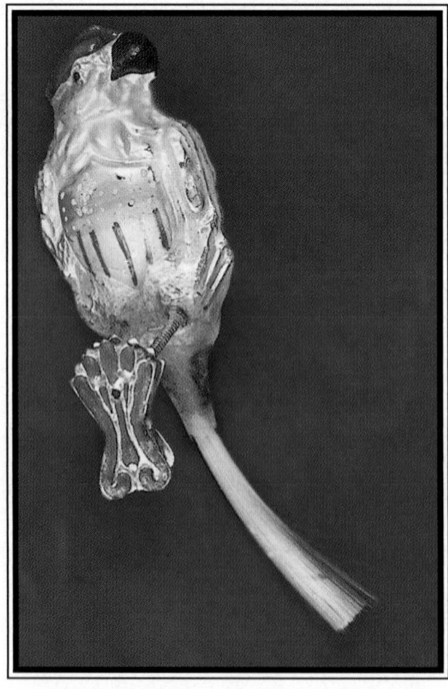

American Eagle with Liberty Shield on its Chest, bottom view.

American Eagle Embossed on a Ball, 2½", circa 1900, double sided [OP-NP (1994), R2]. **$325.00–400.00.**

Eagle with Liberty Shield on Chest (Type II), 4" [OP, R1+]. **$500.00–600.00.**

Eagle with Liberty Shield on Its Chest (Type II), 4" [OP, R1+]. **$500.00–600.00.**

Radko Eagle with Liberty Shield, approx. 5". The ornament of the month for July 2001 — "Freedom's Wings" [NP, R2]. **$60.00–85.00.**

A. Eagle on Top of a Ball, approx. 5½" [German, OP-NP (1970s), R1]. **$150.00–175.00.** 1970s version (shown), **$10.00–20.00.** B. Molded Duck, 2¾" (shown) & 3" [German, OP-NP (1950s & 1970s), R3]. **$25.00–35.00.** C. Swan, approx. 3", "Germany" is embossed on the chest [German, OP, R2]. **$30.00–35.00.** D. Rooster Embossed on an Oval, approx. 2" [OP, R3-4]. **$15.00–20.00.** E. Songbird with a Berry in its Mouth, approx. 4" [OP, R3]. **$65.00–85.00.**

German Free-blown Birds with Annealed Legs, from the Artistic Period (1920s –1930s), sizes may vary: A. Flamingo, 6½". **$60.00–80.00.** B. Stork, 3¼". **$30.00–40.00.** C. Flamingo (4¾"), **$40.00–60.00.**

Ostrich, large, 6¼" [OP, R1]. **$375.00–425.00.**

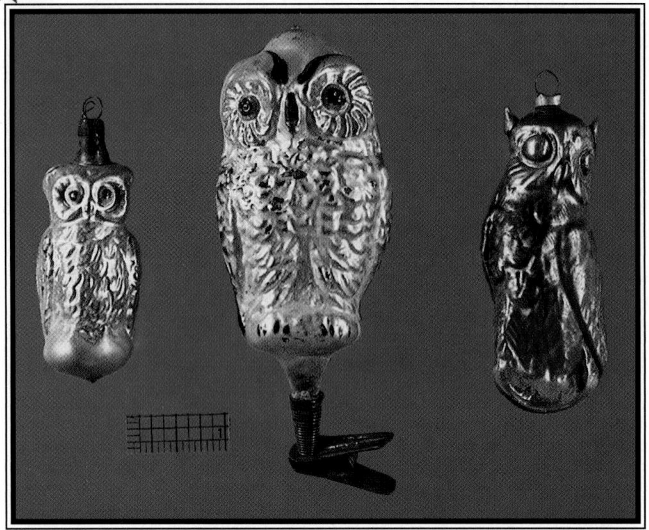

A & B. Standard Form Owls, approx. 2" (shown), 2¾", 3¼" (shown), 3¾", & 4¼" [various countires, OP-NP (continuing), R4]. Small, **$25.00–35.00.** Medium, **$35.00–50.00.** Large, **$45.00–65.00.** C. Owl, horned, 3" [OP, R2]. **$100.00–125.00.**

A. Owl, standard form, 4¼" [OP-NP, R4]. Large, **$45.00–65.00.** B. Miniature Duck, 2" [OP-R2]. **$20.00–25.00.** C. Owl with Large Eyes, 3¾" [OP, R2]. **$60.00–80.00.**

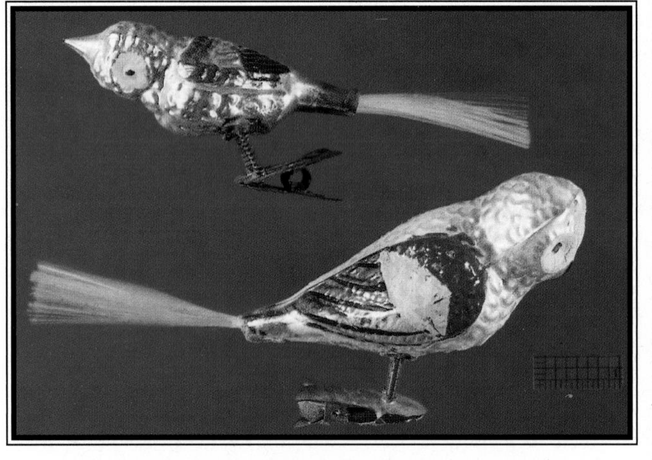

Owls with SG Tail (Type I), 3" and 3¾" [OP, R3]. Medium, **$25.00–30.00.** Large, **$35.00–45.00.**

Owl Wearing a Bonnet, 3½" [OP, R1]. **$200.00–250.00.**

Parrot in a Glass Ring, 3" [OP, R2]. **$70.00–90.00.**

Parrot in a Ball, 4½" [OP, R1]. **$250.00–300.00.**

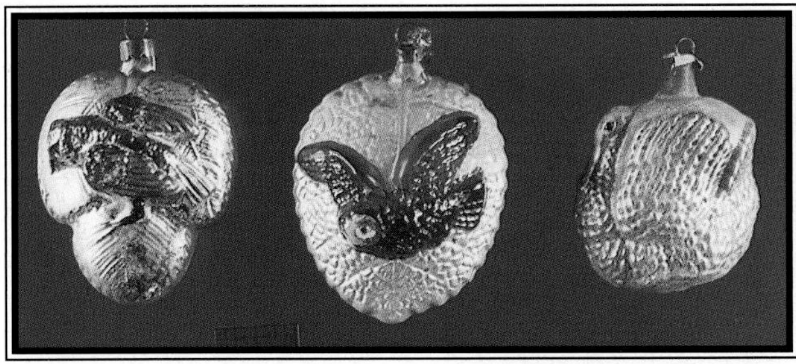

A. Bird on Three Pine Cones, approx. 2¼" & 2¾" [OP, R2-3]. Small, **$15.00–25.00.** Large, **$30.00–40.00.** B. Owl on a Leaf, approx. 3" [German, OP-NP (1970s), R2]. **$125.00–150.00.** C. Turkey (Type II), also called a Swan, approx. 2" [German, OP, R2]. **$100.00–150.00.**

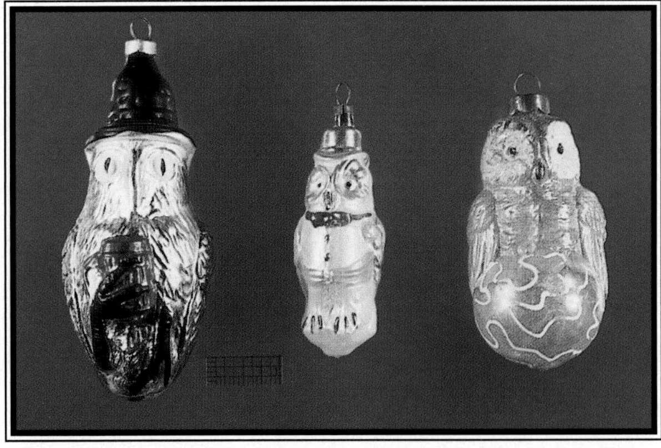

A. Owl with a Top Hat & Beer Stein, approx. 4½" [German, OP-NP (1980s), R1]. Old, **$275.00–300.00.** 1980's version, **$50.00–75.00.** B. Owl with a Top Hat & Vest, approx. 3¼" [German, OP-NP (1950s), R2-3]. **$80.00–95.00.** C. Owl on a Ball, 3¼" (shown) & 4" [German, OP-NP (Radko, 1995, 4"), R2-3]. **$75.00–100.00.**

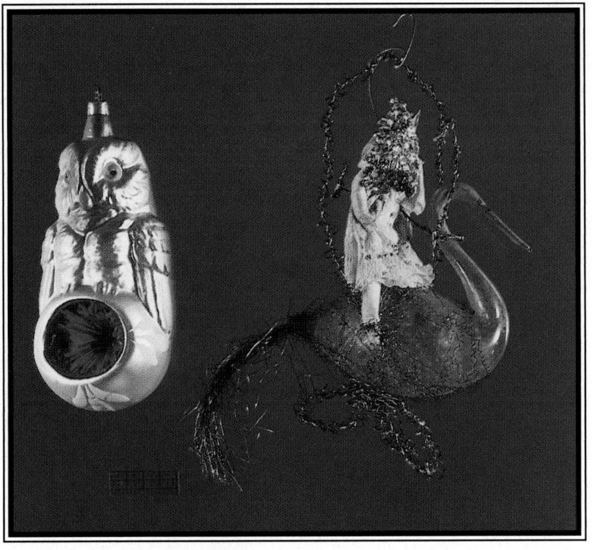

A. Owl on an Indented Ball, approx. 3¼" [German, OP, R2]. **$100.00–125.00.** B. Swan with Spun Cotton Girl Rider, approx. 4" [OP, R1]. **$350.00–400.00.**

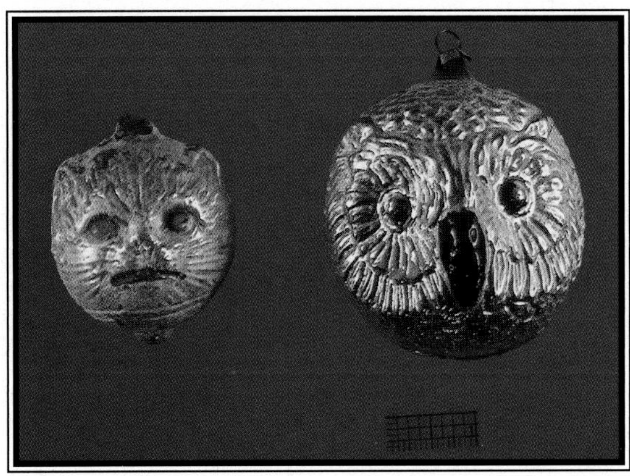

A. Cat Head, approx. 1¾" (shown) & 2½" [German, OP-NP (1991), R2-3]. Small, **$175.00–200.00.** Large, **$250.00–300.00.** B. Owl Head (Type I), approx. 2¾" & 3½" (shown) [German, OP, R2-3]. Small, **$100.00–125.00.** Large, **$150.00–175.00.**

A. Owl Head (Type II), approx. 3" [OP, R2]. **$175.00–200.00.** B. Parrot Head, approx. 3" [German, OP, R1-2]. **$225.00–250.00.**

Various Standard Form Parrots, approx. 3", 3½", 3¾", 4", 4½", & 5½" glass body only [German, OP-NP (1980s), R4]. Small, **$20.00–25.00.** Medium, **$25.00–30.00.** Large, **$35.00–50.00.**

A. Parrot, 4½" [OP-NP (1980s), R3]. Unsilvered medium, **$35.00–45.00.** B. Two Pine Cones on a Feather Branch, 4½" [OP, R1-2]. **$20.00–30.00.**

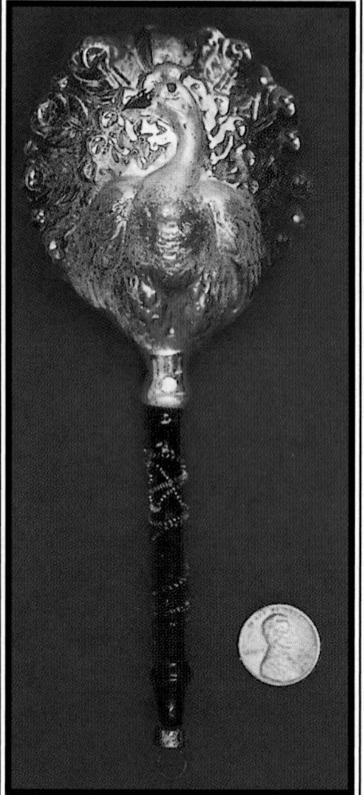

Peacock Baby Rattle, front view, approx. 8" [German, OP, R1+]. **$600.00–750.00.**

A. Pheasant, 4½" [OP, R2]. **$65.00–85.00.** B. Parrot with SG Wings, 3" [OP, R2]. **$65.00–85.00.**

Peacock Baby Rattle, back view.

A & D. Peacocks, standard form, 1½" – 7" glass body only [German, Czech, Austrian; OP-NP (continuing), R5]. Small, **$10.00–15.00.** Medium, **$20.00–25.00.** Large, **$30.00–50.00.** B. Peacock with a Fanned-out Tail, approx. 2¾" [OP, R2]. **$35.00–50.00.** C. Peacock with a Trailing Tail, approx. 3¼" glass body, overall size can vary with the tail [OP, R2-3]. **$20.00–35.00.** E. Two Peacocks on a Clip-on, approx. 2" glass bodies [OP, R3]. **$50.00–75.00.**

Peacock, art glass, 6½" tail span [OP-NP (1979), R1]. Old version, **$300.00–350.00.** 1979 version, **$75.00–100.00.**

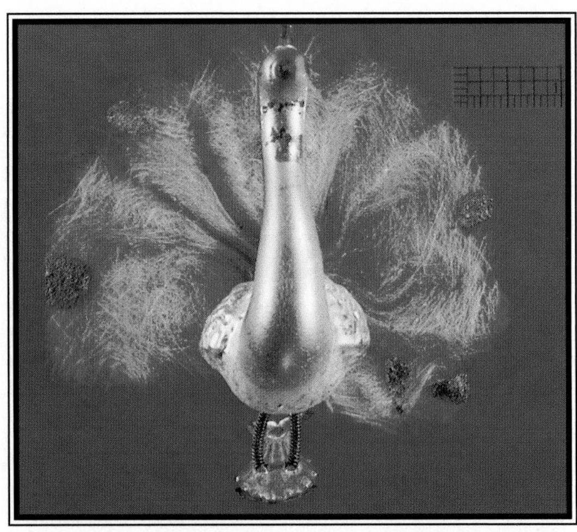

Peacock with Fanned-out Tail and Dresden Trim, 3" [OP, R2]. **$35.00–50.00.**

A. Molded Peacock, approx. 2¼", 2¾", 3½" (shown), & 3¾" [German, OP-NP (1980s), R4-5]. Small, **$15.00–25.00.** Medium, **$25.00–35.00.** Large, **$35.00–50.00.** B. Swan with SG Wings, approx. 3½" glass body [OP, R2-3]. **$50.00–75.00.**

A. Peacock on a Ball, 3½" [German, OP-NP, R2]. **$75.00–100.00.** B. Birdhouse, 2¾" [OP-NP (1950s), R4]. 1950s version (shown) has a "bumpy" pattern. **$25.00–35.00.**

A. Comic Hummingbird, 3½" [OP, R1-2]. **$50.00–75.00.** B. Peacock with Annealed Wings, 3" [OP, R2]. **$20.00–30.00.** C. Stork, standard form, 3 - 4½" (3½" shown), [OP-NP (continuing), R4]. Small, **$30.00 – 40.00.** Medium (3½"), **$40.00–50.00.** Large, **$50.00–60.00.**

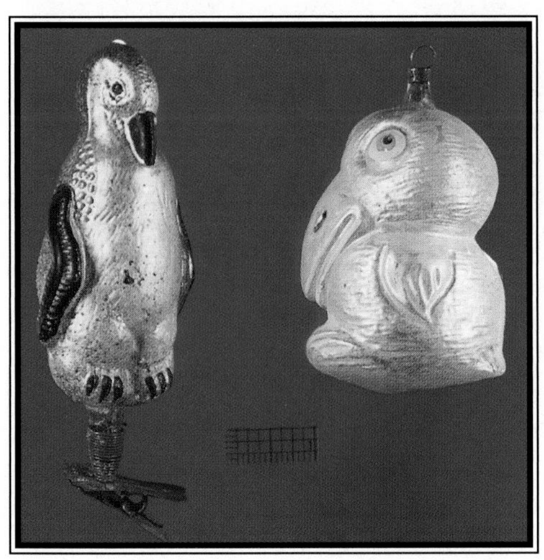

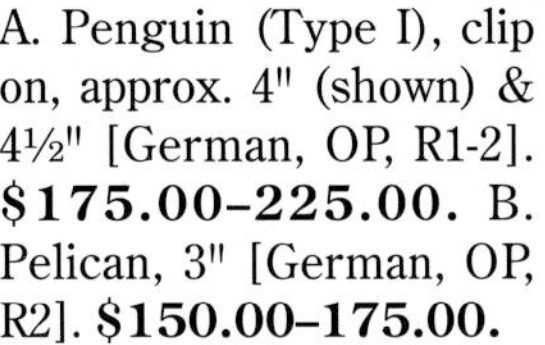

A. Penguin (Type I), clip on, approx. 4" (shown) & 4½" [German, OP, R1-2]. **$175.00–225.00.** B. Pelican, 3" [German, OP, R2]. **$150.00–175.00.**

A. Penguin (Type II), approx. 3½" [OP, R2]. **$75.00–100.00.** B. Free-blown Art Glass Penguin, approx. 1¾" & 4½" (shown) [German, OP (1920s), R3]. Small, **$25.00–35.00.** Large, **$40.00–65.00.**

A. Pigeon with Glass Eyes, 4½" [OP, R2]. **$75.00-100.00.** B. Songbird with a Berry (Type II), 4½" [OP, R1-2]. **$65.00–85.00.**

A. Songbird with an Open Beak, 3¾" [OP, R1-2]. **$45.00–55.00.** B. Songbird with a Key, 4¼" [OP, R1-2]. **$75.00–100.00.**

A Collection of Common Songbirds, approx. 1¼" – 4½" (3" – 3½" shown) glass bodies [German, Czech, Austrian; OP-NP (continuing), R5+]: Small, **$15.00–20.00.** Medium, **$20.00–30.00.** Large, **$25.00–35.00.**

A. Owl (Type I), clip on, approx. 3¼" [OP, R3]. **$25.00–30.00.** B. Two Songbirds on a Clip, approx. 2" – 3" [OP-NP (1970s, small), R3]. **$55.00–75.00.** C. Songbird with a Top Knot & Turned Head, approx. 5" [OP, R1-2]. **$40.00–50.00.** D. Soaring Dove, approx. 4½", the wings are raised as if flying or soaring [German, OP, R1]. **$60.00–85.00.**

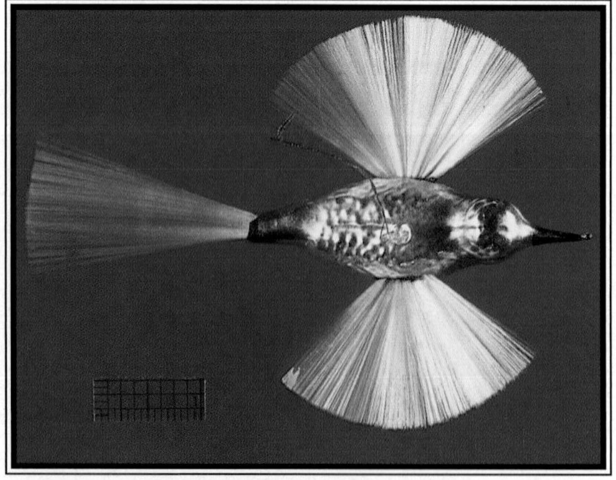

Songbird with SG Wings, also called a Hummingbird, approx. 2½", 3½" (shown), & 3¾" [German, Czech, Austrian; OP-NP (1980s), R3]. **$40.00–50.00.**

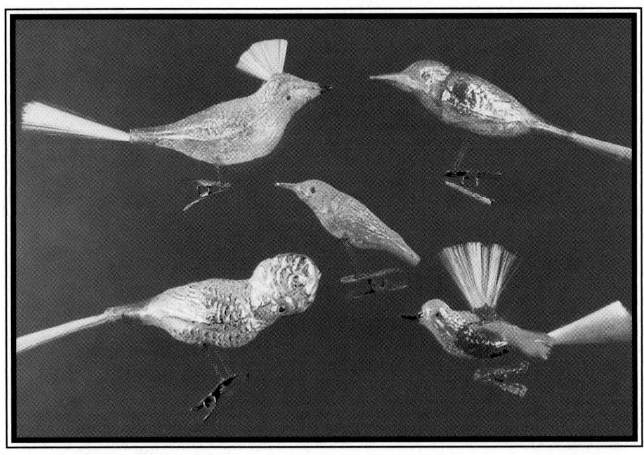

A. Songbird with SG Crest, 3½" [OP-NP, R3]. **$15.00–20.00.** B & C. Songbirds, standard form, 3½" and 2½" [OP-NP, R5+]. **$10.00–15.00.** D. Cockatoo, 3½" [OP-NP, R3-4]. **$20.00–25.00.** E. Songbird with SG Wings, 2½" [OP-NP, R3]. **$20.00–30.00.**

A & C. Cockatiels, approx. 3" & 4" (both shown) [German, OP, R3-4]. Small, **$20.00–25.00.** Large, **$25.00–30.00.** B. Milk Glass Stork, approx. 4" [OP, R2-3]. **$50.00–60.00.** C. Stork, standard form, approx. 3" & 4" (shown) & 4½" glass body [German, Czech, Austrian, OP-NP (continuing), R4]. Small, **$30.00–40.00.** Medium, **$40.00–50.00.** Large, **$50.00–60.00.**

A. Two Storks on a Clip-on, approx. 2" glass bodies [OP, R2]. **$50.00–65.00.** B. Stork with a Wax Baby, approx. 3½" [OP, R1]. **$175.00–200.00.** C. Ostrich, approx. 3¼" (shown) & 6¼" [OP, R1-2]. Small, **$150.00–175.00.** Large, **$375.00–425.00.**

A. Mother and Baby Storks, 3½" [German, OP-NP (1980s), R2]. Old, **$90.00–110.00.** B. Mother and Baby Peacocks, 3" [OP, R2-3]. **$50.00–75.00.**

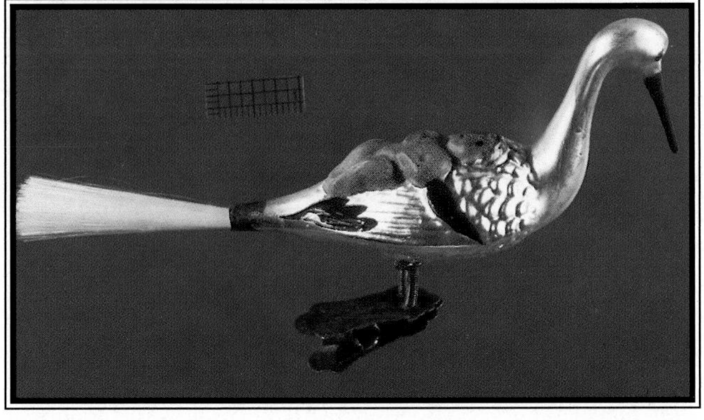

Stork with a Baby on its Back, 4½" [OP, R1]. **$250.00–275.00.**

A. Bird and Branch on a Disk, double, 2¾" [OP-NP (1970s), R2]. **$25.00–35.00.** B. Swan on a Pond, 3" [OP-NP (1980s), R2]. **$40.00–50.00.** C. Stork on a Cylinder, embossed, 2¾" [OP-NP (1980s), R2]. Old, **$30.00–40.00.**

Free-blown Swan Boat, approx. 3¾" – 8¾" (shown) [OP-NP (1990s, small only), R2-3]. Small, **$50.00–75.00.** Medium, **$75.00–100.00.** Large, **$150.00–200.00.**

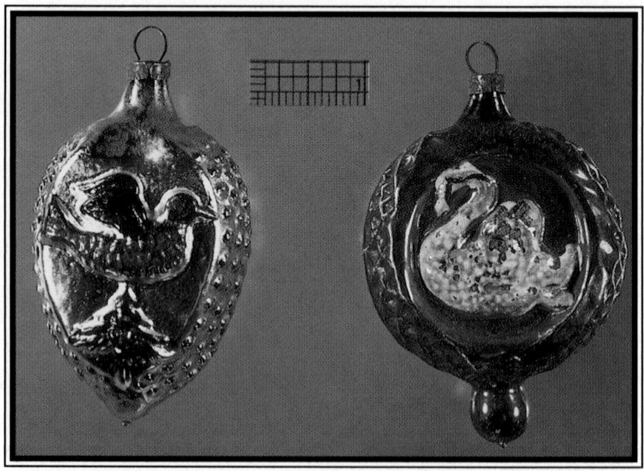

A. Bird and Pine Tree, embossed, 2¾" [OP-NP (1950s), R2-3]. **$15.00–20.00.** B. Swan Indent, 2¾" [OP, R3]. **$30.00–45.00.**

A. Swan with SG Wings, 3½"L [OP, R2-3]. **$50.00–75.00.** B. Swan with Molded Body, 2¾" (shown) & 3" [OP, R4]. **$15.00–25.00.**

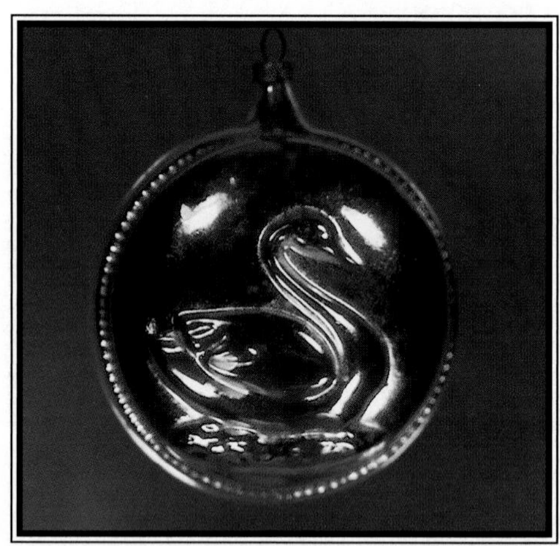

Swan on a Disk, 3", made during the mid-to-late 1930s [German, OP, R1-2]. This style is sometimes referred to as a Nazi ornament. **$90.00–110.00.**

Reverse of Swan on a Disk.

Swans, approx. 1½" – 8½" (2½" – 4" are the most common), all approx. 4" (shown) [OP-NP, R5]: A. Standard Form. Small, **$8.00–12.00.** Medium, **$15.00–20.00.** Large, **$25.00–35.00.** Very large (7"+), **$60.00–90.00.** B. Molded Body. **$15.00–20.00.** C. Swan in Tinsel. **$25.00–35.00.** D. Swan with Tinsel Wings. **$25.00–35.00.** E. Swan with Indents or Reflectors. **$12.00–18.00.**

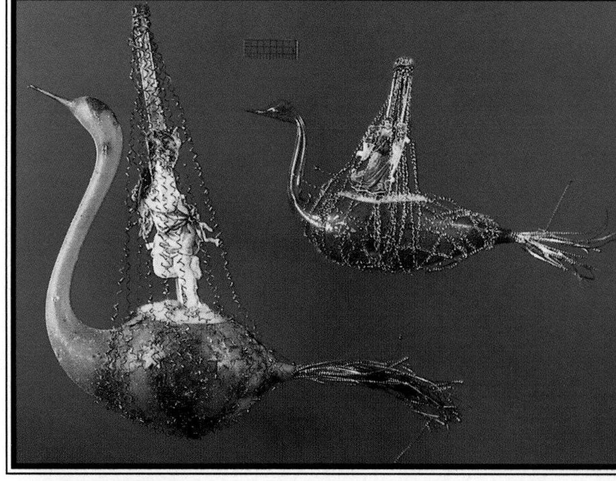

Swan Boats, approx. 3¾" – 8¾" (8" & 5¼" shown) [OP-NP (1990), R2-3]. Small (shown), **$50.00–75.00.** Medium, **$75.00–100.00.** Large (shown), **$150.00–200.00.**

Free-blown Swans with Scrap Riders, approx. 4" - 7" [OP, R3-4]. Small (shown), **$40.00–50.00.** Medium (shown), **$75.00–85.00.** Large, **$100.00–150.00.**

Free-blown Swan Sleigh with a Cotton Rider, approx. 6½" [OP, R1]. **$350.00–400.00.**

Swan Boat with Scrap Sails, approx. 5" [OP, R1]. **$200.00–250.00.**

A. Swan on a Ball, embossed, 3" [OP, R2]. **$35.00–50.00.** B. Hyacinths in a Pot, approx. 3¾" (shown) & 5" [OP, R2-3]. **$70.00–90.00.**

A. Tropical Bird with a Long Beak, approx. 6" [OP, R1]. **$125.00–150.00.** B. Mallard Duck, approx. 3½" [OP, R1]. **$75.00–100.00.**

A. Turkey, double sided, 3¾" [OP, R2]. **$200.00–275.00.** B. Turkey with SG Feathers, 3¾"L [OP, R2]. **$175.00–200.00.**

Two Examples of Art Glass Ornaments: A. Cat in a Glass Ring, 2¾" [German, OP, R2]. **$75.00–100.00.** B. Swan in a Glass Ring, 2¾" [German, OP, R1-2]. **$65.00–85.00.**

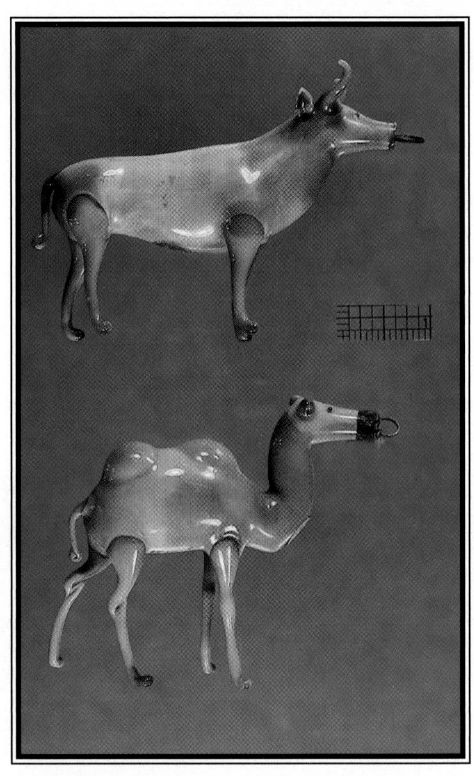

A. Bull, art glass, 3¾" [German, OP, R1]. **$125.00–150.00.** B. Camel, art glass, 3½" [German, OP, R1]. **$125.00–150.00.**

Three-Faced Ornament — Owl Side, approx. 2¼", 2½" (shown), & 3½" [German, OP-NP (1985, small; 1991, large), R2]. Small, **$200.00–250.00.** Medium, **$275.00–350.00.** Large, **$400.00–550.00.**

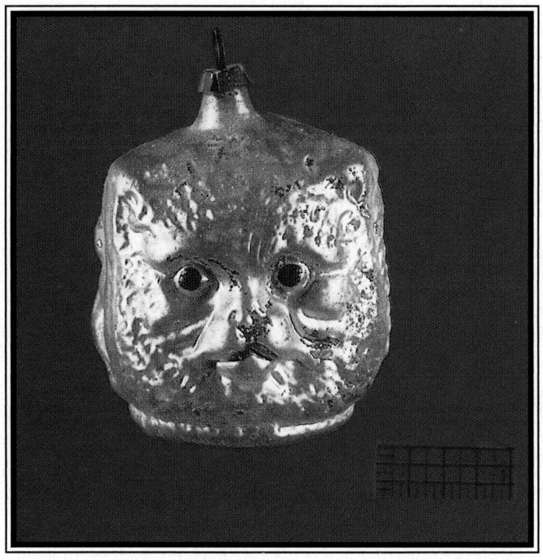

Three-faced Ornament — Cat Side, approx. 2¼", 2½" (shown), & 3½" [German, OP-NP (1985, small; 1991, large), R2]. Small, **$200.00–250.00.** Medium, **$275.00–300.00.** Large, **$400.00–500.00.**

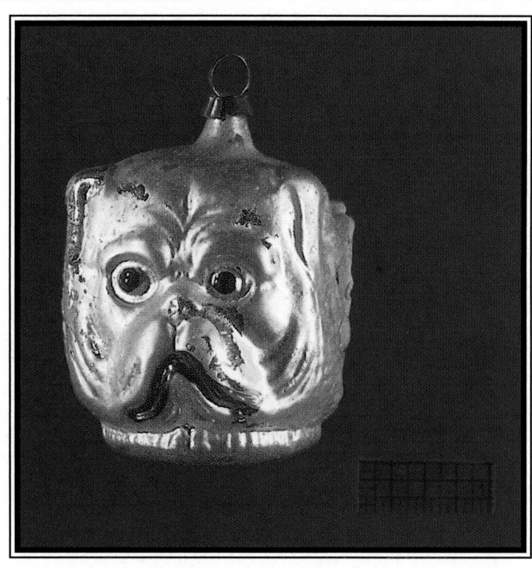

Three-faced Ornament — Bulldog Side, approx. 2¼", 2½" (shown), & 3½" [German, OP-NP (1985, small; 1991, large), R2]. Small, **$200.00–250.00.** Medium, **$275.00–300.00.** Large, **$400.00–500.00.**

A. Stag and Doe, embossed, 2¼" [OP, R2]. **$20.00–25.00.** B. Cat Head, approx. 1¾" (shown) & 2½" [German, OP-NP (1991), R2-3]. Small, **$175.00–200.00.** Large, **$250.00–300.00.**

Cat in a Bag, approx. 3½" & 4" (shown) [German, OP-NP (1985), R3]. Small, **$100.00–125.00.** Large, **$125.00–150.00.**

A. Puss 'n Boots with Chenille Legs and Wax Boots, 4½" overall [German, OP, R1+]. **$450.00–500.00.** B. Cat, ball shaped, 2½" [OP-NP, R1]. **$175.00–225.00.**

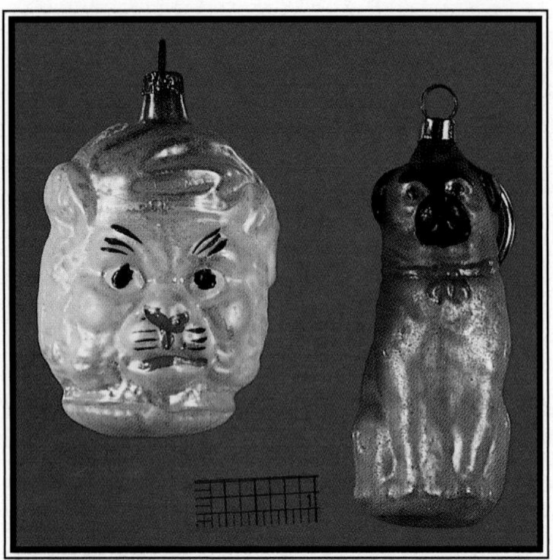

A. Cat Head in a Night Cap, approx. 2¼" (shown) & 3" [German, OP, R2]. **$200.00–250.00.** Large, **$275.00–325.00.** B. Sitting Pug Dog, 3" [German, OP-NP (circa 1991), R2-3]. Old, **$90.00–110.00.**

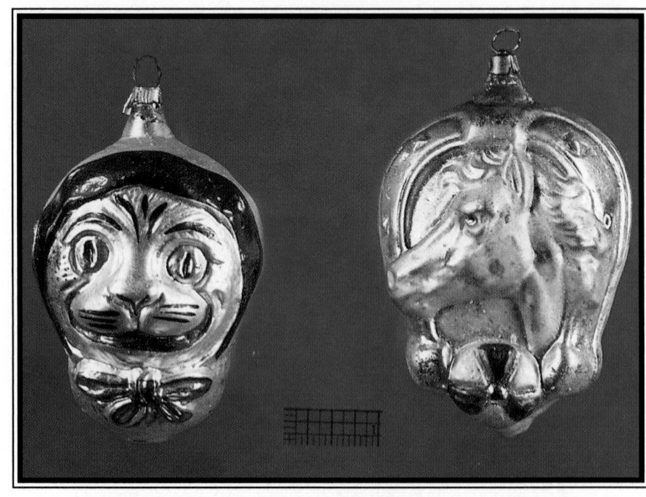

A. Cat in a Bonnet, 3" [OP, R1]. **$300.00–375.00.** B. Horse Head in a Horseshoe (Type II), 3¼" [OP, R1]. **$200.00–275.00.**

A. Sitting Cat (Type I), approx. 3¾" & 4" (shown) [German, OP, R2]. Small, **$175.00–225.00.** Large, **$350.00–450.00.** B. Monkey, "Radio," approx. 3½" & 4½" (shown) [German, OP-NP (Radko, 1993), R2]. Small, **$150.00–175.00.** Large, **$225.00–275.00.**

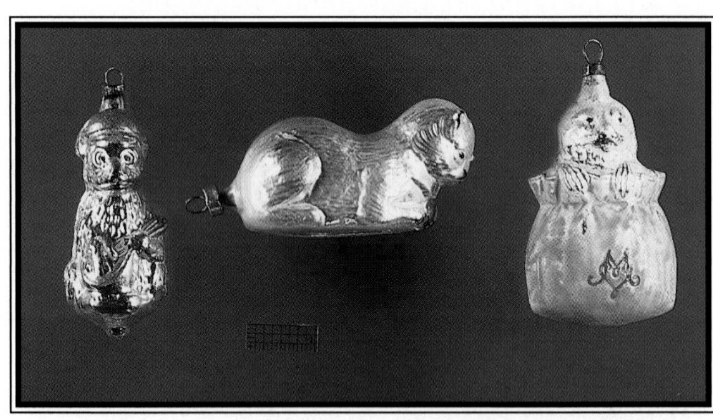

A. "Student" Cat with a Mandolin, approx. 3½" [German, OP, R2]. **$125.00–150.00.** B. Crouched Cat Playing with a Ball, approx. 3¾" [German, OP-NP (1985), R1]. **$275.00–300.00.** C. Cat in a Bag, approx. 3½" (shown) & 4" [German, OP-NP (1985), R3]. Small, **$100.00–125.00.** Large, **$150.00–175.00.**

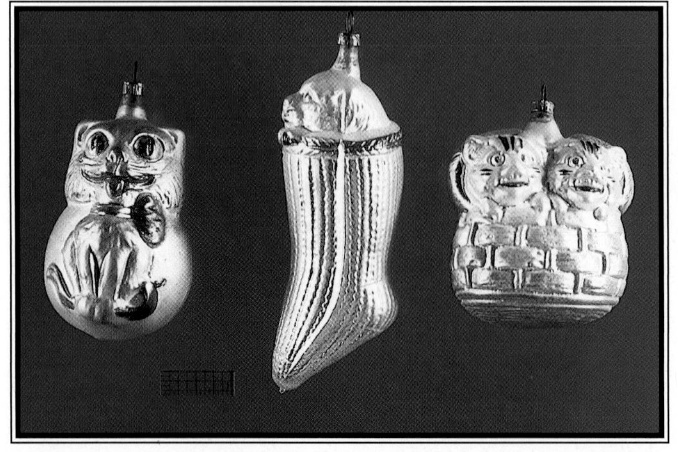

A. Roly-Poly Cat, approx. 3¼". During the 1990s it was reproduced painted orange and sold as a Halloween ornament [OP-NP (1994), R1-2]. **$200.00–250.00.** B. Cat or Dog in a Stocking, approx. 4½" [OP, R1]. **$350.00–450.00.** C. Two Kittens in a Basket, approx. 2" & 2¾" (shown) [Czech, OP-NP (1980s), R2]. Small, **$60.00–75.00.** Large, **$125.00–175.00.**

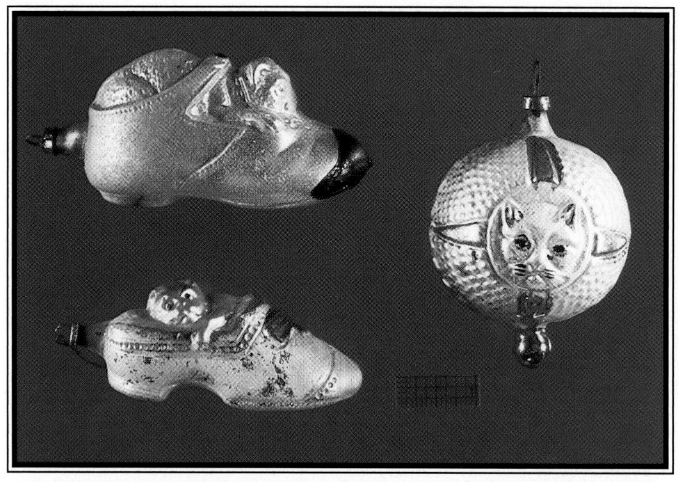

A. Cat in a Shoe, approx. 3" & 3½" (shown) [German, OP-NP (1980s – 1990s), R3]. Both sizes **$175.00–200.00.** B. Sleeping Cat in a Shoe (Type I), approx. 3½" [German, OP-NP (1990), R3]. **$100.00–150.00.** C. Cat in a "Window," approx. 2", double sided [OP, R2-3]. **$125.00–150.00.**

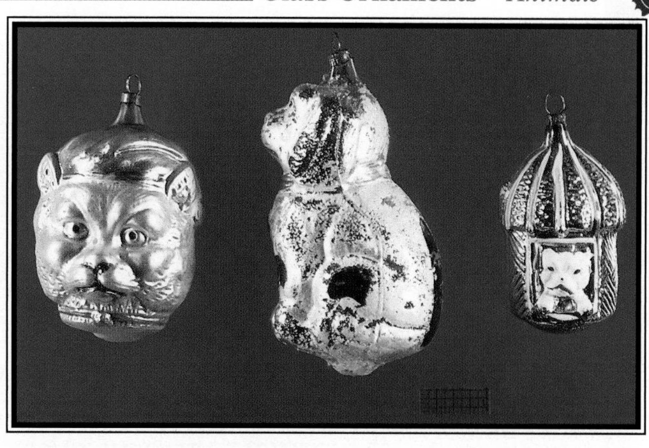

A. Cat in a Nightcap, approx. 2¼" & 3" (shown) [German, OP, R2]. Small, **$200.00–250.00.** Large, **$275.00–325.00.** B. Sitting Spaniel, approx. 2½", 3", & 4¼" (shown) [German, OP-NP (1991), R3]. Small, **$40.00–50.00.** Medium, **$75.00–100.00.** Large, **$200.00–250.00.** C. Dog in a Dog House, approx. 2½" & 3" (shown) [German, OP-NP (1990s), R2]. **$150.00–175.00.**

A. Cat with a Mandolin (Type II), 3½" [German, OP-NP (Radko, 1994), R1]. **$250.00–275.00.** B. Sitting Cat, (Type I), approx. 3¾" & 4" (shown) [German, OP, R2]. Small, **$175.00–225.00.** Large, **$350.00–450.00.**

Cat, popcorn head, 4" [OP, R1]. **$400.00–475.00.**

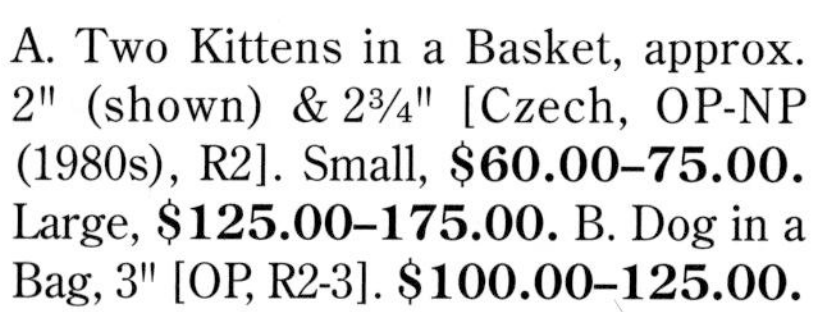

A. Two Kittens in a Basket, approx. 2" (shown) & 2¾" [Czech, OP-NP (1980s), R2]. Small, **$60.00–75.00.** Large, **$125.00–175.00.** B. Dog in a Bag, 3" [OP, R2-3]. **$100.00–125.00.**

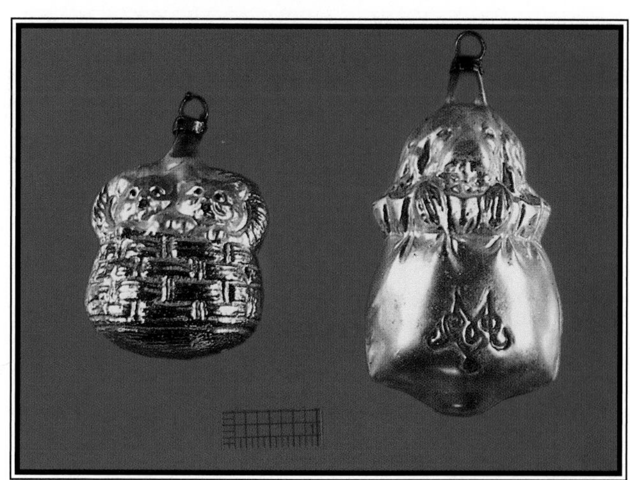

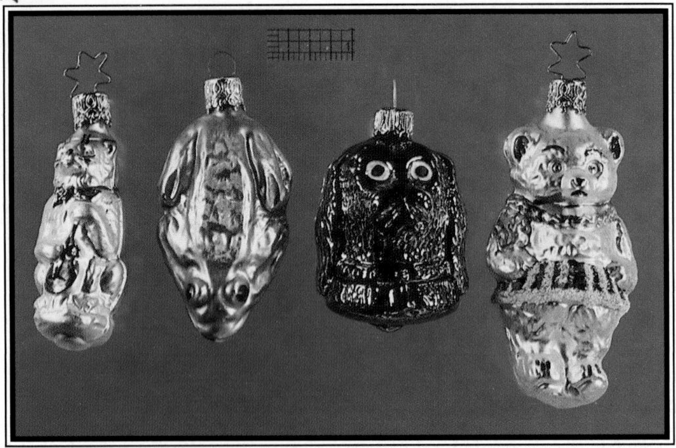

Ornament Reproductions from Antique Molds: A. Cat with a Mandolin (Type III), 2½" [OP-NP (1990s), R1]. **$10.00–15.00.** B. Flat Frog, 2½" [OP-NP (1991), R1-2]. **$10.00–15.00.** C. Spaniel Head, 2" [OP-NP (1993), R1]. **$15.00–20.00.** D. Mama Bear, Inge-glas, 3¼" [OP-NP (1990s), R1]. **$10.00–15.00.**

German Art Glass Animals, circa 1920: A. Black Cat, 2¾" [R1-2]. **$40.00–50.00.** B. Elephant, 4" [R1]. **$45.00–55.00.** C. Pheasant, 5¼" [R1-2]. **$60.00–85.00.** D. Colored Glass Horse, 3" [German, R3]. **$50.00–65.00.**

Cow Head, "Elsie," 2½" [OP, R1]. **$200.00–225.00.**

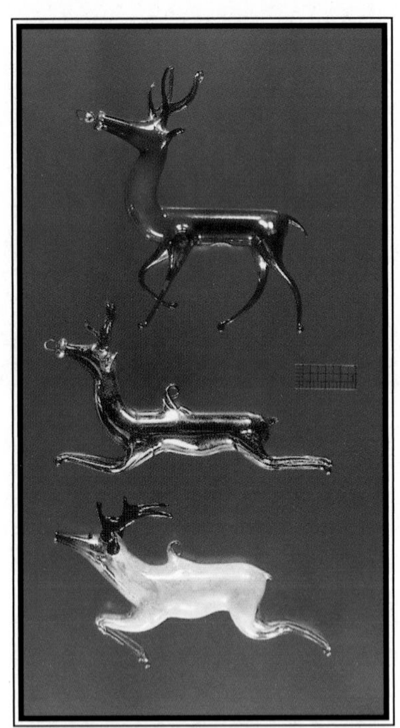

Colored Art Glass: A. Standing Blue Deer, 4" [OP, R3]. **$50.00–75.00.** B. Leaping Gold Deer, 4½" [OP, R3]. **$50.00–75.00.** C. Leaping Silver Deer, 4½" [German, OP-NP, R3]. **$50.00–60.00.**

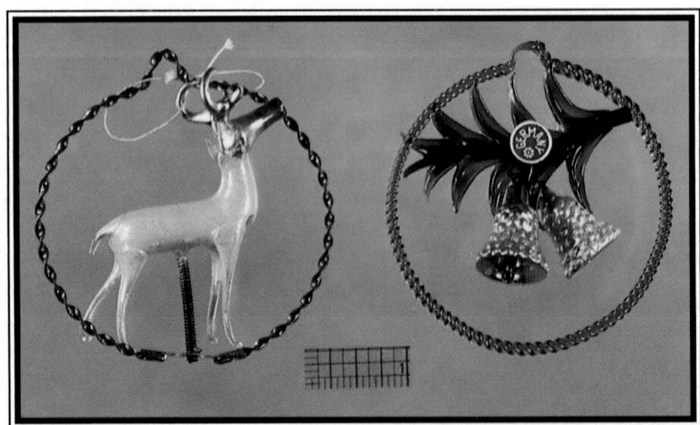

A. Deer Standing in Metal Ring, 3" [OP, R1-2]. **$45.00–55.00.** B. Bells in a Glass Ring, 3" [OP, R1-2]. **$40.00–50.00.**

A. Begging Dog in a Patriotic Hat (Type II), 2¾" glass, 3½" overall [OP, R1]. **$275.00–300.00.** B. Rabbit in an Egg, approx. 3" (shown) & 3½" [OP, R1]. Small, **$175.00–200.00.** Large, **$250.00–300.00.**

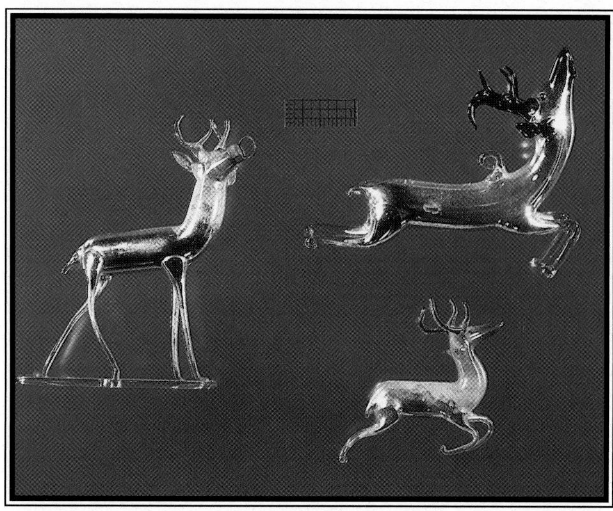

Art Glass Deer, circa 1920: A. Standing Deer, approx. 3" – 7½". Sizes vary because they are free blown, 3" – 4" (shown) are the most common [German, OP-NP (1993, Radko), R4]. Small, **$30.00–50.00.** Medium, **$50.00–100.00.** Large, **$125.00–150.00.** B & C. Leaping Deer, 3½" (shown) and 4½" (shown) are common, but sizes vary [German, OP-NP (1993), R3]. 3½", **$30.00–50.00.** 4½", **$50.00–75.00.**

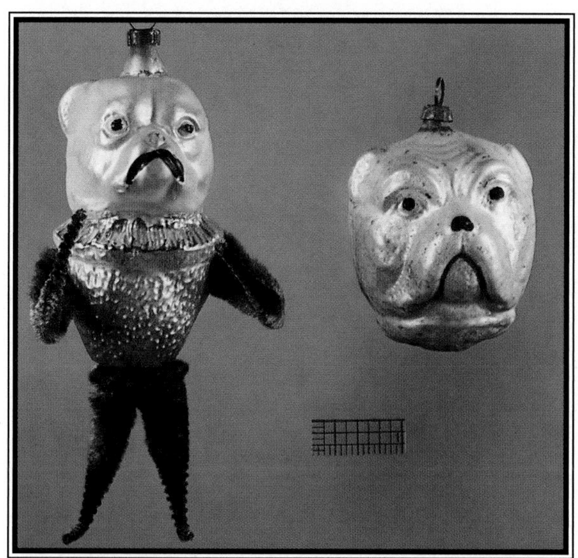

A. Bulldog with Chenille Arms and Legs, 3" glass, 4¾" overall [OP, R1]. **$450.00–550.00.** B. Bulldog Head, approx. 1½", 2¼", & 3" (shown) [German, OP, R2-3]. Small, **$125.00–150.00.** Medium, **$150.00–175.00.** Large, **$200.00–225.00.**

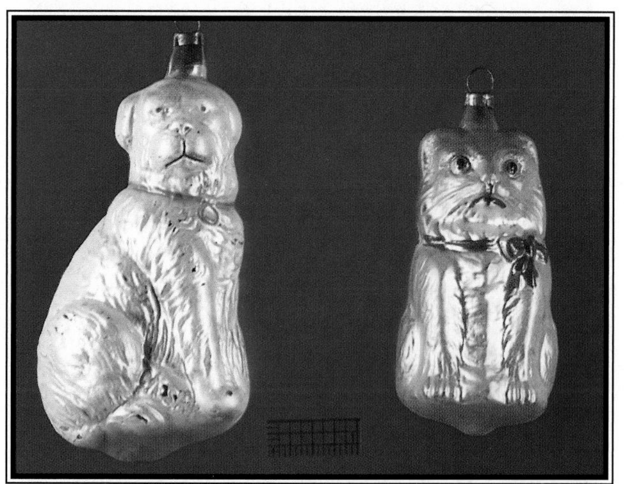

A. Dog, "Caesar," approx. 3½" & 4" (shown). "Caesar" is embossed at the feet; it was the name of Queen Victoria's dog [German, OP, R1-2]. Small, **$175.00–200.00.** Large, **$200.00–250.00.** B. Sitting Cat (Type II), 3¼" [OP, R2]. **$175.00–225.00.**

A. Mouse with a Guitar, 3" [OP, R1]. **$200.00–250.00.** B. Dog Head, double faced, 1½" [OP-NP (1995), R1]. Old, **$80.00–100.00.**

A. Dog in a Conical Hat, 4" [German, OP-NP (1950s & 1990s), R2-3]. Old, **$100.00–150.00.** 1950s, **$50.00–75.00.** B. Spaniel Head, approx. 1½" & 2" (shown) [German, OP-NP (1993), R1-2]. Small, **$90.00–110.00.** Large, **$175.00–200.00.** C. Fantasy Porpoise, approx. 4½" (shown), 5", & 6½" [German, OP-NP (1993), R1-2]. Small, **$150.00–175.00.** Medium, **$200.00–225.00.** Large, **$275.00–300.00.**

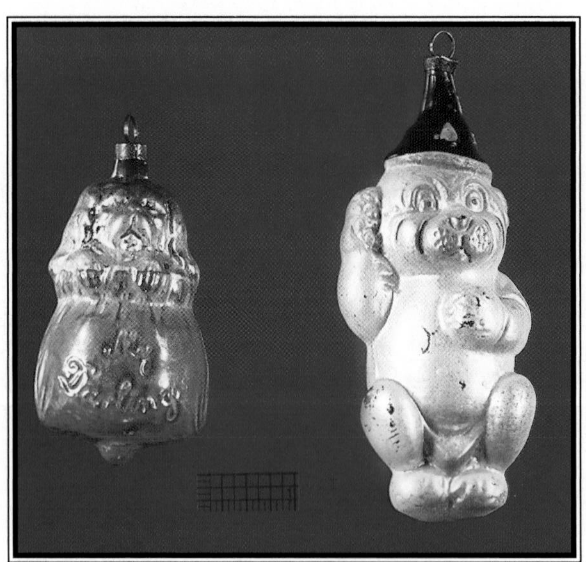

A. Dog in a Bag, "My Darling," approx. 2½", 2¾" (shown), & 3" [German, OP-NP (1970s), R3-4]. Small & medium, **$60.00–75.00.** Large, **$75.00–100.00.** B. Dog in a Conical Hat, 4" [German, OP-NP (1950 & 1990s), R2-3]. Old (shown), **$100.00–150.00.** 1950s, **$50.00–75.00.**

Sitting Dog, "Poor Poochie," 3¼" [OP, R1+]. **$350.00–400.00.**

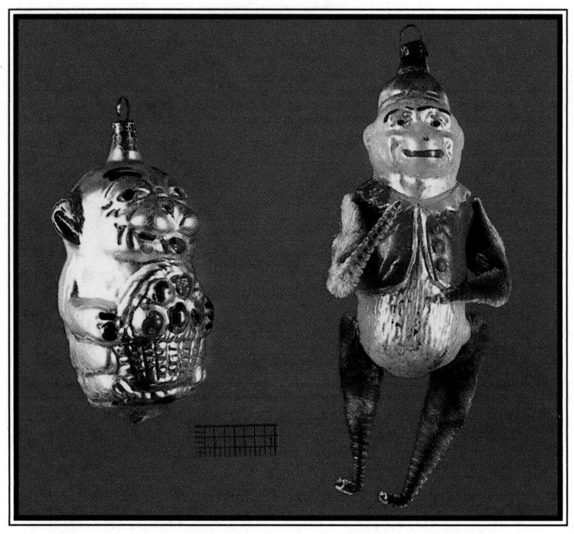

A. Comic Begging Dog with a Basket, approx. 3" (shown) & 4¾" [German, OP-NP (1991), R1-2]. Small, **$175.00–200.00.** Large, **$225.00–275.00.** B. Monkey with Chenille Arms and Legs, 3½" glass, 5½" overall [OP, R1]. **$500.00–600.00.**

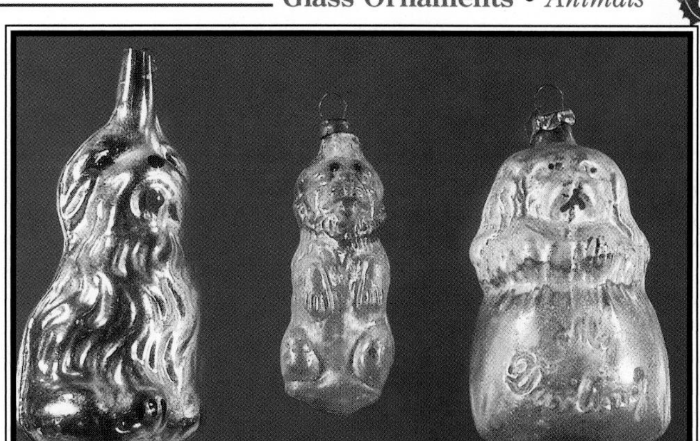

A. Sitting Sheepdog, 3" [OP, R2]. **$50.00–75.00.** B. Begging Lion, 2½" [OP-NP (1991), R1-2]. **$70.00–80.00.** C. Dog in a Bag, "My Darling"; 2½", 2¾", & 3" (shown) [German, OP-NP (1970s), R4]. Large, **$75.00–100.00.**

Free-blown and Annealed Milk Glass Animals, all German, circa 1925: A. Cat, approx. 3" [R2]. **$40.00–60.00.** B & C. Whippets, approx. 3" [R2]. **$40.00–60.00.** D. Swan, approx. 2¾" [R2-3]. **$30.00–40.00.**

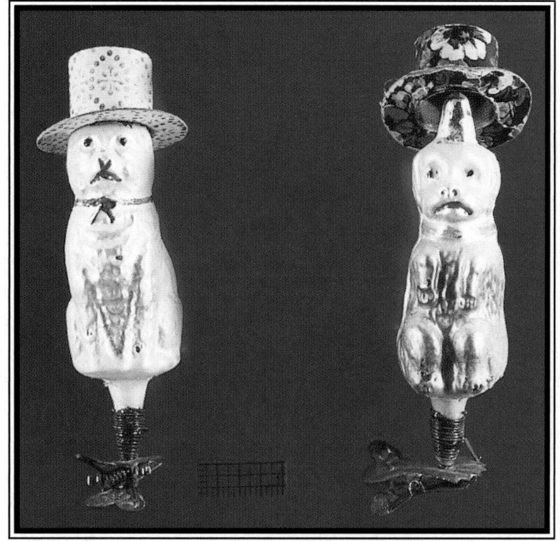

Cat and Dog with Cardboard Hats [both German, OP, R1]: A. Cat, approx. 3½". **$275.00–300.00.** B. Dog, 3½". **$275.00–300.00.**

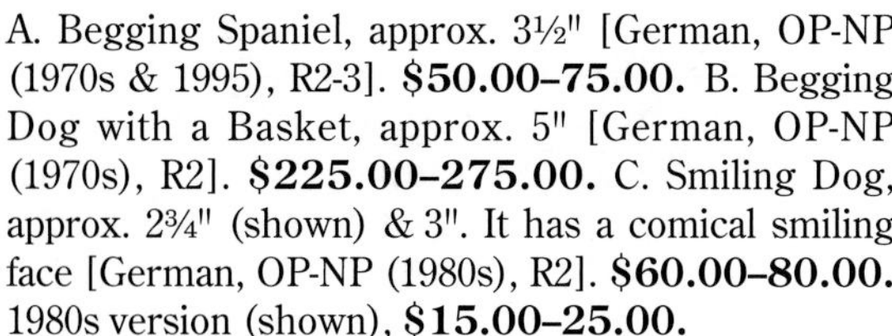

A. Begging Spaniel, approx. 3½" [German, OP-NP (1970s & 1995), R2-3]. **$50.00–75.00.** B. Begging Dog with a Basket, approx. 5" [German, OP-NP (1970s), R2]. **$225.00–275.00.** C. Smiling Dog, approx. 2¾" (shown) & 3". It has a comical smiling face [German, OP-NP (1980s), R2]. **$60.00–80.00.** 1980s version (shown), **$15.00–25.00.**

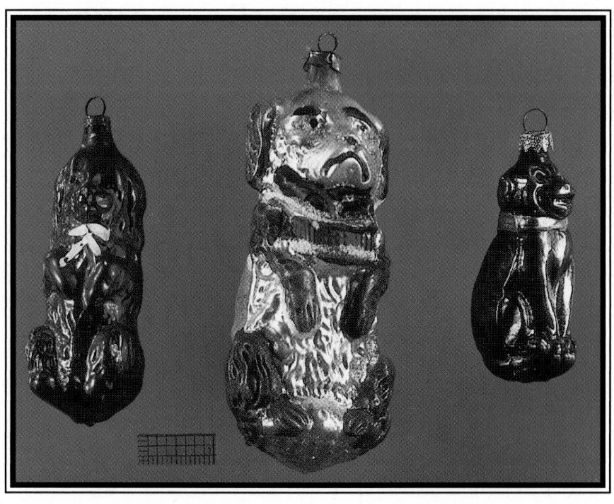

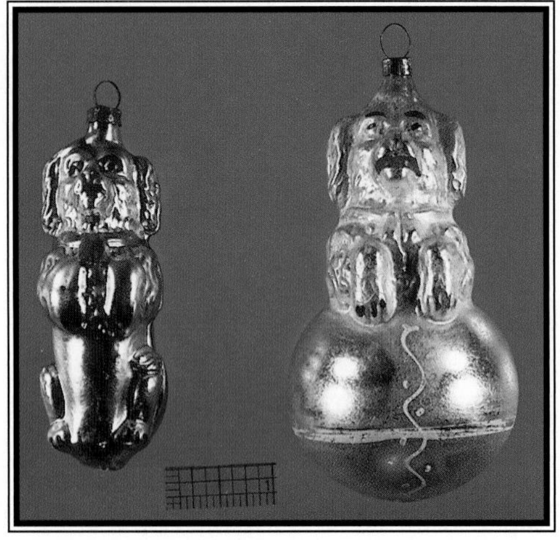

A. Begging Dog (Type I), approx. 3". This mold was used to make the Dog in a Ball [OP-NP (1980s), R2]. **$80.00–90.00.** B. Begging Dog in a Ball, approx. 3½" – 4", size varies with ball [OP-NP (1950s), R3-4]. **$100.00–125.00.**

A. Dog Blowing a Horn, approx. 3" & 3½" (shown) [German, OP-NP (1991), R2]. Small, **$130.00–150.00.** Large, **$200.00–250.00.** B & C. Sitting Spaniels, approx. 2½" (shown), 3" (shown), & 4" [German, OP-NP (1991), R3]. Small, **$40.00–50.00.** Medium, **$75.00–100.00.** Large, **$200.00–250.00.**

Cigar Smoking Dog (cigar is missing), approx. 4¾". He is Bozo from the comic strip by George Studdy. [OP (circa 1915), R1]. **$325.00–400.00.**

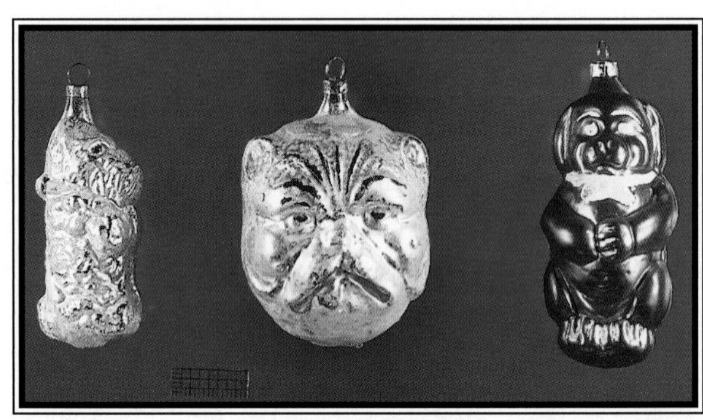

A. Scotty Dog, approx. 3" (shown) & 3½" [German, OP, R2-3]. Small, **$70.00–90.00.** Large, **$100.00–125.00.** B. Bulldog Head, approx. 3" [Germany, OP-NP (1970s), R1-2]. **$200.00–225.00.** C. Standing Dog, approx. 4" [German, OP-NP (1960s & 1970s), R2]. **$100.00–125.00.** 1970s version (shown), **$20.00–25.00.**

A. Elf on a Stump, embossed, approx. 2½" [German, OP-NP (1970s, 1980s, & 1990s), R3]. **$50.00–75.00.** 1970s–1990s version, **$20.00–30.00.** B. Begging Dog (Type II), approx. 2¾" & 3½" (shown) [OP, R2]. Small, **$75.00–100.00.** Large, **$100.00–125.00.**

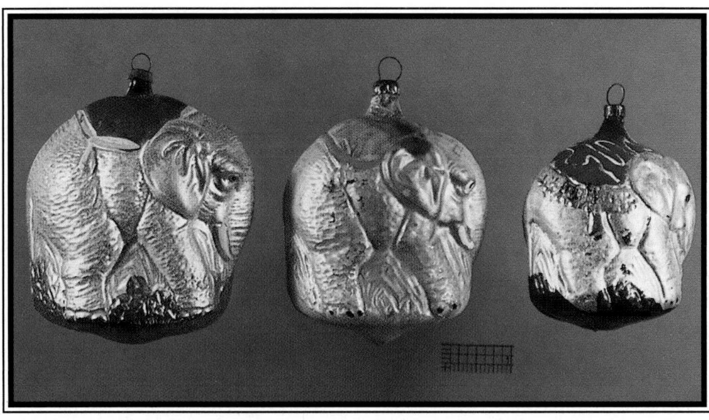

A & B. Walking Elephants, standard form, approx. 2½", 2¾" (shown), 3", 3¼" (shown), & 3¾" [German, OP-NP (1980s – 1990s), R2-3]. Small, **$75.00–90.00.** Medium, **$90.00–110.00.** Large, **$125.00–150.00.** C. Elephant with a Fringed Blanket, approx. 2½" & 2¾" (shown) [German, OP-NP (1991, small only), R2-3]. Both sizes **$75.00–90.00.**

Rare Elephant with Howdah on Its Back, 4¾" [OP, R1+]. **$650.00–750.00.**

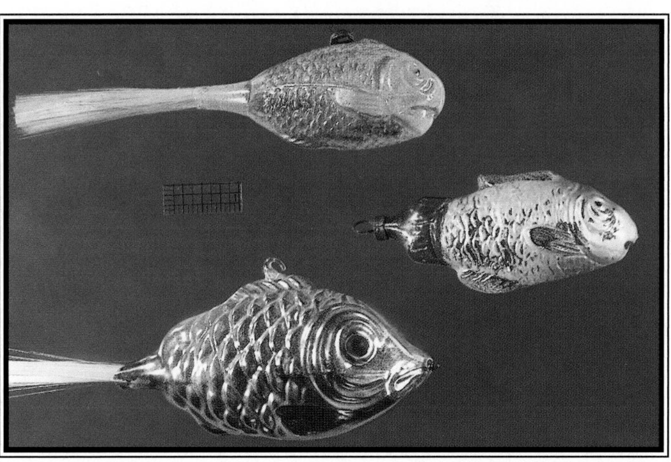

A, B, D, E. All Variations of Standard Form Fish, sizes for the glass body can vary from 2" to 6". Sizes shown: 3½", 3", & 2¾" [German, Czech, Austrian, & Japanese; OP-NP (continuing), R4]. Small, **$15.00–25.00.** Medium, **$25.00–35.00.** Large (4"), **$40.00–75.00.** C. Fish with a Curved Body, approx. 3½" & 4" (shown) [OP-NP (1970s, small only), R3]. Small, **$40.00–60.00.** Large, **$75.00–100.00.**

Three Variations of the Standard Form Fish: 3", 3¼", & 4½" [OP-NP (1950s & 1990s), R3-4]. Small, **$15.00–25.00.** Medium (all shown are medium), **$25.00–35.00.** Large, **$40.00–75.00.**

A. Russian Bear with an Accordion, 2¾" [OP-NP, R3]. **$45.00–50.00.** B. Fish with an Embossed Tail, 3" [OP, R1-2]. **$50.00–75.00.**

Fish with Embossed Waves, approx. 4½" [OP, R3]. **$60.00–75.00.**

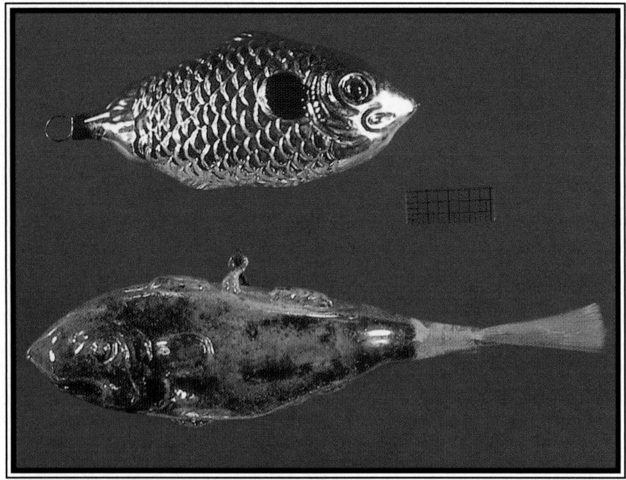

A. Fish, standard form, medium. **$25.00–35.00.** B. Shark, approx. 4½" [German, OP-NP (Radko, 1995), R2-3]. **$100.00–125.00.**

A & B. Fish, standard form, 4½" & 4" [OP-NP, R4]. Both shown are large. **$40.00–60.00.** C. Clamshell, approx. 2" [OP-NP (1970s), R3]. **$25.00–35.00.** D. Lobster, approx. 3¼" (shown) & 3¾" [German, OP-NP (1970s, small; 1991, large), R1]. Old, **$200.00–225.00.** 1970s version (shown), **$25.00–35.00.**

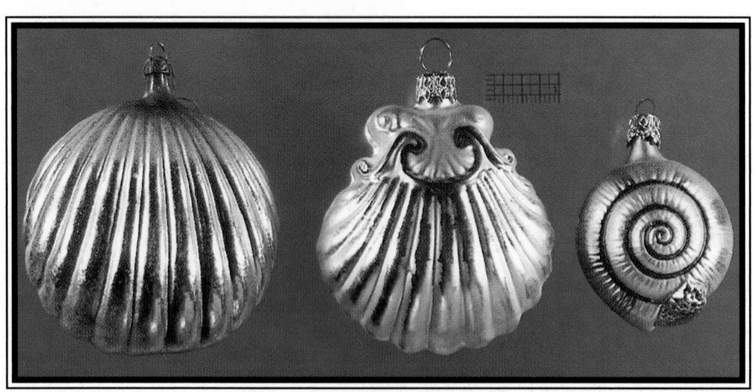

A. Large Shell, 3" [OP, R2]. **$40.00–50.00.** B. Shell, stylized, approx. 3" & 3¼" (shown) [German, Polish, Chinese; OP-NP (1990s), R2]. Old, **$40.00–50.00.** 1990s version (shown), **$8.00–10.00.** C. Shell with a Snail, approx. 2¼" [German, OP-NP (1980s & 1991), R1]. Old, **$100.00–125.00.** 1980s version (shown), **$8.00–15.00.**

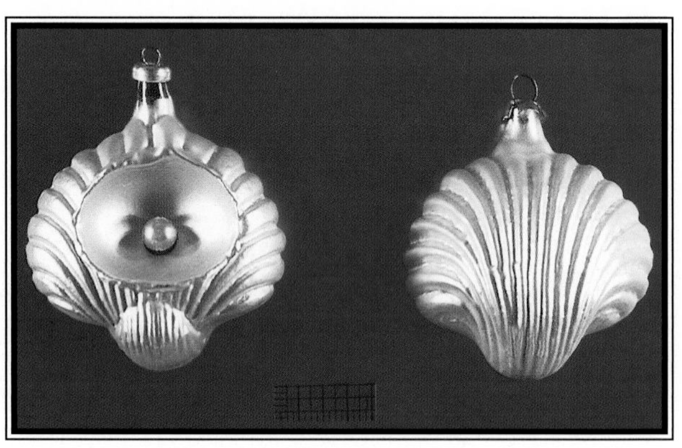

Two Views of an Oyster Shell with a Pearl, approx. 2½" [NP (Italian, 1950s), R2-3]. **$75.00–90.00.**

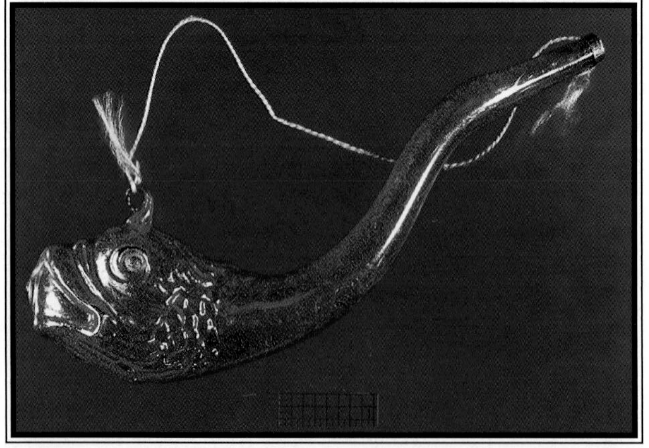

Fantasy Porpoise, large, approx. 4½", 5", & 6½" (shown) [OP-NP (1993), R2]. Small, **$150.00–175.00.** Medium, **$200.00–225.00.** Large, **$275.00–300.00.**

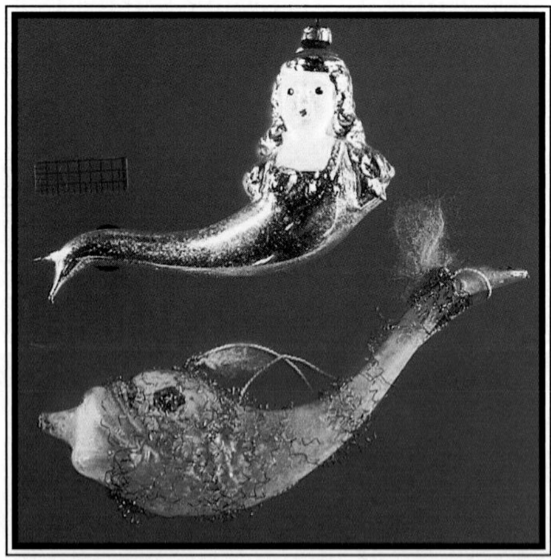

A. Goldilocks Mermaid, approx. 4" [Germany, OP, R1]. **$225.00–300.00.** B. Early Wire-wrapped Porpoise, approx. 4½", 5", & 6½". Sizes may vary because of the free-blown tail; may be silvered or unsilvered [German, OP-NP (1993), R2]. Small, **$150.00–175.00.** Medium, **$200.00–225.00.** Large, **$275.00–300.00.**

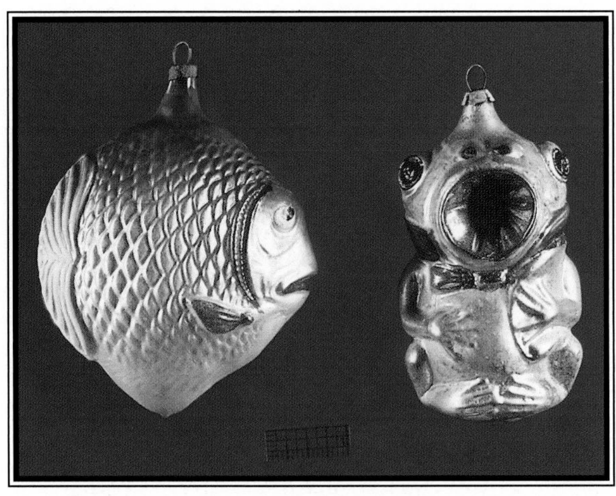

A. Angel Fish, approx. 2½", 3½", & 4½" (shown) [OP-NP (1990s), R2-3]. Small, **$100.00–125.00.** Medium, **$150.00–175.00.** Large, **$200.00–225.00.** B. Singing Frog, approx. 2¾" & 3½" (shown) [OP, R2]. Small, **$125.00–150.00.** Large, **$150.00–185.00.**

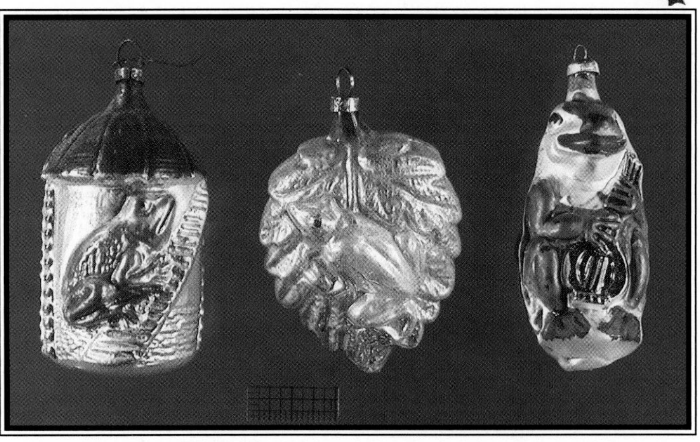

A. Frog Climbing a Ladder (Type I), embossed, 3" [German, OP-NP (1980s), R1-2]. Old, **$90.00–100.00.** B. Frog on Leaves, 2¾" [OP, R2-3]. **$35.00–50.00.** C. Frog with a Banjo (Type II), 2¾" [German, OP-NP (1980s & 1990s), R1-2]. Old, **$90.00–115.00.** 1980s (shown), **$10.00–20.00.**

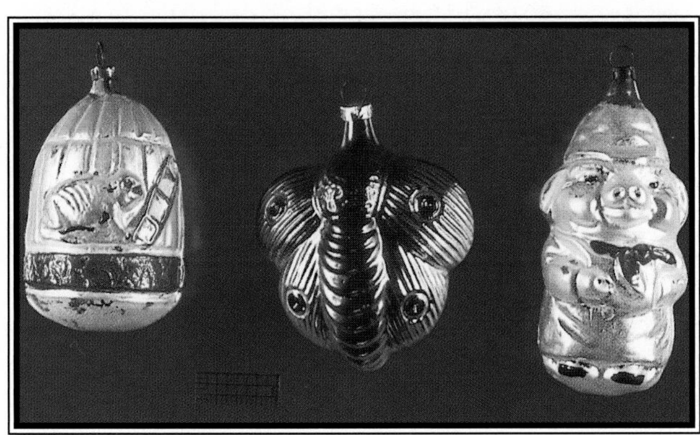

A. Frog Climbing a Ladder (Type II), 2¼" [OP, R2]. **$80.00–90.00.** B. Moth, embossed, approx. 2¼" & 2¾" (shown) [OP-NP (1950s – 1960s, & 1995), R3]. Small, **$20.00–25.00.** Large, **$25.00–35.00.** Large 1950s version (shown), **$25.00–35.00.** C. Builder pig, 3¼" & 3½" [OP, R2]. **$200.00–225.00.**

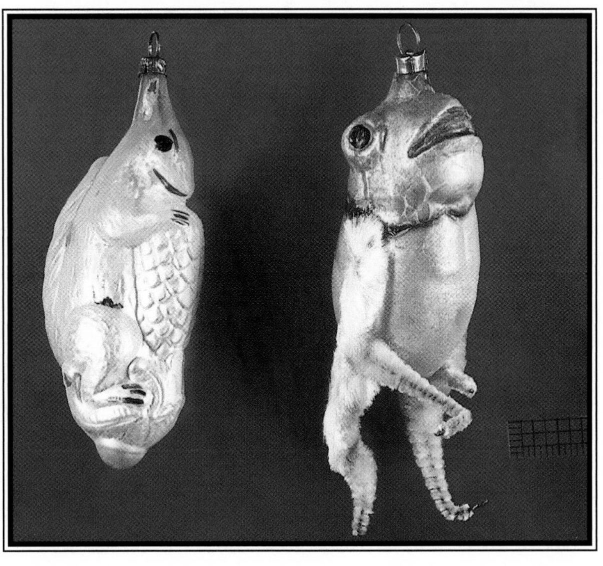

A. Squirrel with a Pine Cone, 4½" [OP, R1-2], **$175.00–225.00.** B. Frog with Chenille Arms and Legs, 3¼" glass, 5" overall [OP, R1+]. **$650.00–800.00.**

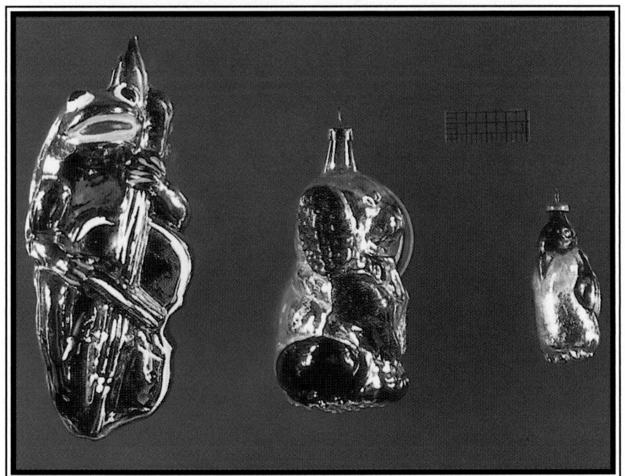

A. Frog Playing a Bass Violin, approx. 4¼" (shown) & 5" [NP (1940s – 1950s), R2]. **$45.00–65.00.** B. Sitting Spaniel with Bumps, approx. 2½". A bumpy pattern on the base & ears shows this to be a 1950s piece [R3]. **$35.00–45.00.** C. Miniature Penguin, 1¾" [OP, R2]. **$25.00–35.00.**

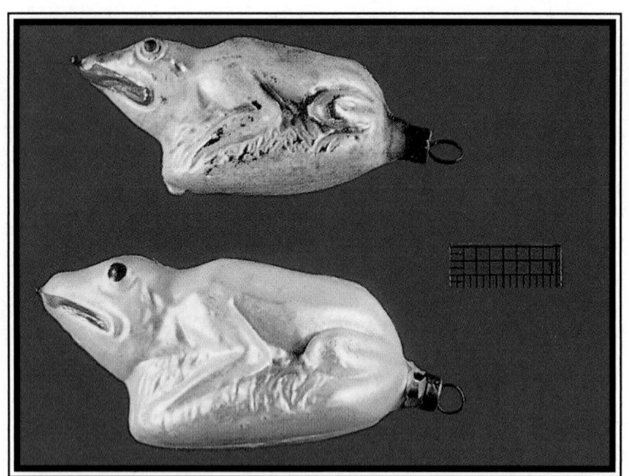

A & B. Hopping Frogs, approx. 2¾", 3" (shown), & 3½" (shown) [OP-NP (1990s, large only), R2-3]. Small, **$60.00–70.00.** Medium, **$75.00–100.00.** Large, **$125.00–150.00.**

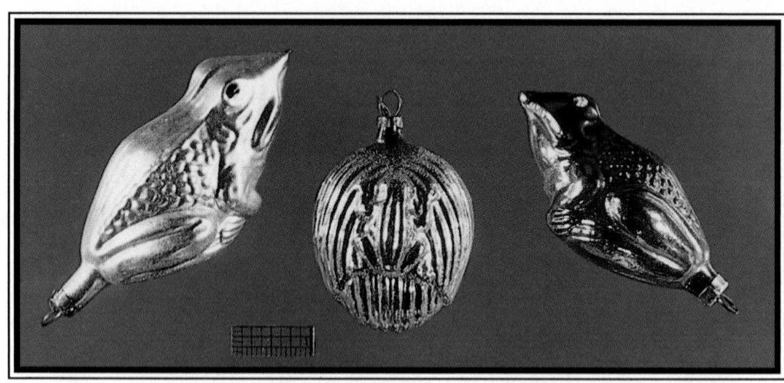

A & C. Frogs, approx. 2½", 2¾", 3" (shown), 3½", & 4" (shown) [German, OP-NP (1950s, 1970s, & 1990s), R3]. Small, **$30.00–40.00.** Medium, **$40.00–50.00.** Large, **$50.00–60.00.** B. Frog on a Leaf, sometimes called a Frog on a Tulip, approx. 2½" [German, OP-NP (1991), R2-3]. **$50.00–75.00.**

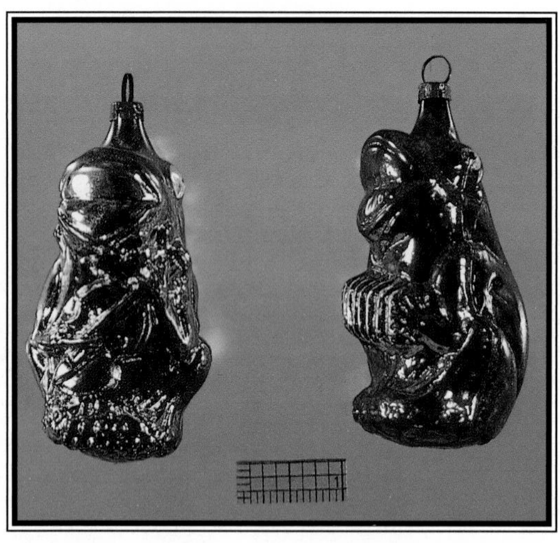

A. Frog Playing a Violin, approx. 2¾" [OP, R2]. **$125.00–175.00.** B. Frog Playing a Concertina, approx. 2¾" [OP, R2]. **$125.00–175.00.**

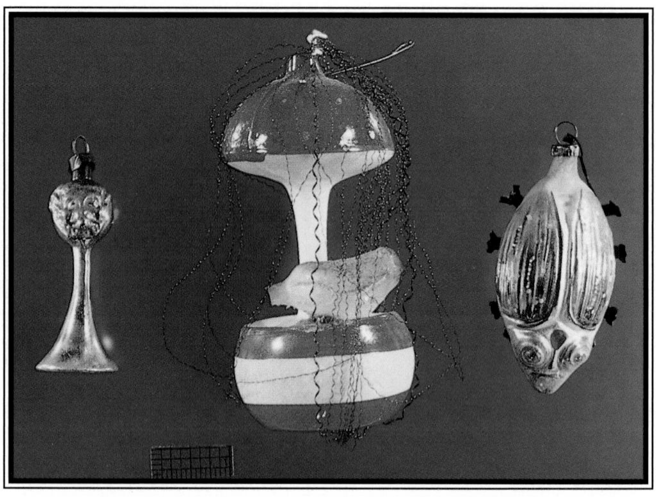

A. Horn with Cat and Dog Heads, one face on each side, approx. 2½" [OP, R1]. **$175.00–200.00.** B. Frog Under a Mushroom, approx. 4" [OP, R1]. **$200.00–225.00.** C. Beetle with Paper Legs, approx. 3" [OP, R2]. **$90.00–100.00.**

Rearing Horse on a Disk, mid-to-late 1930s; this style is sometimes called a Nazi ornament [OP, R1-2]. **$90.00–110.00.**

Reverse of disk.

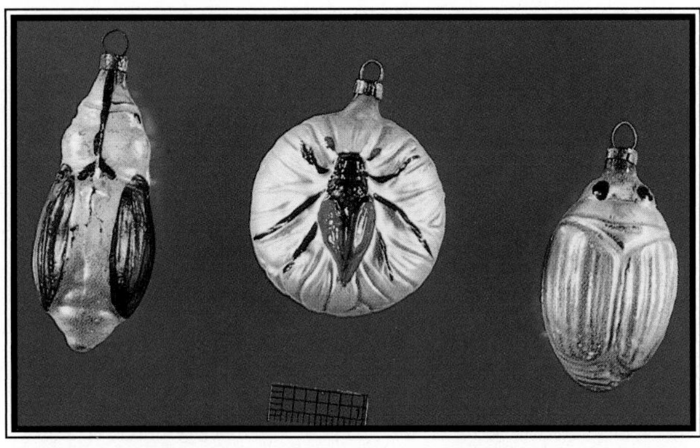

A. Beetle (Type II), approx. 2¾" [OP, R2]. **$65.00–75.00.** B. Bee on a Flower, approx. 2". It has mistakenly been called a Spider in a Web [OP, R3]. **$150.00–175.00.** C. Beetle (Type I), approx. 2", 2¼" (shown), & 3" [OP-NP (Inge-glas, 1990s), R3]. **$55.00–65.00.**

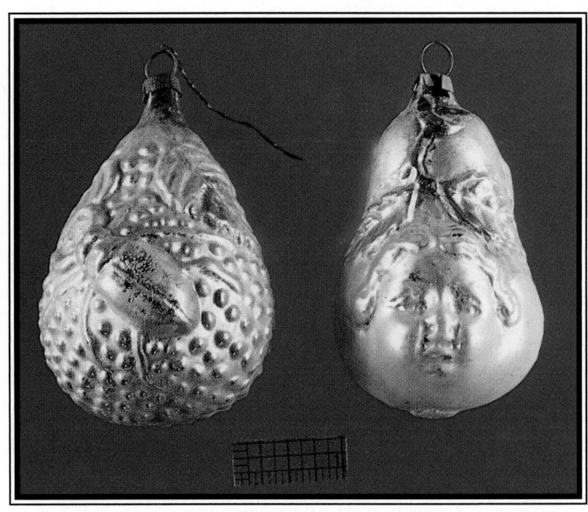

A. Beetle on a Pear, approx. 3" [OP, R2]. **$150.00–175.00.** B. Girl's Head on a Pear, approx. 3" [German, OP-NP (1970s), R1-2]. **$175.00–200.00.**

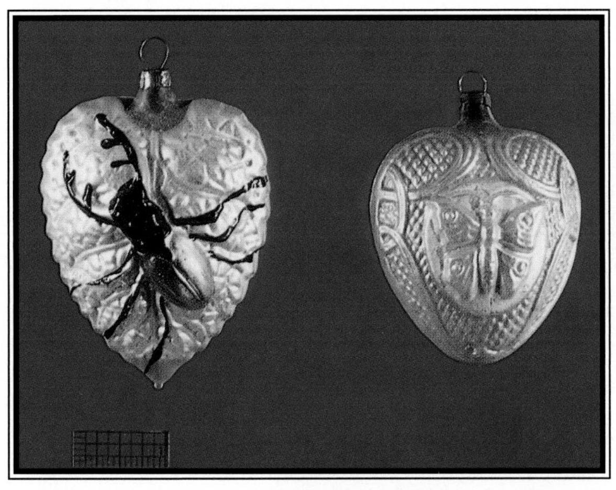

A. Beetle on a Leaf, 3" [OP, R2]. **$175.00–200.00.** B. Butterfly on a Victorian Heart, 2½" [German, OP-NP (1990s), R2]. **$30.00–40.00.**

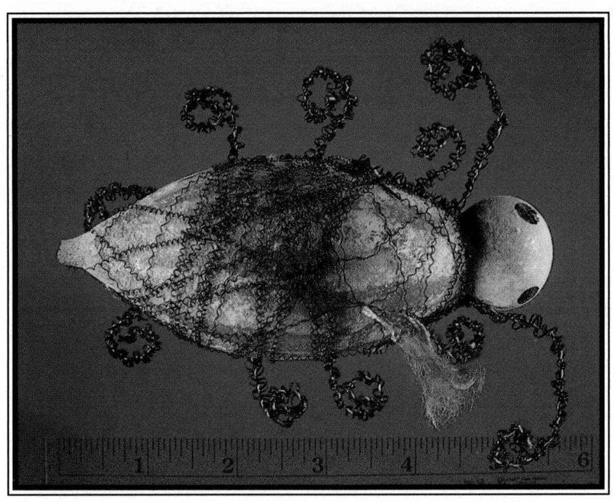

Beetle, free-blown, 5½" [OP, R1]. **$275.00–300.00.**

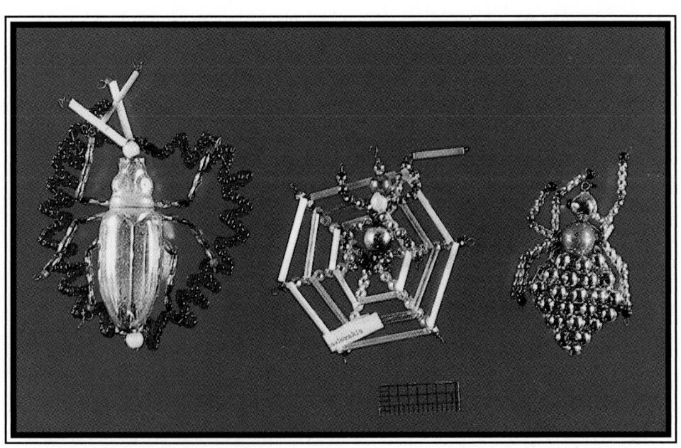

Three Czechoslovakian Beaded Ornaments: A. Beetle in a Beaded Ring, 3½" [Czech, OP, R2]. **$40.00–55.00.** B. Spider in a Web, beaded, 2¾" [Czech, OP, R2]. **$30.00–40.00.** C. Spider, beaded, 2½" [OP, R2]. **$15.00–25.00.**

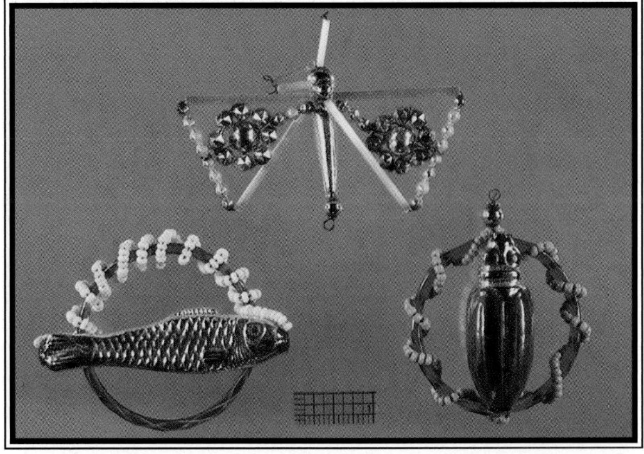

Three Czech Beaded Ornaments: A. Butterfly, beaded, large, 3½" [OP, R2]. **$20.00–30.00.** B. Fish on a Ring, beaded, 3" dia. [OP, R1-2]. **$40.00–55.00.** C. Beetle on a Glass Ring, 2¼" dia. [Czech, OP, R1-2]. **$40.00–55.00.**

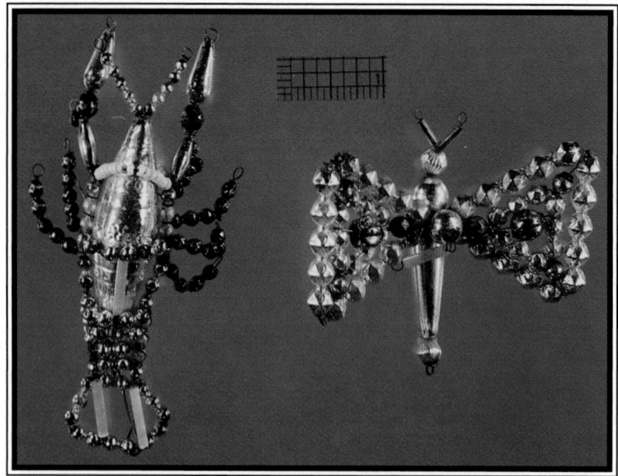

A. Lobster/Crayfish, beaded, approx. 3¾" (shown) & 4½" [Czech, OP-R2]. Small, **$50.00–60.00.** Large, **$60.00–75.00.** B. Butterfly, beaded, small, 2¾" [OP, R2]. **$20.00–30.00.**

Three sizes of Moths with beautiful SG wings, approx. 2", 2½", & 3¼" body sizes, overall size may vary with the size of the wings. Moths/Butterflies with unpainted wings are worth less than those with painted wings. These have mistakenly been called Butterflies [OP-NP (1990s), R2-3]: Small, **$125.00–150.00.** Medium, **$150.00–175.00.** Large, **$175.00–225.00.**

A & B. Two Butterflies with SG wings, art glass bodies, 1¾" & 3½", wing span 5¼" & 5½" [German, OP-NP (1990s), R2-3]. Old, **$100.00–125.00.** C. Moth with SG wings, larger, 3¼" body [OP-NP, R2-3]. **$150.00–175.00.**

Moth with SG wings, 2½" body, rarer clip-on version [OP-NP (1990s), R2-3]. **$175.00–225.00.**

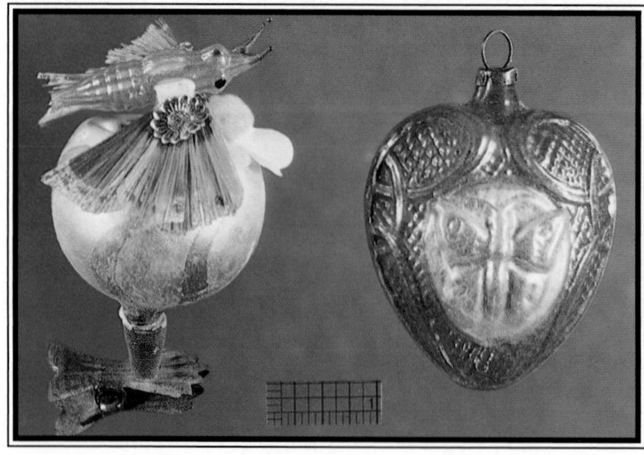

A. Butterfly and a Flower, approx. 2½" [OP, R1]. **$200.00–250.00.** B. Butterfly on a Victorian Heart, 2½" [German, OP-NP (1990s), R2]. **$30.00–40.00.**

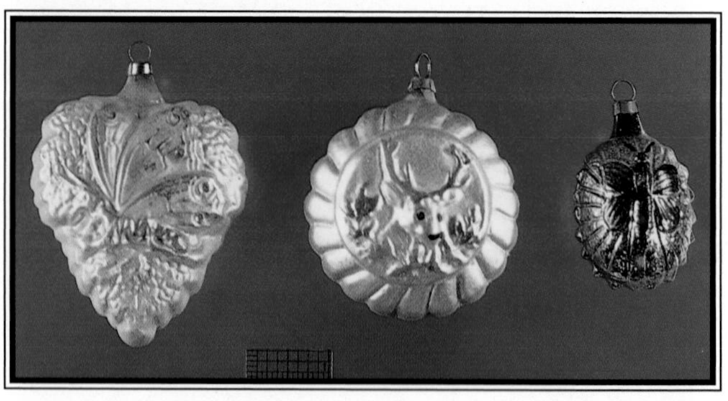

A. Butterfly on a Leaf, embossed, approx. 3" (shown) & 3½" [German, OP-NP (Inge-glas, Radko, & Lauscha Glas; 1993 – 1995), R2-3]. Old, **$80.00–90.00.** B. Deer Head on a Disk, 2½" [German, OP, R2-3]. **$50.00–75.00.** C. Butterfly, embossed onto an oval, 1¾" [German, OP-NP (1980s – 1990s), R3-4]. Old, **$25.00–35.00.**

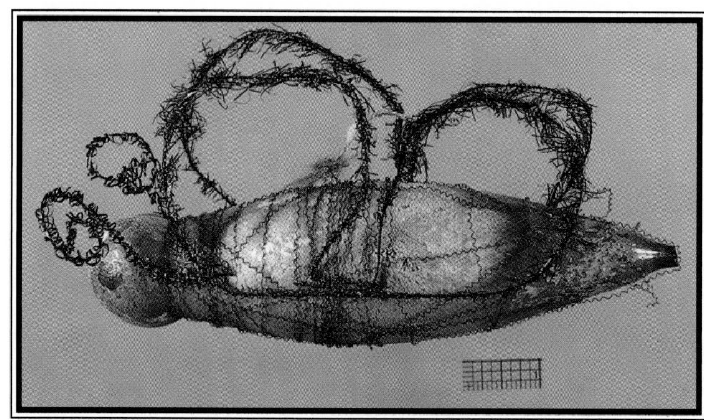

Butterfly, free-blown, large, 7¼" [OP, R1]. **$275.00–325.00.**

Dragonfly, approx. 6½" [OP, R1+]. **$275.00–300.00.**

A. Spider in a Web (Type I), approx. 4½" [OP, R1-2]. **$100.00–125.00.** B. Spider in a Web (Type II), approx. 5½" [OP, R1-2]. **$125.00–150.00.**

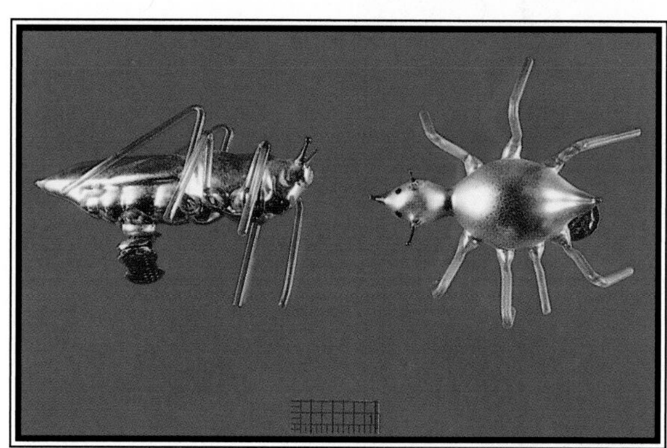

A. Grasshopper, 3" [Italian, NP (1950s), R2-3]. **$75.00–100.00.** B. Spider with Annealed Legs, 2¾" [Italian, NP (1950s), R2-3]. **$60.00–80.00.**

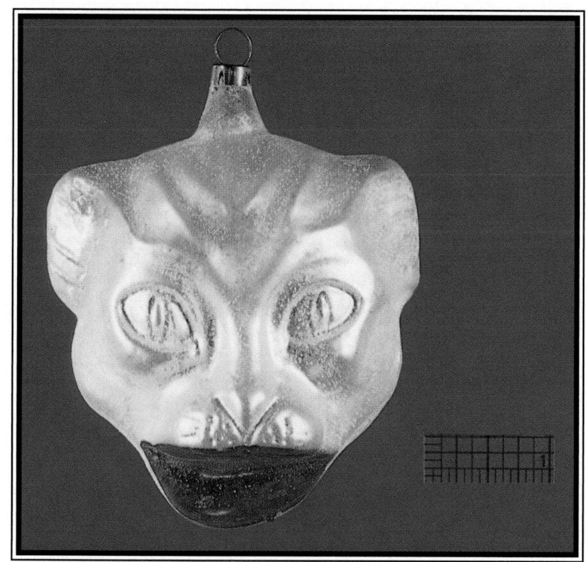

Leopard Head, approx. 2¾" [OP, R1]. **$400.00–500.00.**

A. Lion Head (Type I), 2¾" [OP, R1]. **$375.00–450.00.** B. "Teddy" Lion, 2½", name embossed on rim under lion's chin [OP, R1-2]. **$325.00–400.00.**

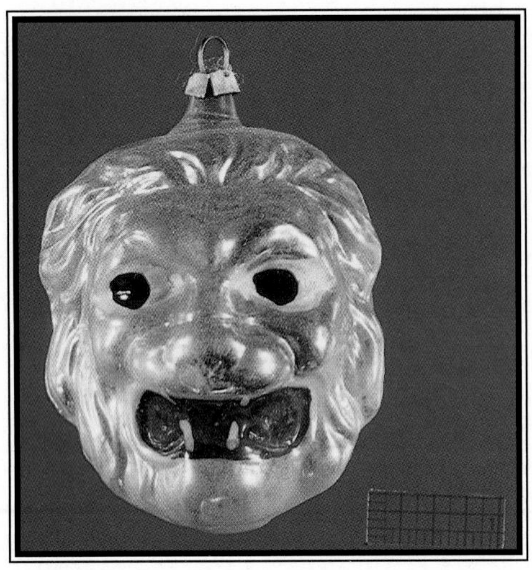

Roaring Lion Head, approx. 2½" & 3" (shown) [OP, R2]. Small, **$175.00–200.00.** Large, **$250.00–275.00.**

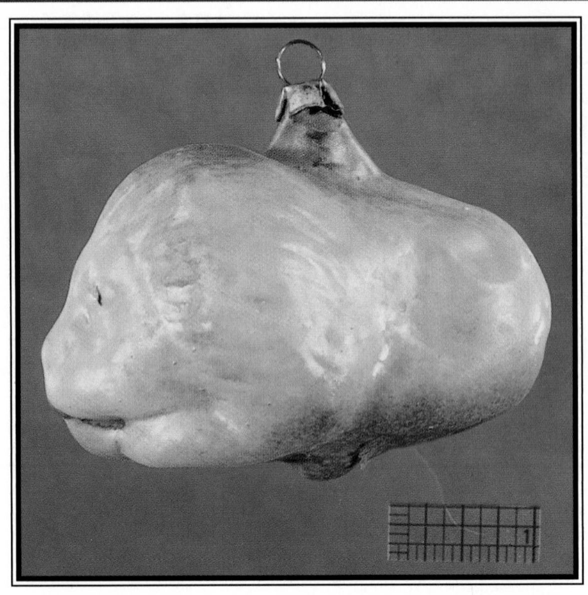

Crouching Lion, approx. 3¼" [OP, R1+]. **$500.00–600.00.**

Sitting Lion, 3¼" [OP, R1]. **$325.00–375.00.**

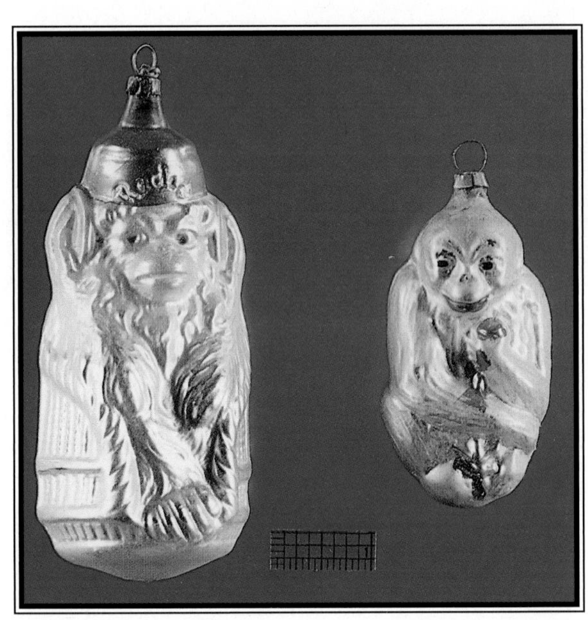

A. Monkey, "Radio," approx. 3½" & 4½" (shown) [German, OP-NP (Radko, 1993), R2]. Small, **$125.00–150.00.** Large, **$200.00–225.00.** B. Monkey with a Vine, approx. 2¾" & 3¼" (shown) [German, OP, R2]. Small, **$120.00–140.00.** Large, **$175.00–200.00.**

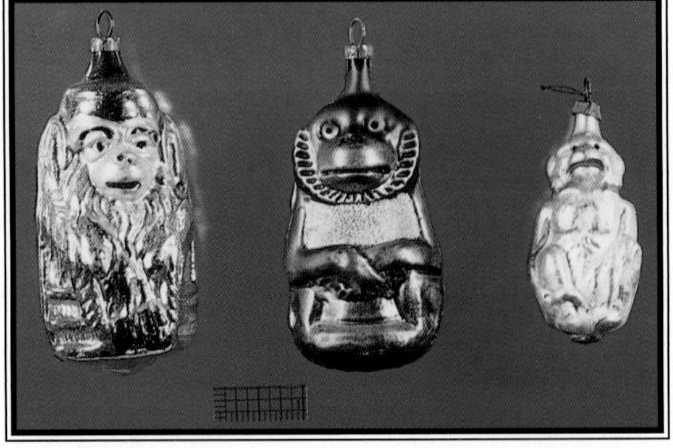

A. Monkey, "Radio," approx. 3½" (shown) & 4½" [German, OP-NP (Radko, 1993), R2]. Small, **$125.00–150.00.** Large, **$200.00–225.00.** B. Monkey with a Fur Ruffle, approx. 3" [German, OP-NP (1980s), R1] **$125.00–150.00.** C. Squatting Monkey, approx. 2½" [German, OP-NP (late 1980s), R1-2]. **$100.00–125.00.**

Monkey in a Clown Suit, approx. 3" [OP, R1+]. **$300.00–350.00.**

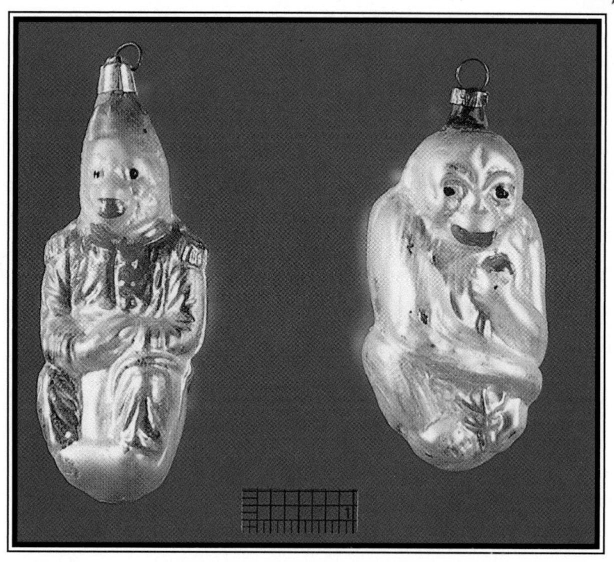

A. Monkey in Drum Major Outfit, 3¼" [OP, R1]. **$350.00–425.00.** B. Monkey Holding a Vine, approx. 2¾" (shown) & 3¼" [German, OP, R2]. Small, **$120.00–140.00.** Large, **$175.00–200.00.**

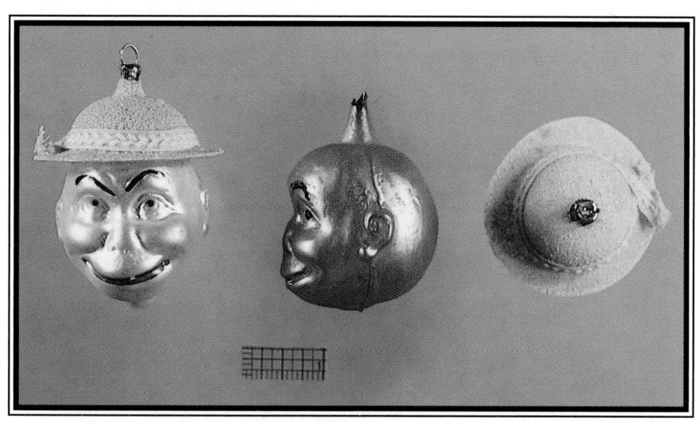

A. Monkey Head with Glass Hat, 2½" [OP, R1]. **$350.00–450.00.** B. Same piece separated.

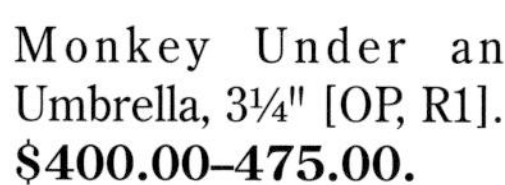

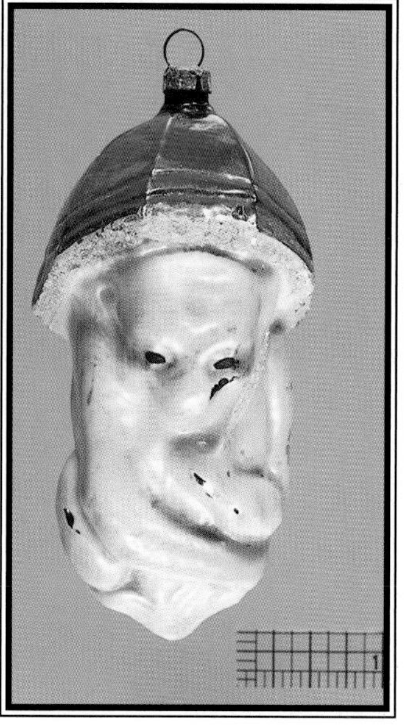

Monkey Under an Umbrella, 3¼" [OP, R1]. **$400.00–475.00.**

Mouse, 3", circa 1890 [R1]. **$350.00–450.00.**

Mickey Mouse, 3½" [German, OP-NP (1980s), R1]. Old, **$350.00–400.00.**

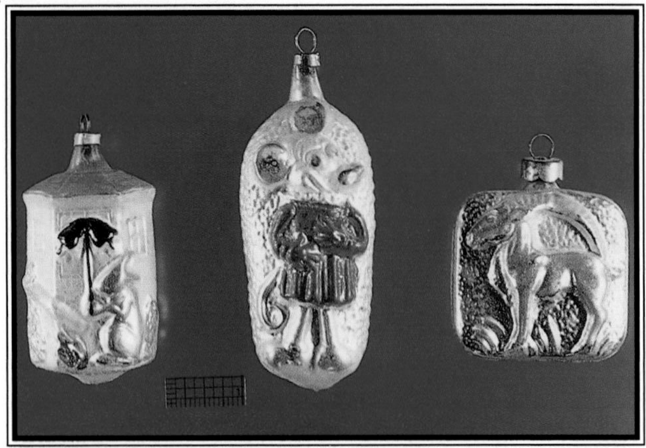

A. Rabbit with an Umbrella, embossed onto a six-sided house, approx. 3" [German, OP-NP (Inge-Glas, 1993), R2]. **$50.00–75.00.** B. Minnie Mouse, embossed, approx. 3½" [German, OP, R1-2]. **$300.00–375.00.** C. Antelope, embossed onto a square, approx. 2" [OP, R1-2]. **$60.00–85.00.**

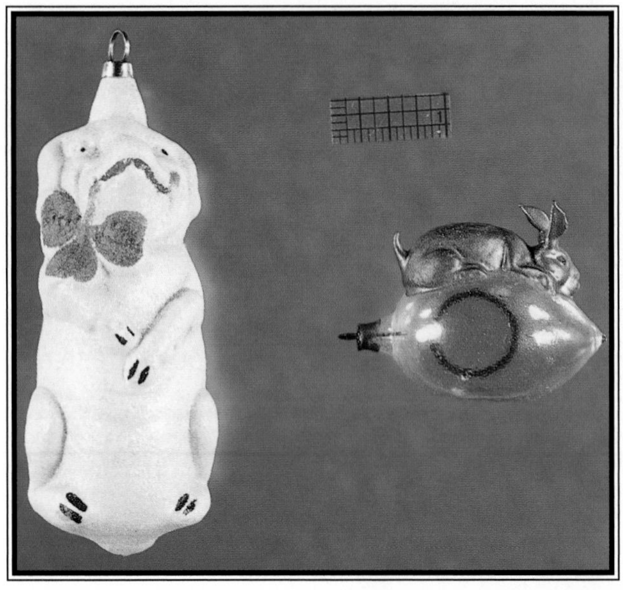

A. Begging Pig with Clover in its Mouth, 3½" [OP, R2]. **$175.00–225.00.** B. Rabbit on an Egg, sold as both a perfume bottle and an ornament, 2" [OP, R1-2]. **$90.00–110.00.**

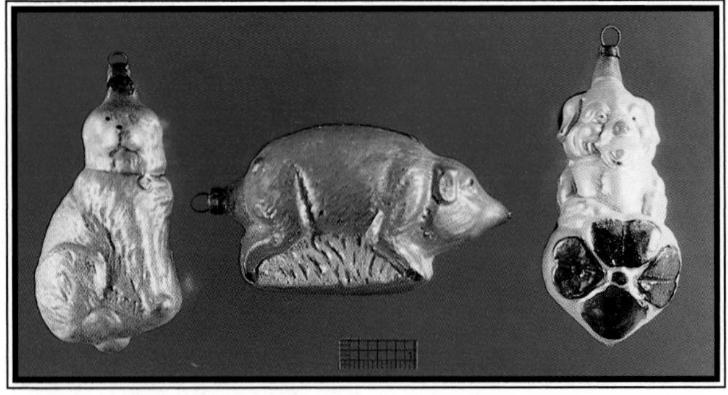

A. Dog, "Caesar," also called a Staffordshire Dog, approx. 3½" (shown) & 4". "Caesar," the name of Queen Victoria's dog, is embossed at the feet [German, OP, R1-2]. Small, **$175.00–200.00.** Large, **$200.00–250.00.** B. Hedgehog or Pig, approx. 4" [OP, R1-2]. **$250.00–300.00.** C. Pig in Clover, approx. 3¾". [German, OP-NP (Inge-glas, 1991), R1]. **$175.00–200.00.**

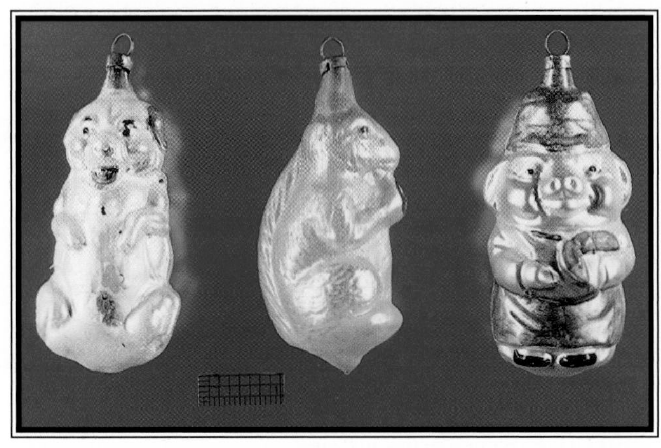

A. Begging Pig, approx. 3¼" [OP, R2-3]. **$100.00–125.00.** B. Squirrel Eating a Nut (Type I), approx. 2½" & 3¼" (shown), [OP-NP (1991), R3-4 small, R2 large]. Small, **$45.00–55.00.** Large, **$65.00–85.00.** C. Builder Pig, approx. 3¼" & 3½" (shown), one of the Three Little Pigs [OP, R2]. **$200.00–225.00.**

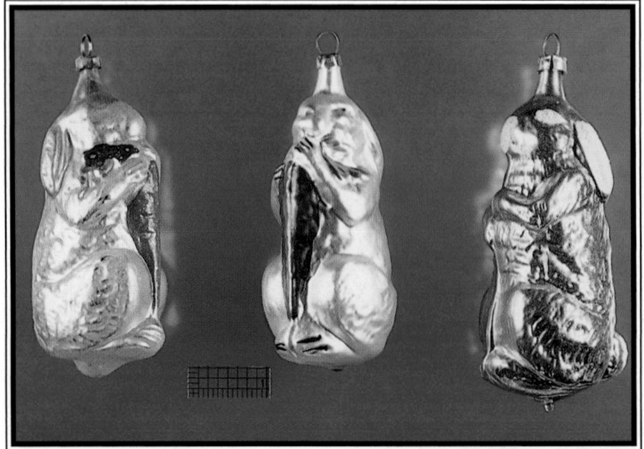

A. & B. Rabbit Eating a Carrot, front (new) and side (old) view, approx. 3" & 3½" (shown) [German, OP-NP (1980s), R3-4]. Both sizes **$60.00–75.00.** C. Rabbit without a Carrot, approx. 3¾" [German, OP-NP (1970s), R2]. **$60.00–80.00.**

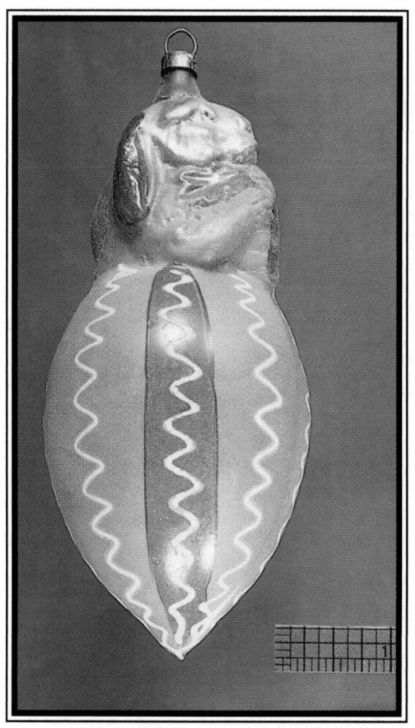

Very Rare Rabbit Emerging from an Egg, 5½" [OP, R1+]. **$450.00–550.00.**

Bunny, 5½" [OP, R1+]. **$700.00–800.00.**

Bunny, side view.

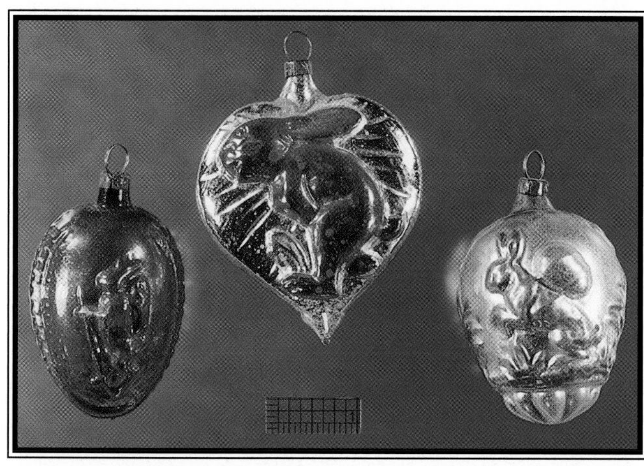

A. Walking Rabbit, embossed, 2" [OP, R2-3]. **$25.00–35.00.** B. Running Rabbit on a Heart, 2¾" [OP-NP (1991), R1-2]. **$100.00–125.00.** C. Easter Bunny, embossed, 2" [OP, R2-3]. **$30.00–40.00.**

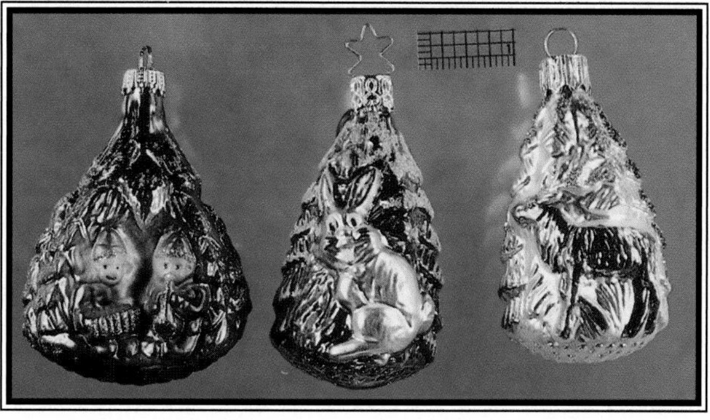

A. Gnomes on a Pine Tree, 2¾" [German, OP-NP (1993), R1]. Old, **$100.00–125.00.** 1993 version (shown), **$10.00–15.00.** B. Rabbit on a Pine Tree, embossed, 2½" [German, OP-NP (1980s), R1]. Old, **$80.00–100.00.** 1980s version (shown), **$10.00–15.00.** C. Deer on a Pine Tree, 2½" [German, OP-NP (1980s), R1]. Old, **$80.00–100.00.** 1980s version (shown), **$10.00–15.00.**

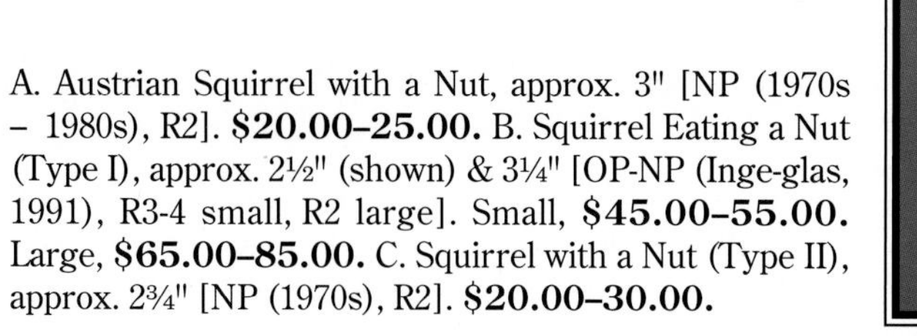

A. Austrian Squirrel with a Nut, approx. 3" [NP (1970s – 1980s), R2]. **$20.00–25.00.** B. Squirrel Eating a Nut (Type I), approx. 2½" (shown) & 3¼" [OP-NP (Inge-glas, 1991), R3-4 small, R2 large]. Small, **$45.00–55.00.** Large, **$65.00–85.00.** C. Squirrel with a Nut (Type II), approx. 2¾" [NP (1970s), R2]. **$20.00–30.00.**

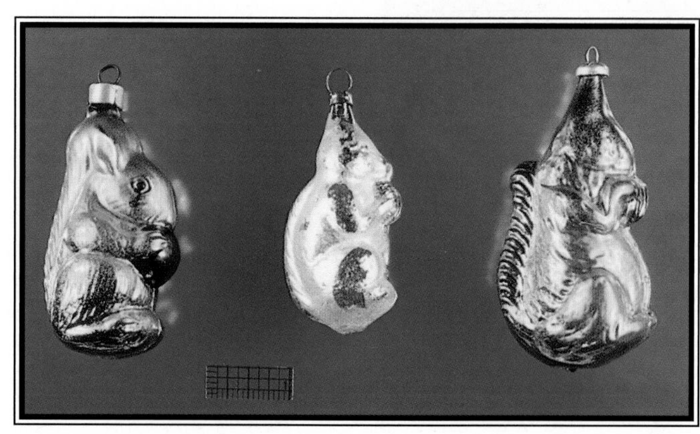

Radko Ornaments: A. Cat Head Rattle, large, 6½" [NP, (1992) R3-4]. **$25.00–35.00.** B. Tiger Head, 2¾" [NP (1990), R3-4]. **$40.00–45.00.** C. Calla Lily, 3" [NP (1992), R3-4]. **$20.00–30.00.**

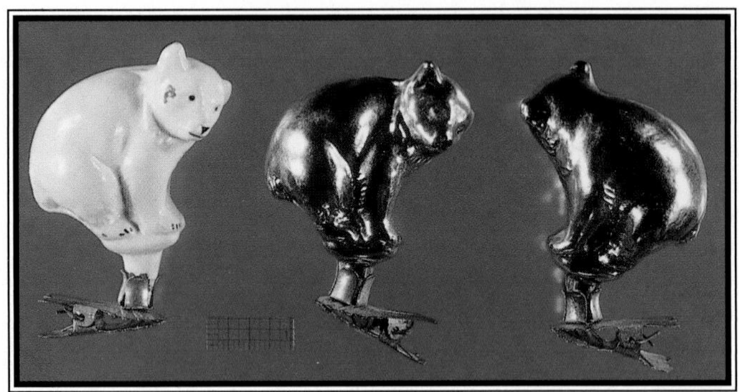

Russian-made Polar Bear, 2¾", unsilvered, silvered, and back side [OP-NP, R3]. **$65.00–75.00.**

A. Russian-made Sitting Bear, 2¾" [OP-NP, R3]. **$65.00–75.00.** B. Russian Dancing Bear, 3" [USSR, OP-NP, R3]. **$45.00–50.00.**

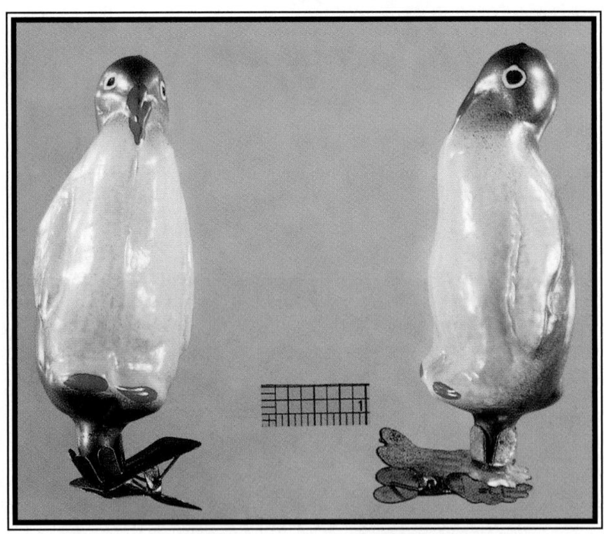

Two Views of Russian Penguin, 3½" [USSR, OP-NP, R3]. **$35.00–45.00.**

Russian Duck in a Scarf, 3¾" [USSR, OP-NP, R3]. **$60.00–75.00.**

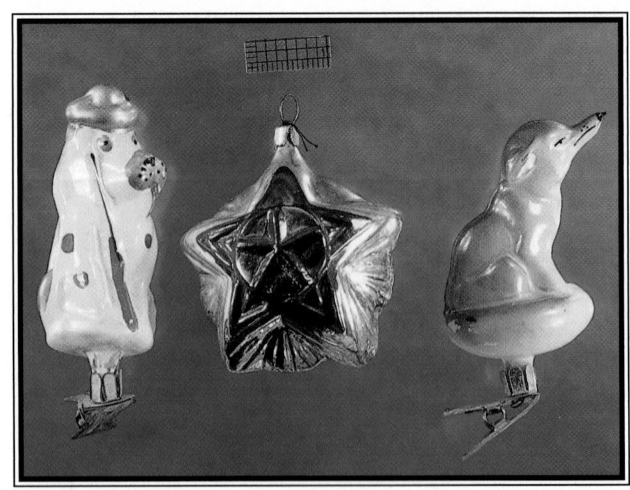

Russian Ornaments: A. Hunting Dog, 3¼" [OP-NP, R3]. **$60.00–70.00.** B. Star, 2½" [OP-NP, R3]. **$40.00–50.00.** C. Fox, 3" [USSR, OP, R2-3]. **$60.00–70.00.**

Chains of Beads

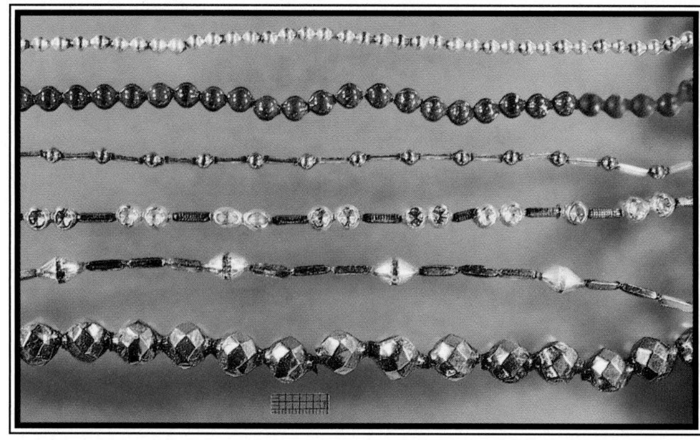

A & B. Common Chains of Japanese Beads, ¼" – ½" [OP-NP, R4-5]. **$1.25–1.50** per foot. C. Bead and Tube [OP-NP, R4]. **$1.50–1.75** per foot. D. Indents [OP-NP, R3-4]. **$3.00–4.00** per foot. E. Molded [OP-NP, R3-4]. **$3.00–4.00** per foot. F. Faceted, 1" [OP-NP, R1-2]. **$5.00–6.00** per foot.

A. Painted Beads [OP, R2-3]. **$10.00–12.00** per foot. B. Oblong Colored Glass Beads [OP, R2]. **$9.00–10.00** per foot. C. Wire-wrapped Unsilvered [OP, R2]. **$12.00–18.00** per foot. D. Wire-wrapped Silvered [OP, R2]. **$12.00–18.00** per foot.

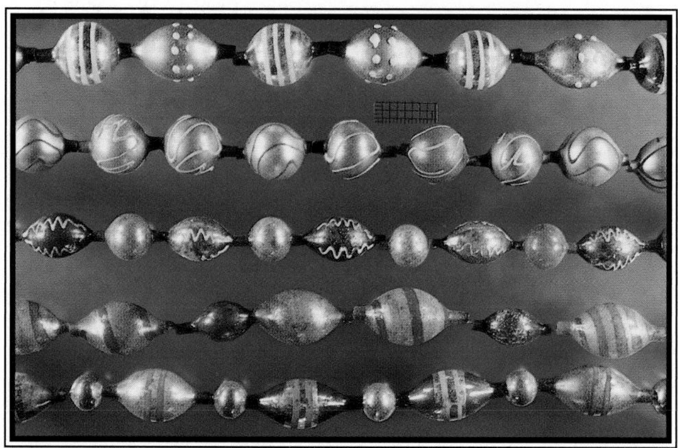

A, C, D, E. Painted Beads and Oblongs [OP, R3-4]. **$15.00–18.00** per foot. B. Painted Round Beads [OP, R2-3]. **$15.00–18.00** per foot.

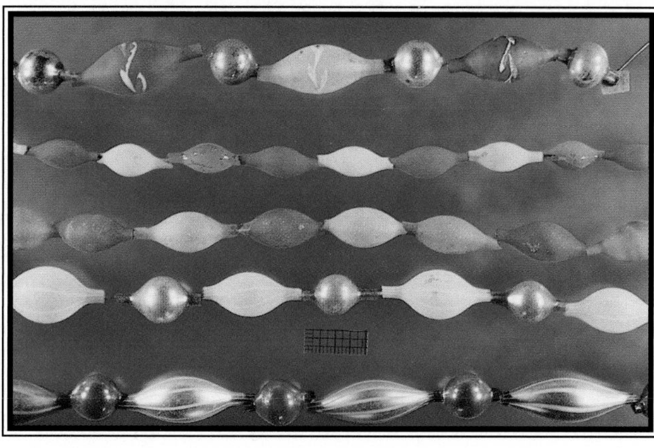

A. Oblong & Round [OP, R3]. **$10.00–12.00** per foot. B. Oblong, small [OP, R3-4]. **$8.00–10.00** per foot. C. Oblong, small [OP, R3-4]. **$8.00–10.00** per foot. D. Oblong & Round [OP, R3-4]. **$8.00–10.00** per foot. E. Oblong and Round with Colored Glass (not painted) Stripes [OP, R2]. **$15.00–20.00** per foot.

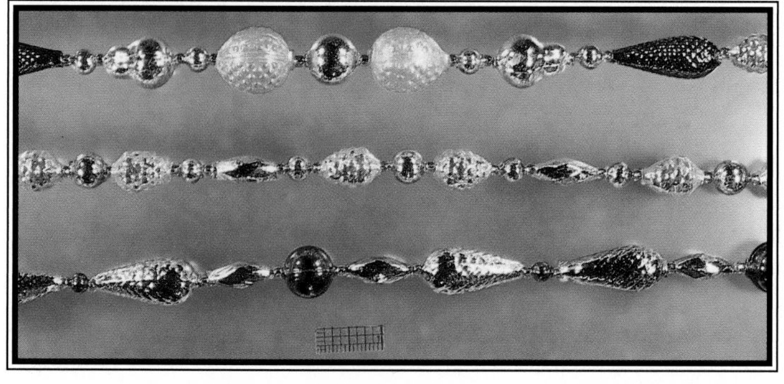

All Made by D. Blumchen & Co.: A. Berries, large [NP (1990 – 1994), R3-4]. **$50.00–70.00** per chain. B. Berries, small [NP, R3-4]. **$50.00–70.00** per chain. C. Ice Cream Cones [NP, R3-4]. **$50.00–70.00** per chain.

A. Umbrella/Ice Cream Cone, 3" & 1½", indented balls [OP, R2-3]. **$20.00–25.00** per foot. B. Fancy Shapes and Balls, 1½" [OP, R3]. **$15.00–20.00** per foot. C. Round Painted Balls, ¾" [OP, R2-3]. **$10.00–15.00** per foot. D. Oblong Beads, small, ½" [OP, R3-4]. **$2.00–3.00** per foot.

A. Umbrella/Ice Cream Cone [OP, R2-3], **$20.00–25.00** per foot. B. Lantern, Japanese, ribbed [OP, R2], **$15.00–20.00** per foot. C. Skeins of Yarn [OP, R1-2], **$25.00–30.00** per foot. D. Double Acorn [OP, R1-2], **$45.00–55.00** per foot.

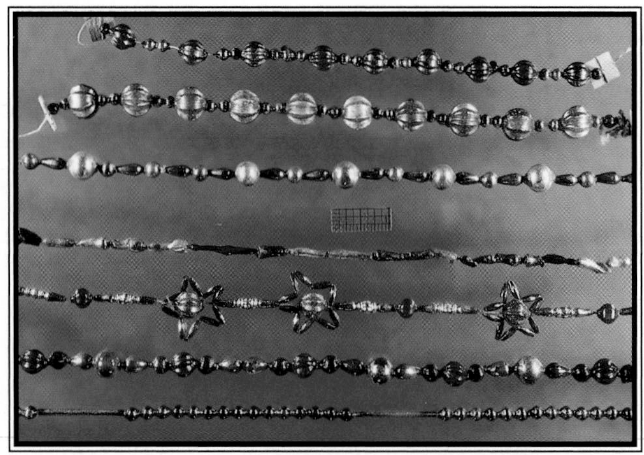

A & B. Faceted Beads, small [OP-NP, R3-4]. **$3.00–4.00** per foot. C, D, E, F, G. Molded Shapes, small [OP-NP, R3-4]. **$3.00–4.00** per foot.

A. Acorns [OP, R2]. **$45.00–55.00** per foot. B. Painted Ball Shapes [OP, R2-3]. C. Fancy Shapes [OP-NP, R3]. **$18.00–25.00** per foot.

Black Man's Head, double-faced [OP, R1]. **$400.00–450.00** per foot.

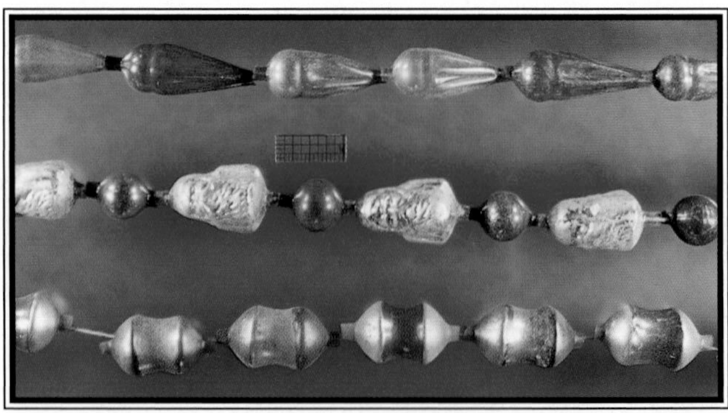

Ice Cream Cone [OP, R2-3]. **$20.00–25.00** per foot. B. Double Bust of Santa, [OP, R1]. **$300.00–325.00** per foot. C. Apple Core [OP, R1-2]. **$25.00–30.00** per foot.

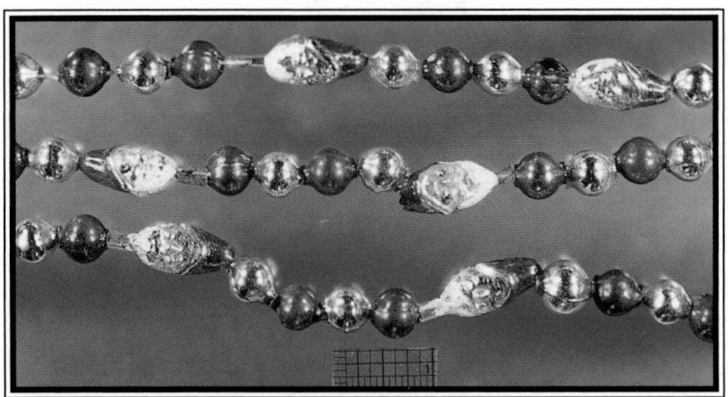

Santa Heads [OP, R1-2]. **$50.00–60.00** per foot.

Radko Beads Made in Antique Czech Molds: A. Beetle Front and Back [OP-NP, R3-4]. **$80.00–110.00** per chain. B. Owl Front and Back. [OP-NP, R3-4]. **$80.00–110.00** per chain.

Radko Chains Made in Antique Czech Molds (1990 – 1995): A. Bat and Ball [OP-NP, R3-4]. **$60.00–75.00** per chain. B. Train Chain, "Christmas Express" [OP-NP, R3-4]. **$90.00–110.00** per chain. C. Santa and Oblongs [OP-NP, R3-4]. **$80.00–100.00** per chain. D. Starburst [OP-NP, R3-4]. **$70.00–90.00** per chain.

Three Inge-glas Chains [All NP (1995), R3-4]. **$80.00–110.00** per chain: A. Man in Crescent Moon and Star. B. Fish and Frog, large. C . Santa and Oblong.

Three Christopher Radko Chains Made from Old Czech Molds (1990 – 1995) [All OP-NP, R3-4]. **$85.00–110.00** per chain: A. St. Nicholas. B. Three Types of Fish. C. Partridge and Pear.

Two Strings of Japanese Beads in Original Packages: A. Round, small [OP-NP, R4-5]. **$1.25–1.50** per foot. B. Molded Shapes [OP-NP, R3]. **$3.00–4.00** per foot.

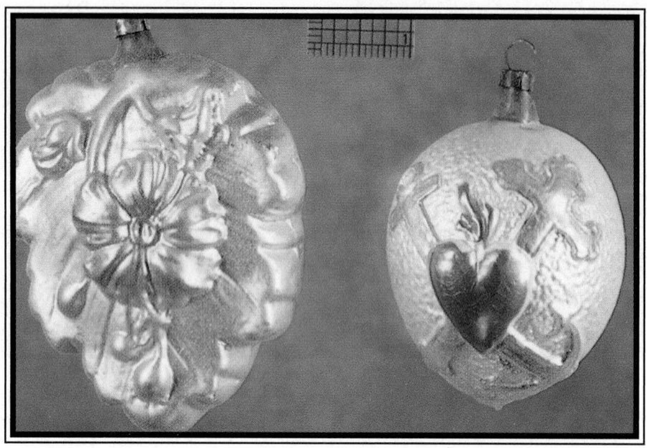

A. Flower Blossom on a Leaf, 3½" [OP, R1]. **$75.00-100.00.** B. Heart, Cross, and Anchor on a Ball, 2½" [OP, R1]. **$100.00-125.00.**

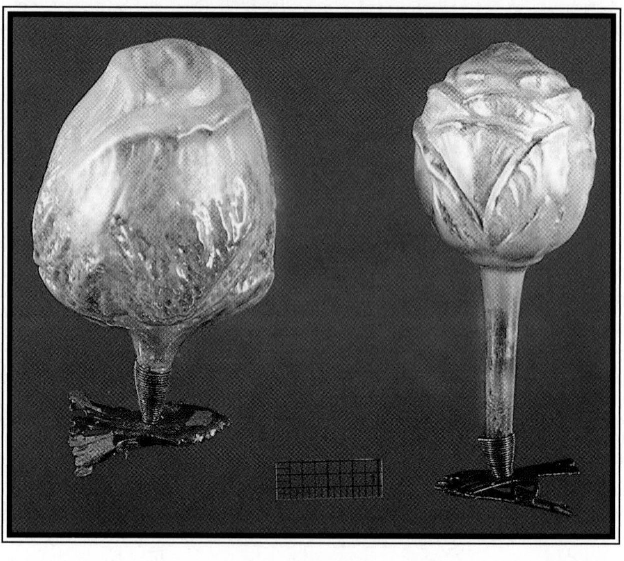

A. Rosebud, generic, large, 2¾" [OP-NP, R3-4]. **$40.00-50.00.** B. Open Rose with a Long Stem, 3½" [OP, R1]. **$75.00-100.00.**

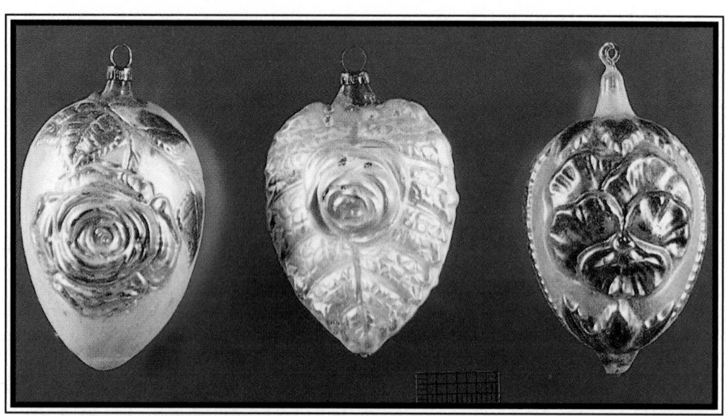

A. Rose Embossed Onto a Shape, large, 3¼" [OP-NP (1980s - 1990s, R4]. **$30.00-40.00.** B. Rose on a Leaf, approx. 2¾" & 3" (shown) [German, OP, R2-3]. **$80.00-90.00.** C. Pansy on an Egg Shape, embossed, 3" [OP-NP (1990s), R2]. **$30.00-40.00.**

A & E. Front & Back View of Rose & Daisy Double-sided Ornament, approx. 2" [OP, R2]. **$30.00-45.00.** B, D, F. Small Embossed Daisies, approx. 1" - 3" [OP-NP, R4-5]. 2" sizes shown, **$10.00-15.00.** C. Small Rosebud, approx. 2" [OP-NP, R4-5]. **$10.00-15.00.** G. Padula, or Generic Stylized Flower, approx. 2" [OP-NP, R4-5]. **$10.00-15.00.**

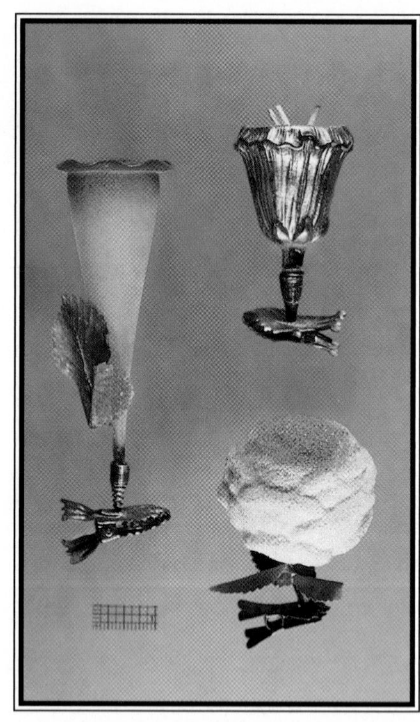

A. Trumpet Flower, free-blown, 4½" [OP, R2-3]. **$125.00-150.00.** B. Morning Glory with Stamens, 1¾" [OP, R2]. **$50.00-75.00.** C. Open Rose, large, 2¼" [OP-NP, R5]. **$30.00-40.00.**

A, C, D, E. Various Styles of Embossed Daisies, approx. 2¼", 1½", 1¾", & 2" (shown) [OP-NP (continuing), R4-5]. Sizes shown, **$10.00–15.00.** B. Cherries Embossed on a Ball, approx. 2" [OP-NP, R3-4]. **$10.00–15.00.**

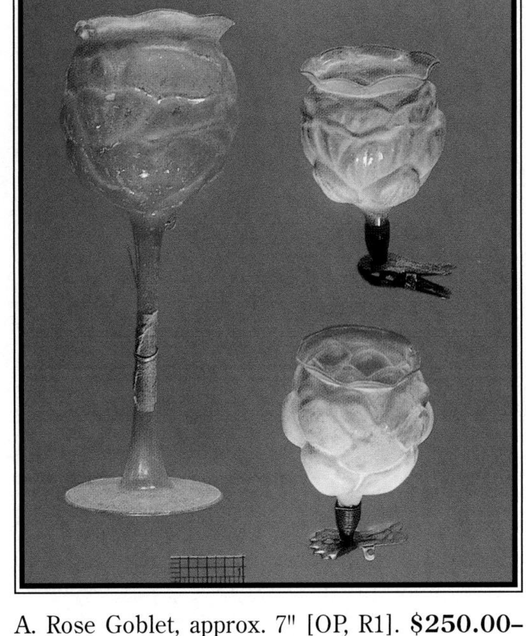

A. Rose Goblet, approx. 7" [OP, R1]. **$250.00–275.00.** B. Hollow Rose, clip-on, approx. 2" [OP, R2-3]. **$75.00–85.00.** C. Hollow Artichoke, approx. 2" [OP, R2]. **$75.00–85.00.**

A Variety of Roses: A. Rosebud, generic style, approx. 1¾" (shown) – 3" [OP-NP (1980s – 1990s), R4]. Small (1¼" – 2"), **$8.00–12.00.** Medium (2" – 2½"), **$12.00–15.00.** Large (2½" – 3"), **$25.00–40.00.** B, C, D, E, G. Various Open Roses, approx. 1¼" – 2¾" [OP-NP (continuing), R5]. Small, **$8.00–12.00.** Medium, **$12.00–20.00.** Large, **$20.00–30.00.** F. Rosette, approx. 2¼", 3", & 3¾" (shown). Made of paper-thin glass, this piece is early and unsilvered [German, OP, R2-3]. Small, **$20.00–25.00.** Medium, **$25.00–35.00.** Large, **$40.00–50.00.**

A & D. Tulips, approx. 2" (shown), 3", & 3¼" (shown) [OP-NP (1980s – 1990s), R3]: A. Small Clip-on. **$30.00–40.00.** D. Large, indented, with inserted paper stamens. **$40.00–50.00.** B & C. Rosebuds, generic style, approx. 1¼" – 3" (both shown are 3") [OP-NP (1980s & 1990s), R4]. Small (1¼" – 2"), **$8.00–12.00.** Medium (2" – 2½"), **$12.00–15.00.** Large (2½" – 3"), **$25.00–40.00.** Two examples shown, **$25.00–30.00.**

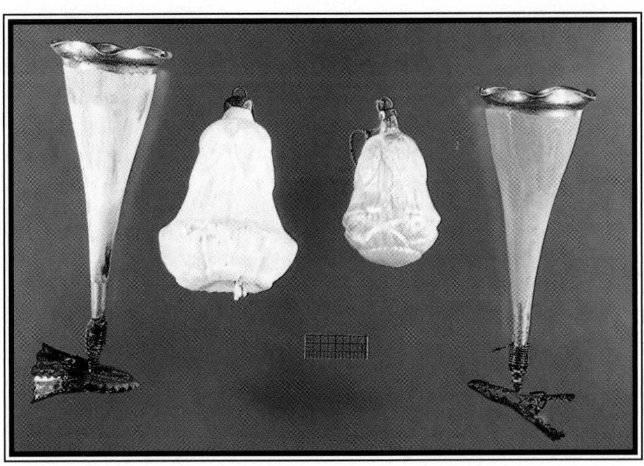

A & D. Free-blown Trumpet Flowers, approx. 4" – 5" (4¼" & 4" shown) [OP, R2-3]. **$100.00–125.00.** B & C. Lotus Flowers, approx. 2" & 2½" (shown) [OP-NP (1980s), R3]. Small, **$15.00–20.00.** Large, **$25.00–35.00.**

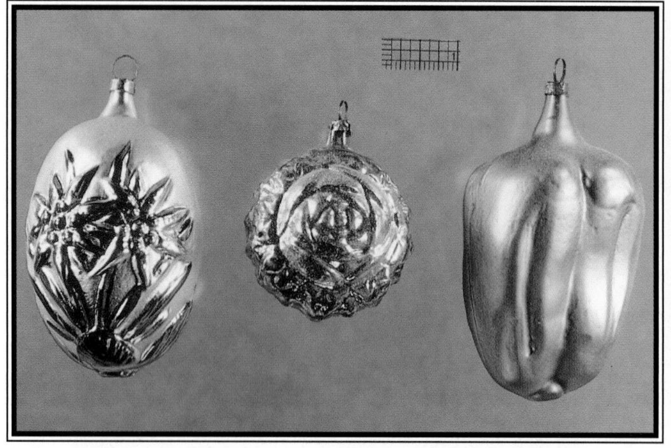

A. Edelweiss on an Egg, 3¼" [OP-NP (1980s), R1]. **$40.00–50.00.** B. Rosette, small, 2¼" [OP, R2-3]. **$20.00–25.00.** C. Pepper, 3½"; despite old cap, probably 1980s piece [NP, R3]. **$8.00–12.00.**

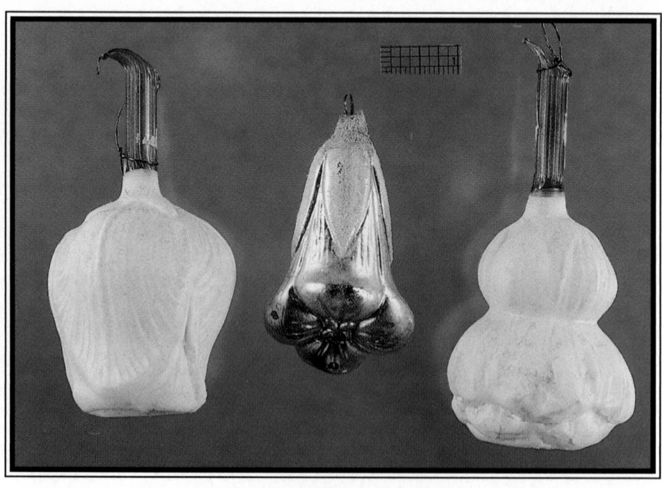

A. Tulip with a Stem, 4½" [OP, R1]. **$75.00–100.00.** B. Foxglove, 3¼" [OP-NP, R2]. **$50.00–60.00.** C. Rose with a Stem and a Hip of Leaves, 5" [OP, R1]. **$75.00–100.00.**

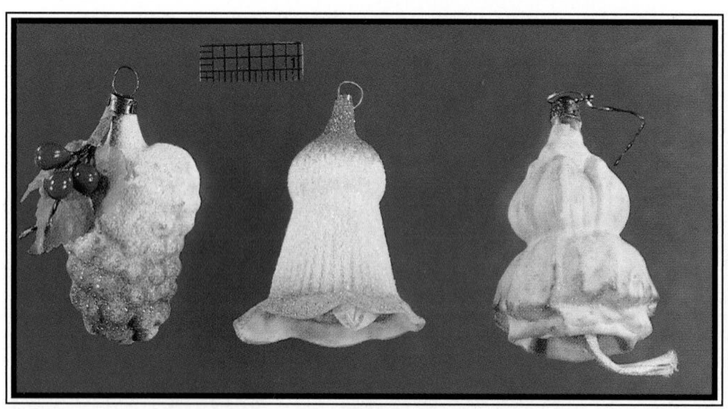

A. Bunch of Grapes, standard form, approx. 2¼" (shown), 2¾", 3¼" [German, OP-NP, R4]. Small, **$15.00–20.00.** Medium, **$30.00–40.00.** Large, **$30.00–40.00.** B. Hollow Trumpet Flower (Type II), 2" [OP, R1-2]. **$125.00–150.00.** C. Rose with Stamens and a Hip of Leaves, 2" [OP, R2-3]. **$50.00–60.00.**

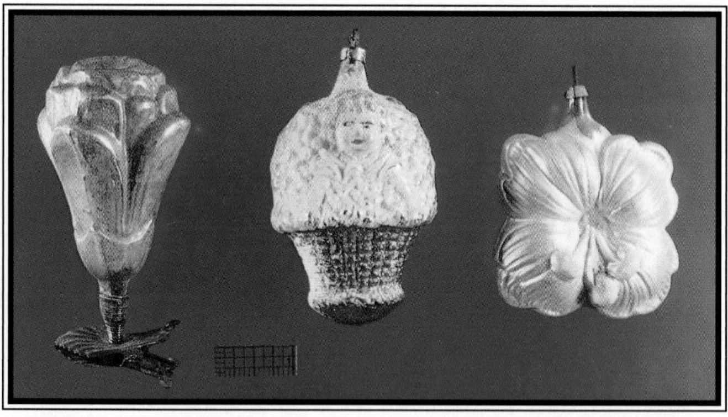

A. Molded Trumpet Flower, approx. 2¾" [OP, R2-3]. **$45.00–55.00.** B. Girl/Angel in a Basket of Flowers, approx. 2¾" (shown) & 3" [German, OP-NP (Lauscha-glas, 1994; Radko, 1995), R2]. **$200.00–275.00.** C. "Pillow" Flower, approx. 2" [OP, R1-2]. **$90.00–110.00.**

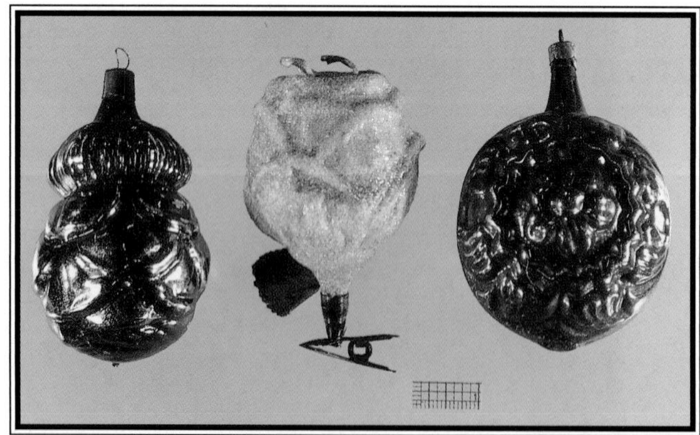

A. Rose with a Hip of Leaves, approx. 2" – 4" (shown) [OP-NP, R3-4]. Small, **$20.00–25.00.** Medium, **$25.00–35.00.** Large, **$35.00–45.00.** B. Open Rose with Stamens, approx. 3¼" [OP, R2]. **$60.00–75.00.** C. Embossed Rose, approx. 3½" [OP, R2-3]. **$25.00 -35.00.**

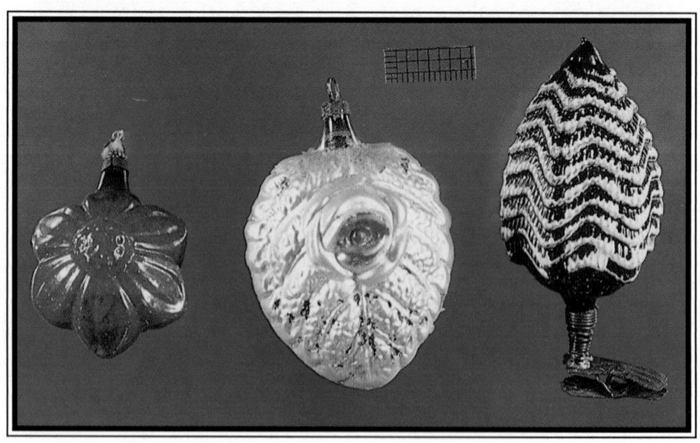

A. Daisy, approx. 1¾" [OP, R3-4]. **$10.00–15.00.** B. Rose on a Leaf, 2¾" (shown) & 3" [Germany, OP, R2-3]. Either size, **$80.00–90.00.** C. Tree with Narrow Limbs, approx. 2¾" [German, OP, R3]. **$25.00–35.00.**

A, B, C. Three Sizes of Rose Baskets (Type I), approx. 1½", 2", & 2¼" (all shown) [German, OP-NP (continuing), R5]. Small, **$5.00–10.00.** Medium, **$10.00–12.00.** Large, **$12.00–18.00.** D. Round Basket of Fruit (Type II), approx. 2½" [OP, R3] **$25.00–35.00.** E. Basket of Daisies, approx. 2" (shown) & 2¾" [German, OP-NP (1980s), R3]. Small, **$20.00–25.00.** Large, **$30.00–40.00.** F. Basket of Apples & Grapes, approx. 2½" [German, OP-NP (1980s), R3]. **$25.00–35.00.** 1980s version (shown), **$12.00–15.00.**

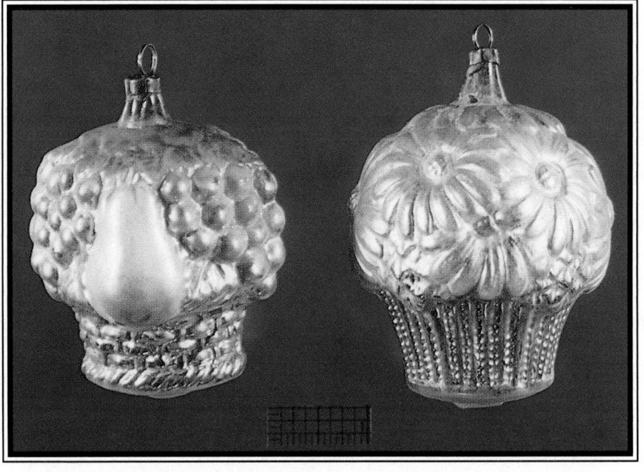

A. Basket of Grapes and Pears, approx. 2½" (shown) & 3" [OP-NP (1993), R3]. Small, **$30.00–40.00.** Large, **$50.00–65.00.** B. Basket of Daisies, approx. 2" & 2¾" (shown) [German, OP-NP (1980s), R3]. Small, **$20.00–25.00.** Large, **$35.00–50.00.**

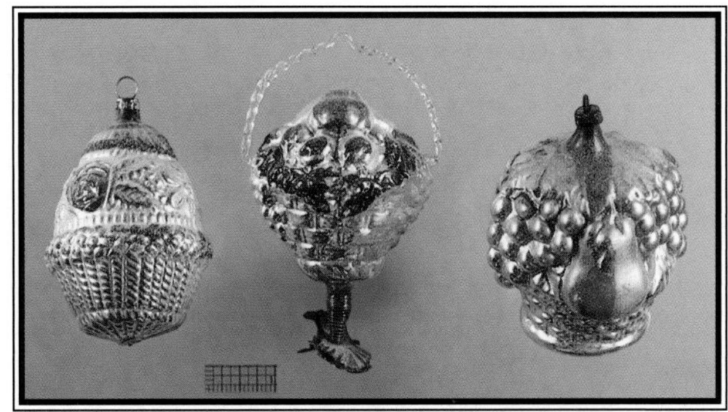

A. Basket of Roses and Daisies, 3" [OP, R2-3]. **$25.00–30.00.** B. Basket of Fruit with Glass Handle, 3½" [OP, R1]. **$200.00–250.00.** C. Basket of Grapes and Pears, approx. 2½" & 3" (shown) [OP-NP (1993), R3]. Small, **$30.00–40.00.** Large, **$50.00–65.00.**

A. Basket of Grapes, round, 3½" [OP, R1]. **$50.00–65.00.** B. Basket with Fabric Flowers, by Blumchen, circa 1989 [R3]. **$25.00–35.00.** C. Basket of Flowers, hooded, 2" [OP, R2]. **$25.00–35.00.**

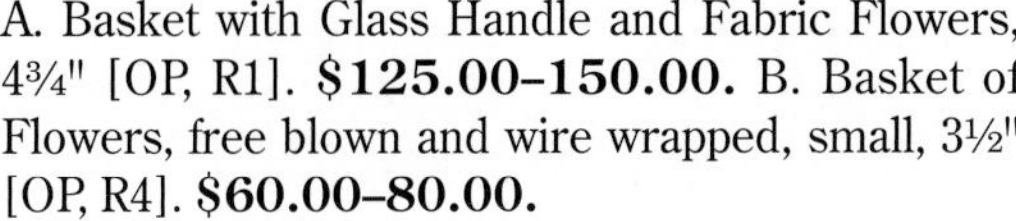

A. Basket with Glass Handle and Fabric Flowers, 4¾" [OP, R1]. **$125.00–150.00.** B. Basket of Flowers, free blown and wire wrapped, small, 3½" [OP, R4]. **$60.00–80.00.**

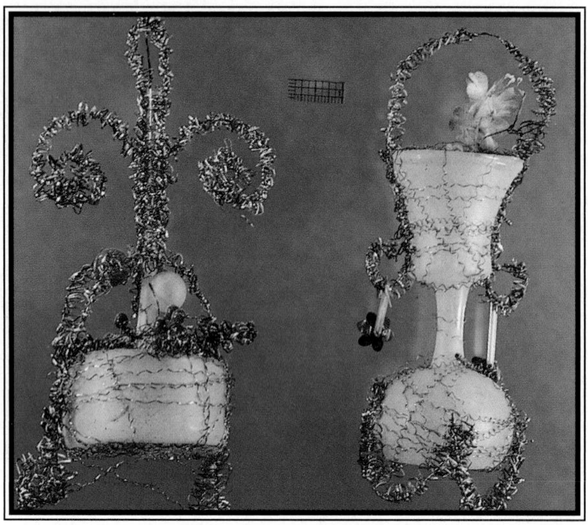

A. Flower Basket, free blown and wire wrapped, elaborate, 8½" overall [OP, R2]. **$150.00–175.00.** B. Flower Vase, elaborate, 8" overall [OP, R2]. **$150.00–175.00.**

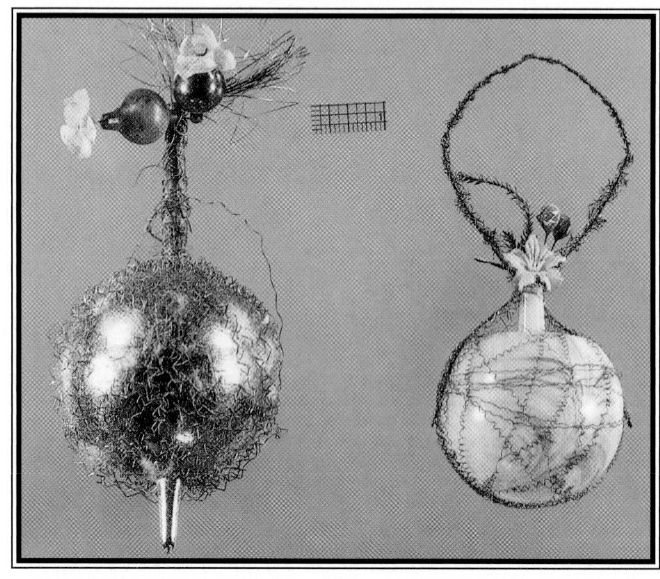

Two Baskets of Flowers, free blown and wire wrapped: A. 6½" [OP, R2]. **$80.00–90.00.** B. End-of-Day Glass, 4" [OP, R4]. **$50.00–75.00.**

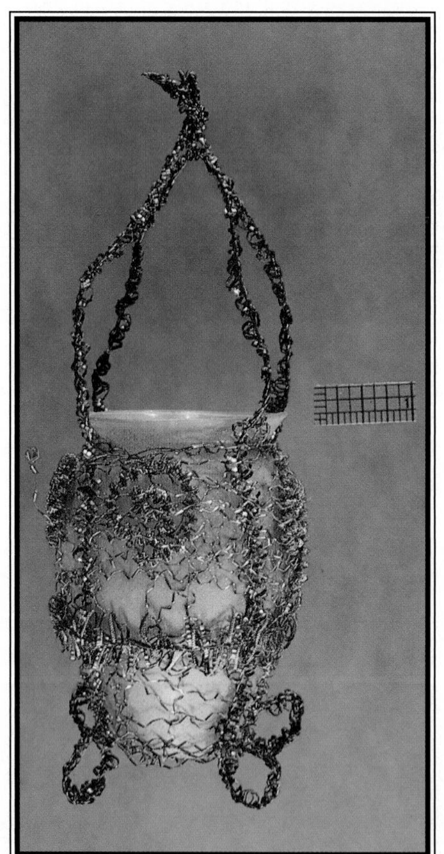

Basket, egg shaped, hollow, 3½" glass [OP, R1-2]. **$150.00–175.00.**

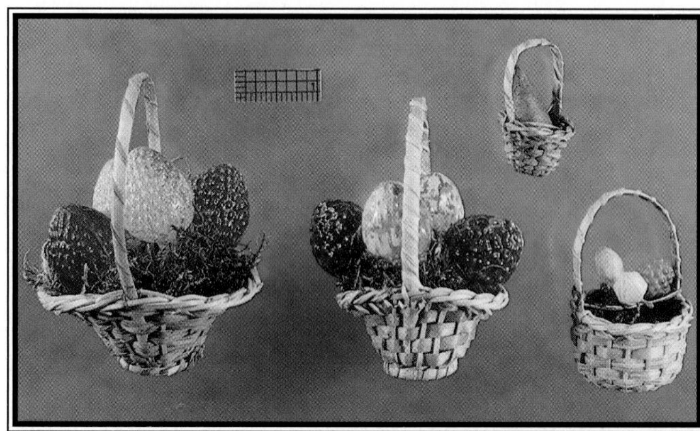

Wooden Baskets with Glass Fruit [all OP, R3]: A. Small at Top (width of basket), 1". **$15.00–20.00.** B. 2½". **$50.00–75.00.** C. 2". **$45.00–65.00.** D. 1½". **$15.00–20.00.**

Wooden Baskets with Glass Fruit [all OP, R3]: A. 3". **$60.00–80.00.** B. 4½". **$100.00–125.00.** C. 4¼". **$125.00–150.00.**

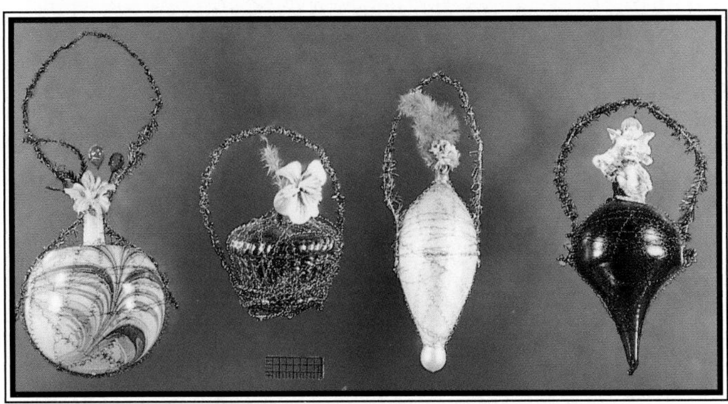

Wire-wrapped Flower Baskets, approx. 3¼", 2", 3½", & 3¼" glass (shown): A. End-of-Day Glass-Hanging Flower Basket. **$50.00–75.00.** B. Molded Basket with Fabric Flower. **$25.00–35.00.** C. Free-blown Hanging Flower Basket, egg shaped. **$40.00–45.00.** D. Hanging Flower Basket with Mirror Image Scrap Angels. **$40.00–45.00.**

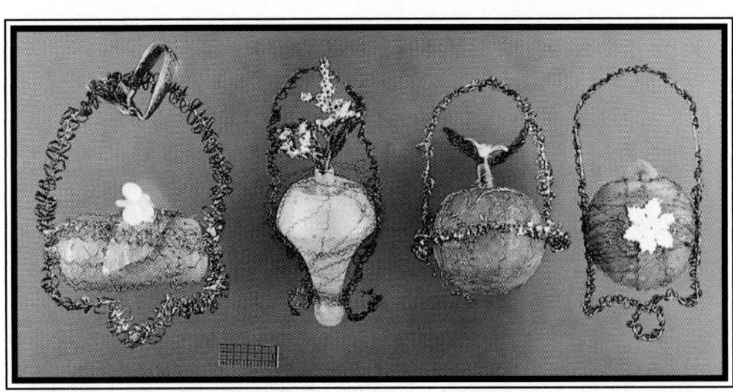

Varying Designs of the Free-blown Hanging Flower Basket. All are early wire wrapped and unsilvered. Approx. 2" – 9" (3", 3", 2", & 2" shown) [German, Austrian, Czech, OP-NP (1950s – 1980s), R4]. Small (2" – 3", shown), **$35.00–50.00.** Medium (3" – 5"), **$40.00–60.00.** Large (5" – 7"), **$65.00–110.00.** Extra large (8"+), **$150.00–175.00.**

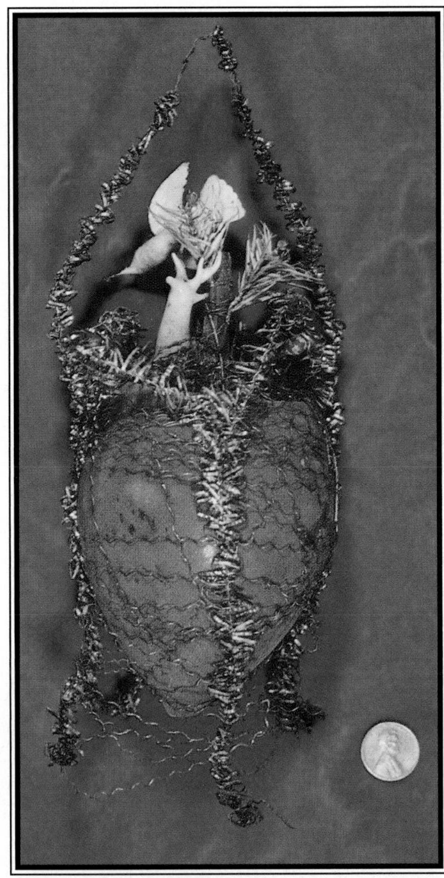

Large Egg-shaped Basket, approx. 6½", an early unsilvered and wire-wrapped piece [German, OP, R1]. **$250.00–300.00.**

Two Large Free-blown Flower Baskets, approx. (in general) 2" – 9" (5½" & 5" shown) [German, Austrian, Czech; OP-NP (1950s – 1980s), R4]. Small (2" – 3"), **$30.00–40.00.** Medium (3" – 5"), **$40.00–60.00.** Large (5" – 7"), **$65.00–110.00.** Extra large (8"+), **$150.00–175.00.** A. **$80.00–90.00.** B. **$50.00–60.00.**

Fruits & Vegetables

A, B, D. Generic Berries, approx. 1" – 2¼" [German, Czech, Austrian, Japanese, American; OP-NP, R5]. **$10.00–15.00.** C & E. Strawberries, approx. 1¾" (shown), 2" (shown), 2¼", 2¾", & 3¾" [OP-NP (1990s), R4]. Small (shown), **$10.00–15.00.** Medium, **$15.00–25.00.** Large, **$25.00–40.00.** F. Round Bunch of Grapes, approx. 2", 2½" (shown), 2¾", & 3" [OP-NP (continuing), R5]. Small, **$8.00–12.00.** Medium, **$10.00–15.00.** Large, **$15.00–20.00.** G. Generic Bunch of Grapes, approx. 1" – 4" (2" shown) [German, Czech, Austrian, Japanese, American; OP-NP, R5]. Small, **$5.00–8.00.** Medium, **$8.00–10.00.** Large, **$10.00–12.00.** H. Bunch of Grapes, standard form, approx. 2¼", 2¾" (shown), & 3¼" [German, OP-NP, R4]. Small, **$15.00–20.00.** Medium, **$20.00–25.00.** Large, **$30.00–40.00.**

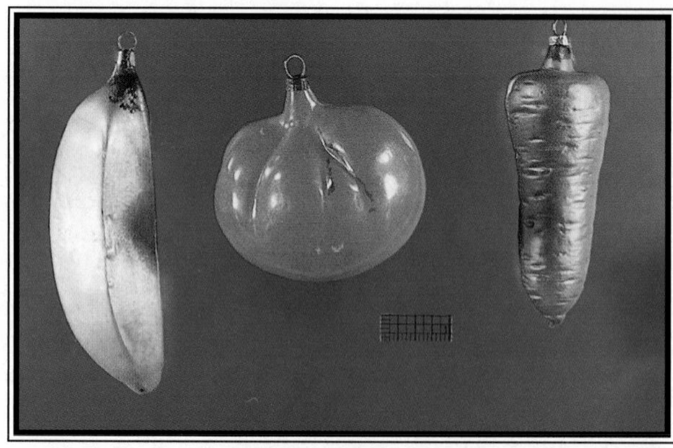

A. Banana (Type II), approx. 3", 3¾", & 4½" (shown) [OP, R2]. Small, **$40.00–50.00.** Medium, **$50.00–60.00.** Large, **$70.00–80.00.** B. Tomato, approx. 2", 2½", 2¾" (shown) [German, OP, R3]. Small, **$30.00–40.00.** Medium, **$50.00–60.00.** Large, **$70.00–80.00.** C. Carrot (Type I), approx. 3½" (shown), 3¾", 4", & 4¼" [German, OP-NP (1991), R3]. Small, **$25.00–35.00.** Medium, **$30.00–40.00.** Large, **$40.00–50.00.**

Artistic Period (1920s) Fruit, all are silvered, some have blushing [R1-2]: A. Plum, approx. 2¼". **$35.00–50.00.** B. Peach, approx. 2¾". **$50.00–60.00.** C. Banana, approx. 6". **$90.00–100.00.** D. Pear, approx. 4½". **$75.00–100.00.** E. Apple, approx. 2¾". **$75.00–100.00.**

A. Free-blown Radish, approx. 2½" [OP, R2-3]. **$20.00–30.00.** B. Squash, approx. 3¼" [OP, R2]. **$25.00–35.00.** C. Carrot (Type II), approx. 2¾", 3" (shown), 4", & 5½" [German, OP-NP (1988), R2]. Small, **$30.00–35.00.** Medium, **$35.00–50.00.** Large, **$50.00–75.00.**

More Artistic Period Fruit: A. Tomato, approx. 2½". **$75.00–85.00.** B. Crabapple, approx. 1½". **$30.00–40.00.** Strawberry, approx. 2½". **$40.00–50.00.**

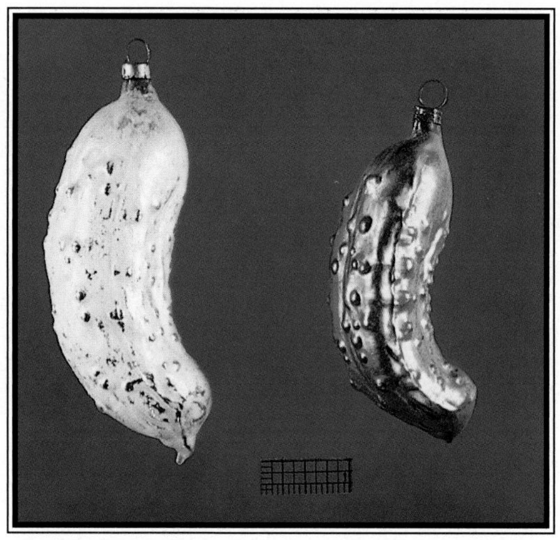

Gherkin Pickle, approx. 1½", 2", 2½", 3¼", 3½" (shown), 4" (shown), & 4½". This pickle has an identifiable curve [German, OP-NP (prolifically reproduced during the 1990s), R3 (for old pieces)]. Miniature, **$25.00–35.00.** Small, **$40.00–50.00.** Medium, **$50.00–60.00.** Large, **$75.00–95.00.** 1990s version, **$8.00–10.00.**

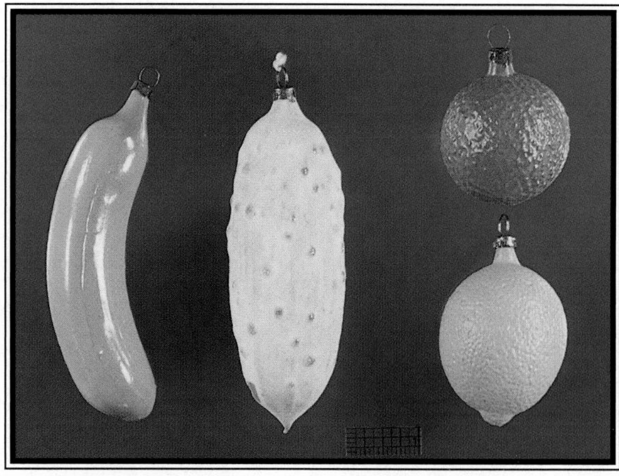

A. Banana (Type I), approx. 3" & 4" (shown) [German, OP, R3]. Small, **$45.00–55.00.** Large, **$60.00–75.00.** B. "Heinz" Pickle, approx. 3½", 3¾", a straight pickle form [Czech, OP-NP (1985, small), R2]. Both sizes **$75.00–100.00.** C. Small Unsilvered Orange, approx. 1¾" (shown), 2½", & 3" [German, OP-NP (1991), R3]. Small, **$20.00–30.00.** Medium, **$40.00–50.00.** Large, **$50.00–75.00.** D. Small Unsilvered Lemon, approx. 2", 2¼" (shown), 2¾", & 3½" [German, OP, R3]. Small, **$20.00–30.00.** Medium, **$30.00–40.00.** Large, **$40.00–55.00.**

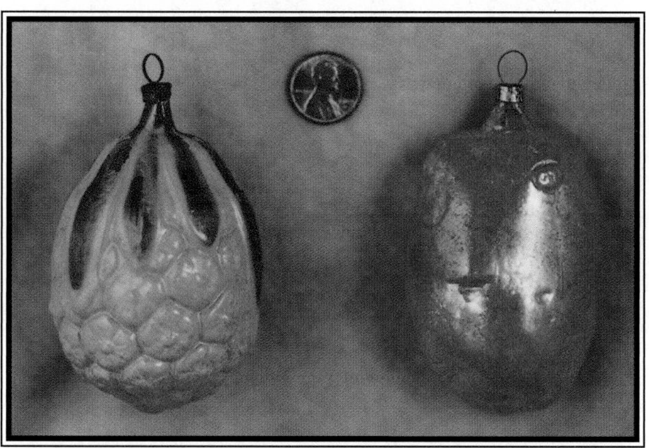

A. Pineapple, approx. 3", unsilvered and painted [OP, R2]. **$125.00–150.00.** B. Potato (Type I), approx. 2¾", 3" (shown), & 3½" [OP, R2]. Small, **$70.00–80.00.** Medium, **$80.00–90.00.** Large, **$90.00–110.00.**

An Assortment of Pears: A. Ribbed Pear, approx. 2½" [OP, R2-3]. **$20.00–30.00.** B. Free-blown Pear Covered with Crushed Glass, 2" – 4" (2" shown) [OP-NP, R4-5]. Small, **$10.00–20.00.** Medium, **$15.00–25.00.** Large, **$20.00–35.00.** C. Pear Half, unsilvered, approx. 3½" [OP-NP (1995), R1-2]. **$70.00–90.00.** D & E. Molded pears, approx. 1½" – 5" (3" & 4" shown) [OP-NP (continuing), R4-5]. Small, **$15.00–25.00.** Medium, **$25.00–40.00.** Large, **$50.00–75.00.**

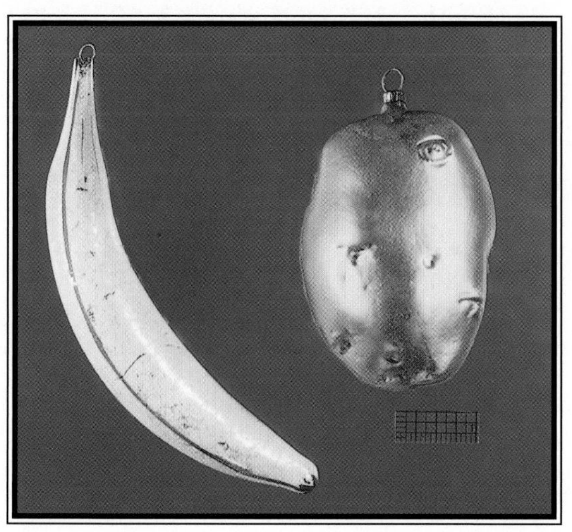

A. Banana (Type III), 6" [OP-R1-2]. **$90.00–100.00.** B. Potato (Type I), approx. 2¾", 3", & 3½" (shown) [OP, R2]. Small, **$70.00–80.00.** Medium, **$80.00–90.00.** Large, **$90.00–110.00.**

A. Carrot (Type I), painted as a parsnip, small, 3½" [German, OP, R2-3]. **$25.00–35.00.** B. Watermelon Slice (Type I); 3½", 4½", & 5" (shown) [German, OP, R2-3]. Small, **$80.00–100.00.** Medium, **$100.00–120.00.** Large, **$150.00–175.00.** C. Carrot (Type I), 4" [German, OP-NP (1990s), R3]. Small, **$25.00–35.00.** Medium, **$30.00–40.00.** Large, **$40.00–50.00.**

A. Ear of Corn without Leaves, approx. 3" & 4" (shown) [OP, R2]. Small, **$30.00–40.00.** Large, **$40.00–50.00.** B, C, D. Three Ears of Corn with Leaves [German, OP-NP (1990s), R3-4]: B. Medium, 3½". **$40.00–50.00.** C. Medium, 3". **$35.00–45.00.** D. Small, 1½". **$20.00–30.00.**

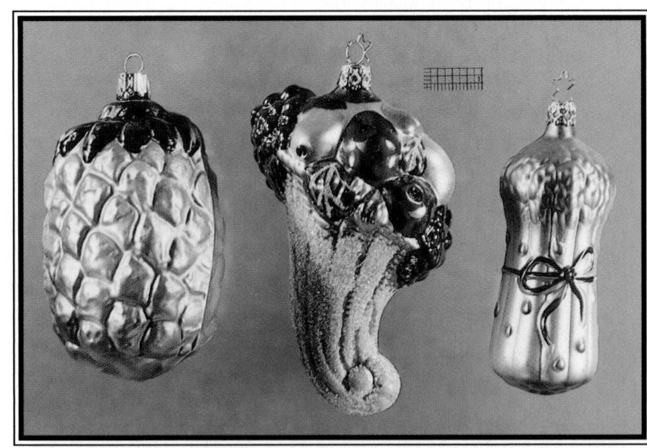

A. Pineapple, large, 4½" [NP (1993), R3-4]. **$10.00–15.00.** B. Cornucopia of Fruit, 5½" [NP (circa 1993)]. **$20.00–30.00.** C. Asparagus Stalks, 4½" [NP (circa 1993), R3-4]. **$15.00–20.00.**

Peas in a Pod, 2½" glass, 3¾" overall [OP, R1+]. **$400.00–500.00.**

A. Grapefruit Half, 3¼" [German, NP (1990s), R3-4]. **$12.00–15.00.** B. Peas in a Pod, large, 5" [NP (1993), R3-4]. **$8.00–12.00.** C. Apple Half, 2½" [OP-NP, R1]. Old, **$100.00–125.00.** 1993 version (shown), **$8.00–12.00.**

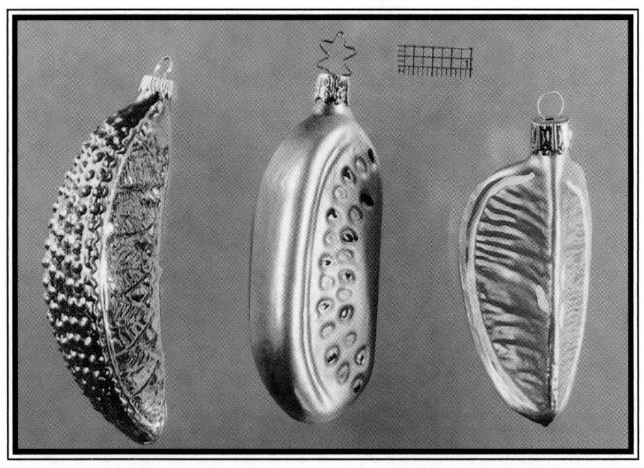

A. Pineapple Slice, 4½" [NP (1990s), R3-4]. **$10.00–15.00.** B. Watermelon Slice (Type II), 4" [NP (1990s), R3-4]. **$10.00–20.00.** C. Orange Slice, 3½" [OP-NP (1990s), R1]. **$30.00–40.00.** 1990s version (shown), **$10.00–15.00.**

A. Bunch of Grapes Embossed onto a Heart, approx. 2¾" [German, OP, R3]. **$25.00–35.00.** B. Watermelon Slice (Type I), approx. 3½", 4½" (shown), & 5" [German, OP, R2-3]. Small, **$80.00–100.00.** Medium, **$100.00–120.00.** Large, **$150.00–175.00.**

A. Unsilvered Orange, approx. 1¾", 2½", & 3" (shown) [German, OP-NP (1991), R3]. Small, **$20.00–30.00.** Medium, **$40.00–50.00.** Large, **$50.00–75.00.** B. Watermelon Slice (Type I), approx. 3½" (shown), 4½", & 5" [German, OP, R2-3]. Small, **$80.00–100.00.** Medium, **$100.00–120.00.** Large, **$150.00–175.00.**

A. Giant Walnut, 4½"H x 3½"W [OP, R2]. **$40.00–50.00.** B. Free-blown Apple, approx. 1" – 2" diameter, sizes vary because pieces are free-blown [OP-NP, R4]. **$20.00–30.00.** C. Lemon, approx. 2", 2¼" (shown), 2¾", & 3½", covered with starch "snow" [German, OP, R3]. Small, **$20.00–30.00.** Medium, **$30.00–40.00.** Large, **$40.00–55.00.** D. Strawberry, approx. 1¾", 2" (shown), 2¼", 2¾", 3¾" [OP-NP (1990s)]. Small, **$10.00–15.00.** Medium, **$15.00–25.00.** Large, **$25.00–40.00.**

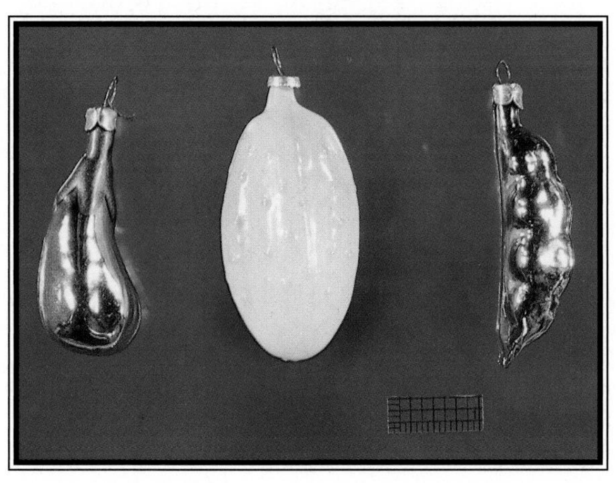

Russian Ornaments: A. Eggplant, 2¾" [OP-NP, R3-4]. **$20.00–25.00.** B. Pickle, milk glass, 3¼" [OP-NP, R3-4]. **$25.00–35.00.** C. Peas in a Pod, 3" [USSR, OP-NP, R3-4]. **$20.00–25.00.**

Hearts

A. Heart with a Pansy, 2¼" [OP, R2]. **$15.00–25.00.** B. Heart with a Daisy (Type II), 2¼" [OP, R2]. **$10.00–15.00.** C. Egg with a Heart and Flame, 2¾" [OP, R1-2]. **$25.00–35.00.** D. Heart with a Church and "Merry Christmas," 2½" [OP-NP (1995), R2-3]. **$40.00–50.00.**

A. Heart on a Quilted Heart, 2" [OP, R3]. **$10.00–18.00.** B. Heart with a Bee, 2" [OP, R1]. **$35.00–45.00.** C. Heart with an Indented Flower, 2¾" [OP, R2-3]. **$10.00–20.00.** D. Heart with an Indented Circle, 2¼" [OP, R2-3]. **$12.00–18.00.** E. Heart with an Indented Star (Type I), 2¼" [OP, R2]. **$12.00–15.00.**

A. Heart on a Heart, approx. 2" [German, OP, R3-4]. **$10.00–18.00.** B. Berries on a Heart, approx. 1¾" [OP, R3-4]. **$8.00–12.00.** C. Heart with Embossed Stars as a Wire-wrapped Flower Basket, approx. 2" glass heart [German, OP, R2-3]. **$25.00–35.00.** D. Daisy on a Heart (Type I), approx. 2¼" [OP, R3-4]. **$10.00–15.00.** E. Iris on a Heart, approx. 2½" [OP, R3-4]. **$20.00–30.00.**

A & D. Quilted Heart, approx. 1¾" (shown) & 2½" (shown) [OP-NP (1980s), R4]. Small, **$5.00–10.00.** Large, **$15.00–20.00.** B. Indented Heart, approx. 1¾" [OP, R3]. **$5.00–10.00.** C. Heart with a Bumpy Pattern, approx. 2½" & 2¾" (shown) [OP-NP (1970s), R4]. Small, **$8.00–10.00.** Large, **$10.00–15.00.**

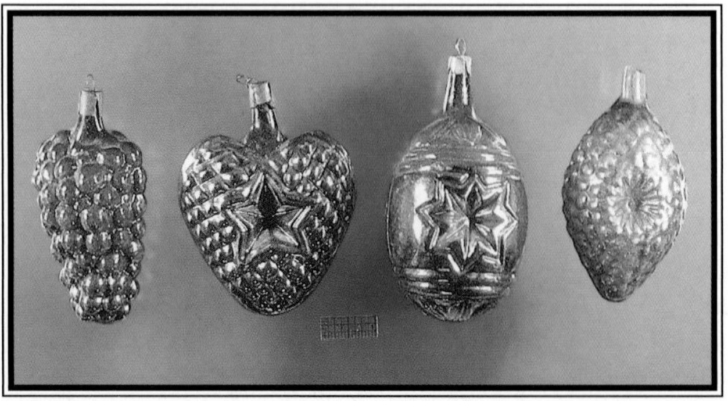

These Four Crude Pieces, all made of heavy glass, are from the same unknown early manufacturer: A. Heavy Glass Grapes, approx. 3½" [OP, R3]. **$20.00–25.00.** B. Heavy Glass Heart, approx. 3½" [OP, R3]. **$20.00–25.00.** C. Heavy Indented Barrel, approx. 3½" [OP, R3]. **$20.00–25.00.** D. Heavy Indent, approx. 3½" [OP, R3]. **$20.00–25.00.**

Heavenly Bodies

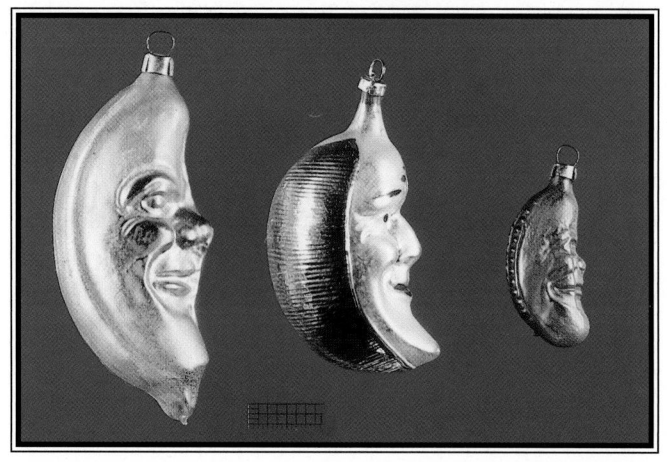

A. Man in the Moon (Type I), approx. 2¾" & 4" (shown) [German, OP-NP (1970s), R2-3]. Small, **$50.00–75.00.** Large, **$100.00–125.00.** B. Man in the Moon (Type III), approx. 3" & 3½" [OP-NP (1950s, 1980s, & 1990s), R3]. Small, **$80.00–100.00.** Large, **$125.00–150.00.** C. Man in the Moon (Type II), approx. 2" (shown) & 2¾" [German, OP-NP (1970s), R2-3]. Small, **$25.00–35.00.** Large, **$50.00–65.00.**

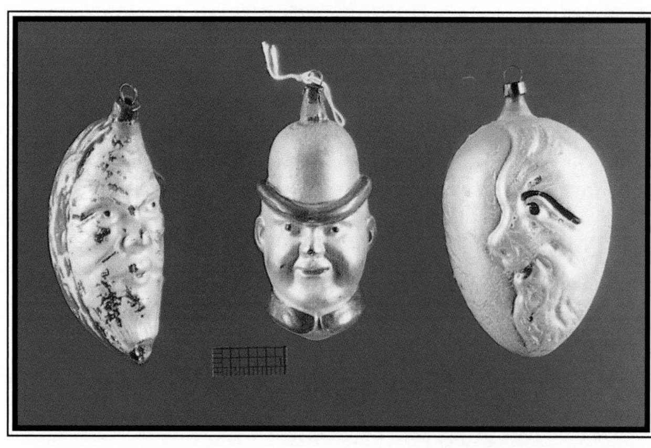

A. Man in the Moon (Type I), approx. 2¾" (shown) & 4" [German, OP-NP (1970s), R2-3]. Small, **$50.00–75.00.** B. Man in a Derby Hat, approx. 3" [OP, R1]. **$250.00–300.00.** C. The North Wind, approx. 3" [OP, R1-2]. **$250.00–300.00.**

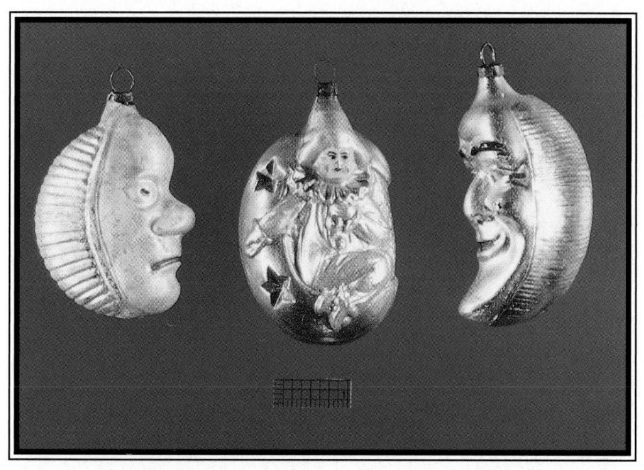

A. Frowning Man in the Moon, approx. 2¾" [OP, R1-2]. **$100.00–125.00.** B. Boy Clown in the Moon, approx. 3" (shown) & 3½" [German OP-NP (1990s), R3]. Small, **$100.00–125.00.** Large, **$175.00–200.00.** C. Man in the Moon (Type III), approx. 3" [OP-NP (1950s, 1980s, & 1990s), R3]. Small, **$80.00–100.00.**

A. Comet, approx. 3¼" [OP, R2]. **$35.00–45.00.** B. Small Molded Star, approx. 1½" (shown) & 2½" [OP-NP (1970s), R3-4]. Small, **$8.00–10.00.** Large, **$15.00–20.00.** C. Sun & Moon Face on a Ball, approx. 2" [German, OP-NP (1970s), R3]. **$90.00–110.00.**

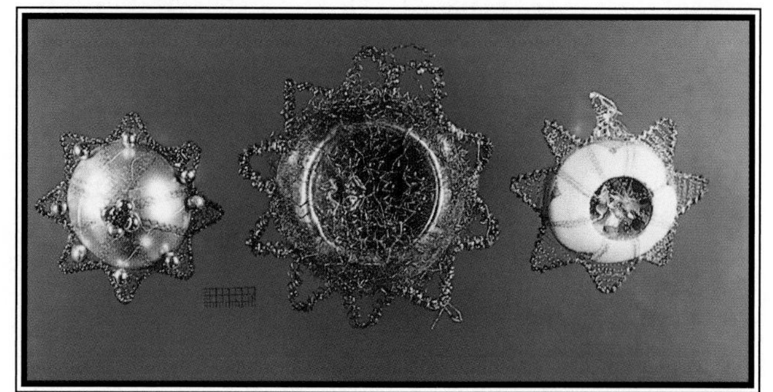

Wire-wrapped Stars, approx. 2" – 3½" [German, Czech, OP-NP (1950s), R3-4]. Small, **$20.00–25.00.** Medium, **$25.00–35.00.** Large, **$50.00–75.00.**

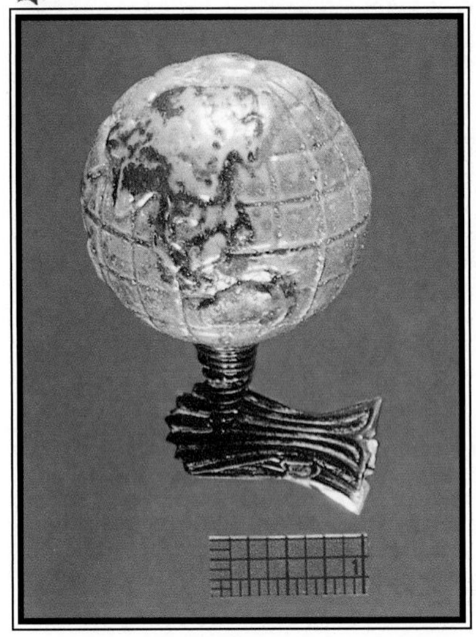

Globe (Type I), small, 1¾" [OP-NP (1990s), R1]. **$300.00–350.00.**

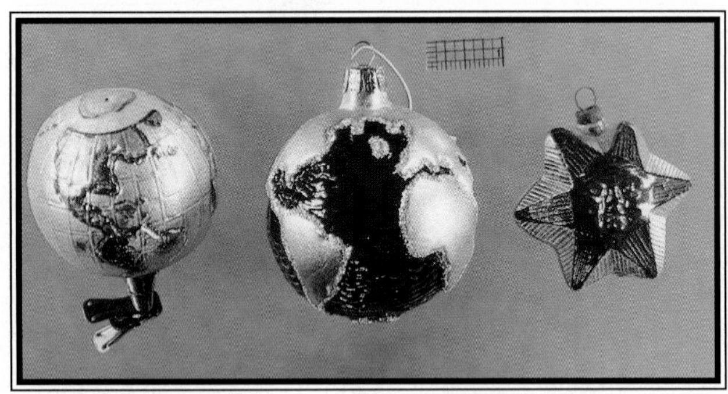

A. Globe (Type 1), 2¼", Lauscha Glas [NP, (1994)]. **$15.00–20.00.** B. Globe (Type II), 2¼" [Czech, NP (1990s), R3-4]. **$10.00–12.00.** C. Star with a Face, double sided, 2¼" [OP, R2]. **$40.00–55.00.**

A. Pear Face, approx. 2" & 2¾" (shown) [German, OP-NP (1980s), R2]. Small, **$100.00–125.00.** Large, **$150.00–175.00.** B. Sunface (Type I), double, 2¼" [OP, R2]. **$100.00–125.00.**

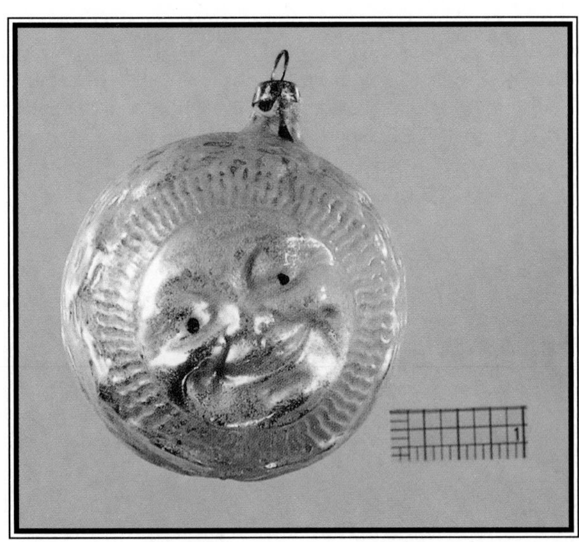

Sunface and Sun in Clouds, 2¼" [German, OP-NP (1992), R1-2]. **$125.00–150.00.**

Reverse Side of Sunface and Sun in Clouds.

Two Round-faced Men in the Moon, both are double faced: A. Type I, 2¼" [German, OP, R1]. **$150.00–200.00.** B. Type II, 2½" [OP, R1-2]. **$150.00–175.00.**

A. Cottage with a Mill Wheel, large, 3" [OP-NP, R2]. **$50.00–75.00.** B. Cuckoo Clock (Type II), 2¾" [OP, R1-2]. **$60.00–85.00.**

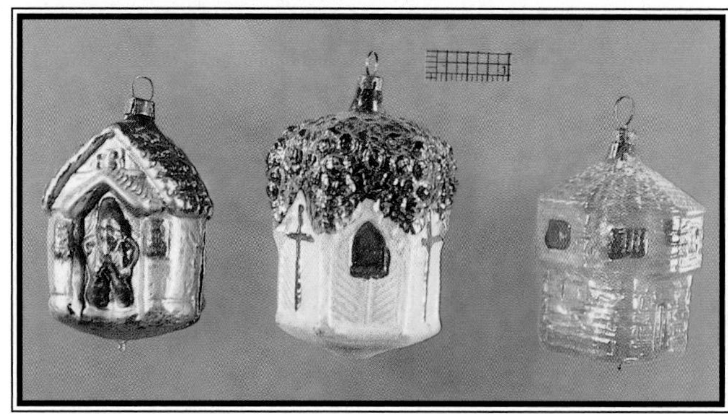

A. House with Elf at the Door, 2½" [OP, R2]. **$30.00–40.00.** B. "Chapel in the Wood," approx. 2½" & 3" (shown) [OP-NP (1995), R2-3]. Small, **$25.00–35.00.** Large, **$35.00–50.00.** C. House/Stockade, 2½" [OP, R1-2]. **$50.00–60.00.**

A. "Blumchen Cathedral," 7" [NP (1993), R2]. **$50.00–75.00.** B. Domed Cathedral, 4½" [Polish, NP (1993), R3-4]. **$15.00–20.00.**

A. Church on an Egg, 3½" [OP, R2-3]. **$60.00–90.00.** B. Church on a Disk, approx. 2" & 2½" (shown) [OP-NP (1991), R2-3]. Small, **$20.00–30.00.** Large, **$30.00–40.00.**

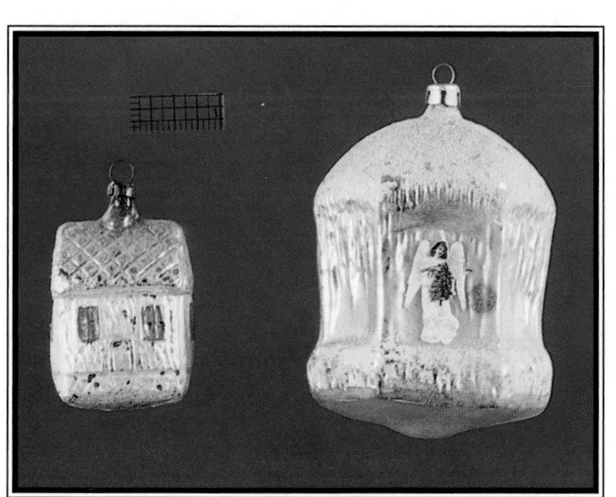

A. Peasant's Cottage, 1¾" [OP, R2-3]. **$20.00–25.00.** B. Ice House, 3" [OP, R1-2]. **$50.00–75.00.**

A. Town Hall Building, approx. 1½", 2', & 2½" (shown) [German, OP-NP (Inge-glas, 1991), R3]. Small, **$15.00–20.00.** Medium, **$20.00–30.00.** Large, **$30.00–40.00.** B. Town House, 2½" [OP, R2-3]. **$20.00–25.00.** C. Czech House with a Turkey, approx. 2½" (shown) and 3" [Czech, OP-NP (1980s), R3]. Small, **$20.00–25.00.** Large, **$40.00–60.00.**

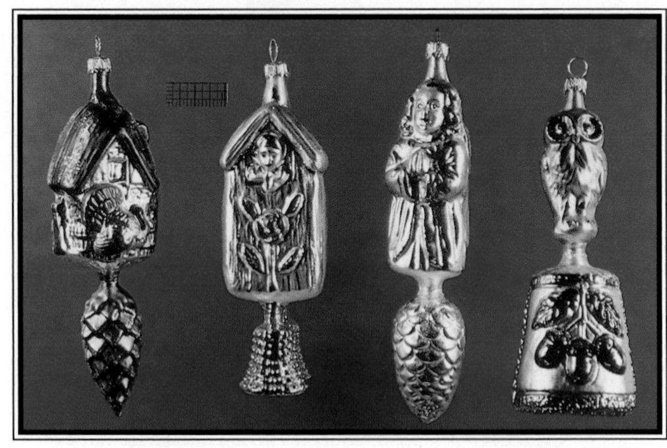

Four Christopher Radko Ornaments Combining Two Old German Molds on Each Piece [NP (ca. 1994), R3]: A. Turkey and House on a Pine Cone, 5". **$25.00–35.00.** B. Elf, Flower, and House on a Bell, 5". **$25.00–35.00.** C. Angel with Folded Wings Standing on a Pine Cone, 5½". **$30.00–40.00.** D. Owl on Top of a Bell, 5". **$25.00–35.00.**

A. Round Snow-covered House, approx. 2½", 3½" (shown), & 4" [German, OP, R2-3]. Small, **$25.00–35.00.** Medium, **$35.00–45.00.** Large, **$50.00–60.00.** B. Windmill on a Disc, approx. 2¼" [OP, R3]. **$30.00–40.00.** C. Church on an Egg, approx. 3½" [OP, R2-3]. **$60.00–90.00.**

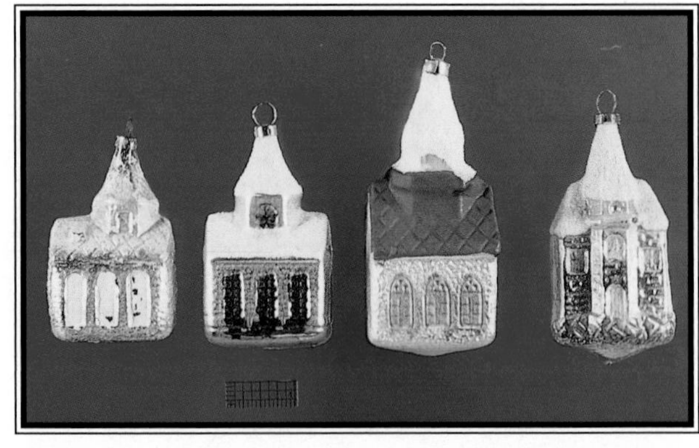

A. German Church, approx. 3" [OP-NP (Inge-glas, 1991), R3]. **$30.00–40.00.** B. Czech Church, approx. 3" [OP-NP (1975), R3]. **$30.00–40.00.** C. German Church, approx. 4" [OP-NP (1975), R3]. **$35.00–50.00.** D. Victorian House, approx. 3¼" [OP-NP (1990s), R2-3]. **$35.00–45.00.**

A. Church on a Disc, approx. 2" & 2½" (shown) [OP-NP (1991), R2-3]. Small, **$20.00–30.00.** Large, **$30.00–40.00.** B. House with a Turkey, approx. 2" (shown), 2½", & 2¾" [German & Austrian, OP-NP (1980s), R3-4]. Small, **$15.00–20.00.** Medium, **$25.00–35.00.** Large, **$40.00–60.00.** There are slight variations among the German, Czeck, and Austrian pieces.

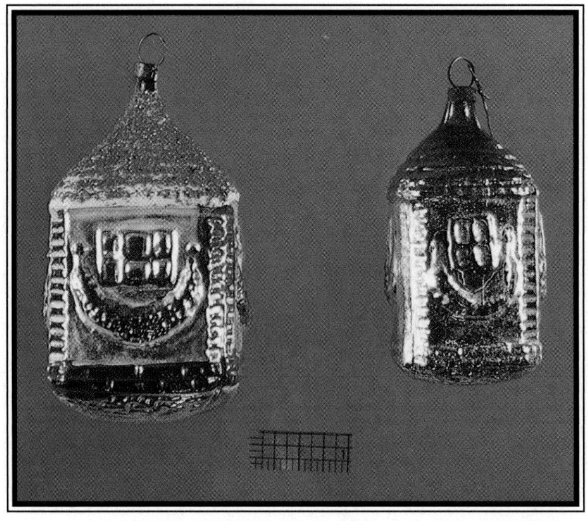

Houses with Pine Roping, approx. 1½", 2", 2½" (shown), & 3" (shown) [German, OP-NP (1990s), R4]. Small, **$10.00-15.00.** Medium, **$15.00-20.00.** Large, **$20.00-30.00.**

A. House with Pine Roping, 2" (shown) [German, OP-NP (1990s), R4]. Small, **$10.00-15.00.** B. Tall House, approx. 3" [German, OP-NP (Inge-glas, 1991), R3]. **$20.00-30.00.** C. Square House, approx. 2½" (shown) & 2¾" [German, OP-NP (1950s & 1990s), R4]. Small, **$15.00-20.00.** Large, **$20.00-30.00.**

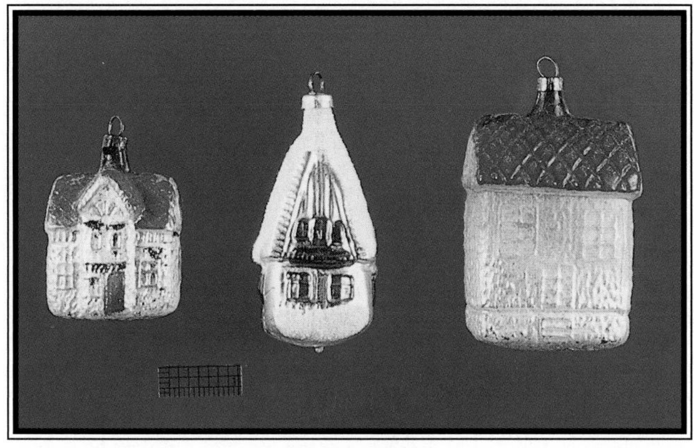

A. Town Hall Building, approx. 1½" (shown), 2", & 2½" [German, OP-NP (1991), R3]. Small, **$15.00-20.00.** Medium, **$20.00-30.00.** Large, **$30.00-40.00.** B. Chalet, approx. 2¾" [OP-NP (1985), R2-3]. **$20.00-30.00.** 1980s version (shown), **$15.00-18.00.** C. Large Stucco House, approx. 3" [Czech, OP, R2-3]. **$35.00-45.00.**

A. House with a Turkey, 2½" [German, OP-NP, R3-4]. Medium, **$25.00-35.00.** B. Molded Windmill (Type II), approx. 3¾" [OP-NP (1950s - 1960s), R2-3]. **$75.00-100.00.** 1950s - 1960s version (shown), **$40.00-50.00.** C. House with a Turkey, approx. 2½" [Austrian, OP-NP (1970s), R3-4]. Medium, **$25.00-35.00.** 1970s version (shown), **$12.00-15.00.**

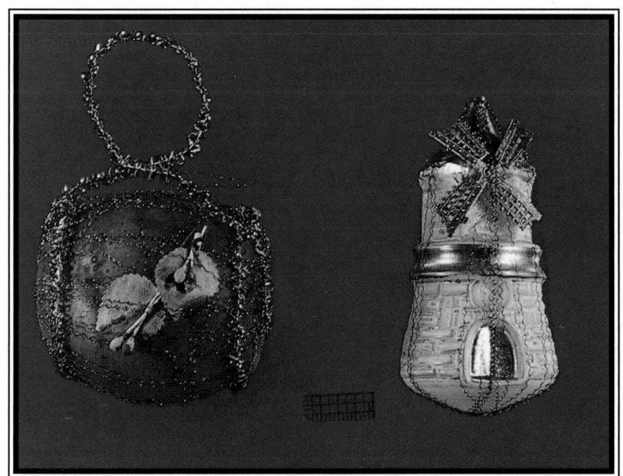

A. Free-blown Wire-wrapped Barrel, approx. 3¼" [OP, R2]. **$110.00-135.00.** B. Molded Windmill (Type I), approx. 4¼" [German, OP, R2]. **$75.00-100.00.**

A. Molded Windmill (Type I), approx. 4¼", missing paper arms [German, OP, R2]. **$75.00–100.00.** B. Free-blown Windmill (Type II) [OP, R2-3]. **$60.00–85.00.**

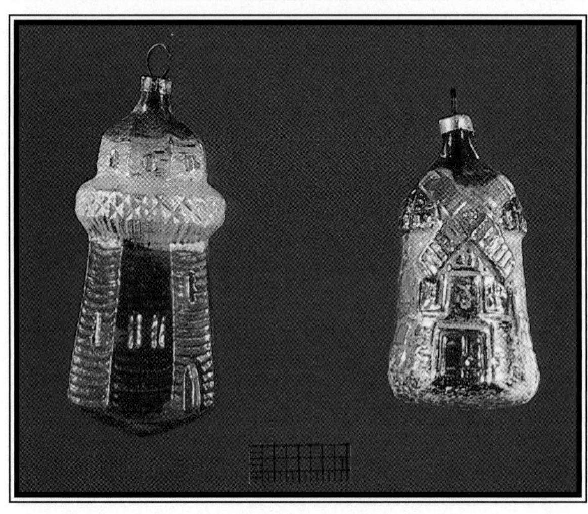

A. Lighthouse, approx. 3" [OP-NP (1950s – 1960s), R3-4]. **$40.00–60.00.** B. Windmill with Embossed Arms, approx. 2¼" [OP-NP (1950s), R3]. **$25.00–35.00.**

Early Wire-wrapped Free-blown Windmill (Type I), unsilvered, approx. 5" [OP, R1-2]. **$150.00–175.00.**

A & B. Front & Back View of the Standard Form Cottage, approx. 1¾", 2", 2¼" (shown), 2½", 2¾" (shown), & 3" [German, OP-NP (continuing), R5]. Small, **$8.00–12.00.** Medium, **$12.00–18.00.** Large, **$20.00–25.00.** C. Tree House (Type I), approx. 2½" [OP, R2]. **$45.00–65.00.**

A. Gingerbread House, approx. 3" [OP, R2]. **$40.00–50.00.** B. Castle Tower, approx. 4" [OP-NP (1991), R2]. **$100.00–140.00.** C. Town Hall Building, approx. 2" [German, OP-NP (1991), R3]. Medium, **$20.00–30.00.**

A. House with Pine Roping and Extended Arms, "The Village," 5¾" [German, OP, R1]. **$200.00–275.00.** B. House with Pine Roping and Indented Star, 5¼" [German, OP, R1-2]. **$125.00–150.00.**

A. House with Pine Roping and Free-blown Star, 3¾" [German, OP, R2]. **$50.00–75.00.** B. Crossed American Flags, embossed, small, 2½" [NP (1950s), R2]. **$100.00–125.00.** C. Purse with Embossed Flower, 2" [OP, R3]. **$25.00–35.00.**

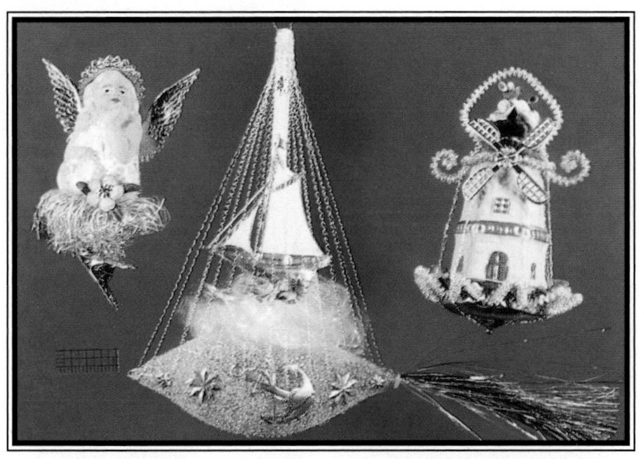

Three Ornaments by D. Blumchen & Co [all NP (1992), R2-3]: A. Raphael Angel, 2¼". **$50.00–75.00.** B. Sailboat with Sails, 6½". **$50.00–75.00.** C. Windmill (Type III), 4½". **$65.00–85.00.**

A. Windmill with Embossed Arms, Dresden arms added, 2¼" [OP-NP, R3]. **$50.00–75.00.** B. Top Hat, hollow, 2½" [OP, R1]. **$175.00–200.00.** C. Windmill on a Bell, 2¼" [OP, R2-3]. **$30.00–40.00.**

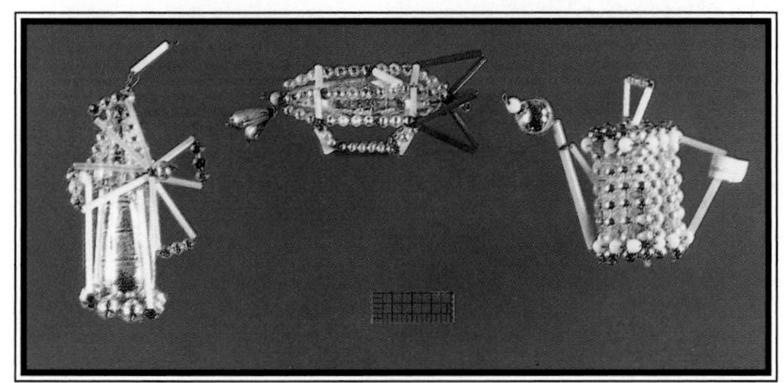

Three Beaded Ornaments, probably Czech: A. Windmill, 3½" [OP, R2]. **$25.00–35.00.** B. Dirigible, 3¼" [OP, R2]. **$30.00–40.00.** C. Water Can, 2¼" [OP, R2]. **$25.00–35.00.**

Household Items

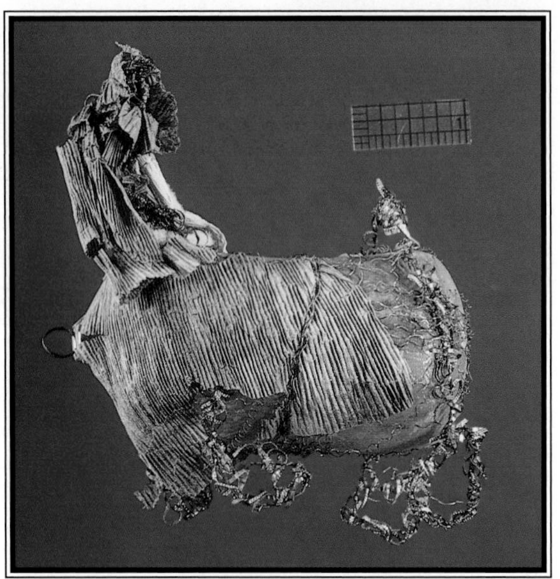

Free-blown Baby Cradle, approx. 3¼", holds a chenille baby [OP, R1]. **$275.00-300.00.**

"Merry Xmas" Baby Rattle, approx. 5" [OP, R2]. **$150.00-175.00.**

Barrel Baby Rattle or Gavel, approx. 6½", wire wrapped, unsilvered [OP, R1]. **$175.00-200.00.**

A. Champagne Bottle in a Bucket, approx. 4" [Italian, NP (1950s), R1]. **$125.00-150.00.** B. Two Rabbits on an Egg, 3¼" [OP, R1-2]. **$40.00-55.00.**

Bottles with Paper Labels, approx. 2" - 5" (2" - 3" are the most common) [OP, R2]. A. "ERDENER" label, 2¾". **$75.00-100.00.** B. No label, 2¾", missing labels greatly affect value. Without label, **$45.00-55.00.** With label, **$90.00-110.00.** C. "MALAZA" label, 3". **$75.00-100.00.**

A. Free-blown Wire-wrapped bottle, approx. 4" – 6", sizes may vary (5½" shown) [OP, R3]. **$75.00–100.00.** B. Molded Coffee Pot with a Rose, approx. 3¼" [OP, R2-3]. **$40.00–50.00.** C. Free-blown Flask with Scrap, Wire, & Fabric Decorations, 4" – 7", sizes may vary (5½" shown) [OP, R3]. **$75.00–100.00.**

A. Reverse Carousel, approx. 2½" & 2¾" (shown). The animals face left instead of right (as in all other carousels) [OP, R2-3]. Either size, **$90.00–110.00.** B. Carousel, standard form, approx. 2½" (shown) & 3" [German, OP-NP (1980s), R3]. Small, **$50.00–60.00.** Large, **$70.00–90.00.** C. Small Carousel, approx. 2½" [OP-NP (1980s), R2]. **$40.00–50.00.** 1980s version (shown), **$15.00–20.00.**

Carousel with Round Top, 3¼" [OP, R2-3]. **$50.00–75.00.** B. Transportation Carousel, 2¼" [OP, R1-2]. **$125.00–150.00.**

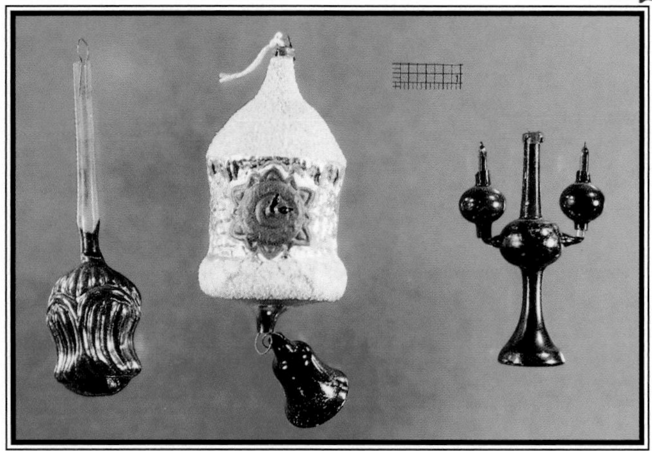

A. Broom, 4½" [OP, R1-2]. **$30.00–35.00.** B. Clock Tower with a Bell, 5¼" [OP, R1]. **$100.00–125.00.** C. Candle Lamp, 3¼" [OP, R1-2]. **$75.00–90.00.**

A. Lighthouse, approx. 3" [OP-NP (1950s – 1960s), R3-4]. **$40.00–60.00.** B. Carousel with a Round Top, approx. 3¼", 3½" (shown), and 4" [OP, R2-3]. Medium and large, **$65.00–85.00.**

Clocks with Paper Dials: A. Wall Clock, approx. 3¾" [German, OP, R2]. **$75.00–100.00.** B. Pocket Watch, approx. 1¾" [OP, R2]. **$45.00–55.00.** C. Cuckoo Clock, approx. 2¾" & 3½" (shown) [German, OP-NP (1950s & 1990s, small), R3]. Small, **$25.00–35.00.** Large with paper face, **$75.00–100.00.**

A. Pocket Watch with an Embossed Face (Type I), approx. 1¾" [OP, R2]. **$50.00–60.00.** B. Cuckoo Clock with Paper Face, approx. 2¾" & 3½" (shown) [German, OP-NP (1950s & 1990s, small), R3]. Large with paper face, **$80.00–100.00.** Small, **$30.00–45.00.** C. Telephone, approx. 1¾" [NP (1950s & 1990s — this version does not have the handset), R2]. **$70.00–90.00.**

A. Clock and Sundial, approx. 2½". The sundial is on the back [OP, R2]. **$100.00–150.00.** B. Rectangular Wall Clock, approx. 3" [German, OP-NP (1980s), R2]. **$75.00–100.00.**

A. Alarm Clock, 3½" [OP, R1-2]. **$100.00–125.00.** B. Pocket Watch (Type II), small, 1¾" [German, OP-NP (1980s), R2]. **$50.00–75.00.**

A. Pocket Watch with a Head, 3¾" [NP (Radko, 1993) R3-4]. **$30.00–40.00.** B. Barrel with Grapes, 3" [OP-NP, R2]. Old, **$60.00–75.00.** 1989 version (shown), **$12.00–18.00.** C. Clown Head, "Bozo," 1¾" [OP, R1-2]. **$125.00–150.00.**

A. Early Free-blown Gramophone, approx. 4½" [OP, R1-2]. **$200.00–275.00.** B. Unsilvered and Unusual Basket of Flowers, approx. 4½". **$150.00–175.00.**

A. Free-blown Wine Glass, approx. 5¾", unsilvered & wire wrapped [OP, R2]. **$100.00–125.00.** B. Champagne or Wine Glass, approx. 5½" [OP, R2]. **$100.00–125.00.**

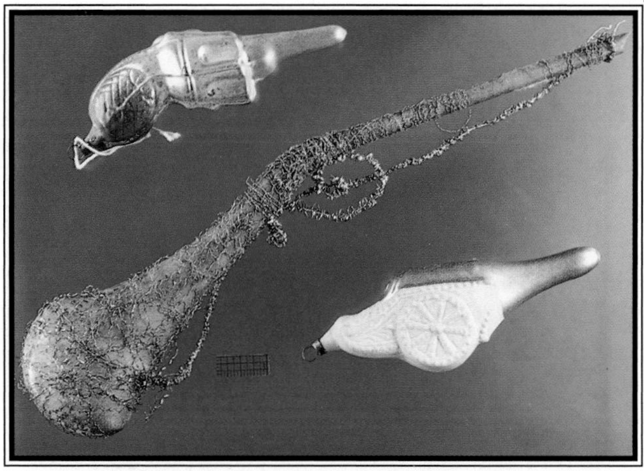

A. Revolver, approx. 5" [OP, R2]. **$225.00–275.00.** B. Free-blown & Wire-wrapped Rifle, approx. 12" [OP, R1-2]. **$325.00–400.00.** C. Cannon, approx. 5½" [OP, R1]. **$250.00–350.00.**

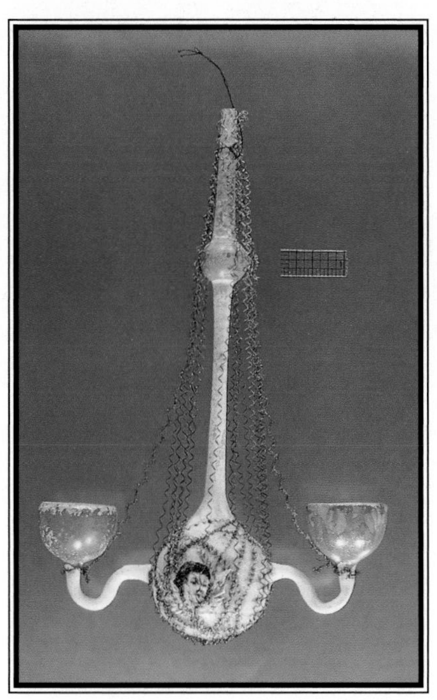

Gas Lamp Chandelier (Type I), approx. 7¾" [German, OP-NP (2003), R1]. **$275.00–375.00.**

Gas Lamp Chandelier (Type I), 7" [OP, R1-2]. **$300.00–375.00.**

A. Banquet Lamp, large, 6" [OP, R3]. **$100.00–125.00.** B. Candelabra, 5½" [OP, R1]. **$150.00–175.00.** C. Art Glass Banquet Lamp, 3½" [OP-NP]. Old, **$50.00–75.00.** 1990s form (shown), **$15.00–20.00.**

A & C. Banquet Lamps with Attached Globes: A. 5¼" [OP-NP (1950s), R3]. **$65.00–85.00.** C. 4" [OP-NP, R3], **$25.00–35.00.** B. Table Lamp with Molded Shade, 4¼" [OP, R2-3]. **$25.00–35.00.**

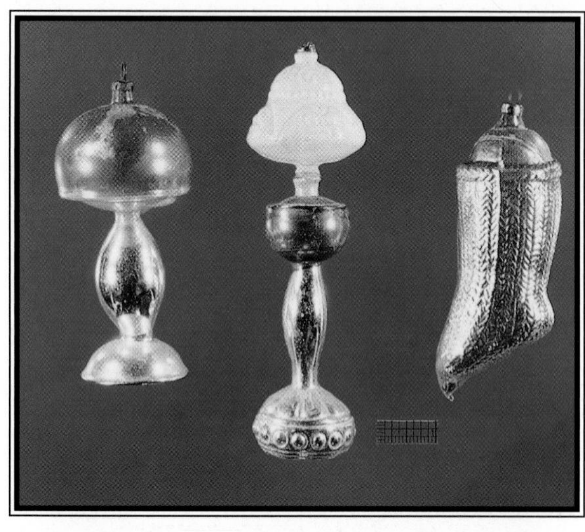

A. Table Lamp, approx. 4½" [OP-NP (1980s), R4-5]. **$30.00–35.00.** B. Banquet Lamp with Molded Milk Glass Shade, approx. 6½" [OP, R2-3]. **$110.00–135.00.** C. Knit Stocking with a Ball, approx. 4¼" [OP, R1-2]. **$150.00–175.00.**

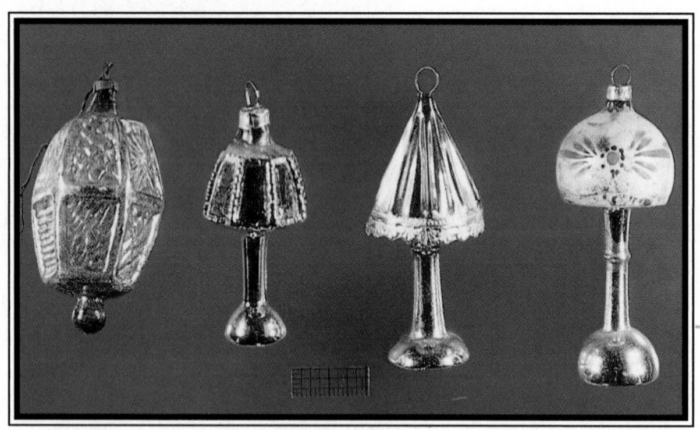

A. Paneled Lantern, approx. 3½". B, C, D. Various Styles of Table Lamps, approx. 3" – 5" (3", 4¼", & 4½" shown) [OP-NP (1980s), R4-5]. Small, **$12.00–18.00.** Medium, **$20.00–30.00.** Large, **$30.00–40.00.**

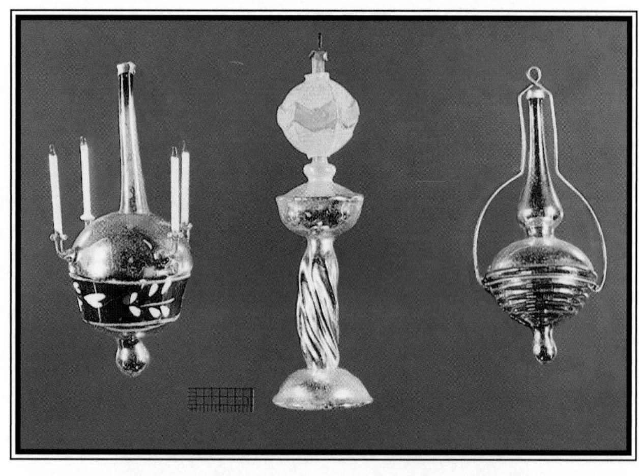

A. Candle Chandelier, approx. 5" [OP, R2-3]. **$50.00–75.00.** B. Banquet Lamp with Molded Shade, approx. 6½" [OP, R2-3]. **$90.00–110.00.** C. Hanging Oil Lamp with a Metal Hanging Bracket (Type I), approx. 4½" (glass only) [OP, R1-2]. **$40.00–50.00.**

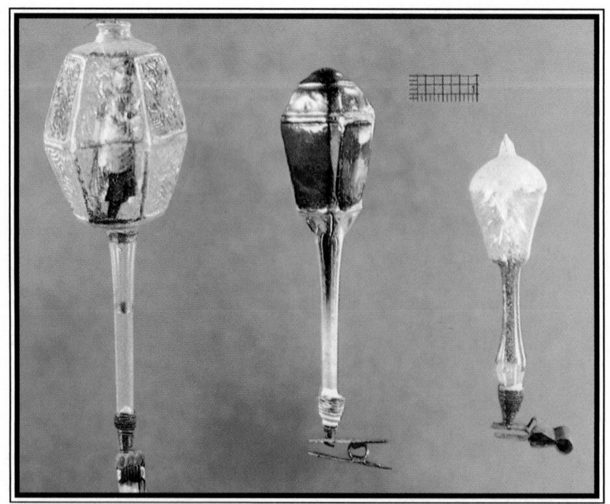

Street lights: A. Twelve-paneled with Scraps Inside, 5½" [OP, R1]. **$75.00–100.00.** B. Four-paneled with Domed Top, 4½" [OP-NP, R2]. **$35.00–45.00.** C. Round Lamp, 3¾" [OP, R1-2]. **$40.00–50.00.**

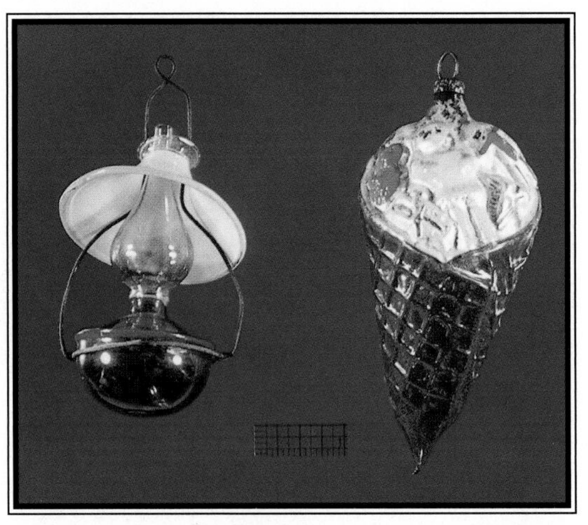

A. Hanging Oil Lamp (Type II), 4" [OP, R2]. **$70.00-90.00.** B. Cornucopia of Toys, approx. 3¼", 3¾" (shown), & 4" [OP-NP (1980s), R2-3]. Small, **$100.00-125.00.** Medium, **$150.00-175.00.** Large, **$200.00-250.00.**

German Pipe, 11½", extra large [OP, R1]. **$350.00-450.00.**

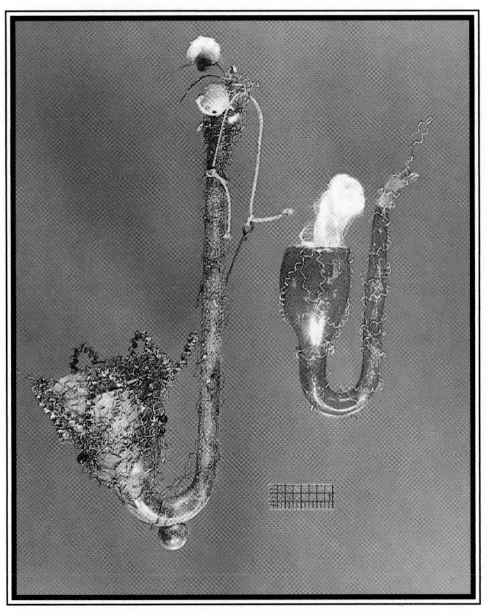

A. German Pipe, approx. 7½" [OP, R1]. **$150.00-175.00.** B. German Pipe with Smoke, approx. 3¼" [OP, R1-2]. **$50.00-75.00.**

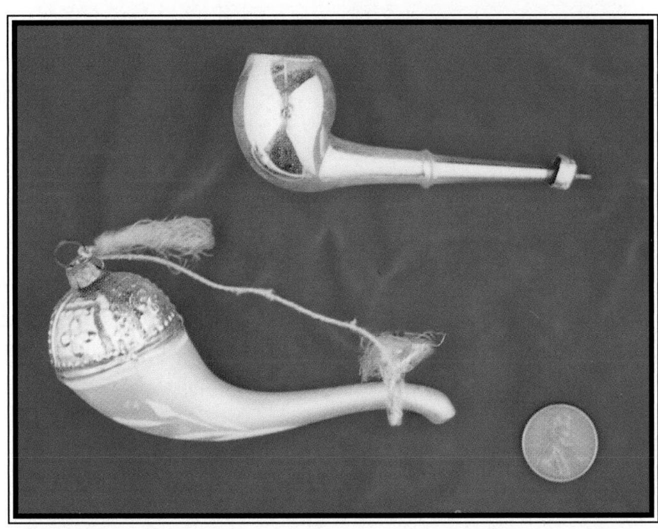

A. Straight-stemmed Pipe, 3" (shown) – 10", sizes vary (3" – 5" is typical) [OP-NP (continuing), R4]. Small (3" – 5"), **$15.00-25.00.** Medium (5" – 8"), **$75.00-100.00.** Large (8"+), **$175.00-200.00.** B. Dublin Pipe, 3" – 6", sizes vary (3" shown) [OP, R4]. Small, **$25.00-35.00.** Medium, **$40.00-60.00.** Large, **$60.00-80.00.**

Bubble Pipe, 5¼" [NP (1950s & 1960s), R1]. **$40.00-50.00.**

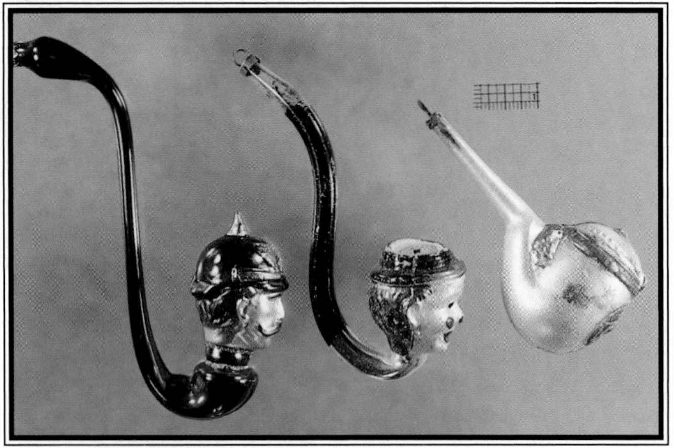

A. Kaiser Head Pipe, 7" [NP (Radko, 1994), R3-4]. **$50.00–75.00.** B. Hans Head Pipe, 5¼", [NP (1950s), R2]. **$150.00–175.00.** C. Pipe, decorative, 4" [OP, R1]. **$35.00–50.00.**

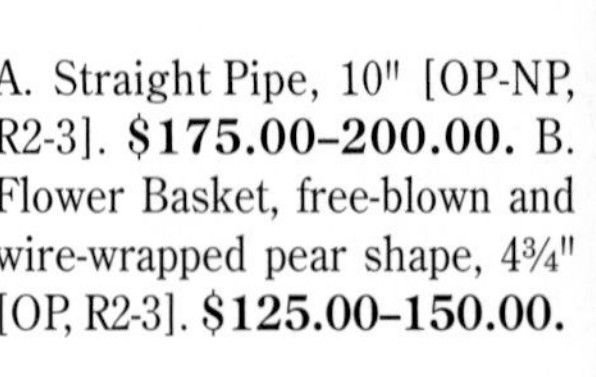

A. Straight Pipe, 10" [OP-NP, R2-3]. **$175.00–200.00.** B. Flower Basket, free-blown and wire-wrapped pear shape, 4¾" [OP, R2-3]. **$125.00–150.00.**

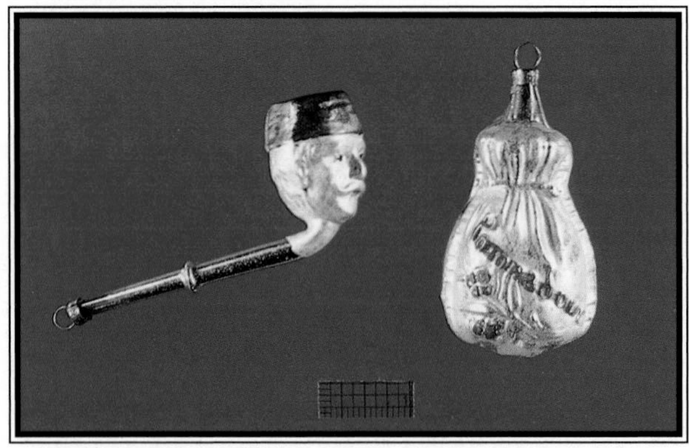

A. Man's Head Pipe (Type I), 1½" head, approx. 3¾" overall [German, OP, R1-2]. **$200.00–250.00.** B. Pompadour Bag, approx. 2½" [OP-NP (1990s), R1-2]. **$100.00–135.00.**

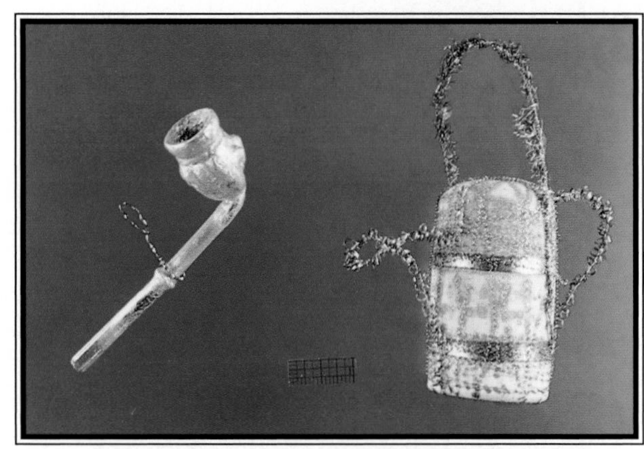

A. Man's Head Pipe (Type II), 1½" head, approx. 3¾" overall [OP, R1-2]. **$200.00–225.00.** B. Free-blown and Wire-wrapped Watering Can, approx. 3½" [OP, R1-2]. **$125.00–150.00.**

A. Quilted Pillow (Type I), approx. 3½" [German, OP, R3]. **$30.00–40.00.** B. Die, approx. 1¾" & 2" (shown) [German, OP-NP (1970s), R2]. Small, **$50.00–65.00.** Large, **$75.00–90.00.** C. Quilted Pillow (Type II), approx. 3¼" [German, OP-NP (1970s), R3]. **$30.00–40.00.**

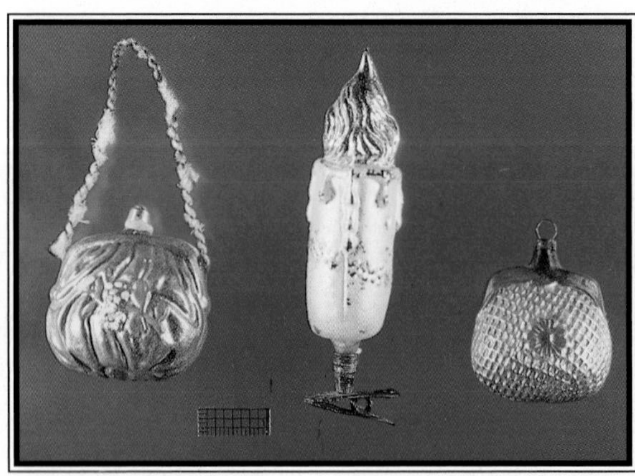

A. Wrinkled Purse, approx. 2½" [OP, R2]. **$70.00–90.00.** B. Clip-on Molded Candle, approx. 4" (glass only) [German, OP-NP (Inge-glas, 1980s & 1990s), R2]. **$125.00–175.00.** C. Purse with an Embossed Flower, approx. 2" [OP, R3]. **$25.00–35.00.**

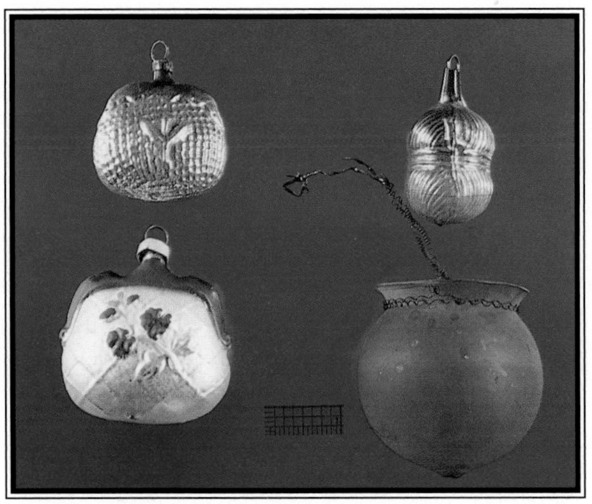

A. Purse with Embossed Leaves, approx. 1¾"W [OP-NP (1980s), R1-2]. **$25.00–35.00.** B. Skein of Yarn, approx. 1¾" (shown) & 2¼" [German, OP, R2]. Small, **$20.00–30.00.** Large, **$30.00–40.00.** C. Purse with Embossed Roses, approx. 2¼" [German, OP-NP (1970s – 1980s), R2]. **$50.00–75.00.** D. Free-blown and Hollow Cauldron, approx. 1½", 3½", & 2¾" (shown) [OP, R3]. Small, **$25.00–40.00.** Medium, **$40.00–65.00.** Large, **$75.00–125.00.**

A. Baseball with an Anchor, 2½" [OP, R1-2]. **$175.00–225.00.** B. Wicker Basket Purse, 1¾" [OP, R1-2]. **$100.00–135.00.**

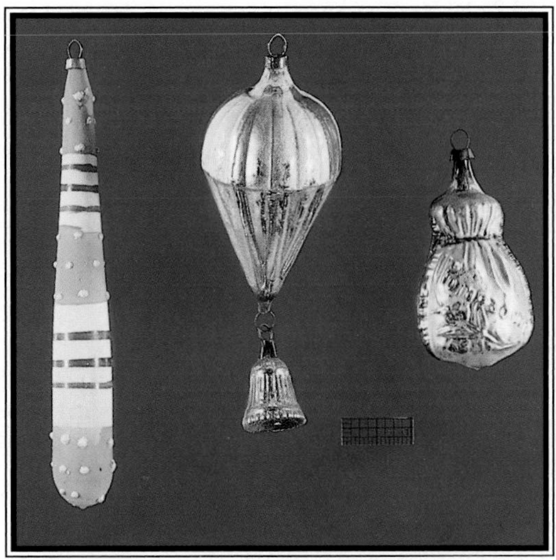

A. Baseball Bat, 6" [OP, R2-3]. **$100.00–125.00.** B. Parachute with Bell, 4½" [OP, R1]. **$75.00–100.00.** C. Pompadour Bag, 2½" [OP-NP (1990s), R1-2]. **$100.00–135.00.**

Three Radko Ornaments [all NP, R3-4]: A. "Drapper Shoe," double strapped, large, 5", 1991. **$40.00–50.00.** B. Girl Holding a Puppy, "Madeline's Puppy," 4", 1992. **$40.00–50.00.** C. Purse, "Her Purse," large, 3½", 1991. **$30.00–40.00.**

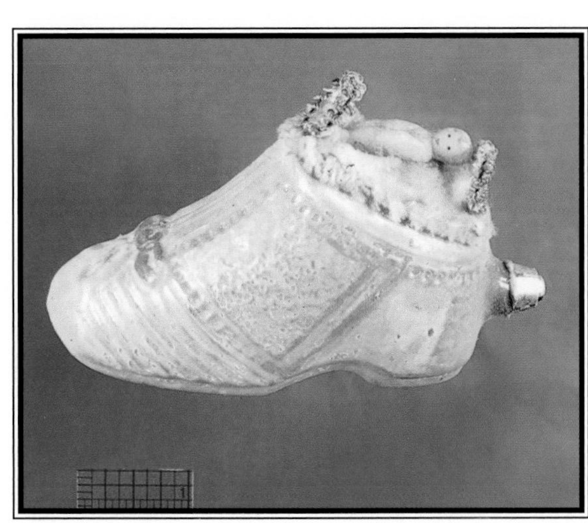

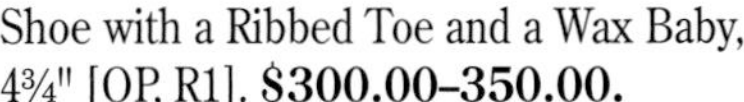

Shoe with a Ribbed Toe and a Wax Baby, 4¾" [OP, R1]. **$300.00–350.00.**

A. Cat Sleeping in a Shoe (Type II), approx. 3½" [German, OP-NP (1960s & 1970s), R3]. **$100.00–150.00.** B & D. Standard Form Shoes, approx. 1¾", 2", 3" (shown), & 3½" (shown) [German, OP-NP (continuing), R4] Small, **$15.00–20.00.** Medium, **$20.00–25.00.** Large, **$30.00–40.00.** C. Baby Shoe with a Scrap Baby Face, approx. 3" [OP, R1-2]. **$150.00–175.00.**

A. Roller Skate, 3¾" [OP, R1]. **$150.00–200.00.** B. Shoe with a Poinsettia, 3½" [German, OP-NP (Matthaei, 1993), R1]. Old, **$100.00–125.00.** 1993 version (shown), **$15.00–20.00.** C. Beer Stein, 4" [German, OP-NP (1980s – 1995), R1]. **$175.00–200.00.**

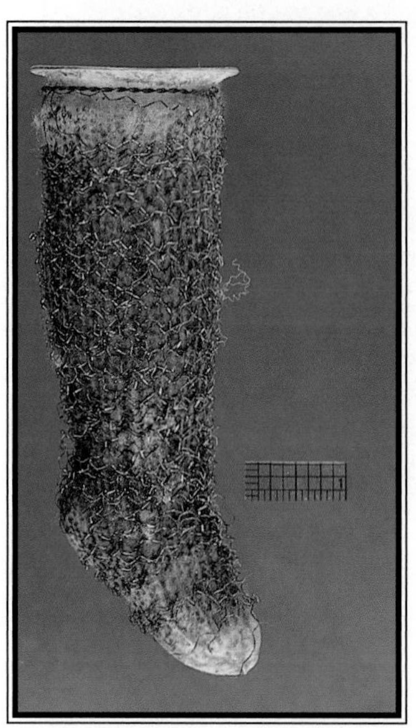

Hollow Stocking, 6¼", unsilvered and wire wrapped [OP, R1]. **$350.00–400.00.**

Christmas Stocking, approx. 4¼" [OP, R2]. **$175.00–200.00.**

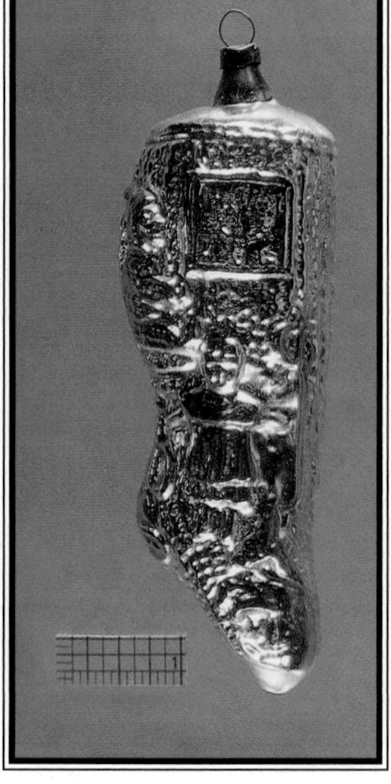

A. Stocking with Toys, 5" [German, NP (ca. 1975), R3]. **$15.00–20.00.** B. Knitted Stocking, 6" [OP-NP, R1-2]. Old, **$125.00–150.00.** 1980s version (shown), **$10.00–15.00.** C. Railroad Lantern, 2¾" [OP-NP (1980s), R1-2]. **$75.00–90.00.**

A. Free-blown Urn or Sugar Pot, approx. 2½" [OP-NP, R4-5]. **$15.00–25.00.** B. Free-blown Coffee Pot, approx. 3½" [OP-NP, R4-5]. **$15.00–25.00.** C. Teapot, approx. 1½" [OP-NP, R4-5]. **$15.00–25.00.**

A. Coffee Pot, 2¾" [OP-NP, R4-5]. **$20.00–35.00.** B. Teapot, 2¼" [NP (1950s), R4-5]. **$15.00–20.00.** C. "Medoc" Bottle with Paper Label, 2½" [OP, R2]. **$100.00–125.00.**

Closed Umbrellas, approx. 4¼", 10", & 7¼" (all shown), but sizes vary [OP-NP, R4]. Prices vary with added decoration. Prices for pieces shown: A. **$10.00–12.00.** B. **$20.00–25.00.** C. **$18.00–20.00.**

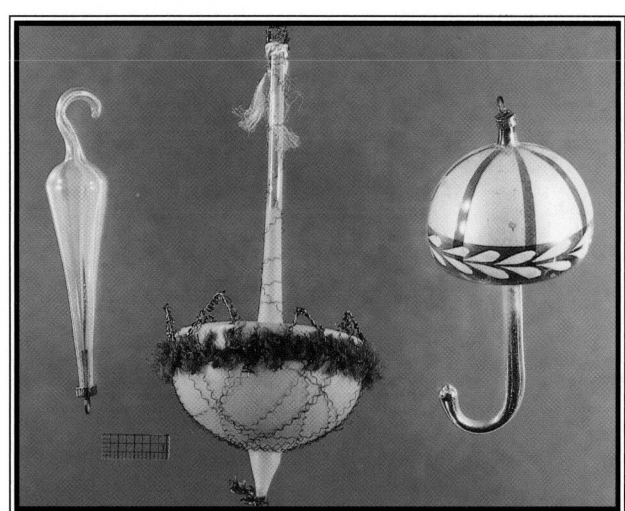

A. Closed Umbrella, art glass, 4½" [OP, R2]. **$30.00–40.00.** B. Open Umbrella, wire wrapped, 8" [OP-NP, R3]. **$80.00–100.00.** C. Open Umbrella with Handle, 5" [OP, R2]. **$60.00–75.00.**

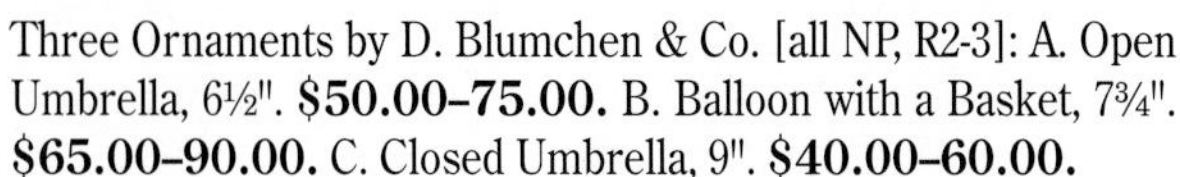

Three Ornaments by D. Blumchen & Co. [all NP, R2-3]: A. Open Umbrella, 6½". **$50.00–75.00.** B. Balloon with a Basket, 7¾". **$65.00–90.00.** C. Closed Umbrella, 9". **$40.00–60.00.**

Kugels

Kugel Balls, small, 2" – 2½", various shades of green [OP, R3]. **$40.00–65.00.**

Rare Kugel Balls: A. Miniature red, 1¾" [OP, R3]. **$70.00–90.00.** B. Amethyst, small, 3" [OP, R1+]. **$500.00–600.00.** C. Amethyst, labeled "Made in France," 2½" [OP, R1+]. **$400.00–500.00.**

Reproduction Kugel Balls from India — note cap designs [NP, R3-4]. **$8.00–12.00.**

Kugel Shapes: A. Ribbed Ball, small, 2" [OP, R1-2]. **$200.00–250.00.** B. Red Ball, miniature, 1½" [OP, R3]. **$70.00–90.00.** C. Gold Ribbed Egg, medium, 3" [OP, R1]. **$225.00–275.00.** D. Gold Ball, small, 2½" [OP, R3]. **$35.00–50.00.** E. Silver Ribbed Ball, 3" [OP, R1-2]. **$250.00–300.00.**

A. Miniature Blue Kugel, 1½" [OP, R1]. **$40.00–50.00.** B. Early Egg Shape with a Pike and a Cork-and-Wire Hanger, 1¾" [OP, R1-2]. **$125.00–150.00.** C. Early Egg Shape with a Cork-and-Wire Hanger, 2¼" [OP, R1-2]. **$125.00–150.00.** D. Miniature Green Kugel Ball, 1¼" [OP, R2]. **$40.00–50.00.**

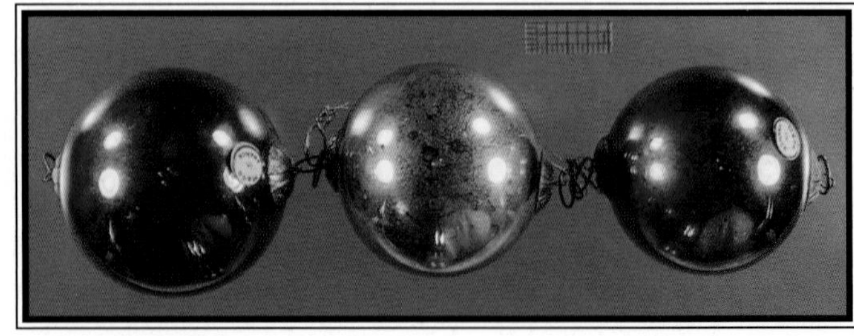

Kugel Balls with Double Hangers, 2½" dia. [OP, R1+]: A. Green. **$250.00–275.00** each. B. Blue, paper label reads "Made in France." **$250.00–300.00** each.

Kugel End-of-Day Glass. Color is glass, not paint, 3" [OP, R1+]. **$750.00–900.00.**

Kugel Balls Painted with Flowers [OP, R1]: A. Blue, small, 2⅞". **$200.00–250.00.** B. Silver with Stripes and Flowers, small, 2¾" [OP, R1]. **$250.00–275.00.**

Kugel Balls with Painted Decorations: A. Green Ball with Flower, medium, 3½" [OP, R1]. **$250.00–350.00.** B. Gold Ball with Stripes, 3⅛" [OP, R1]. **$250.00–275.00.**

Artichoke-shaped Kugel, 3" [OP, R1+}. **$1,200.00–1,500.00.**

Three Egg and Teardrop Shapes: A. Blue Egg, small, 2¾" [OP, R2]. **$160.00–185.00.** B. Gold Egg, medium, 3½" [OP, R2]. **$150.00–200.00.** C. Gold Teardrop, 3¼" [OP, R2]. **$150.00–200.00.**

Ball of Clustered Berries [both OP, R1-2]: A. Green, 4". **$750.00–900.00.** B. Gold, 3¾". **$700.00–800.00.**

Kugel Grapes: A. Standard Grape Cluster, blue, 4" [OP, R3]. **$250.00-300.00.** B. Standard Grape Cluster, gold, 4½" [OP, R3]. **$200.00-250.00.** C. Grapes in Oval Cluster, green, small, 3½" [Indian, OP-NP (1990s), R1-2]. **$175.00-200.00.**

A. Schecken Kugel, approx. 4½". The interior is decorated with paint and wax [OP, R1]. **$700.00-850.00.** B. Early Kugel with Pike, approx. 4", rare ruby red [OP, R1+]. **$500.00-650.00.**

Kugel Grapes in an Oval Cluster, 3" [OP, R2]. **$175.00-200.00.**

Kugel Grapes, gold, 4½" [OP, R3]. **$200.00-250.00.**

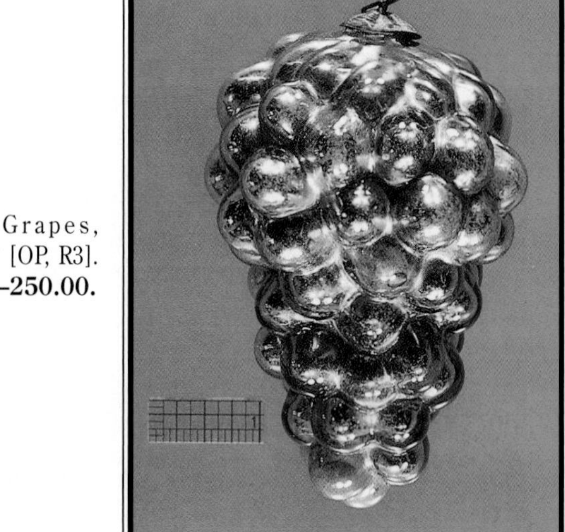

Three Sizes and Colors of the Standard Grape Cluster [all OP, R3]: A. Green, 6". **$500.00-550.00.** B. Blue, 4½". **$275.00-350.00.** C. Gold, medium, 4". **$175.00-225.00.**

Grapes in an Oval Cluster [all OP-NP, R1-2]: A. Green, small, 3½". **$175.00-200.00.** B. Green, 3". **$175.00-200.00.** C. Blue, small, 3½". **$175.00-200.00.** D. Silver, medium, 4". **$125.00-150.00.** E. Gold, small, 3½". **$125.00-150.00.**

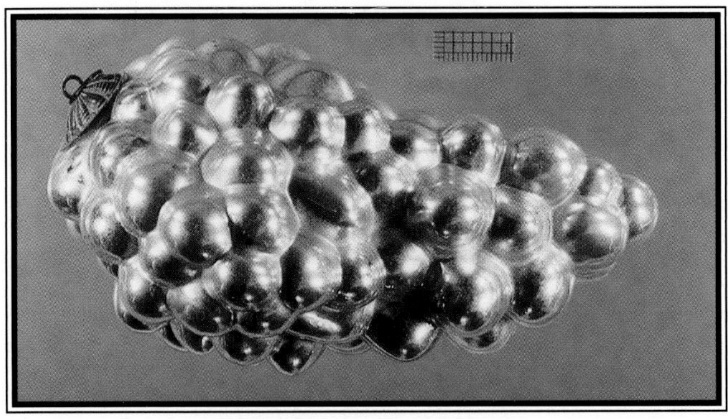

Curved Bunch of Grapes, rare, 7¼" [OP, R1+]. **$2,000.00–2,500.00.**

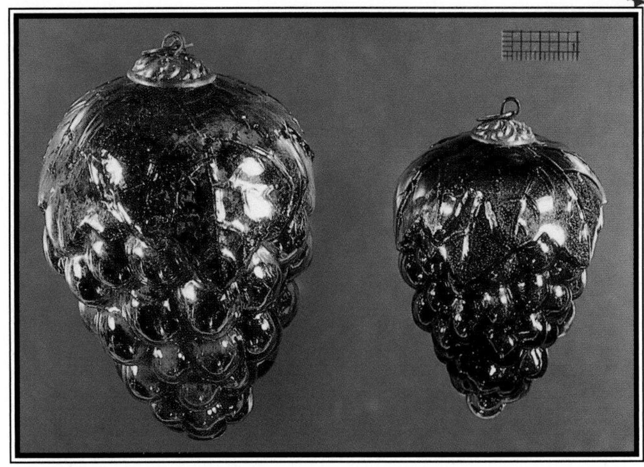

Grapes with Leaves, both marked "Depose" in leaves [both OP, R1]: A. Gold, large, 4¾". **$450.00–600.00.** B. Green, small, 4". **$500.00–600.00.**

Grapes with Embossed Leaves, extra large, 7¼" [OP, R1]. **$900.00–1,000.00.**

Reproduction Kugels from India: A. Red Grapes with Embossed Leaves, 4" [NP]. **$8.00–10.00.** B, C, D. Silver, Gold, and Cobalt Grapes in Oval Cluster, 2¾" [NP]. **$8.00–10.00.** Note the small pikes.

Pine Cone with Leaves, rare, 4¼" [OP, R1+]. **$1,200.00–1,500.00.**

Round Kugel Pine Cone, rare, blue, 4½" [OP, R1+]. **$1,200.00–1,500.00.**

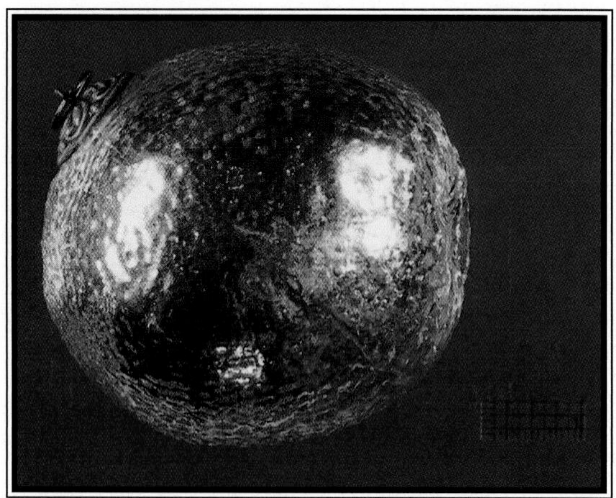

Kugel Orange, silver, 3½" [OP, R1]. **$900.00-1,000.00.**

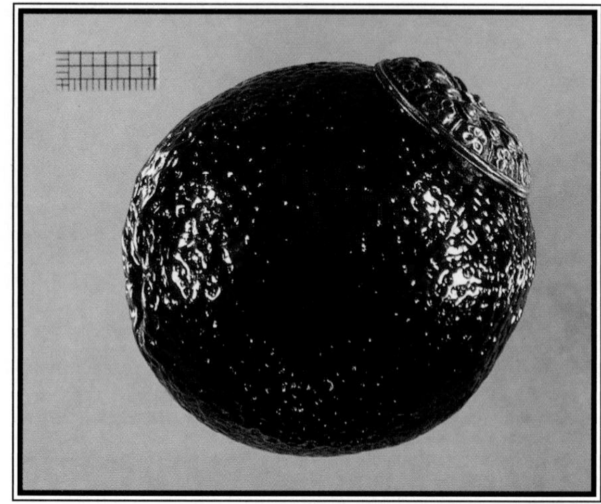

Kugel Orange or Lemon, unsilvered, 3½", amethyst colored [OP, R1]. **$1,100.00-1,300.00.**

Kugel Strawberry, rare, 4¼", cobalt blue [OP, R1+]. **$2,500.00-3,000.00.**

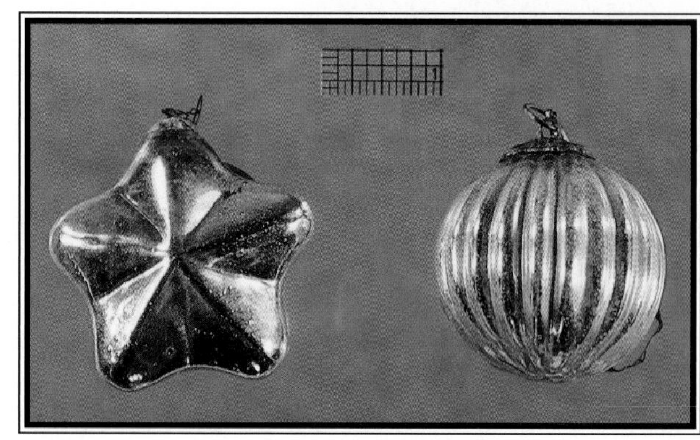

A. Kugel Star, 2¼" [OP, R1+]. **$350.00-450.00.** B. Ribbed Kugel Ball, small, 1¾", silver [OP, R1-2]. **$175.00-200.00.**

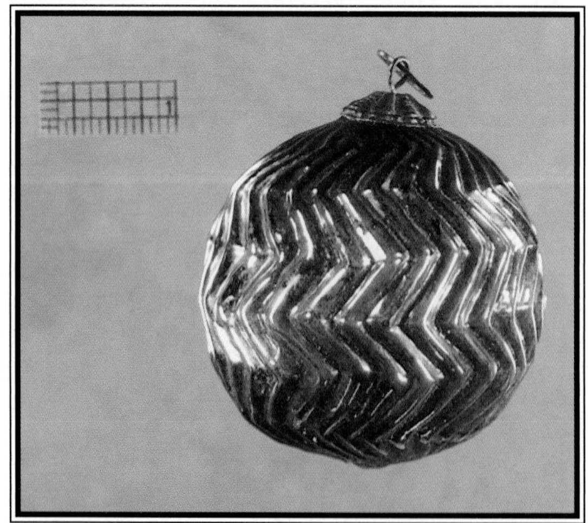

Kugel Ball with Zigzag patterns, amethyst, 2". Lighter glass may mean this is a transition style [OP, R1+]. **$300.00-350.00.**

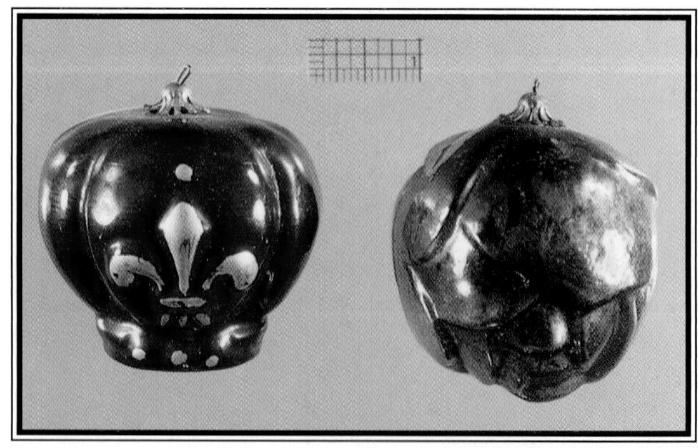

Heavy Glass Kugel-likes with Unusual Caps: A. Crown, 2" [OP, R1]. **$100.00-125.00.** B. Rose, 2¼" [OP, R1]. **$100.00-125.00.**

Mushrooms

A & C. Mushrooms, standard form, 3" [OP-NP, R4]. **$15.00–25.00.** B. Standard Mushroom and a Clay Gnome, 3", clay gnome is 2" [OP, R2]. **$75.00–100.00.**

Also see pages 113–114 for mushroom people.

Free-blown Mushrooms, standard form, approx. 2¼", 2", 3", & 1½" (shown) [OP-NP (continuing), R4]. Small (1" – 2"), **$10.00–15.00.** Medium (2" – 3"), **$10.00–15.00.** Large (3" – 4"), **$20.00–30.00.**

Musical Instruments

A. Bell with Embossed Flowers, Lily-of-the-Valley, 2¼" [OP-NP, R4]. **$10.00–15.00.** B. Bell with Santa Faces, 2¾" [OP, R1-2]. **$100.00–125.00.** C. Bell with an Embossed Windmill, 2¼" [OP, R2-3]. **$30.00–40.00.**

A. Bell with an Embossed Church, approx. 2½" [OP, R3]. **$20.00–30.00.** B. Bell with Flowers, approx. 1½" (shown) & 2½" [German, Czech, Austrian; OP-NP, R4]. **$10.00–15.00.** C. Bell with Geometric Designs, approx. 1½" & 3½" (shown) [German, Czech, Austrian; OP-NP, R4-5]. **$10.00–15.00.** D. Bell with a Crown (Type II), approx. 3" [OP, R2-3]. **$35.00–45.00.** E. Hand Bell (Type I), approx. 4" [OP-NP, R3]. **$20.00–30.00.** F. Bell with a Crown (Type I), approx. 3¾" [German, OP, R2-3]. **$50.00–75.00.**

A. Bell with a Crown (Type I), approx. 3¾" [German, OP, R2-3]. **$50.00–75.00.** B. Common Bell with Scrap Decoration, approx. 2", but size can vary. **$15.00–20.00.** C. Bell with an Embossed Eagle, approx. 4" [German, OP, R2]. **$100.00–125.00.**

A. Cello, wire-wrapped, 6½" [OP-NP, R3-4] **$65.00–85.00.** B. Free-blown Mandolin, 9" [OP, R3]. **$150.00–175.00.**

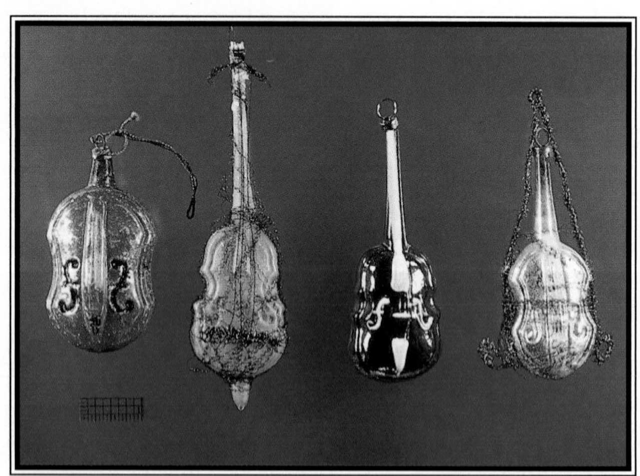

A & B. Cellos, molded, approx. 3" – 6½" (3¼" & 6" shown) [OP-NP (continuing), R3-4]. Small, **$15.00–20.00.** Medium, **$20.00–30.00.** Large, **$40.00–50.00.** C & D. Violins, molded, approx. 3" – 6½" (5¼" & 4" shown) [OP-NP (1950s – 1990s), R3-4]. Small, **$15.00–20.00.** Medium, **$20.00–30.00.** Large, **$35.00–50.00.**

Drum, approx. 2" & 2½" (shown) [German, OP-NP (continuing)]. **$20.00-25.00.** B & C. French Horns or Tubas, approx. 2½" - 6" (4½" & 5¾" shown), sizes vary [OP-NP (continuing), R4-5]. Small, **$8.00-12.00.** Medium, **$12.00-18.00.** Large, **$25.00-35.00.**

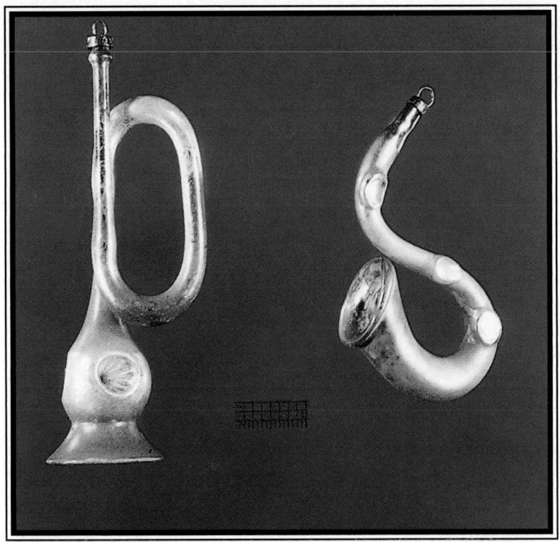

A. Trumpet with Indents, approx. 5½" [OP, R3]. **$20.00-30.00.** B. Saxophone, approx. 4" [German, OP, R2]. **$40.00-50.00.**

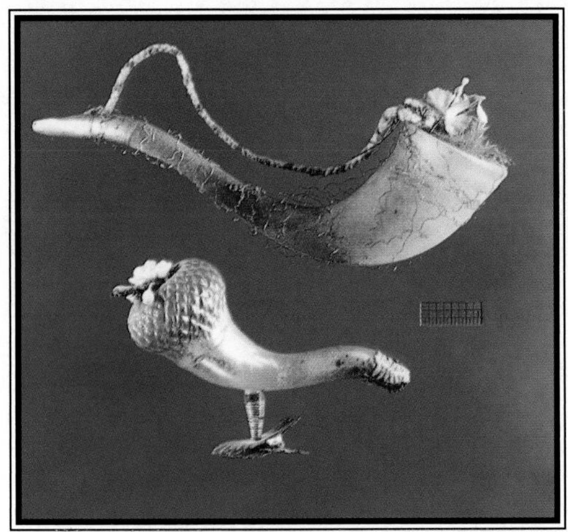

A. Hollow Hunting Horn, approx. 8" [OP, R2]. **$150.00-175.00.** B. Clip-on Hunting Horn, approx. 4½" [OP, R1]. **$125.00-150.00.**

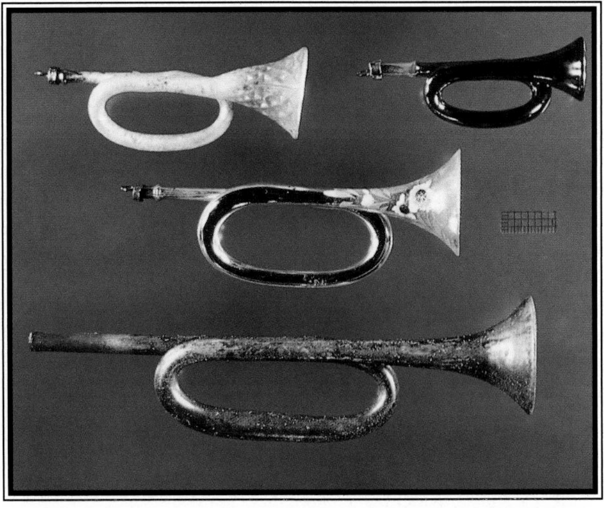

A. Trumpet Variation with Molded Bell, approx. 4½" [OP, R3]. **$15.00-20.00.** B, C, D. Free-blown Trumpets, approx. 3" - 8½" (3¼", 5¼", & 7¾" shown) [OP-NP (continuing), R5]. Small, **$8.00-12.00.** Medium, **$12.00-20.00.** Large (7"+), **$30.00-50.00.**

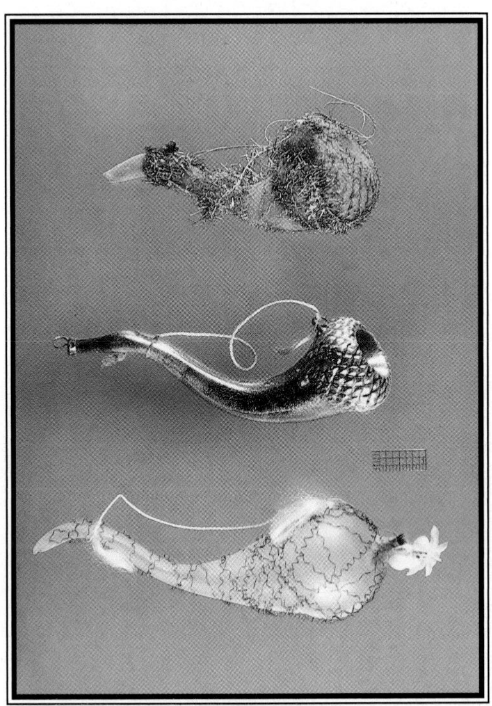

Three Types of Hunting Horns, sizes vary from 4" to 8": A. Free-blown & Molded, approx. 4¾", unsilvered, wire wrapped [OP, R3]. **$90.00-110.00.** B. Free-blown & Molded, approx. 6", silvered [OP, R3]. **$90.00-110.00.** C. Free-blown & Unsilvered, approx. 6¾" [OP, R3]. **$125.00-150.00.**

A, B, C. Lyres, free-blown, annealed, approx. 2¾" – 4½" (2¾", 4½", & 4" shown) [OP-NP (1950s – 1960s), R3-4]: A. **$25.00-30.00.** B. **$40.00-50.00.** C. **$25.00-30.00.**

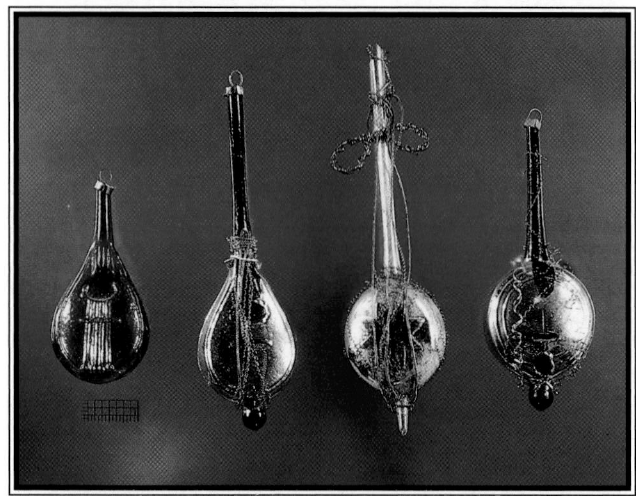

A & B. Mandolins, approx. 3¼" – 6" (3¼" & 5½" shown), sizes vary, [OP, R4]. Small, **$10.00-12.00.** Medium, **$15.00-20.00.** Large, **$20.00-25.00.** C. Free-blown Banjo, approx. 5" – 10" (6½" shown) [OP, R2-3]. Small, **$25.00-35.00.** Medium, **$35.00-50.00.** Large, **$75.00-100.00.** Large with extra decoration, **$100.00-175.00.** D. Molded Banjo, approx. 4" [German, OP-NP (1991), R2]. **$35.00-50.00.**

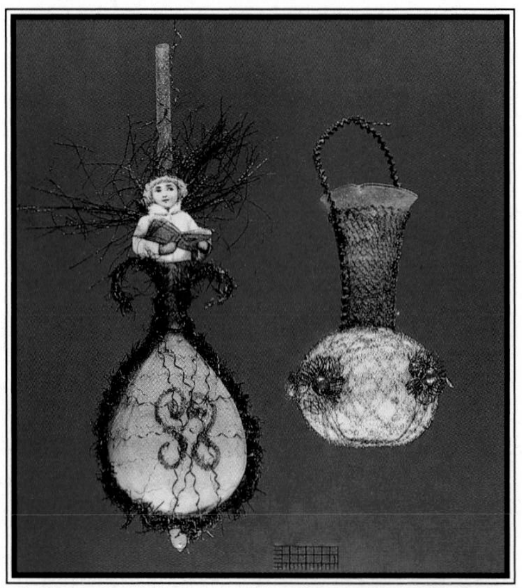

A. Mandolin, free-blown, wire-wrapped, 7½" [OP, R3]. **$125.00–150.00.** B. Basket/Vase, free-blown, wire-wrapped, 4" [OP, R3]. **$125.00–150.00.**

Early Free-blown Large Musical Instruments, all are wire wrapped and unsilvered. A. Banjo, approx. 10¾" [OP, R1]. **$175.00-200.00.** B. Mandolin, approx. 9¼" [OP, R2-3]. **$125.00-150.00.** C. Clarinet, approx. 9" [OP, R1]. **$125.00-150.00.** D. Mandolin, approx. 10¾" [OP, R2-3]. **$150.00-175.00.**

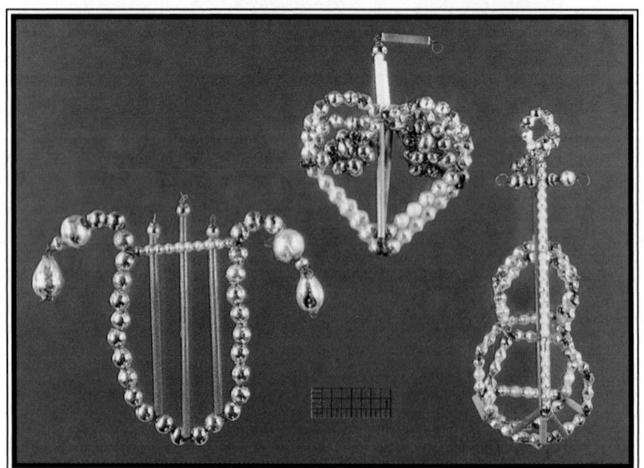

Beaded Ornaments: A. Heart, 2¾" [OP, R2]. **$12.00-18.00.** B. Lyre, 2¾" [OP, R2]. **$10.00-15.00.** C. Guitar, 4" [OP, R2]. **$25.00-30.00.**

Nuts, Acorns, and Pines Cones

A. Acorn Chain, approx. 18" [OP, R2]. **$90.00-150.00.** B. Acorn, approx. 1½" [OP-NP, R4]. **$10.00-12.00.** C. Acorn, approx. 2" [OP-NP, R4]. **$15.00-20.00.**

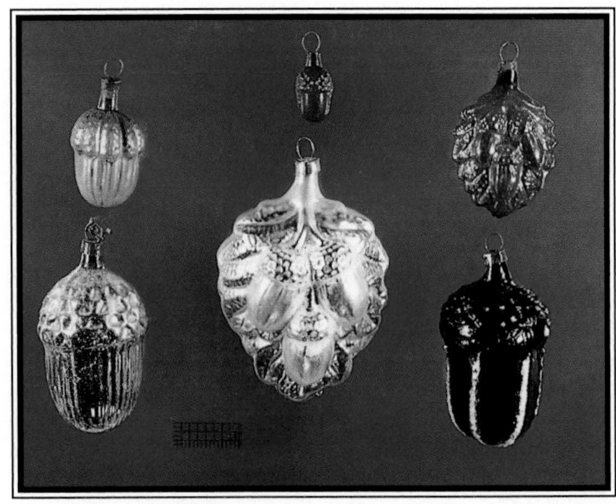

A, B, D, F. Acorns, approx. 1½",¾", 2¼", & 2½" (shown) [German, Austrian, Japanese; OP-NP (1990s), R4]. Small (1" - 2"), **$8.00-12.00.** Medium (2" - 3"), **$15.00-20.00.** Large (3" - 4"), **$20.00-25.00.** C & E. Acorns on an Oak Leaf, 1¾" (shown) & 2¾" (shown) [German, OP-NP (1970s), R3-4]. Small, **$12.00-18.00.** Large, **$20.00-30.00.**

A. Real Nut that Has Been Silvered. **$1.00-2.00.** B. Real Nut that Has Been Gilded. **$.50-1.00.** C. Small Glass Walnut, **$10.00-15.00.** D. Half Walnut Shell Decorated with fabric and a Tiny Wax Baby Jesus. **$50.00-75.00.** Real Walnut Purse, Victorian homemade Decoration, **$90.00-110.00.**

A Collection of Various Sizes and Styles of Pine Cones, approx. 1" - 6" (1" - 4" shown) [American, German, Austrian, Japanese, Czech; OP-NP (continuing), R5]. Small (1" - 2"), **$5.00-10.00.** Medium (2" - 4"), **$10.00-15.00.** Large (4" - 6"), **$20.00-30.00.**

Various Forms and Sizes of the Standard Walnut, approx. 1", 1¼", 1¼", 2½", 1¾", 2¼" & 2¼" (all shown) [German, Czech, Austrian; OP-NP (1980s - 1990s), R4-5] A, B, C. **$8.00-12.00** each. D. **$35.00-45.00.** E. **$10.00-15.00.** F. **$20.00-25.00.** G. **$25.00-35.00.**

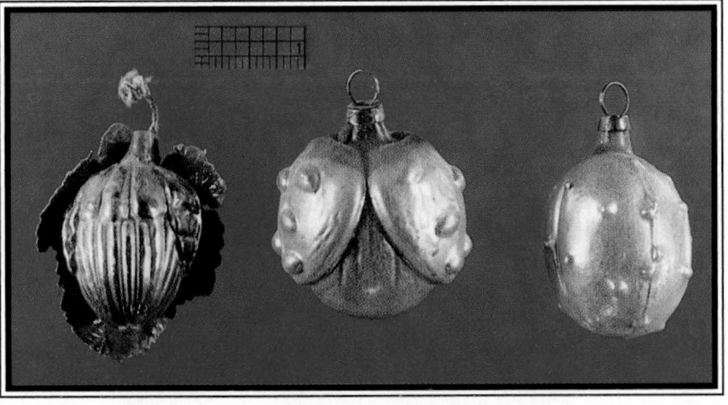

A. Standard Acorn on a Fabric Leaf, 1½" [OP, R2]. **$15.00-18.00.** B. Open Chestnut, 1½" [OP, R1-2]. **$30.00-35.00.** C. Closed Chestnut , 1½" [OP, R1-2]. **$15.00-20.00.**

Patriotic Items

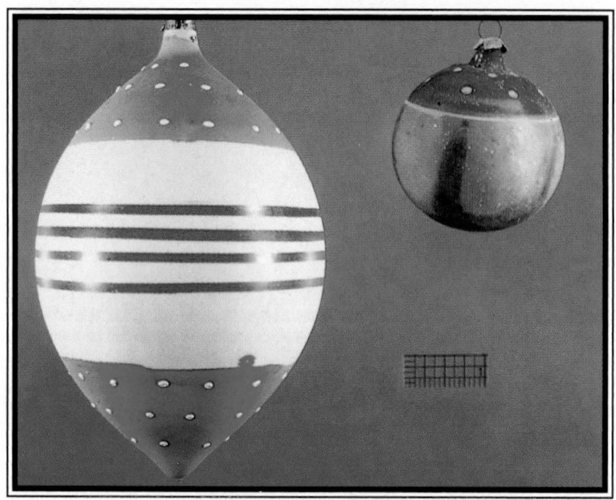

Free-blown Patriotic Shapes: A. Oval, large, 4¾" [OP, R2]. **$60.00–85.00.** B. Ball, small, 2" [OP, R3]. **$25.00–35.00.**

A. Flag on a Ball, 2¾" [OP, R1]. **$175.00–200.00.** B. Oval Rattle with Stars and Stripes, 10½" [OP, R1]. **$200.00–250.00.** C. Oval with Stars and Stripes, 3" [OP, R1]. **$100.00–150.00.**

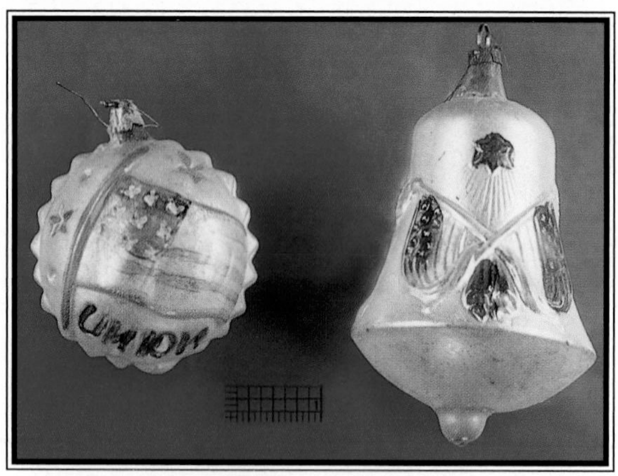

A. Flag, 2½" [OP, R1]. The word "Union," with a backwards *n,* is embossed below the flag. **$250.00–300.00.** B. Bell with an Embossed Eagle and Flags, approx. 3½" & 4" (shown) [German, OP, R1]. Small, **$175.00–200.00.** Large, **$250.00–300.00.**

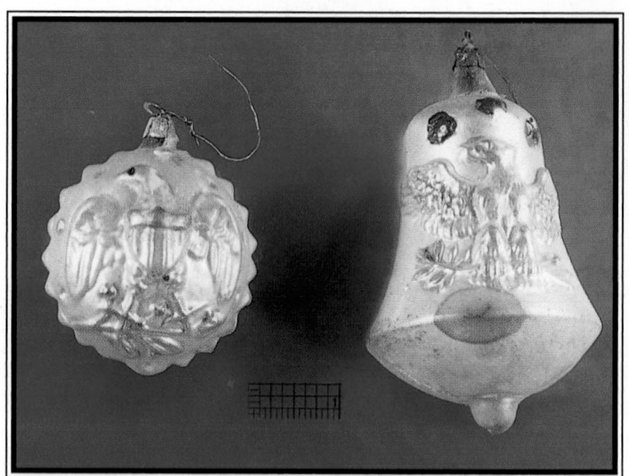

Reverse of both the "Union" Flag and the Bell with the Embossed Eagle and Flags.

A. Miss Liberty Head, approx. 3¾". The back of the head shows her hair in a bun [probably German, NP (ca. 2001) R2-3]. **$20.00–30.00.** B. Statue of Liberty, approx. 6½". Clouds form behind the head and upraised arm [Polish, NP (ca. 2001), R2-3]. **$20.00–25.00.**

Other patriotic pieces on p 16-17.

People

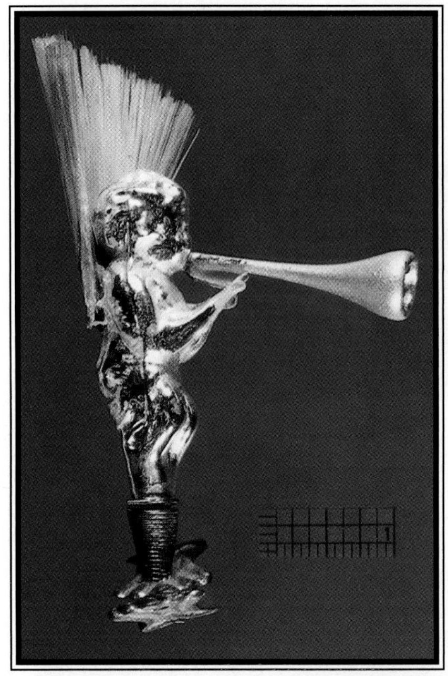

Cherub Blowing a Trumpet (Type II), 2¼" [OP, R1-2]. **$250.00–300.00.**

A. Cherub on a Ball (Type I), approx. 4½" [German, OP, R1-2]. **$150.00–175.00.** B. Standing Angel Tree Topper (Type I), approx. 7" [German, OP, R2]. **$325.00–400.00.** Standing Angel, approx. 3½" (shown) & 4" [German, OP-NP (Radko, 1994, 4" size), R2]. Small, **$150.00–175.00.** Large, **$175.00–200.00.**

A. Beautiful Angel Bust, approx 4" [German, OP-NP (1980s)]. Old, **$200.00–250.00.** 1980s version (shown), **$15.00–20.00.** B. Raphael Angel on a Cloud, a 1980s production. Approx. 4" [German, NP, R4-5]. **$10.00–15.00.**

A. Mother and Child Angels, approx. 3¾" [OP, R2]. **$275.00–325.00.** B. Raphael Angel Bust, approx. 2¼", 2½", 3" (shown), & 4". There are several slightly different versions [German, OP-NP (1980s & 1990s), R2-3]. Small, **$125.00–150.00.** Medium, **$175.00–225.00.** Large, **$275.00–300.00.** C. Kneeling Angel (Type I), approx. 3¼" [German, OP-NP (1970s), R3]. **$175.00–200.00.**

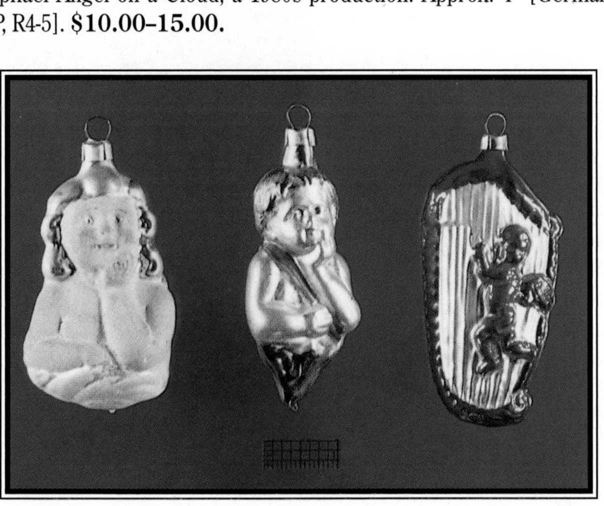

A. Raphael Angel Bust, approx. 2¼", 2½", 3" (shown), & 4" [German, OP-NP (1980s – 1990s), R2-3]. Small, **$125.00–150.00.** Medium, **$175.00–225.00.** Large, **$275.00–300.00.** B. Boy Cherub, approx. 3½" [German, OP-NP (1970s), R1-2]. **$175.00–200.00.** C. Angel on a Harp, approx. 3½" [German, OP-NP (1970s), R2]. **$100.00–125.00.**

A. Angel on a Heart, 2½" & 3" [German, OP-NP (1960s & 1990s, 2½"), R2]. **$60.00–85.00.** B. Raphael Angel on an Egg, approx. 3¼" [OP, R1-2]. **$100.00–150.00.** C. Baby Jesus on a Leaf, approx. 3" [German, OP-NP (1990s), R1-2]. **$175.00–200.00.** D. Angel Head, double faced, approx. 2¾" [OP, R2]. **$200.00–250.00.** E. Angel Flying on a Disc, approx. 2" diameter [OP, R2]. **$45.00–60.00.**

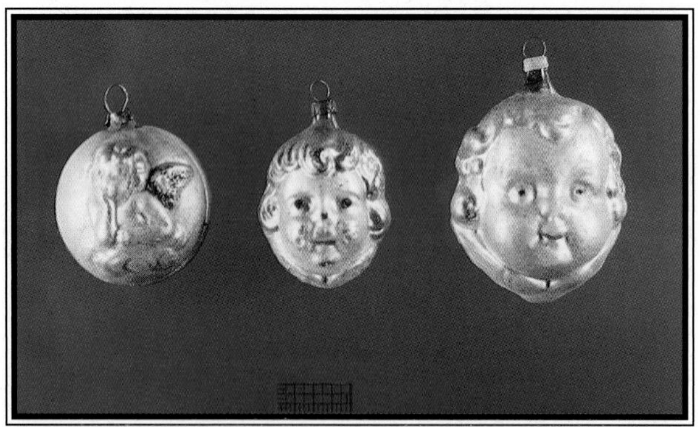

A. Raphael Angel on a Disc, approx. 2" [OP, R2-3]. **$45.00–65.00.** B & C. Putti Angel Heads, approx. 2" (shown), 2½", & 3" (shown). Wings show under the chin. [German, OP-NP (1970s), R2-3]. Small, **$40.00–50.00.** Medium, **$50.00–75.00.** Large, **$90.00–110.00.**

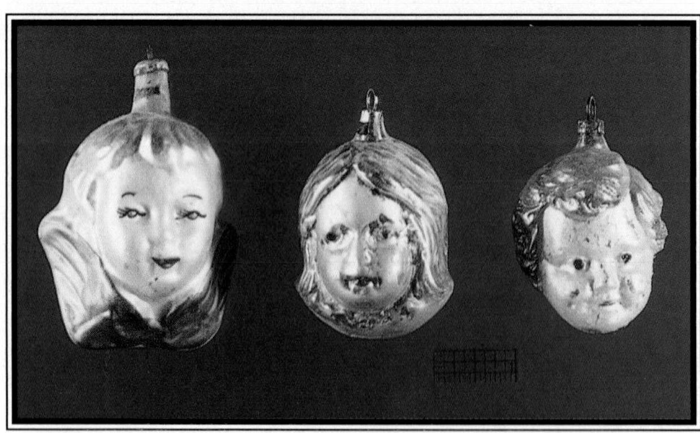

A. Italian Angel Head with Large Wings, approx. 2½" [NP (1950s), R3]. **$30.00–40.00.** B. Girl's Head (Type III), approx. 2¼" [OP, R2]. **$100.00–125.00.** C. Baby Jesus Head/Baby Boy Head, approx. 2", 2¼" (shown), & 3" [German, OP, R2-3]. Small, **$60.00–90.00.** Medium, **$100.00–125.00.** Large, **$150.00–175.00.**

A. Angel Blowing a Trumpet, approx. 5" [NP (1950s only), R2-3]. **$100.00–150.00.** B. Standing Angel with Folded Wings, approx. 3" (shown) & 3½" [German, OP-NP (1990s), R4]. **$60.00–75.00.**

A. Angel Head Embossed on a Disc, approx. 2" [OP-NP (1950s), R3]. **$30.00–40.00.** B. Putti Angel Head, approx. 2" [German, OP-NP (1970s), R2-3]. Small, **$40.00–50.00.**

Angel Bust, 2½" (shown missing paper wings) & 4" [OP-NP (1980s, large), R2]. Small, **$125.00–150.00.** Large, **$200.00–250.00.**

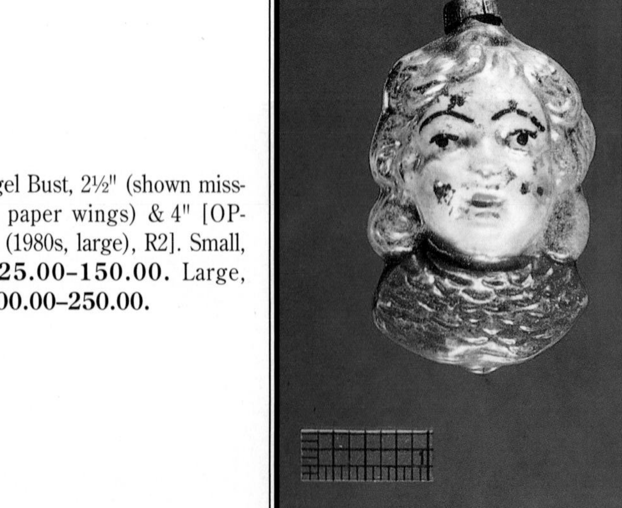

A. Angel Bust, a second version, 2½" [OP-NP (1980s), R2]. Small, **$275.00–325.00.** B. Fairy Head with Glass Eyes, 3¾" [OP, R1-2]. **$250.00–300.00.**

A. Angel in a Basket, triple indent, 2¼" [OP, R1]. **$100.00–150.00.** B. Angel with a Mandolin, triple indent, 3¾" [OP, R1]. **$100.00–150.00.** C. Baby Face, four faces indent, 2¼" [OP, R1-2]. **$200.00–250.00.**

A. Cherub on a Bell, 4" [German, OP, R1]. **$150.00–175.00.** B. Girl's Head with Leaves, 2½" [OP, R1]. **$150.00–200.00.**

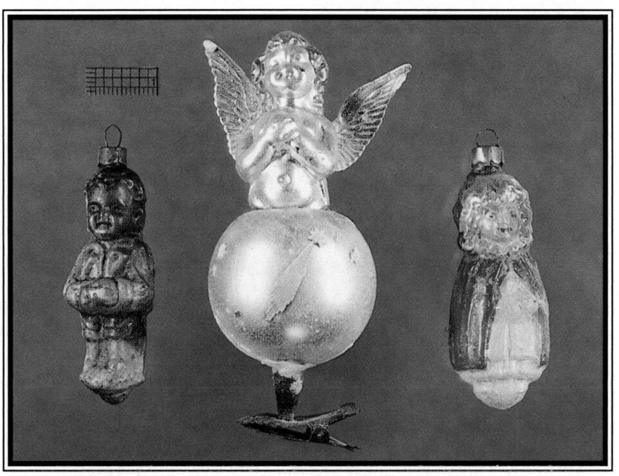

A. Boy with a Wine Bottle, 3" [OP, R1]. **$175.00–200.00.** B. Cherub on a Ball (Type II), 4½" [OP, R1-2]. **$200.00–250.00.** C. Little Red Riding Hood, 3" [German, OP-NP (1990s), R1]. Old, **$175.00–200.00.**

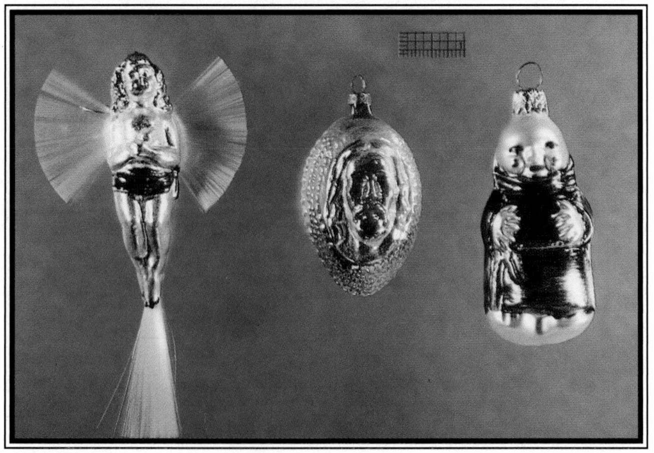

A. Flying Cherub, 3¾" [OP, R1]. **$175.00–225.00.** B. Jesus Face in an Egg Shape, 2¾" [German, OP-NP (1990), R1]. Old, **$200.00–225.00.** C. Monk, "Friar Fulk," 3½" [NP (1990s), R3]. **$15.00–20.00.**

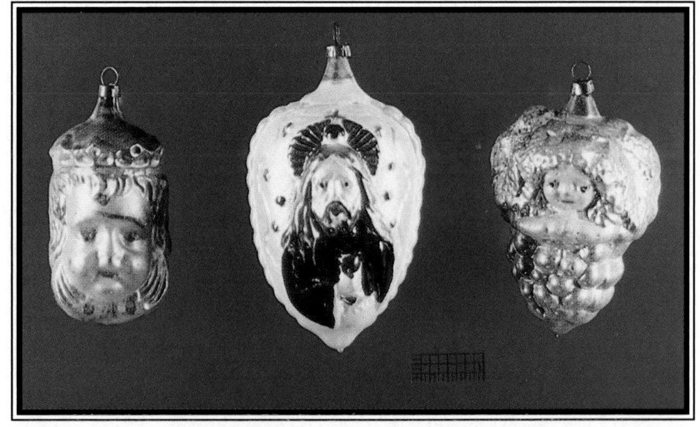

A. Angel Head with a Crown, double sided, 2½" [OP, R1]. **$175.00–200.00.** B. Jesus Bust on an Egg Shape, 3¼" [German, OP-NP (1990s), R2]. Old, **$225.00–250.00.** C. Grapes with a Girl's Face, 3" [OP, R2-3]. **$175.00–225.00.**

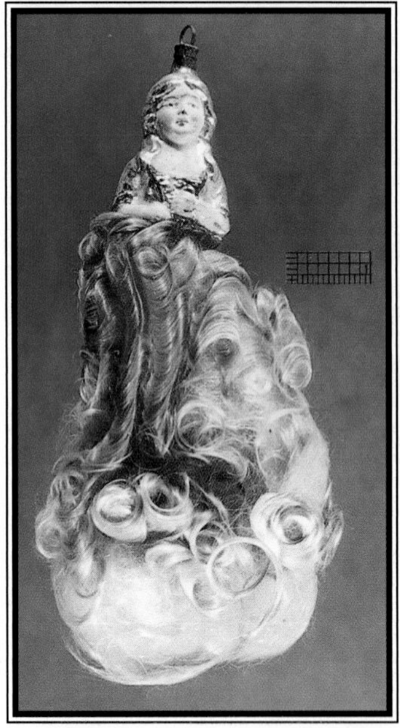

Angel on an SG Cloud (Type I), 4". "DHL" is embossed into the back of Type I pieces [OP, R1-2]. **$325.00–375.00.**

A. Snow Angel with a Basket of Flowers, approx. 3" [German, OP-NP (1970s), R1]. **$150.00–175.00.** B. Angel in a Hoop Skirt, approx. 4½" [NP (1950s), R2-3]. **$50.00–75.00.** C. Standing Angel (Type I), approx. 4" [German, OP-NP (1980s), R2-3]. **$150.00–175.00.** 1980s version (shown), **$10.00–18.00.**

A. Kneeling Angel with Molded Wings, approx. 3½" [German, OP-NP (1970s), R2-3]. **$65.00–85.00.** B. Angel with a Tree and Horn, approx. 4" [German, OP-NP (1950s & 1970s), R3]. **$75.00–90.00.** C. Angel with a Tree, approx. 4" [German, OP-NP (1980s), R1]. Old, **$150.00–175.00.** 1980s, **$20.00-30.00.**

A & B. Angel & Santa Double-sided Ornaments, approx. 3½". Santa is a standard form [German, OP-NP (1950s & 1970s), R1]. Old, **$300.00–350.00.** 1950s & 1970s (shown), **$50.00–75.00.**

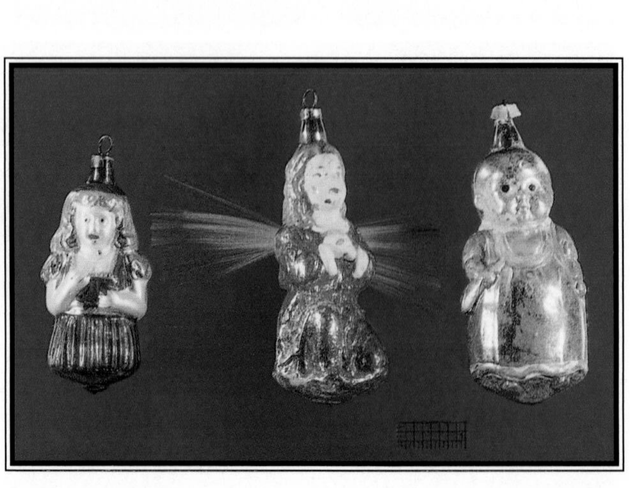

A. Goldilocks, approx. 3" [German, OP-NP (1970s), R3-4]. **$50.00–65.00.** B. Kneeling Angel (Type II), approx. 3¾" [OP, R2-3]. **$175.00–200.00.** C. Baby with a Bottle, approx. 3½" [OP, R1]. **$300.00–350.00.**

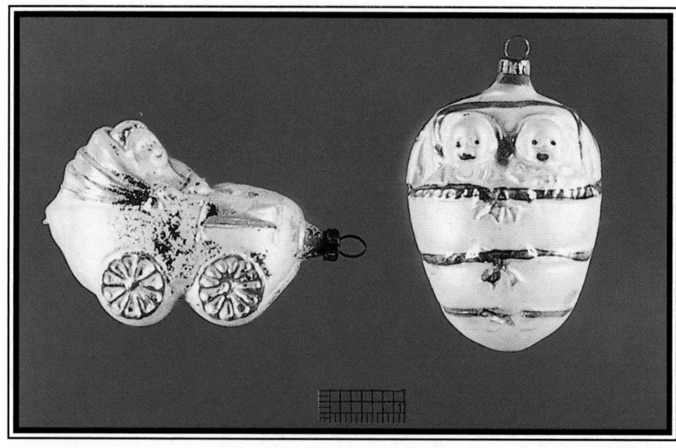

A. Baby in a Buggy, approx. 2¼", 2¾", & 3" (shown) [German, OP-NP (1980s), R2-3]. Small, **$100.00–125.00.** Medium, **$150.00–175.00.** Large, **$200.00–225.00.** B. Twin Babies in Bunting, approx. 3" [German, OP, R1-2]. **$160.00–190.00.**

A. Scrap-faced Baby in a Lady's Shoe, approx. 4½" [German, OP, R1]. **$300.00–375.00.** B. Baby in a Bathtub, approx. 2¾" [German, OP, R1+]. **$500.00–650.00.** C. Baby in Bunting with a Scrap Face, approx. 2½" & 3½" (shown) [OP, R2]. Small, **$175.00-200.00.** Large, **$200.00–225.00.**

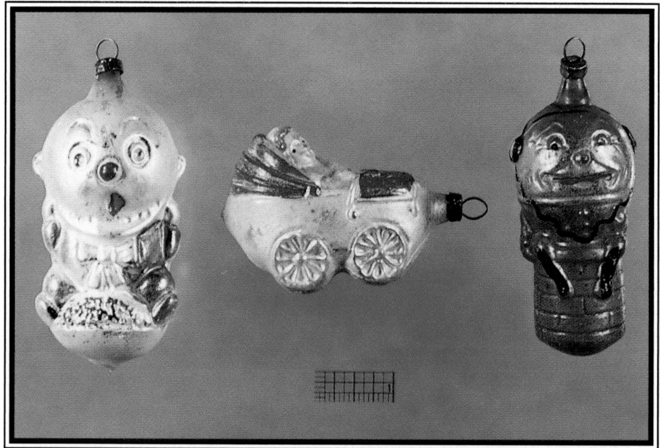

A. Large-headed Baby, 3¼" [OP-NP (1990s), R2]. Old, **$200.00–250.00.** B. Baby in a Buggy, approx. 2¼", 2¾" (shown), & 3" [German, OP-NP (1980s), R2-3]. Small, **$100.00–125.00.** Medium, **$150.00–175.00.** Large, **$200.00–225.00.** C. Humpty Dumpty on a Wall, 3" [OP, R1-2]. **$200.00–275.00.**

Baby Face Indents in a Double Shape, 5" [OP, R1]. **$300.00-350.00.**

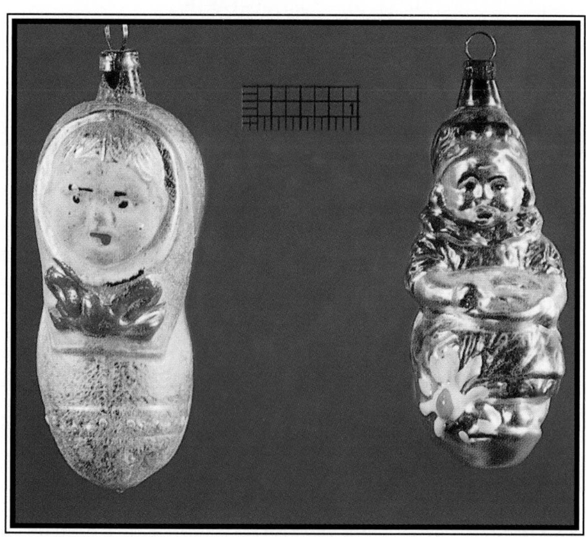

A. Baby Face in a Shoe (Type I), 3½" [OP, R1]. **$300.00–350.00.** B. Little Miss Muffet (Type II), 3" [OP-NP (1994), R1]. Old, **$200.00–250.00.**

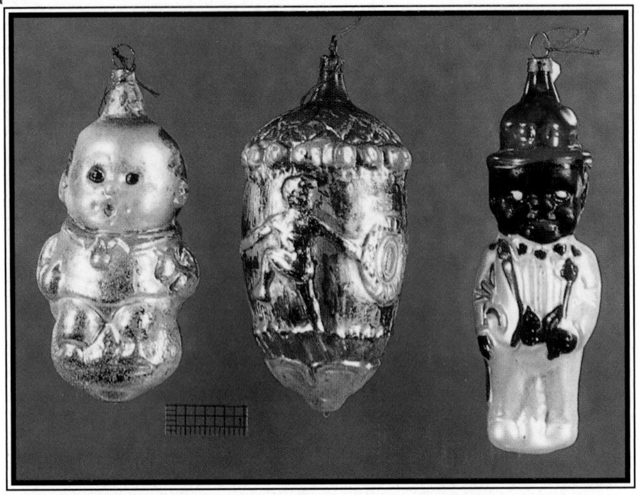

A. Pudgy Sitting Baby, 3¾" [OP, R1]. **$250.00–300.00.** B. Boys Dancing on a Top, 3¾" [OP, R1-2]. **$175.00–200.00.** Al Jolson in a Tuxedo, 4½" [OP, R1]. **$375.00–425.00.**

A. Boy Clown Head; 2½", 3" (shown), 3½", & 4" [German, OP-NP (1980 – 1990s), R3-4]. Old painted face, **$150.00–175.00.** B. Baby Head in a Bonnet, 2½" [OP, R1-2]. **$200.00–275.00.**

A. Scrap-faced Baby in Bunting, approx. 2½" (shown) & 3½" [OP, R2]. Small, **$175.00–200.00.** Large, **$200.00–225.00.** B. Madonna, standing, 4" [OP, R1]. **$250.00–300.00.** C. Boy Playing a Concertina, 2½" [OP-NP (1992), R2-3]. **$75.00–85.00.**

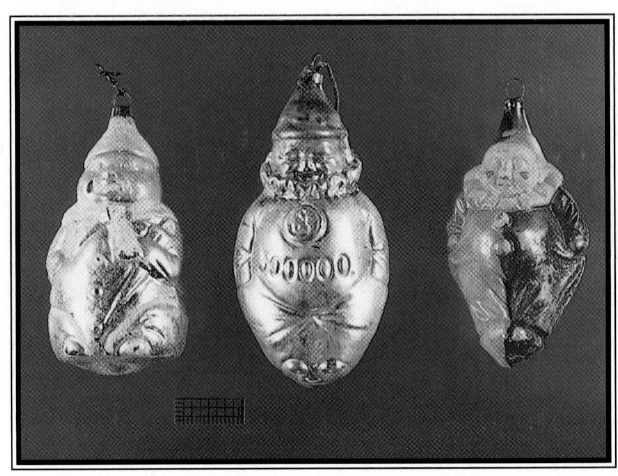

A. Snowman with an Umbrella, 3¾" [OP, R1-2]. **$300.00–350.00.** B. 500,000 Clown; 3", 3¾", 4¼", & 4¾" (shown) [German, OP-NP (1990), R3-4]. Small **$75.00–100.00.** Medium, **$100.00–125.00.** Large, **$140.00–175.00.** C. Potbellied Clown, medium, 3¼" & 3½" (shown) [OP-NP (1970s), R3]. **$45.00–60.00.**

A. Clown Playing a Bass Fiddle, large, approx. 3½" (shown) & 4½" [NP (1950s), R3]. Small, **$30.00–40.00.** Large, **$35.00–45.00.** B. Girl Bell, approx. 3" [OP, R1]. **$175.00–225.00.** C. Baby with a Pacifier in Bunting, large, approx. 2½" & 3½" (shown) [German, OP-NP (1970), R2-3]. Small, **$100.00–135.00.** Large, **$150.00–180.00.**

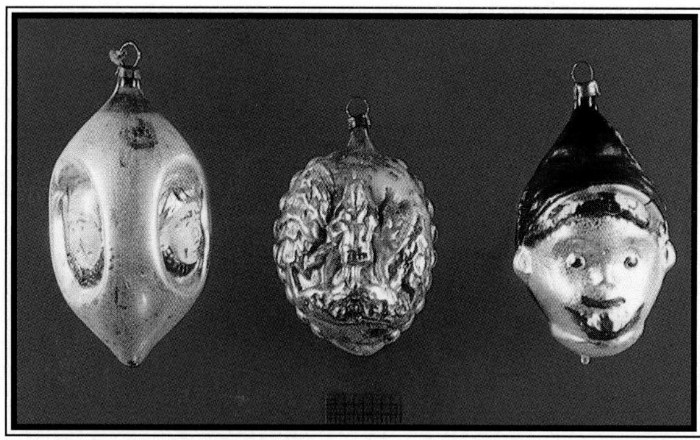

A. Three-faced Baby Indent, approx. 3½". One baby cries, one smiles, and one is "normal" [OP, R2]. **$200.00–250.00.** B. Red Riding Hood & Wolf, embossed. **$75.00–100.00.** C. Elf Head, approx. 3" [German, NP (1970s), R2]. **$25.00–35.00.**

A. Boy Clown Head, 3" [German, OP-NP (1980s – 1990s), R3-4]. Old, **$75.00–85.00.** B. Boy Clown Head with Free-blown Hat, 4" [German, OP, R1]. **$125.00–175.00.** C. Clown Head in a Beehive Hat, 3" [OP, R1-2]. **$200.00–250.00.**

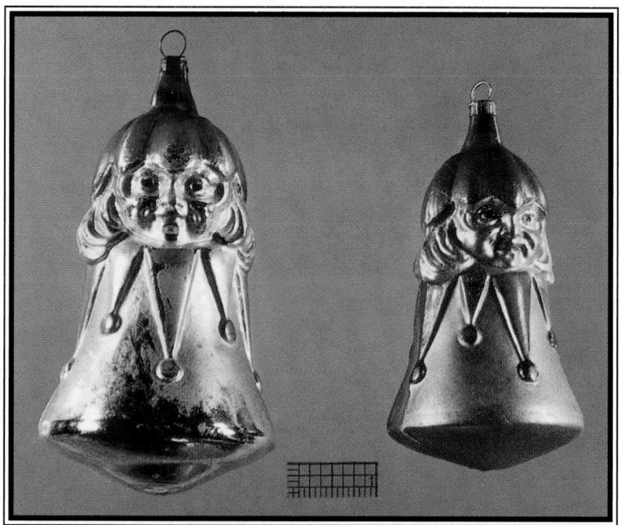

Girl Jesters (Type I), approx. 2¾", 3¼", 3¾" (shown), & 4¼" (shown) [German, OP-NP (Inge-glas, 1993, 2¾"), R3]. Small (2¾"), **$75.00–100.00.** Medium, **$100.00–125.00.** Large (3¾"), **$150.00–175.00.** Large (4¼"), **$200.00–275.00.**

A. Clown, "Smiling Tom," 4" [OP, R2-3]. **$150.00–200.00.** B. 500,000 Clown, medium, 4¼" [OP-NP (1990), R3-4]. **$100.00–125.00.**

Grinning Clown Head, approx. 2¾", 3½", 4" (shown), 4½", & 5" (shown) [OP, R2]. Small, **$250.00–300.00.** Medium (4"), **$350.00–400.00.** Large (5"), **$400.00–500.00.**

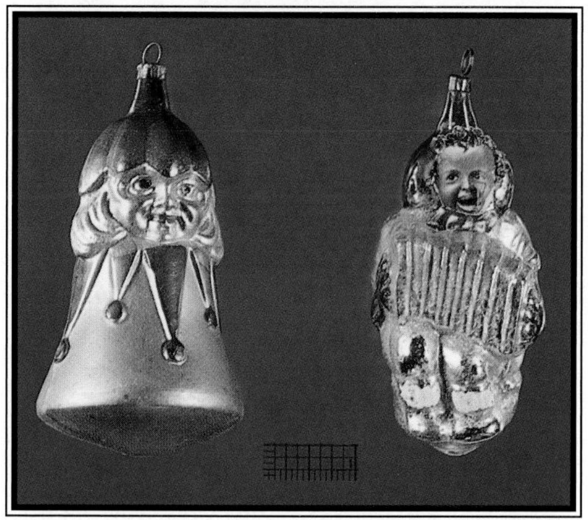

A. Girl Jester (Type I), small, 3¼" [OP-NP, R3]. **$100.00–125.00.** B. Black Boy with a Scrap Face Playing an Accordion, 3¼" [OP, R1]. **$275.00–300.00.**

A. Dutch Girl with a Purse, 3½" [OP, R2-3]. **$125.00–150.00.** B. Girl Jester (Type II), 3¼" [NP (1950s), R2]. **$30.00–40.00.**

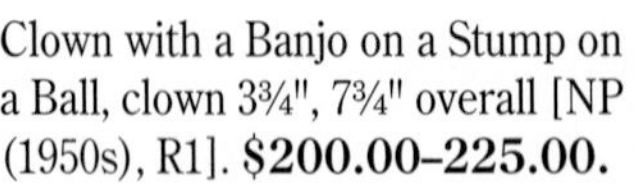

Clown with a Banjo on a Stump on a Ball, clown 3¾", 7¾" overall [NP (1950s), R1]. **$200.00–225.00.**

A. Clown on a Comet Ball, 3¼" [OP-NP (1950s & 1990s), R2-3]. Old, **$125.00–150.00.** B. Baby Jesus Head/Baby Boy Head, approx. 2" (shown), 2¼", & 3" [German, OP, R2-3]. Small, **$50.00–75.00.** Medium, **$75.00–100.00.** Large, **$125.00–150.00.** C. Glass Shape with Decoration Inside, 4¾", scrap dwarf inside [OP-NP (1950s), R3]. 1950s version. **$45.00–65.00.**

Hans Head Chandelier, 3½" [OP-NP (1950s), R1]. Old, **$200.00–250.00.** 1950s version, **$175.00–200.00.**

A. Joey Clown Head, large, 2¼" & 3½" (shown) [German, OP-NP (1950s & 1990)]. Small, **$50.00–75.00.** Large, **$75.00–95.00.** B. Joey Clown Head with a Spun Glass Collar, 3" head, approx. 6" overall [German, OP, R1-2]. **$250.00–300.00.**

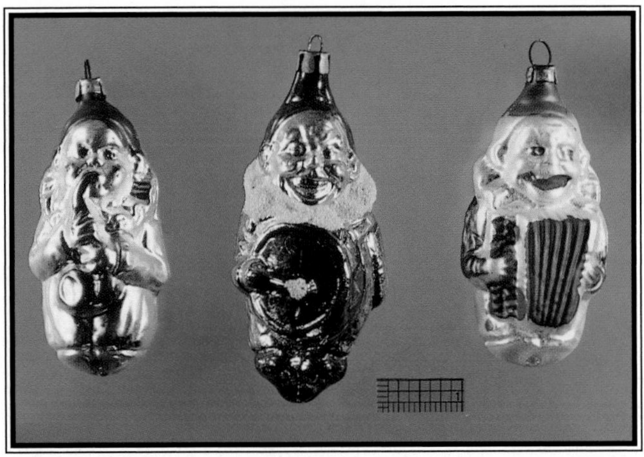

Three Joey Clowns: A. With a Saxophone, approx. 3¼" [German, OP-NP [1950s & 1970s), R2-3]. **$50.00–75.00.** B. With a Drum, approx. 3½" [German, OP-NP (1950s), R4]. **$50.00–75.00.** C. With an Accordion, approx. 3¼" [German, OP-NP (1950s), R3]. **$50.00–75.00.**

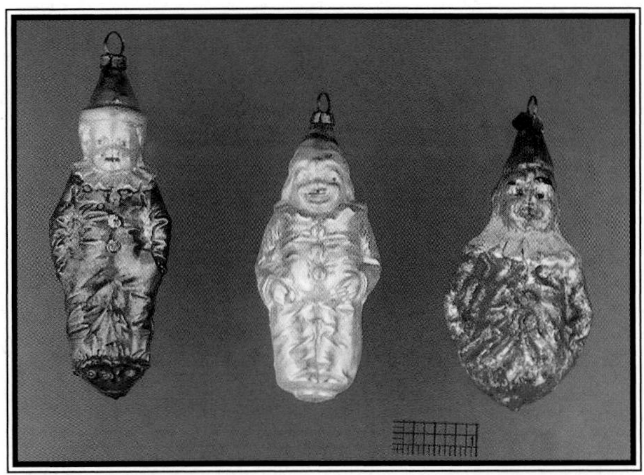

A. Boy Clown, approx. 3¼" & 4" (shown) [German, OP, R2-3]. Small, **$50.00–75.00.** Large, **$75.00–100.00.** B. Standard Form Clown (Type III), approx. 3" [OP, R3]. **$50.00–75.00.** C. Clown Torso (Type I), approx. 3" [OP-NP, R2-3]. **$40.00–65.00.**

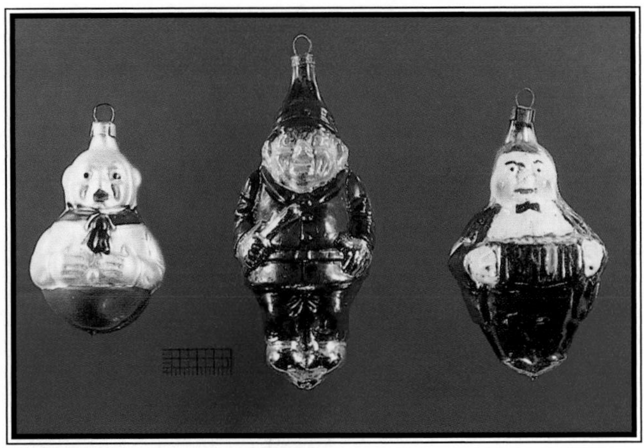

A. Roly-Poly Clown, approx. 2½", also called Tweedle Dee [German, OP-NP (1950s & 1980s), R2-3]. **$90.00–110.00.** B. Comic Keystone Cop, approx. 4½" [German, OP, R2]. **$130.00–175.00.** C. Fat Man Playing a Concertina, 3½" [German, OP-NP (1950s), R3]. 1950s version (shown), **$40.00–55.00.**

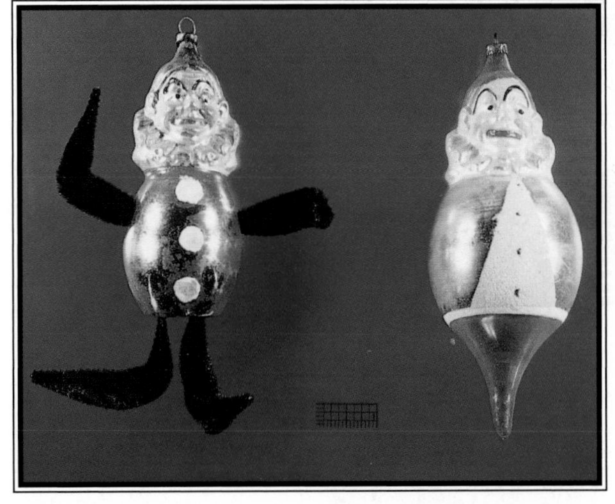

A. Joey Clown with Chenille Arms & Legs, 4" glass body, approx. 5½" overall [German, OP-NP (Radko, 1993), R2]. **$200.00–275.00.** B. Joey Clown with a Stylized Body, approx. 6" [German, OP-NP (Radko, 1990s), R2-3]. **$125.00–175.00.**

A. Boy Clown on a Ball, approx. 4" [NP (1940s – 1950s), R3]. **$50.00–75.00.** B, C, D. Standard Form Clowns, small & medium, approx. 3" – 4" [German, Czech, Austrian; OP-NP (1950s – 1990s), R4-5]. Small, **$35.00–50.00.** Medium, **$50.00–75.00.** Large, **$75.00–100.00.**

A. Judy Bell, double faced, approx. 5". Judy is half of the famous Punch & Judy clowns [German, OP, R1-2]. **$150.00–175.00.** B. Hans Clown Head or Foxy Grandpa on a Spike, approx. sizes vary with the free-blown spike (5" shown) [German, OP, R2-3]. **$150.00–175.00.**

A. Clown Playing a Concertina, approx. 3½" [Czech, OP-NP (1980), R2]. **$65.00–85.00.** B. 500,000 Clown, approx. 3", 3¾", 4¼" (shown), & 4¾" [German, OP-NP (Inge-glas, 1990), R3]. Small, **$75.00–100.00.** Medium, **$100.00–125.00.** Large, **$140.00–175.00.** C. Clown in a Boot, approx. 3" [German, OP-NP (1980s), R1]. **$150.00–175.00.**

Boy Clown on an Indent, 4" head, approx. 6" overall [German, OP, R1-2]. **$200.00–250.00.**

Clown Head, double faced, approx. 3½". The opposite side is the same [OP, R1]. **$200.00–275.00.**

A. Punch & Judy Show (Type I), approx. 3" [German, OP, R2]. **$125.00–150.00.** B. Punch & Judy Show (Type III), approx. 3" [German, OP, R2]. **$100.00–125.00.** C. Punch & Judy Show (Type II), approx. 3" [German, OP-NP (Inge-glas, 1970s), R2]. Old, **$125.00–150.00.** 1970s, **$20.00–30.00.**

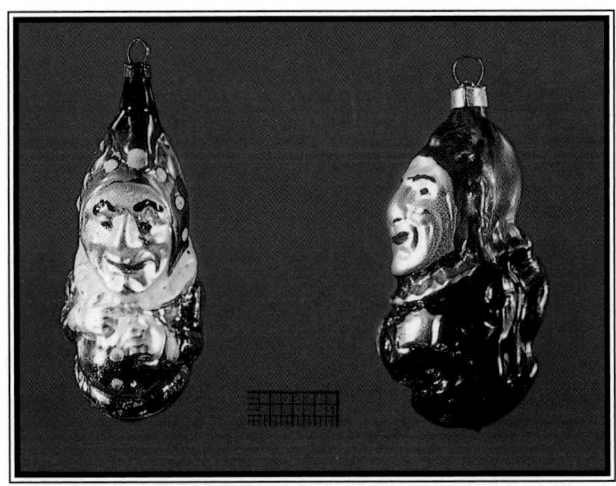

Front & Side View of Punch Clown, approx. 3½" [German, OP-NP (1970), R2]. **$150.00–175.00.**

A. Double-faced Judy Clown on a Stylized Body, approx. 5¼" [German, OP, R1-2]. **$200.00–250.00.** B. Clown Head Indented into a Free-blown Shape, 1½" clown head, approx. 4" overall [OP, R2-3]. **$100.00–125.00.**

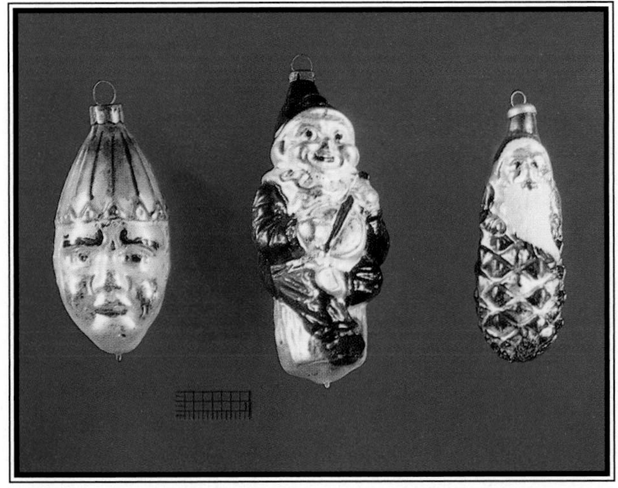

A. Judy Clown Head, single sided, approx. 3" [German, OP, R2-3]. **$100.00–125.00.** B. Clown on a Stump Playing a Banjo, approx. 3", 3¾", & 4¾" (shown) [German, OP-NP (1950s & 1980s), R4]. Small & Medium, **$40.00–50.00.** Large, **$50.00–75.00.** C. Santa or Dwarf in a Pine Cone [OP-NP (1970s & 1980s), R1]. Old, **$125.00–150.00.** 1970s, **$20.00–30.00.**

A & B. Two Diamond Clowns, so named because of their shape. **$40.00–65.00.** C. Comic Figure, approx. 3" [OP, R2-3]. **$125.00–150.00.**

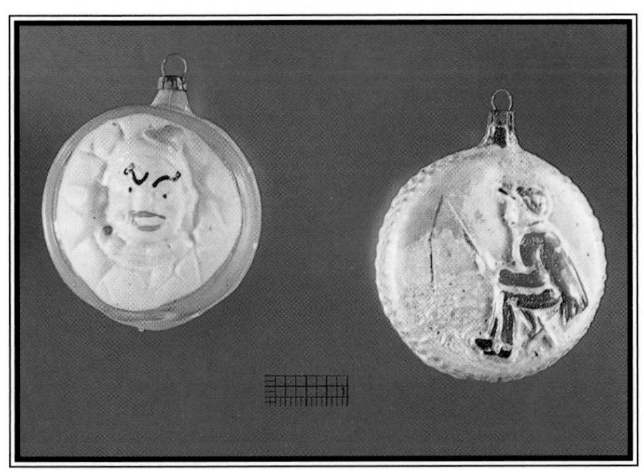

A. Clown in a Drum, approx. 1½" & 2½" (shown) [German, OP-NP (1980s, both sizes), R2]. Small, **$50.00–75.00.** Large, **$125.00–175.00.** B. "The Fisherman," embossed, approx. 2½" [OP, R2]. **$100.00–125.00.**

A. Clown on a Log Playing a Banjo, approx. 4" [NP (1950s), R3-4]. **$35.00–45.00.** B. Snowman Clown, approx. 4¼" [Germany, OP-NP (1950s), R3-4]. **$100.00–125.00.** 1950s version (shown), **$25.00–35.00.** C. Large-headed Clown (Type II), approx. 3¼" [OP, R2-3]. **$75.00–100.00.**

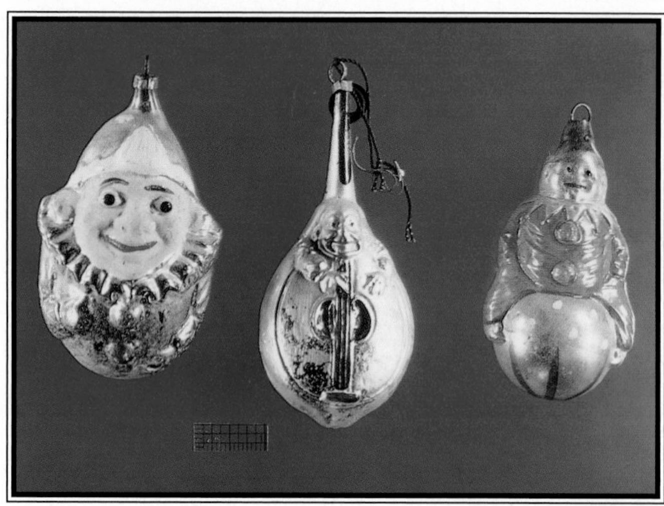

A. Clown Head with Glass Eyes, approx. 3¾" [German, OP, R1]. **$325.00–375.00.** B. Clown in a Mandolin (Type I), approx. 5½" [OP, R2-3]. **$125.00–175.00.** C. Clown Sitting on a Ball, approx. 3½" [German, OP, R2-3]. **$150.00–175.00.**

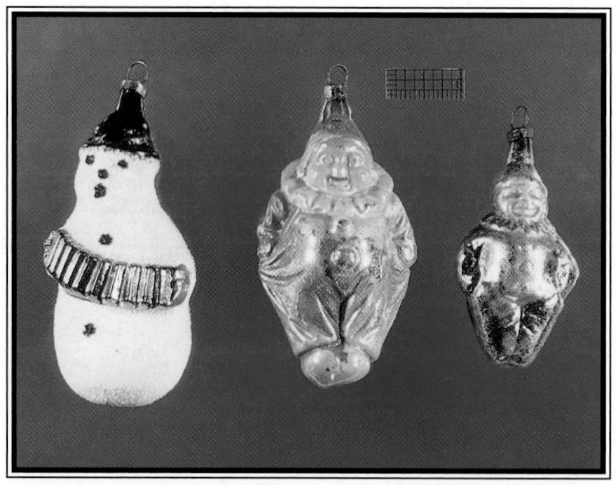

A. Snowman with a Concertina, approx. 4" [German, OP-NP (1950s & 1990s), R3]. **$50.00–75.00.** B. Clown with a Potbelly, approx. 3½" [OP-NP (1970s), R3]. **$45.00–60.00.** C. Standard Form Clown, approx. 2½" [OP-NP (1950s – 1990s), R4-5]. Small, **$30.00–45.00.**

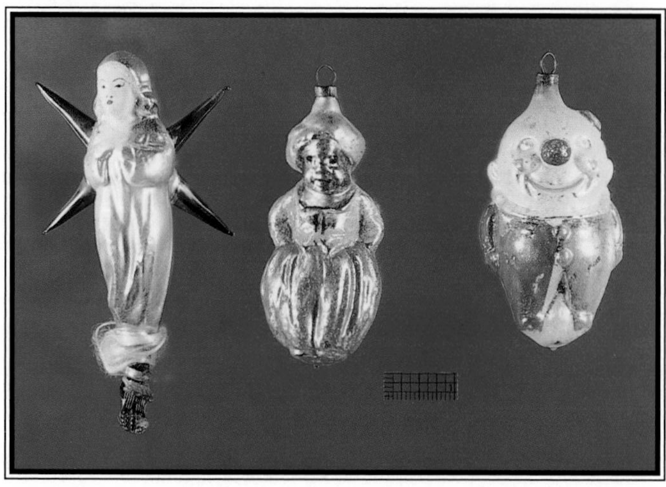

A. Standing Angel with Spike Wings, approx. 4¼" [OP, R2]. **$225.00–275.00.** B. Aladdin, approx. 3½" [German, OP-NP (1970s), R1-2]. **$325.00–375.00.** C. Clown with a Strawberry Nose, approx. 3½" [German, OP-NP (1980s & 1995), R2]. **$150.00–175.00.**

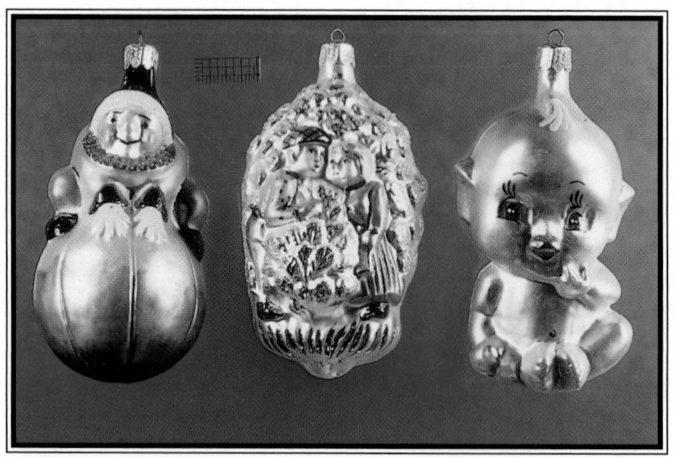

Radko Ornaments: A. Clown Sitting on a Ball, 4½" [NP (1991), R3-4]. **$45.00–55.00.** B. Man and Woman Kissing over a Bush, large, 4½" [OP-NP (1991), R3-4]. **$30.00–40.00.** C. Baby with a Large Head, 4½" [NP (1991), R3-4]. **$35.00–45.00.**

Two Joey Clowns: A. Joey Clown with Chenille Arms and Legs, 4" glass, 5½" overall [OP-NP, R1-2]. **$175.00–250.00.** B. Joey Clown in a "Waffle" Coat, 3" glass, 5" overall [OP, R2]. **$250.00–325.00.**

Joey Clown on a Cone, 5" [German, OP-NP (ca. 1950s), R1-2]. **$100.00–125.00.** B. Joey Clown Head, small, 2¼" [OP-NP (continuing), R3-4]. Small, **$55.00–65.00.**

A. Frog on a Ball, 2¾" frog, 5" overall [OP, R1]. **$175.00–225.00.** B. Joey Clown on a Cone, 4¼" [OP-NP (1950s), R1-2]. **$100.00–125.00.**

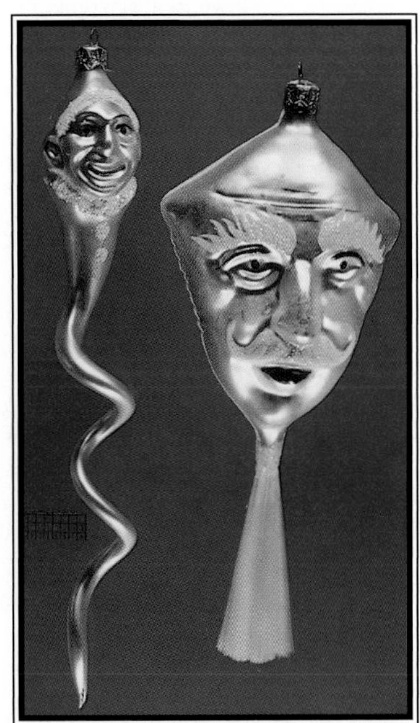

A. Joey-Clown-headed Snake, 9", Radko version [NP (1989), R2]. **$40.00–50.00.** B. Einstein Kite, 4½", Radko version [NP (1980s), R2]. **$40.00–50.00.**

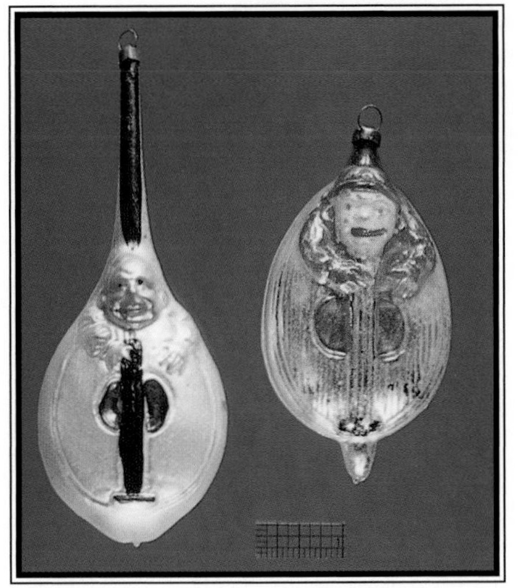

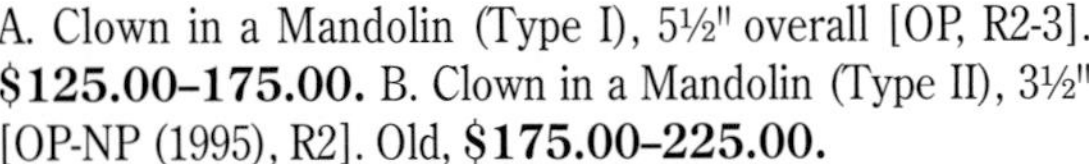

A. Clown in a Mandolin (Type I), 5½" overall [OP, R2-3]. **$125.00–175.00.** B. Clown in a Mandolin (Type II), 3½" [OP-NP (1995), R2]. Old, **$175.00–225.00.**

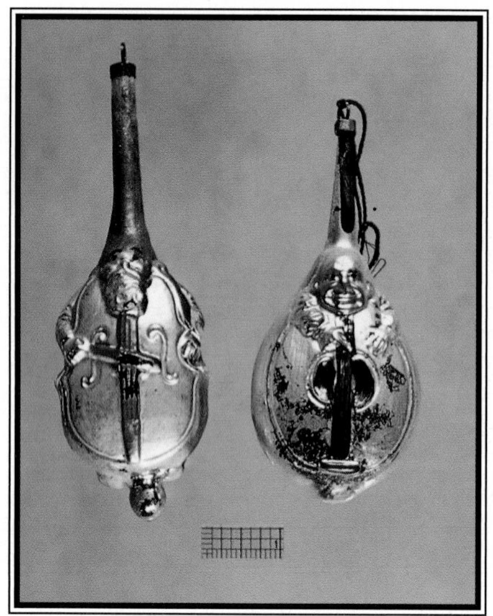

A. Man in a Cello, 3½" without pike, 5½" overall [OP-NP (1980), R1]. Old, **$250.00–300.00.** B. Clown in a Mandolin (Type I), 5½" [OP, R2-3]. **$125.00–175.00.**

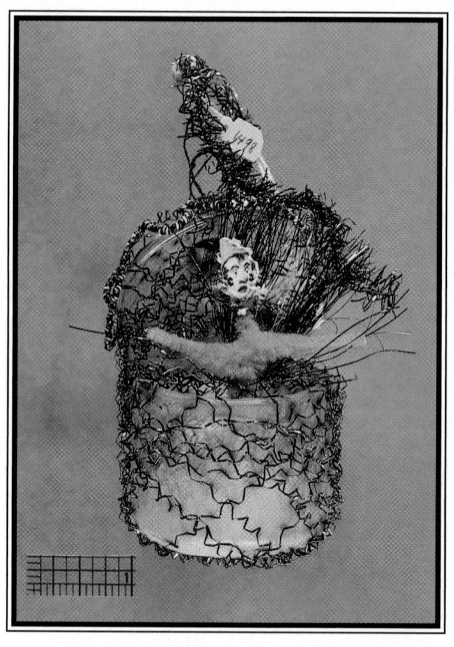

Jack-in-the-Box Clown, 3" [OP, R1]. **$325.00–375.00.**

A. Roly-Poly or Tweedle Dee Clown, 2½" [German, OP-NP (1950s & 1980s), R2-3]. **$100.00–135.00.** 1950s version (shown), **$40.00–50.00.** B. Indian Standing Smoking a Pipe, 3½" (shown) & 4" [German, OP-NP (1950s & 1980s), R3]. Old, **$250.00–275.00.** 1950s version (shown), **$50.00–75.00.** C. Angel Bust with SG Wings, 3" [OP, R2]. **$90.00–110.00.**

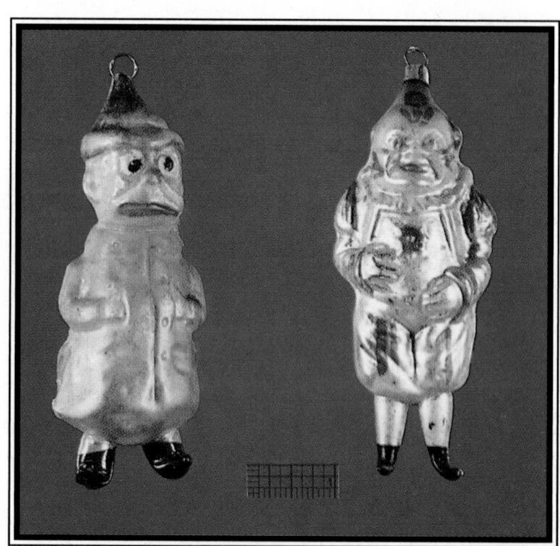

A. Yellow Kid with Annealed Legs, 3½" body, 4" overall [OP, R1+]. **$950.00–1,100.00.** B. Clown with Annealed Legs, 3¼" body, 4¼" overall [OP, R1+]. **$850.00–1,000.00.**

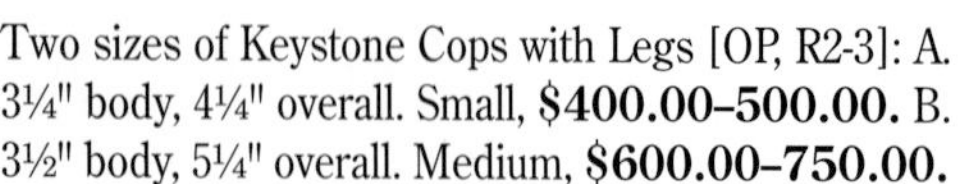

Two sizes of Keystone Cops with Legs [OP, R2-3]: A. 3¼" body, 4¼" overall. Small, **$400.00–500.00.** B. 3½" body, 5¼" overall. Medium, **$600.00–750.00.**

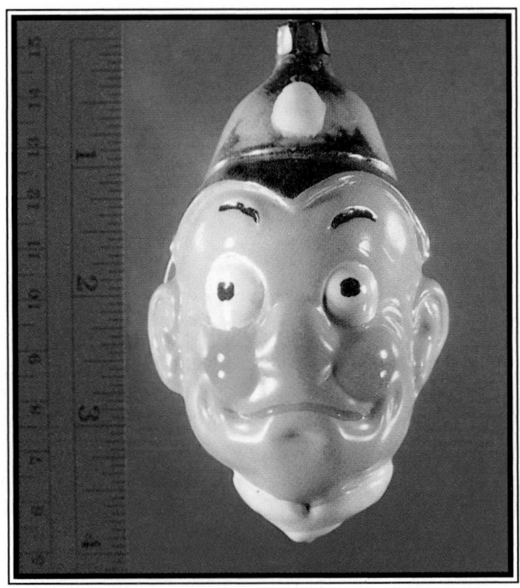

Keystone Cop Head, comic, 3¾" [OP, R1]. **$180.00–200.00.**

A. Tin Man, 5¼" [OP, R2]. **$100.00–125.00.** B. Keystone Cop with Stylized Body and Chenille Arms and Legs, 4½" glass, 6" overall [OP, R1]. **$300.00–350.00.**

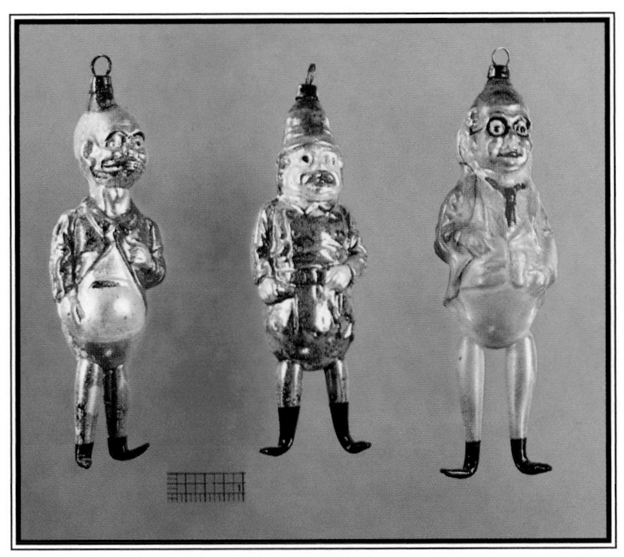

The Three Most Commonly Found Legged Figures: A. Happy Hooligan (Type I), 4½" [OP, R3]. **$350.00–450.00.** B. Keystone Cop, medium, 3½" body size without legs [OP, R2-3]. **$400.00–500.00.** C. Foxy Grandpa with Annealed Legs (Type I), 4½" [OP, R2-3]. **$400.00–500.00.**

A. Man in a Fez Hat, double faced, 2½". The other side shows a smiling face [OP, R1]. **$350.00–400.00.** B. Happy Hooligan Head, 2¾" [OP, R1]. **$300.00–350.00.**

A. Boy in a Night Cap, 3" [OP-NP (1980s), R1-2 for clip-on]. Clip-on price, **$175.00–225.00.** B. Clip-on Happy Hooligan Head, 2¾" [OP, R1]. **$300.00–350.00.** C. Buster Brown Head, 2¾" [OP, R1]. **$275.00–300.00.**

A. Foxy Grandpa (Type II), 3½" [OP, R2]. Without legs, **$200.00–250.00.** With legs, **$400.00–450.00.** B. Man's Head with Mutton Chops, 3¼" [OP, R1-2]. **$250.00–300.00.**

A & B. Comic Man with an Umbrella, approx. 3½" (shown), 4" (shown), & 4½". Also called a Peasant Man [German, OP-NP (1980s – 1990s), R2-3]. Small, **$125.00–150.00.** Medium, **$175.00–200.00.** Large, **$225.00–275.00.** C. Winston Churchill or Palmer Cox Brownie, approx. 3½" [OP-NP (1950s), R1-2]. **$250.00–275.00.**

A. Palmer Cox Brownie with Crossed Arms (Type I), 3" or 3½" body, approx. 5" overall [German, OP, R1-2]. **$1,000.00–1,200.00.** B. Happy Hooligan (Type II), 4¼" body, 5¾" overall [German, OP, R1]. **$850.00–1,000.00.** C. Mary Pickford with Annealed Legs, approx. 4¼" [German, OP-NP (1950s, without legs), R1]. **$500.00–600.00.**

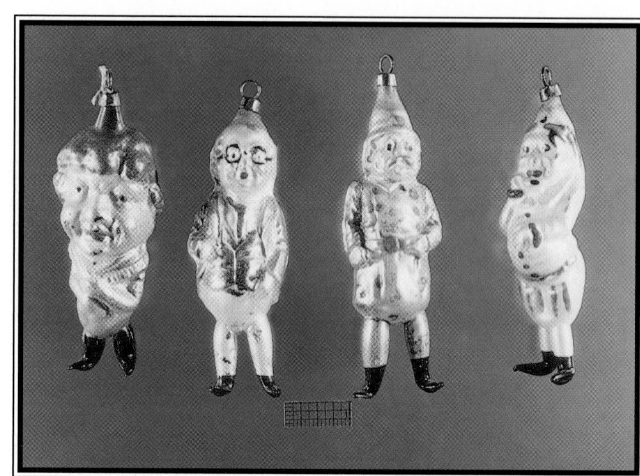

Four Figures with Annealed Glass Legs: A. "ZaZu" Large-headed Women with Annealed Legs, approx. 3½" (shown) & 4¼" [German, OP, R1]. Small, **$900.00–1,100.00.** Large, **$1,250.00–1,500.00.** B. Foxy Grandpa (Type I), approx. 4½" [OP, R2-3]. **$350.00–450.00.** C. Keystone Cop with Annealed Legs, 4" body size without legs [German, OP, R2]. Without legs. **$225.00–275.00.** With legs, **$550.00–650.00.** D. Punch Clown, 3½" body, approx. 4" overall [German, OP, R1+]. **$900.00–1,100.00.**

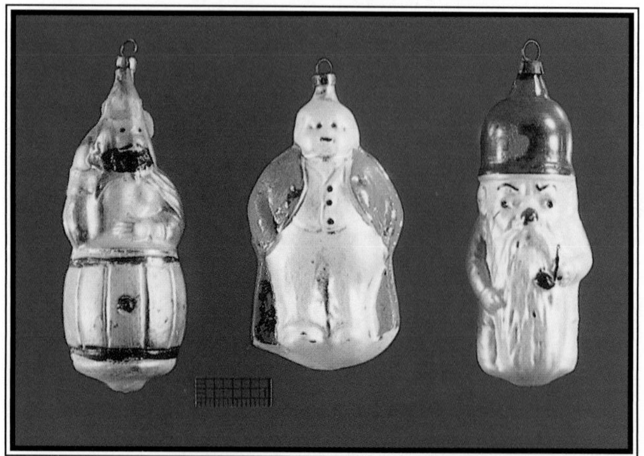

A. Ali Baba in a Barrel, approx. 4" [German, OP, R1]. **$400.00–500.00.** B. "The Ringmaster," approx. 3¾" [OP, R1]. **$350.00–400.00.** C. Gnome in a Large Hat, approx. 4" [OP, R1-2]. **$275.00–325.00.**

A. Bust of John Bull with Chenille Arms and Legs, approx. 2¾" & 3" (shown), glass body, wax hands and boots [German, OP-NP (1995), R1-2]. **$450.00–550.00.** B. Eddie Cantor with Chenille Arms & Legs, 4" glass body, approx. 5½" overall [German, OP, R1-2]. **$550.00–650.00.** C. Comic Keystone Cop with Chenille Legs, 3" glass body, approx. 4½" overall [German, OP, R1]. **$450.00–550.00.**

A. Squatting Black Boy, approx. 3¼", also called Black Peter [German, OP-NP (1990), R2]. **$250.00–300.00.** B. Pinocchio, approx. 4" [German, OP-NP (1950s & 1990s), R2]. **$75.00–100.00.** C. Smitty (Type II), approx. 3½", also called Skippy [German, OP, R2]. **$200.00–225.00.**

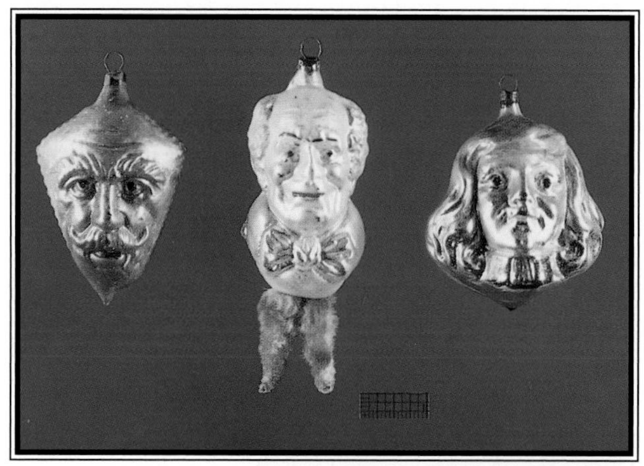

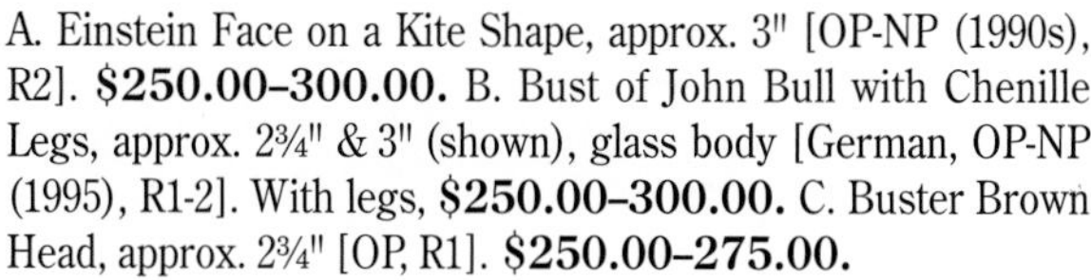

A. Einstein Face on a Kite Shape, approx. 3" [OP-NP (1990s), R2]. **$250.00–300.00.** B. Bust of John Bull with Chenille Legs, approx. 2¾" & 3" (shown), glass body [German, OP-NP (1995), R1-2]. With legs, **$250.00–300.00.** C. Buster Brown Head, approx. 2¾" [OP, R1]. **$250.00–275.00.**

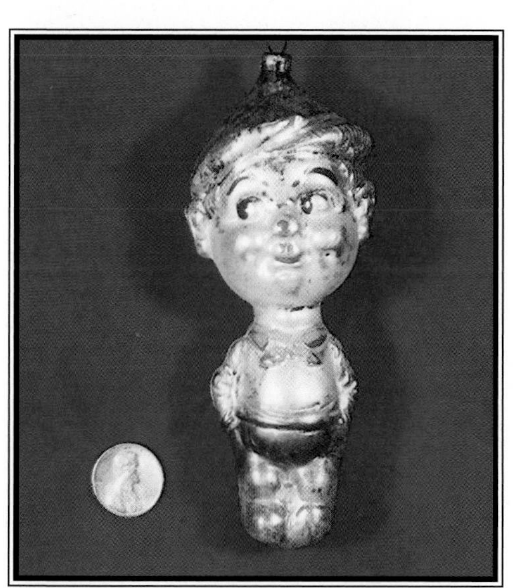

Smitty (Type I), approx. 4½" [German, OP-NP (Radko, 1990s), R1-2]. **$225.00–275.00.**

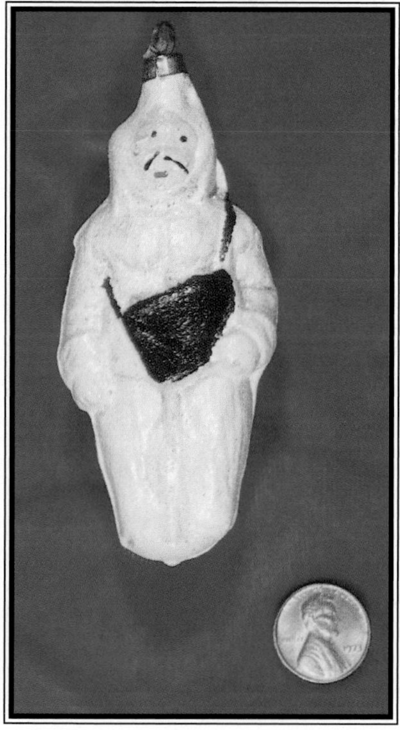

The Explorer, also called Amelia Earhart or Admiral Perry, approx. 3½" & 3¾" (shown); this version with a moustache looks more like Perry in his Arctic outfit [German, OP, R2-3]. **$150.00–200.00.**

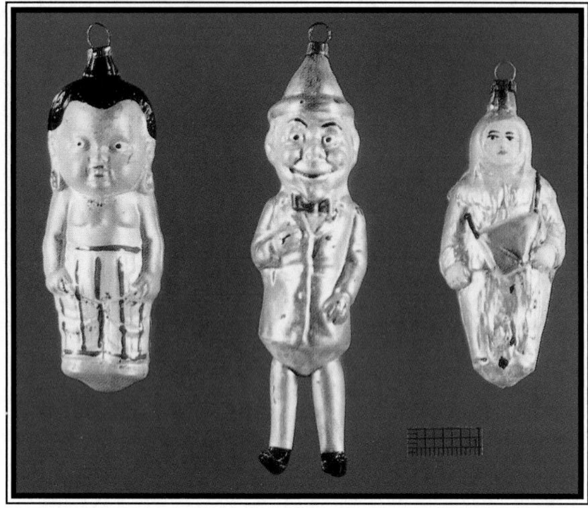

A. Little Black Sambo, approx. 4¼" [German, OP, R1-2]. **$400.00–475.00.** B. Moon Mullins with Annealed Legs (Type II), approx. 5½" [German, OP, R1-2]. **$1,000.00–1,200.00.** Without legs, **$250.00–300.00.** C. The Explorer, also called Amelia Earhart or Admiral Perry, approx. 3½" (shown) & 3¾". This version looks more like Earhart [OP, R2-3]. **$150.00–200.00.**

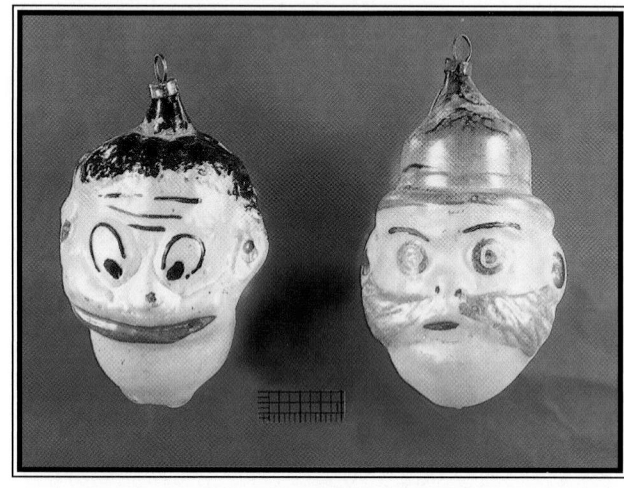

A. Flip Head, 4" [OP, R1+]. **$450.00–550.00.** B. Man's Head with Mutton Chops, 3¼" [OP, R1-2]. **$250.00–300.00.**

Flip from the comic strip *Little Nemo*: A. Type I, 3" [OP, R1-2]. **$500.00–600.00.** B. Type II, 3½" [OP, R1-2]. **$550.00–700.00.**

Flip, 3½", can have annealed legs [OP, R1+]. Without legs, **$550.00–700.00.** With legs, **$1,000.00–1,300.00.**

Dagwood, 3½" [OP, R1+]. **$450.00–550.00.**

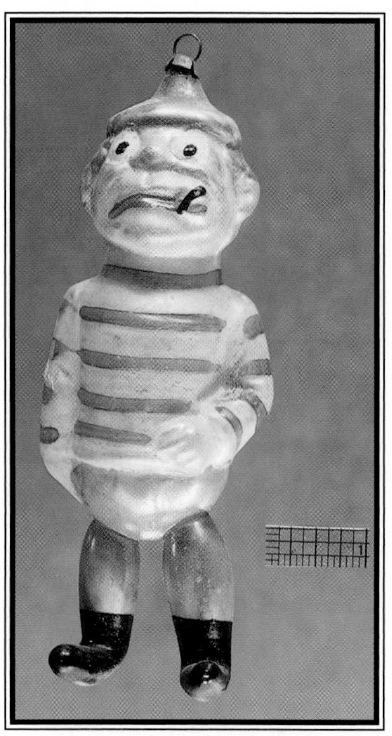

Popeye or Longshoreman with Annealed Legs, large, 5¾" [OP, R1-2]. **$700.00–800.00.**

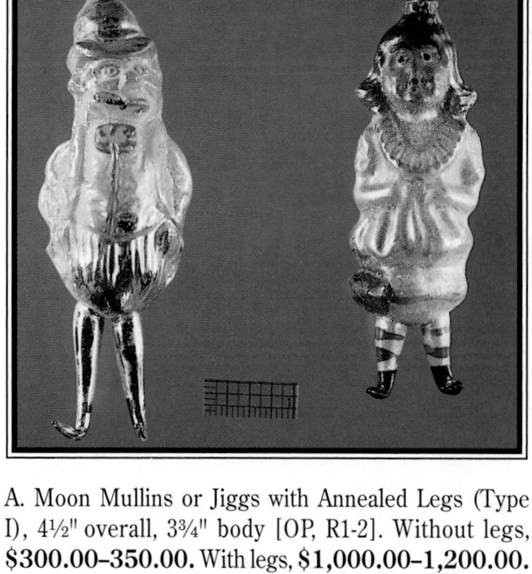

A. Moon Mullins or Jiggs with Annealed Legs (Type I), 4½" overall, 3¾" body [OP, R1-2]. Without legs, **$300.00–350.00.** With legs, **$1,000.00–1,200.00.** English Lady with Annealed Legs, 2¾" body, 3½" – 4" overall [OP-NP (1970s & 1990s, no legs), R1]. Old with legs, **$850.00–1,000.00.**

A. Man in a Barrel, 3" [OP, R1-2]. **$275.00–300.00.** B. Jiggs, 3¼" [OP, R1]. **$300.00–350.00.** C. Bowling Pin Man, 3¼" [OP-NP (1980s), R2-3]. Old, **$150.00–175.00.**

A. Grinning Clown Head, 2¾", unsilvered with tinsel sprig [OP, R1-2]. Small, **$200.00–225.00.** B. Devil "Klabubau" Head, 2¼" [OP, R1]. **$150.00–175.00.**

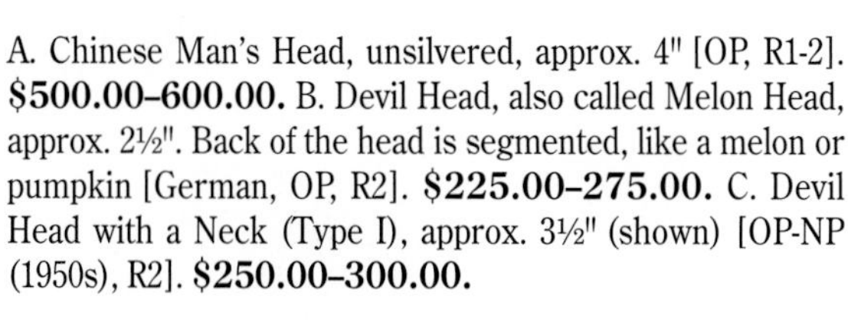

A. Chinese Man's Head, unsilvered, approx. 4" [OP, R1-2]. **$500.00–600.00.** B. Devil Head, also called Melon Head, approx. 2½". Back of the head is segmented, like a melon or pumpkin [German, OP, R2]. **$225.00–275.00.** C. Devil Head with a Neck (Type I), approx. 3½" (shown) [OP-NP (1950s), R2]. **$250.00–300.00.**

Devil Head Pendent, approx. 12" overall [German, OP, R1+]. **$1,100.00–1,300.00.**

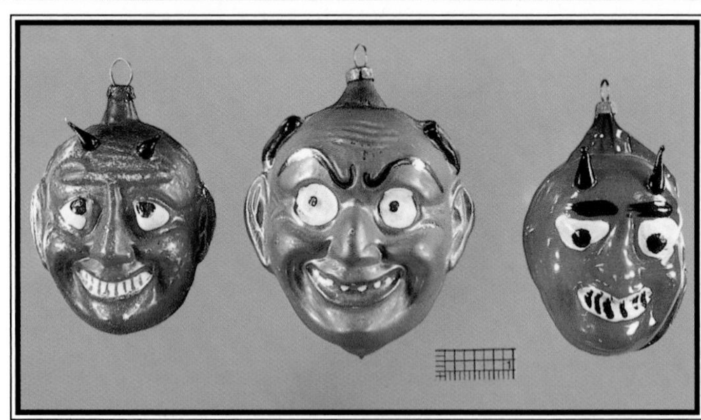

A. Devil Head with Annealed Horns (Type II), 2¼" [OP, R1]. **$225.00–250.00.** B. Devil Head with Molded Horns, 2½" & 3" (shown) [German, OP-NP (Inge-glas 1980s & 1990s) R1-2]. Old, Small, **$200.00–225.00.** Large, **300.00–350.00.**. C. Devil Head with Annealed Horns (Type I) [OP, R1-2]. **$200.00–225.00.**

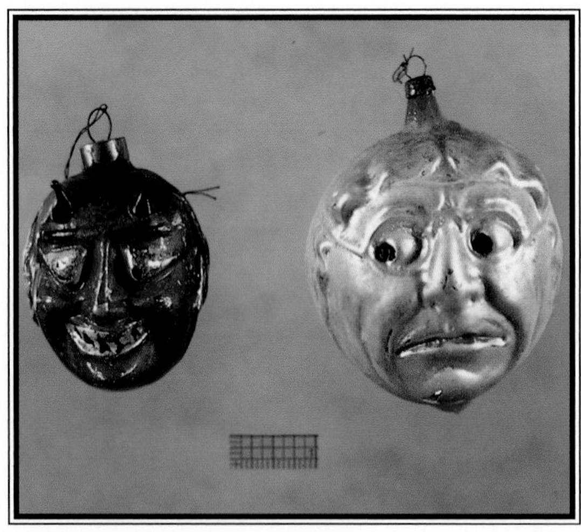

A. Devil Head with Annealed Horns (Type I), 2½" [OP, R2]. **$225.00–250.00.** B. Mr. Rose Head, 3¼", open rose on reverse [OP, R1]. **$225.00–275.00.**

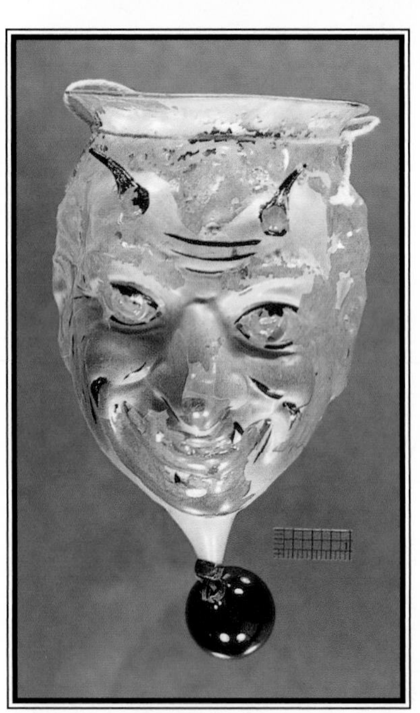

Devil/Krampus, hollow, large, 7" overall, 5½" head [OP, R1+]. Large, **$750.00–900.00.**

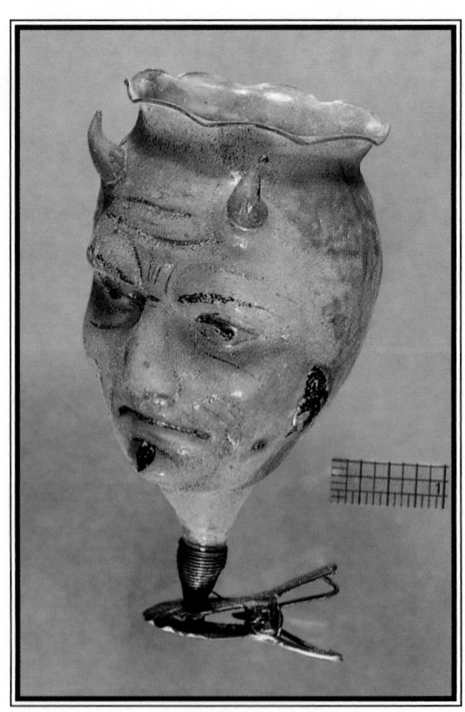

Devil/Krampus Head, hollow, blown, small [OP, R1]. **$450.00–550.00.**

A. Hansel, approx. 3", 3½", & 4½" (shown) [German, OP-NP (1990s), R2-3]. Large size, **$150.00–250.00.** B. Mother and Child Angels, 3¾" [OP, R2]. **$275.00–325.00.**

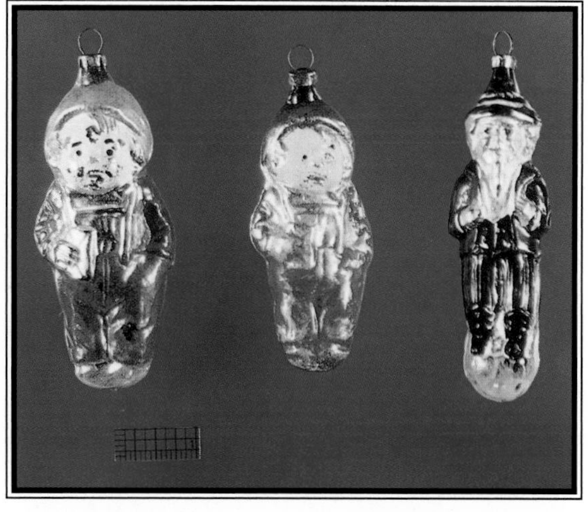

A & B. Hansel [German, OP-NP (1990s), R2-3]. Small (3"), **$60.00–70.00.** Medium (3½"), **$75.00–100.00.** C. Standing Uncle Sam, 3½" [OP, R2]. **$150.00–175.00.**

A. Goldilocks, clip on, 3" [OP-NP (1970s), R3-4]. Old, **$100.00–125.00.** B. Man Skiing, embossed, double sided, 3½" [OP, R1-2]. **$75.00–100.00.**

A. Goldilocks Head (Type I), 2½" [OP-NP, R3]. Small, **$125.00–150.00.** B. Goldilocks Head (Type II), 2¾" [OP, R2]. **$125.00–150.00.**

A. Goldilocks Head (Type I), 2½", with painted face [OP-NP, R3]. Old small, **$150.00–175.00.** B. Monkey-faced Man's Head, 2½" [OP-NP (1950s), R2]. Old, **$150.00–175.00.** 1950s version (shown), **$50.00–75.00.** C. Boy's Head, comic, 2" [OP, R1-2]. **$100.00–125.00.**

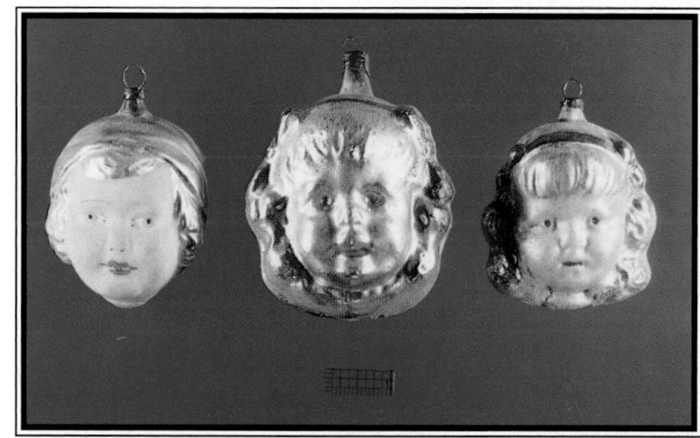

A. Flapper Girl Head, approx. 2½", 2¾" (shown), & 3¾" [German, OP, R2-3]. Small, **$100.00–150.00.** Medium, **$150.00–200.00.** Large, **$200.00–250.00.** B & C. Goldilocks Heads, approx. 2½" (shown) & 3" (shown) [German, OP-NP (Lauscha Glas, 1995), R3 small, R2 large]. Small, **$125.00–150.00.** Large, **$150.00–175.00.**

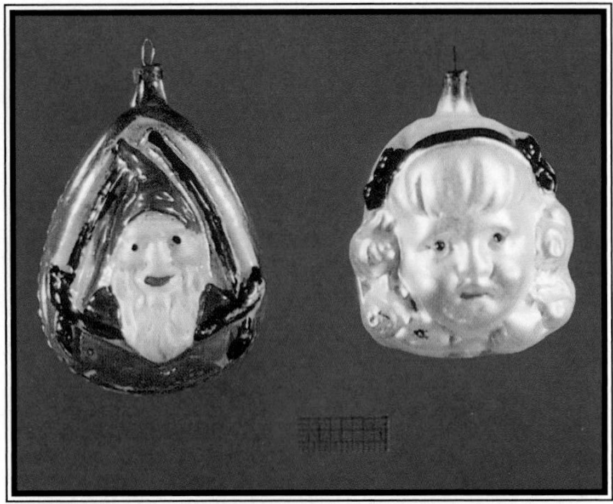

A. Gnome in a Triangle Window, approx. 2¼" & 3½" (shown) [German, OP-NP (1950s), R3]. 1950s version (shown), **$55.00–65.00.** B. Goldilocks Head, approx. 2½" [German, OP-NP, R3]. **$125.00–150.00.**

A. Little Miss Muffet (Type I), approx. 2", 2½", 3", 3½", & 4" (shown) [German, OP-NP (1990s, two smallest sizes), R3-4]. Small (2"), **$35.00–50.00.** Medium (2½" - 3"), **$55.00–65.00.** Medium (3½"), **$90.00–110.00.** Large (4"), **$125.00–150.00.** B. Chubby Boy in a Toboggan Hat, also called Whistling Boy, approx. 2¾", 3", 3¼", 3¾", & 4" (shown) [German, OP-NP (1950s & 1990s), R3-4]. Small & Medium, **$75.00–100.00.** Large (3¾" & 4"), **$125.00–150.00.**

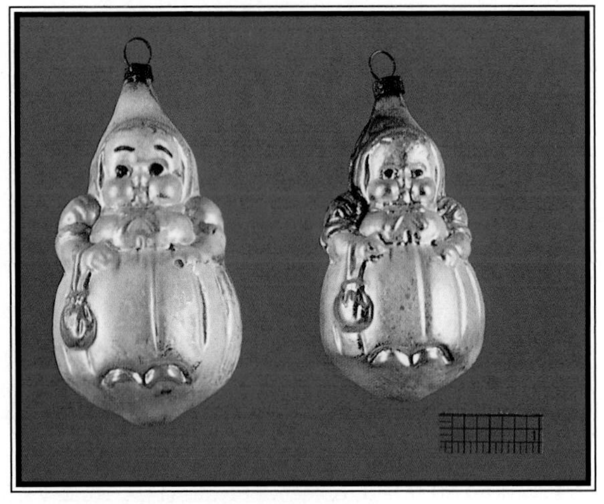

A & B. Little Miss Muffet, approx. 2", 2½", 3" (shown), 3½" (shown), & 4" [German, OP-NP (1990s, two smallest sizes), R3-4]. Small (2"), **$35.00–50.00.** Medium (2½" – 3"), **$55.00–65.00.** Medium (3½"), **$90.00–110.00.** Large (4"), **$125.00–150.00.**

Witch Head Goblet, 4½" [OP, R1]. **$550.00–700.00.**

Witch, 3½" [OP, R1-2]. **$400.00–500.00.**

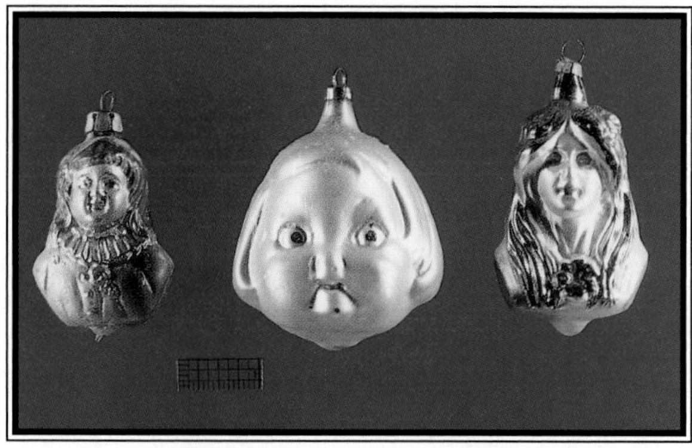

A. Indian Princess Bust, approx. 2½" [OP, R2]. **$135.00–160.00.** B. Dolly Dingle Head, approx. 3" [OP, R1-2]. **$175.00–225.00.** C. Art Nouveau Bust of Lady, approx. 3" [OP, R1]. **$200.00–250.00.**

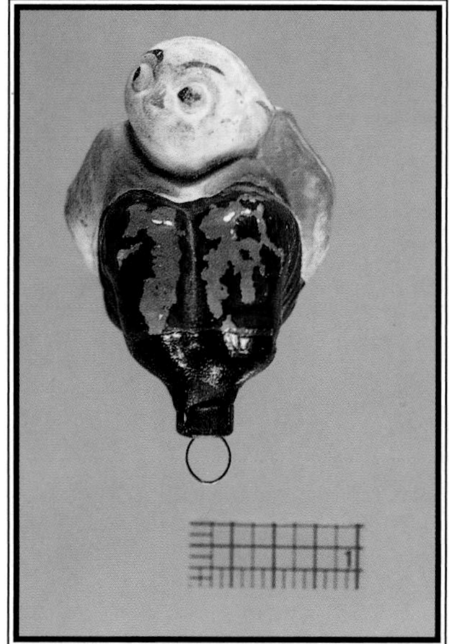

Mooning Brownie, *Der Geld Schizer*, unsilvered, front view, 2" [OP, R1+]. **$450.00–550.00.**

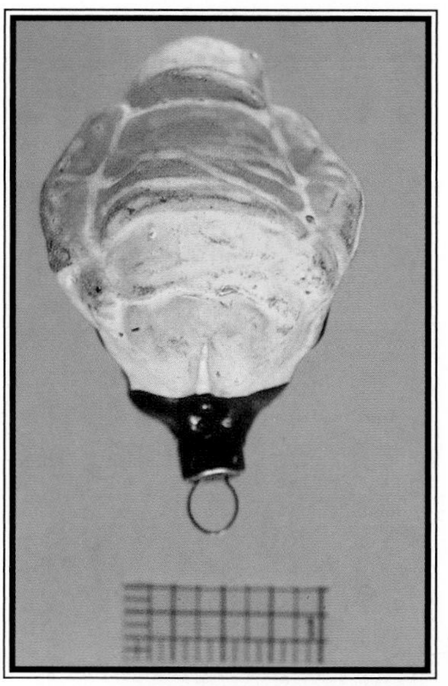

Rear view of preceding photo.

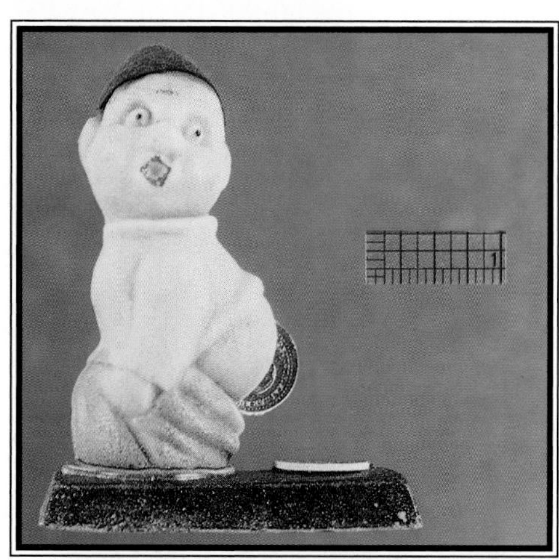

Marzipan *Der Geld Schizer* showing the original concept for the Mooning Brownie in the preceding pictured.

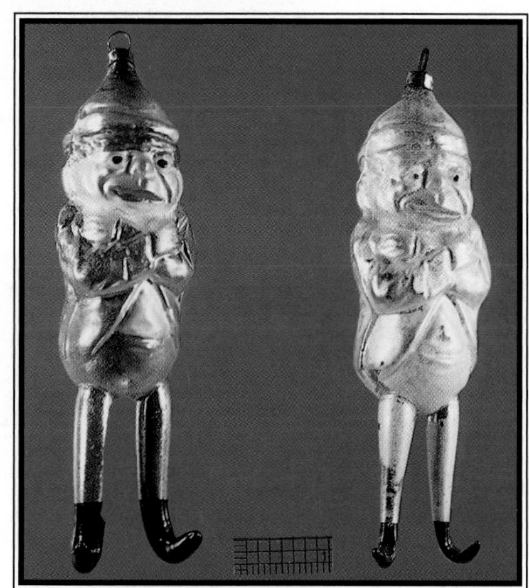

Palmer Cox Brownie (Type I), 3½" body, 5" overall. This picture shows the difference a paint job makes [OP, R1-2]. Large without legs, **$200.00–225.00.** Large with legs, **$800.00–1,000.00.**

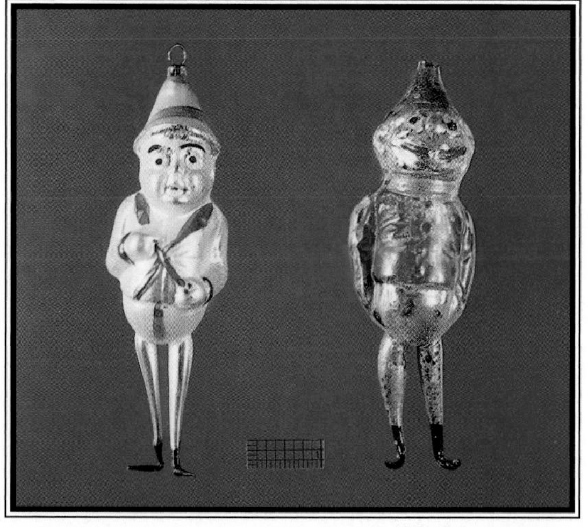

Palmer Cox Brownies: A. Type III, 3¼" body, 5" overall [OP, R1-2]. Without legs, **$250.00–275.00.** With legs, **$750.00–900.00.** B. Type IV, 3" body, 4½" overall [OP, R2]. Without legs, **$175.00-200.00.** With legs, **$700.00–800.00.**

A. Palmer Cox Brownie (Type II), 3¾" body, 5½" overall [OP, R1]. **$750.00–900.00.** B. Mary Pickford with Annealed Legs, 3" body, 4½" overall [OP-NP, R1]. Without legs, **$125.00–150.00.** With legs, **$500.00–600.00.**

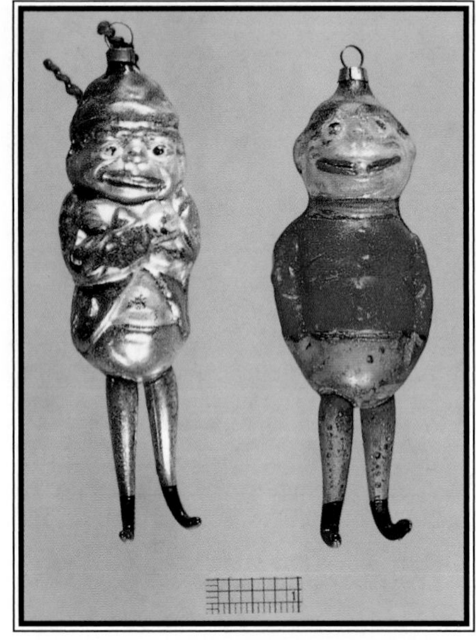

A. Palmer Cox Brownie with Crossed Arms (Type I), 3" body, 4¾" overall [OP, R1-2]. Without legs, **$150.00–175.00.** Small with legs, **$800.00–1,000.00.** B. Palmer Cox Brownie (Type IV), arms straight, 3" body, 4½" overall [OP, R2]. With legs, **$700.00–800.00.**

Dwarf with Annealed Arms and Legs, 2¼" body, 3¾" overall [OP, R1+]. **$2,000.00–2,500.00.**

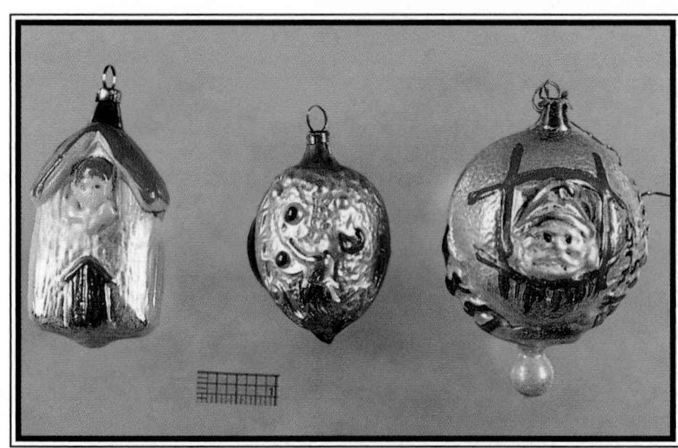

A. Elf in a House, 2¾" [OP, R2]. **$90.00–110.00.** B. Elves on a Walnut, 2¼" [OP, R1]. **$40.00–50.00.** C. Santa or Elf in a Window, 3½" [German, OP, R2]. **$125.00–150.00.**

A. Elf on a Stump, embossed, approx. 2½" [German, OP-NP (1950s, 1970s, 1980s, & 1990s), R3-4]. **$65.00–85.00.** B. Gnome Playing a Concertina, approx. 3¾" [German, OP-NP (1950s, 1980s, & 1990s), R2-3]. 1950s & 1980s version shows bumps at the ends of the log – old version shows rings. 1990s Radko also shows rings. Old, **$125.00–150.00.** 1950s version, **$45.00–60.00.** C. Elf Atop a Mushroom, approx. 3½" [OP, R1]. **$200.00–250.00.**

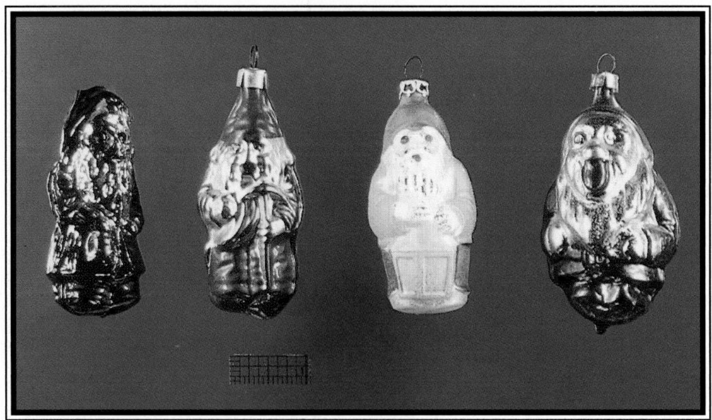

A. Dwarf with a Money Bag, approx. 2¾" [German, OP-NP (1980s), R1]. **$100.00–135.00.** B. Dwarf with a Pick, approx. 2½" [German, OP-NP (1980), R1-2]. **$90.00–110.00.** C. Dwarf with a Lantern, approx. 2½" [German, NP (1970s), R2-3]. **$15.00–25.00.** D. Singing Dwarf, approx. 2½" [German, OP-NP (1980s), R1]. **$100.00–125.00.**

Set of Doubl-Glo's Snow White and the Seven Dwarfs, American made. **$400.00–450.00.**

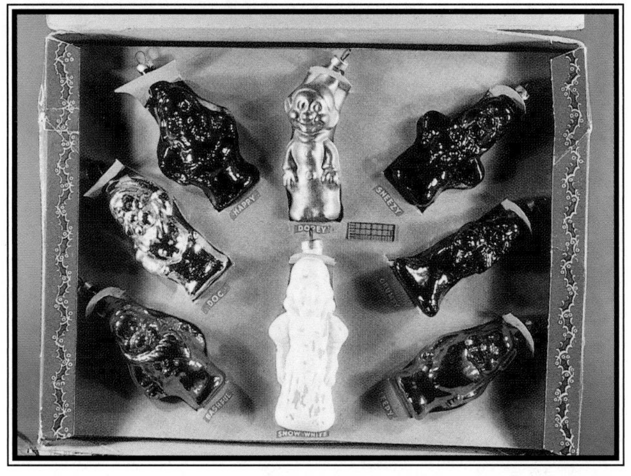

Doubl-Glo's Snow White and the Seven Dwarfs. Dwarfs approx. 3¼", Snow White 4" [American, OP, R3 as individual pieces, R1 as a boxed set]. **$35.00–45.00** each. Boxed set, **$400.00–450.00.**

Fairy Head, 3¾", missing glass eyes [OP, R1-2]. Missing eyes lower the price. **$250.00–275.00.**

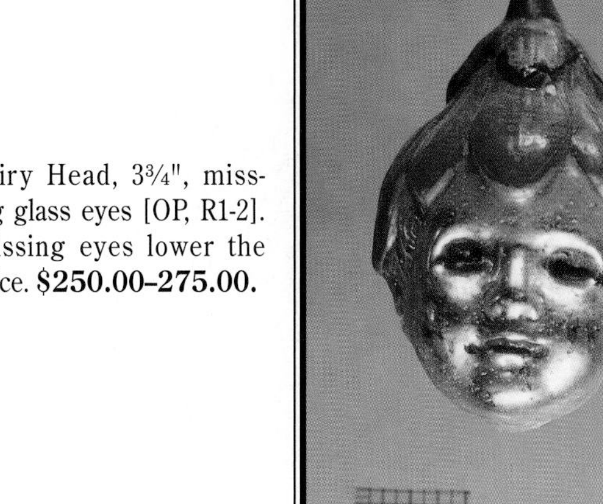

A. Mushroom Man with a Pipe and Walking Stick, approx. 3¾" [German, OP, R1-2]. **$125.00–150.00.** B. Mushroom Man with a Money Bag [OP, R1-2]. **$175.00–200.00.** C. Mushroom Girl with a Pipe, approx. 4" [OP, R1-2]. **$125.00–150.00.**

Front and Side Views of a Mushroom Man, approx. 3½" [German, OP-NP (1990), R3]. **$80.00–100.00.**

A. Mushroom Girl (Type II), approx. 3½" [German, OP-NP (1970s), R2]. **$125.00–150.00.** 1970s version (shown), **$30.00–40.00.** B. Elf Under a Mushroom [German, OP-NP (1971), R2]. **$60.00–75.00.** 1970s version (shown), **$25.00–35.00.** C. Mushroom Girl (Type I), approx. 3½" [OP, R2-3]. **$90.00–110.00.**

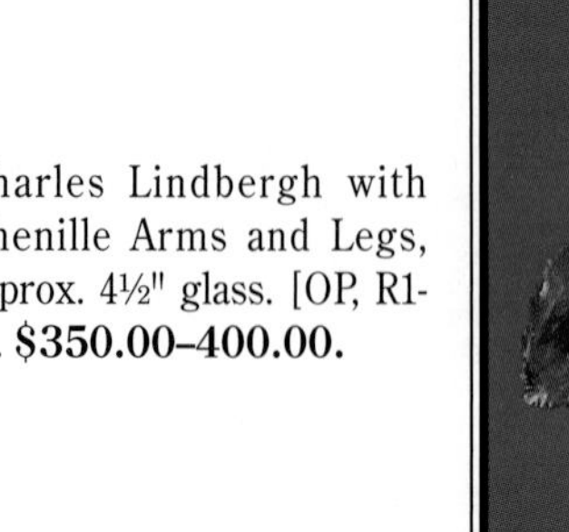

Charles Lindbergh with Chenille Arms and Legs, approx. 4½" glass. [OP, R1-2]. **$350.00–400.00.**

A. Barney Google Head, approx. 2¼" [OP, R1]. **$350.00–400.00.** B. Joan of Arc Head, approx. 2½" [German, OP, R2-3]. **$100.00–125.00.** C. Charlie Chaplin Head, approx. 2⅝", 3½" (shown), & 6" (made by Inge-glas in 1995) [German, OP-NP, R1-2]. Small, **$300.00–350.00.** Large, **$400.00–475.00.** 6", **$35.00–40.00.**

A Rare and Beautiful Bust of Jesus, approx. 3", circa 1890 [German, OP-NP (Matthai and Inge-glas, 1990s), R1+]. **$400.00–450.00.**

A. Standing Madonna & Child (Type I), 2½" & 3" (shown) [German, OP-NP (1994, small), R1]. Small, **$175.00–200.00.** Large, **$250.00–300.00.** B. Bust of Madonna & Child, approx. 2½" [OP, R1-2]. **$175.00–200.00.**

A. Standing Madonna & Child (Type II), approx. 5½" [NP (1950s), R2-3]. **$50.00–75.00.** B. Madonna & Child, approx. 3½" [German, OP-NP (1980s), R2]. **$175.00–225.00.**

A. Al Jolson Head, 3½" [German, OP, R1]. **$300.00–350.00.** B. Black Man's Head with Bumpy Pattern, 3" [OP-NP (1990s), R1-2]. Old, **$125.00–175.00.** C. Raspberry Face, 2½" [OP, R1-2]. **$100.00–125.00.**

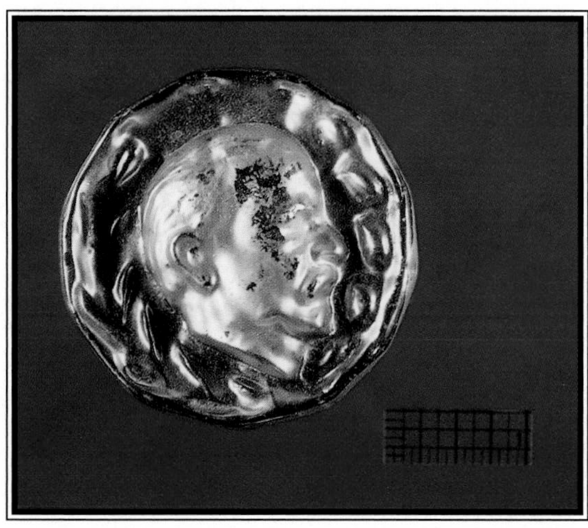

Lenin Head Medallion, clip in rear, 2½" [OP, R1+]. **$275.00–325.00.**

Two U.S. Presidents [both NP (1990s), R3]: A. Radko George Washington Head, approx. 5". B. Radko Lincoln Bust, approx. 4¾". **$45.00–70.00** each.

A. Martha Washington, 3¾" [Italian, NP (1950s), R3]. B. George Washington, 5" [Italian, NP (1950s), R3]. **$45.00–65.00** each. Pair, **$100.00–125.00.**

A. Uncle Sam on a Boot, 4¼" [German, OP-NP (1994), R1-2]. Old, **$450.00–550.00.** B. Ben Franklin, 2¾" [German, OP, R1-2]. **$450.00–550.00.**

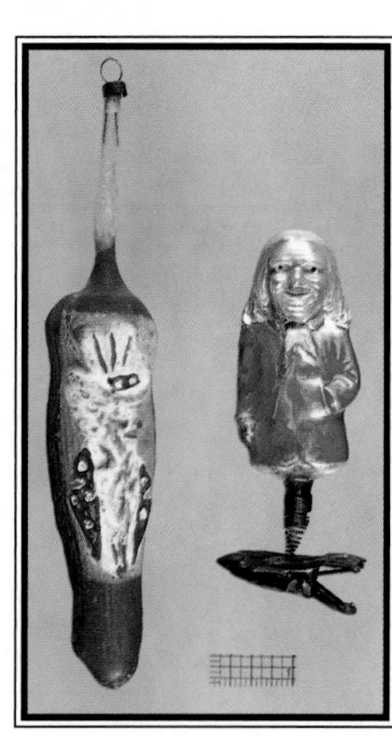

A. Happy Hooligan (Type I), 4½" [German, OP, R3]. With clip, **$150.00–175.00.** With legs, **$350.00–400.00.** B. Standing Indian with Annealed Legs, 5" [German, OP, R1]. **$850.00–950.00.**

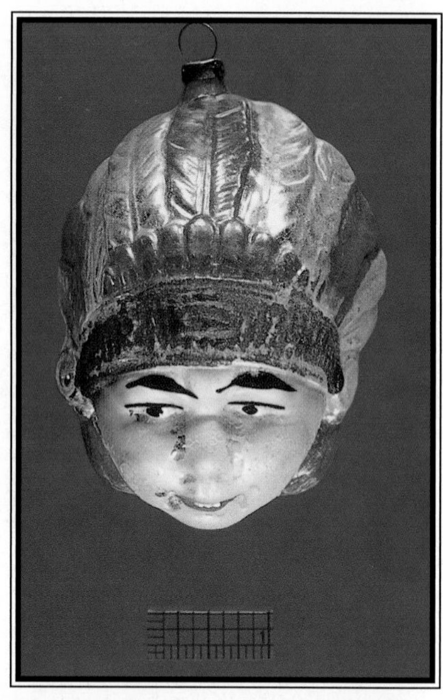

Indian Boy in a Headdress, 3¼" [OP, R1]. **$400.00–475.00.**

A. Grim-faced Indian with War Paint, 3¼" [OP, R1-2] **$350.00–400.00.** B. Indian Head on a Pine Cone, approx. 2¾", 3", 3¾" (shown), & 4" [German, OP, R2]. Small, **$275.00–300.00.** Medium, **$350.00–400.00.** Large, **$400.00–450.00.**

A. Indian Head on a Pine Cone, 3¾" [German, OP, R2]. Medium, **$350.00–400.00.** B. Grim-faced Indian with a Headdress, stylized body, 1¾" head, 6" overall [German, OP, R2]. **$350.00–450.00.** C. Indian Head in Headdress (Type I), approx. 3" & 3½" (shown) [German, OP-NP (1990), R2]. Old, **$300.00–325.00.**

A. Indian Head in a Headdress (Type I), approx. 3" & 3½" (shown) [German, OP-NP (1990s), R2]. **$300.00–325.00.** B. Grim-faced Indian with a Headdress (Type I), approx. 1¾" & 2¼" (shown) [German, OP, R2]. Small, **$175.00–200.00.** Large, **$250.00–300.00.** C. Indian in Bust Form, approx. 3¾" [German, OP-NP (1940s – 1950s, & 1990s), R2-3]. **$275.00–350.00.**

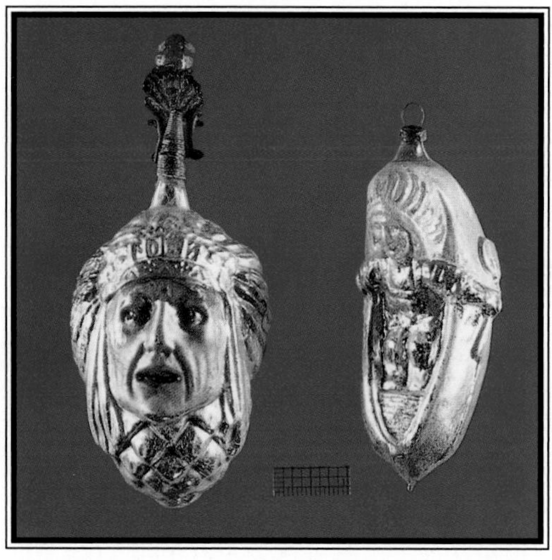

A. Indian Head on a Pine Cone, approx. 3", 3¾", & 4" (shown) [German, OP, R2]. **$350.00-400.00.** B. Indian in a Canoe, approx. 3¾" (shown) & 4¼" [German, OP-NP (1970 & 1990), R2]. **$250.00-300.00.**

A. Standing Indian Smoking a Pipe, approx. 3½" (shown) and 4" [German, OP-NP (1950s & 1980s), R2]. **$250.00-300.00.** 1980s version (shown), **$15.00-25.00.** B. Indian in a Headdress (Type II), approx. 3¾" [German, NP (1950s & 1970s), R2]. 1950s version, **$75.00-100.00.** 1970s version (shown), **$20.00-30.00.** C. Indian Head, approx. 3" [NP (1970s), R1-2]. **$25.00-40.00.**

Grim-faced Indian in War Paint, approx. 3¼" (Type II) [German, OP, R1-2]. **$350.00-400.00.**

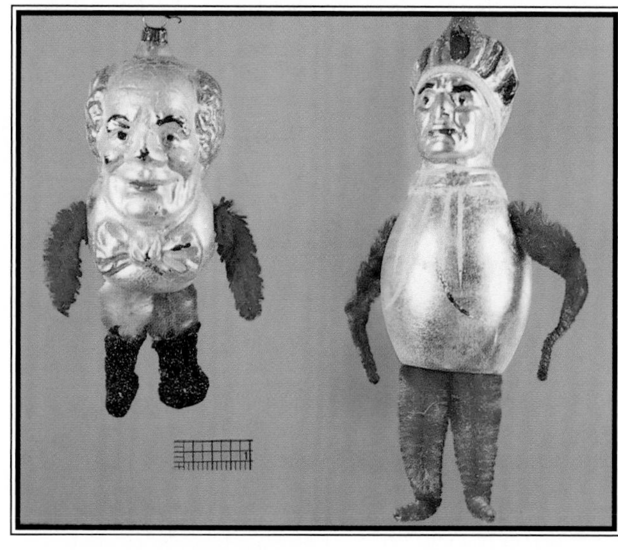

A. Bust of John Bull with Chenille Arms and Legs, 2¾" body, 4¼" overall [German, OP-NP (1995), R1]. Old, **$400.00-550.00.** B. Grim-faced Indian with Headdress and Chenille Arms and Legs, 6" overall, 4¼" glass body [German, OP, R1]. **$500.00-650.00.**

A. Grotesque Uncle Sam, approx. 6¾", 9" with glass hat attached. This piece has been identified as Uncle Sam from old ornament ads [German, OP, R1+]. **$1,500.00-1,750.00** with hat. **$800.00-900.00** without hat. B. Joey-Clown-headed Snake, 2" molded clown head, approx. 7" - 9" overall [German, OP-NP (Radko, 1989; Inge-glas, 1995), R2]. Old version, **$200.00-250.00.**

The hat that goes with the grotesque Uncle Sam in the preceding photo [OP, R1]. Hat alone, **$200.00–225.00.**

A. Child in a Snowsuit, approx. 4", may have metal skis attached [German, OP-NP (Radko, 1990s), R3]. **$60.00–75.00.** With skis, **$90.00–110.00.** Radko version, **$30.00–40.00.** B. Miss Liberty, approx. 3" [German, OP, R2]. **$250.00–300.00.** C. Miss Liberty in a Flag, approx. 3½" [German, OP-NP (1970s & 1980s), R1+]. **$300.00–400.00.** 1970s & 1980s version (shown), **$30.00–40.00.** D. Boy in a Flower Basket, approx. 2¼" (shown) & 3½" [German, OP-NP (1990), R3]. Small, **$50.00–65.00.** Large, **$80.00–90.00.**

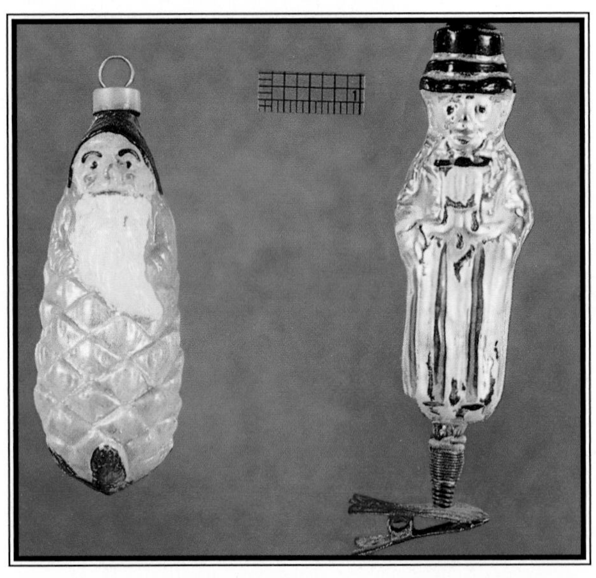

A. Dwarf or Santa in a Pine Cone, 3½" [OP-NP (1980s), R2]. Old, **$100.00–125.00.** B. Uncle Sam Boy, clip on, 3" & 3¾" (shown) [OP-NP (1990s), R2]. Small, **$175.00–225.00.** Old large, **$300.00–350.00.**

A. Joan of Arc Head, 2½" [German, OP, R2-3]. **$100.00–125.00.** B. Joan of Arc, clip on [German, OP, R2-3]. **$150.00–200.00.** C. Red Riding Hood Head, approx. 1¾" (shown) & 2½". The small head is more rare than the large [OP, R3-4]. **$65.00–85.00.**

Hindenburg Bust, 4½" [German, NP (1992), R4]. **$15.00–25.00.** B. Graf Zeppelin Head, 3" [German, OP-NP (Inge-glas, 1980s), R1]. Old large, **$250.00–300.00.** C. Boy's Head with Small Hat, 2½" [OP-NP (1980s), R1]. Old, **$150.00–175.00.** 1980s version (shown), **$15.00–20.00.**

A. Goofy Clown, 4" [OP, R2]. **$200.00–250.00.** B. Kaiser Wilhelm, 3½" [OP, R1]. **$300.00–400.00.**

Jesus Bust with Glass Eyes, 3¼" [OP, R1+]. **$700.00–775.00.**

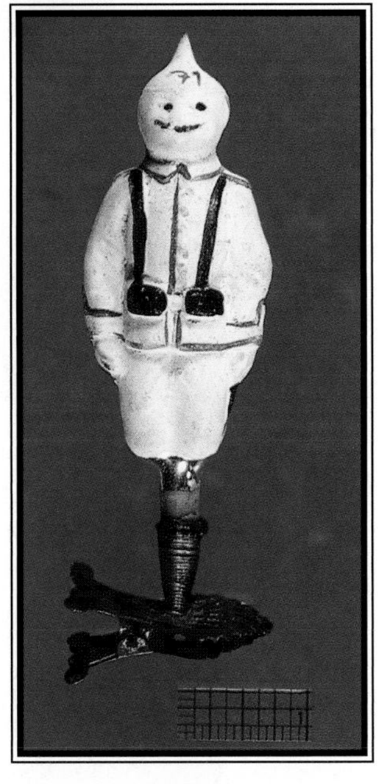

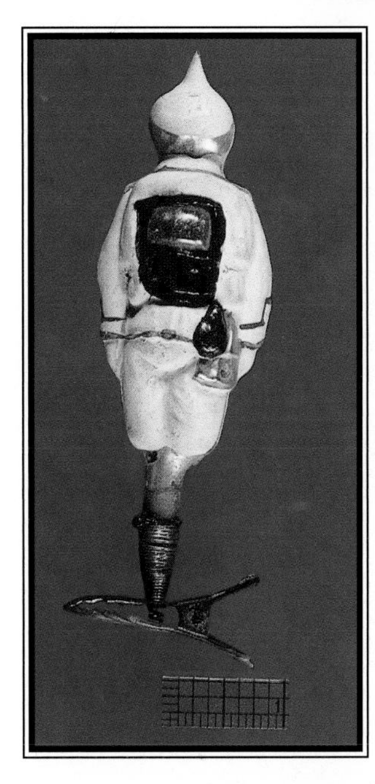

Above: Two Views of a German WWI Soldier on a Clip, approx. 4" (glass only). He wears a German uniform with a spiked helmet. Both front and back views are shown [German, OP, R1+]. **$750.00–1,000.00.**

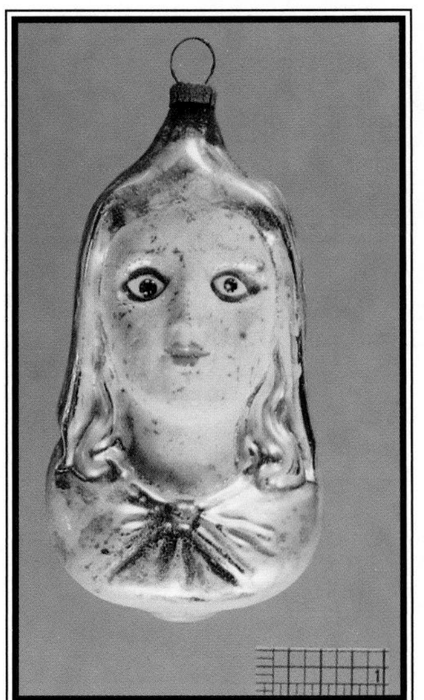

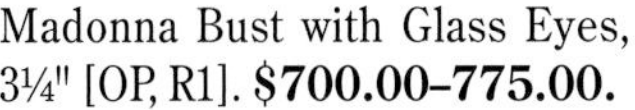

Madonna Bust with Glass Eyes, 3¼" [OP, R1]. **$700.00–775.00.**

A. Madonna and Child, Radko, 4¼" [Polish, NP (1991), R3]. **$40.00–65.00.** B. Angel Torso with Present, 4½" [OP-NP (1990s), R1]. Old, **$250.00–300.00.** 1990s version (shown), **$25.00–35.00.**

A. Comic Clown or Cat Head on a Ball, 4" [OP, R1]. **$175.00–200.00.** B. Cardinal Richelieu Face, 3½" [OP, R1]. **$300.00–350.00.**

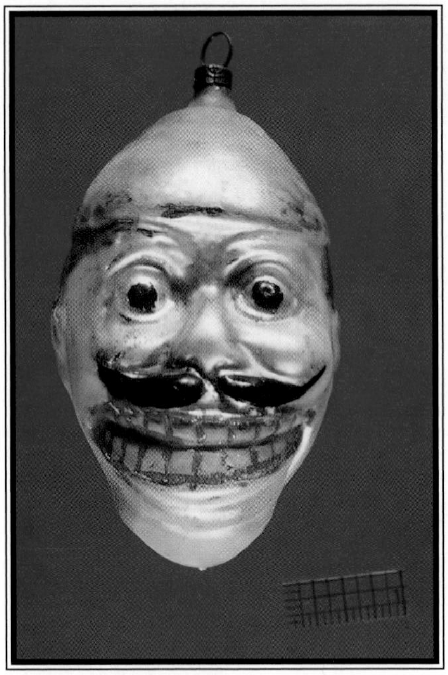

Jerry Colona Head, 3½" [OP, R1]. **$450.00–550.00.**

Uncle Sam Bust, 3½" [German, OP-NP (2000) R1+]. **$700.00–800.00.**

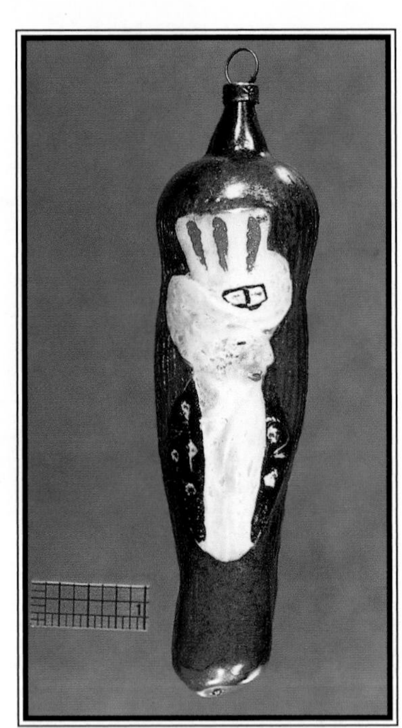

Uncle Sam on a Boot, approx. 4¼" (shown), 4½", 5", & 6½" [German, OP-NP (Radko, 1994), R1-2]. All sizes, **$450.00–550.00.**

A. Uncle Sam Boy, 3" (shown) & 3¾" [OP-NP (1990s), R2]. Small, **$200.00–250.00.** Large, **$250.00–300.00.** B. Angel on an SG Cloud (Type II), 1¾" body, 2¾" – 4" overall, also called Marie Antoinette, Martha Washington, or Madame Pompadour [OP, R1]. Size can vary with spun glass skirt. **$350.00–425.00.**

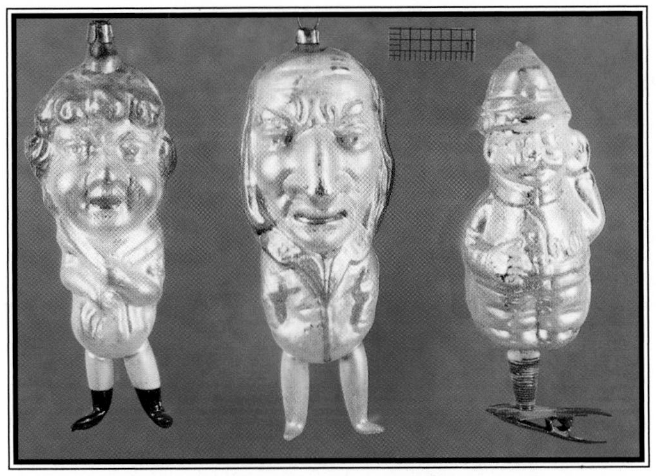

A. "ZaZu" Woman with Large Head and Annealed Legs, 3½" & 4¼" (shown) [OP, R1]. Small, **$900.00–1,100.00.** Large, **$1,200.00–1,500.00.** B. Disraeli with Annealed Legs, 4½" [OP, R1+]. **$1,200.00–1,500.00.** C. Policeman, "Stop Cop," 3½" [German, OP-NP (1980s), R1-2]. **$300.00–350.00.**

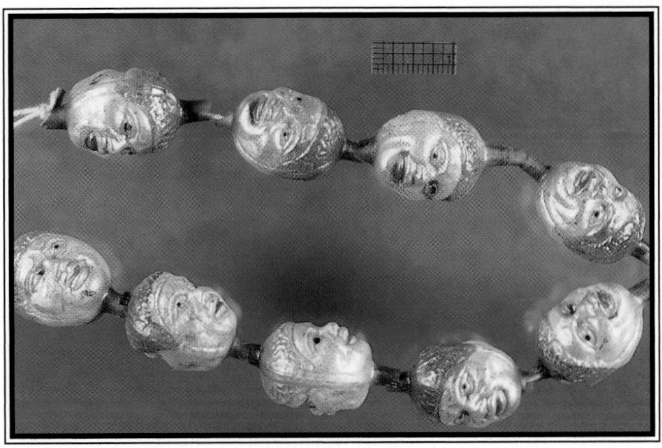

Double-faced Chain of Black Man's Heads, 18" overall, 1¾" each head [OP, R1]. Chain of 9, **$550.00–650.00.**

A. Prince Head on a Cone, 2" head, 6½" overall [OP, R1-2]. **$150.00–200.00.** B. Girl's Head on a Cylinder, 1½" head, 3¾" overall [OP, R1]. **$125.00–150.00.**

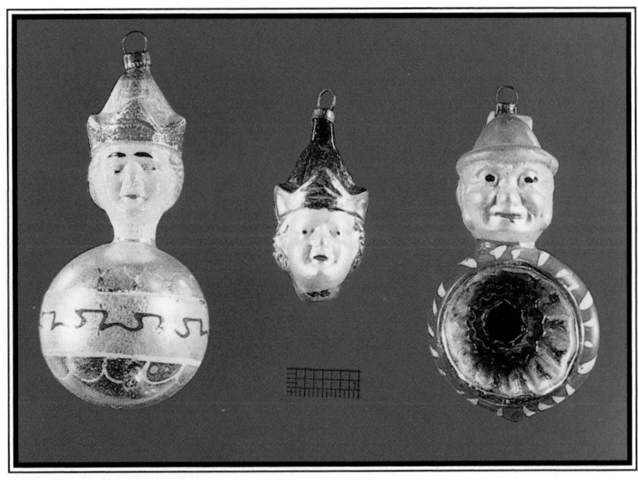

A. Prince Head on a Ball, approx. 4½", but sizes can vary with the free-blown ball [German, OP, R2]. **$150.00–175.00.** B. Boy's Head with a Crown, also known as The Prince, approx. 2¼" [German, OP, R2]. **$80.00–90.00.** C. Hans Clown Head on an Indent, also known as Foxy Grandpa, approx. 3¾" [German, OP, R2-3]. **$125.00–150.00.**

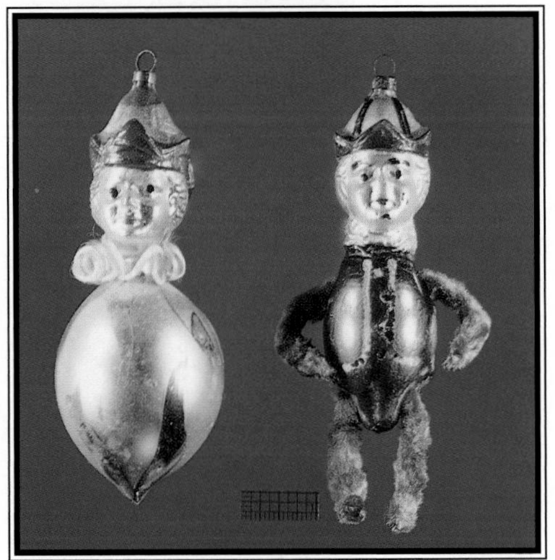

A. The Prince on a Stylized Body, approx. 5¼". Sizes can vary with the free-blown ball [German, OP, R1-2]. **$175.00–200.00.** B. The Prince with Chenille Arms and Legs, 4¼" glass body, approx. 5½" overall [German, OP-NP (Radko & Inge-glas, 1995), R1-2]. **$300.00–400.00.**

Two ornaments made by Radko: A. Boy's Head in a Trumpet, "Trumpet Player," double faced, 8¼" [NP (1990), R3]. **$40.00–50.00.** B. Man's Double-faced Head in a Pipe, 5¼" [NP (1991 & 1993), R3]. **$35.00–45.00.**

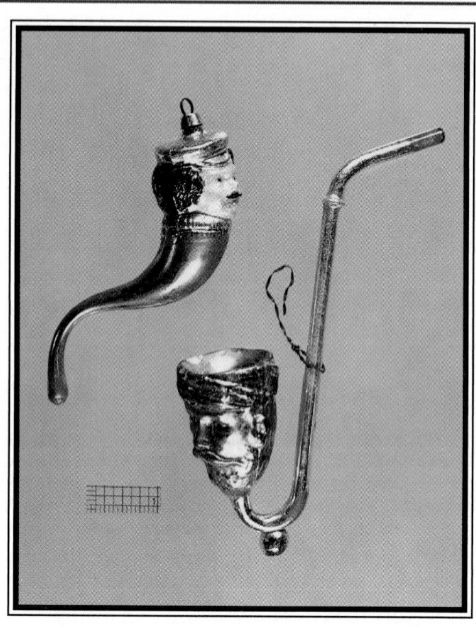

A. Sailor's Head Dublin Pipe, 1¼" head, 3½" & 4½" (shown) overall [OP, R1]. Small, **$175.00–200.00.** Medium, **$200.00–250.00.** Large, **$225.00–250.00.** B. Santa Head Pipe, 6" [German, OP, R1]. **$350.00–400.00.**

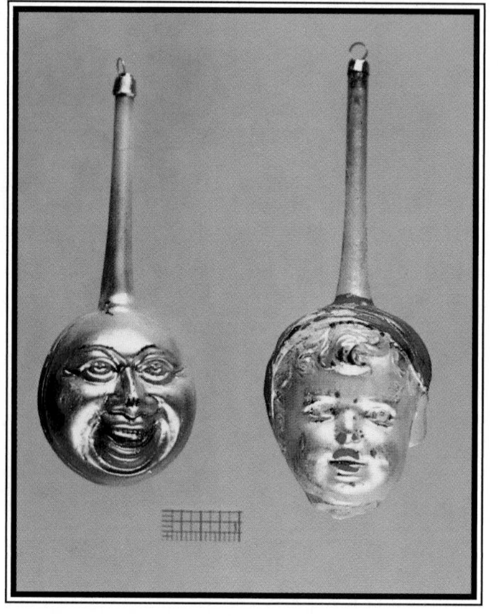

A. Double Sun Face Rattle, 2¼" face, 5" overall [OP, R1-2]. **$275.00–350.00.** B. Boy in a Nightcap Rattle, 2½" head, 5½" overall [Czech, OP, R1-2]. **$275.00–350.00.**

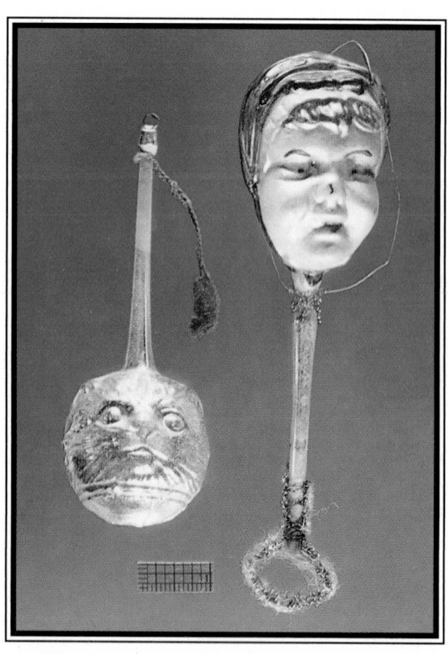

Left & Right: A. Cat Head Rattle, 1¾" cat head, approx. 5½" overall [German, OP, R1]. **$275.00–300.00.** B. Boy's Head or Baby's Head Rattle, 2½" head, approx. 6½" overall. The head is double sided, showing smiling and crying faces [OP, R1+]. **$400.00–450.00.**

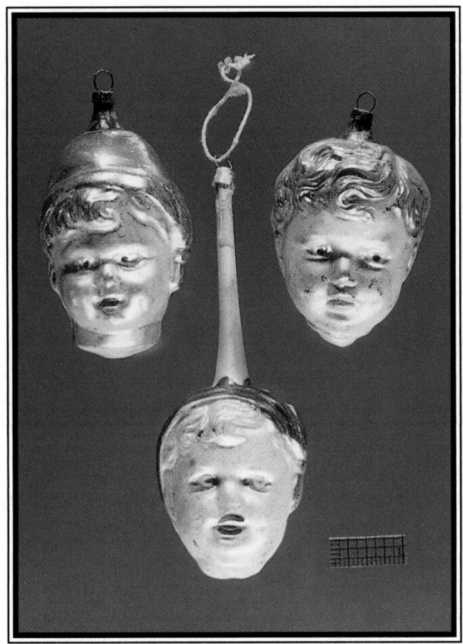

A. Boy with a Neck in a Nightcap, approx. 3" [OP-NP (1990s), R2]. **$125.00–150.00.** B. Boy in a Nightcap Baby Rattle, 2½" head, approx. 5½" overall [Czech, OP, R1-2]. **$275.00–350.00.** C. Boy's Head (Type II), approx. 2¾" [OP, R2-3]. **$100.00–125.00.**

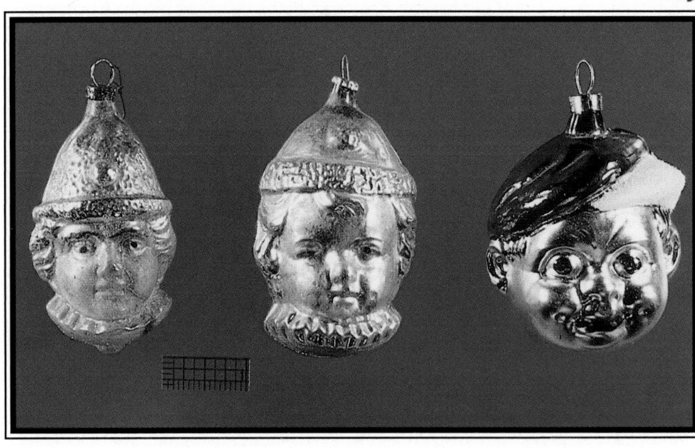

A. Boy Clown Head, approx 2½", 3", (shown) 3½", & 4". (medium) [German, OP-NP (1980s – 1990s, 3½"), R3-4]. Small, **$65.00–75.00.** Medium **$100.00–125.00.** Large, **$125.00–150.00.** B. Boy's Head in a Toboggan Hat, approx. 3" [OP, R3]. **$100.00–125.00.** C. Smitty Head, approx. 2½" [German, OP-NP (1980s), R1]. **$150.00–175.00.** 1980s version (shown), **$20.00–30.00.**

A. Round Man in the Moon, double faced, approx. 2¼" [German, OP, R1]. **$150.00–200.00.** B. Thor Face, approx. 3", spun glass beard is missing [German, OP, R1]. **$275.00–325.00.** C. Al Jolson Head in Blackface, approx. 2¾" [OP, R1]. **$200.00–250.00.** D. Small Chinese Man's Head, approx. 2½" [OP, R2]. **$75.00–100.00.** E. Double-faced Boy's Head, also called a Negro Head or Aunt Jemima's Head, approx. 2" [OP, R2-3]. **$75.00–100.00.**

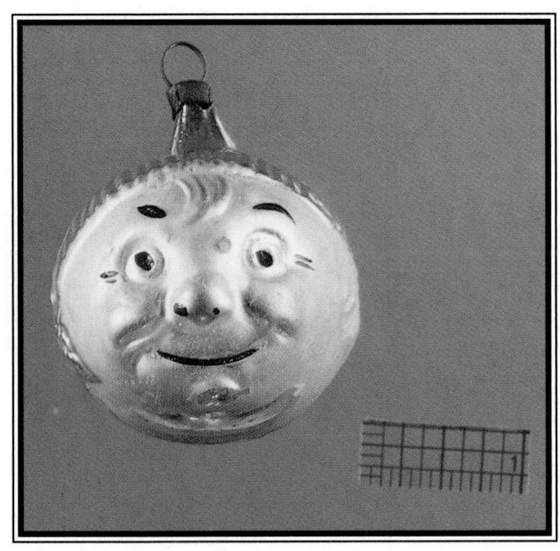

Comic Baby Boy's Head, approx. 1½" & 2" (shown) [OP-NP (1990), R2]. Small, **$75.00–100.00.** Large, **$125.00–150.00.**

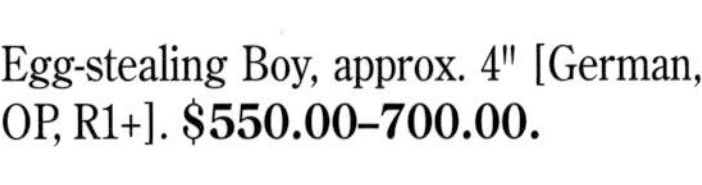

Egg-stealing Boy, approx. 4" [German, OP, R1+]. **$550.00–700.00.**

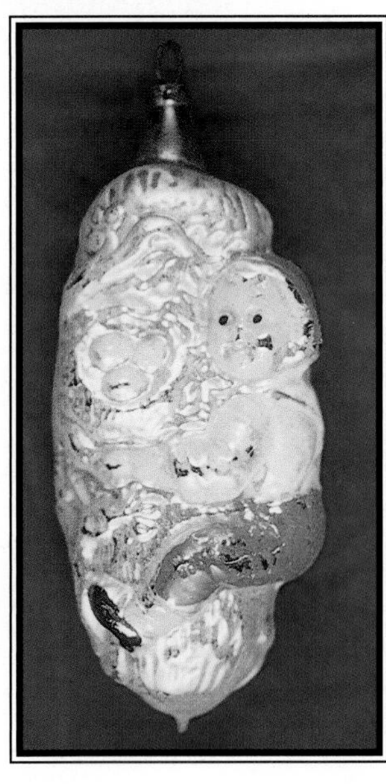

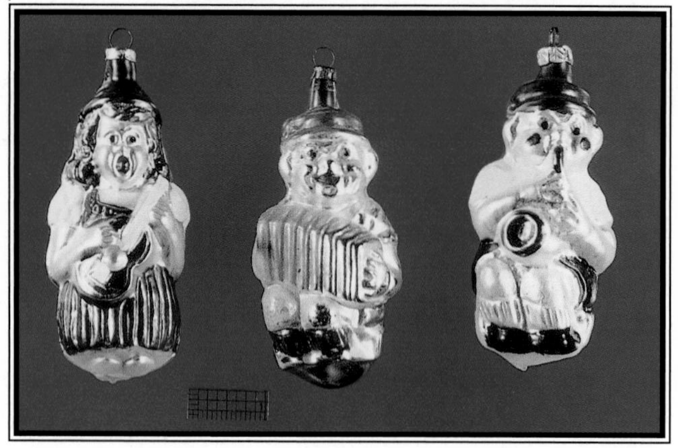

A. Woman Playing a Guitar, approx. 3¾" [German, OP-NP (early 1980s), R1]. **$250.00-300.00.** 1980s version (shown), **$20.00-25.00.** B. Man Playing an Accordion, approx. 3¼" [German, OP, R3]. **$50.00-75.00.** C. Man Playing a Saxophone, approx. 3¾" [German, OP-NP (1980s), R1-2]. **$150.00-175.00.** 1980s version (shown), **$15.00-20.00.**

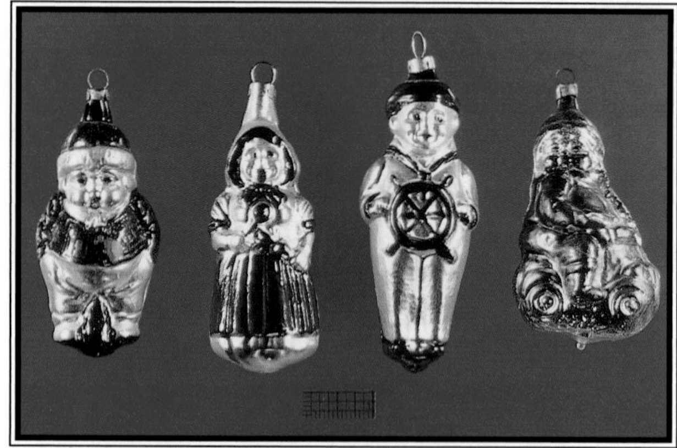

A. Chubby Boy in a Toboggan Hat, approx. 2¾", 3", 3¼" (shown), 3¾", & 4" [German, OP-NP (1950s & 1990s), R3-4]. Small (2¾" - 3¼"), **$75.00-100.00.** Large (3¾" - 4"), **$125.00-150.00.** B. Peasant Woman with a Spoon, approx. 3½" [Czech, OP-NP (1950s & 1980s), R2]. **$100.00-125.00.** 1980s version (shown), **$10.00-20.00.** C. Sailor with a Pilot's Wheel, approx. 4" [Czech, OP-NP (1980s), R1-2]. **$125.00-150.00.** 1970s version (shown), **$20.00-25.00.** D. Chubby Boy Riding a Toy Car, approx. 2¾" & 3¼" (shown) [German, OP-NP (1960s & 1990s, small), R1-2]. **$125.00-150.00.** 1960s version (shown), **$40.00-55.00.**

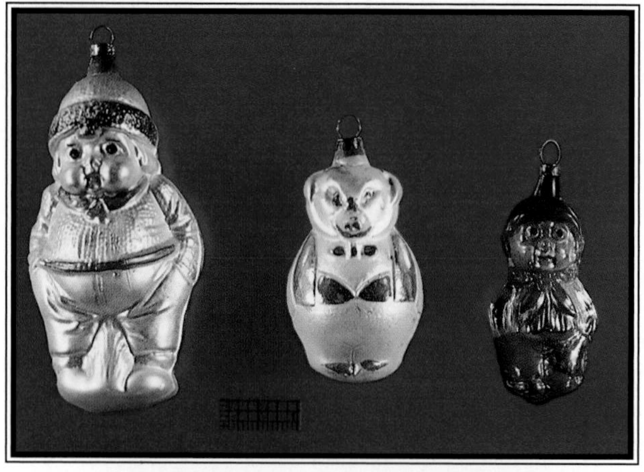

A. Chubby Boy in a Toboggan Cap, also called Whistling Boy, approx. 2¾", 3", 3¼", 3¾" (shown), & 4" [German, OP-NP (1950s & 1990s), R3-4]. Small (2¾" - 3¼"), **$75.00-100.00.** Large (3¾" - 4"), **$125.00-150.00.** B. Pig in a Tuxedo, approx. 2¼" & 2¾" (shown) [OP, R2]. **$100.00-135.00.** C. Kayo, approx. 2½", from the *Moon Mullins* comic strip [OP, R2]. **$70.00-90.00.**

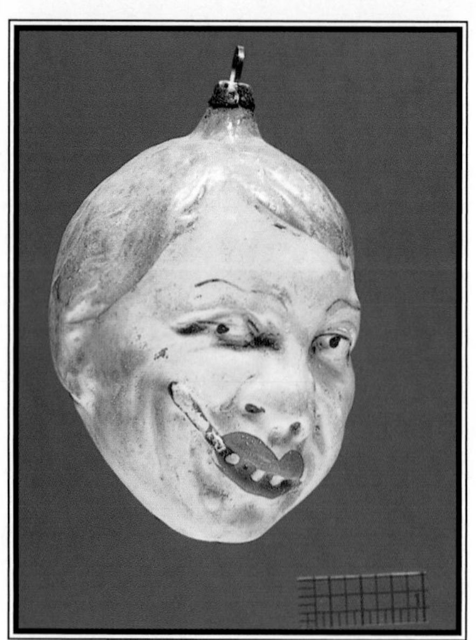

Man Smoking a Cigarette, 2¾" [OP, R1+]. **$800.00-950.00.**

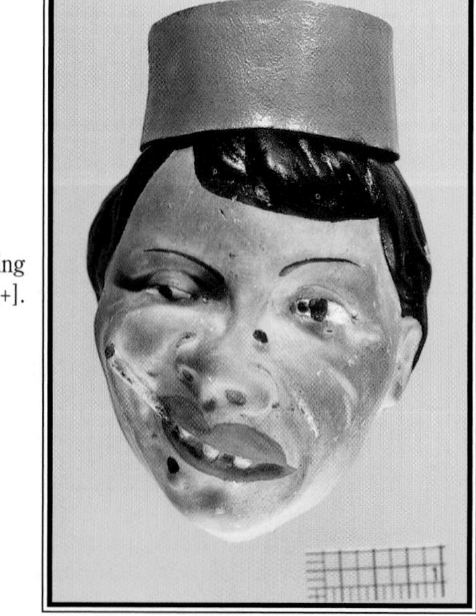

Black Man in a Fez Smoking a Cigarette, 2¾" [OP, R1+]. **$900.00-1,100.00.**

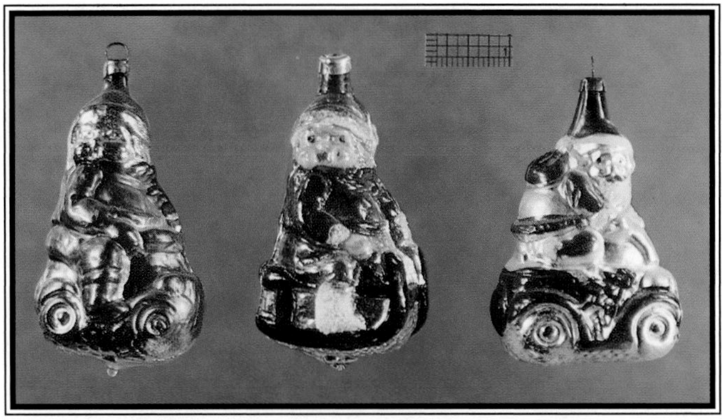

A. Chubby Boy Riding a Toy Car, 2¾" & 3¼" (shown) [OP-NP (1960 & 1990), R1-2]. Small, **$50.00–75.00.** Large, **$125.00–150.00.** B. Chubby Boy Riding a Sled, 3¼" [OP-NP (1950s), R1]. Old, **$125.00–150.00.** C. Santa in a Toy Car, 3" [OP-NP (1950s), R1]. 1950s, (shown), **$150.00–175.00.**

A. Boy Aviator with Chenille Legs, 3" body, 4½" overall [German, OP-NP (1990s), R1]. Old, **$300.00–375.00.** B. Man and Woman Kissing, 3¼" [OP, R1]. A windmill is on the back. **$150.00–175.00.**

A. Boy Feeding a Dog, embossed, 3" [OP-NP (Inge-glas, 1992), R1-2]. Old, **$125.00–150.00.** 1992 version (shown), **$10.00–15.00.** B. Boy Feeding a Chicken, embossed, 3" [OP, R2]. **$125.00–150.00.** C. Boy Scout, 3¼" [OP-NP (Inge-glas, 1993), R1]. Old, **$225.00–275.00.** 1993 version (shown), **$10.00–15.00.**

A. Chimney Sweep (Type II), 3" [OP, R2]. **$100.00–125.00.** B. Old Bald Man, "Mr. Jingles," 3¾" [NP (1950s – 1960s), R2]. **$35.00–50.00.** C. Chubby Girl Angel with a Star, 2¾" & 3½" (shown) [German, OP-NP (1950s, 1980s, & 1990s; small only), R2-3]. Small, **$75.00–90.00.** Large, **$90.00–110.00.**

Chimney Sweep on a Ball, 7½" [NP (1950s), R1-2]. **$175.00–200.00.**

A. Man with Mutton Chops, approx. 4", 4½" & 5" (shown) [OP, R2]. Small, **$150.00–175.00.** Medium, **$175.00–200.00.** Large, **$250.00–275.00.** B. Man with a Fiddle, 4" [OP, R1]. **$200.00–250.00.**

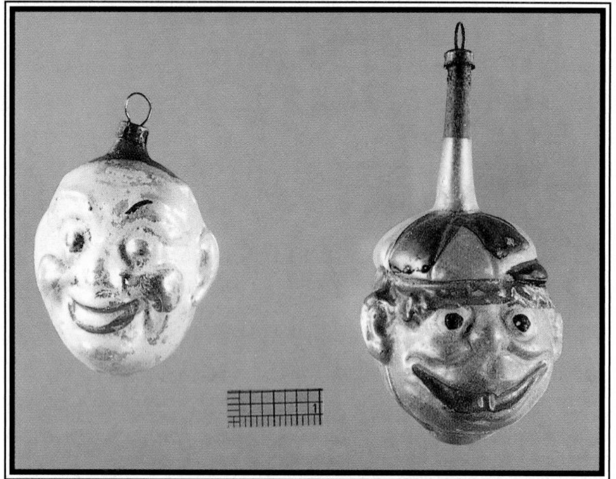

A. Man's Head with a Bone in the Nose, 2¼" [OP, R1]. **$150.00–175.00.** B. Monkey-faced Man's Head Rattle, 2½" head, 3¾" overall [OP, R1]. **$250.00–300.00.**

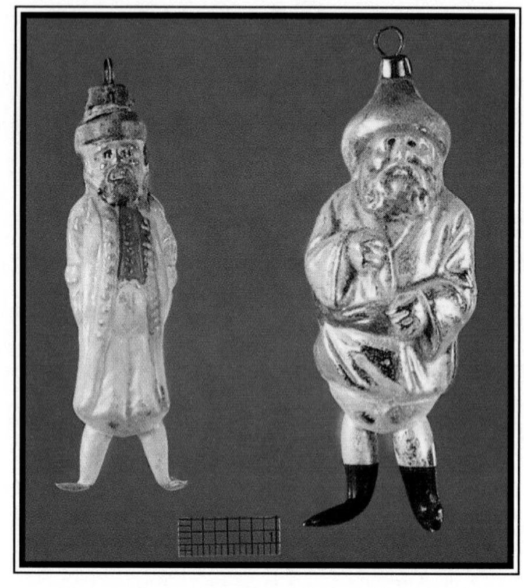

A. Man with Annealed Legs in a Long Coat, 3" body, 3¾" overall [OP, R1]. Without legs, **$250.00–300.00.** With legs, **$850.00–950.00.** B. Bearded Man with Annealed Legs, sometimes called Ali Baba, 3" body, 4½" overall [OP, R1]. **$800.00–900.00.**

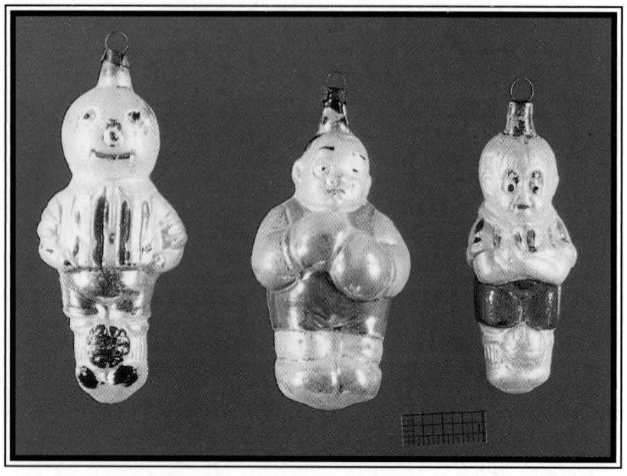

A. Soccer Ball Boy, approx. 3¾", head is a soccer ball [OP-NP (1990s), R2]. **$200.00–250.00.** B. The Boxer, approx. 2¾" & 3¼" (shown) [OP-NP (1950s & 1990s), R2]. **$200.00–250.00.** C. Soccer Boy, approx. 3" [OP, R2]. **$200.00–250.00.**

A. The Roly-Poly Boxer, approx. 4¼" [OP, R1]. **$225.00–275.00.** B. Clown, clip on, approx. 3" [OP, R1-2]. **$100.00–125.00.**

Man with Pipe and Keys, *Burgermiester*, 4¼" [OP, R1-2]. **$250.00–300.00.**

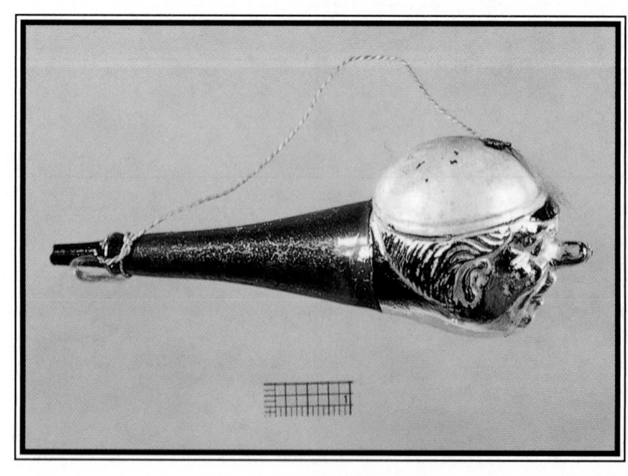

Jockey Head in a Horn, 6¼" [German, OP, R2]. **$300.00–375.00.**

Jockey Head on a Pipe, 6", 2" head [German, OP-NP (Radko, 1994), R2]. **$300.00–375.00.**

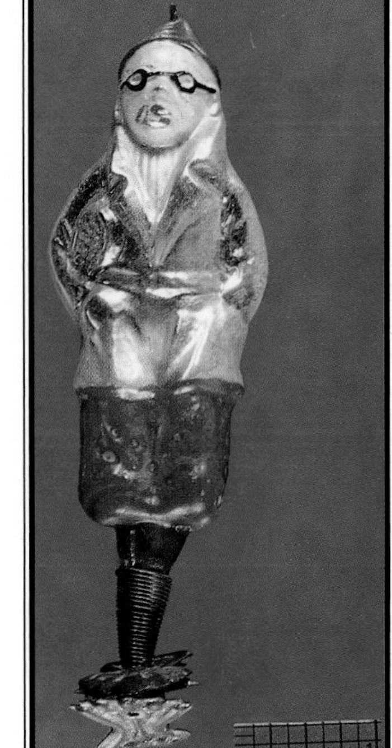

Tennis Player, 3¾" [OP, R1+]. **$500.00–650.00.**

Deep Sea Diver, 4½" [OP, R1]. **$350.00–400.00.**

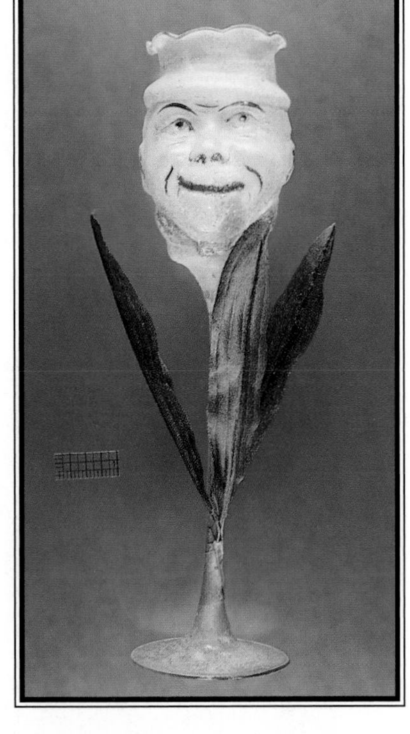

Man with a Bow Tie, goblet, also a candle shade, 8⅞" [OP, R2]. **$600.00–700.00.**

Uncle Mistletoe & Aunt Holly, approx. 4", 5" (shown), & 5¼". Made exclusively for Marshall Field Department Stores, 1930s – 1950s. A. Uncle Mistletoe, 5" [OP-NP (1950s & 1970s), R2-3]. **$50.00–75.00.** B. Aunt Holly, 5" [OP-NP (1950s), R2-3]. **$50.00–75.00.** Set shown is marked "Germany – US Zone." Set in box, **$150.00–175.00.**

A. Man and Woman Kissing over a Bush, 3½" [German, OP-NP (1991), R1]. **$300.00–350.00.** B. German Couple, 3" [OP, R1]. **$400.00–450.00.**

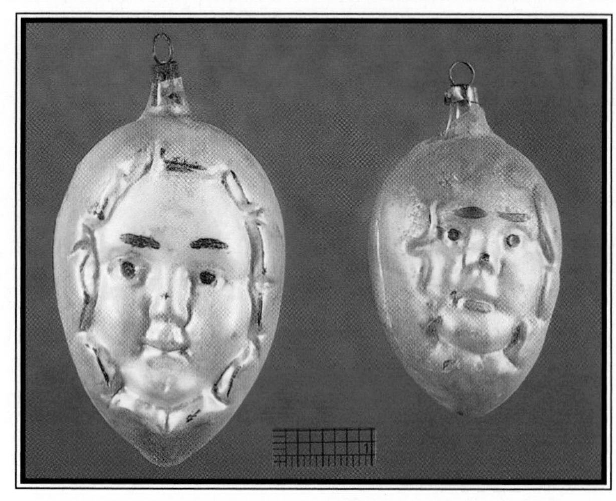

Girls' Faces in an Egg, double sided, 2 sizes [both OP, R1-2]: A. 3¼". **$225.00–250.00.** B. 2½". **$175.00–200.00.**

A. Girl with a Hat in a Tulip, 3¼" [German, OP, R2]. **$175.00–225.00.** B. Girl's Head on a Rose, 2½" [OP, R1-2]. **$175.00–225.00.** C. Girl in a Basket of Flowers, approx. 2¾" (shown) & 3" [OP-NP (1994), R2]. **$200.00–275.00.**

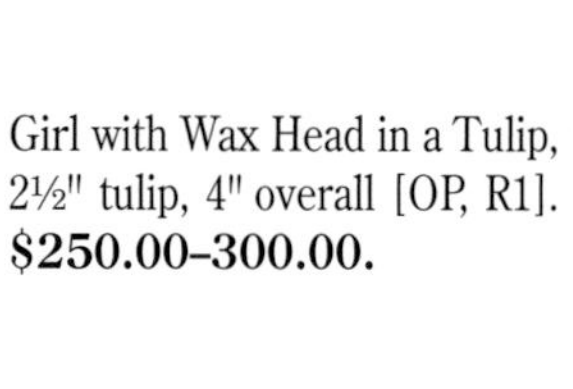

Girl with Wax Head in a Tulip, 2½" tulip, 4" overall [OP, R1]. **$250.00–300.00.**

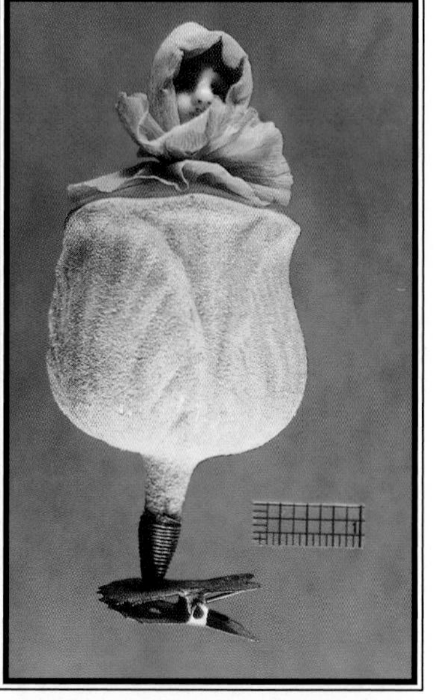

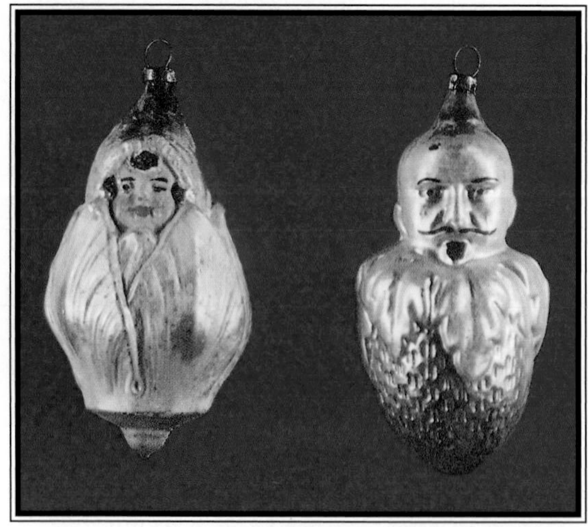

A. Girl with a Hat in a Tulip, approx. 3¼" [German, OP, R2]. **$175.00–225.00.** B. Pierre Strawberry, approx. 3½" [German, OP, R1+]. **$600.00–750.00.**

Radko Polish Versions of: A. Pierre Strawberry, 3¾" [NP (1991), R3]. **$35.00–45.00.** B. Girl's Head in Large-petaled Flower, 3½" [NP (1980s), R2-3]. **$35.00–45.00.**

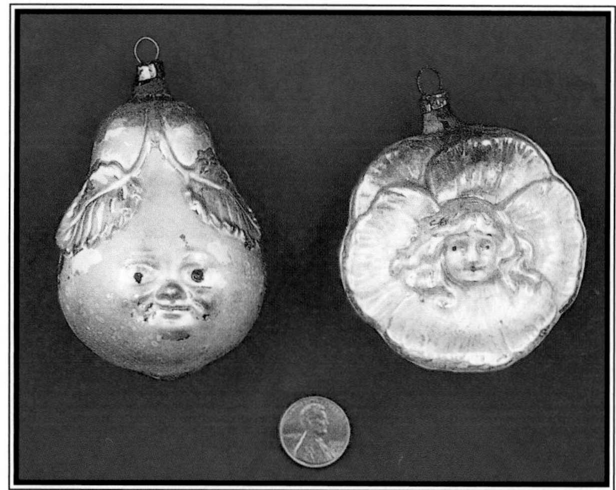

A. Pear Face with Leaves, approx. 2" & 2¾" (shown) [German, OP-NP (1950s, 1970s, & 1980s), R2-3]. Small, **$100.00–125.00.** Large, **$150.00–175.00.** B. Girl's Head in a Large-petaled Flower, approx. 2½" [German, OP, R2]. **$200.00–250.00.**

A. Pear with a Clown Face, approx. 2½" [OP, R1]. **$200.00–250.00.** B. Standard Mold-blown Pear, approx. 1½" – 5" (2½" shown) [OP-NP (continuing), R4-5]. Small (shown), **$15.00–25.00.** Medium, **$25.00–40.00.** Large, **$50.00–75.00.**

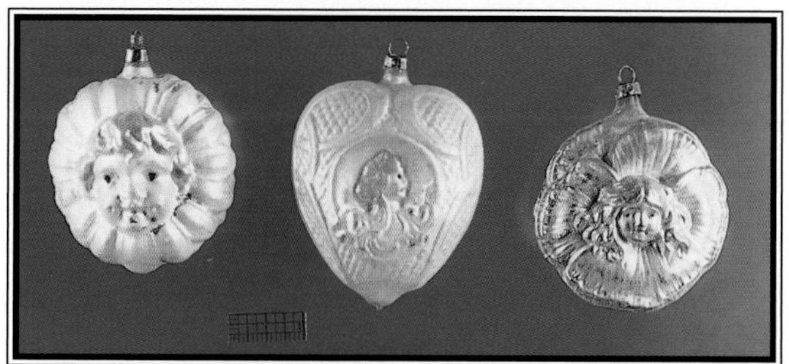

A. Girl's Head in a Daisy, 2½" [German, OP-NP (1990), R1]. **$175.00–200.00.** B. Bust of a Victorian Lady in a Heart; another head is on the other side, 3" [OP, R2] **$90.00–110.00.** C. Girl's Head in a Large-petaled Flower, 2½" [German, OP-NP (Radko), R2-3] **$200.00–250.00.**

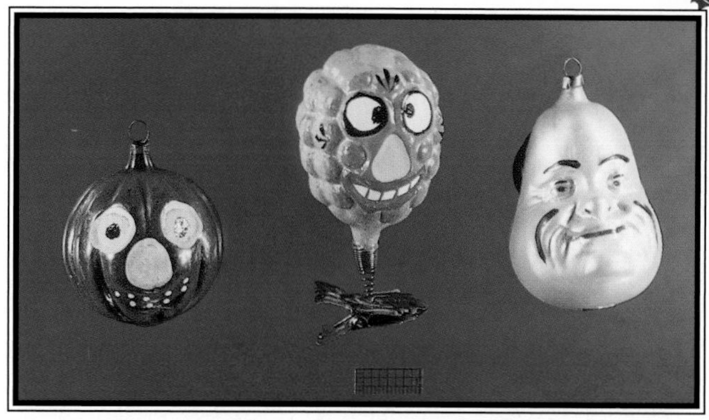

A. Jack-o'-Lantern, approx. 2¼", 2½" (shown), 3", & 4½" [OP-NP (1980s – 1990s, large), R2]. Small (shown), **$125.00–150.00.** Medium, **$150.00–175.00.** 1980s version (large), **$25.00–35.00.** B. Popcorn Head, approx. 2½" [German, OP, R2]. **$300.00–375.00.** C. Pear Man, approx. 3" [German, OP, R1-2]. **$200.00–250.00.**

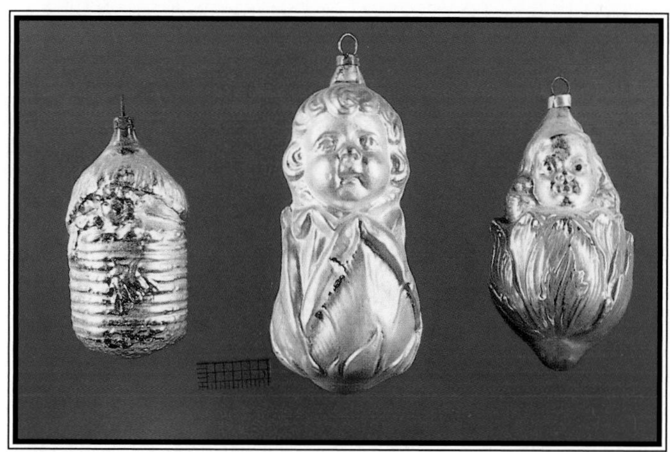

A. Girl in a Beehive, approx. 2¼", 2¾", & 3" (shown) [German, OP-NP (1994), R2]. Small, **$70.00–80.00.** Medium, **$90.00–110.00.** Large, **$125.00–175.00.** B. Angel in a Tulip, approx. 4" [German, OP, R1+]. **$350.00–400.00.** C. Girl in a Tulip, approx. 3½" [German, OP, R2]. **$175.00–225.00.**

A. Girl's Head in a Water Lily, 2¾" [German, OP-NP (1990), R1]. **$125.00–150.00.** B. Girl's Bust in a Sunflower, 3¼" [German, OP-NP, R1]. Old, **$150.00–175.00.** East German 1988 or 1989 version (shown), **$20.00–30.00.** C. Girl's Head in Grapes, 3" [German, OP-NP (1994), R1]. Old, **$300.00–375.00.** 1994 version (shown), **$10.00–15.00.**

A. Sour Grapes, large, 4" (shown) [OP, R1-2]. **$275.00–325.00.** B. Grapes with Girl's Face, 3" [OP, R2-3]. **$175.00–225.00.** C. Grapes with a Bacchus Face, 2½" [German, OP-NP (1997), R2]. **$175.00–200.00.**

A. Pumpkin Man with Legs (Type II), 3½" body, 5½" overall [OP, R1]. **$600.00–700.00.** B. Pumpkin Man with Legs (Type I), 3¼" body, 4¾" overall [OP, R1]. **$600.00–750.00.** C. Variation of Type II, with holes for chenille arms [OP, R1]. **$600.00–700.00.**

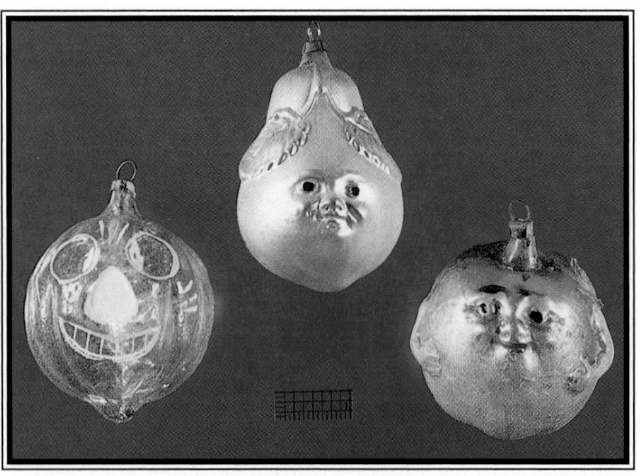

A. Jack-o'-Lantern, approx. 2¼", 2½" (shown), 3½", & 4½" [OP-NP (1993), R2]. Medium, **$150.00–175.00.** B. Pear Face, approx. 2" & 2¾" (shown) [German, OP-NP (1980 – 1990), R2-3]. Small, **$100.00–125.00.** Large, **$150.00–175.00.** C. Apple with Face and Arms, approx. 2¼" (shown) & 2¾" [German, OP-NP (1980s), R1-2]. Small, **$125.00–150.00.** Large, **$175.00–200.00.**

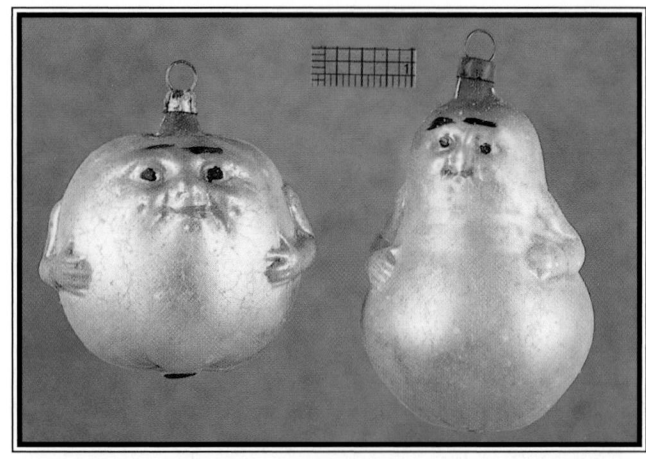

A. Apple Face with Arms, 2¼" (shown) & 2¾" [German, OP-NP (1980s), R1-2]. Small, **$125.00–150.00.** Large, **$175.00–200.00.** B. Pear with a Face and Arms, 3¼" [German, OP-NP (1980s), R1-2]. **$200.00–250.00.**

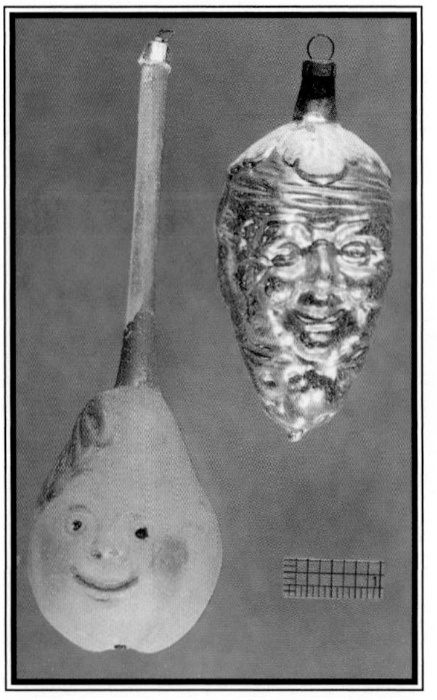

A. Pear Face Rattle, 6" [OP, R1]. **$300.00–350.00.** B. Parsnip Face, 3" (shown) & 4" [German, OP-NP (1998), R1-2]. Small, **$200.00–250.00.** Large, **$350.00–400.00.**

A. Apple with Face, 3" [OP, R1]. **$250.00–300.00.** B. Pine Cone Man, 3" & 3½" (shown) [German, OP, R1]. Small, **$175.00–200.00.** Large, **$225.00–275.00.**

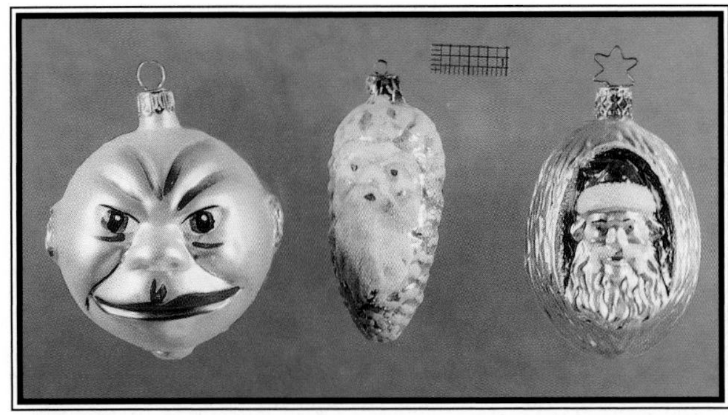

A. Onion Head, 3" (shown) & 3¾" [OP-NP (1994), R1]. Old, **$250.00–300.00.** 1994 version (shown), **$20.00–30.00.** B. Face in Pine Cone (Type II), 3" [OP, R2-3]. **$75.00–100.00.** C. Gnome Head in a Walnut, 3" [German, OP-NP (Inge-glas, 1993), R1]. **$175.00–200.00.** 1993 version (shown), **$15.00–25.00.**

A & B. Face in a Curved Pine Cone (Type I), approx. 2¾" (shown), 3½" (shown), & 4½". Also called Jack Frost [German, OP-NP (1950s & 1990s), R3]. Small, **$80.00–100.00.** Medium, **$125.00–150.00.** Large, **$175.00–225.00.** B. Jack Frost Head, approx. 2½" (shown) & 3½" [German, OP-NP (1980s – 1990s), R3]. Small, **$40.00–60.00.** Large, **$100.00–125.00.**

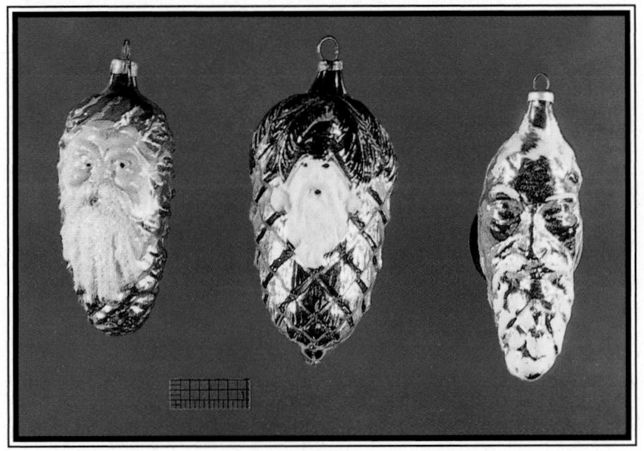

A. Face in a Pine Cone, Type I, approx. 3" (shown), & 3½" [German, OP-NP (1980s), R3]. **$80.00–90.00.** B. Small Santa Head on a Pine Cone, 3½" [OP, R2] **$125.00–150.00.** C. Face in a Curved Pine Cone (Type II), 3¼" [OP-NP (1960s), R1]. Old, **$90.00–110.00.**

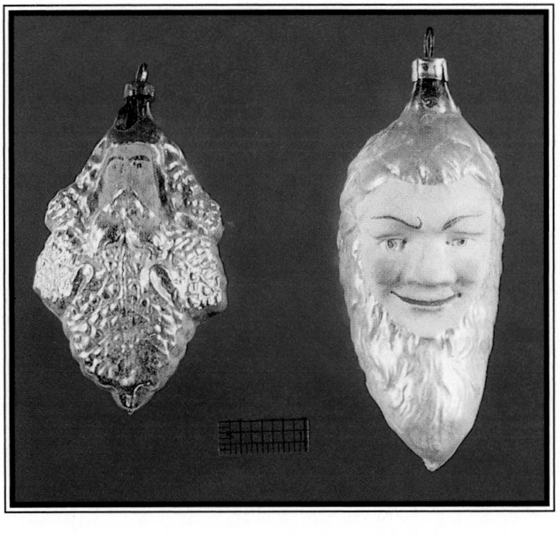

A. Grape Leaves with Old Man's Face, 3½" [OP-NP (Radko, 1995, newly molded 5" size), R1]. Old, **$275.00–325.00.** B. Face in a Curved Pine Cone (Type I), large, 4½" [OP, R2-3]. **$175.00–225.00.**

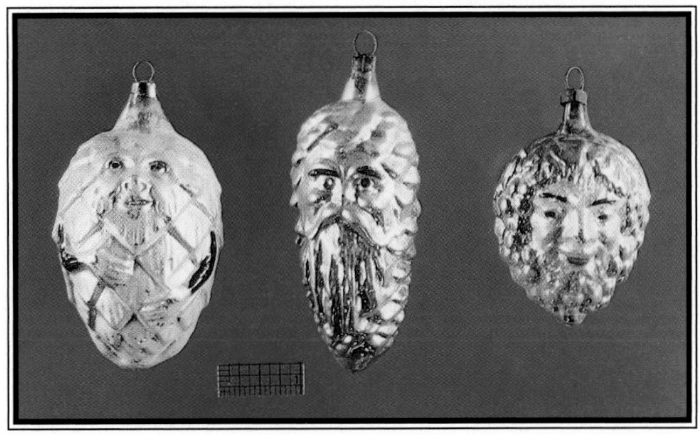

A. Pine Cone Man, approx. 3" (shown) & 3½" [German, OP, R1]. Small, **$175.00–200.00.** Large, **$225.00–275.00.** B. Face in a Pine Cone (Type I), approx 3" & 3½" (shown) [German, OP-NP (1980s), R3]. Small, **$80.00–100.00.** Large, **$125.00–150.00.** C. Bacchus Face in a Bunch of Grapes, approx. 2½" [German, OP-NP (1997), R2]. **$175.00–200.00.**

Parsnip Face, approx. 3" – 4" (shown) [German, OP-NP (1998), R1-2]. Small, **$200.00–250.00.** Large, **$350.00–400.00.**

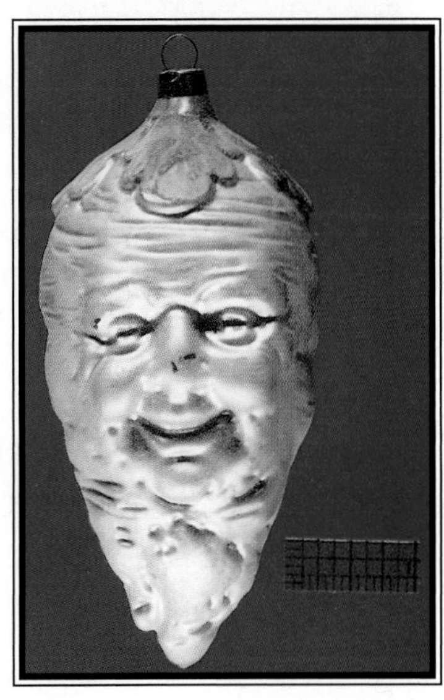

Popcorn Heads [both OP, R2]: A. Large, 3¼". **$375.00–425.00.** B. Medium, 3". **$325.00–375.00.**

A. Daisy Man with a Top Hat, approx. 2" [OP, R1]. **$75.00–100.00.** B. Santa Face in a Pine Tree, approx. 3" (shown) & 3¾" [OP-NP (1980 – 1990), R2]. Small, **$75.00–100.00.** Large, **$100.00–125.00.** C. Horse Head in a Horseshoe (Type I), approx. 2½" [OP, R1-2]. **$175.00–200.00.**

A. Onion Head, large, approx. 3" & 3¾" (shown) [OP-NP (1994, 3"), R1]. **$250.00–300.00.** B. Priest's Head, large, approx. 3", 3½", & 4¼" (shown) [German, OP, R1]. Small, **$225.00–250.00.** Medium, **$275.00–325.00.** Large, **$375.00–400.00.** C. Ringmaster's Head, also called Charlie McCarthy, large, approx. 3¾", the eyes are original [OP, R1-2]. **$275.00–325.00.**

Four Variations of the Standard Form Snowman, approx. 2¾", 3", 3½", & 4" [OP-NP (1950s & 1970s), R4]. Small, **$20.00–30.00.** Medium, **$35.00–45.00.** Large, **$50.00–75.00.**

A. Snowman with a Broom in a Ball, approx. 4" overall [German, OP, R1-2]. **$125.00–150.00.** B. Walking Snowman, approx. 4½" [NP (1950s only), R3]. **$50.00–75.00.** C. American Snowman, approx. 3½" [American, OP, R1-2]. **$50.00–75.00.**

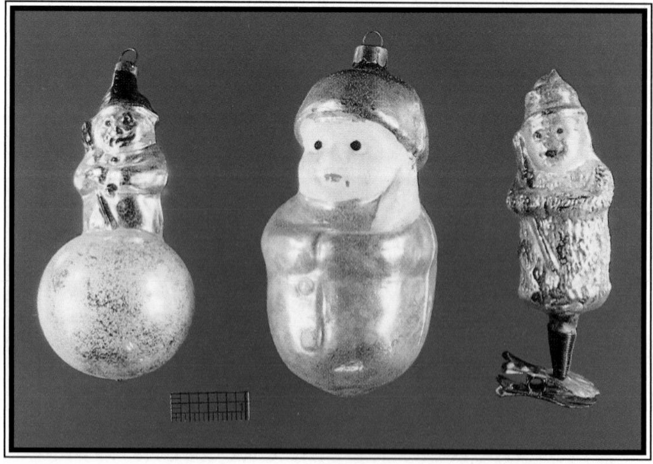

A. Snowman on a Ball, approx. 3¾" (shown) & 5¾" [German, OP, R2]. Small, **$125.00–150.00.** Large, **$175.00–200.00.** B. Snow Boy, approx. 4" [OP, R1-2]. **$275.00–300.00.** C. Dimpled Snowman on a Clip, approx. 3" (glass only) [OP, R3]. **$90.00–110.00.**

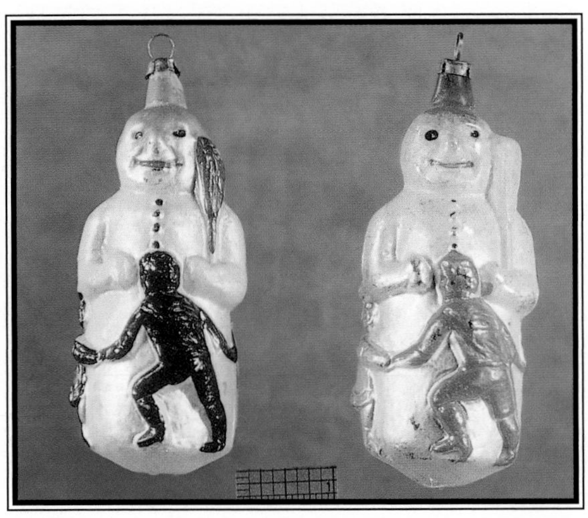

Snowmen with Dancing Children, 3¾" [OP, R1]. **$900.00-1,1000.00.** Snowman with Black Children is more rare.

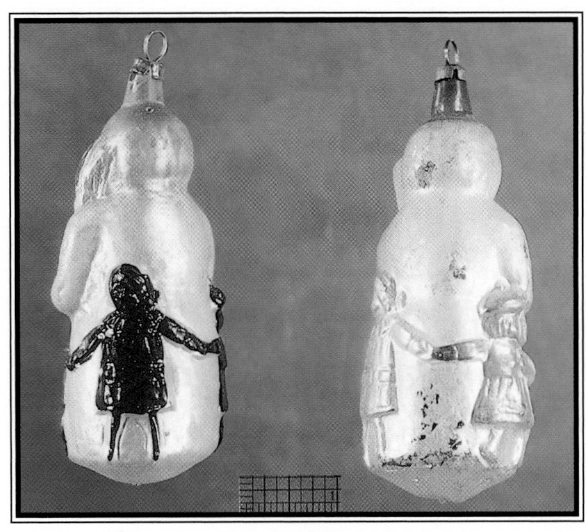

Snowmen with Dancing Children, reverse.

Snowman in a Ball, 3" snowman, approx. 5" overall [OP, R2]. **$180.00-200.00.**

A. Radish Head, approx. 3" (shown) - 4"; sizes may vary because they are free blown [OP, R2-3]. Small, **$100.00-125.00.** B. Snowman on a Ball, 5¾" [OP, R2]. Large, **$175.00-200.00.**

A. Girl's Head (Type I), approx. 2" (shown) & 2½" [German, OP, R2-3]. Small, **$90.00-100.00.** Large, **$100.00-125.00.** B. Snowman with a Walking Stick, 3" [German, OP-NP (Inge-glas, 1991), R2]. Old, **$80.00-100.00.**

A. Girl in a Fur Coat, approx. 3½" (shown) & 3¾" [OP, R2]. Small, **$175.00-200.00.** Large, **$200.00-225.00.** B. Snowman with a Top Hat, 3¼" [OP, R2]. Clip-on, **$125.00-150.00.** C. Girl Clown, "My Darling," approx. 3¾" (shown) & 4¼" [German, OP-NP (Radko, 1994), R2-3]. Small, **$100.00-125.00.** Large, **$150.00-200.00.**

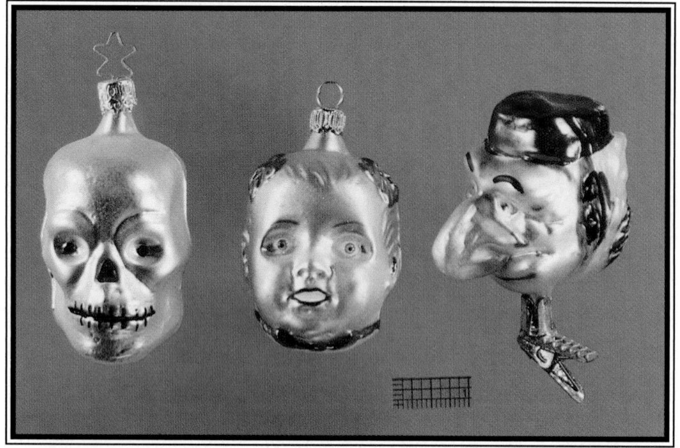

A. Skull, 2¾" [German, OP-NP (Inge-glas, 1980s), R1+]. Old, **$400.00-500.00.** 1980s version (shown), **$20.00-30.00.** B. Baby Girl's Head (Type I), 2½" [OP-NP (1994), R2-3]. Radko version, **$35.00-45.00.** C. Man's Head, "Mr. Big Nose," 2½" [German, OP-NP (1980s), R1]. Old, **$400.00-450.00.** 1980s version (shown), **$25.00-35.00.**

A. Girl's Head in a Toboggan Cap, 2½" [OP,R2-3]. **$125.00-150.00.** B. Baby Girl's Head (Type II), 2¾" [German, OP, R2-3]. **$100.00-150.00.**

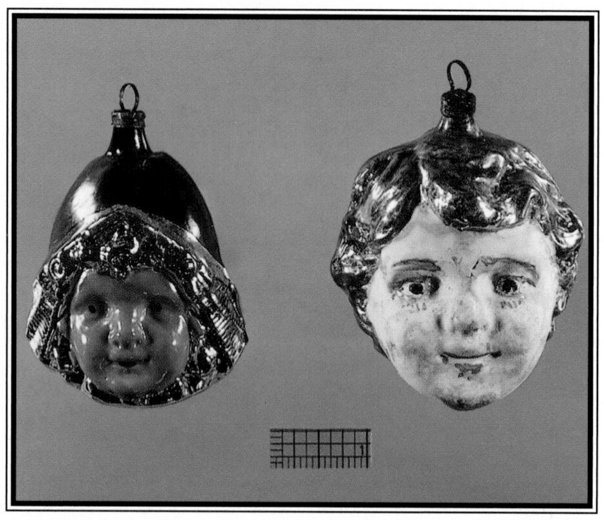

A. Dutch Girl's Head, approx. 2", 2½" (shown), 3", & 3½" [Czech, OP-NP (1950s & 1980s, small & medium), R2-3]. Small, **$90.00-110.00.** Medium, **$125.00-175.00.** Large, **$200.00-250.00.** 1950s (shown), **$40.00-55.00.** B. Boy's Head (Type I), approx. 2½" [OP, R2]. **$125.00-150.00.**

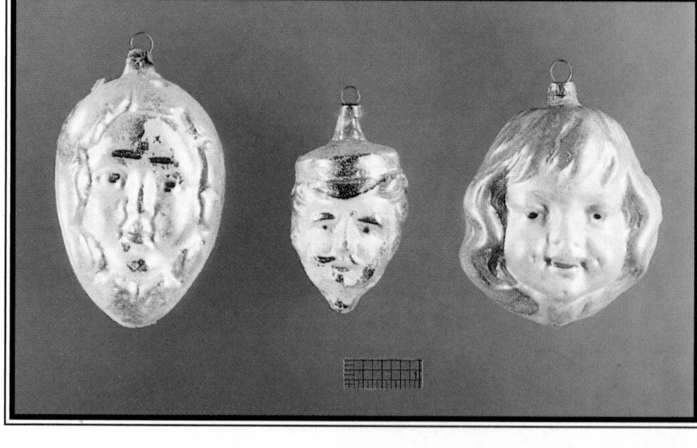

A. Girls' Faces in an Egg (double sided), approx. 2½" & 3¼" (shown) [OP, R1-2]. Small, **$175.00-200.00.** Large, **$225.00-250.00.** B. "The Conductor" Head, approx. 2¼" [OP, R1-2]. **$175.00-200.00.** C. Girl's Head (Type II), approx. 2¾" [OP, R1-2]. **$125.00-175.00.**

A. Mrs. Santa Claus, approx. 4¼" [German, OP-NP (1990s), R2]. **$250.00-275.00.** B. Girl's Torso and a Present, approx. 4½" [OP-NP (1990s), R1]. **$300.00-375.00.** C. Peasant Lady, approx. 3¾" & 4¼" (shown) [German, OP, R2]. Small, **$200.00-225.00.** Large, **$225.00-250.00.**

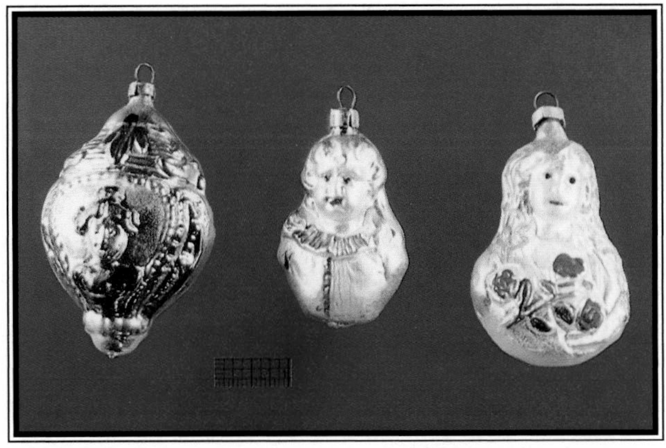

A. Victorian Lady on an Urn, approx. 3¼" [German, OP-NP (1960s & 1970s), R2-3]. **$50.00–75.00.** B. Bust of a Victorian Girl, approx. 2¾" [German, OP-NP (1970s), R1]. **$150.00–175.00.** C. Bust of a Lady with Flowers, approx. 3¼" [German, OP-NP (1970s), R1]. **$150.00–175.00.**

A. Snow Girl with a Rose, approx. 3" [OP, R1]. **$150.00–175.00.** B. Girl's Head on a Heart, approx. 3½" [OP, R2]. **$100.00–125.00.** C. Angelic Girl, approx. 3½" [OP, R2]. **$200.00–250.00.**

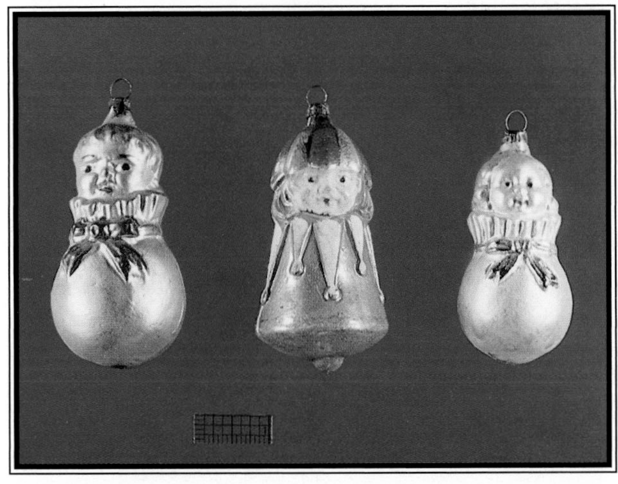

A. Boy in a Bag, approx. 3" (shown) & 3½" [German, OP, R3]. Small, **$75.00–100.00.** Large, **$100.00–125.00.** B. Girl Jester (Type I), approx. 3¼" [German, OP-NP, R3]. Medium, **$100.00–125.00.** C. Girl in a Bag, approx. 2¾" (shown) & 3¼" [German, OP, R3]. Small, **$75.00–100.00.** Large, **$100.00–125.00.**

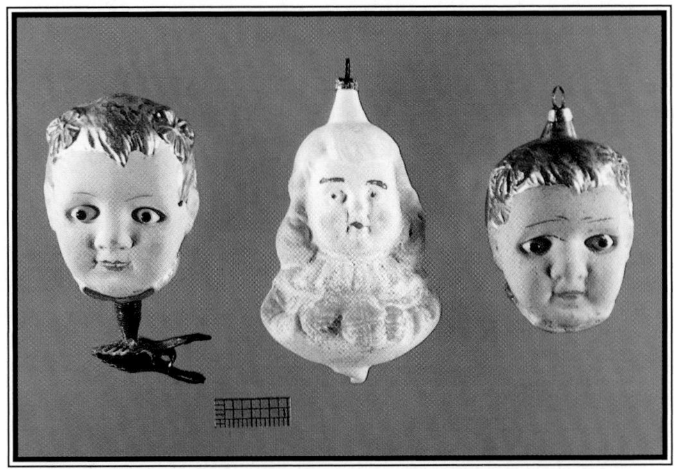

A & C. Baby Girl's Heads (Type I), clip on and hanging, 2½" [German, OP-NP (1994), R2-3]. Old, **$90.00–110.00.** Clip-on, **$150.00–175.00.** B. Bust of Girl Holding a Ball, 3¼" [OP, R1-2]. **$200.00–250.00.**

Woman with Apron and Extended Legs, 3" body, 3½" overall [OP, R1]. **$700.00–800.00.**

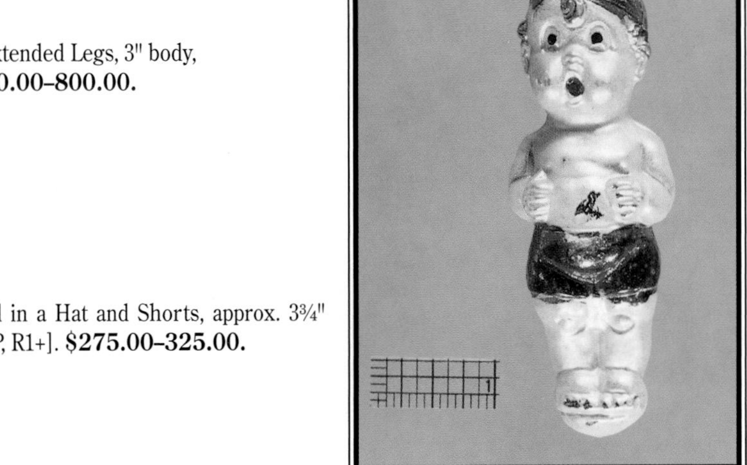

Girl in a Hat and Shorts, approx. 3¾" [OP, R1+]. **$275.00–325.00.**

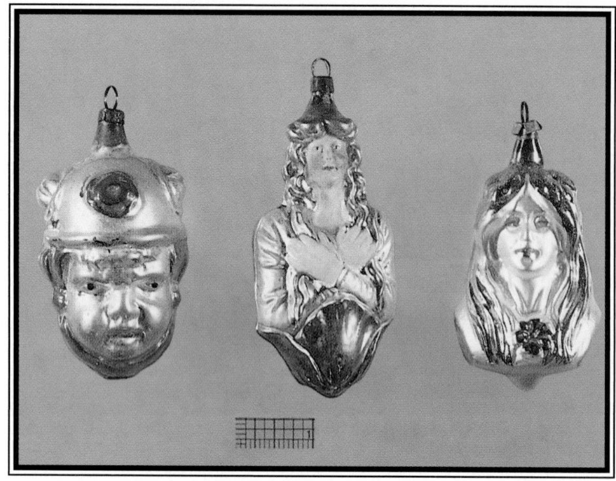

A. Girl's Head in a Bonnet, double faced, 2¾" [OP, R1-2]. **$200.00–225.00.** B. Woman with Crossed Arms in a Flower, 3½" [OP, R1-2]. **$300.00–350.00.** C. Art Nouveau Bust of Lady, 3" [OP, R1]. **$225.00–250.00.**

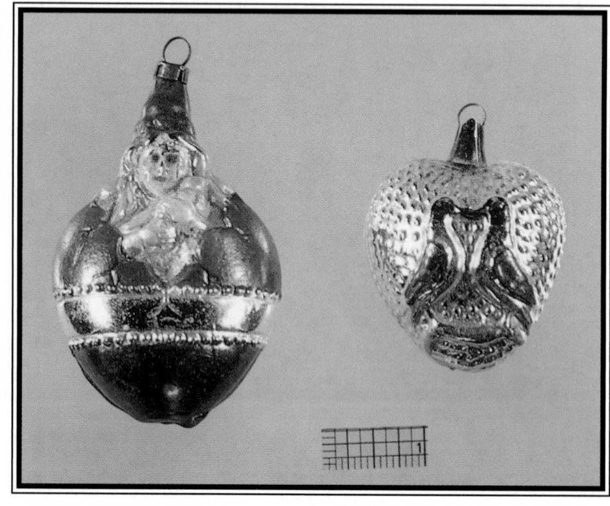

A. Girl in a Broken Heart, 3" [German, OP-NP (1990s), R1-2]. Old, **$200.00–250.00.** B. Love Birds on a Heart, 2" [OP, R2]. **$20.00–25.00.**

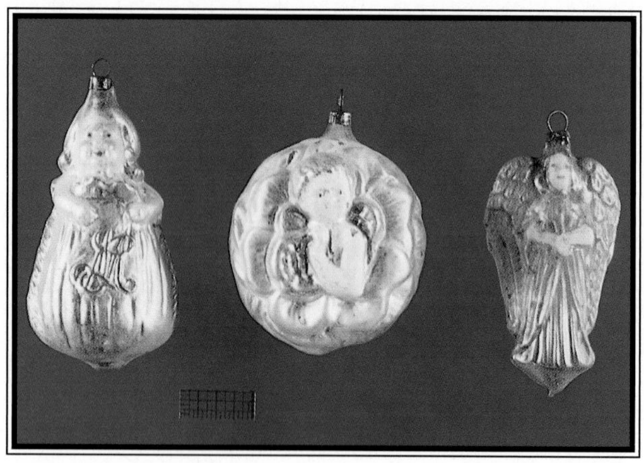

A. Girl in a Sack Monagrammed "LM," 3¾" [German, OP, R2]. **$125.00–150.00.** B. Bust of a Girl in a Rose, approx. 3" (shown) & 3½". May be found as double or single-sided pieces [OP-NP (1980s, large), R2]. Small, **$80.00–90.00.** Double, **$100.00–110.00.** Large, **$160.00–185.00.** Double, **$150.00–175.00.** C. Angel Standing with Flowers, 3½" [OP, R2]. **$125.00–150.00.**

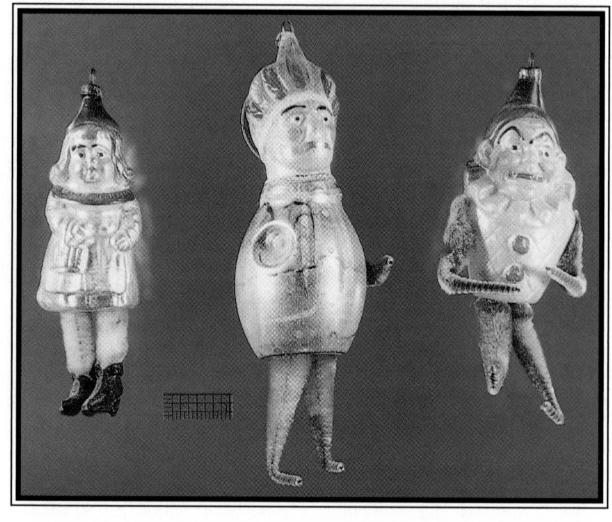

A. Girl with Chenille Legs and a Basket, 3" glass, 4½" overall [German, OP-NP (Inge-glas, 1990s), R1]. Without legs, **$125.00–150.00.** Old with legs, **$300.00–350.00.** B. Grim-faced Indian with Chenille Arm and Legs, 6" [German, OP, R1]. **$500.00–650.00.** C. Joey Clown in a Waffle Coat, 3" glass, 5" overall [OP, R2]. **$250.00–325.00.**

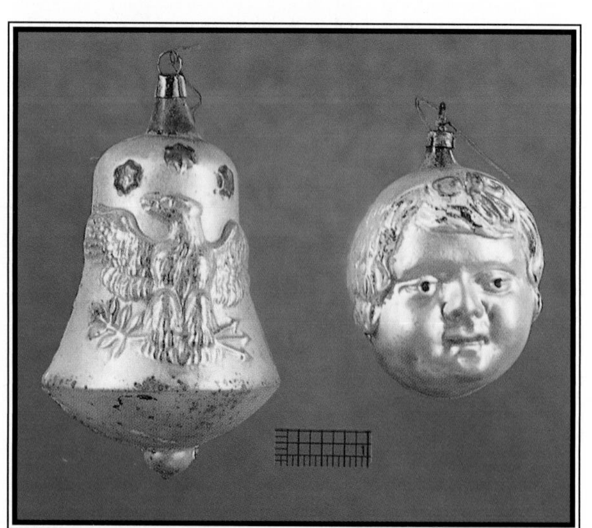

A. Bell with Embossed Eagle and Flags, approx. 3½" (shown) & 4" [German, OP, R1]. Small, **$175.00–200.00.** Large, **$250.00–300.00.** B. Baby Girl's Head, double faced, 2¼" [OP, R1]. **$300.00–375.00.**

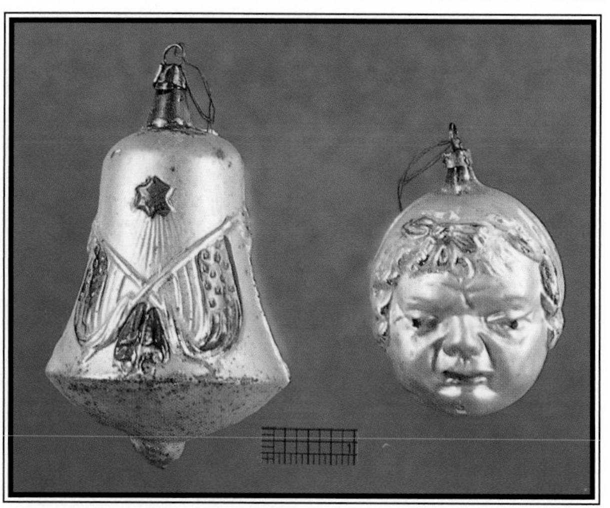

Reverse of preceding photo.

A. Peasant Woman with a Spoon, 3½" [Czech, OP-NP (1950s & 1980s), R2]. Old, **$125.00–150.00.** B. Roly-Poly Policeman, 3¼" [OP-NP (1980s), R2]. Old, **$175.00–225.00.** C. Snow Baby, 2½" [German, OP, R1-2]. **$100.00–125.00.**

A. Boy with a Crown, double faced, 2¾" [OP, R1-2]. **$200.00–225.00.** B. Bust of Girl with Glass Eyes, 3½" [OP, R2]. **$325.00–375.00.** C. Girl's Head in Tam Hat, 2¼" [OP, R2]. **$125.00–150.00.**

A. Kate Greenaway Girl, approx. 3" & 4" (shown) [German, OP, R2]. Small, **$100.00–125.00.** Large, **$200.00–250.00.** B. Long-haired Boy, approx. 2¾" [OP, R2]. **$90.00–110.00.** C. Angel with Lithographed Paper Face, approx. 3" & 3½" (shown) [OP, R2]. Small, **$150.00–175.00.** Large, **$225.00–275.00.**

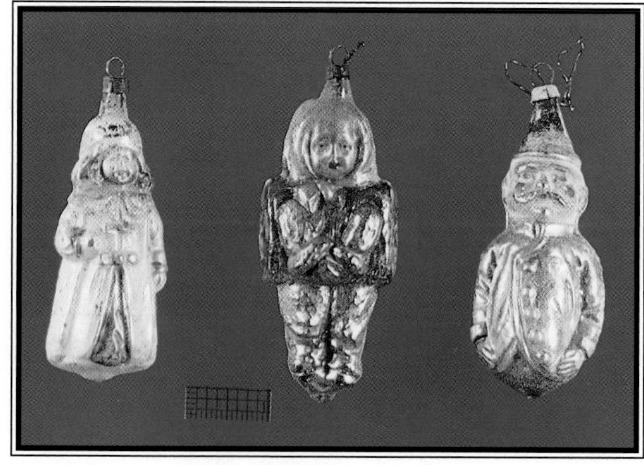

A. Kate Greenaway Girl, approx. 3" (shown) & 4" [German, OP, R2]. Small, **$100.00–125.00.** Large, **$200.00–250.00.** B. Girl in a Fur Coat, approx. 3½" & 3¾" (shown) [OP, R2]. Small, **$175.00–200.00.** Large, **$200.00–225.00.** C. Bismarck, approx. 3" [German, OP, R1]. **$250.00–300.00.**

A. Angel with Lithographed Face, approx. 3" (shown) & 3½" [OP, R2]. Small, **$150.00–175.00.** Large, **$175.00–200.00.** B. Scrap Girl with a Blown Glass Skirt. **$150.00–175.00.** C. Santa with a Scrap Face (Type I), approx. 3" [German, OP, R1-2]. **$150.00–175.00.**

A. Chimney Sweep (Type I), approx. 4" & 4½" (shown) [German, OP-NP (Inge-glas, 1970s), R1]. **$125.00–150.00.** 1970s version (shown), **$20.00–25.00.** B. Baby Girl Carrying a Tree, approx. 2", 2½", & 3½" (shown) [German, OP-NP (1980s & 1990s), R1]. Small, **$90.00–110.00.** Medium, **$150.00–175.00.** Large, **$200.00–250.00.** 1980s version (shown), **$10.00–15.00.** C. Angel Under a Tree, also called Fluffy, approx. 3½" [German, OP-NP (1970s & 1990s), R1]. **$250.00–300.00.**

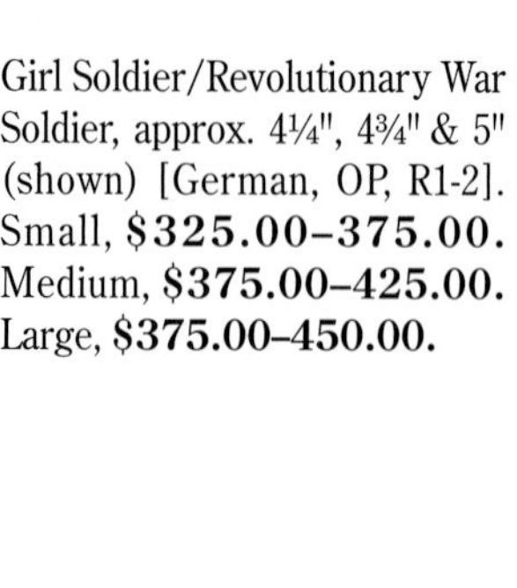

Girl Soldier/Revolutionary War Soldier, approx. 4¼", 4¾" & 5" (shown) [German, OP, R1-2]. Small, **$325.00–375.00.** Medium, **$375.00–425.00.** Large, **$375.00–450.00.**

Girl's Head (Type I), approx. 2" & 2½" (shown) [German, OP, R2-3]. Small, **$100.00–125.00.** Large, **$125.00–150.00.** Clip-on, **$175.00–225.00.**

A. German Military Helmet, 2¼" x 1¾" [OP-NP (Germany & Radko, 1994), R1]. Old, **$300.00–325.00.** B. Girl on a Toboggan Sled, 3½" [German, OP-NP (1980s), R1]. Old, **$500.00–600.00.**

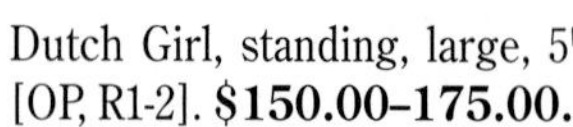

Dutch Girl, standing, large, 5" [OP, R1-2]. **$150.00–175.00.**

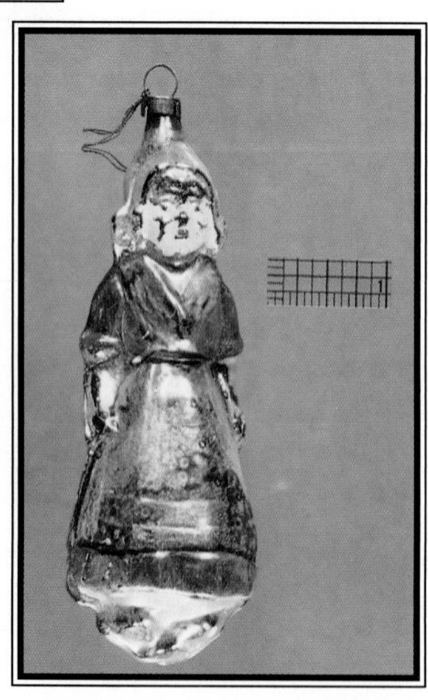

Girl Kewpie Doll, 4½" [OP, R1-2]. **$175.00–225.00.**

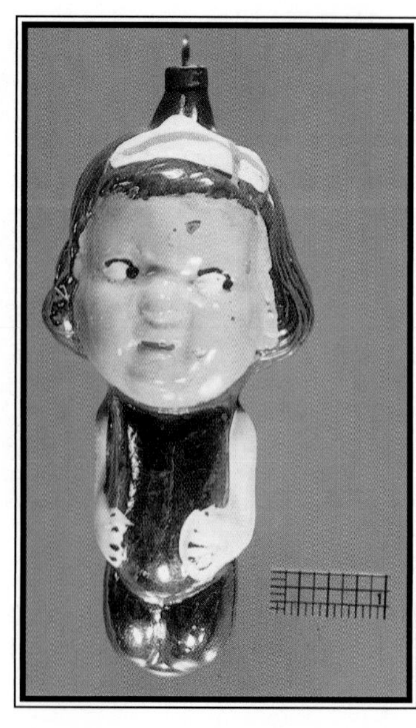

A. Peasant Lady, 3¾" & 4¼" (shown) [German, OP, R2]. Small, **$200.00–225.00.** Large, **$250.00–275.00.** B. Comic Man with Umbrella; 3½", 4, & 4½" (shown) [German, OP-NP (1980s & 1990s), R2-3]. Small, **$125.00–150.00.** Medium, **$175.00–200.00.** Large, **$225.00–275.00.** Possibly companion pieces.

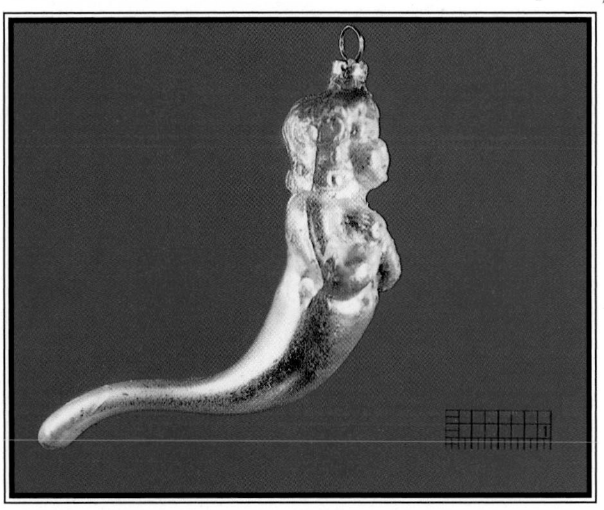

Angelic Mermaid, approx. 4". The upper torso is molded from an angel ornament [German, OP, R1-2]. **$150.00–175.00.**

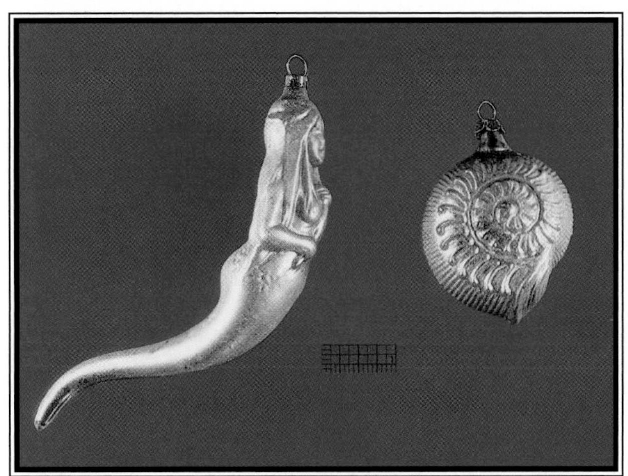

A. Mermaid (Type II), 6" [OP, R1+]. **$400.00–475.00.** B. Nautilus Shell (Type I), 2" [OP, R2]. **$125.00–150.00.**

Mermaid (Type I), 3¾" [OP, R1]. **$300.00–400.00.**

Russian Grandaughter Frost, 4¼" [USSR, OP, R2-3]. **$50.00–60.00.**

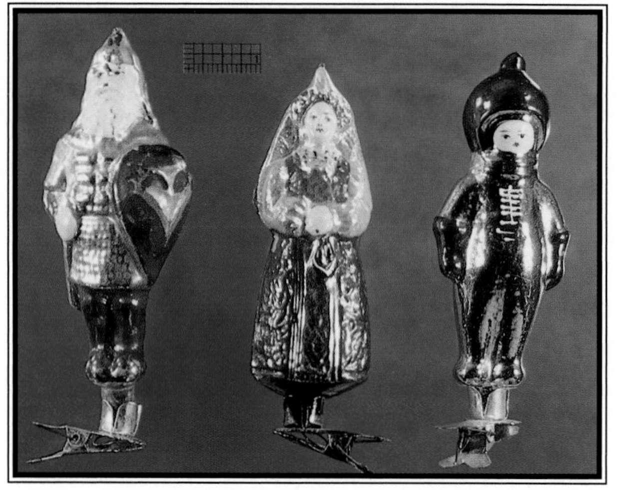

Three Russian Ornaments: A. Knight with Shield, 4½" [OP, R2-3]. **$60.00–75.00.** B. Fairy Princess, 4¼" [OP, R2-3]. **$60.00–75.00.** C. Astronaut, 4¼" [NP (1960s), R2-3]. **$20.00–30.00.**

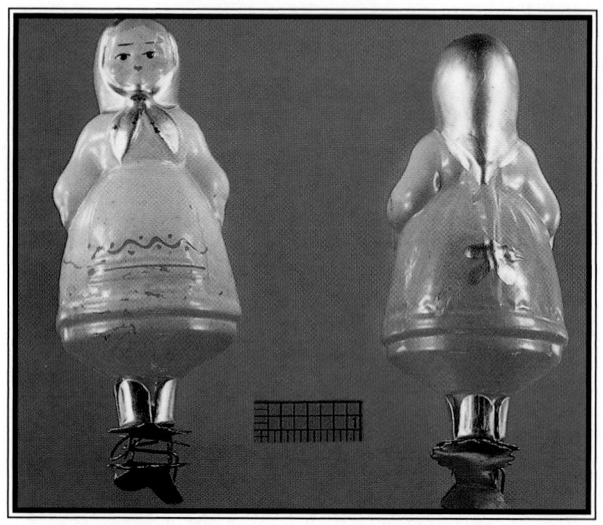

Peasant Girl in an Apron, front and back, 3¼" [OP, R2-3]. **$50.00–60.00.**

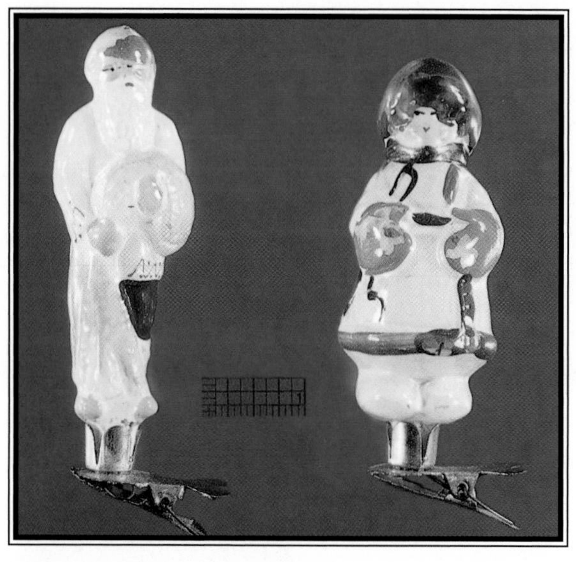

A. Old Fisherman, 3¾" [OP, R2]. **$55.00–70.00.** B. Girl in a Snowsuit, 3½" [OP, R2-3]. **$40.00–50.00.**

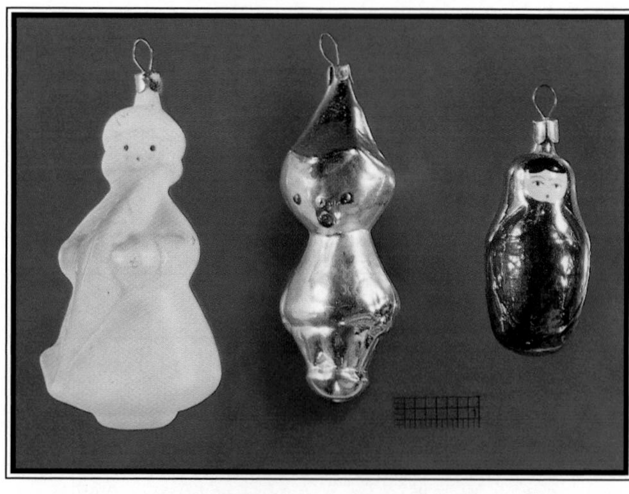

A. Fishwife, 4" [NP (1950s), R2-3]. **$20.00–30.00.** B. Boy in a Cone Hat, 4¼" [NP (1960s – 1970s), R2-3]. **$15.00–20.00.** C. Peasant Woman Nesting Doll, 2¾" [OP, R2-3]. **$15.00–25.00.**

A. Grandfather Frost, large, 4½" [OP, R2-3]. **$55.00–70.00.** B. Granddaughter Frost, large, 4" [OP, R2-3]. **$50.00–65.00.** C. Grandfather Frost, small, 3¼" [OP, R2-3]. **$45.00–60.00.** D. Granddaughter Frost, small, 3¼" [OP, R2-3]. **$30.00–40.00.**

Pilot, 3¾" [OP, R2-3]. **$55.00–70.00.**

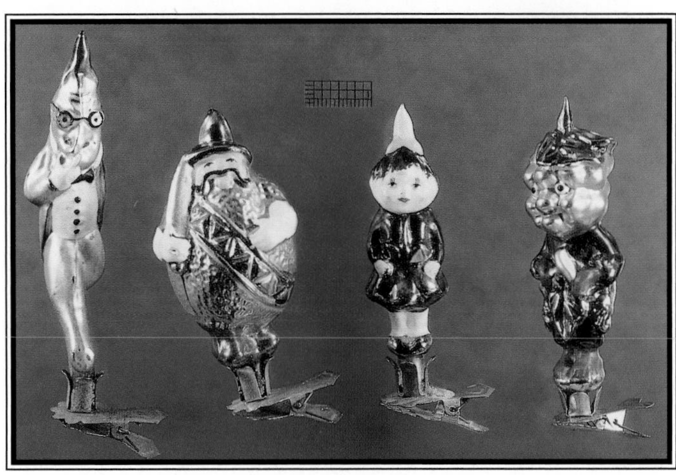

A. Peaman, 5" [OP, R2-3]. **$60.00–75.00.** B. Lemon Man, 3½" [OP, R2-3]. **$70.00–80.00.** C. Strawberry Girl, 3½" [OP, R2-3]. **$60.00–75.00.** D. Raspberry Boy, 4" [OP, R2-3]. **$60.00–75.00.**

A. Pumpkin Man, 4½" [OP, R2-3]. **$60.00–75.00.** B. Onion Boy, 4" [OP, R2-3]. **$60.00–75.00.** C. Radish Girl, 4" [OP, R2-3]. **$60.00–75.00.**

Wiseman, 3¼" [OP, R2-3]. **$50.00–60.00.**

Santas

Standard Form Santa Claus [both OP-NP, R4]: A. Red, 4½". **$45.00–60.00.** B. Gold, 4½". **$55.00–70.00.**

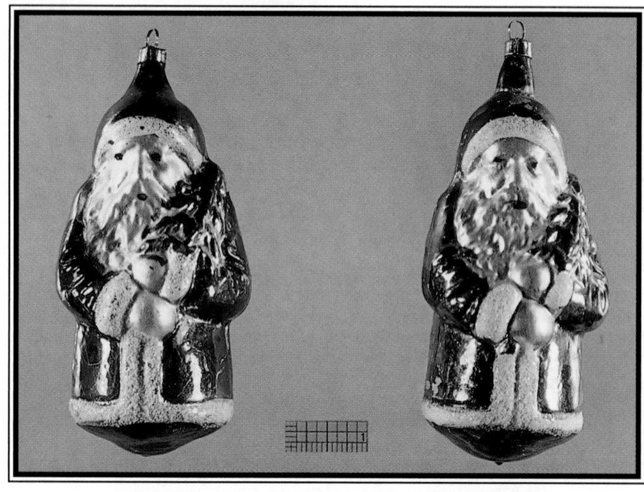

Standard Form Santa Claus, various colors [both OP-NP, R4]: A. Blue, 4½". **$55.00–70.00.** B. Green, 4½". **$55.00–70.00.**

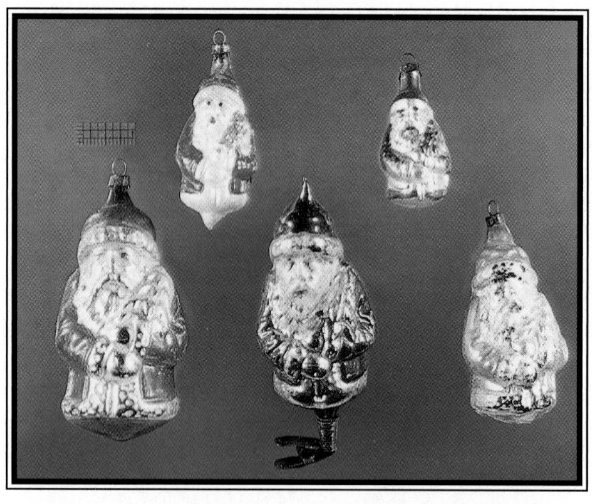

A–E. Various Forms and Sizes of the Standard Form Santa, approx. 2" – 5½", sizes and exact moldings vary greatly (2½" – 3½" are the most common sizes) [German, Czech, Austrian; OP-NP (continuing), R5]. Small (2" – 3"), **$15.00–25.00.** Medium (3"–4"), **$30.00–40.00.** Large (4" – 5½"), **$45.00–65.00.** Clip-on, **add $10.00.** Color other than red, **add $10.00.**

Santa in a Balloon, Santa 2", approx. 4½" overall, circa 1890 [OP-NP (Radko, 1990s), R1+]. **$350.00–400.00.**

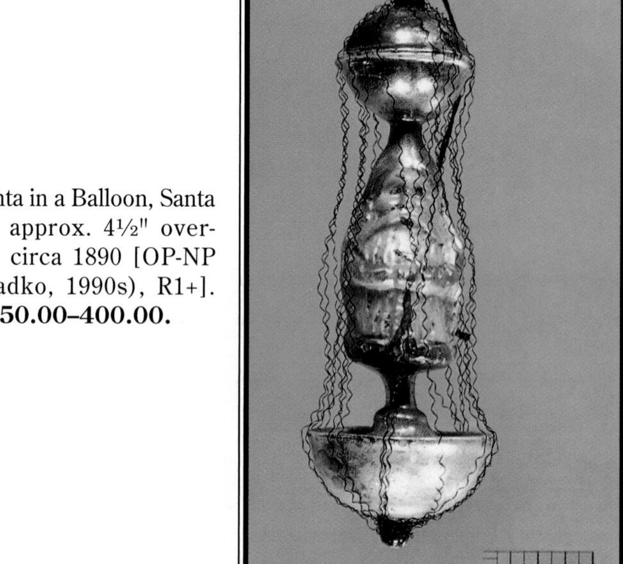

A. Standard Form Santa, approx. 3" [OP-NP (continuing), R4-5]. **$50.00–65.00.** B. Standard Form Santa in a Tinsel Wreath, approx. 2½", glass only [OP, R2]. **$75.00–100.00.** C. Santa with a Large Bag (no tree), approx. 3" [German, OP-NP (1980), R2]. **$30.00–40.00.** 1980s version (shown), **$12.00–18.00.**

A. Father Christmas Holding a Small Bag (Type II), approx. 3½" & 4½" (shown) [Czech, OP-NP (1990s), R2-3]. Small, **$50.00–75.00.** Large, **$75.00–100.00.** B. "Square" Santa with a Tree & a Bag, approx. 4" & 4½" (shown) [German, OP-NP (1994), R3]. Small, **$75.00–90.00.** Large, **$100.00–125.00.** C. Santa with a Bag & Toys, approx. 3" & 3¾" (shown) [OP, R3-4]. Small, **$50.00–75.00.** Large, **$75.00–100.00.**

A. Stooped-over Father Christmas; 2½", 2¾", & 3½" (shown) [German, OP, R2-3]. Small, **$50.00–75.00.** Medium, **$75.00–85.00.** Large, **$85.00–95.00.** B. Standard Form Santa, 4" [German, OP, R4]. **$45.00–65.00.** C. Frowning Santa with a Basket, approx. 3" [OP, R3]. **$40.00–60.00.**

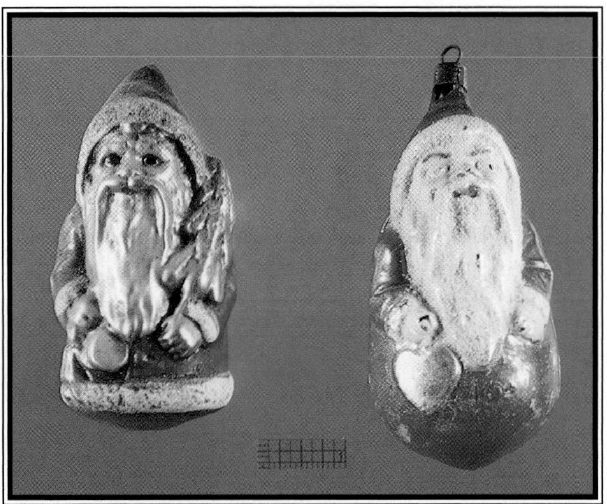

A. Santa with a Tree & a Drum, approx. 3¾" [OP, R2]. **$100.00–125.00.** B. Roly-Poly Santa with a Heart, approx. 4" [OP, R2]. **$125.00–150.00.**

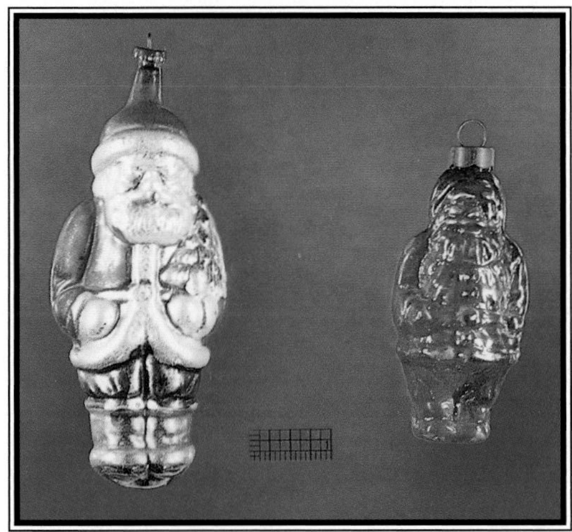

A. "American" Santa with a Tree, approx. 4½" [German, OP-NP (1995), R2]. **$65.00–85.00.** B. American Santa, approx. 3", made by Corning Glass [American, OP, R1-2]. **$50.00–75.00.**

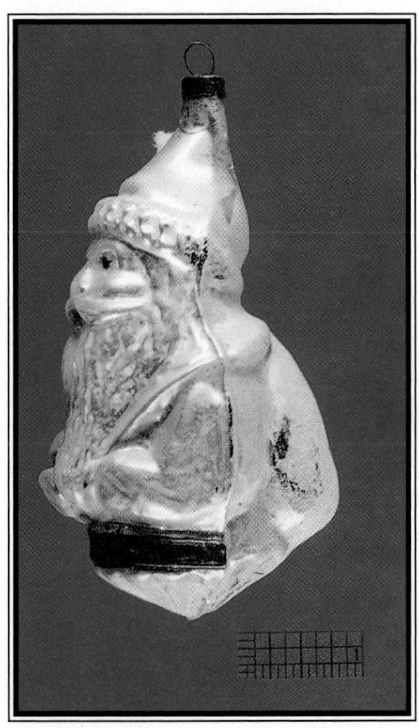

Chubby Santa with a Yellow Pack, approx. 3¾". Both his hands are at his waist [OP, R1]. **$150.00–175.00.**

Santa with Legs and with His Hands on His Hips, approx. 5¼" [Probably German, OP, R1]. **$125.00–150.00.**

Chubby Santa in a Blue Coat, approx. 3½" [OP, R1]. **$125.00–150.00.**

Molded Glass Santas, approx. 1", circa 1920, probably German [R1]. **$45.00–55.00.**

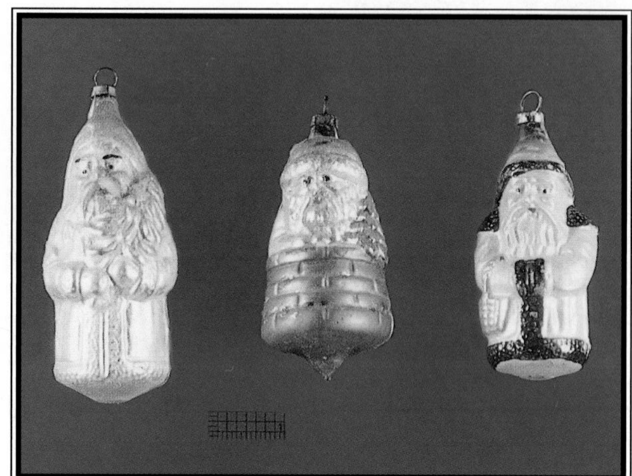

A. Standard Form Father Christmas, 3¾" [OP-NP, R4]. **$30.00–40.00.** B. Santa in Chimney (Type II), 2¾" (shown) & 3" [German, OP-NP (Lauscha Glas, 1994 & 1995), R3-4]. Small, **$50.00–60.00.** Large, **$60.00–70.00.** C. Santa with Basket (Type II), small, 3" [OP, R2-3]. **$65.00–85.00.**

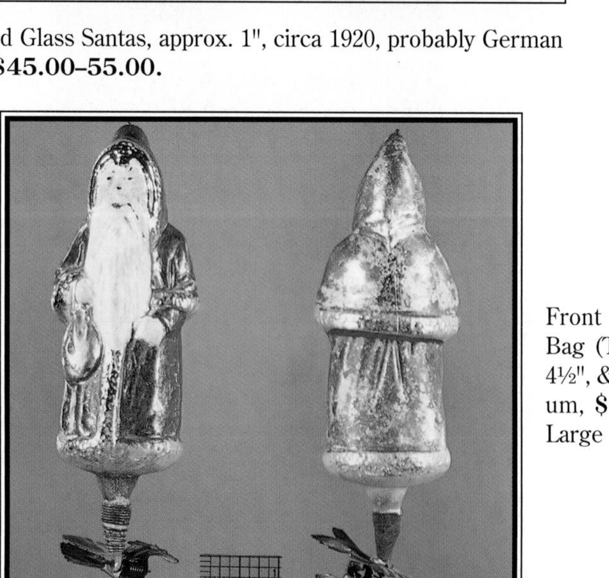

Front and Back View of Father Christmas Holding a Small Bag (Type I), also called *Wienachtsman*; 3¼", 4¼" (shown), 4½", & 4¾" [German, OP, R3]. Small, **$75.00–85.00.** Medium, **$90.00–100.00.** Large (4½"), **$100.00–125.00.** Large (4¾"), **$150.00–175.00.**

A. Santa with a Basket (Type II), 4" [OP, R2-3]. **$65.00–85.00.** B. Santa with a Scrap Face and a Hood and Cape, 3" [OP, R1-2]. **$150.00–175.00.**

Santa with a Doll in a Bag, 3½" [OP, R1]. **$350.00–450.00.**

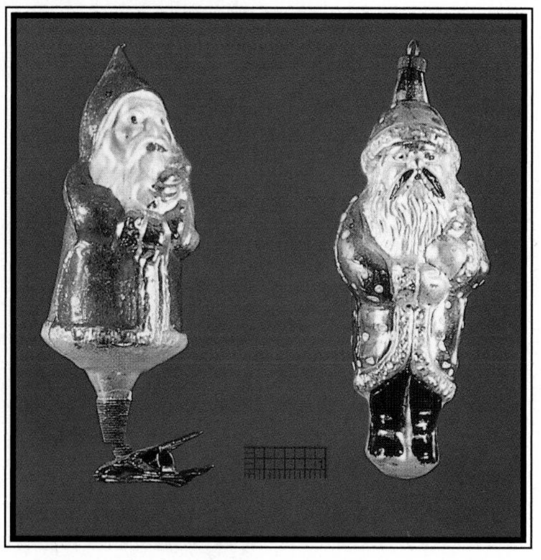

A. Standard Form Father Christmas, 3½" [OP-NP, R4]. **$35.00–45.00.** B. Pere Noel, approx. 4½" (shown) & 4¾" [German, OP-NP (Inge-glas, 1990s), R1-2]. Small, **$75.00–100.00.** Large, **$150.00–175.00.**

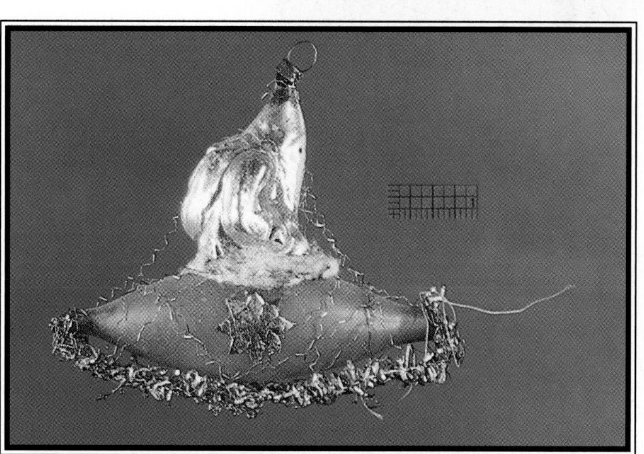

Santa on a Sled, 4" x 3¼" [OP, R1]. **$225.00–275.00.**

Sitting Santa on a Sled, 3¼" [OP, R1+]. **$550.00–600.00.**

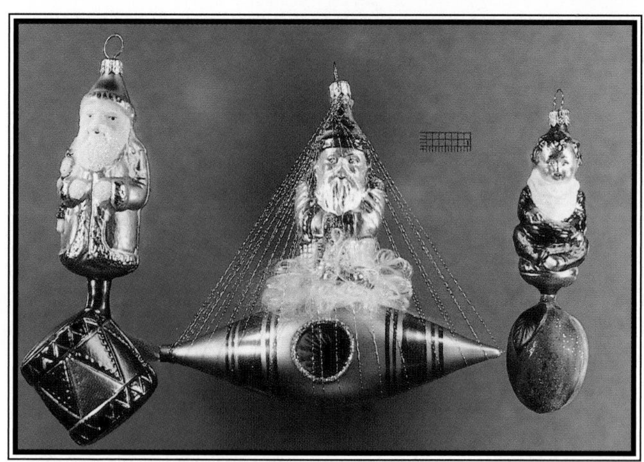

All by Radko: A. Santa on a Drum, 7" [NP (1995), R3-4]. **$35.00–50.00.** B. Santa on a Sailboat, 5½" [NP (1994), R3-4]. **$75.00–100.00.** C. Little Jack Horner on a Plum, 5½" [NP (1995), R3-4]. **$35.00–45.00.**

Santa with a Large Head, 4¼" [OP, R1-2]. **$275.00–350.00.**

A. Santa Under a Tree, 3½" [German, OP-NP (Inge-glas, 1980s), R2]. Old, **$200.00–250.00.** B. Father Christmas with a Staff, 3¾" [OP, R1-2]. **$100.00–125.00.** C. Santa on a Square Cookie, 3¼" [OP-NP (1995), R1]. Old, **$200.00–250.00.**

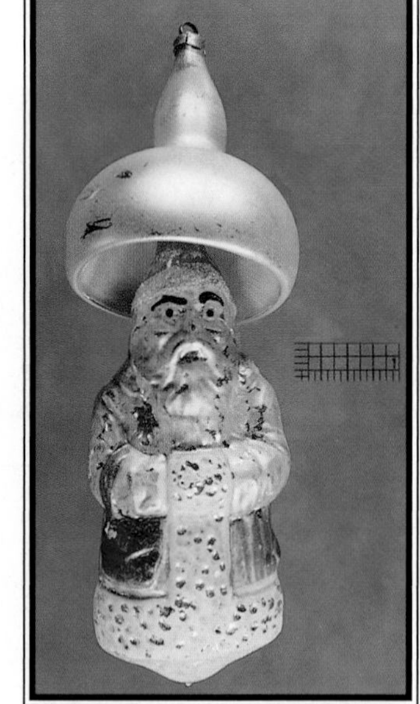

Santa under a Mushroom Cap (Type II), 6" [OP, R1]. **$250.00–275.00.**

A. Santa Under an Umbrella, 8" [NP, Radko (1990s), R3]. **$45.00–65.00.** B. Peacock on a Ball, 7¼" [NP (Radko, 1992), R2]. **$30.00–40.00.**

A. Santa Under Mushroom Cap (Type I), 4¾" [OP, R2]. **$275.00–325.00.** B. Belsnickle Santa, 3¼" [OP, R1+]. **$250.00–300.00.**

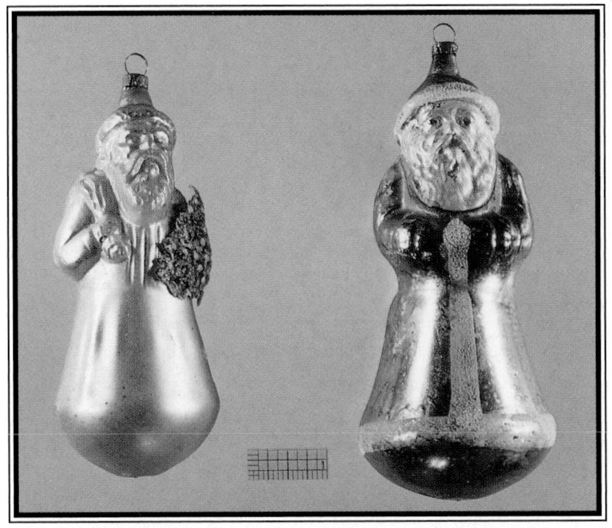

A. Santa with a Bell Bottom Belsnickle Form, 2½" molded, 4" – 4½" (shown) overall [OP, R2]. **$300.00–400.00.** B. Santa with a Bell Bottom Belsnickle Form and Arms in Sleeves, 2½" molded, 5" overall [OP, R1-2]. **$350.00–400.00.**

A. Santa with a Bell Bottom Belsnickle Form, 4" (shown) to 4½" [OP, R2]. **$250.00–300.00.** B. Stocking, knitted, 3½" [OP-NP, R2]. Small, **$100.00–125.00.** B. Man with Pipe and Keys, *Burgermiester*, 4¼" [OP, R2]. **$250.00–300.00.**

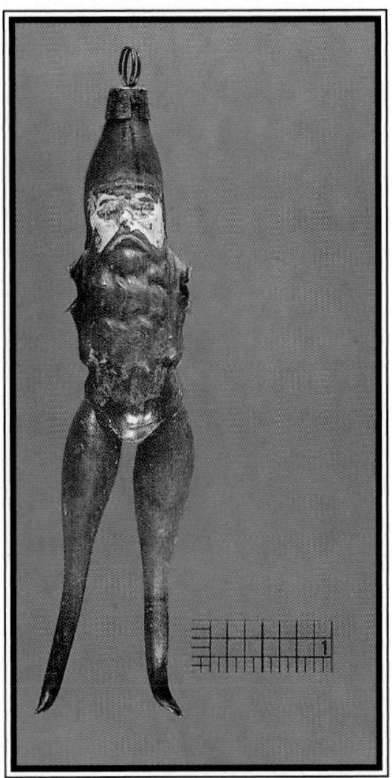

Santa with Annealed Arms and Legs, 2" molded, 4" overall [OP, R1+]. Undamaged, **$2,000.00–2,500.00.**

Radko Santas: A. Santa on an Icicle, 9½" [NP (1992), R3-4]. **$30.00–40.00.** B. "Russian" Santa, 7" [NP (1991), R4]. **$35.00–50.00.** C. Poinsettia Santa, 4¾" [NP (1993), R3-4]. **$40.00–50.00.**

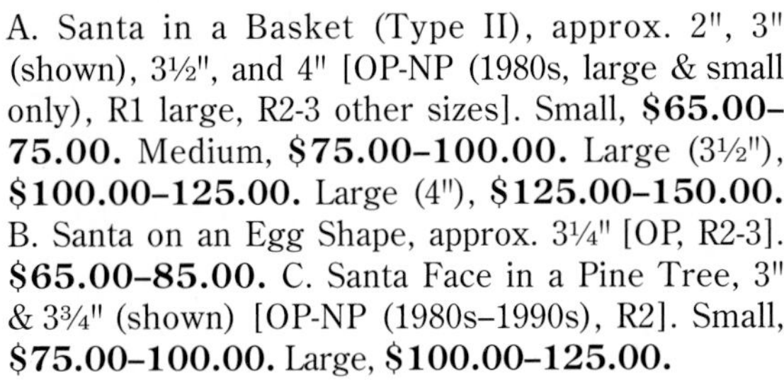

A. Santa in a Basket (Type II), approx. 2", 3" (shown), 3½", and 4" [OP-NP (1980s, large & small only), R1 large, R2-3 other sizes]. Small, **$65.00–75.00.** Medium, **$75.00–100.00.** Large (3½"), **$100.00–125.00.** Large (4"), **$125.00–150.00.** B. Santa on an Egg Shape, approx. 3¼" [OP, R2-3]. **$65.00–85.00.** C. Santa Face in a Pine Tree, 3" & 3¾" (shown) [OP-NP (1980s–1990s), R2]. Small, **$75.00–100.00.** Large, **$100.00–125.00.**

A. Father Christmas on an Egg Shape, approx. 2¾" & 3½" (shown) [German, OP, R2-3]. Small, **$90.00–110.00.** Large, **$150.00–175.00.** B. Santa in a Window, approx. 3" [German, OP, R2]. **$100.00–135.00.** C. Santa Head on an Egg Shape, approx. 2½" [OP, R1-2]. **$100.00–125.00.**

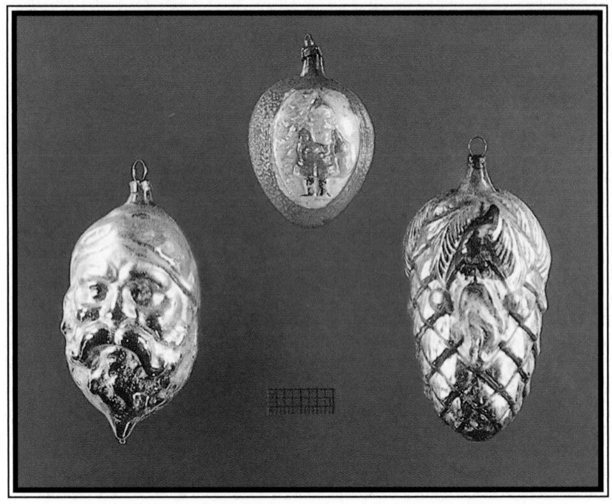

A. Santa Head with a Cap, approx. 3" (shown) & 4" [German, OP-NP (1980s), R2-3]. Small, **$75.00–100.00.** Large, **$150.00–175.00.** B. Santa on an Oval Shape, approx. 2½". The reverse shows a tree with candles [OP, R2-3]. **$65.00–85.00.** C. Small Santa Head on a Pine Cone, approx. 3½" [OP, R2]. **$125.00–150.00.**

A. Santa Indent, approx. 4", sizes vary with the size of the free-blown ball. The number of indents may vary from 1 to 2 (shown) or 3 [German, OP, R2]. 1 indent, **$50.00–75.00.** 2 indents, **$100.00–125.00.** 3 indents, **$150.00–175.00.** B. Father Christmas on an Oak Leaf, approx. 3½" [American, OP, R3]. **$40.00–50.00.**

A. Santa on a Leaf, approx. 3". This is a double-sided piece — the back is the same [OP, R2-3]. **$50.00–75.00.** B. Santa or Father Christmas on a Pine Cone, approx. 2¾", 3¾", & 4½" (shown) [OP, R2-3]. Small, **$65.00–80.00.** Medium, **$100.00–125.00.** Large, **$150.00–200.00.** C. Santa or Father Christmas on an Egg Shape, approx. 2¾" & 3½" (shown). The reverse shows a branch [German, OP, R2-3]. Small, **$90.00–110.00.** Large, **$150.00–175.00.**

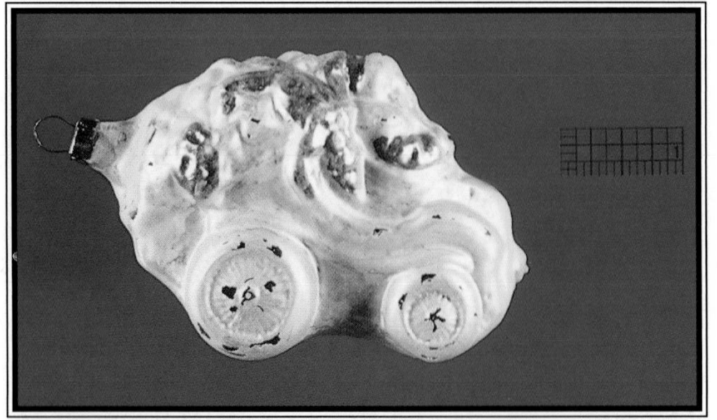

Santa in an Automobile, approx. 3¼" [OP, R1]. **$400.00–500.00.**

A. "The Parachutist," approx. 4¼" [German, OP-NP (East German, 1970), R1]. **$200.00–250.00.** 1970s version (shown), **$25.00–30.00.** B. Santa in a Coach, approx. 3"H & 2½"W [German, OP-NP (1976), R1+]. **$350.00–450.00.** 1976 version (shown), **$40.00–50.00.** C. Santa in a Parachute, approx. 3" [German, OP-NP (1980s & 1990s), R1]. **$175.00–200.00.** 1980s (shown), **$15.00–25.00.**

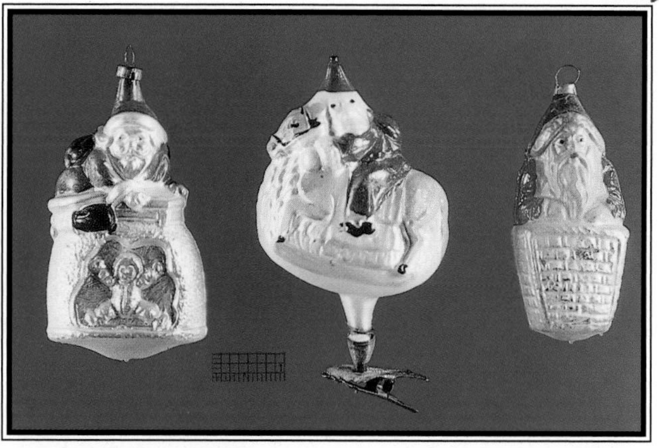

A. Santa on the Chimney, approx. 3" [German, OP-NP (1993), R1]. **$275.00–325.00.** B. Santa Riding on a Horse, approx. 3"H & 2½"L [German, OP-NP (1970s), R1+]. **$400.00–500.00.** C. Santa in a Basket (Type II), approx. 2", 3" (shown), 3½", and 4" [OP-NP (1980s, small & large only), R1 large, R2-3 other sizes]. Small, **$65.00–75.00.** Medium, **$75.00–100.00.** Large (3½"), **$100.00–125.00.** Large (4"), **$125.00–150.00.**

A. Santa with His Hands in His Sleeves, 2" [OP, R4]. **$20.00–30.00.** B. Santa in a Glass Triangle, approx. 3" [German, OP, R1-2]. **$65.00–90.00.** C. Miniature Gnome, 2" [OP, R1-2]. **$75.00–100.00.** D. Santa on an Egg Shape, 2½" [OP, R3]. **$50.00–75.00.**

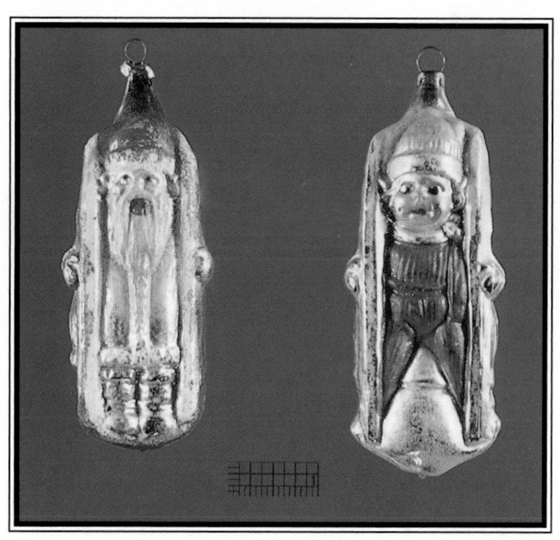

A. Santa in a Sled, 3½" [German, OP-NP (1993), R1]. **$325.00–375.00.** B. Boy in a Sled, 3½" & 4" (shown) [German, OP-NP (East German, 1980s), R2]. Small, **$150.00–175.00.** Large, **$175.00–225.00.**

A. Santa Head on a Heart, approx. 3" [German, OP-NP (1970s), R1]. **$175.00–200.00.** B. Santa Face Under a Pine Tree, approx. 3½" [German, OP, R3]. **$75.00–90.00.** C. Santa in a Basket (Type I); 2½", 3" (shown), & 3½" [German, OP-NP (1986), R3]. Small, **$75.00–85.00.** Medium, **$85.00–95.00.** Large, **$125.00–150.00.**

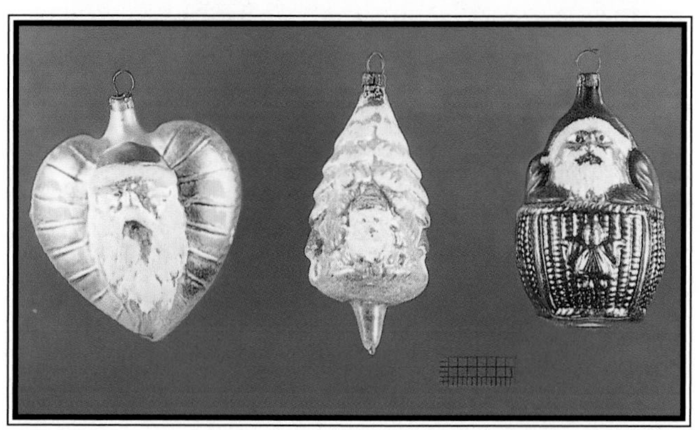

A. Santa on a Ball (Type IV), approx. 3¾" [German, OP, R2]. **$125.00–150.00.** B. Santa in a Stocking, approx. 3½" [Czech, OP-NP (1980s), R1-2]. **$175.00–200.00.** C. Santa in an Acorn Cap, approx. 4" [OP, R2-3]. **$90.00–110.00.**

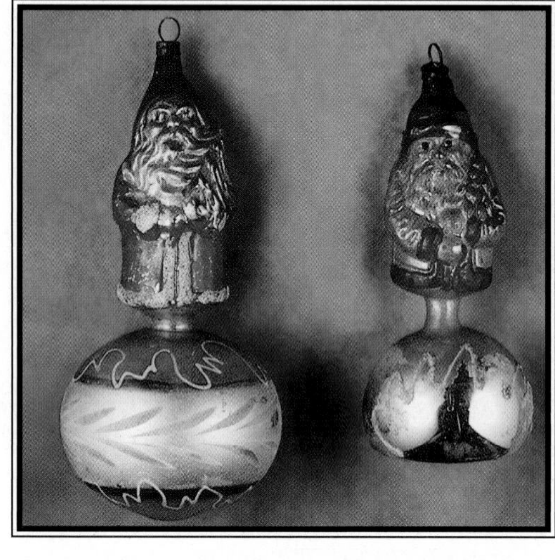

A. Santa on a Ball (Type I), approx. 5", sizes may vary with the free-blown ball [OP-NP (1990s), R3]. **$150.00–200.00.** B. Santa on a Ball/Bell, approx. 4½" [OP, R2-3]. **$150.00–175.00.**

Three variations of a Santa in a Ball, approx. 2½" –4", sizes vary with the size of the free-blown ball: A. Type II [OP, R3]. **$100.00–125.00.** B. Type I, approx. 3½" [OP, R3]. **$90.00–110.00.** C. Type III, approx. 3¾" [OP, R3]. **$90.00–110.00.**

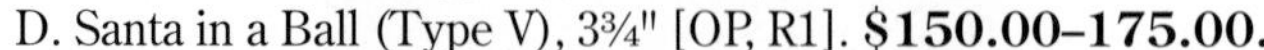

A. Santa Bust, double sided, 1½" [OP, R2-3]. **$35.00–50.00.** B. Santa in a Ball (Type III), 3¾" [OP, R3]. **$90.00–110.00.** C. Santa in a Ball (Type I), 2¾" [OP, R3-4]. **$90.00–110.00.** D. Santa in a Ball (Type V), 3¾" [OP, R1]. **$150.00–175.00.**

A. Santa in a Cone, 5" [OP, R1]. **$150.00–175.00.** B. Santa Head on a Ball, 4" [OP, R1]. **$150.00–175.00.**

A. Snowman in a Chimney, approx. 3" [German, OP-NP (1990s), R1-2]. **$200.00–250.00.** B. Santa in a Chimney (Type II), approx. 2¾" (shown) & 3" [German, OP-NP (1995), R3-4]. Small, **$50.00–60.00.** Large, **$60.00–70.00.** C. Santa in a Chimney (Type I), approx. 2¾" & 3" (shown). The second row of bricks form a ledge [German, OP-NP (1950s & 1980s), R3-4]. Small, **$60.00–70.00.** Large, **$65.00–85.00.**

A. Roly-Poly Santa, approx. 3" [OP, R1-2]. **$125.00–175.00.** B. Mushroom with a Face, approx. 2¾" [OP, R1-2]. **$175.00–200.00.**

A & B. Two Sizes of Santa with Chenille Legs & Wax Boots, approx. 3½", 4½" (shown), & 5" (shown) [German, OP, R3 medium size, R2 small & large size]. Small, **$125.00–135.00.** Medium, **$125.00–150.00.** Large, **$150.00–175.00.** C. Jolly Santa in a Tassel Cap (Type I), approx. 2¾" & 3½" (shown) [OP-NP (1950s), R3-4]. Small, **$65.00–85.00.** Large, **$90.00–110.00.**

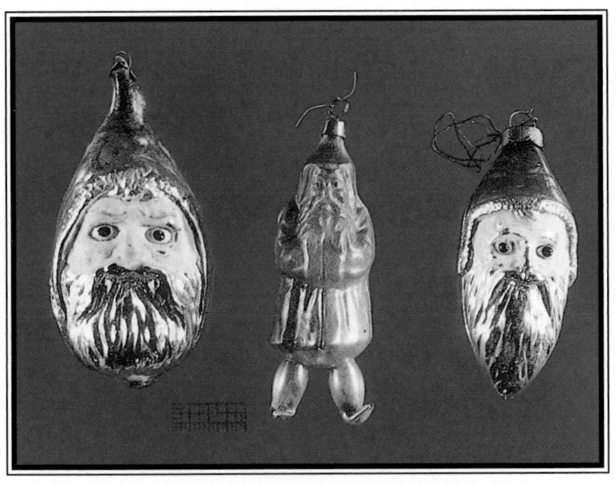

Father Christmas Head with Glass Eyes, approx. 3½" [German, OP, R2]. **$300.00–350.00.** B. Santa with Annealed Legs, approx. 3¾" [OP, R1]. **$650.00–750.00.** C. Santa Head with Glass Eyes, approx. 3½" [German, OP, R1]. **$325.00–375.00.**

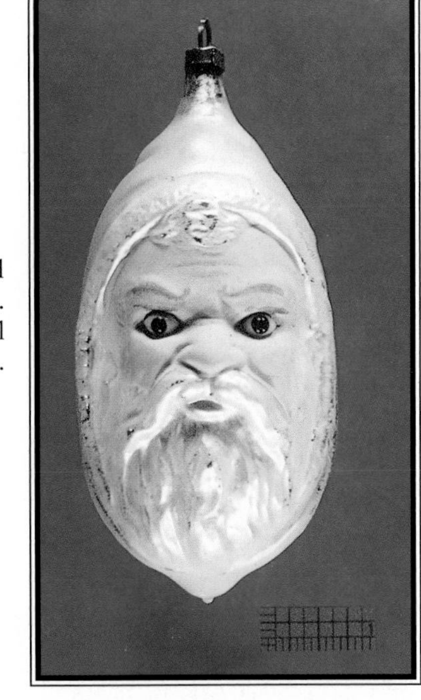

Father Christmas Head with Glass Eyes, approx. 3¾". He has an unusual yellow hood [OP, R1]. **$300.00–350.00.**

A. Father Christmas Head with Glass Eyes (eyes missing), approx. 3½". Clip-ons add slightly to the price; missing glass eyes seriously hurt the price [German, OP, R2]. **$300.00–350.00.** B & C. Two versions of the Standard Form Father Christmas Head, approx. 1½" (shown), 2½", 3", 3½" (shown), & 4" [German, OP-NP (1940s–1950s, medium), R3-4]. Small (1½"–2½"), **$45.00–55.00.** Medium (3" & 3½"), **$55.00–75.00.** Large (4"), **$90.00–110.00.** D. Jolly Santa Head in a Tassel Cap (Type I), approx. 2¾" & 3½" (shown) [OP-NP (1950s), R3-4]. Small, **$65.00–85.00.** Large, **$90.00–110.00.**

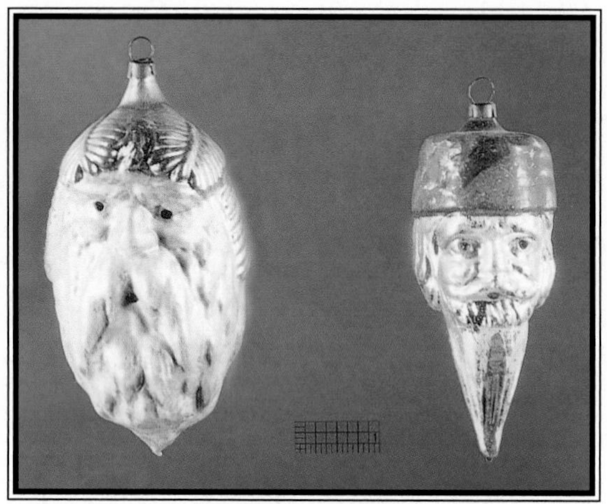

A. Santa Head with a Leaf Cap, approx. 4" [German, OP, R2]. **$275.00–325.00.** B. Santa in a Fur Cap on a Pike, approx. 3¾" [OP, R1-2]. **$200.00–250.00.**

A. Czech Santa, approx. 3" [NP (1980s), R2]. **$20.00–30.00.** B & C. Standard Father Christmas Heads, both approx. 2½" [German, OP-NP (1940s–1950s), R3-4]. **$45.00–55.00** each. D. Jolly Santa in a Tassel Cap (Type II), 3½" [German, OP-NP (1980s), R1]. **$75.00–100.00.** 1980s version (shown), **$12.00–18.00.** E & F. *Weihnachtsmann* Head, approx. 2", 3", 3½" (shown), 3¾", & 4" (shown). *E* is German and *F* is Czech [German & Czech, OP-NP (1970s–1980s), R4]. Small (2"–3"), **$50.00–75.00.** Medium (3½" – 3¾"), **$100.00–125.00.** Large (4"), **$125.00–150.00.**

A. Santa on a Ball/Bell (Type II), 4½" [OP, R2-3]. **$150.00–175.00.** B. Santa Bell, 2¼" [German, OP-NP (Inge-glas, 1995), R2]. **$100.00–125.00.**

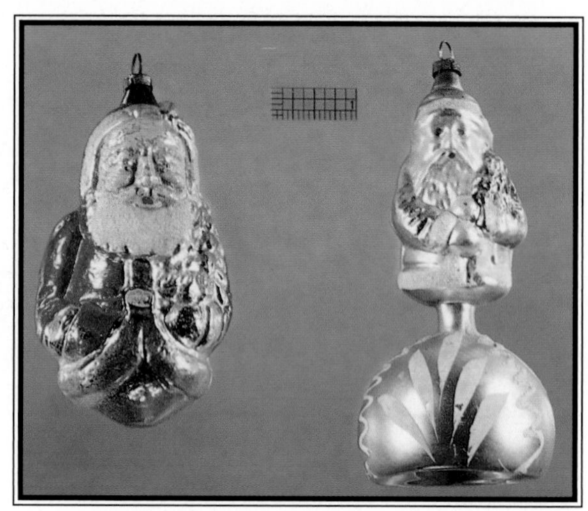

A. Santa with Tree and Holly Sprig, 3¾" [German, OP-NP (1990s), R2]. **$100.00–125.00.** B. Santa on a Ball/Bell (Type II), 4" [OP, R3 ball, R2 bell]. **$150.00–175.00.**

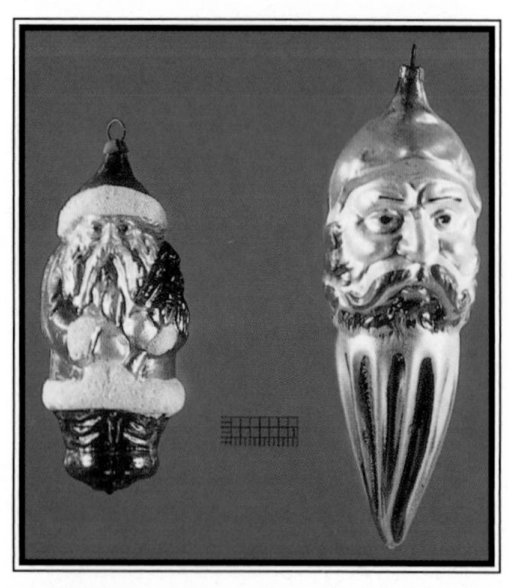

A. Santa with Legs, approx. 3¼", 3½", 4" (shown), & 4½" [German, OP, R3-4]. Small, **$30.00–40.00** Medium, **$40.00–50.00.** Large (4"), **$75.00–100.00.** Large (4½"), **$150.00–200.00.** B. Santa Head with Cap on a Pike, 5½" [OP, R2]. **$250.00–300.00.**

Standard Form Father Christmas Heads [OP-NP]: A. 4" [R3]. Large, **$150.00–200.00.** B. 3" [R3-4]. Medium, **$75.00–100.00.**

Airplane with Wheels, free-blown, large, 7" [OP, R2]. **$300.00–400.00.** Medium, 5" –6". **$250.00–300.00.**

Airplane with a Plaster/Cotton Santa, 7¼", Blumchen, circa 1993–1994 [R2-3]. **$125.00–175.00.**

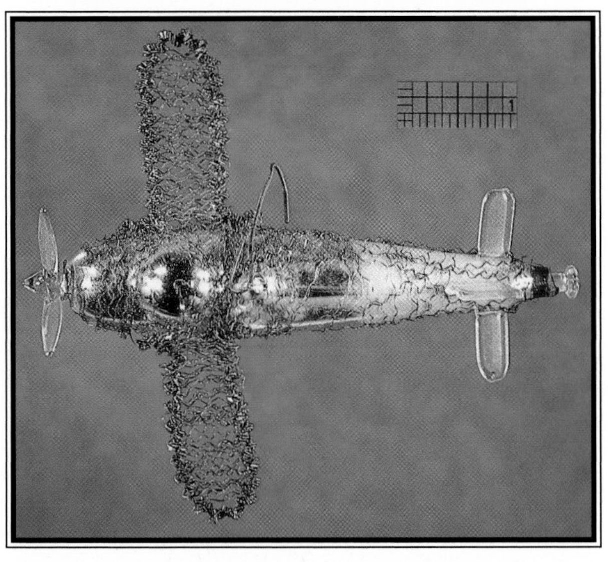

Rare and Unusual Airplane with Glass Propeller, 4¼". The propeller is attached to a glass rod that runs the length of the plane and is turned by the small knob at the rear [OP, R1+]. **$850.00–1,000.00.**

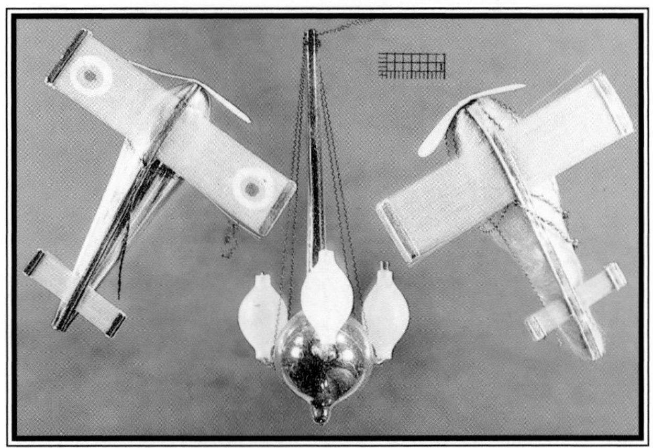

A. *Spirit of St. Louis*, large, 4½" [OP, R2-3]. **$150.00–175.00.** B. Gas Chandelier (Type II), three globes, 5½" [OP, R1-2]. **$75.00–100.00.** C. Variation, SG wrapped, 4½" [OP, R1]. **$200.00–250.00.**

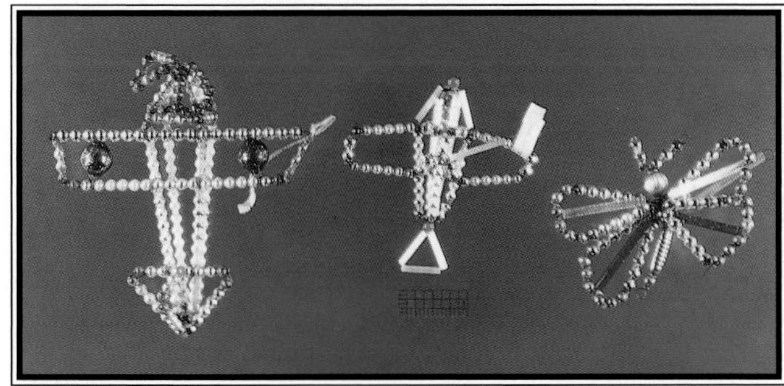

A & B. Airplanes, beaded: A. 4" [Czech, OP, R2-3]. **$30.00–40.00.** B. 2½" [OP, R2-3]. **$25.00–35.00.** C. Butterfly, beaded, 2¾" wing span [Czech, OP, R2]. **$20.00–30.00.**

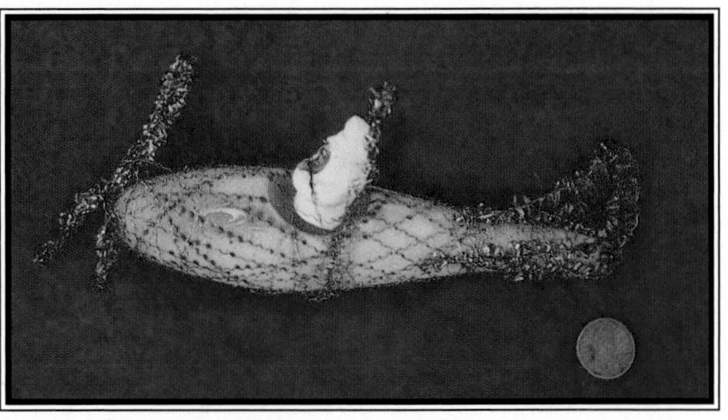

Airplane with a Plaster Santa, approx. 7½", circa 1900 [OP, R1]. **$300.00–400.00.**

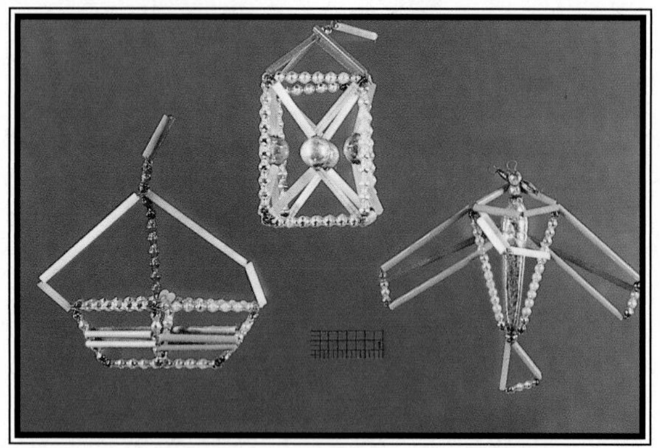

Beaded Ornaments: A. Lantern, 2½" [OP, R2]. **$8.00–12.00.** B. Sailboat, 2¾" [OP, R2]. **$10.00–16.00.** C. Jet Airplane, 3" [OP, R2]. **$15.00–25.00.**

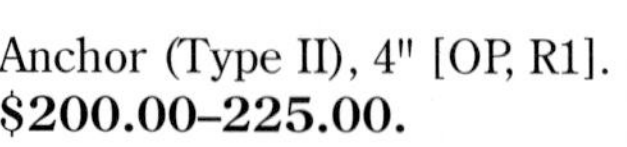

Anchor (Type II), 4" [OP, R1]. **$200.00–225.00.**

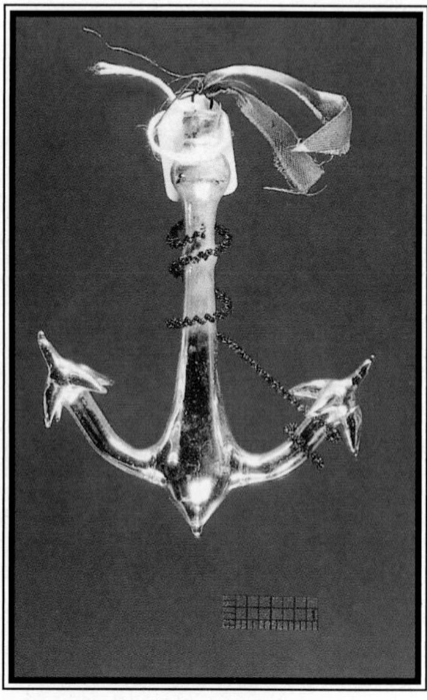

Anchor (Type III), large, 6½", three arms [OP-NP (1950s), R2]. **$150.00–175.00.**

A. Shell, indented, 1¾" [OP-NP (1950s), R1]. **$30.00–35.00.** B. Anchor, indented, 5½" [OP, R2]. **$125.00–150.00.**

Free-blown Car with Metal Wheels, 4½" [OP, R1]. **$350.00–425.00.**

A. Automobile (Type I), 3" [OP, R2-3]. **$80.00–90.00.** B. VW Car, small, 2¾", 1950s [R3]. **$30.00–40.00.** C. Touring Car (Type II), 3" [OP, R2]. **$125.00–150.00.** D. Square Car, large, 2¼" & 2¾" (shown) [OP, R2-3]. Small, **$90.00–100.00.** Large, **$100.00–125.00.** E. Automobile (Type II), 3" [OP, R2-3]. **$125.00–150.00.**

A. Automobile (Type II), 3" [OP, R2-3]. **$125.00–150.00.** B. Touring Car (Type I), 2¾" [OP, R2]. **$125.00–150.00.**

A. Touring Car (Type II), approx. 3" [OP, R2]. **$125.00–150.00.** B. Truck, 2½" [OP, R1-2]. **$150.00–175.00.** C. Comic Car, approx. 2½" [OP, R1-2]. **$125.00–140.00.**

A. VW Car, approx. 2¾", 3½" (shown), & 3¾" [German, NP (1950s, 1970s and 1980s), R3]. Small, **$30.00–40.00.** Medium, **$40.00–50.00.** Large, **$40.00–50.00.** B. Locomotive, 3" [German, OP-NP (1950s & 1970s), R2]. **$90.00–110.00.** 1950s version (shown), **$25.00–35.00.** C. Automobile (Type II), 3" [OP, R2-3]. **$125.00–150.00.** D. Covered Wagon, 2" [German, NP (1950s), R2]. **$30.00–40.00.**

A. Truck, 2½" [OP, R1–2]. **$150.00–175.00.** B. Bus, 2¾" & 3"(shown) [OP–NP (Inge-glas, 1992), R1]. Small, **$125.00–150.00.** Large, **$150.00–175.00.**

Molded Single Balloon by Blumchen, 8¾", circa 1990 [R3]. **$75.00–95.00.**

Single Balloon, indented, large, 7½" [OP-NP, R2-3]. **$100.00–125.00.**

Single Balloon, approx. 8¾", large, mold blown [OP-NP (1970s), R3]. **$125.00–150.00.**

A–E. Various sizes & styles of "Single Balloons," approx. 2¾"–12". Sizes vary with the size of the free-blown ball and the length of the attached glass pike; 4"–7" are common sizes [OP-NP (continues), R4]: A. 8¾". **$100.00–125.00.** B. 6¾". **$60.00–75.00.** C. 5¾". **$50.00–60.00.** D. 4". **$25.00–35.00.** E. 2¾". **$20.00–25.00.** In general, small balloons (2¾"–4") are **$20.00–40.00.** Medium balloons (5" –7"), **$50.00–75.00.** Large balloons (8"–10"), **$100.00–150.00.** Extra Large (11"–12"), **$150.00–200.00.**

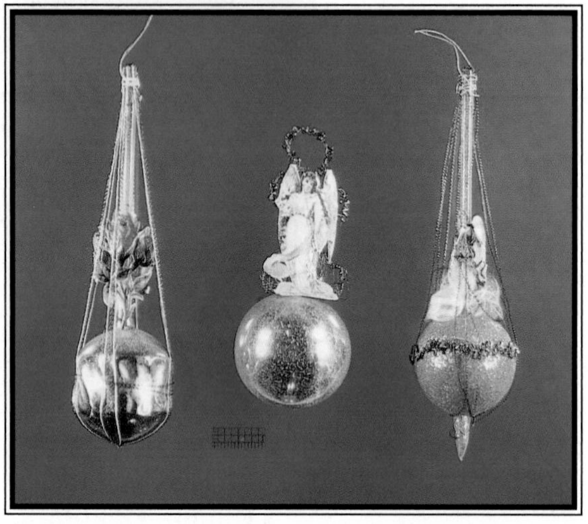

Variations of Free-blown Single Balloon: A. 6½". **$55.00–65.00.** B. 4½". **$40.00–55.00.** C. 6¾". **$70.00–85.00.**

A, B, C. Double Balloons, approx. 2½" to 18". The most common sizes are 4" to 8". Sizes vary because they are free-blown. 12"–18" versions were made in the early 1990s. Values are greatly affected by the wire wrapping, scraps, and extras that are added [OP-NP (1950s, 1980s, & 1990s), R3-4]: A. 4¼". **$45.00–55.00.** B. 9". **$175.00–200.00.** C. 4". **$50.00–60.00.** In general, small balloons (2½"–4") are **$35.00–70.00.** Medium balloons (5" –6"), **$100.00–150.00.** Large balloons (7" – 9"), **$150.00–250.00.** Extra large balloons (12"–18", 1990s), **$150.00–175.00.**

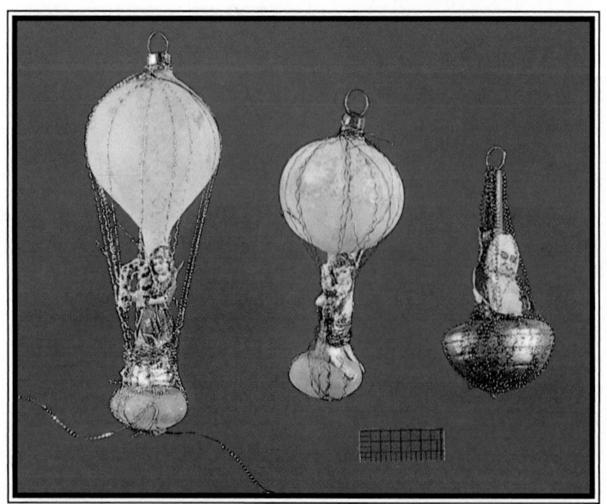

A & B. Double Balloons, 4½" & 3¼" [OP, R3-4]: A. **$70.00–80.00.** B. **$40.00–50.00.** C. Molded Single Balloon or a Gondola with a Pike, 2½"H [OP-NP (1970s), R2]. **$30.00–40.00.**

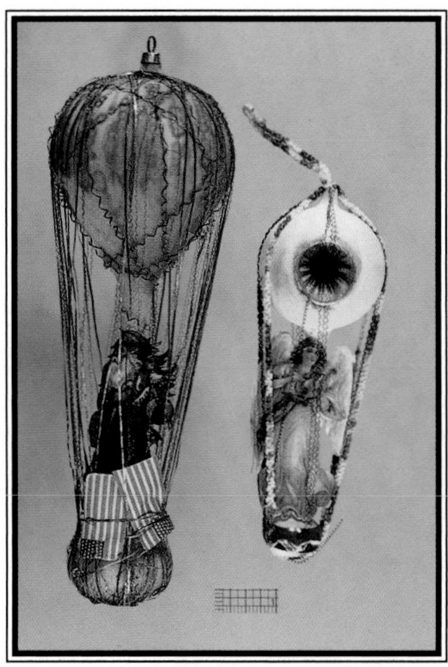

A. Patriotic Double Balloon, large, 8" [OP, R2-3]. **$225.00–250.00.** B. Double Balloon, indented, large and elaborately wrapped, 5½" [OP, R1-2]. **$90.00–125.00.**

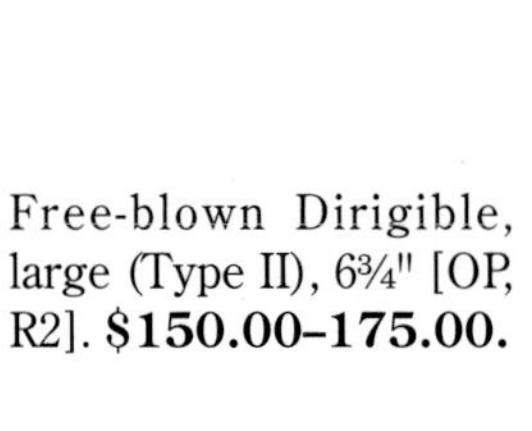

Free-blown Dirigible, large (Type II), 6¾" [OP, R2]. **$150.00–175.00.**

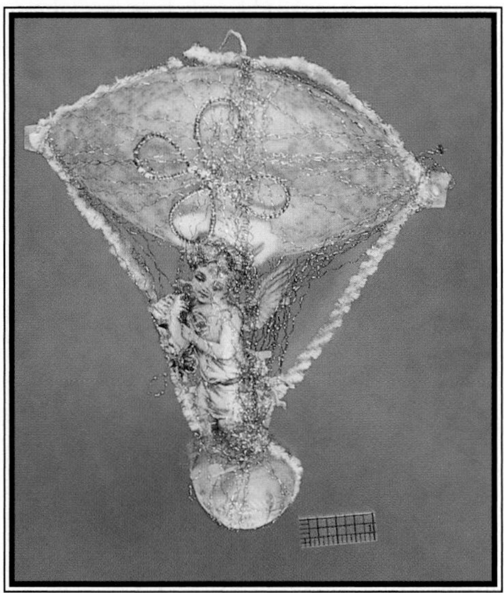

Wire-wrapped Dirigible with Scrap Angel (Type II), approx. 6"H and 5"W [German, OP, R2-3]. **$150.00–175.00.**

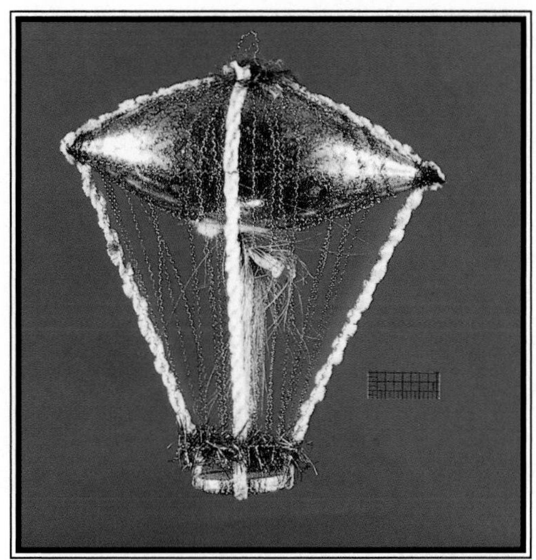

Free-blown Dirigible (Type II), 5½"H x 5"W [OP, R2]. **$90.00–110.00.**

A, B, C. Three Versions of the Free-blown Gondola, all 3½" – 4" [OP, R3]. **$60.00–90.00.**

Czech Beaded Ornaments: A. Spider Web, approx. 2¼" [OP-NP (1950s), R2]. **$30.00–40.00.** B. Bicycle, 3½" [NP (1950s), R2]. **$75.00–100.00.**

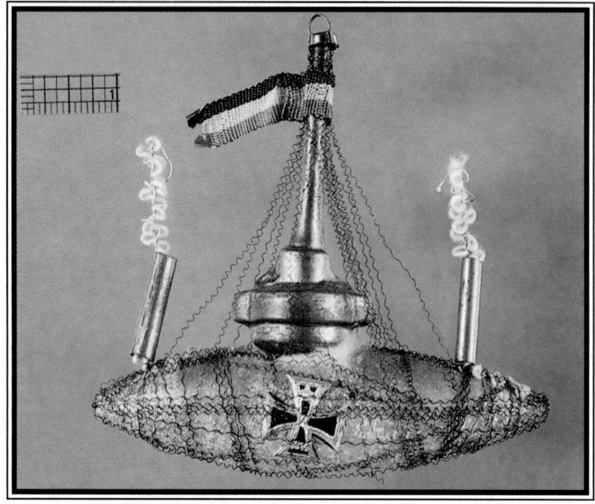

Steamship with an Iron Cross, 4½"L x 4"H [OP, R1+]. **$375.00–425.00.**

Sailing Ship, approx. 6½"H. This classic eighteenth century ship was made in Germany, in the late 1990s [R2-3]. **$20.00–30.00.**

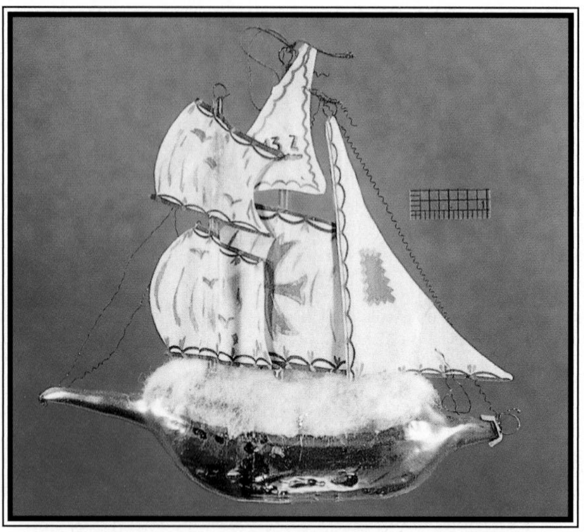

Three-masted Ship with Sails, 5¾"L x 5½"H [OP-NP (possibly Italian, 1950s), R1]. **$150.00–175.00.**

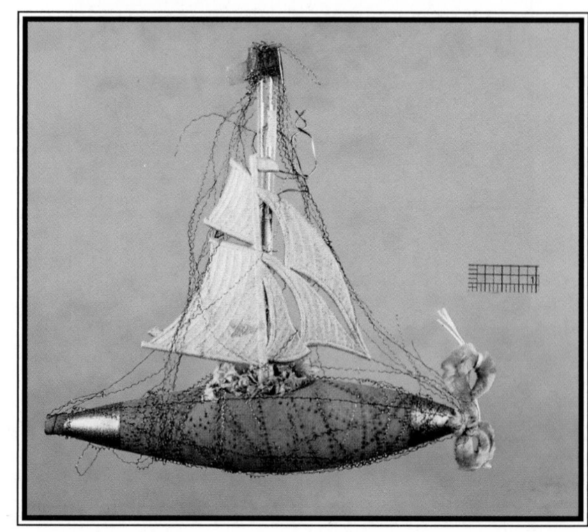

Sailboat with Paper Sails, medium, 6½"L [OP, R2]. **$175.00–200.00.**

Sailboat with Sails, large, 10", replaced sails hurt value [OP, R1]. With replaced sails, **$80.00–90.00.** With original sails, **$175.00–200.00.**

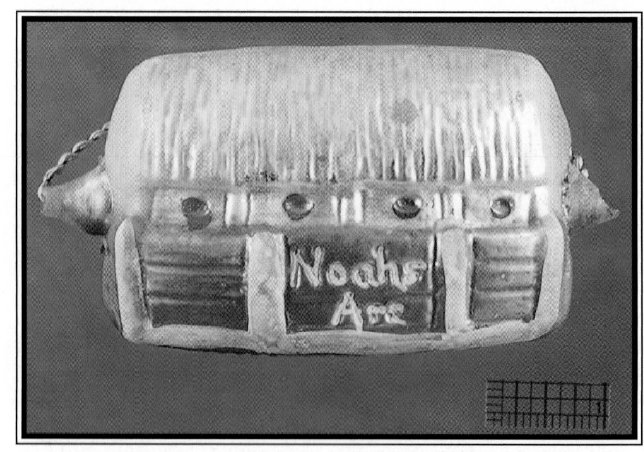

Noah's Ark, 3¾" [OP, R1+]. **$1,200.00–1,500.00.**

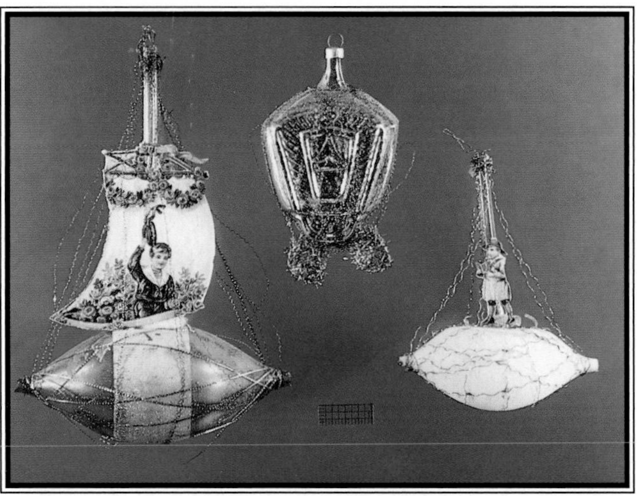

A. Patriotic Sailboat, 5½" [OP, R1-2]. **$150.00–175.00.** B. Cinderella's Carriage, 3" [German, OP, R3]. **$50.00–60.00.** C. Sailboat, 4" hull [OP, R4]. **$50.00–75.00.**

"Crown" Sailboat, approx. 5", patriotic version [German, OP, R2-3]. **$200.00–225.00.**

Free-blown Steamship, approx. 4½"–5½", wire wrapped [OP, R1-2]. **$200.00–225.00.**

A–E. Free-blown Sailboats, approx. 3"–10". Sizes vary because they are free-blown; 3½" –6½" are the most common sizes [OP-NP (1950s, 1970s–1990s), R3-4]. A. 3¼"L. **$60.00–75.00.** B. 3¼" L. **$50.00–60.00.** C. 8½"H. **$125.00–150.00.** D. 6". **$125.00–150.00.** E. 5½". **$100.00–110.00.** In general, small boats (3"–4") are **$40.00–75.00.** Medium boats (5"–7"), **$125.00–150.00.** Large boats (8"–10"), **$200.00–250.00.**

A & B. Sailboats with Paper Sails, 3½"–4" hulls. Paper sails add value to the piece [OP-NP (1980s), R2-3]. **$65.00–85.00** each.

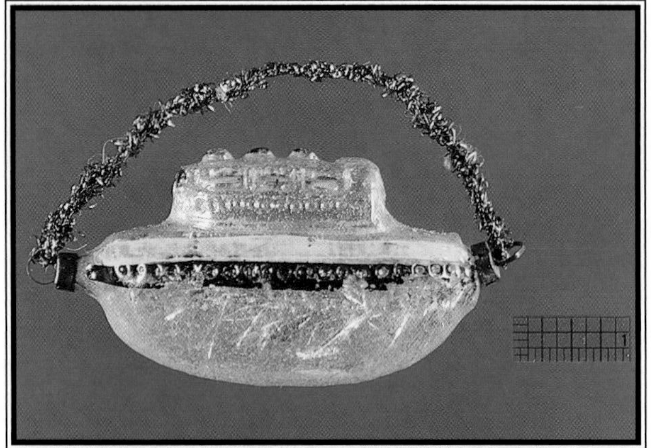

Bremen Steamship, approx. 3¾". "Bremen" is embossed on the hull [German, OP, R1]. **$325.00–375.00.**

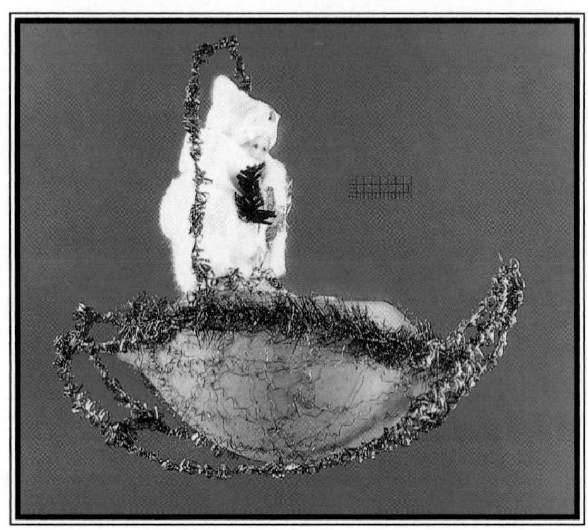

Sleigh with a Cotton Batting Rider, approx. 6" [OP, R1]. **$350.00–400.00.**

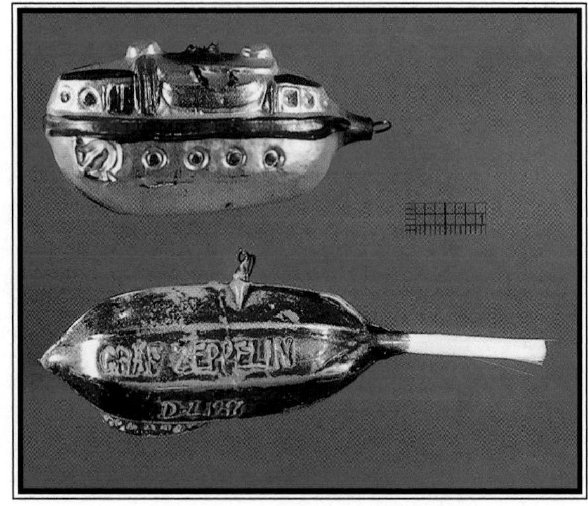

A. Passenger Ship, 3½" [German, OP-NP (1950s), R3]. **$80.00–110.00.** B. Graf Zeppelin "DL 127," approx. 3½" [German, OP, R2-3]. **$200.00–275.00.**

A. Graf Zeppelin "DL 127," approx. 3½" [German, OP, R2-3]. **$200.00–275.00.** B. Graf Zeppelin with an American Flag, approx. 5¼" [German, OP, R2-3]. **$125.00–150.00.** C. "Los Angeles" Zeppelin, approx. 4" [German, OP, R2]. **$300.00–350.00.**

Zeppelin "ZR III" with Motor Crown, approx. 5¾" [German, OP, R1+]. **$300.00–350.00.**

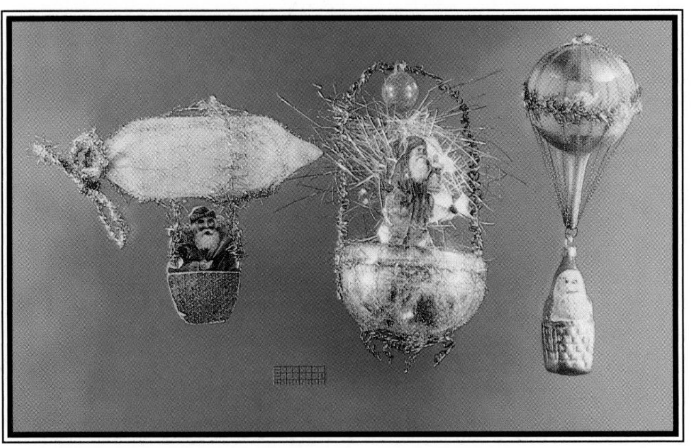

A. Free-blown Zeppelin with Santa Rider, approx. 5" glass body [OP, R3]. **$200.00–225.00.** B. Santa in a Large Gondola, 6" [OP, R2-3]. **$175.00–200.00.** C. Balloon Riding Santa, approx. 6½" [OP, R1-2]. **$175.00–200.00.**

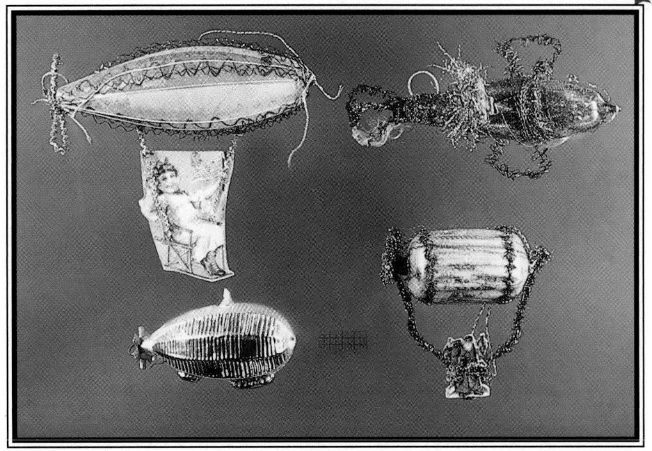

A. Free-blown Patriotic Zeppelin, 5½" glass body [OP, R2]. **$200.00–225.00.** B. Free-blown Wire-wrapped Airplane, 5½"L [German, OP, R2]. **$150.00–175.00.** C. Zeppelin (Type II), approx. 3½" (shown) & 5" [German, OP-NP (1950s, 1980s & 1990s), R2]. **$75.00–100.00.** 1950s version (shown), **$35.00–45.00.** D. Small Free-blown Dirigible, approx. 3" glass body [OP, R2]. **$85.00–90.00.**

Gondola with "Barber" Poles, 4½" [OP, R2]. **$125.00–150.00.**

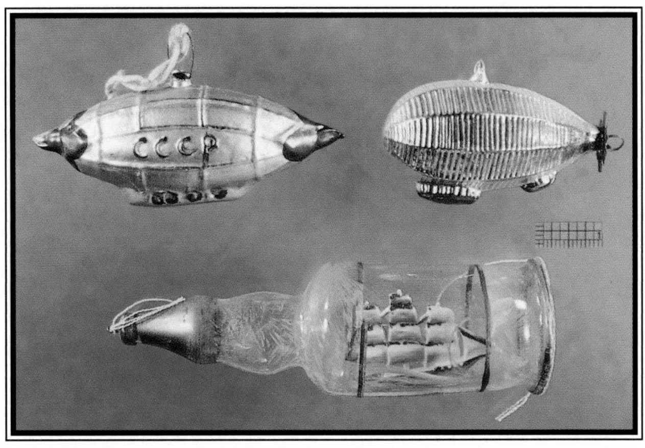

A. Russian Zeppelin, embossed "CCCP," 4½" [OP, R2]. **$75.00–100.00.** B. Zeppelin (Type II), small, 3½" [German, OP-NP (1950s, 1980s, & 1990s), R2]. Old, **$75.00–100.00.** 1980s version (shown), **$25.00–35.00.** C. Ship in a Bottle, 6" [OP, R1]. **$125.00–150.00.**

"Los Angeles"-Zeppelin, approx. 4¾" & 6" (shown). Also issued as a 4¾" size, with "LZ 127" embossed on it [German, OP-NP (Lauscha Glas 1995), R1]. Small, **$275.00–300.00.** Large, **$300.00–350.00.**

New Zeppelins Blown in Old Molds: A. Zeppelin with Two Heads, embossed, 4½" [German, OP-NP, R1+]. Old, **$650.00–750.00.** 1993 version, **$25.00–30.00.** B. Zeppelin (Type II), "Z R III," 3¼" [OP-NP, R1-2]. Old, **$75.00–85.00.** 1980s version **$15.00–20.00.** C. Zeppelin (Type I), embossed as such, 4" [OP-NP, R1-2]. Old, **$300.00–350.00.** 1992 version (shown), **$15.00–20.00.**

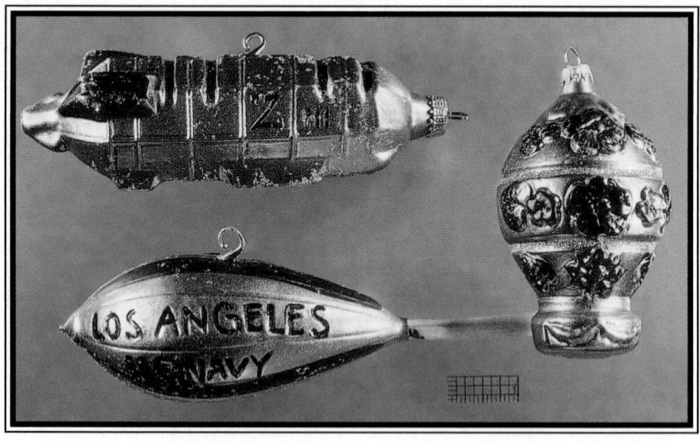

New Airships Blown in old Molds: A. Zeppelin, embossed "Z III," 5¾" [OP-NP (Lauscha Glas, 1994), R1+]. Old, **$350.00–400.00.** 1994 version, **$15.00–20.00.** B. Balloon, "Montgolfiere 1783," 3½" [OP-NP, R1+]. Old, **$350.00–400.00.** 1994 version, **$15.00–18.00.** C. Zeppelin, "Los Angeles U.S. Navy," 4¾" [German, OP-NP, R1]. Old, **$450.00–600.00.** 1994 version, **$15.00–20.00.**

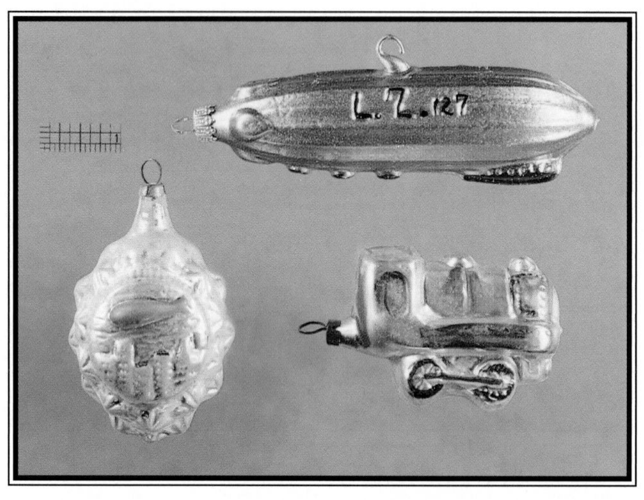

A. Zeppelin, "LZ 127," approx. 4¾" (shown) & 6" [German, OP-NP (Lauscha Glas, 1995), R1]. Old, **$275.00–325.00.** 1995 version (shown), **$20.00–25.00.** B. *Hindenburg* over New York, embossed, 2½" [OP-NP (1980s), R1-2]. **$125.00–150.00.** C. Locomotive (Type II), 2½" [OP-NP, R1-2]. Old, **$100.00–125.00.** 1980s version (shown), **$15.00–20.00.**

A. Locomotive (Type I), 3" [OP-NP (1950s), R1]. **$90.00–110.00.** B. Train, Passenger Cars, 1¾" [OP-NP, (1950s) R1]. **$30.00–45.00** each.

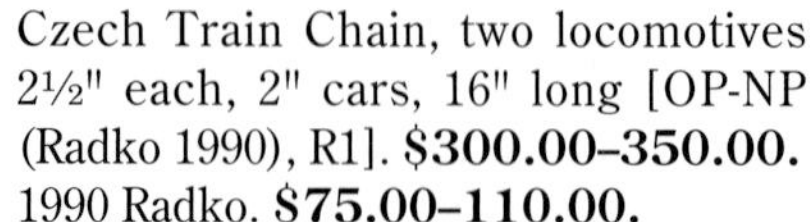

Czech Train Chain, two locomotives 2½" each, 2" cars, 16" long [OP-NP (Radko 1990), R1]. **$300.00–350.00.** 1990 Radko. **$75.00–110.00.**

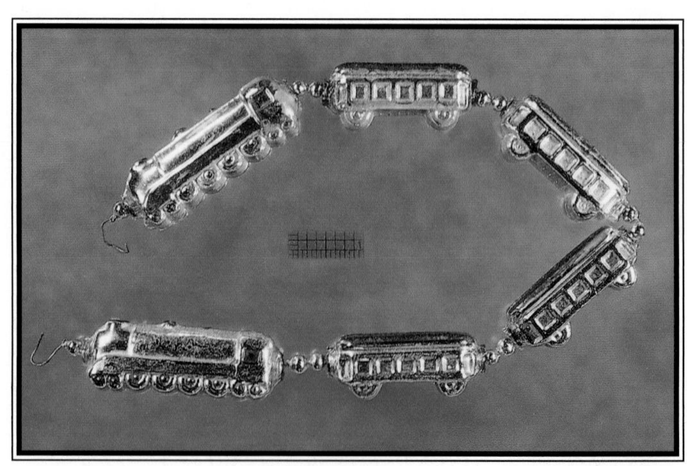

Trees

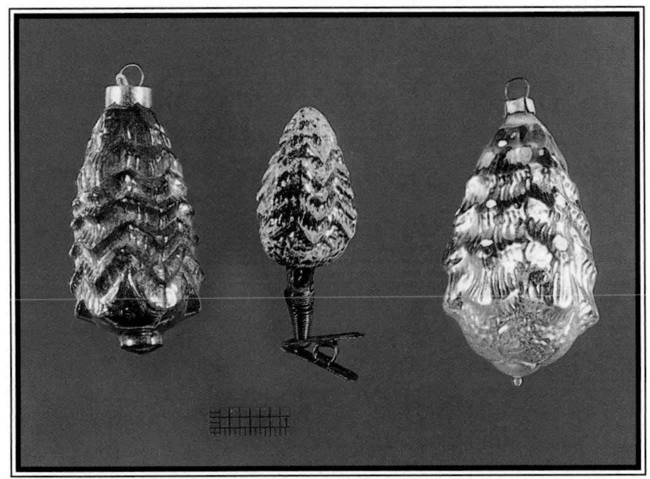

A. American Tree, approx. 3", made by Corning Glass [American, OP, R2]. **$25.00–35.00.** B. Standard Form Tree; 1¾", 2" (shown), 2½", 3", and 3½" [German, OP-NP (1970s), R3-4]. Small, **$15.00–25.00.** Medium, **$20.00–25.00.** Large, **$30.00–40.00.** For clip-ons add **$10.00.** C. "Decorated" tree, 3" [German, OP-NP (1970s), R3]. **$30.00–35.00.**

A. Standard Form Tree, clip on, 3½" [German, OP-NP (1970s), R3-4]. **$30.00–40.00.** B. House Under a Tree, approx. 3" [OP-NP (1980s), R2]. **$65.00–85.00.** C. Santa Face Under a Pine Tree, 3½" [German, OP, R3]. **$75.00–90.00.**

A. Tree on a Ball, 5¼" [OP, R2-3]. **$125.00–150.00.** B. Tree on a Three-sided Ornament, 2½" [OP, R1-2]. **$30.00–45.00.** C. Tree with a Trunk, small, 2¾" [OP, R3]. **$12.00–18.00.**

Tree Chandelier, 4" [OP, R1+]. **$200.00–250.00.**

Miscellaneous

American Made War Ornaments, circa 1942 – 1943 [R3-4]. Balls, **$3.00–4.00.** Fancy shapes, **$5.00–8.00.**

Ball Shape Variations: American War Ornaments, circa 1944 – 1945, note paper caps [R3-4]. **$6.00–8.00** (only with paper caps).

Balls with Stencil Decoration, circa 1950s [R5]. **$1.00–2.00.**

Balls with Decal Decorations, all circa 1950s: A. Mickey Mouse [R2]. **$18.00–25.00.** B. Angel [R2]. **$5.00–10.00.** C. Donald Duck [R2]. **$18.00–25.00.**

A & C. Two Glass Balls with Colored Glass Stripes [OP, R2]. Large (3"), **$25.00–35.00.** Small (1¾"), **$15.00–25.00.** B. Fancy Molded Shape, 2½" [OP-NP, R5]. Medium, **$6.00–12.00.**

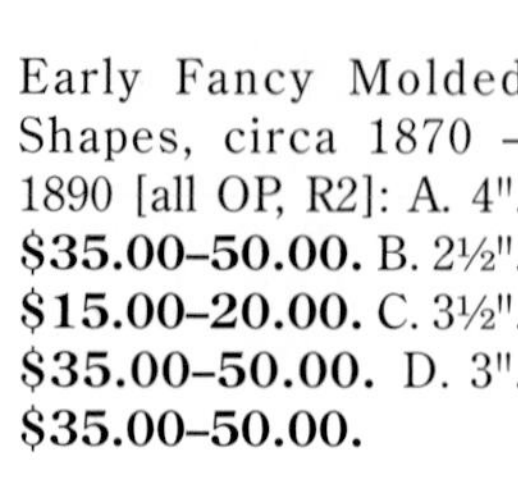

Early Fancy Molded Shapes, circa 1870 – 1890 [all OP, R2]: A. 4". **$35.00–50.00.** B. 2½". **$15.00–20.00.** C. 3½". **$35.00–50.00.** D. 3". **$35.00–50.00.**

Six Fancy Molded Shapes, small, approx. 2" [OP-NP, R5]. **$3.00–8.00** each.

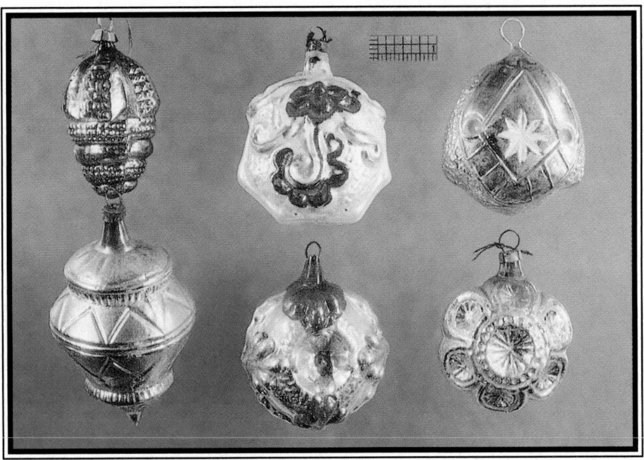

German Fancy Molded Shapes, all approx. 2", better quality [OP-NP, R5]. **$10.00–15.00** each.

Fancy Molded Shapes, 2½" – 3" [OP-NP, R5]. **$15.00–25.00.**

Fancy Molded Shapes, American made, circa 1930 – 1940, approx. 2" – 2½" [OP, R3-4]. **$5.00–10.00.**

A Selection of Fancy German Shapes, all mold made, approx. 2" – 2½" [German, OP, R4]. **$5.00–10.00.**

A Collection of Fancy American Shapes: All of these are mold made circa 1935 – 1940. The two cylindrical, pleated-looking shapes are *Odawara*-type Japanese lanterns. Approx. 2" – 3" [OP, R4-5]. **$4.00–7.00.**

A Collection of American Fancy Molded Ornaments, circa 1935 – 1940: A. Fruit Basket, 2" [R2]. **$10.00–15.00.** B. Guitar, 2" [R2]. **$5.00–10.00.** C. Rose with a Hip of Leaves, 2½" [R3]. **$4.00–6.00.** D. Square Lantern, 2¾" [R3]. **$3.00–5.00.** E & F. Large & Small Gifu Lanterns, 3" & 2½". **$3.00–8.00.** G, H, I. Bells; 2", 2½", & 2¾" [R5]. **$1.00–3.00.** J. Candle, 3½" [R4]. **$2.00–3.00.**

A Collection of American Figural Ornaments, all circa 1930 – 1940s: A. Santa, 3" [R2]. **$75.00–90.00.** B. Grapes on a Heart, 3" [R2]. **$20.00–30.00.** C. Father Christmas on a Leaf, 3½" [R3]. **$40.00–50.00.** D. Pine Tree, 3" [R2]. **$25.00–35.00.** E. Bunch of Grapes (Type II), 3" [R3]. **$5.00–8.00.** F. Small Bunch of Grapes (Type I), 1½" [R5]. **$2.00–3.00.** G & H. Pine Cones, 1¾" & 2¾" [R3-4]. **$5.00–10.00.**

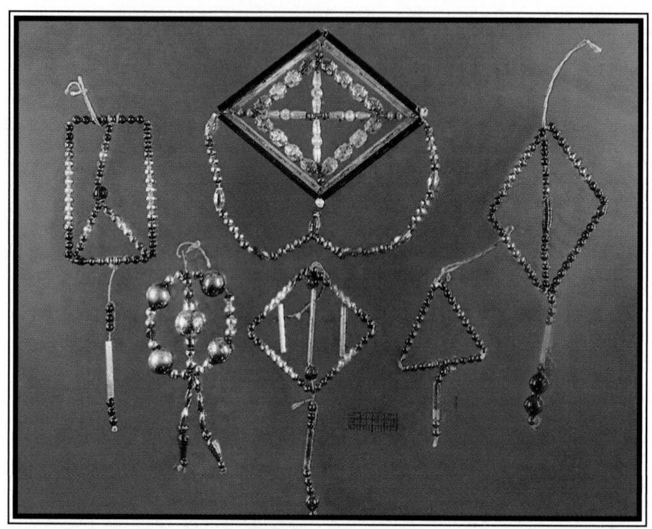

A Collection of Various Czech Beaded Ornaments in Geometric Shapes [OP, R4]: Diamond-shaped pendant (center top), **$25.00–35.00.** Others, **$5.00–10.00.**

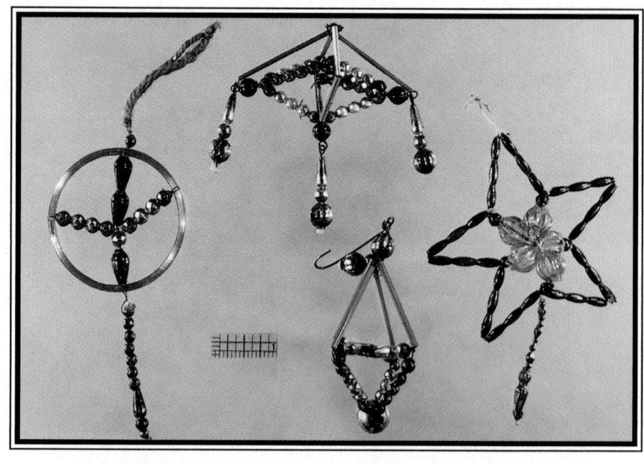

Beaded Ornament Shapes [probably Czech, OP-NP, R4]. **$5.00–10.00.**

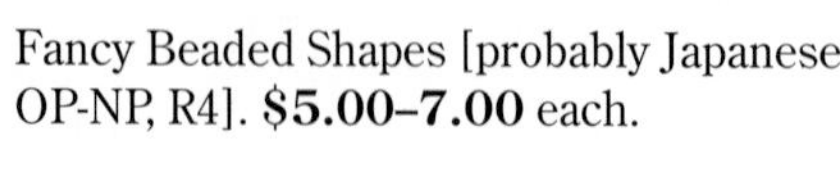

Fancy Beaded Shapes [probably Japanese OP-NP, R4]. **$5.00–7.00** each.

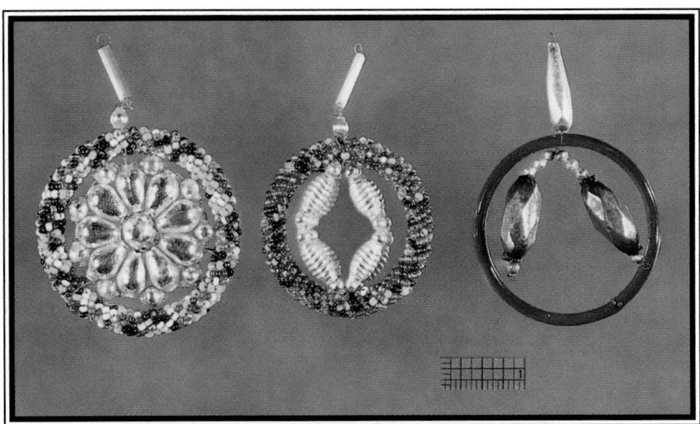

Czech Glass Ring Ornaments, all made circa 1920–1930 of decorated glass rings; in *A* & *B*, the rings are wrapped with strands of tiny glass beads: A. Beaded Ring with Silver Flower Center, approx. 2¼" dia. [R1]. **$35.00–45.00.** B. Beaded Ring with a Silver Oval, approx. 2" dia. [R1]. **$30.00–35.00.** C. Ring with Blue Faceted Dangles, approx. 2¼" [R2-3]. **$15.00–20.00.**

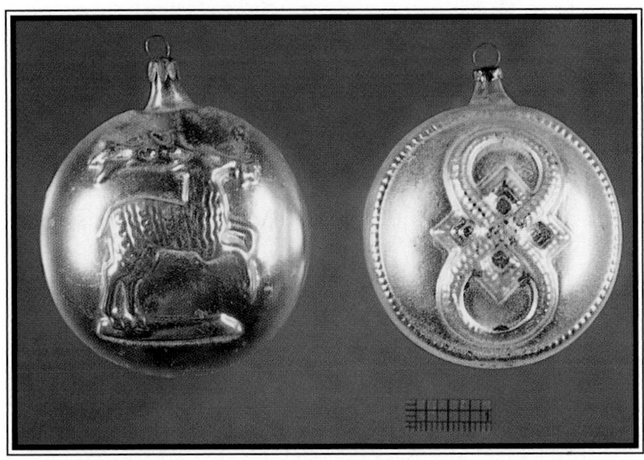

Nazi and Glass Runic Ornaments, approx. 1¾" dia. The stag ornament has a stylized stag head on the back. The same runic design is embossed on both sides of the second ornament. They were produced in the 1930 – 1940s and called *Julschmuck,* or "Yule ornaments." Each rune had a specific meaning [R1]. **$90.00–110.00** each.

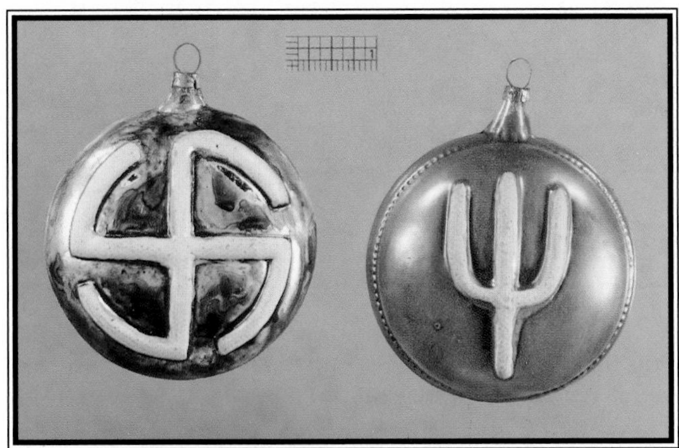

Nazi ornaments: A. Swastika Ornament, 2" [OP, R1+]. **$175.00–200.00.** B. Runic Ornament, 2" [OP, R1]. **$90.00–110.00.**

Czech Fluorescent Glass Ornaments. The insides of the glass beads are coated with a fluorescent impregnated wax so that they will glow in the dark. All made circa 1930 [R1+]: A. Berry, approx. 2¼". **$50.00–75.00.** B. Faceted Dangle, approx. 1⅛". **$30.00–45.00.** C. Oblong, approx. 3"L x 2½"H. **$50.00–60.00.**

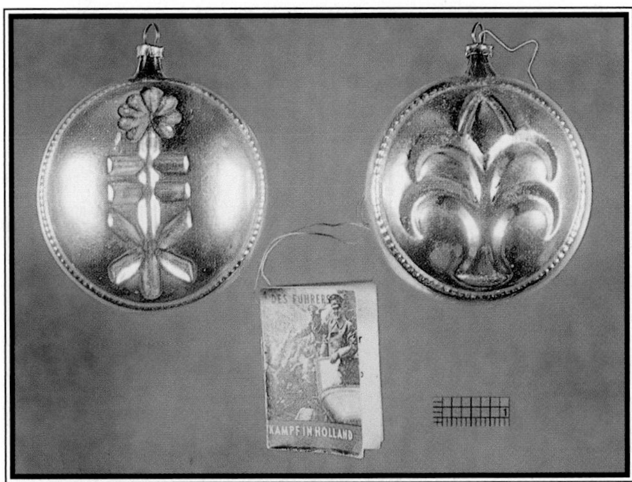

A & B. Nazi Ornament and Glass Runic Ornament, each approx. 1¾" dia. The same runic design is embossed on both sides of the glass ornaments. They were produced in the 1930 – 1940s, and called *Julschmuck,* or "Yule ornaments," instead of Christmas ornaments. Each rune had a specific meaning [R1]. **$90.00–110.00** each. C. Paper Book about Adolf Hitler, approx. 2". A whole series of these were produced for children and were hung on trees during the war years. They glorified the Nazi leaders and war campaigns [R1]. **$40.00–60.00.**

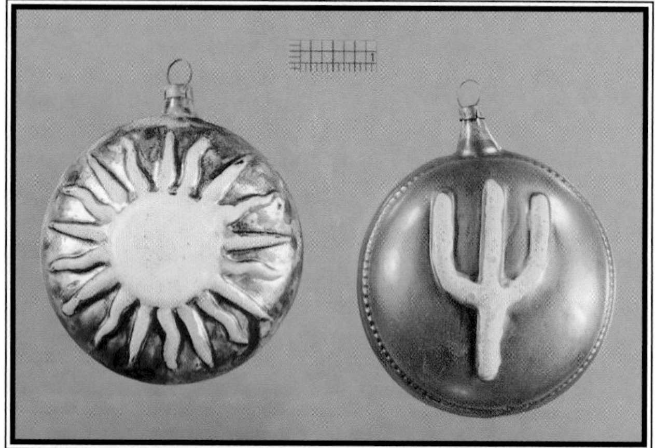

Nazi ornaments: A. Swastika reverse. B. Runic reverse.

Bomb, approx. 1¾". This could more accurately be described as an artillery shell. The number embossed at the top represents the size of the shell. The other design is perhaps the German Imperial Eagle. These were produced during World War I [German, OP, R1]. **$200.00–250.00.**

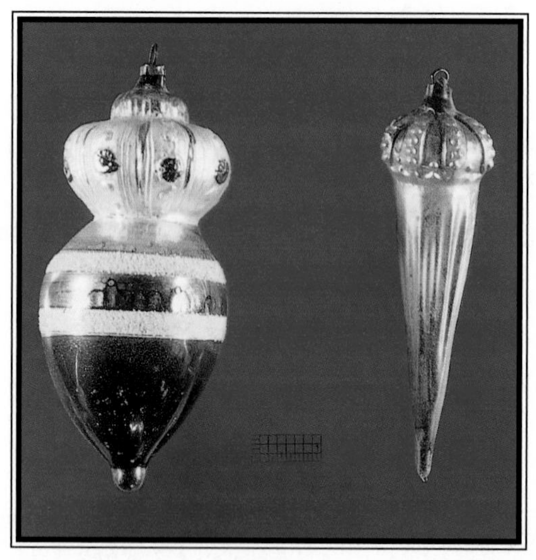

A. Crown on an Egg, large, 5½" [OP, R1-2]. **$75.00–100.00.** B. Crown on a Cone, 5¼" [OP, R2]. **$50.00–75.00.**

A. Indented Ornament with a Daisy, 5½", circa 1890 [OP, R2]. **$60.00–85.00.** B. French Crown on a Pike, 2½" crown, 5½" overall [OP, R1]. **$75.00–100.00.**

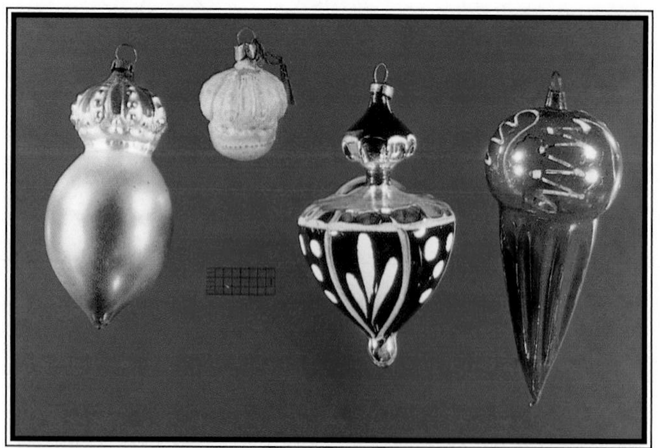

A. Crown on an Egg, 3½" [German, OP, R1-2]. **$40.00–60.00.** B. Crown, 1¼" [OP, R3]. **$15.00–20.00.** C. Toy Top, 3½" [OP, R3-4]. **$5.00–10.00.** C. Ice Cream Cone, 4" [OP, R4]. **$5.00–10.00.**

Glass balls with decorations inside: A. Cardboard Church, 3¼" [OP, R3]. **$25.00–30.00.** B. Celluloid Deer and Trees, 3¼" [R3]. **$15.00–20.00.**

Glass Shapes with Decorations Inside: A. Oblong and Ball with Dresden Angel, 3½" [OP, R2]. **$50.00–75.00.** B. Egg Shape with Jesus in Manger, with scrap, 4¼" [OP, R2]. **$50.00–75.00.**

Glass Balls with Miniature Ornaments Inside, 1½" ornaments inside, approx. 2½" overall [German, OP, R1-2]. A. Bird. **$90.00–110.00.** B. Santa. **$90.00–110.00.** C. Swan. **$90.00–110.00.**

Three Scrap and Glass Ornaments. The scraps are enclosed in the ornaments and seen through clear glass windows: A. Angel, 3". **$50.00–75.00.** B. Children, 2". **$50.00–75.00.** C. Jesus, 3". **$50.00–75.00.**

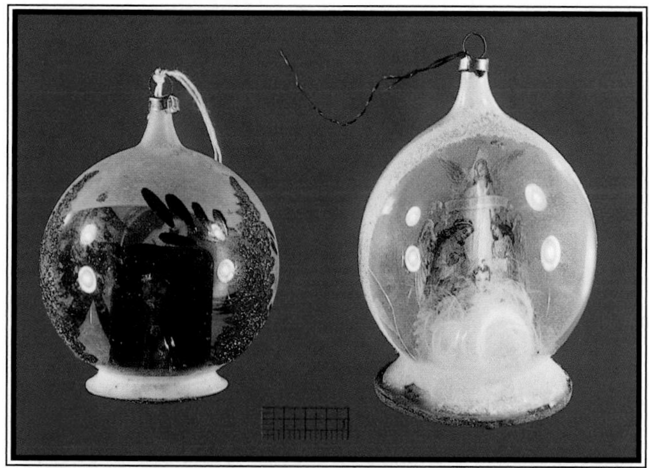

Glass Balls with Decorations Inside: A. Composition Angel (Type I), 3" [R2]. **$30.00–50.00.** B. Scrap Nativity, 3½" [OP, R2]. **$40.00–55.00.**

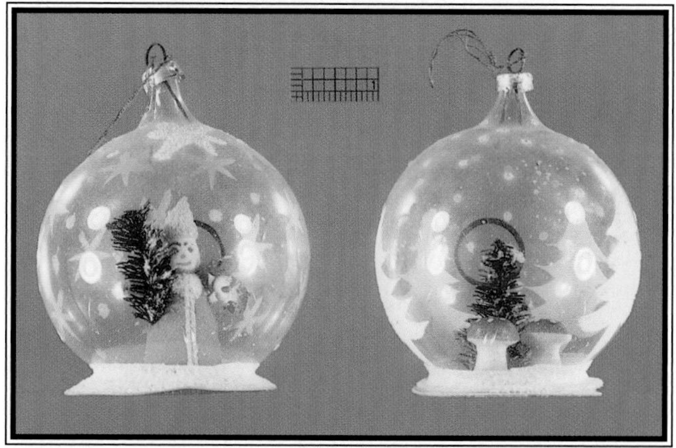

Glass Balls with Decorations Inside: A. Snow Girl, cotton, 3" [R2]. **$15.00–20.00.** B. Celluloid Mushrooms, 3", circa 1950 [R3]. **$25.00–30.00.**

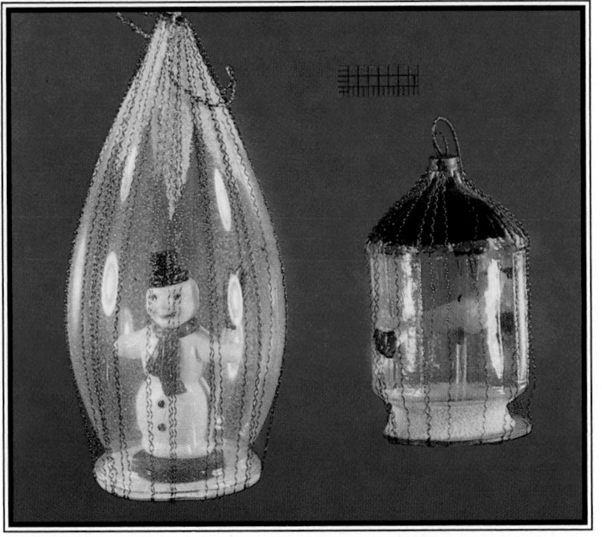

Glass Shapes with Decoration Inside: A. Oblong Shape with Celluloid Snowman, 6", circa 1950 [R3]. **$25.00–30.00.** B. Birdcage with Molded Glass Bird, 3½" [OP, R1-2]. **$75.00–100.00.**

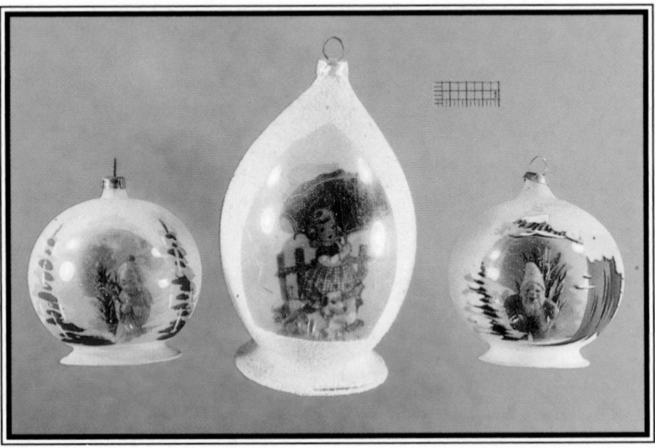

Ornaments with Decorations Inside: A. Angel (Type II), composition, 2½" [OP, R2]. **$30.00–40.00.** B. Egg Shape with Scrap of Girl and Umbrella, circa 1950s, 4½" [R2-3]. **$25.00–35.00.** C. Dwarf, composition, 3" [OP, R2]. **$40.00–50.00.**

Acorn with Extended Arms, 4½" [OP, R2]. **$200.00–250.00.**

A. Bell with Embossed Cherries and Extended Arms, 2¾" [OP, R2]. **$150.00–175.00.** B. Cupcake with Extended Arms, 3½" [OP, R2]. **$100.00–125.00.**

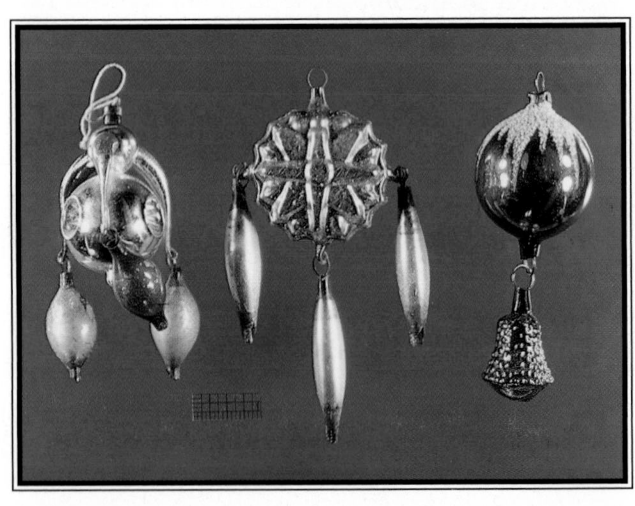

A. Indented Ball with Three Extended Arms, approx. 3" [OP, R2]. **$100.00–125.00.** B. Sunburst with Hanging Ornaments, approx. 4" [OP, R1-2]. **$50.00–75.00.** C. Ball with a Hanging Bell, approx. 3½" [OP, R2]. **$30.00–40.00.**

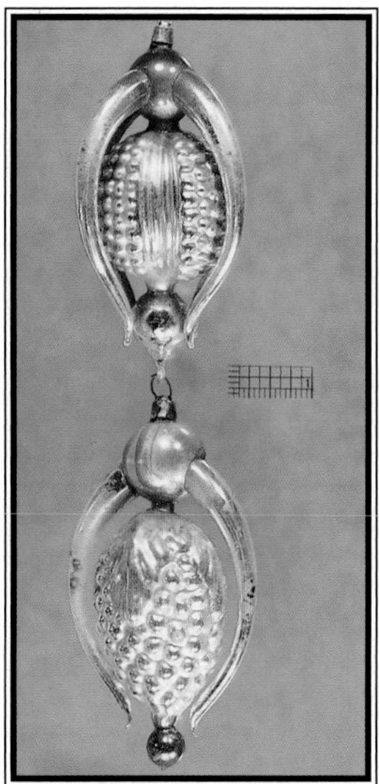

Double Fantasy with Extended Arms, circa 1890, 8¼" [OP, R1+]. **$275.00–350.00.**

Ornaments with Extended Arms: A. Pine Cones, three arms, 3½" [OP, R1-2]. **$150.00–200.00.** Indented Ball, three arms, 4" [OP, R2]. **$125.00–150.00.**

Water Fountain, approx. 4¾"H. Made of free-blown and annealed glass, this is probably Italian, circa late 1940s – 1950s [R2]. **$65.00–85.00.**

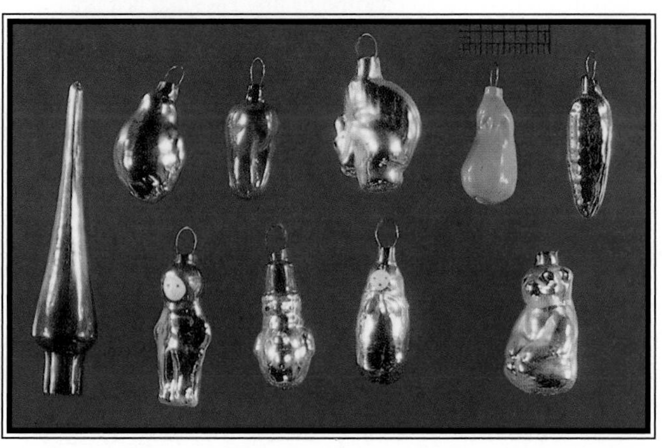

Russian Miniature Ornaments and Original Box, approx. 1" – 1½", circa 1950s – 1960s [R1]. Ten ornaments in original box labeled simply "tree decorations," **$50.00–75.00.**

Dresden Ornaments

Dresden embossed cardboard ornaments are some of the most beautiful, durable, and cleverly made ornaments to adorn the Christmas tree. Since they were never as popular in the United States as they were in Germany, they also remain some of the rarest and most expensive of Christmas ornaments.

The name *Dresden* came about because most of these pieces were produced by approximately nine companies in the Dresden-Leipzig-Furth area of Germany, from about 1880 until the time of World War II. During this time, a vast variety of shapes and sizes were produced. Although many were only 2-3 inches in size and embossed in a metallic gold or silver, others were considerably larger and realistically painted.The term *Dresden* is often incorrectly applied to any cardboard die-cut or embossed paper item. It should only refer to that type of German paper ornament that has been embossed and cut from detailed dies, and not merely constructed of cardboard.

Stamping a 1/32-inch sheet of cardboard between two dies produced Dresden ornaments. One die was the stamping die, and the other the receiving die, which was like a negative. Each minutely detailed area on the stamping die was raised, and the corresponding area on the recieving die was depressed. Thus, a double-sided ornament would require four separate dies, since each side is the reverse, or mirror image, of the other. And each three-dimensional ornament would require two separate dies for each applied piece. This intricate die work gave the ornament its charming detail. After embossing and cutting, cottage laborers then gently glued and assembled the applied pieces, and painted them when necessary.

The more intricate a piece was, the more labor was involved, and the more expensive the piece became. Cost is one reason for the scarcity of Dresden in this country; these ornaments did not compete well against the cheaper glass ornaments. One would assume that the highly elaborate three-dimensional pieces such as carriages, locomotives, passenger ships, etc., cost around thirty-five cents apiece at the turn of the century. At the same time, fancy glass ornaments were selling at a penny or less apiece.

The Dresden ornament is usually found in one of three forms:

1. Flat: This type of ornament is designed to be printed and embossed on only one side. The reverse side can be plain card board, but was usually painted with gold or silver ink to avoid a plain cardboard look if the ornament were to turn with the air current or the back be seen through the tree. This Dresden may be nearly flat with shallow embossing or may be deeply pressed and embossed to give a more rounded look. The flat could be embellished with scraps or lithographs, or with touches of lacquered color. Because of its simple form, the flat tends to be the least expensive.
2. Double: This type of ornament is embossed and colored on two sides. In one style, matching mirror images have been glued together so that the piece gives the same appearance from either side. In a second style, one can see the front and back of an animal, person, etc., not just the mirror image of it. A double is usually about 1/8" to 1/2" thick and made of only two pieces. Generally, they are not wide enough to stand up by themselves; in fact, many may be found as flats, because doubles sometimes became separated through the years and are now often sold as separate pieces.
3. Three-dimensional: This elaborate type of ornament is more like a small model and was usually made up of many small detailed pieces glued together. Most three-dimensional ornaments will stand up by themselves, so they will have a width of 1/2" or more. This form is the most rare, desirable, intricate, beautiful, and expensive.

Any of these types of Dresdens could have been stamped from gold or silver paper, or readily been painted a natural color. Many come with a small loop of string or thread from which they were hung.

Flat, double, and three-dimensional Dresdens have all been reproduced in limited amounts and limited styles. It appears that small, delicate trim pieces have been in almost continuous production.

Russian Dresdens appear to have been made only as doubles, finished in gold, silver, and natural paints. The gold is a brass color, the silver is an aluminum leaf, and the paints are muted pastels that are finely done. It is currently believed that production of Russian Dresdens began in the 1920s and ran through the 1970s. As a group, the Dresdens create a shimmering magic that was once the glory of the Christmas tree.

Explanation of Abbreviations and Terms:

Applied	Pieces that were molded separately and glued on or applied to the ornament.
G/S	Gold or silver. The object is embossed and coated with a gold or silver metallic leaf, for an original bright, shiny finish.
Natural	The ornament has been painted in a realistic or natural manner.
Flat	The described ornament is printed on one side only.
Double	The ornament is made of at least two mirror images glued together.
3-D	The ornament is three-dimensional and does not have a flat appearance.
Gelatin	Colored cellophane, often placed behind the open spaces on the ornament to give the appearance of a colored background. It was also added to colorful rosettes, stars, etc.; many times this gelatin will be found torn or taken completely off the ornament.
[R1]	The rarity of the item is rated as a one.
OP	All pieces are before 1940 unless otherwise noted.

A. Gecko, 4" [OP, R1]. **$850.00–950.00.** B. Alligator, 4" [OP, R2]. **$450.00–500.00.** C. Frog, 2" [OP, R2]. **$400.00–475.00.**

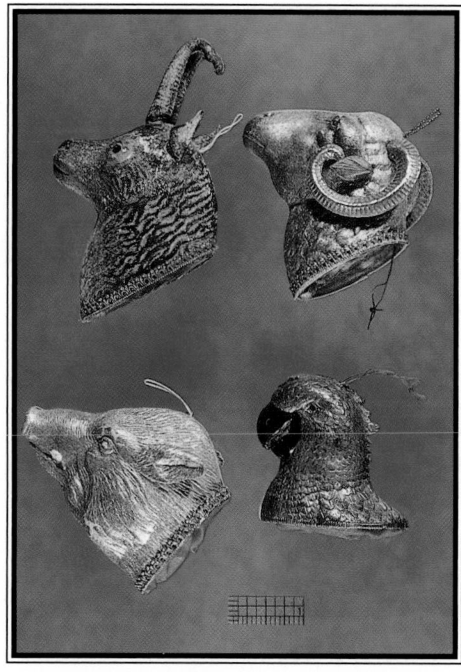

Dresden Candy Containers [all OP, R1]: A. Antelope, 3¾". **$1,200.00–1,500.00.** B. Ram, 2½". **$1,200.00–1,500.00.** C. Boar, 2½". **$1,600.00–1,800.00.** D. Parrot, 1¾". **$1,600.00–1,800.00.**

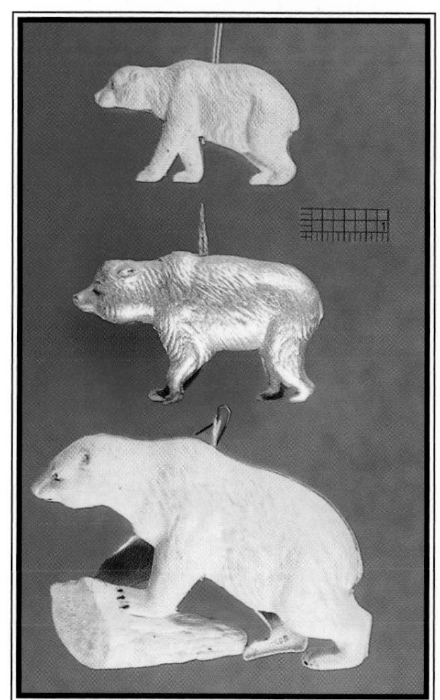

A. Polar Bear, 2¾" [OP, R2]. **$350.00–450.00.** B. Polar Bear, 3" [OP, R1-2]. **$450.00–550.00.** C. Polar Bear on a Rock, 4"L x 2¾"H [OP, R1]. **$600.00–750.00.**

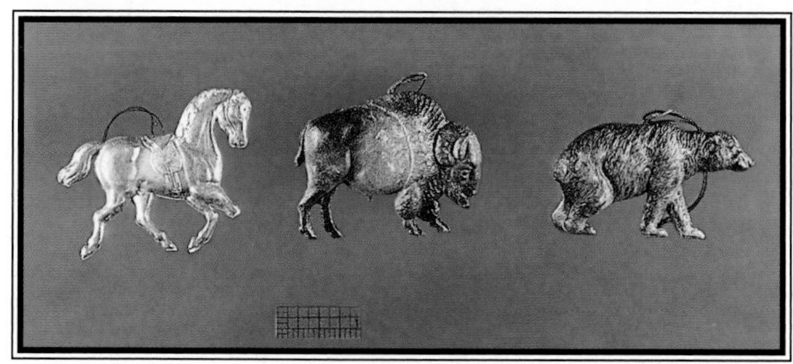

A. Prancing Horse (Type II), 2¼" [OP, R2]. **$160.00–180.00.** B. Buffalo, double, 2¼" [OP, R2]. **$275.00–300.00.** C. Brown Bear, double, 2½" [OP, R2–3]. **$275.00–325.00.**

A. Dancing Bear with Stick, 3¼" [OP, R1]. **$800.00–900.00.** B. Polar Bear on Ice, 2"W [OP, R1–2]. **$275.00–300.00.** C. Bear with Trainer, 3"L x 2"H [OP, R1+]. **$1,700.00–2,000.00.**

A. Running Dog, 3"L [OP, R2]. **$375.00–425.00.** B. Flying Eagle, small, 3¾" wing span [OP, R2]. **$475.00–525.00.**

A. Ostrich (Type I), 4" [OP, R1–2]. **$500.00–650.00.** B. Flying Eagle, large, 6¼" wing span [OP, R2]. **$650.00–750.00.** C. Stork (Type I), 4"H [OP, R2–3]. **$250.00–300.00.**

A. Cockatiel, 2½" [OP, R1]. **$1,600.00–1,800.00.** B. Horse, 3" [OP–NP, R2]. **$1,200.00–1,400.00.** C. Rooster (Type II), 3" [OP, R1]. **$1,500.00–1,650.00.**

A. Opera Glasses Candy Container, 3"W x 2"H [OP, R1–2]. **$500.00–650.00.** B. Sparrow, 4"L [OP, R1–2]. **$200.00–225.00.** C. Poulter Pigeon, 3½" [R1–2]. **$200.00–225.00.**

A. Homing Pigeon, 3"L x 2¾"H [OP, R2]. **$350.00–425.00.** B. Flamingo, 4"H [R1]. **$425.00–475.00.** C. Condor, 3"H [R1]. **$425.00–475.00.**

A. Gold Finch, 2½"L [OP, R1–2]. **$325.00–375.00.** B. Ostrich (Type II), 4½"L [R1–2]. **$600.00–750.00.** C. Birdie on a Branch, 3"L [OP, R1]. **$400.00–450.00.**

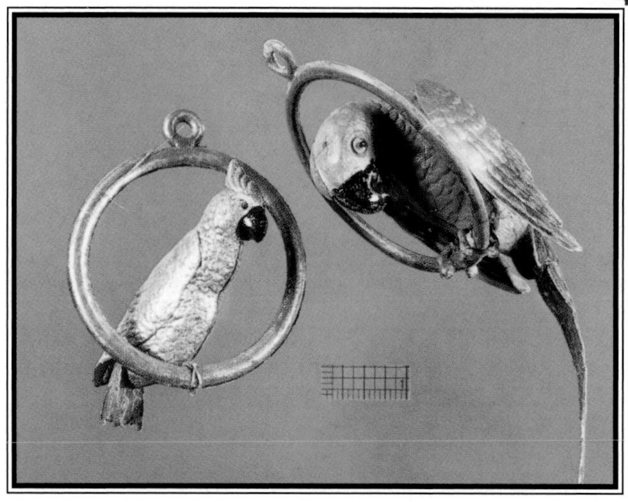

A. Cockatiel on a Swing, 3¾" [OP, R1]. **$575.00–675.00.** B. Parrot on a Swing, 6"L [OP, R1]. **$650.00–750.00.**

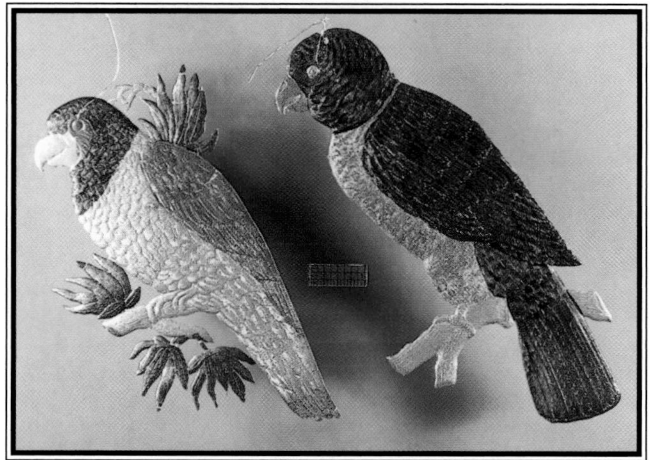

A. Parrot on a Branch with Leaves, flat, 7¾"L [OP, R2]. **$150.00–175.00.** B. Parrot on a Branch (Type II), flat, 9"L [OP, R2]. **$150.00–175.00.**

Peacock, flat, 7"H [OP, R2]. **$150.00–175.00.** B. Pheasant, flat, 6"H [OP, R2]. **$150.00–175.00.**

A. Duck (Type II), 3"H [OP, R2–3]. **$450.00–550.00.** B. Turkey, hen, 2¾"L [OP, R2]. **$425.00–500.00.** C. Tom Turkey, 2¼" [OP, R2]. **$450.00–550.00.**

A. Turkey Candy Container, 4" x 3½" [OP, R1–2]. **$450.00–550.00.** B. Swan Candy Container, 2¾" x 3" [OP, R1–2]. **$450.00–550.00.**

A. Moose, double, 2¼" x 2¼" [R2–3]. **$125.00–175.00.** B. Turkey, 2½" x 2½" [R2–3]. **$90.00–120.00.** C. Comet with Embossed Tail, double [OP, R2]. **$65.00–75.00.**

A. Duck (Type I), 3–D, approx. 2½"H x 3"L [German, OP, R2]. **$450.00–550.00.** B. Rooster, 3–D, approx. 3"H [German, OP, R2]. **$500.00–575.00.**

A. Chinese Rooster, 4½"L [OP, R1]. **$450.00–550.00.** B. Perch, 3½"L; Dresden fish are so accurately molded they can be identified as to type [OP, R3]. **$300.00–325.00.**

Birdcage, large, flat, 7¼"L (shown) & 4½"L [OP, R3]. Small, **$90.00–110.00.** Large, **$110.00–135.00.**

Rooster Candy Container, 3–D, 2¾"H & 3¼" [OP, R1–2]. Small, **$900.00–1,000.00.** Large, **$1,000.00–1,200.00.**

A. Owl on a Crescent Moon, 5¾" [OP, R2]. **$140.00–160.00.** B. Rooster Head, 5½" [OP, R1-2]. **$125.00–150.00.**

A. Perch, 3½" [OP, R3]. **$300.00–325.00.** B. Geometric Shape Candy Container, 3–D, 2¼" [OP, R1]. **$150.00–175.00.** C. Flying Songbird, 3¼" [OP, R1]. **$550.00–600.00.**

A. Rooster Dressed in Crepe Paper, 2¼" [OP, R1]. **$700.00–800.00.** B. Puss 'n Boots, 3" [OP, R1]. **$750.00–850.00.** C. Donkey (Type I), 3–D, 2" [OP, R2–3]. **$350.00–425.00.**

A. Proud Peacock, 3–D, 4¼"H [OP, R2–3]. **$600.00–700.00.** B. Black Cat, arched back, 3–D, 4"H, also used as a Halloween favor [OP, R2]. **$500.00–600.00.**

A. Sitting Owl, 3–D, small, 3¼" [OP–NP (1990s), R1–2]. **$450.00–550.00.** B. Charging Bull, 2"H x 3¼"L [OP, R1]. **$500.00–650.00.** C. Standing Dachshund, 2¼"H x 4½"L [OP, R1–2]. **$475.00–550.00.**

A. Camel, flat, 4¾" x 3¼"H [OP, R3]. **$140.00–160.00.** B. Camel with Packages, flat, 3¾"H [OP, R2]. **$125.00–150.00.**

A. Camel with Arab Rider, small, 3½" x 3¼" [OP, R1–2]. **$750.00–850.00.** B. Dresden–like Jockey on a Horse, 4½" x 3¾" [OP, R1]. **$175.00–200.00.**

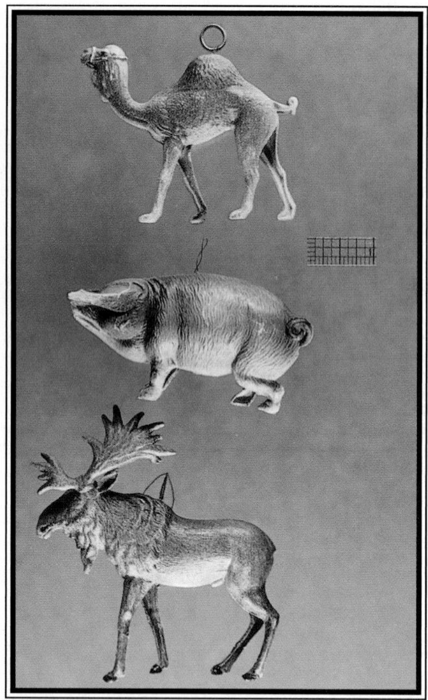

A. Walking Camel, 3–D, 3"W x 2½"H [OP, R2]. **$175.00–200.00.** B. Pig, 3–D, 3½" [OP, R2]. **$450.00–600.00.** C. Moose, 3–D, small, 3½"H [OP, R3]. **$350.00–400.00.**

A. Mooing Cow, 3"H x 5¼"W [R2]. **$95.00–115.00.** B. Cow, 6½"W x 4½"H [R2–3]. **$125.00–150.00.**

Two Dresden Flats: A. Racehorse and Rider, approx. 5" [OP, R2]. **$100.00–125.00.** Cow with a Milk Pail, approx. 4¼" [OP, R2]. **$95.00–115.00.**

A. Walking Lion, double, 3½"L [OP–NP, R2]. **$125.00–150.00.** B. Reindeer or Stag, double, 2"L [OP, R2–3]. **$125.00–150.00.**

A. Reindeer or Stag, 3–D, 3½" [OP, R3]. **$275.00–325.00.** B. Salamander, 3–D, 4" [OP, R1]. **$400.00–450.00.**

A. Stag, flat, 5"H [OP, R2]. **$125.00–150.00.** B. Insect Larva, double, 4"L [OP, R1–2]. **$120.00–140.00.** C. Mallard Duck, flat, 4½"H [OP, R2]. **$125.00–150.00.**

A. Pug with Muzzle and Leash, 3½" [OP, R1]. **$550.00–600.00.** B. Standing Dachshund, 4½"L [OP, R1–2]. **$400.00–475.00.**

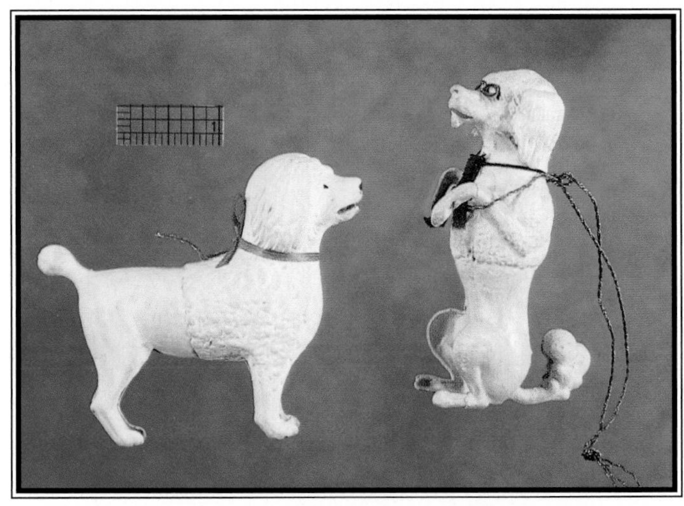

A. Poodle, 3¼"L [OP, R1–2]. **$450.00–525.00.** B. Begging Poodle with Glasses and Tie, 3¼" [OP, R1]. **$500.00–550.00.**

A. Doghouse Candy Container, 1¾"H x 2¼"L [OP, R1]. **$300.00–400.00.** B. Weimeraner, 3"H x 3½"L [OP, R1–2]. **$450.00–500.00.**

A. Dwarf with a Money Bag, 3-D, 3½" [OP, R1–2]. **$700.00–800.00.** B. Crouched Cat, 3-D, 3¼" [OP, R2–3]. **$550.00–600.00.** C. Sitting Spaniel, 3-D, 2¾" [OP, R2]. **$500.00–550.00.**

A. Sitting Spaniel, 3-D, 2¾" [OP, R2]. **$500.00–550.00.** B. Standing Rabbit, flat, 4½" [OP, R2–3]. **$90.00–110.00.**

A. Barking Bulldog, double, 3¾"L [OP, R2]. **$450.00–475.00.** B. Stork (Type II), 3–D, 3½"H [OP, R2–3]. **$250.00–300.00.**

Dog and Doghouse, 3–D, approx. 2"W x 1¾"H [German, OP, R1–2]. **$750.00–850.00.**

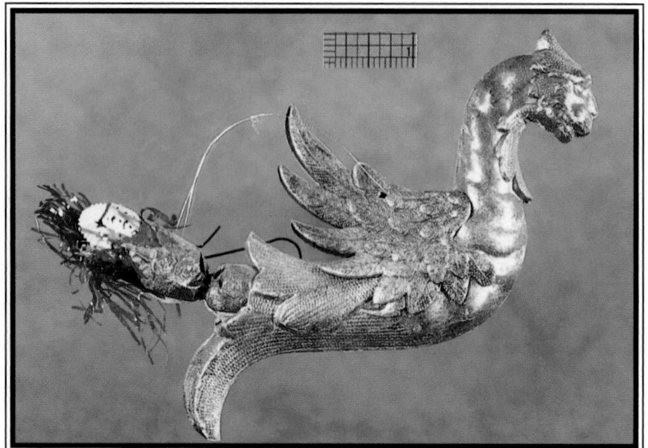

Flying Dragon Candy Container, 6"L [OP, R1]. **$1,200.00–1,400.00.**

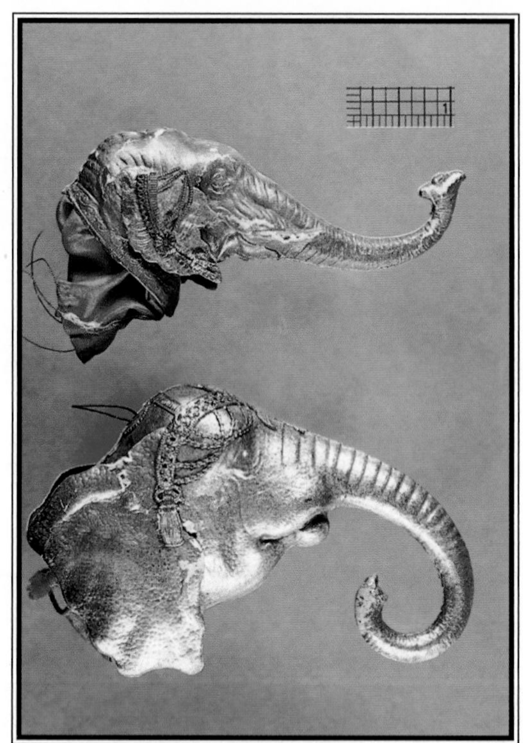

A. Circus Elephant Head Candy Container with Extended Trunk, 4"L [OP, R1]. **$1,400.00–1,600.00.** B. Circus Elephant Head Candy Container, 3⅞"L [OP, R1–2]. **$1,500.00–1,800.00.**

A. Elephant, "Jumbo," 3"H x 4"L [OP, R1–2]. **$100.00–115.00.** B. Donkey Carrying a Basket, 3½"H x 4¾"L [OP, R2]. **$110.00–125.00.** C. Cow with Milk Pail, 3"H x 5"L [OP, R2]. **$100.00–120.00.**

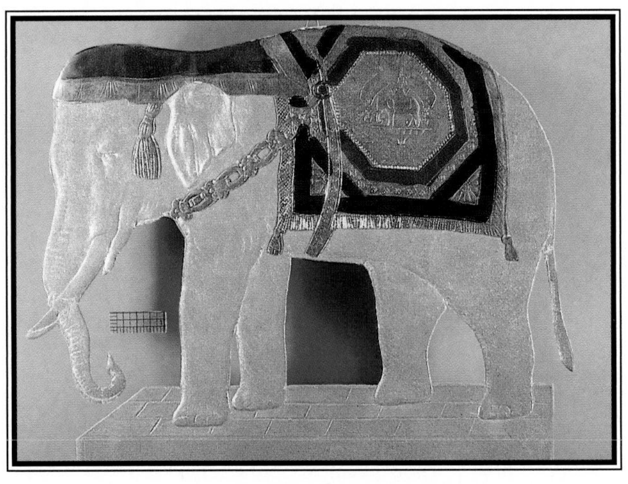

Circus Elephant with a Blanket, flat, 8¼"H x 9½"L [OP, R2]. **$120.00–140.00.**

A. Giraffe, flat, 6½"H [OP, R2]. **$125.00–135.00.** B. Elephant Pull Toy, flat, 4"H x 5½"W [OP, R2]. **$125.00–140.00.**

A. Elephant with a Dog on Its Back, 3–D, 2¾"H x 3"W [OP, R1]. **$700.00–850.00.** B. Racehorse, 3–D, 3½" x 3½" [R2–3]. **$450.00–500.00.**

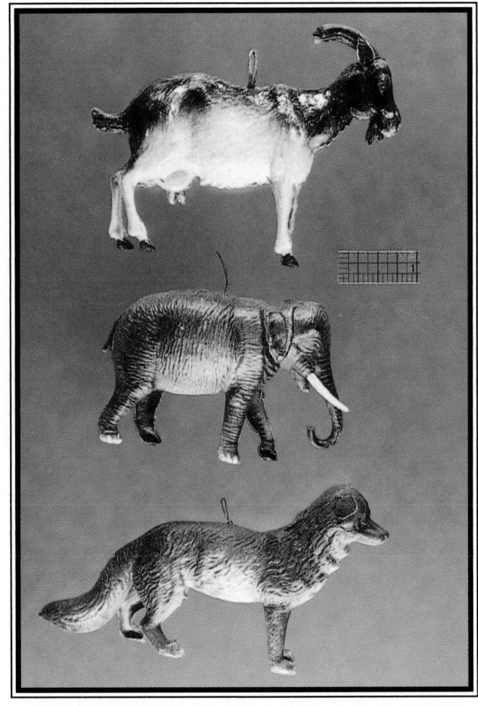

A. Nanny Goat, 3–D, large, 4" [OP, R2–3]. **$400.00–500.00.** B. Walking Elephant, 3–D, 3" [OP, R2–3]. **$375.00–425.00.** C. Fox, 3–D, large, 4¾" [OP, R2]. **$375.00–425.00.**

A. Elephant with its Trunk Up, double, 3½"H [OP, R2]. **$275.00–300.00.** B. Terrapin/Turtle, 3–D, 3½" [OP, R1–2]. **$375.00–400.00.** C. Arched-back Cat, double, 2½" [OP, R2–3]. **$200.00–250.00.**

Swimming Carp, 6¼" [OP, R1–2]. **$500.00–650.00.**

A. Fantasy Fish Porpoise Candy Container, 4" [OP–NP (2000), R1]. **$550.00–650.00.** B. Bluegill (Type II), 4¼" [OP, R2]. **$200.00–250.00.** C. Large Carp, 7½" [OP, R1]. **$550.00–650.00.**

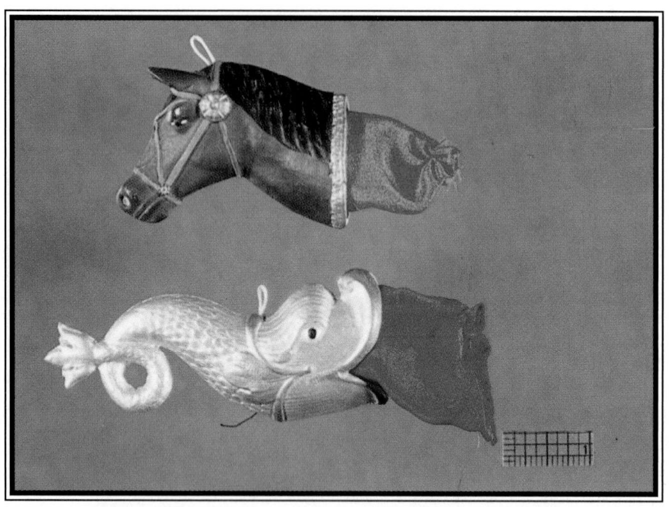

A. Reproduction Dresden Candy Containers, both American made by Kummerow, circa 2001. **$75.00–100.00** each: Horse Head, approx. 2¾". B. Fantasy Porpoise, approx. 4".

Large Carp Candy Container, 7¼" x 3¾" [OP, R1]. **$700.00–800.00.**

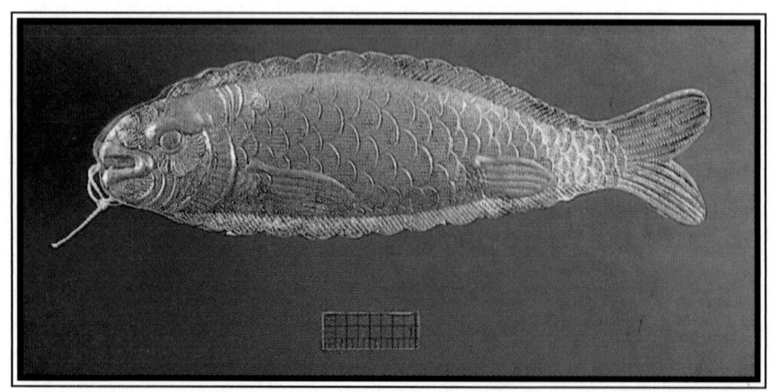

Fish, single or double sided, 6½" [OP, R3]. Single, **$75.00–100.00.** Double, **$150.00–175.00.**

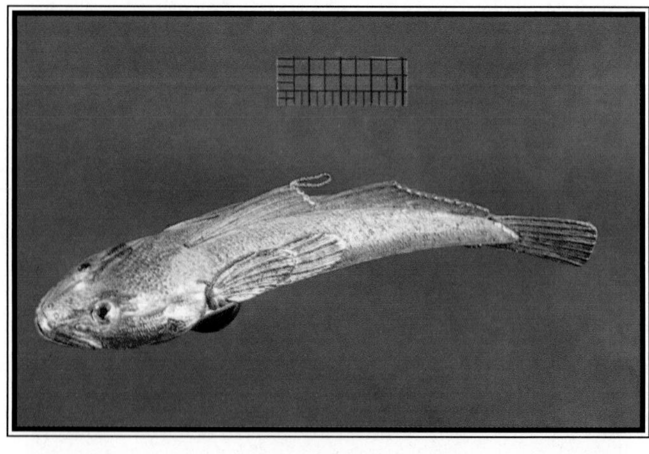

Swimming Catfish , 3–D, 5" [OP, R1]. **$1,000.00–1,200.00.**

A. Large Halibut, double, 9" [OP, R3]. **$175.00–200.00.** B. Rooster. (Type II), flat, 3" [OP, R2]. **$95.00–110.00.** C. Lion, flat, 4¼"L [OP, R2–3]. **$110.00–125.00.**

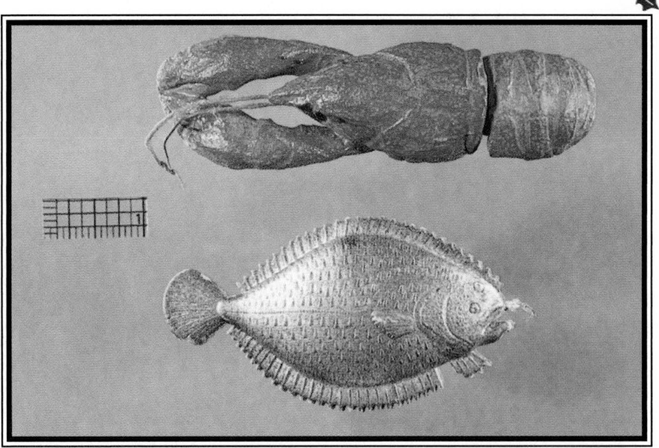

A. Lobster Candy Container, 3–D, 4½", large [OP, R2]. **$325.00–350.00.** B. Flounder, double, 3½" [OP, R2]. **$400.00–450.00.**

A. Generic Fish, flat, 5" [OP, R3]. **$65.00–85.00.** B. Bluegill, double, 5⅛" [OP, R3]. **$225.00–300.00.**

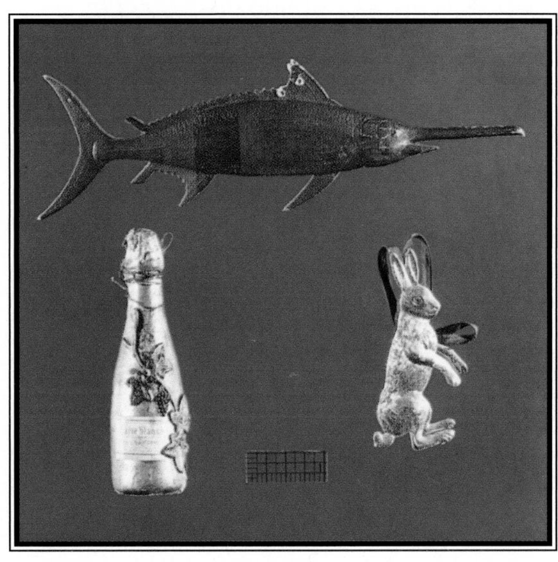

A. Swordfish, double, 6½" [OP, R1–2]. **$375.00–400.00.** B. "Carte Blanche" Champagne Bottle, 3–D, 3¼" [OP, R2]. **$275.00–300.00.** C. Standing Rabbit, flat, 2½" [OP–NP, R3]. **$50.00–65.00.**

A. Nautilus Shell Candy Container, small, 3" [OP, R1]. **$450.00–500.00.** B. Sea Horse, 3" [OP, R1]. **$325.00–350.00.** C. Scallop Shell Candy Container, 2½" [OP, R1–2]. **$400.00–500.00.**

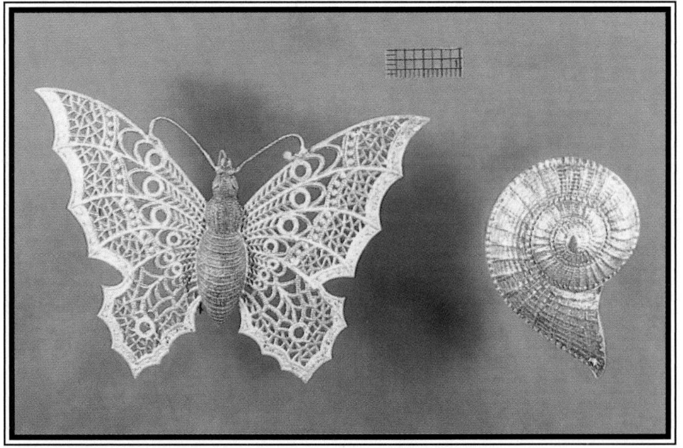

A. Butterfly with Filigree Wings (Type I), large, 5¼" [OP, R2]. **$300.00–400.00.** B. Nautilus Shell Candy Container, large, 3½" [OP, R1]. **$475.00–550.00.**

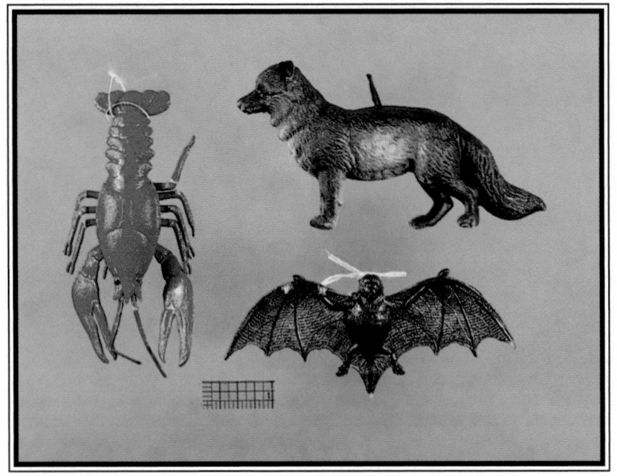

A. Lobster or Crayfish, 3–D, 4" [OP, R2]. **$400.00–450.00.** B. Fox, 3–D, large, 4¾"L [OP, R2]. **$375.00–425.00.** C. Bat, 3–D, 4¾"L [OP, R1]. **$2,000.00–2,500.00.**

A. Two Goats at a Barrel Candy Container, 3"W x 2½"H [OP, R1–2]. **$650.00–800.00.** B. Mountain Goat Charging, 4¾"W x 3¼"H [OP, R1–2]. **$775.00–875.00.**

A. Hen Candy Container, 2½" [OP, R1]. **$375.00–450.00.** B. Nanny Goat, small, 3¾"L x 3"H [OP, R2–3]. **$400.00–450.00.** C. Charging Buffalo, double, 3¾" [OP, R1–2]. **$300.00–375.00.**

Animal Head Candy Containers: A. Cow, 2¾" [OP, R1]. **$1,500.00–1,700.00.** B. Horse, 3" [OP–NP, R2]. **$1,200.00–1,400.00.** C. Dog Head, 2½" [OP, R1]. **$1,500.00–1,700.00.** D. Rooster (Type I), 3" [OP, R1]. **$2,500.00–3,000.00.**

A. Horse with a Lady Rider, 3–D, large, 3" [OP, R2]. **$650.00–750.00.** B. Horse with a Gentleman Rider, 3–D, 3" [OP, R1–2]. **$650.00–750.00.**

A. Donkey with Jockey Rider, 3–D, 3" [OP, R1–2]. **$450.00–475.00.** B. Horse's Leg Candy Container, 3–D, 3" [OP, R1–2]. **$375.00–450.00.**

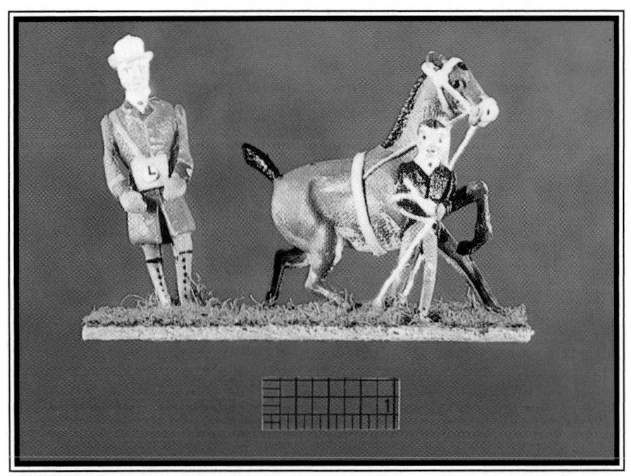

Racehorse, Owner, and Stableboy, 3–D [OP, R1]. **$1,400.00–1,600.00.**

A. Horse with a Blanket, 2¾"H x 3"W [OP, R2]. **$450.00–500.00.** B. Rocking Horse (Type I), small, 2"H x 2½"W [OP, R1]. **$350.00–450.00.** C. Rocking Horse (Type II), large, 5"L x 2¾"H [OP, R1–2]. **$400.00–450.00.**

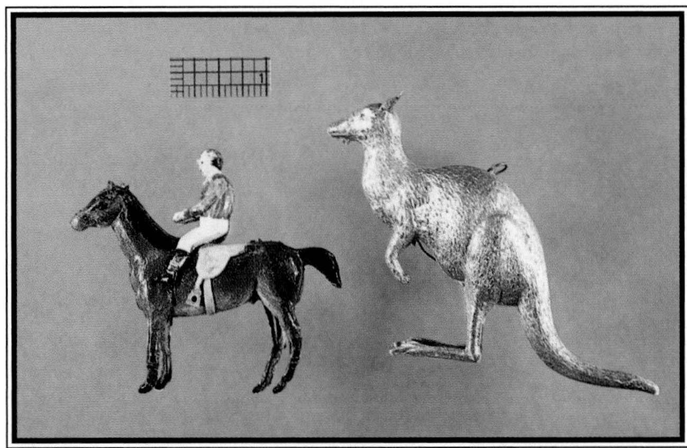

A. Horse with Jockey, 3–D, 2¾" H x 2¾" L [OP, R2–3]. **$400.00–450.00.** B. Kangaroo, 3–D, 4" head to tail [OP, R1–2]. **$500.00–650.00.**

A. Holstein Cow, 3–D, 2¾" [OP, R2]. **$350.00–375.00.** B. Racehorse, 3–D, 3½"H, marked "Germany" on the stomach [OP, R2]. **$400.00–450.00.** C. Prancing Horse (Type I), double, 3½" [OP, R2]. **$180.00–200.00.**

A. Horse with Jockey, 3–D, 3¼"H x 3½"L [OP, R2–3]. **$400.00–500.00.** B. Moth, 3–D, 5" [OP, R1]. **$500.00–600.00.**

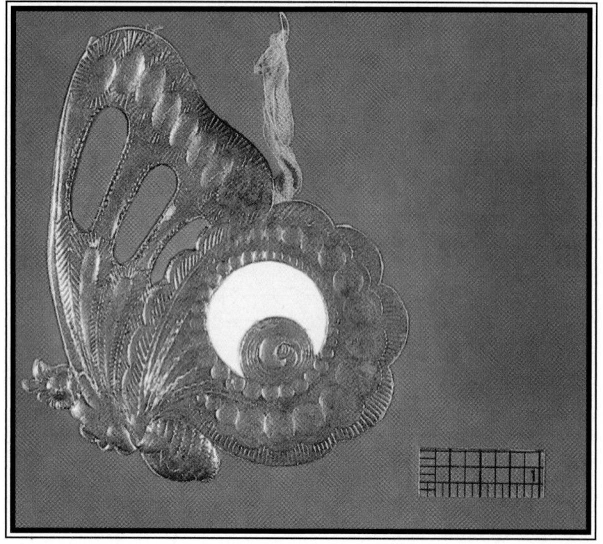

Butterfly, G/S, double, approx. 3½". The wings open along the backside to allow small items such as money to be inserted inside [OP, R1]. **$200.00–225.00.**

Butterfly with Cast Lead Body, flat, 4" [OP, R1]. **$225.00–300.00.**

Three Treatments of Butterflies with Filigree Wings, small, 1½" – 2½", flats [OP–NP, R3–4]: A. **$70.00–90.00.** B & C. Decorative Backs. **$75.00–100.00** each.

All new Dresdens. **$5.00–8.00** each: A. Walking Lion, 3½". B. Poodle, double, 2½". C. Dragonfly, 2¾" wing span. D. Mouse/ Rat, double, 3¾". E. Ladybug, 2½". F. Lobster, 2½".

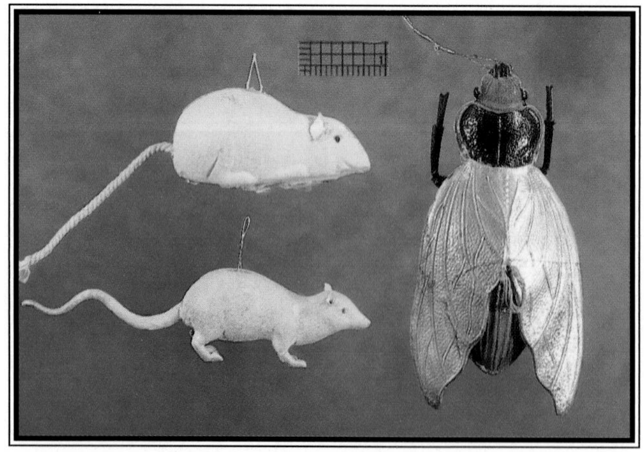

A. Mouse Candy Container, 2½" [OP, R1]. **$475.00–575.00.** B. Opossum, 4" [OP, R1]. **$375.00–475.00.** C. Beetle, large, 4" [OP, R1–2]. **$650.00–750.00.**

A. Walking Pig (Type I), double, 2½" [OP, R1–2]. **$150.00–175.00.** B. Walking Lion (Type I), double, 3½"L [OP–NP, R2]. **$125.00–150.00.** C. Sturgeon, 3–D, approx. 5¼" [OP, R1]. **$250.00–325.00.**

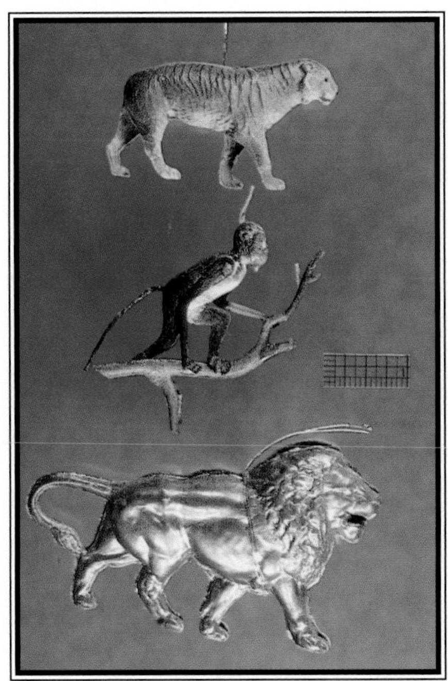

A. Tiger, 2½" [OP, R1–2]. **$500.00–600.00.** B. Monkey on a Branch, 3½" [OP, R1]. **$750.00–900.00.** C. Walking Lion (Type II), 4¼"L x 2½"H [OP, R2]. **$200.00–275.00.**

A. Monkey Climbing a Vine, flat, 5½" [OP, R2]. **$125.00–135.00.** B. Six-pointed Star, 3-D, small, 3¼" [OP, R3]. **$95.00–110.00.** C. Eagle on a Branch with Spread Wings, flat, 5½" [OP, R2–3]. **$90.00–110.00.**

Moose, 3-D, 3½"H x 3½"L [OP, R3]. **$350.00–400.00.**

A. Rabbit Candy Container, 2" [OP, R2]. **$650.00–750.00.** B. Cornucopia Candy Container, 4¼" [OP, R2]. **$125.00–140.00.** C. Heart Candy Container, 2½" [OP, R2]. **$140.00–160.00.**

A. Standing Ram, flat, 4"L x 3½"H [OP, R2–3]. **$110.00–125.00.** B. Pug Dog, flat, 2"W x 2¼"H [OP, R1–2]. **$95.00–110.00.** C. Sheep, flat, 2½" [OP, R1–2]. **$70.00–80.00.**

A. Diamond-back Terrapin Candy Container (Type I), 3½" [OP, R2]. **$450.00–550.00.** B. Turtle Candy Container (Type II), small, 3½" [OP, R2]. **$450.00–550.00.** C. Turtle (Type II), 4" [OP, R2]. **$475.00–550.00.** D. Turtle Candy Container (Type I), large, 6" [OP, R2]. **$600.00–700.00.**

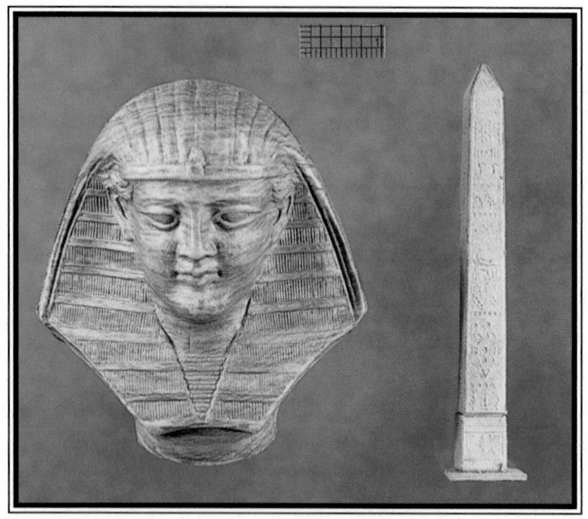

A. Sphinx Head Candy Container, 4¼" [OP, R1]. **$750.00–850.00.** B. Obelisk Candy Container, 5" [OP, R1]. **$500.00–600.00.**

A. Flowers and Ribbon, flat, 7½" [OP, R1–2]. **$150.00–175.00.** B. "Merry Christmas" Banner, flat, 6¼" [OP, R1–2]. **$150.00–175.00.**

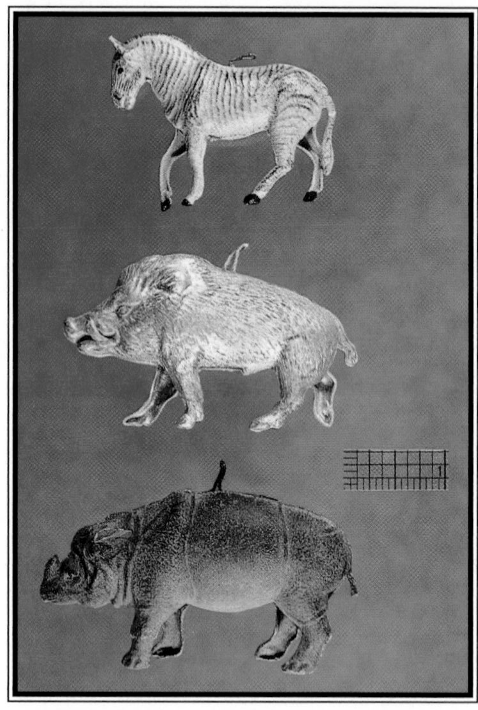

A. Zebra, 3-D, 2¼" [OP, R1–2]. **$450.00–550.00.** B. Boar, 3-D, 3"L [OP, R1]. **$650.00–750.00.** C. Rhinoceros, 3-D, 3¼"L [OP, R1–2]. **$600.00–700.00.**

A. Flower Basket with Daisies, 5¾"L [OP, R1–2]. **$125.00–150.00.** B. Flower Basket with Handle, 4¾"H [OP, R2]. **$120.00–135.00.** C. Flower Basket Hanging, 6¾"H [OP, R2]. **$125.00–150.00.**

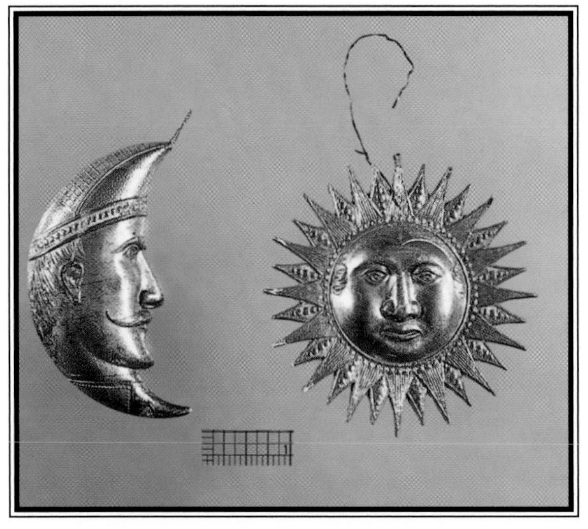

A. Man in the Moon with Phrygian Hat, 3–D, 3" [OP, R2]. **$750.00–900.00.** B. Man in the Sun (Type II), 3–D, 3" [OP, R2]. **$750.00–900.00.**

A. Crescent Moon with Scrap Angel, 4½" [OP, R2–3]. **$100.00–135.00.** B. Horseshoe, "Good Luck," 2¾"H [OP, R2]. **$75.00–95.00.**

A. Crescent Moon with Scrap Angel, flat, 4½" [OP, R2–3]. **$100.00–135.00.** B. Bicycle, 3–D, 3½" [OP, R1]. **$700.00 – 800.00** in good condition. C. High Top Shoe, flat, 3½"H [OP, R2]. **$65.00–85.00.**

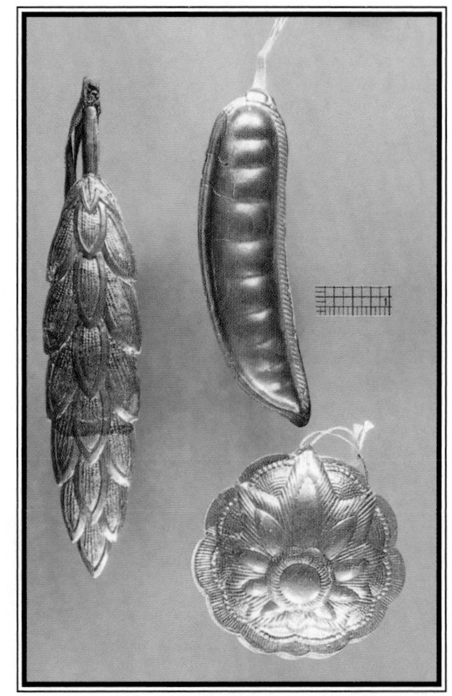

A. Stalk of Wheat, double, 6"L [OP, R1–2]. **$200.00–225.00.** B. Peas in a Pod, double, large, 4⅜" [OP, R2]. **$225.00–275.00.** C. Flower Design Purse, 2¾" [OP, R2]. **$150.00–175.00.**

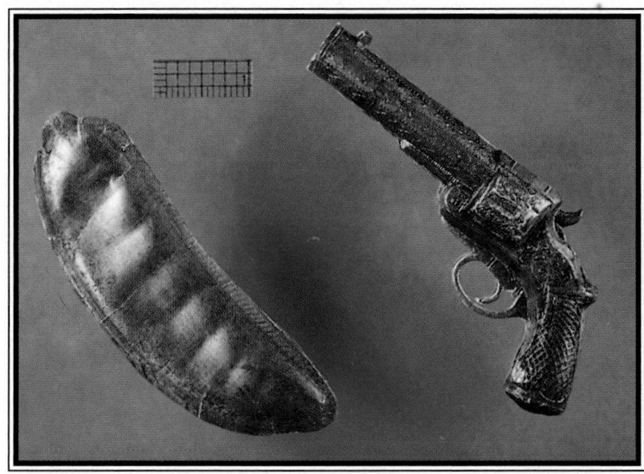

A. Peas in a Pod, double, small, 4¼" [OP, R2]. **$200.00–250.00.** B. Cowboy Revolver Candy Container, 3–D, large, 4¼"H [OP, R2]. **$450.00–600.00.**

A. Cannon, 3½" [OP, R1]. **$700.00–800.00.** B. Windmill Candy Container, 3¼" [OP, R1]. **$400.00–500.00.** C. Bell Candy Container, 2½" [OP, R1]. **$400.00–425.00.**

Dresden House, 2" [OP, R1]. **$500.00–600.00.**

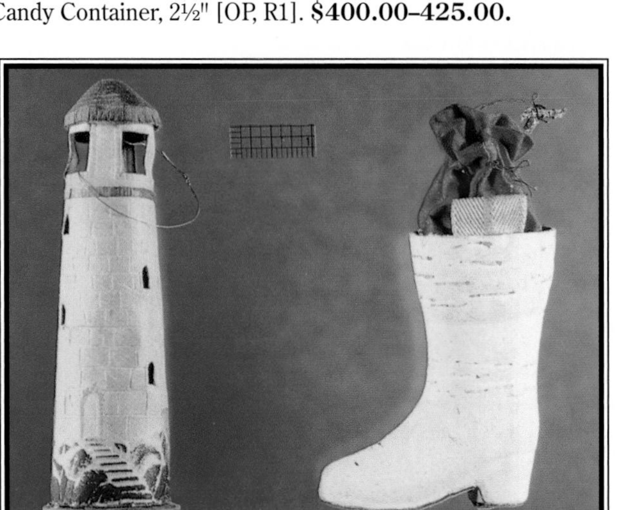

A. Lighthouse Candy Container, 6" [OP, R1–2]. **$275.00–350.00.** B. Riding Boot Candy Container, non-Dresden, 3½" [OP, R2]. **$175.00–200.00.**

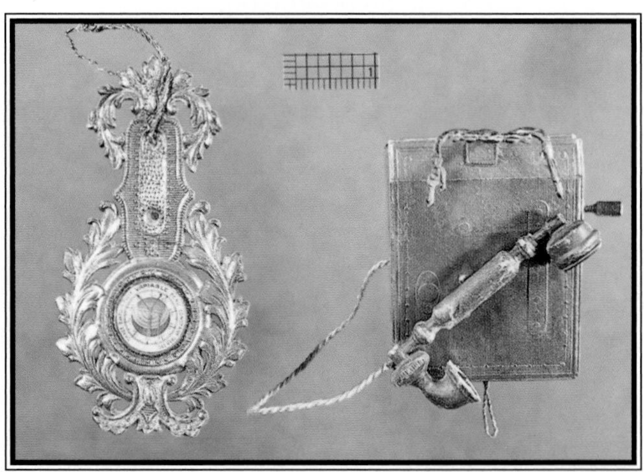

A. Barometer Candy Container, 3¾" [OP, R1]. **$1,000.00–1,200.00.** B. Telephone Candy Container, 2½" [OP, R1]. **$1,200.00–1,500.00.**

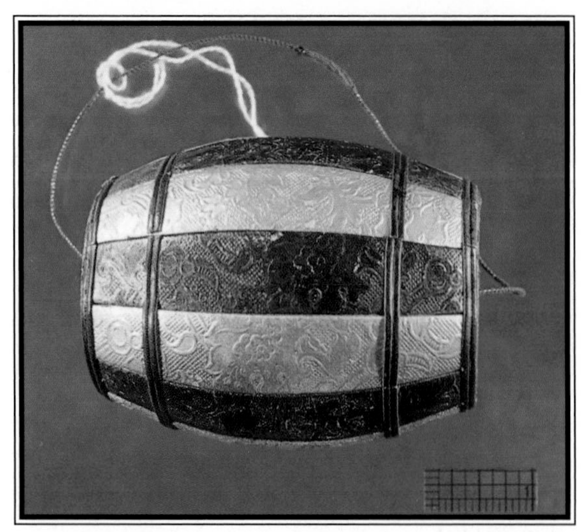

Barrel Candy Container, 3¼"L, 2" dia. [OP, R2]. **$250.00–275.00.**

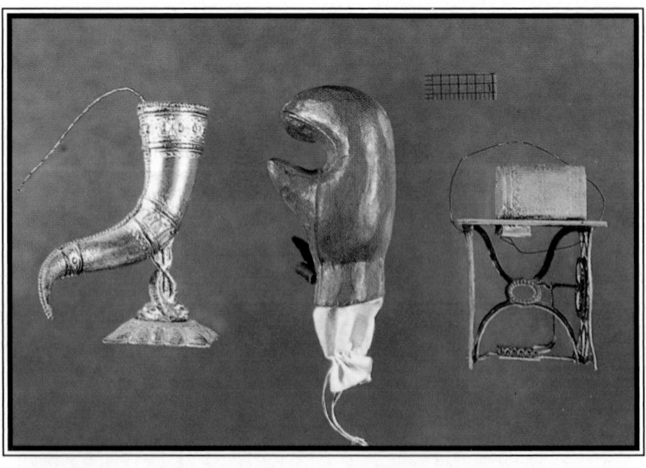

A. Drinking Horn Candy Container, 3¼" [OP, R1]. **$650.00–750.00.** B. Boxing Glove Candy Container, 3" [OP, R1]. **$400.00–500.00.** C. Sewing Machine, 2¾" [OP, R1]. **$450.00–550.00.**

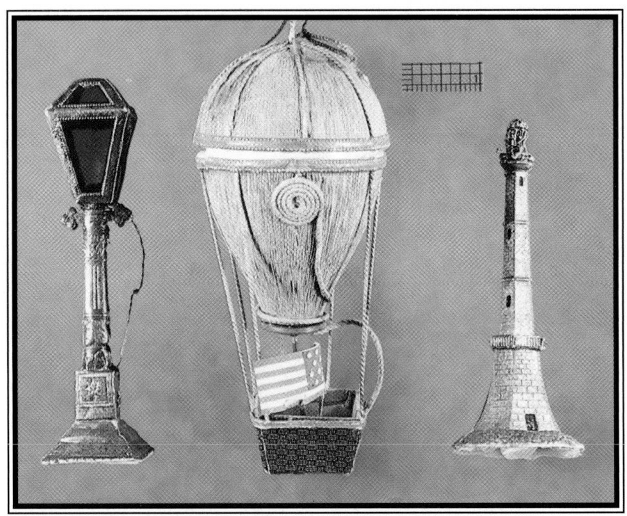

A. Street Lamp, 4¾" [OP, R1]. **$350.00–450.00.** B. Hot Air Balloon Candy Container, non–Dresden, 5" [OP, R1]. **$450.00–500.00.** C. Lighthouse Tower Candy Container, 4" [OP, R1]. **$375.00–475.00.**

Two Dresden Candy Containers: A. Candy Basket, approx. 2¼"H [OP, R2–3]. **$150.00–185.00.** B. Tea Cup and Saucer, approx. 1¾"H [OP, R1]. **$350.00–425.00.**

Two Dresden Candy Containers: A. Decorated Box, approx. 2¼"H [OP, R2]. **$125.00–145.00.** B. Milk Can, approx. 3¾" [OP, R1]. **$400.00–550.00.**

Coal Scuttle Candy Container, 3-D, approx. 3⅛". It opens on the bottom to hold candy [OP, R1]. **$350.00–400.00.**

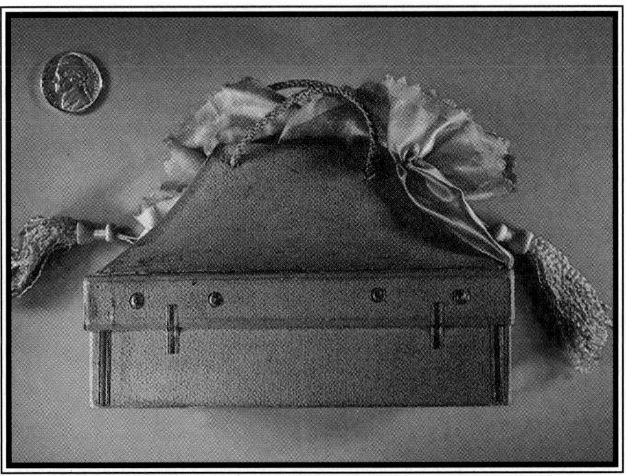

Luggage Candy Container, approx. 4¾"W. This piece has an unusual shape and a large ribbon tied around it [OP, R1]. **$450.00–550.00.**

Lantern Candy Containers: A. Six-sided (Type I), 3" [OP, R1–2]. **$225.00–275.00.** B. Four-sided, small, 2¼" [OP, R1–2]. **$200.00–250.00.** C. Four-sided, large, 3½" [OP, R1–2]. **$325.00–400.00.** D. Six-sided (Type II), 3¾" [OP, R1–2]. **$225.00–275.00.**

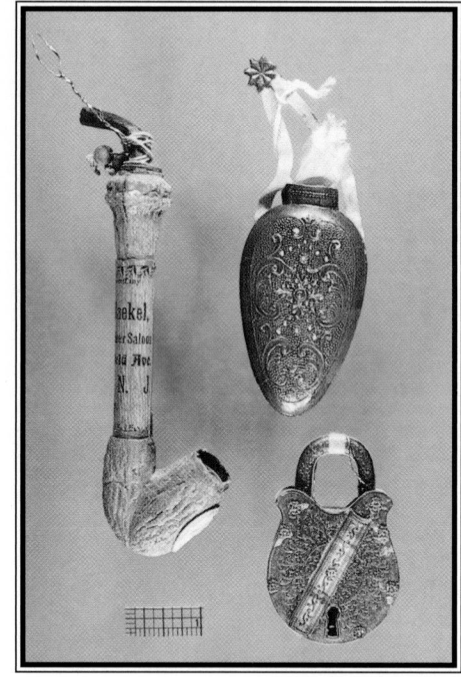

A. Long-stemmed Pipe Candy Container, 6"H [OP, R1]. **$375.00–425.00.** B. Flask Candy Container, 3" [OP, R1–2]. **$325.00–375.00.** C. Padlock Candy Container, 2½" [OP, R1–2]. **$400.00–500.00.**

A. Jeweled Dagger Candy Container, 5½" [OP, R1]. **$900.00–1,100.00.** B. Pipe with Lady's Head Candy Container, 7" [OP, R1]. **$1,000.00–1,200.00.**

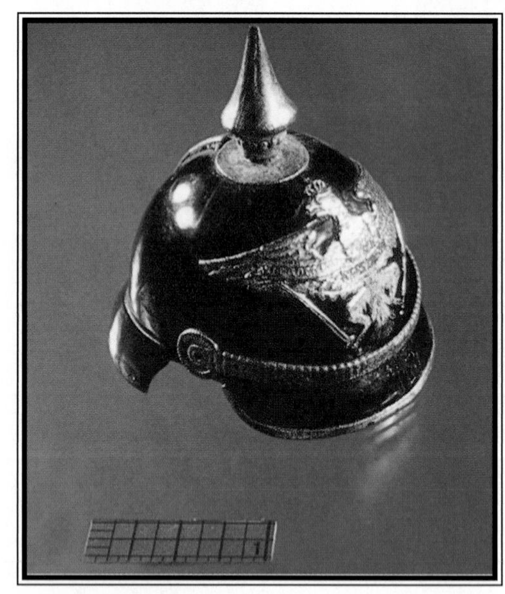

Prussian Spiked Helmet Candy Container, 2½" [OP, R1]. **$450.00–600.00.**

A. Helmet with Short Bill Candy Container, 3¼" [OP, R1]. **$275.00–350.00.** B. Roman Gladiator Candy Container, 3¼" [OP, R1]. **$250.00–275.00.** C. Conquistador Helmet Candy Container, 4¼" [OP, R1]. **$350.00–400.00.**

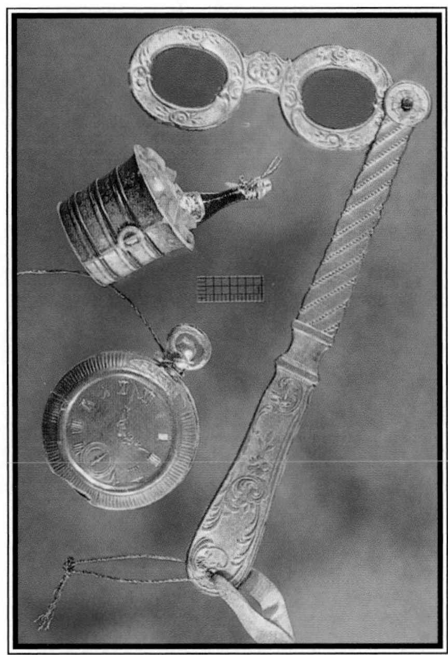

A Night at the Opera: A. Champagne Bottle in a Bucket Candy Container, large, 3" [OP, R2]. **$400.00–425.00.** B. Pocket Watch, 3" [OP, R1–2]. **$250.00–300.00.** C. Opera Glasses with Handle, 8½" [OP, R1]. **$400.00–450.00.**

A. Ice Skate Candy Container, 2¾" [OP, R1]. **$550.00–650.00.** B. Lady's Boot with Slip Candy Container, 3½" [OP, R1]. **$550.00–600.00.** C. Lady's Boot Roller Skate Candy Container, 4"H [OP, R1]. **$650.00–800.00.**

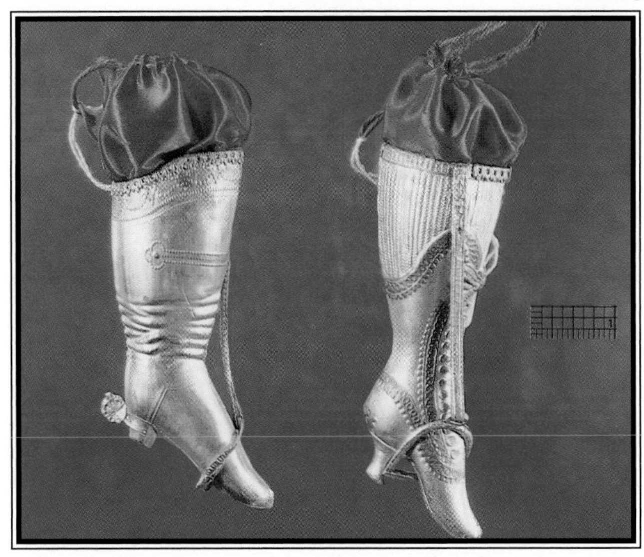

A. Riding Boot in Stirrup Candy Container, 4" [OP, R1–2]. **$650.00–750.00.** B. Lady's Boot with Stocking in Stirrup Candy Container, 4" [OP, R1]. **$650.00–750.00.**

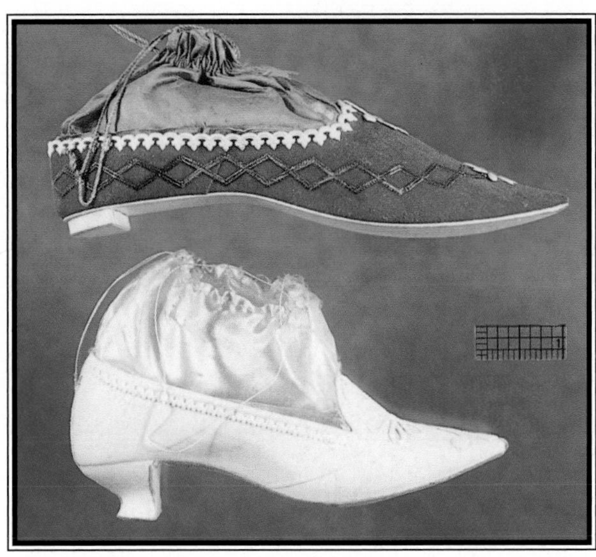

A. Red Fabric Slipper Candy Container, 5½" [OP, R1–2]. **$275.00–300.00.** B. Wedding Slipper Candy Container, large, 4¾" [OP, R2]. **$375.00–400.00.**

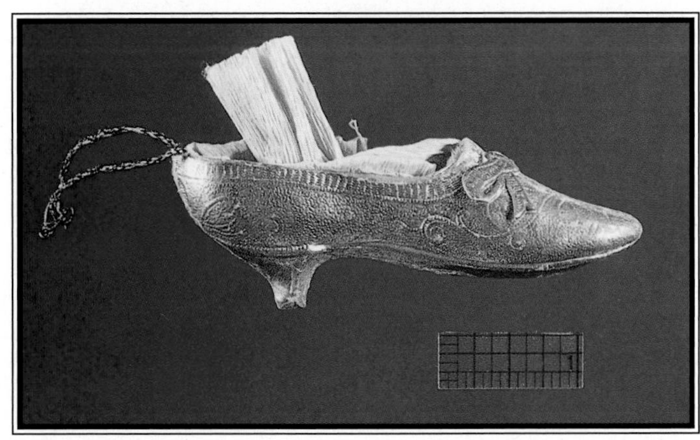

Lady's Slipper Candy Container [OP, R2–3]. Small (2"), **$225.00–250.00.** Medium (3½"), **$275.00–300.00.** Large (4"), **$375.00–400.00.**

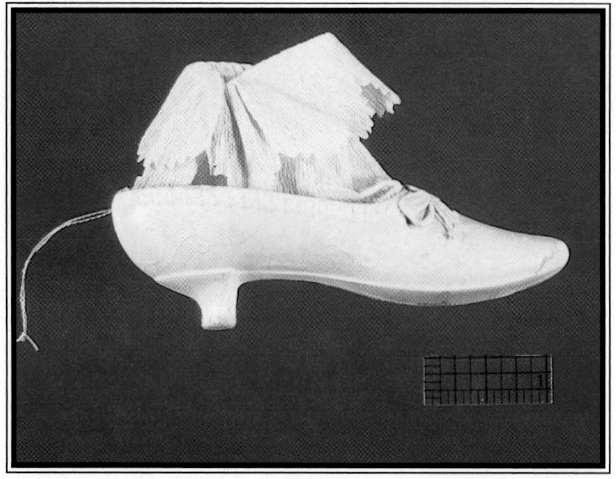

Wedding Slipper Candy Container [OP, R2]. Small, **$225.00–250.00.** Medium (3¾"), **$275.00–325.00.** Large (4"), **$375.00–400.00.**

A. Dresden Postal Horn or Hunting Horn Candy Container, 3¾" [OP, R2]. **$350.00–375.00.** B. Fabric–covered Women's Shoe Candy Container, non–Dresden [OP, R2]. Small (2¾"), **$175.00–200.00.** Large, **$200.00–250.00.**

A. Purse Candy Container, 2½"H [OP, R2]. **$225.00–250.00.** B. Flower Basket, 5" [OP, R2]. **$110.00–125.00.** C. Icicle, double, 5" [OP, R2]. **$100.00–125.00.**

Medals or Medallions, multilayer, 2"–4" [OP, R2]: A. Three Layers. **$75.00–100.00.** B. Two Layers. **$40.00–50.00.** C. Three Layers. **$75.00–100.00.** D.Three and Four Layers, large. **$125.00–150.00.**

A. Six-pointed Star Medallion, 4" [OP-NP, R1-2]. **$25.00–35.00.** B. Maltese Cross Medallion (Type I), 3¾" [OP-NP, R1-2]. **$25.00–35.00.** C. Triangular Armed Medallion, 3¾" [OP-NP, R1-2]. **$30.00–40.00.** All of these medallions were reissued circa 1988. New versions (shown), **$2.00–4.00.**

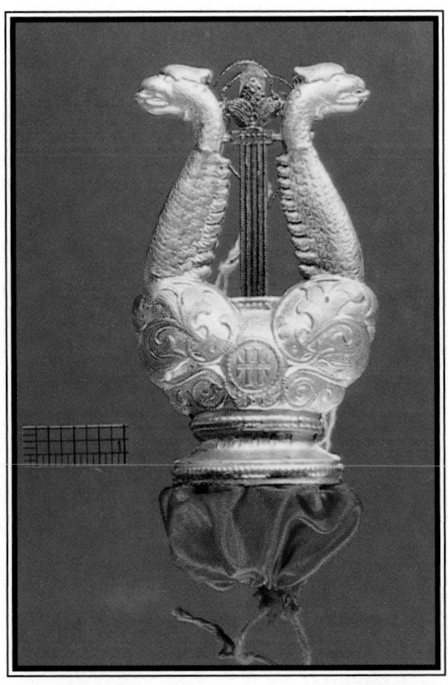

Lyre with Dragon Heads Candy Container [OP, R1-2]. Large (4" x 2½"), **$500.00–600.00.** Small (3"), **$400.00–500.00.**

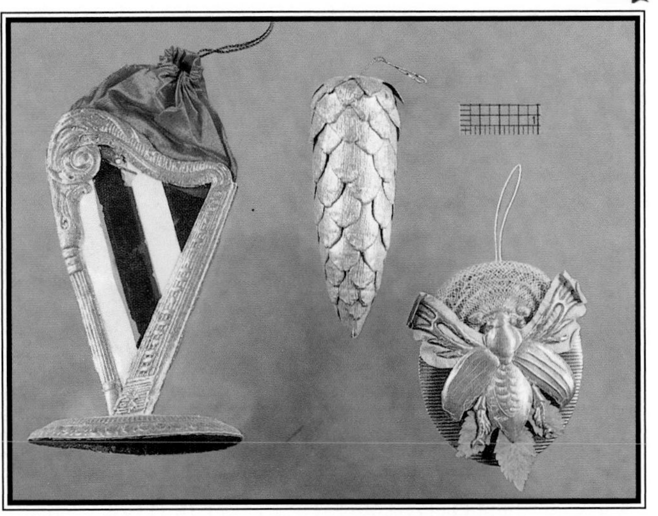

A. Harp Candy Container, 4½" [OP, R1-2]. **$350.00–400.00.** B. Pine Cone Candy Container (Type II), 3¼" [OP, R1-2]. **$250.00–300.00.** C. Bee on a Disk, 3" dia. [OP, R1-2]. **$150.00–175.00.**

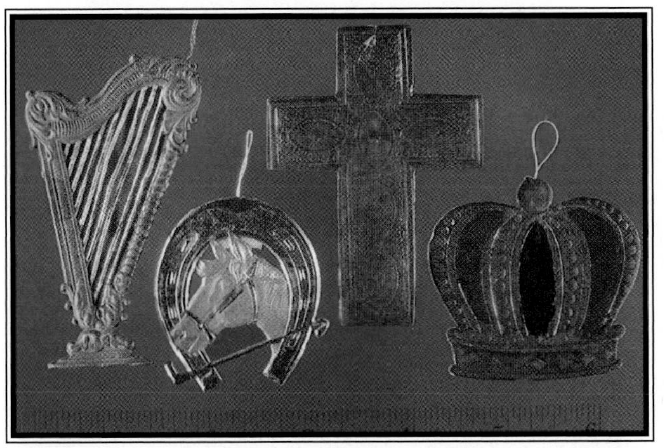

A. Harp, flat, 3½" [OP, R2]. **$75.00–100.00.** B. Horse Head in Horseshoe, flat, 2" [OP, R2]. **$95.00–110.00.** C. Cross, flat, 3½" [OP, R2]. **$60.00–75.00.** D. Crown, flat, 2" [OP, R2]. **$75.00–90.00.**

A. Bell with Holly Rope, flat, 6¾" [OP, R2-3]. **$125.00–150.00.** B. Rocking Horse with Boy Rider, double, 4"H [OP, R1-2]. **$275.00–300.00.** C. Christ's Crown, flat, 6"W [OP, R1-2]. **$115.00–130.00.**

A. Acorn Candy Container, 2¾" [OP, R2]. **$125.00–150.00.** B & C. Dresden Walnut Candy Container, 1½" & 1¾" [OP, R2]. Small, **$45.00–55.00.** Medium, **$75.00–100.00.** D. Dresden Walnut Candy Container, large, 2¾" x 2½" [OP, R2]. **$150.00–200.00.**

A. Flying Angel (Type I), 4½" [OP, R1]. **$1,000.00–1,200.00.** B. F lying Angel (Type II), 4¼" [OP, R1]. **$850.00–950.00.**

A. Angel/Putti Head with Wings, 3¼" [OP, R1]. **$175.00–225.00.** B. Angel/Putti with Scrap Head, 3¼"W [OP, R2-3]. **$75.00–95.00.**

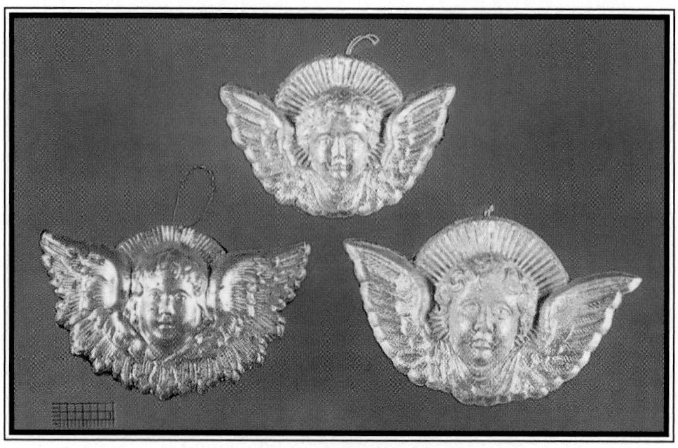

Dresden Putti Angel Heads; the three variations all are double sided [OP, R1-2]: A. Small (3½"), **$200.00–250.00.** B. Medium (4¼"), **$275.00–300.00.** C. Large (4¾"), **$275.00–325.00.**

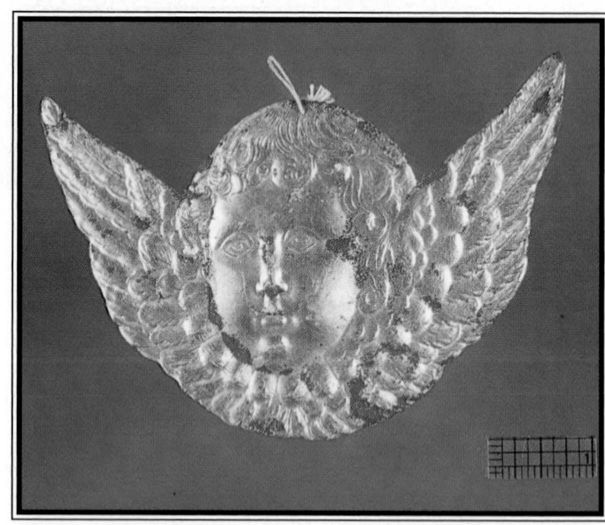

Dresden Putti Angel Head, flat, approx. 5"W [OP, R2]. **$100.00–125.00.**

Angel with Tissue Paper Skirt, G/S, flat, approx. 6" [OP, R2-3]. **$175.00–200.00.**

A. Angel Tree Top, large, 8" [OP, R2]. **$300.00–325.00.** B. Dresden Cornucopia, 6", heavily embossed [OP, R3]. **$75.00–100.00.**

A. Large 3-D Star, 5¾" dia. [OP, R1-2]. **$160.00–185.00.** B. Dresden Angel Tree Top, 6½" [OP, R2-3]. **$275.00–300.00.**

A. Angel/Putti with Scrap Head Candy Container, 4¾"L, Dresden wicker basket on the back [OP, R1]. **$175.00–225.00.** B. Santa with Wicker Basket Candy Container [OP, R1]. **$350.00–400.00.**

A. Angel/Putti Head with Starburst, 5" [OP, R2-3]. **$150.00–175.00.** B. Christmas Tree, 7" [OP, R1-2]. **$175.00–200.00.** C. Angel, flat, 4"H [OP, R2]. **$125.00–150.00.**

A. Wreath, large, flat, 4¼" [OP, R2]. Wreath alone, **$50.00–65.00.** With Santa, **$100.00–125.00.** B. Medal or Medallion, five layers [OP, R1-2]. **$75.00–100.00.** C. Angel with a Palm Branch, flat, 4½" [OP, R2]. **$100.00–125.00.**

A. "Merry Christmas" Hot Air Balloon, flat, 6¾" [OP, R1]. **$175.00–200.00.** B. Angel with Scrap Torso, 7¼" [OP, R1-2]. **$175.00–200.00.**

A. Babies in a Tub, flat, 5"W [OP, R2-3]. **$125.00–150.00.** B. Baby in a Basket, flat, 5"H x 3½"W [OP, R2-3]. **$125.00–150.00.**

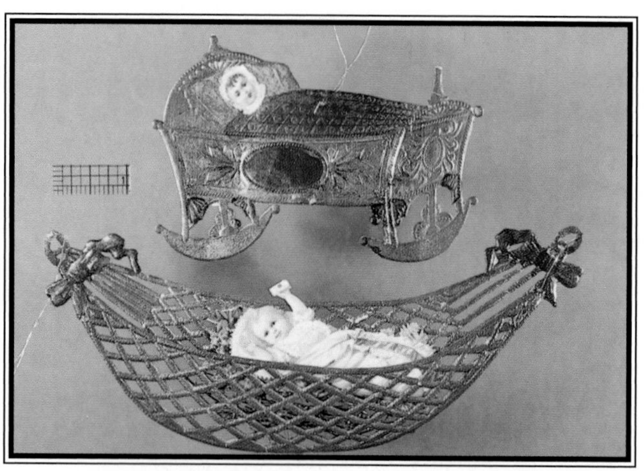

A. Baby in a Cradle, flat, 4¼"L [OP, R1-2]. **$150.00–175.00.** B. Baby in a Hammock, 7¼"L [OP, R2]. **$150.00–175.00.**

Baby in a Buggy, flat, 5½"W x 5¾"H [OP, R2]. **$150.00–175.00.**

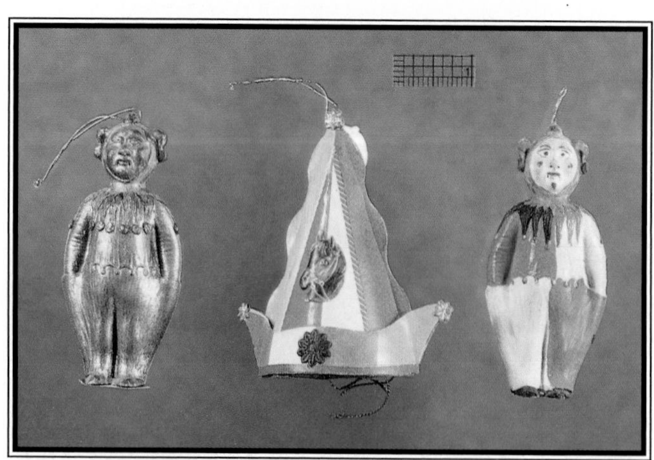

A & C. Standing Jester, 3¼" [OP, R1]. **$800.00–900.00.** B. Clown Hat Candy Container, 3¼", non-Dresden [OP, R1]. **$350.00–450.00.**

A. Clown Face in Frame, 4¾" [OP, R1]. **$600.00–750.00.** B. Man's Face in a Flower, 4" [OP, R1]. **$600.00–750.00.**

A. Dwarf with Money Bag, 3½"H [OP, R1-2]. **$700.00-800.00.** B. Dwarf Riding Reindeer, 3"H x 2¾"L [OP, R1]. **$1,000.00-1,100.00.**

Indian on a Horse, 3-D, 3½"H x 3½"L [OP, R1]. **$1,100.00-1,200.00.**

A. Greek Warrior, flat, 4¾"L [OP, R2-3]. **$150.00-175.00.** B. Bicycle with a Boy Rider, flat, 5"H [OP, R2-3]. **$150.00-175.00.**

Knight, flat, 10¼" [OP, R1]. **$175.00-225.00.**

Civil War Soldier, G/S, flat, approx. 4" [OP, R1]. **$100.00-135.00.**

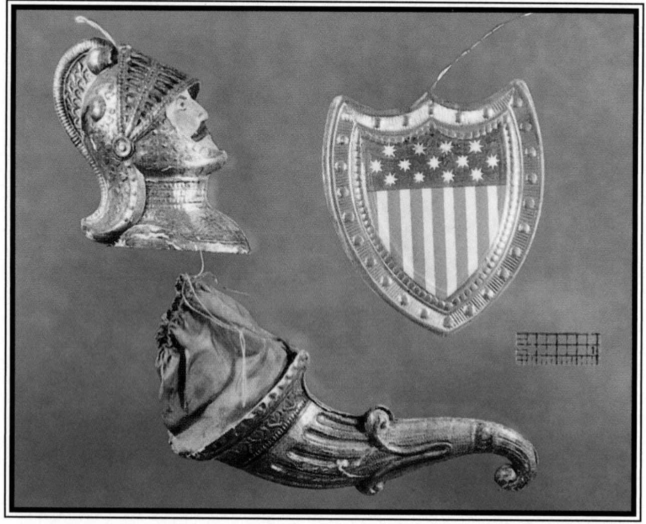

Knight in a Helmet Candy Container, 2¾" [OP, R1]. **$1,000.00–1,100.00.** B. Liberty's Shield Candy Container, 3" [OP, R2]. **$300.00–350.00.** C. Cornucopia Candy Container, 4½"L [OP, R1]. **$400.00–475.00.**

Santa Claus with Children, *Weihnachtsman*, 3¾", both sides shown [OP, R1]. **$1,600.00–1,800.00.**

A. Santa Claus, short coat, flat, 4½" [OP, R2]. **$150.00–175.00.** B. Military Hat, flat, 3¼" [OP, R1-2]. **$90.00–110.00.**

Santa, G/S, flat, approx. 7" [OP, R1]. **$175.00–200.00.**

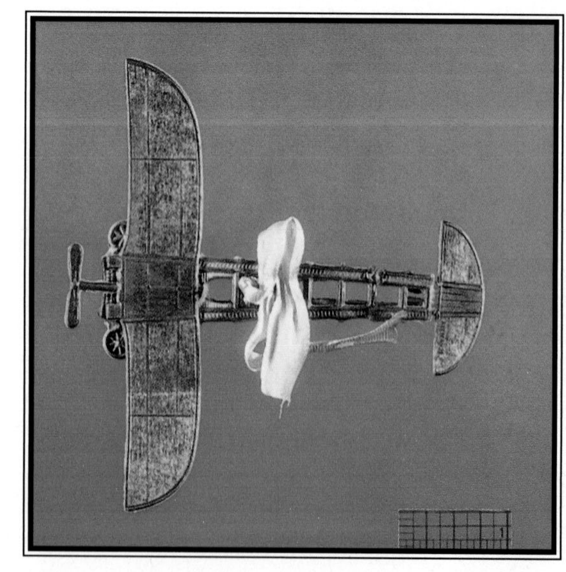

Dresden Airplane, 3-D, 3¾"W [OP, R1]. **$500.00–550.00.**

Two Dresden Transportation Pieces: A. Water Wagon, approx. 2½" [OP, R1]. **$600.00–700.00.** B. Airplane, approx. 2¾" wingspan [OP, R1-2]. **$900.00–1,000.00.**

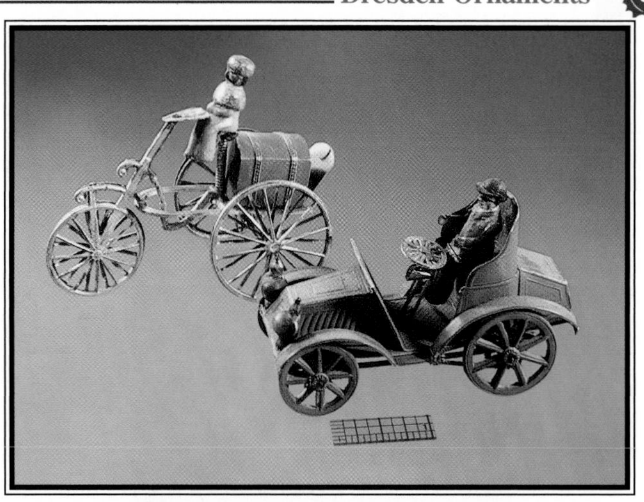

A. Velocipede Tricycle, 3" x 2¾" [OP, R1]. **$1,500.00+.** B. 1903 Winton, 3¼"L [OP, R1+]. **$2,000.00+.**

Gaff-rigged Sailboat, large, 4¼H x 4½"L [OP, R1]. **$800.00–850.00.**

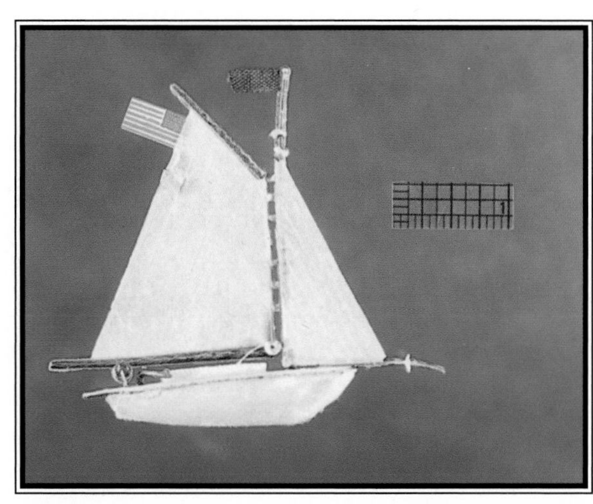

Gaff-rigged Sailboat, small, 3-D, 3¼"L x 3"H [OP, R2]. **$450.00–500.00.**

A. Sailboat, Skiff, 3-D, 3"H x 3"L [OP, R2]. **$450.00–550.00.** B. Cowboy Revolver Candy Container [OP, R2]. Small (3¾"), **$400.00–500.00.** Large (4¼"), **$500.00–650.00.**

Gondola, flat, 8¾"L [OP, R1]. **$200.00–225.00.**

Sailboat with Scrap Figures, flat, 6¾"H x 5"W [OP, R2-3]. **$125.00–135.00.**

Paddle Wheel Boat, 3-D, 3⅞" & 4¼" [OP, R1-2]. **$1,100.00–1,400.00.**

A. Ocean Freighter (Type II), 2¼"H x 6"L [OP, R1]. **$2,500.00+.** B. Ocean Freighter (Type III), 2¼"H x 6"L [OP, R1]. **$2,500.00+.**

A. Zeppelin Candy Container (Type II), 5" [OP, R2]. **$600.00–750.00.** B. Ocean Freighter (Type I), 5½" [OP, R1]. **$2,500.00+.**

A. Wagon with a High Seat, 4½" [OP, R1]. **$900.00–1,100.00.** B. Hansom Cab in Tandem, 6¼" [OP, R1]. **$2,500.00+.**

Gondola Candy Container, 3-D, approx. 4¾"L. The cabin area lifts off to hold candy [OP, R1]. **$1,450.00–1,550.00.**

A. Coronation Coach, 4"L [OP, R1]. Coach only, **$900.00–1,000.00.** With people & horses, **$2,200.00+.** B. Curricle Carriage, 6" [OP, R1]. **$2,500.00+.**

Ram Pulling a Cart, 3-D, 2¼"L ram, approx. 5"L overall [OP, R1]. **$1,200.00–1,300.00.**

Coach Pulled by a Horse, flat, 6½"L [OP, R2]. **$130.00–150.00.**

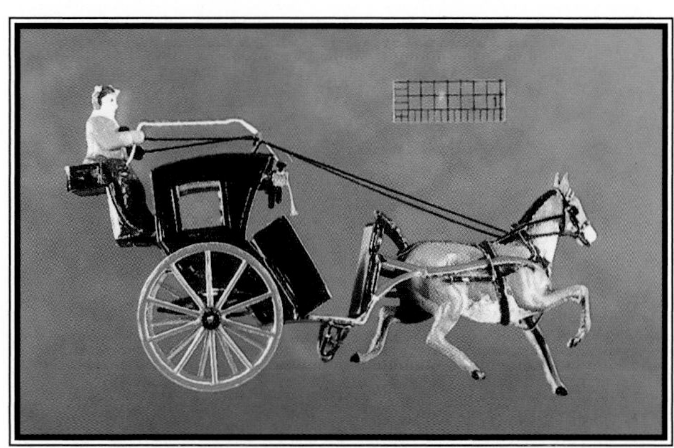

Hansom Cab, 3-D, 5"L [OP, R1]. **$2,200.00+.**

A. Prancing Horse (Type II), small, 1¾"H x 2½"L [OP, R2]. **$160.00–180.00.** B. Chariot with Two Horses Candy Container, 3-D, 3¾" [OP, R2]. **$750.00–850.00.**

A. Zeppelin, 3-D, 5½" [OP, R1]. **$550.00–700.00.** B. Street Car or Trolley marked "Registered 4446 Depose," 3-D, 3" (shown) & 3½" [OP, R3]. **$450.00–500.00.**

A. Streetcar/Trolley Candy Container, small, 3" [OP, R2-3]. **$500.00–550.00.** B. Early Locomotive, 2¾"L [OP, R1-2]. **$1,000.00–1,100.00.** C. Steam Ship Candy Container, 4¼"L [OP, R1]. **$550.00–650.00.**

A. Streetcar/Trolley Candy Container, 3-D, large, 3½"L [OP, R2-3]. **$550.00–625.00.** B. Roller Skates, 3-D, 4" [OP, R1]. **$400.00–550.00.**

Locomotive Candy Container, 4¼" x 2"H [OP, R1]. **$2,500.00+.**

Girl Pushing a Small Sled with a Woman in It, 3-D, 3½"L x 2¼"H [OP, R1]. **$1,000.00–1,150.00.**

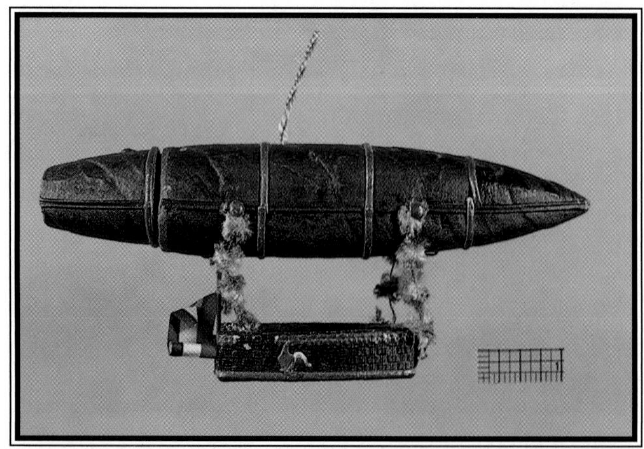

Cigar-shaped Zeppelin Candy Container, 3-D, 6¼" [OP, R1]. **$750.00–850.00.**

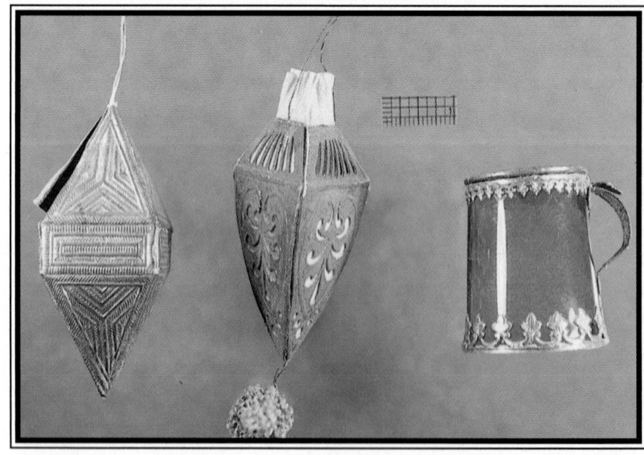

Geometric Shape Candy Containers: A. Double Pyramid Candy Container, 4" [OP, R1-2]. **$175.00–200.00.** B. Three-sided Candy Container, 3¼" [OP, R1-2]. **$175.00–200.00.** C. Stein Candy Container, 2¼" [OP, R1-2]. **$350.00–425.00.**

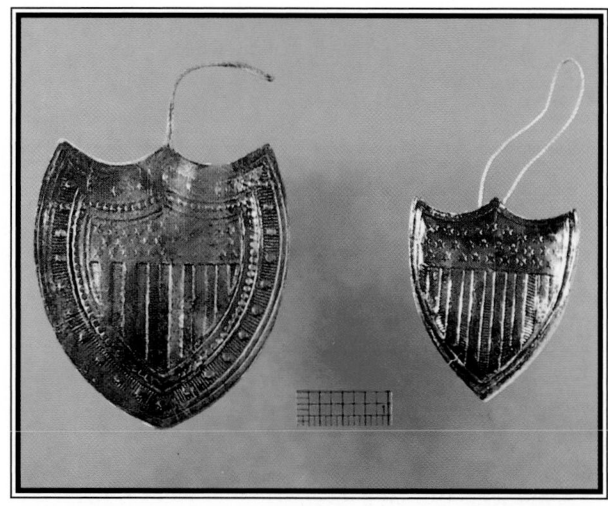

Two Liberty Shields, both double: A. 3½" [OP, R2-3]. **$130.00–160.00.** B. 2½" [OP, R2]. **$125.00–150.00.**

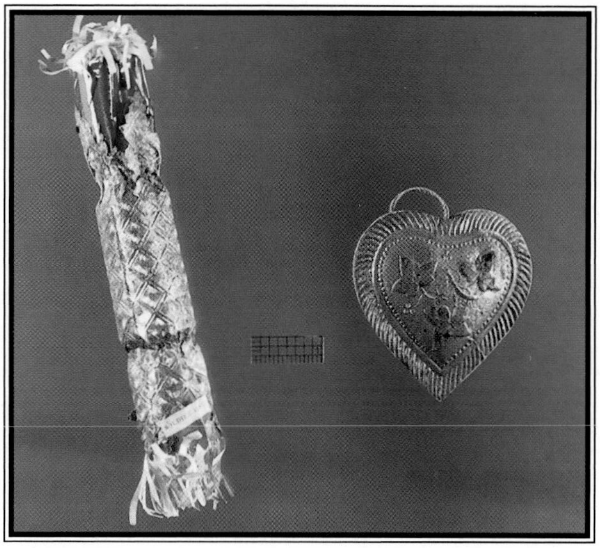

A. Dresden Cracker, 6½". It opens with a "crack" to reveal trinkets inside [OP-NP, R2]. **$75.00–95.00.** B. Heart with Ivy, double, 2½" [OP, R2-3]. **$125.00–150.00.** Flat, **$50.00–75.00.**

A & B. Twelve-pointed Flowers with Scraps, flat [OP-NP, R3]: A. 3". **$40.00–60.00.** B. 3¼". **$40.00–60.00.** C. Horseshoe, "jeweled," 3" [OP, R2]. **$75.00–95.00.** D. Railroad Lantern, flat, 4" [OP, R1-2]. **$100.00–115.00.** E. Postal Horn, flat, 3¼" [OP, R2]. **$100.00–120.00.**

A. Diamond-shaped Medallion, flat, 6½"W [OP, R3-4]. **$85.00–110.00.** B. Flower with Tinsel & Scrap Picture, flat, 2" [OP, R3-4]. **$40.00–60.00.** C. Medallion with a Gelatin Flower, flat [OP-NP, R3]. **$50.00–65.00.** Double-sided, **$125.00–150.00.**

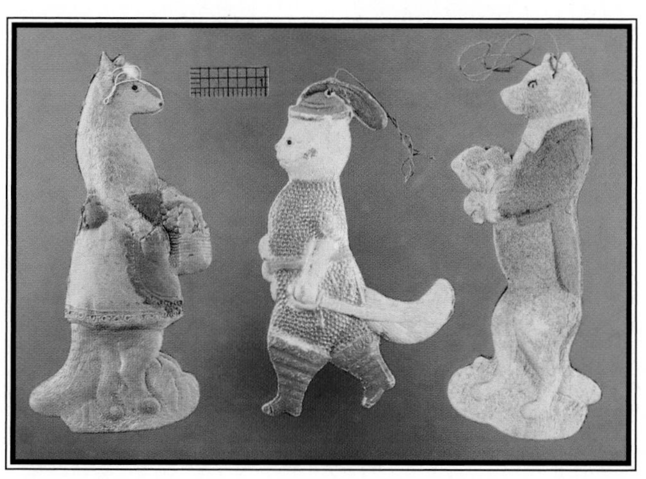

Russian Dresdens, circa 1920: A. Fox Lady, 5" [OP, R2]. **$90.00–100.00.** B. Puss 'N Boots, 4¼" [OP, R2]. **$90.00–100.00.** C. Fox Man, 5" [OP, R2]. **$90.00–100.00.**

Russian Dresdens, circa 1925: A. Frog, 3" [R2]. **$20.00–25.00.** B. Subway Station, [R2]. **$35.00–40.00.** C. Girl with a Lamb, 3¼" [R2]. **$35.00–45.00.**

Russian Dresdens, circa 1935: A. Motorcycle, 2½" [R2-3]. **$20.00–25.00.** B. Man with a Dog, 5" [R2-3]. **$15.00–20.00.** C. Clown Head, 3" [R2-3]. **$15.00–20.00.**

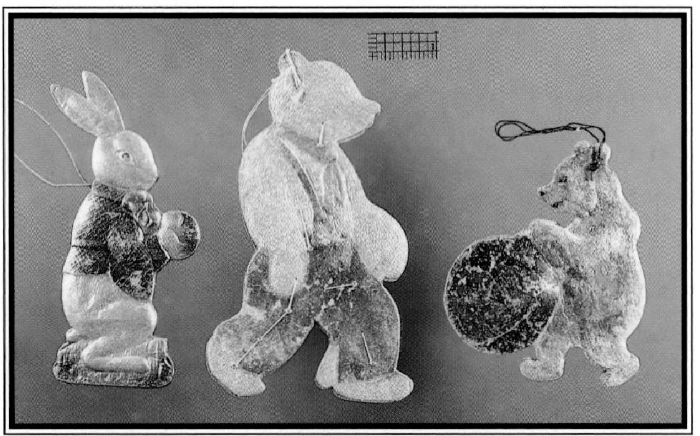

Russian Dresdens, circa 1935: A. Rabbit with Ball, 4½" [R2-3]. **$15.00–20.00.** B. Walking Bear, 4¾" [R2-3]. **$15.00–20.00.** C. Bear with a Ball, 3¾" [R2-3]. **$15.00–20.00.**

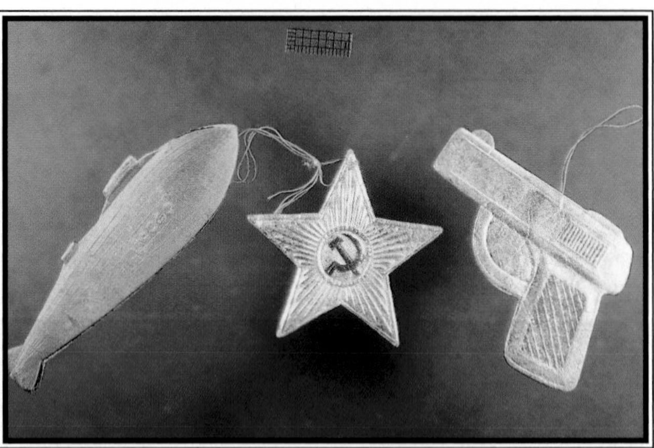

Russian Dresdens, circa 1935. These were made during a militaristic period in the Soviet Union: A. Dirigible or Sub, 5½" [OP, R2]. **$50.00–60.00.** B. Star with Hammer and Sickle, 3½" [OP, R2]. **$30.00–40.00.** C. Pistol, 3¾" [OP, R2]. **$20.00–25.00.**

Russian Dresdens, circa 1960: A. Red Star, 1½" [NP, R3]. **$15.00–20.00.** B. Cosmonaut, 3½" [NP, R3]. **$20.00–30.00.**

Dresden-like Santa Claus, double sided, 3-D, 3½" [OP, R1]. **$400.00–475.00.**

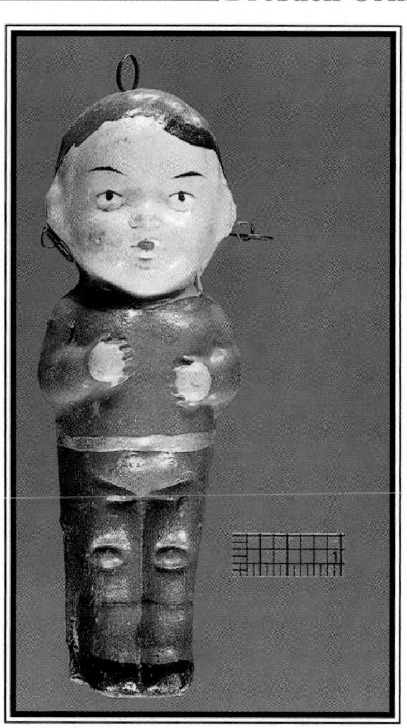

Dresden-like Girl with Earrings, 3-D, 5¼, circa 1920 [R1]. **$300.00–325.00.**

Dresden-like Pine Cone, 3-D, 3½" [OP, R1-2]. **$150.00–175.00.**

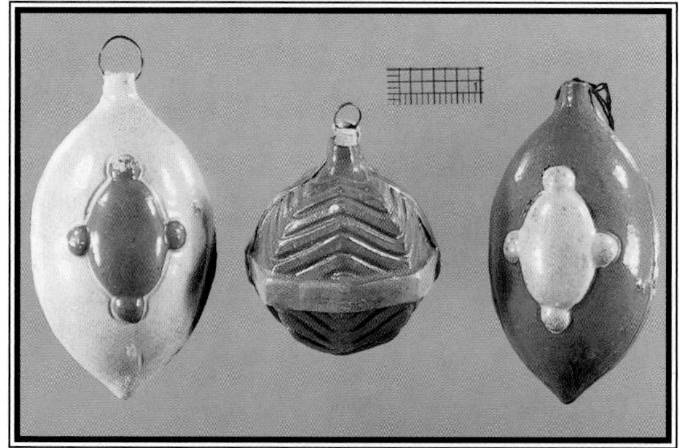

Three Dresden-like Ornaments: A & C. Geometric Oval Within an Oval [OP, R1-2]. **$50.00–60.00** each. B. Geometric Ball with Zigzag Lines, 3-D, 2" [OP, R1-2]. **$50.00–60.00.**

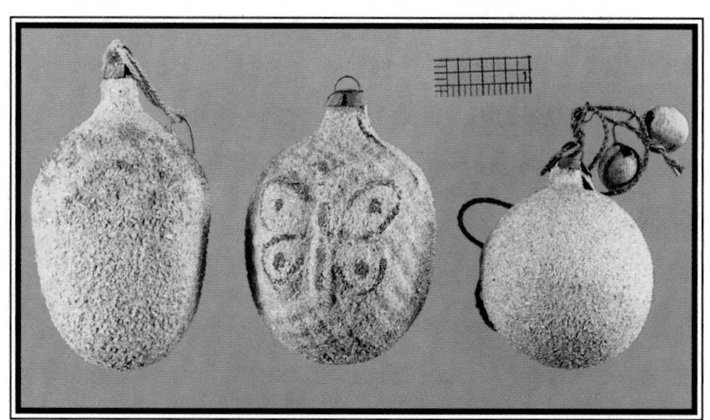

Three Dresden-like Ornaments Covered with Crushed Glass, circa 1910: A. Acorn, 3-D, 2½" [R1-2]. **$60.00–80.00.** B. Butterfly on an Oval, 3-D, 2¼" [R1-2]. **$70.00–90.00.** C. Geometric Ball, 3-D, 2" [R1-2]. **$25.00–30.00.**

Paper Candy Containers

In the past, candy, nuts, fruits, and sweets-in general played a large role as Christmastime gifts. Originally, all these tantalizing goodies were hung on the tree; hence, it received one of its many titles: "the sugar tree."

Perhaps the simplest and most enduring of these candy hanging forms was the cone, or cornucopia. All that was needed to create one was a sheet of paper or cardboard, to be rolled diagonally into a cone shape and then fastened. Many of these cones were decorated with colored paper, tinsel, pictures from scraps, advertisements, or postcards. These early homemade candy containers are extremely difficult to find, because most were used once and thrown away. Later, with the new mechanical processes for stamping, embossing, and shaping cardboard, many imaginative and beautiful candy containers were offered to the eagerly buying public. Some pieces represented common, everyday items like suitcases, but other items represented a way of life about which most people could only dream, a life filled with opera glasses, grand pianos, and crowns.

In their "golden age," from about 1870 to 1929, hundreds and possibly thousands of variations of these ornaments were produced. Many were hung on the tree year after year, long after their sweet contents had disappeared. These beautiful and ingenious pieces of Victorian art are scarce today. At the height of their popularity, their cost was prohibitive to many families. Also, these candy containers were hurt by the high tarrifs and war embargoes of the early twentieth century. Then too, many candy containers also doubled as toys and were never reused as Christmas ornaments; others were simply discarded when their contents were consumed.

The Russian candy container is another unique style of ornament that has recently found its way into Western markets. These pieces appear to be circa 1910–1960 and are made primarily from heavy paper that has printed pictures and designs.

Candy containers were made commercially in a wide variety of materials, including fabrics, metals, and plastics. Fabric containers included net bags, cornucopias, and stockings. Metal candy baskets were popular until the 1920s and 1930s. Foil boots and cornucopias were marketed in the 1950s and 1960s. Plastic Santa, sleigh, and reindeer candy containers were popular in the 1940s, 1950s, and 1960s. Most of the treats that came in these containers were small, hard candies, although some ornaments held small presents instead. Many containers were sold empty and filled at home.

Oval Candy Box, 4½" [OP, R1-2]. **$175.00–225.00.**

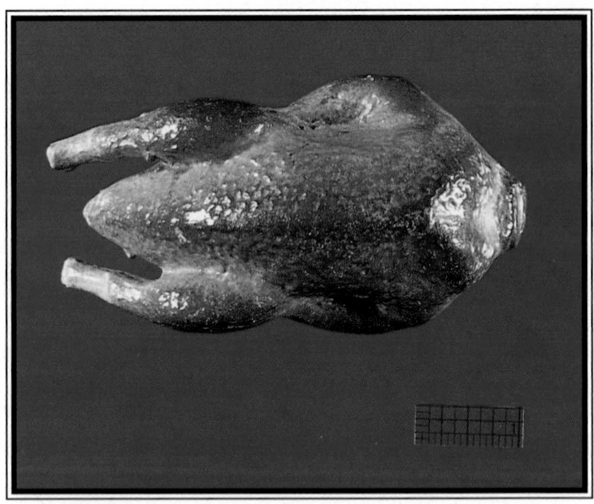

Roasted Turkey Candy Container [OP, R3]. Small (4½"), **$75.00–100.00.** Medium (5" – 8"), **$100.00–125.00.** Large (9"–10"), **$150.00–200.00.**

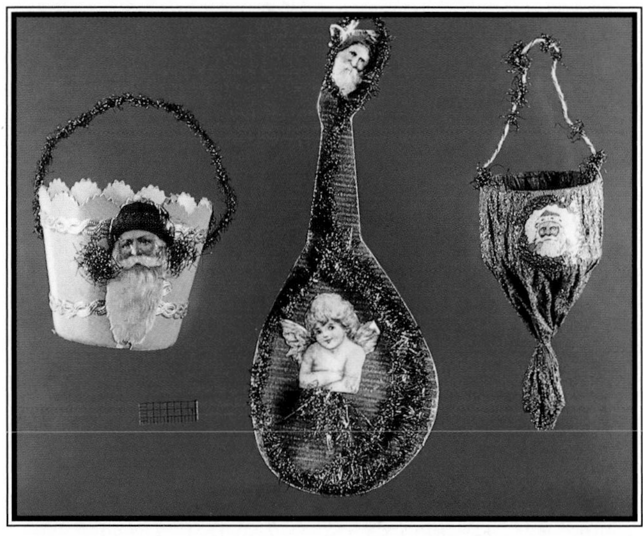

A & C. Candy Baskets or Buckets [OP, R3]. **$75.00–90.00** each: A. 2½". C. 4½", crepe paper stiffened by glue. B. Mandolin (Type II), 7½" [OP, R2-3]. **$100.00–125.00.**

Candy Containers: A. Wicker Basket, round, 2¼" [OP, R1-2]. **$175.00–200.00.** B. Wicker Basket, sewing, 3½" [OP, R1-2]. **$225.00–275.00.** C. Wicker Basket, oval, 3½" [OP, R1-2]. **$225.00–275.00.**

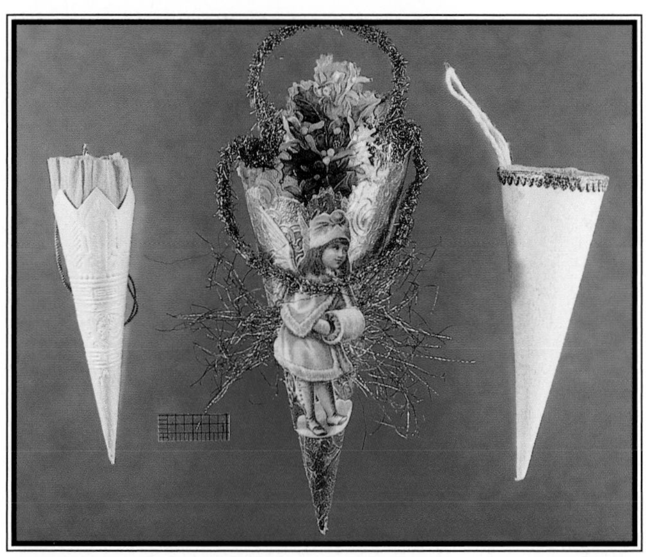

Three Paper Cornucopias: A. Embossed Paper with Medallions, 4½" [OP, R2-3]. **$90.00–110.00.** B. Cornucopia from Dresden Paper, 7½", lightly embossed [OP, R3]. **$125.00–150.00.** C. Plain-colored Paper, 4½" [R3]. **$20.00–30.00.**

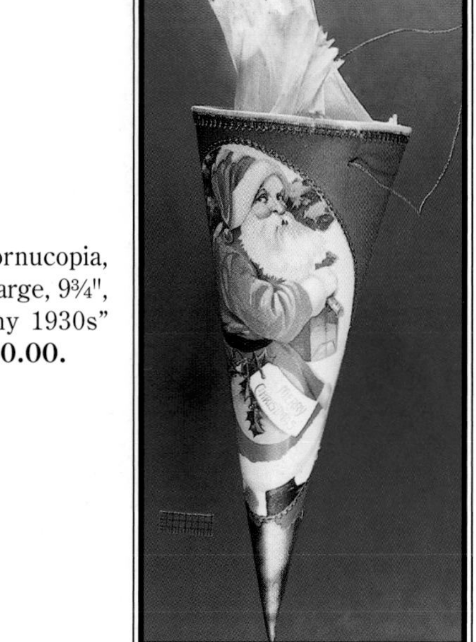

Colored Paper Cornucopia, with Lithograph, large, 9¾", marked "Germany 1930s" [R2-3]. **$60.00–80.00.**

Three Cornucopias: A & B. Dresden Paper, lightly embossed gold, 8". **$75.00–100.00.** B. Silver, 7". **$70.00–90.00.** C. Colored Paper with Lithograph, 6¾". **$35.00–45.00.**

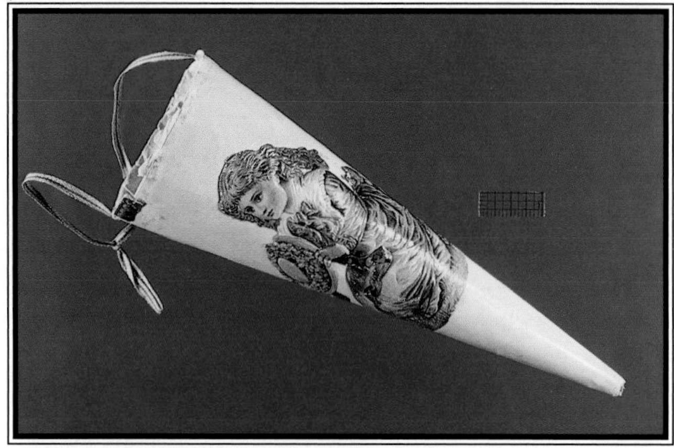

Commercially made Cornucopia with Applied Lithograph, 9¼" [OP, R2]. **$75.00–100.00.**

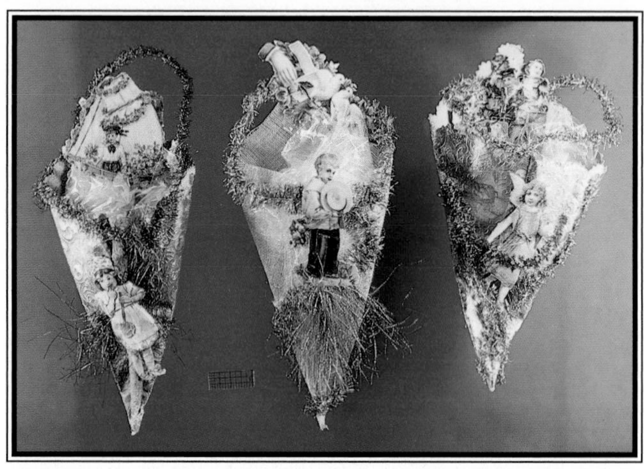

A. Dresden Paper, 8" [OP, R2-3]. **$85.00–115.00.** B. Pink Netting, 8½" [OP, R2-3]. **$55.00–75.00.** C. Dresden Paper, 7¼" [OP, R2-3]. **$95.00–115.00.**

Two Cornucopias, both embossed foil with scrap, both 8½". **$80.00–90.00** each.

Two Paper Cornucopias: A. Commercially Made with Holly Paper & Scraps, 7½" [OP, R3]. **$60.00–85.00.** B. Homemade of Blue Paper and a Scrap, 5" [OP, R2]. **$20.00–25.00.**

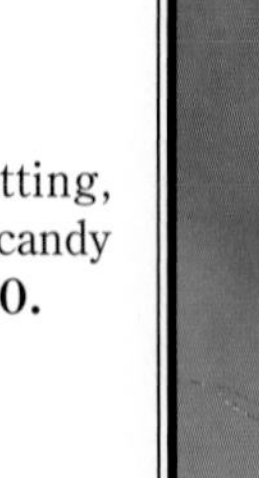

Flat Dresden-like Slipper with Netting, 7¼". The netting turned this into a candy container [OP, R2]. **$100.00–125.00.**

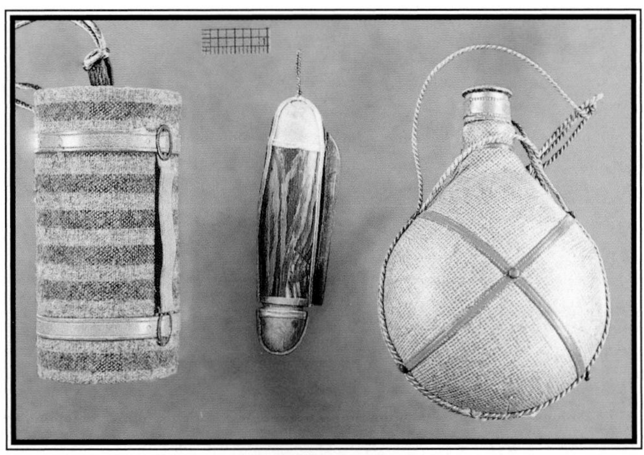

Candy Containers: A. Bed Roll, fabric covered, 4" [OP, R1]. **$350.00–450.00.** B. Pocket Knife, 3¾" [OP, R1]. **$350.00–375.00.** C. Canteen, 4¾" [OP, R1]. **$375.00–450.00.**

A. Dresden Wicker Purse Candy Container, 1½" [OP, R2-3]. **$175.00–200.00.** B. Globe Candy Container, 3", large [OP, R3]. **$175.00–200.00.** Small (2¾"), **$150.00–175.00.**

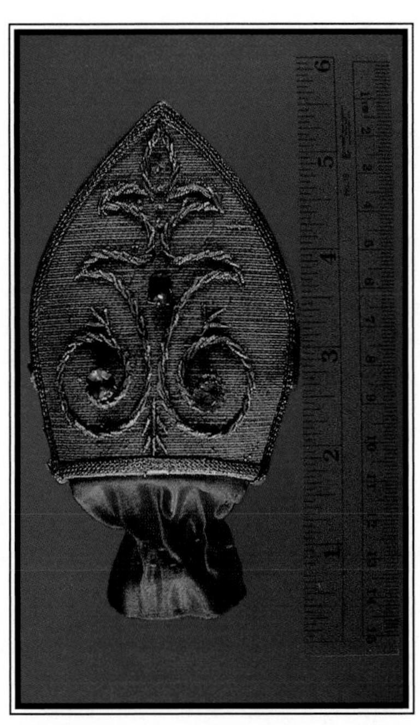

St. Nicholas's Miter, 3¾", fabric over cardboard [OP, R1]. **$400.00–500.00.**

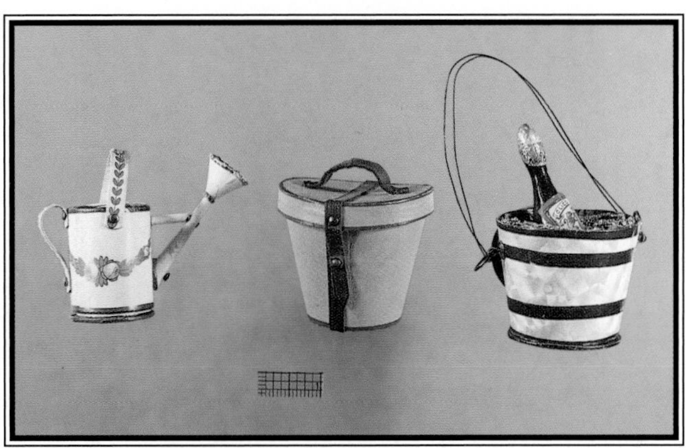

A. Watering Can, 2½" [OP, R2]. **$250.00–275.00.** B. Man's Hat-box, large, 2" [OP, R2-3]. **$125.00–145.00.** C. Champagne in a Bucket Cooler, 3¼" [OP, R2]. **$225.00–250.00.**

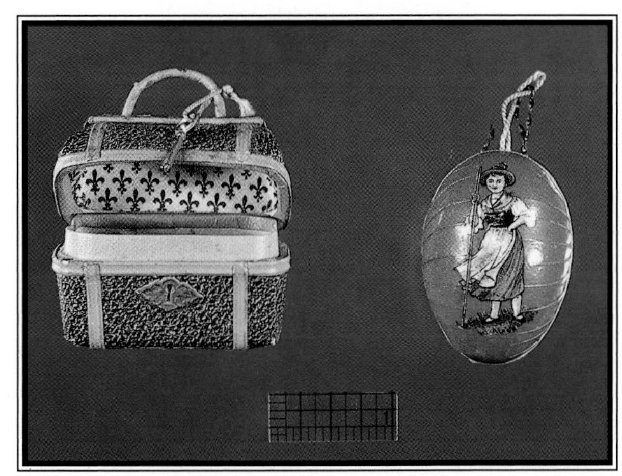

A. Carrying Case, 2", has metal key [OP, R2]. **$150.00–175.00.** B. Egg Shape, 1½". Small, **$20.00–25.00.** Medium, **$30.00–50.00.** Large (7"–10"), **$75.00–150.00.**

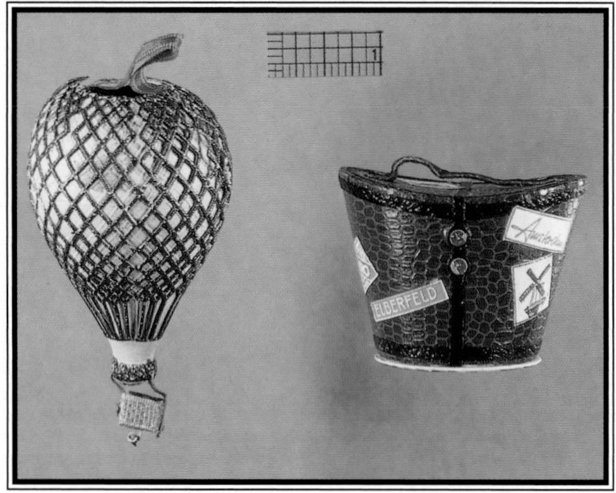

A. Dresden Hot Air Balloon Candy Container, 3" [OP, R2]. **$1,200.00–1,300.00.** B. Man's Hatbox, 1½", printed with foreign labels [OP, R2-3]. **$125.00–145.00.**

Luggage of Printed Paper [OP, R3]: A. Curved Top Trunk, small, 1¾". **$60.00–75.00.** B. Hatbox, small, 1¾". **$75.00–85.00.** C. Round Travel Trunk, 3¼". **$110.00–125.00.** D. Suitcase, 2½". **$75.00–85.00.** E. Satchel, small, 2½", marked "Made in Germany." **$75.00–85.00.**

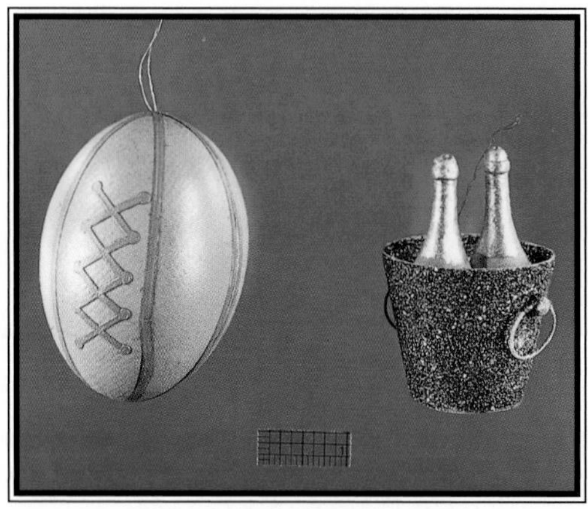

A. Football Candy Container, 3¼" [OP, R3]. **$50.00–60.00.** B. Dresden-like Ice Bucket with Two Champagne Bottles, 3", marked "Made in Paris France" [OP, R1]. **$150.00–200.00.**

A. Guitar Candy Container; 3½", 4" (shown), 4½", 5¾", 6", & 9" [OP, R3]. Small, **$100.00–125.00.** Medium, **$85.00–100.00.** Large, **$100.00–150.00.** B. Banjo, 9" [OP, R1-2]. **$95.00–110.00.** C. Mandolin; 4", 5½" (shown), & 9" [OP, R3]. Small, **$90.00–110.00.** Medium, **$125.00–150.00.** Large, **$175.00–200.00.**

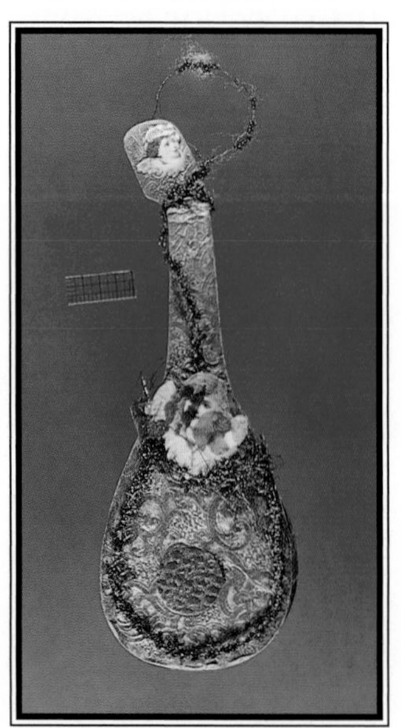

Mandolin Candy Container (Type II), 7½". Pieces of this type are cardboard covered with gold foil. They are NOT Dresden ornaments. They can be homemade or commercial, circa 1925 [R2]. **$100.00–125.00.**

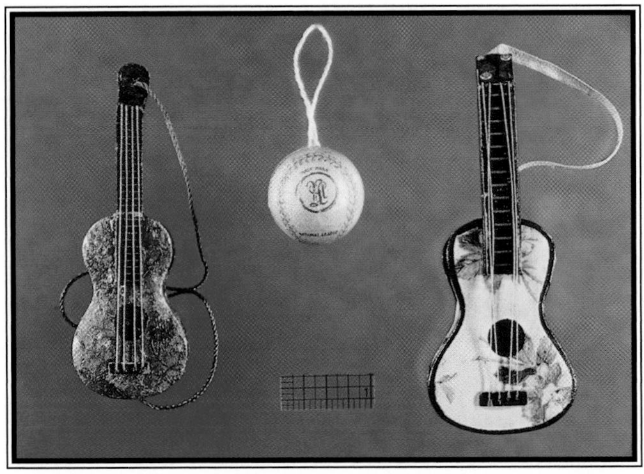

A & C. Guitars (Type I): A. Foil Covered, 3½" [OP, R3-4]. **$75.00–90.00.** C. Printed Paper, medium, 4½". **$150.00–175.00.** B. Baseball, "National League,"-small, 1" [OP, R2]. **$90.00–100.00.**

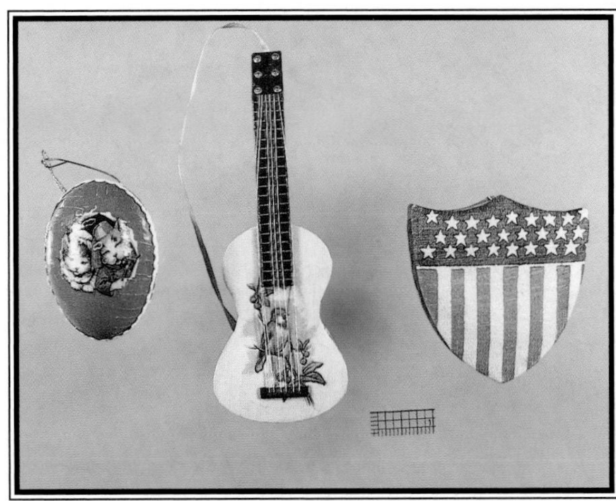

A. Egg-shaped Candy Container, small, 2½" [OP, R3]. **$30.00–40.00.** B. Guitar (Type I), printed paper, medium, 5¾" [OP, R3]. **$100.00–125.00.** C. Liberty Shield Candy Container, fabric covered, 3" [OP, R3]. **$100.00–125.00.**

Two Styles of Drum Candy Containers, medium: A. 2½"H x 3" dia. B. 2"H x 3" dia. **$100.00–125.00.** Larger than 3", **$135.00–160.00.**

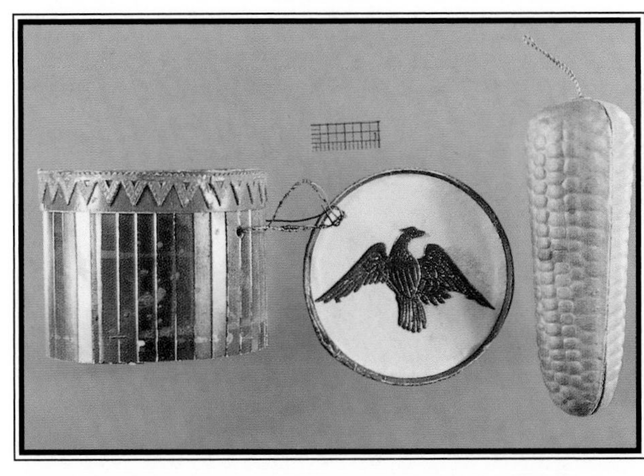

A & B. Drum Candy Container with Dresden Trim, 2½"H x 3" dia. **$125.00–150.00.** C. Ear of Corn Candy Container, 4¾" [OP, R2]. **$150.00–200.00.**

Pine Cone Candy Container, 7", circa 1948 [R2-3]. **$75.00–100.00.**

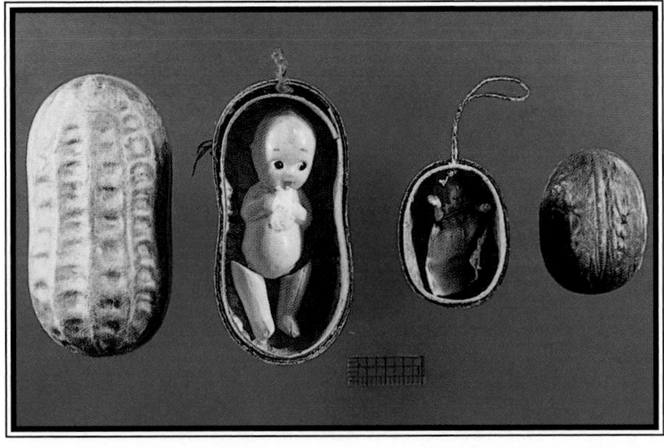

A. Opened Peanut Candy Container with Original Celluloid Doll; 2½", 2¾", 3¾" (shown), & 4¼"; marked "made in Austria" [Austrian & Japanese, OP, R3]. Small, **$45.00–55.00.** Medium, **$55.00–65.00.** Large, **$65.00–75.00.** B. Open Walnut Candy Container with Original Celluloid Toy; 1½", 1¾", & 2" (shown) [OP, R2]. Small, **$45.00–50.00.** Medium, **$50.00–60.00.** Large, **$60.00–75.00.**

A. Basket or Bucket Candy Container, 3½" [OP, R2-3]. **$75.00–100.00.** B & C. Cylinder-shaped Candy Containers: B. 6" [OP, R1]. **$150.00–200.00.** C. 5" [OP, R2]. **$75.00–100.00.**

A & C. Globe Candy Containers; 1½" (shown), 2¾" (shown), & 3" dia. [OP, R3]. Small, **$95.00–110.00.** Medium, **$125.00–150.00.** Large, **$150.00–175.00.** B. Heart Candy Container with an Angel Graphic, 2" [OP, R3]. **$75.00–100.00.**

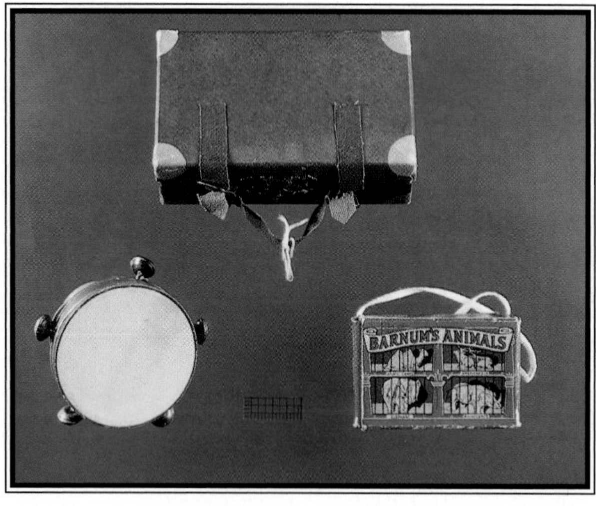

A. Suitcase Candy Container, 4". Pieces like this often ended up as doll accessories [OP, R2]. **$100.00–150.00.** B. Tambourine Candy Container (Type I), 2½" [OP, R2-3]. **$175.00–225.00.** C. Early Animal Crackers Box, 3", probably the longest running candy box designed to hang on the tree. Only the old boxes are collectible [OP, R2]. **$15.00–25.00.**

Two Santa Boot Candy Containers: A. 4", marked "Made in Germany," has a fabric bag [OP, R2-3]. **$25.00–35.00.** B. 3¼" [probably Japanese, OP, R2]. **$10.00–15.00.**

Santa Boots, pressed paper, 6", covered with Venetian dew and Dresden trim [OP-NP (1930s – 1950s), R3]. **$20.00–30.00.**

Feather Tree in a Pot Candy Container, 6" [German, OP, R1-2]. **$200.00–250.00.**

Early Lithographed Candy Boxes, 4½", circa 1880 [R1]. Same design on both. Hand painted, **$90.00–100.00.** Plain, **$70.00–90.00.**

Three Printed Candy Boxes: A. #29, 4¼" [OP, R3]. **$20.00–30.00.** B. #1, "Reindeer," 4½" [OP, R3]. **$8.00–12.00.** C. "Coaster," 4½" [American, OP (circa 1930), R3]. **$8.00–12.00.**

Three Printed Candy Boxes: A. Santa Putting up a Billboard, no title, no number, 3¼" [OP, R3]. **$15.00–20.00.** B. #33, 4¼" [American, OP, R3]. **$15.00–20.00.** C. #85, 4¼", large [American, OP, R3]. **$20.00–30.00.**

Three Printed Candy Boxes: A. "Santa," 5¾" [OP, R3]. **$10.00–12.00.** B. #20, "Secrets," 4¼" [American, OP, R3]. **$12.00–15.00.** C. #19, "Christmas Eve," 4½" [OP, R3]. **$10.00–15.00.**

Three Printed Candy Boxes: A. #34, 4¼" [American, OP, R3]. **$20.00–30.00.** B. Back side of #85 [OP, R3]. **$20.00–30.00.** C. #26, "St. Nick," 4¼" [OP, R3]. **$10.00–15.00.**

Two Candy Boxes: A. #96, "Merry Christmas," 4½" [OP, R3]. **$20.00–30.00.** B. #4, Bust of Santa with Toys, no title [OP, R3]. **$15.00–20.00.**

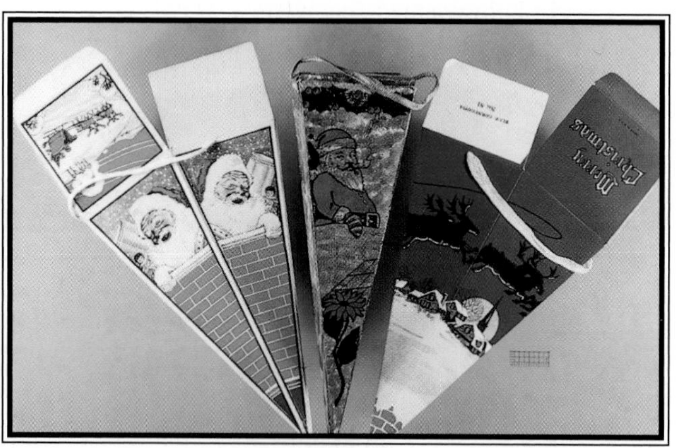

Cornucopias: A. #82, "Red Cornucopia 8" [American, OP, R3]. **$30.00–45.00.** B. Santa at the Chimney, no title, no number, 9", made by U.S. Foil Co. [OP, R3]. **$30.00–45.00.** C. #81, "Blue Cornucopia" [OP, R3]. **$30.00–45.00.**

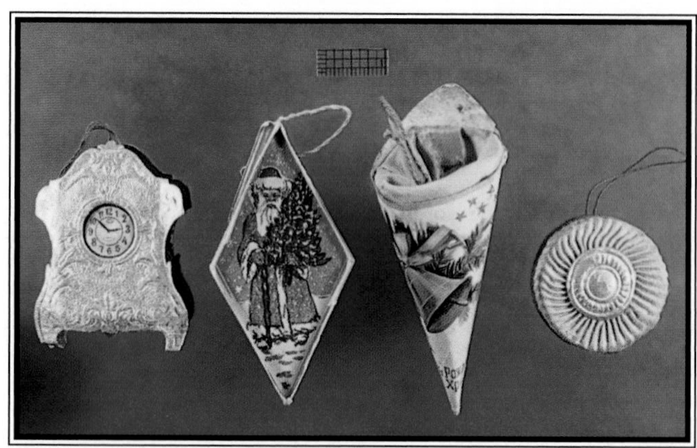

Russian Candy Containers: A. Mantel Clock, 2¾", circa 1925 [R2]. **$60.00–75.00.** B. Santa on a Diamond-shaped Box, circa 1930 [R2]. **$60.00–70.00.** C. Cornucopia, 4¾", circa 1930 [R2]. **$40.00–50.00.** D. Pill Box, 2", circa 1910 [R1]. **$135.00–150.00.**

Russian Candy Containers: A. Three Bears Book, 3¾" [OP, R2]. **$70.00–80.00.** B. Clock, printed paper, 4" [OP, R2]. **$70.00–80.00.** C. Animal Music Book, 3" [OP, R2]. **$70.00–80.00.**

Paper Ornaments

From the earliest descriptions of Christmas trees during the Renaissance until the 1920s, paper played a major role in decorations. The earliest record of a decorated tree, one in Strasbourg in 1605, mentioned paper roses as part of the ornamentation. Paper chains, flowers, and candleholders are depicted on trees from the 1700s and early 1800s. Paper decorations reached the pinnacle of their popularity from the 1870s to 1900. During this time, new printing and embossing processes brought commercially made "fancy German paper" flooding into the international market. While the commercially made decorations are more sought after by collectors, the homemade ones are just as rare.

There were many popular themes in both commercial and homemade paper ornaments. Flowers, stars, crescent moons, crosses, hearts, anchors, horses, horseshoes, lyres, harps, dolls, fairies, sleighs, shoes, boats, trolley cars, Jacob's ladders, hot air balloons, vases, urns, coffee pots, baskets, butterflies, carriages, fish, birds, dogs, cats, and other animals all found their place on the holiday tree. Patriotic themes such as Miss Liberty, Uncle Sam, stars, the American eagle, and shields were popular during the Spanish-American War and World War I. At the turn of the century, tarrifs, embargoes, and anti-German feelings generated by World War I cut deeply into both the supply and the demand for paper ornaments. By the 1920s, the style of decorations changed from predominantly paper to predominantly glass decorations. By the 1940s and 1950s, only paper candy boxes and Moravian stars remained.

Scraps, also known as die-cuts or, more accurately, chromolithographs, were a product of the industrial and technological revolution of the nineteenth century. As Christmas ornaments, scraps are often found as small angels, Santas, or children riders glued onto blown glass airplanes, balloons, dirigibles, sailboats, swan boats, cotton, Dresden ornaments, glass, or other types of material to add fine-colored detail. Sometimes the scrap was not merely added for color, but rather became an integral part of the glass ornament itself. Then too, the scraps themselves often became ornaments. Twists of wire tinsel, colored cellophane, crepe paper, cotton batting, or mica snow might be added for further decoration. Sometimes the scrap was wired or glued onto a simple tinsel ring. Other times, wire loops were pushed through the paper scrap itself. The value of a scrap ornament is not based on whether it is store bought or homemade, but rather on its overall appearance and subject matter. It is generally true that the older the scrap is, the more desirable and valuable it is. There were thousands of different scraps used as Christmas ornaments, and it would be very difficult to catalog them all.

Double scraps, ornaments with scraps on either side (whether exactly the same or different), will be worth more. Mirror image scraps, decorations that have scraps that fit back-to-back perfectly, are even rarer than other doubles. Some scraps were used plain, with only a string or thread hanger. Like other ornaments, the condition of the paper decoration is important. Creases, stains, tears, fading, flaking paint, or ink all substantially reduce the value and desirability of a scrap.

Scrap reproductions have been produced in the past twenty years. Older scraps were generally printed on heavy paper that was sometimes the thickness of light cardboard and was more heavily embossed. The colors on old pieces are also richer and deeper than on new. Modern versions are made by offset printing and not by chromolithography, and thus, they are generally easily recognized from the originals. New prints have been reproduced on thin paper, with shallow embossing and the manufacturer's name printed on the front or reverse. Now that the quality of color photo copying has greatly improved, collectors can reproduce even the rarest of chromos themselves.

The golden age of the richly colored, embossed, and die-cut scrap lasted from about 1870 to 1905. In 1905, tarrifs on "fancy German paper" began to cut back the supply in both the United States and Europe. Whether homemade or commercially produced, scraps once added color and variety to the Victorian tree.

Large Angel with a Palm Branch, 15" [OP, R1]. **$150.00–175.00.**

Angel with a Cornucopia, approx. 4½", 8" (shown), and 9" overall. A wire coil on the back allows this piece to be hung or used as a tree top. Made by Littauer & Boysen, circa 1900 [German, OP, R2]. Medium, **$90.00–110.00.** Large, **$125.00–150.00.**

Angel with a Lily, approx. 7" & 9" (shown), scrap only [German, OP-NP, R2]. Small, **$50.00–60.00.** Large, **$70.00–90.00.**

Praying Angel, 7½" [OP, R1-2]. **$50.00–75.00.**

Two Lady Angels, 3" & 8½" (shown) [OP, R2]. Small, **$20.00–25.00.** Large, **$50.00–75.00.**

Angel with an Open Book, 4½", 10½" overall [OP, R2]. **$60.00–75.00.**

Angel with a Ribbon, 8" scrap, 12" overall [OP, R2]. Scrap, **$30.00–40.00.** With tinsel, **$60.00–75.00.**

Angel with a Decorated Tree, 6½", 9" overall [OP, R2]. Scrap, **$25.00–35.00.** With tinsel, **$60.00–80.00.**

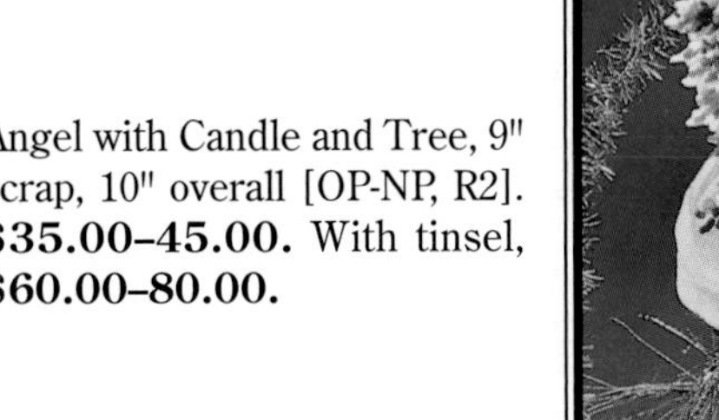

Angel with Candle and Tree, 9" scrap, 10" overall [OP-NP, R2]. **$35.00–45.00.** With tinsel, **$60.00–80.00.**

A. Angel with a Book and Tree, 9" [OP, R1-2]. Scrap, **$40.00–50.00.** With tinsel, **$60.00–70.00.** B. Angel with a Book and Scroll, 9¼" [OP, R1-2]. Scrap, **$35.00–45.00.** With tinsel, **$45.00–60.00.**

Angel Torso with a Banner, 4", 7¼" overall [OP, R2]. Scrap, **$12.00–18.00.** With tinsel, **$40.00–50.00.**

A. Three Angels Standing in a Crescent Moon, small, 2½" scrap, 3" overall [OP, R3]. Scrap, **$15.00–20.00 each.** B. Children, generic, 2¼" [OP-NP]. **$15.00–20.00.** C. Angel Sitting in a Crescent Moon, small, 2¾" [OP, R2]. Scrap, **$8.00–10.00.** With tinsel, **$15.00–20.00.**

Mother and Child Angels, 9¼" scrap, 12" overall [probably English, OP, R1-2]. Scrap, **$20.00–30.00.** With tinsel, **$45.00–55.00.**

Flying Angel with a Basket of Toys, 6¼" scrap, 9" overall. Two scraps appear slightly blurred because they were off register during the printing process [OP, R2]. Scrap, **$30.00–35.00.** With tinsel, **$50.00–60.00.**

Angel in a Crescent Moon, 8¼"H [OP, R2]. **$85.00–110.00.**

Two Girl Angels Ringing a Bell, 7¾" [OP, R2-3]. **$45.00–65.00.**

A. Child Angel in a Banner (Type I), 7" [OP, R1-2]. Scrap, **$25.00–30.00.** With tinsel, **$50.00–65.00.** B. Child Angel in a Banner (Type II), 7" [OP, R1-2]. Scrap, **$25.00–30.00.** With tinsel, **$50.00–65.00.**

Two Angel Children with a Tree, 7" [OP-NP (1990s), R2]. Scrap, **$40.00–50.00.** With tinsel, **$60.00–80.00.**

Angel on a Cloud Praying, 7" scrap, 12" overall [OP, R1]. Scrap, **$25.00–35.00.** With tinsel, **$60.00–70.00.**

Angel with a Violin, 6" scrap, 8½" overall [OP, R2]. Scrap, **$12.00–18.00.** With tinsel, **$40.00–55.00.**

Two Angels in an Eight-pointed Star, 7½" [OP, R1-2]. Scrap, **$30.00–40.00.** With tinsel, **$60.00–80.00.**

A. Nativity Scene, generic, 3" [OP, R3-4]. Scrap, **$3.00–5.00.** With tinsel, **$10.00–15.00.** B. Angel Head, generic, 2½" [OP-NP, R3]. Scrap, **$3.00–5.00.** With Tinsel, **$15.00–20.00.** C. Two Lady Angels with Flowers, small, 3" [OP, R2]. Scrap, **$8.00–12.00.** With tinsel, **$25.00–35.00.**

Angel Heads, generic [OP-NP, R3]: A. 2½" scrap, 6½" overall. **$20.00–25.00.** B. 1¾" scrap, 5½" overall. **$20.00–25.00.** C. 1" scrap, 4½" overall. **$15.00–20.00.**

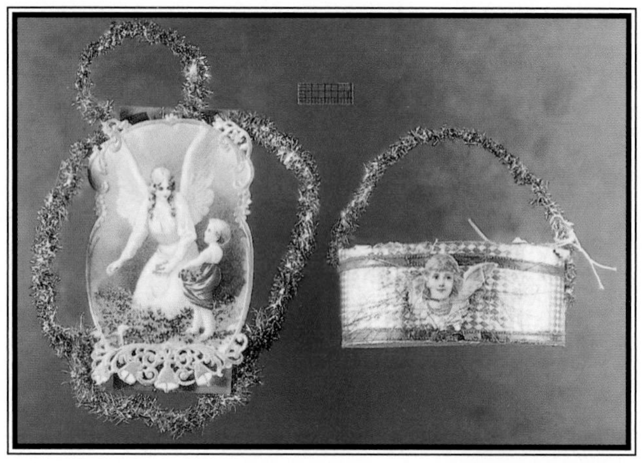

A. Guardian Angel and Boy in a Frame, 5¼" [OP, R1-2]. Scrap, **$30.00–40.00.** With tinsel, **$45.00–55.00.** B. 1" Angel Head Applied to a Candy Bucket, 4¼"L [OP, R3]. **$90.00–125.00.**

Small Generic Angel on a Crepe Paper Oval, Dresden wings, 3½" angel, 5¾" overall [OP, R2-3]. **$35.00–45.00.**

Generic Angels on Crepe Paper and Tarlton Cotton [all OP, R2-3]: A. 2½" scrap, 5¼" overall. **$20.00–25.00.** B. 2¾" scrap, 5¾" overall. **$30.00–35.00.** C.¾" scrap, 2¾" overall. **$15.00–20.00.**

A. Angel with a Cornucopia, small, 4½" [OP, R2]. Scrap, **$20.00–25.00.** With tinsel, **$25.00–30.00.** B. Santa in a Heart Frame, 4½" [OP, R1-2]. Scrap, **$15.00–20.00.** With tinsel, **$25.00–35.00.**

Snow Angel with a Candle, 10" [German, OP-NP, R2-3]. Made by Heymann & Schmidt. Scrap, **$90.00–125.00.**

Snow Angel with Toys and Butterfly, 7" & 10" (shown) [German, OP, R3]. Made by Heymann & Schmidt. Small scrap, **$50.00–60.00.** Large scrap, **$90.00–125.00** .

Snow Angel with Nest of Birds, 10½" [German, OP, R3]. Made by Heymann & Schmidt. Scrap, **$90.00–125.00.**

Snow Angel with Basket of Lilies; 4", 7½", & 9¾" (shown) [German, OP, R2]. Made by Heymann & Schmidt. Small scrap, **$25.00–35.00.** Medium scrap, **$60.00–95.00.** Large scrap, **$90.00–125.00.**

Snow Angel Boy with a Tree, 2½" & 7¾" (shown) [OP, R1-2]. Small, **$10.00–12.00.** Large, **$60.00–80.00.**

Snow Angel with a Letter, 4½" scrap, 6½" overall [OP, R1-2]. Scrap, **$8.00–12.00.** With tinsel, **$40.00–55.00.**

Snow Angel with a Basket of Holly, 4¾" scrap, label reads "Patented June 1898" [OP, R1-2]. Scrap, **$18.00–25.00.** With tinsel, **$40.00–50.00.**

Three Snow Children with Toys, 10" & 12½" (shown) [OP, R1-2]. Small scrap, **$175.00–200.00.** Large scrap, **$275.00–350.00.**

Snow Angel with Hand Bells, 12¾" [OP, R1]. **$175.00–200.00.**

Two Snow Angels made by Littaur & Boyse (1887 – 1927): A. Snow Angel with a Tree & Songbook, 8" [German, OP-NP (1980s – 1990s), R2-3]. **$50.00–75.00.** B. Snow Angel with a Tree, 5" [German, OP-NP (1980s – 1990s), R2-3]. **$50.00–75.00.**

Snow Children in the Forest, 9½" [OP, R2-3]. **$70.00–90.00.**

Snow Children in an Ice Cave, 10½" [OP, R2-3]. **$70.00–90.00.**

Snow Children around a Fire, 10¼" [OP, R2-3]. **$70.00–90.00.**

Snow Children Carrying a Tree, 12" [OP, R1]. Scrap, **$175.00–200.00.**

Large Chromolithograph Snow Girl with Toys, approx. 14¼". Probably German, circa 1880 – 1890 [R1]. **$225.00–275.00.**

Goggle-eyed Children boy approx. 3½" overall, girl approx. 5" overall [both OP, R2]. **$20.00–30.00** each.

Two Scrap and Tinsel Ornaments [both OP, R2]. These were probably manufactured as a set. **$25.00–35.00** each: A. Girl with a Tree, approx. 4½". B. Boy with a Tree, approx. 4".

Three Small Homemade Scraps, all approx. 4½" overall. These are probably homemade using small chromolithograph scraps and blank calling cards, circa 1915 – 1920 [R2-3]. **$8.00–12.00** each.

Five Snow Children with Toys, 7¾" [OP, R1-2]. Scrap, **$75.00–100.00.** With tinsel, **$100.00–125.00.**

A. Boy Clown, 3½" [OP, R3]. **$15.00–20.00.** B. Angel in a Star Medallion, 3½" [OP, R3]. **$15.00–20.00.** C. Boy & Girl in an Oval of Flowers, 3½" [OP, R3]. **$15.00–20.00.**

Nativity Scene with Angels, 6¼" [OP, R1]. Scrap, **$30.00–40.00.** With tinsel, **$45.00–60.00.**

Madonna and Child, 4¾" scrap, 9½" over-all [OP, R2]. Scrap, **$20.00–25.00.** With tinsel, **$40.00–50.00.**

Nativity/Snow Scene, 3-D, 5¼" x 5" [German, OP, R2]. **$30.00–40.00.**

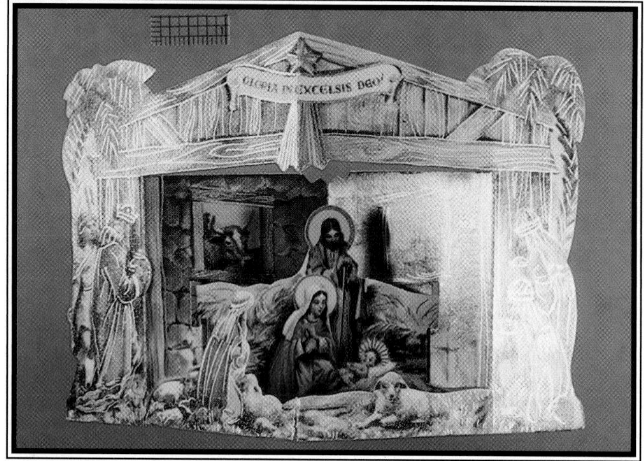

Nativity Scenes Fold-out, 7" x 4½" [German, OP, R2]. **$35.00–45.00.**

Santa with Tree and Toys (Type VIII), 5½" & 11¼" (shown), used as an advertising card [OP, R2-3]. Small scrap, **$20.00–30.00.** Large scrap, **$150.00–175.00.** Small with tinsel, **$30.00–50.00.** Large with tinsel, **$200.00–250.00.**

Santa in a Ring of Dancing Children, 10¾" x 8½" [German, OP, R1-2]. **$200.00–275.00.**

Santa with Children (Type III), 9¾" [OP-NP (1990s), R2]. Scrap, **$175.00–225.00.**

Santa, Child, and Angel, 7" [German, OP, R1]. Scrap, **$90.00–110.00.**

Santa with Children (Type I), 10¼" x 7½" [OP, R2]. Scrap, **$150.00–185.00.** With tinsel, **$150.00–185.00.**

Santa with Toys and Lantern, 9¼", by Raphael Tuck [English, OP, R1]. Scrap, **$140.00–175.00.**

Santa with a Cane, Toys, and a Puppet, 10" [OP, R1]. Scrap, **$175.00–200.00.**

Santa with Toys, "Jolly Elf," 12"H x 6¾"W [OP-NP (1990s), R1-2]. Old, **$175.00–200.00.** New, **$2.00.**

A. Santa with Children Blowing Horns, 6", by Raphael Tuck [OP, R2]. Scrap, **$20.00–30.00.** With tinsel, **$35.00–45.00.** B. Santa with a Cane and Toys, 8¼" x 3½" [possibly English, OP, R2]. Scrap, **$50.00–75.00.** With tinsel, **$75.00–90.00.**

A. Santa with Tree, Toys, and Glasses, 6¾" [probably English by Tuck, OP, R2]. Scrap, **$30.00–40.00.** With tinsel, **$50.00–65.00.** B. Santa with Tree, Toys, and Bundle of Books, 6¾" [OP, R2]. Scrap, **$30.00–40.00.** With tinsel, **$50.00–65.00.** C. Santa with Girl and Lamb, 6" [probably English, OP, R2]. Scrap, **$15.00–18.00.** With tinsel, **$20.00–25.00.**

Swag of Three Scraps of Santa with a Tree and Toys , 6¾" each [OP, R2-3]. Each scrap, **$20.00–25.00.** Each with tinsel, **$35.00–45.00.** Swag of three, **$60.00–75.00.**

Swag of Three Scraps of Walking Santa with a Tree and Toys (Type I), all 4¾" [OP, R1-2]. Each scrap, **$15.00–18.00.** Each with tinsel, **$30.00–40.00.** Swag of three, **$45.00–60.00.**

Santa with a Tree and Toys (Type VI), 9¼" [OP, R2]. Scrap, **$65.00–75.00.** With tinsel, **$75.00–90.00.**

Santa in White with a Tree and Toys, 9¼" [German, OP, R2]. Scrap, **$75.00–90.00.** With tinsel, **$125.00–150.00.**

Santa with a Tree (Type I), 6¼", made by E. Heller of Vienna [Austrian, OP, R2-3]. **$50.00–60.00.**

Santa with a Tree and Toys (Type IV), 3¾" & 6½" (shown) [OP, R2-3]. Small, **$30.00–40.00.** Large, **$60.00–75.00.**

Two Sizes of a Santa with a Tree and Toys (Type II), 6¾" & 4¾". This is a popular image of Santa [OP-NP (1990s), R3]. Small, **$25.00–35.00.** Large, **$50.00–60.00.**

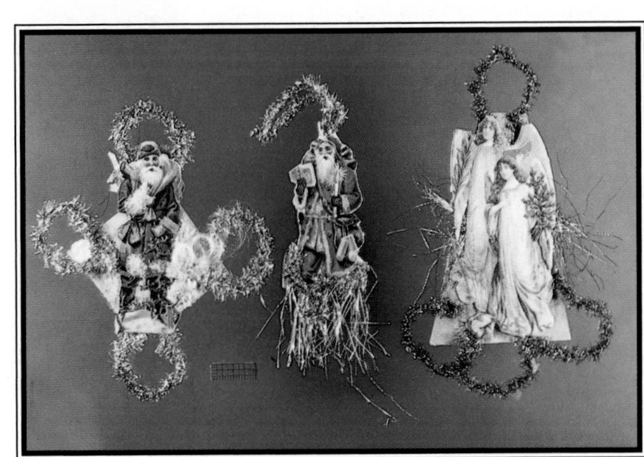

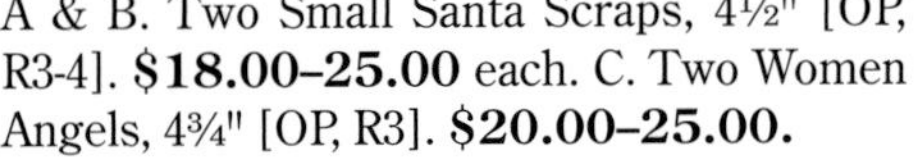

A & B. Two Small Santa Scraps, 4½" [OP, R3-4]. **$18.00–25.00** each. C. Two Women Angels, 4¾" [OP, R3]. **$20.00–25.00.**

Santa with a Tree and Toys (Type III), 6¼" scrap, 9" overall [OP, R2-3]. **$90.00–110.00.**

Santa and Children (Type II), approx. 6½" and 10¼" (shown) [German, OP, R2]. Small, **$75.00–100.00.** Large, **$150.00–175.00.**

Santa in a White Fur Coat and with a Cane, 4½" [OP, R1-2]. Scrap, **$30.00–40.00.** With tinsel, **$50.00–60.00.**

Santa Getting His Picture Taken, 7" [OP, R1]. Scrap, **$50.00–65.00.** With tinsel, **$75.00–90.00.**

A. Santa with a Tree and Toys (Type V), 9¾" [OP, R2]. Scrap, **$65.00–75.00.** With tinsel, **$75.00–90.00.** B. Santa Paper Doll Ornament, Father Christmas with Sad Face and Presents, 6" scrap, 11" overall [OP, R2]. Scrap, **$80.00–100.00.** With skirt, **$225.00–275.00.**

A. Santa with a Tree and a Basket of Toys, 8½" [OP, R2]. Scrap, **$25.00–35.00.** With tinsel, **$50.00–60.00.** B. Santa in Blue with a Tree and a Bag of Toys, 8½" [OP, R2]. Scrap, **$20.00–30.00.** With tinsel, **$50.00–60.00.**

A. Santa with a Tree, Toys, and an Airplane, 9¼" [OP, R2]. Scrap, **$30.00–45.00.** With tinsel, **$50.00–60.00.** B. Santa in Blue with a Tree, Toys, and a Car, 9¼" [OP, R2]. Scrap, **$30.00–45.00.** With tinsel, **$50.00–60.00.**

Swag of Three Scraps of Walking Santa with a Tree and Toys (Type II), 4¾" [OP, R2]. Each scrap, **$12.00–18.00.** Each with tinsel, **$30.00–45.00.** Swag of three, **$40.00–50.00.**

Swag of Four Small Santas, 2" [OP, R2-3]. **$2.00–5.00** each. Swag of four, **$8.00–15.00.**

Father Christmas Head with Holly, 4¼" scrap, 8½" overall [OP, R2-3]. Scrap, **$8.00–10.00.** With tinsel, **$25.00–35.00.**

A. Krampus Heads, 3½" [OP, R3]. Each scrap, **$4.00–5.00.** Each with tinsel, **$10.00–15.00.** B. St. Nicholas Heads, 3¾" [OP, R3]. Each scrap, **$5.00–10.00.** Each with tinsel, **$15.00–25.00.**

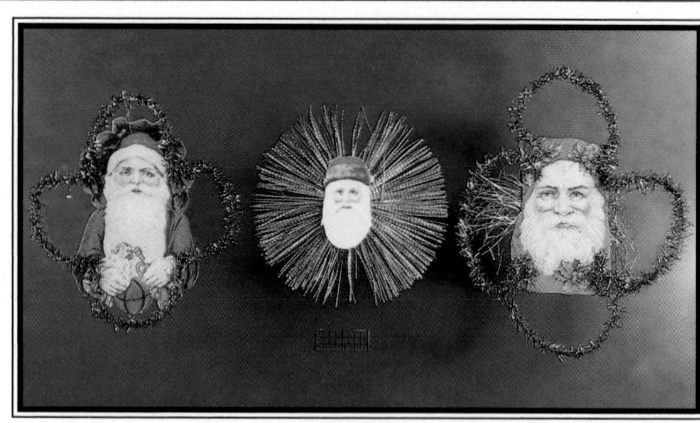

Generic Santa Heads: A. 3½" scrap, 4" overall. **$20.00–25.00.** B. 1½" scrap, 3½" overall. **$15.00–20.00.** C. 2½" scrap, 5" overall. **$20.00–25.00.**

A. Santa Head on a Metal Snowflake, 5" [OP, R2-3]. **$20.00–25.00.** B. Santa Head on a Cardboard Star, with tinsel, 7¼" [OP, R2-3]. **$15.00–20.00.** C. Santa on a Dresden Bird, 6½" [OP, R1]. **$50.00–60.00.**

Two Santas in a Model T Truck, 4½"L [OP-NP (1990s), R2]. **$35.00–45.00.**

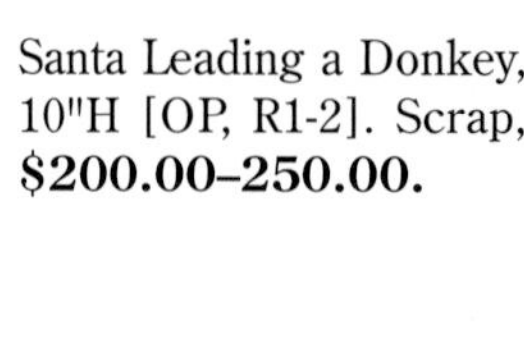

Santa Riding a Donkey (Type II), 9½" scrap, 12" overall [OP, R2]. Scrap, **$50.00–65.00.** With tinsel, **$80.00–90.00.**

Santa Leading a Donkey, 10"H [OP, R1-2]. Scrap, **$200.00–250.00.**

Santa Riding a White Horse, large, 13½" [OP, R1-2]. Scrap, **$650.00–800.00.**

Santa in a Train, 6¾"L [OP, R1]. Scrap, **$75.00–100.00.**

Santa and Children with His Sleigh and Two Reindeer, small, 8"L x 5½"H [OP, R2]. Scrap, **$100.00–135.00.**

Santa with His Sleigh, 10" [OP, R1]. **$300.00–375.00.**

Santa and Children with His Sleigh and One Reindeer, 13½"L x 9"H [OP, R2]. **$275.00–325.00.**

Santa in a Sleigh with Two Horses, 13¼"L x 9¼"W [OP, R1-2]. **$300.00–375.00.**

Decorated Tree (Type II), 8¼" scrap, 10½" overall [OP, R1]. Scrap, **$70.00–80.00.** With tinsel, **$100.00–110.00.**

Decorated Tree on a Table, 13" [OP, R1]. Scrap, **$250.00–300.00.**

A. Angel Sitting in a Crescent Moon, 5½" [OP, R2]. Large scrap, **$20.00–25.00.** With tinsel, **$30.00–40.00.** B. Christ Kindle with Crown of Thorns, 6¾" [OP, R2]. Scrap, **$20.00–25.00.** With tinsel, **$35.00–45.00.** C. Christ Kindle with Sheep and Fruit, 7" [OP, R2]. Scrap, **$20.00–25.00**. With tinsel, **$35.00–45.00.**

Three Christ Kindle Figures: A. Christ Kindle with a Tree and a Lamb (Type I), 7" [OP, R2]. Scrap, **$18.00–25.00.** With tinsel, **$35.00–45.00.** B. Christ Kindle with a Tree and a Basket of Cookies, 7" [OP, R1-2]. Scrap, **$20.00–25.00.** With tinsel, **$35.00–45.00.** C. Christ Kindle with a Tree and a Lamb (Type II) [OP, R2]. Scrap, **$18.00–20.00.**

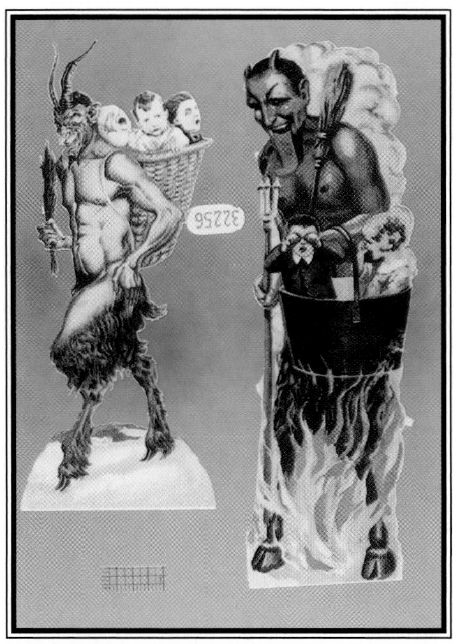

A. Krampus Carrying Off Children, 7¼" [OP, R1-2]. Scrap, **$40.00–50.00.** B. Krampus with Children in a Pot, 8½" [OP, R1-2]. Scrap, **$35.00–45.00.**

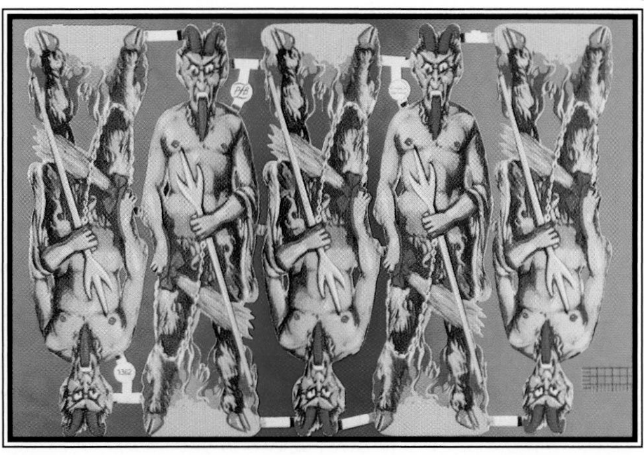

Krampus with Switches and a Pitchfork, large, 6½", by PBZ [OP, R2-3]. Scrap, **$8.00–12.00** each.

Praying Angel with a Cotton Skirt, large, 8¼" scrap, 21" overall [OP, R1-2]. **$250.00–275.00.**

Angel Doll with a Harp, ready for a cotton skirt, 9½" scrap, would make a 15" - 17" doll [OP, R1]. Scrap, **$60.00–80.00.** Doll with skirt, **$200.00–250.00.**

Angel Doll with Cornucopia, large, 9½", doll with skirt could be 15" – 17" long [OP, R1-2]. Scrap, **$60.00–80.00.** Doll with skirt, **$200.00–250.00.**

A & B. Lithographed Woman and Child Doll Ornaments, 6¼" and 3½", circa 1870, fabric and lace skirts [OP, R1]. Woman, **$35.00–45.00.** Child, **$20.00–25.00.**

Lady with Flowers in a Fabric Skirt, approx. 11" overall. The arms are made of white cardboard and probably indicate the piece was homemade, circa 1870 [R1]. **$60.00–90.00.**

Lady in a Fabric Skirt with a Bustle, approx. 10½" overall. The arms are made of white cardboard. This is an early piece and was probably homemade circa 1870 [R1]. **$50.00–75.00.**

Baby with a Bottle and a Cotton Skirt, approx. 25" overall and 14" scrap, circa 1890 [German, OP, R2]. Small, **$225.00–275.00.**

Baby with a Bottle, 15" overall [OP, R1-2]. Scrap, **$40.00–50.00.** With skirt, **$200.00–250.00.**

A. Generic Doll Ornament, Baby in a Cotton Gown, 4½" [OP, R3]. **$30.00–50.00.** B. Nativity Scene in Eight-Pointed Star, 5¼" [OP, R2-3]. Scrap, **$15.00–20.00.** With tinsel, **$25.00–30.00.**

A. Happy and Crying Baby in a Bonnet, 2½", will make a 5" – 6" doll [OP, R3]. Small scrap, **$12.00–18.00.** With skirt, **$75.00–85.00.** B & C. Happy and Crying Baby, 2½" and 4½" [OP, R3]. Large scrap, **$15.00–20.00.** With skirt, **$100.00–150.00.**

Girl in a Cape Coat and a Cotton Skirt, approx. 4½" scrap and 12¼" overall, circa 1890 [R2]. **$100.00–125.00.**

Girl with a Doll and a Cotton Skirt, approx. 18¾". Probably German, circa 1890. **$200.00–250.00.**

Girl with Roses and a Cotton Skirt, approx. 20". She is marked "From Aunt Carrie to Louise Lloyd Dec 25, 1910." Probably German [R2]. **$200.00–275.00.**

Girl in a Bonnet and a Cotton Skirt, approx. 6½" scrap and 17" overall. Probably German, circa 1890 [R2]. **$150.00–200.00.**

Girl Holding Flowers, 6" scrap, 15" overall [OP, R2]. Scrap, **$25.00–35.00.** With skirt, **$175.00–200.00.**

Girl with a Kitten, 5¼" scrap, 11" – 13" overall [OP, R2-3]. Scrap, **$25.00–35.00.** With skirt, **$175.00–200.00.**

Girl with a Doll and a Cotton Skirt, 10" [OP, R2]. **$125.00–150.00.**

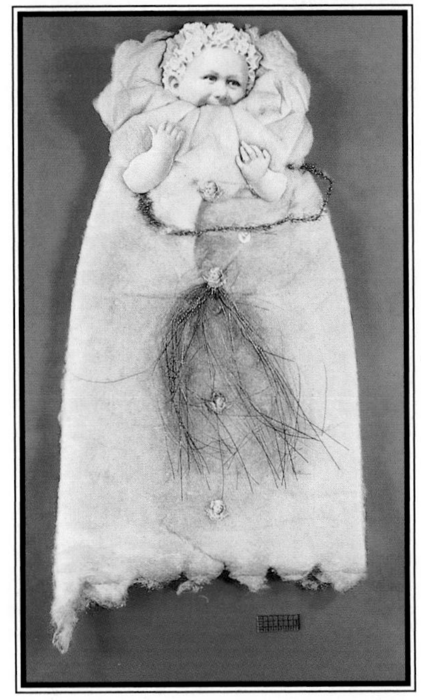

Happy Baby Doll Ornament, scrap with cotton skirt, 4" scrap baby, 14" overall [German, OP, R2]. **$150.00–200.00.**

Miss Liberty Paper Doll Ornament, 9¾" [OP, R2]. **$175.00–200.00.**

Cat with a Ball of Yarn, 18" [probably German, OP, R1]. **$300.00–400.00.**

Monkey with a Tambourine, 18¾" [probably German, OP, R1]. **$300.00–400.00.**

Boy in a Cotton Snowsuit, 8½" [OP, R1]. **$125.00–150.00.**

Jointed Dolls in Crepe Paper Dresses and Tinsel Trim [OP, R2-3]. **$60.00–85.00.**

Scraps on Lace Rosettes, 4½" dia, homemade [OP, R1]. **$40.00–50.00** each.

Busts of Children on Crepe Paper Discs, 5" [OP, R2-3]. **$30.00–40.00.**

A. Snow Girl with a Doll, 4¾" [OP-NP, R2]. Scrap, **$25.00–35.00.** With skirt, **$125.00–150.00.** B. Snow Girl with a Muff, 5" [OP-NP, R2]. Scrap, **$25.00–35.00.** With skirt, **$125.00–150.00.**

Three Sizes of Little Red Riding Hood Scrap Dolls. Made in Germany by Littaur & Boysen, which also produced 2¾" & 3¾" sizes [all R3]: A. 5¾". Scrap, **$20.00–30.00.** With Skirt, **$50.00–80.00.** B. 5". Scrap, **$20.00–30.00.** C. 5¼", full body. Scrap only, **$8.00–10.00.** With tinsel, **$15.00–20.00.**

Two Peasant Ladies with Their Babies, large, 4¼" scrap, 9" overall [R3]. Made in Germany by Littaur & Boysen, which also made a 2¾" size. Scrap, **$20.00–25.00.** With skirt, **$60.00–75.00.**

Snow Girl with a Tree and a Spun Glass Skirt, 4¾" torso, 9½" overall [OP, R1]. Scrap, **$30.00–40.00.** With skirt, **$80.00–90.00.**

Ballerina with Jointed Arms and Legs, approx. 16". The skirt is crepe paper with Dresden trim, and the collar is fabric lace with Dresden trim [OP, R1-2]. **$150.00–175.00.**

Patriotic Lady, 21½" [OP, R1]. **$550.00–700.00.**

Lady in a Rounded Skirt, large, 9½" [OP, R3]. **$70.00–80.00.**

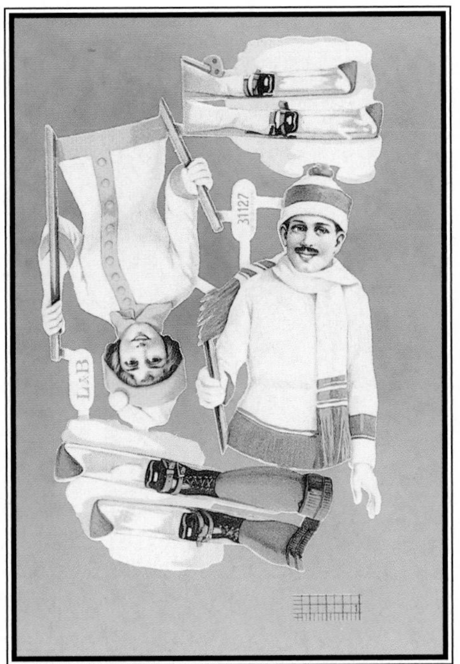

Man and Woman Skiers, both 4¾", made by Littaur and Boysen [German, OP, R2]. Each scrap, **$20.00–25.00.** Each with skirt, **$50.00–75.00.**

Santa with Cotton Skirt (Type III), 4½" head, 17" overall [OP, R1]. **$250.00–300.00.**

Santa with a Pack and a Cotton Skirt, approx. 9½" scrap and 20¼" overall. Probably German made, circa 1900 [R2]. **$225.00–275.00.**

A. Santa in an SG Skirt (Type I), 4½" body, 8¾" overall [OP, R2-3]. Scrap, **$30.00–35.00.** With skirt, **$70.00–90.00.** B. Santa in an SG Skirt (Type III), 2½" body, 5" overall [OP, R2-3]. Scrap, **$20.00–25.00.** With skirt, **$50.00–65.00.**

Santa to be Used with Skirt (Type II), large, 5½" [German, OP, R2-3]. Scrap, **$45.00–55.00.** With skirt, **$150.00–175.00.** This Santa was also made in a 2½" size.

Santa (Type II) with a Cotton Skirt, approx. 2½" & 5½" (shown) scrap, 13" overall [German, OP, R2-3]. **$150.00–175.00.**

Two Santas to be Used with Skirts (Type VI and Type VII, both 2½" torso) [German, OP, R2]. Scrap only, **$15.00–20.00.** With skirt, **$45.00–60.00.**

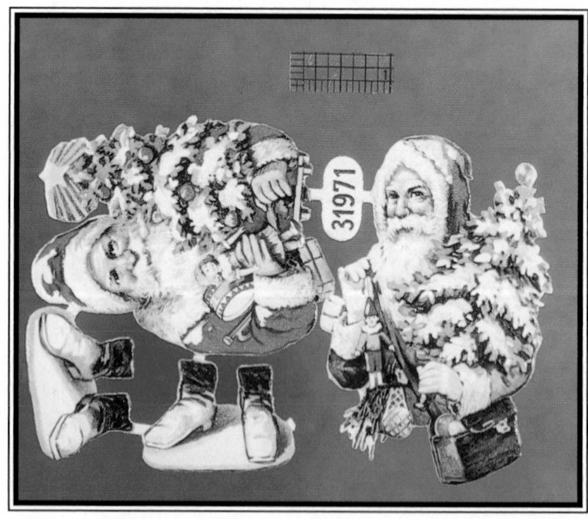

A. Santa to be Used with Skirt (Type IV), 3" torso [German, OP, R2-3]. Scrap only, **$25.00–35.00.** With skirt, **$50.00–90.00.** B. Santa to be Used with Skirt (Type V), 3¼" torso [German, OP, R2-3]. Scrap, **$25.00–35.00.** With skirt, **$80.00–90.00.**

A. Two Santas to be Used with Skirts (Type VIII and IX), both 5", still joined on ladder and ready for spun glass or cotton skirt [both OP, R2]. Scrap, **$30.00–35.00.** With skirt, **$100.00–125.00.** B. Santa Heads (Type IV), 1¼" – 1⅝" [OP, R3]. **$2.00–3.00** each.

Standard Form SG Rosette with Angel in a Flower Frame, large, double sided, 7¾" [OP, R3]. **$70.00–80.00.**

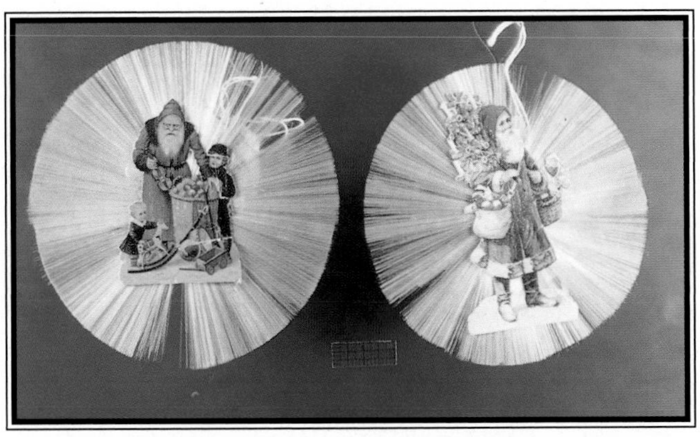

Spun Glass Rosettes with Scrap Santa on both sides: A. Medium, 4¾" dia. **$40.00–50.00.** B. Medium, 4½" dia. **$40.00–50.00.**

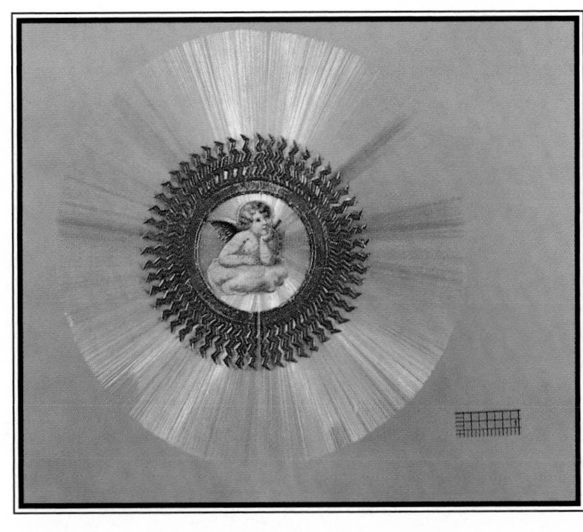

SG Rosette with Raphael Angel in a Dresden Sunburst, large, single sided, 6¾" [OP, R3]. **$55.00–65.00.**

Multicolored SG Rosette with Sun Face, 5" dia. [OP, R1]. The multicolored spun glass is unusual. **$70.00–80.00.**

Santa on a Spun Glass Comet, tinted various colors, 8½"L. The various colors of spun glass make this unusual [OP, R2]. **$60.00–80.00.**

Two Spun Glass Ornaments: A. St. Nicholas and Krampus in a Spun Glass Rosette, approx. 3¼" scraps, 4" dia., German or Austrian, circa 1930 [R2]. **$25.00–30.00.** B. Red Riding Hood with a Spun Glass Skirt, approx. 2½" scrap & 3½" dia. [OP, R2-3]. **$30.00–35.00.**

A. Old Woman in a Bonnet and a Spun Glass Skirt, 2¾" scrap, 6" overall [OP, R1-2]. **$40.00–50.00.** B. Santa with a Spun Glass Skirt (Type III), 6½" overall [OP, R2-3]. **$50.00–75.00.** C. Old Man with a Fez and a Spun Glass Skirt, 2¾" scrap, 6¼" overall [OP, R1-2]. **$40.00–50.00.**

A. Blue Spun Glass Comet, 7", colored spun glass is unusual [OP, R1]. **$60.00–80.00.** B. Spun Glass Rosette with Santa Head, 4" [OP, R3]. **$35.00–40.00.** C. Santa Head Comet, 8¼" [OP, R3]. **$40.00–60.00.** D. Rosette with Angel Head, 4" [OP, R3]. **$30.00–40.00.**

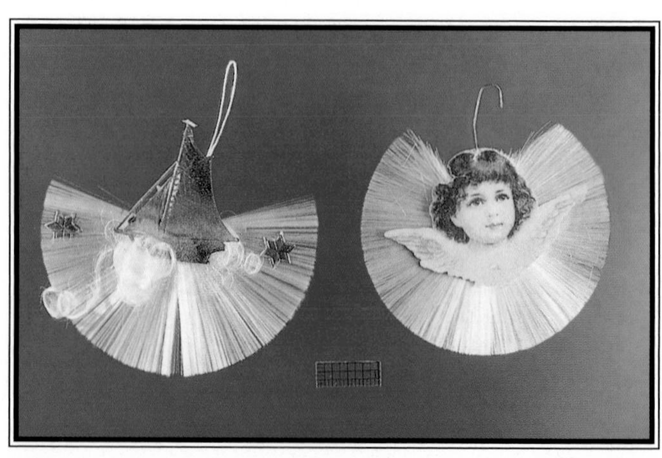

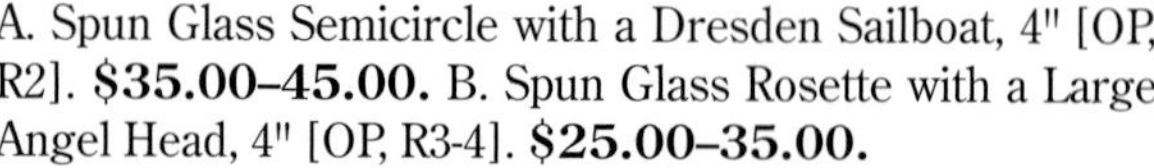

A. Spun Glass Semicircle with a Dresden Sailboat, 4" [OP, R2]. **$35.00–45.00.** B. Spun Glass Rosette with a Large Angel Head, 4" [OP, R3-4]. **$25.00–35.00.**

Spun Glass Semicircle with Angels, 6¾" [OP, R2]. **$50.00–75.00.**

A. Spun Glass Rosette with a Foil Flower, 4" [OP, R2]. **$35.00–40.00.** B. Spun Glass Rosette with a Comet Tail and an Angel Head Scrap, 7" [OP, R3]. **$40.00–50.00.** C. Spun Glass Rosette with a Pink Tint, 3¼" [OP, R2]. **$35.00–40.00.**

A. Boy Angel Walking on a Cloud, 6" [OP, R2-3]. **$25.00–40.00.** B. Angel with SG Wings, 5¼" [OP, R2-3]. **$50.00–60.00.** C. Angel with an SG Body, 4¾" [OP, R2]. **$75.00–85.00.**

Rosette Tree Top with Santa Holding a Child, 7¾" [OP, R1-2]. **$85.00–100.00.**

Standard Form SG Rosette with Walking Angel, large, single side, 7½" [OP, R2-3]. **$65.00–85.00.**

Czech Cardboard Houses, carefully painted and covered with Venetian dew (tiny glass balls) [OP, R3]. A & B. 1¾"H. **$12.00–15.00.** C & D. 3¼"L. **$25.00–30.00.**

Czech Cardboard Houses, 2" – 2¼" [OP, R3]. **$10.00–12.00.**

Czech Cardboard Houses, 1¾" – 2¼", elaborate [OP, R3]. **$15.00–25.00** each.

Czech Cardboard Houses and Churches , 1¾" – 2¼" [OP, R3]. Houses, **$12.00–15.00** each. Church, **$15.00–20.00.**

Czech Cardboard Churches, 2½" [OP, R3]. **$10.00–20.00.**

Czech Cardboard Church Ornaments, 3" – 3¾" [OP, R2]. **$15.00–25.00.**

Japanese Cardboard Houses, painted [OP, R4]. **$5.00–10.00.**

Set of Japanese Cardboard House Ornaments, glitter covered, 2½" church, 1¾" houses [NP (1950 – 1960), R4]. **$5.00–6.00** each. Set, **$20.00–25.00.**

Cardboard Stars with Heads [all OP, R2]: A. Moritiz, 3¾". **$25.00–35.00.** B. Max, 3¾". **$25.00–35.00.** C. Christmas Angel, 3¾". **$25.00–35.00.**

A & C. Cardboard Stars with Heads: A. Santa, 3¾" [OP, R1-2]. **$25.00–35.00.** C. Angel, 3¾" [OP, R1-2]. **$25.00–35.00.** B. Homemade Moravian Star, 4½" [OP-NP, R4-5]. **$0.50–1.00.**

Three Czech Frosted Cardboard Pieces, all covered with crushed glass or Venetian Dew, all circa 1920 – 1930 [R2]. **$20.00–25.00** each: A. Deer, approx. 2⅞"L. B. Angel, approx. 2½"H. C. Duck, approx. 2⅞"L.

Three Czech Frosted Cardboard Pieces, all covered with crushed glass or Venetian Dew, all circa 1920 – 1930 [R2]: A. Disc with Dresden Angel, approx. 2½". **$20.00–25.00.** B. Three-layer Star, approx. 3". **$15.00–20.00.** C. Two-layer Flower, approx. 2½". **$15.00–20.00.**

A. Butterfly with Composition Body, 4" wingspan [OP, R2]. **$110.00–135.00.** B. Cardboard Butterfly with Venetian Dew, 3" [Czech, OP, R1-2]. **$25.00–35.00.**

Flat Cardboard Hot Air Balloon Ornament, medium, 6¾". Ornaments of this type are often called Pennsylvania Dutch ornaments. **$90.00–110.00.**

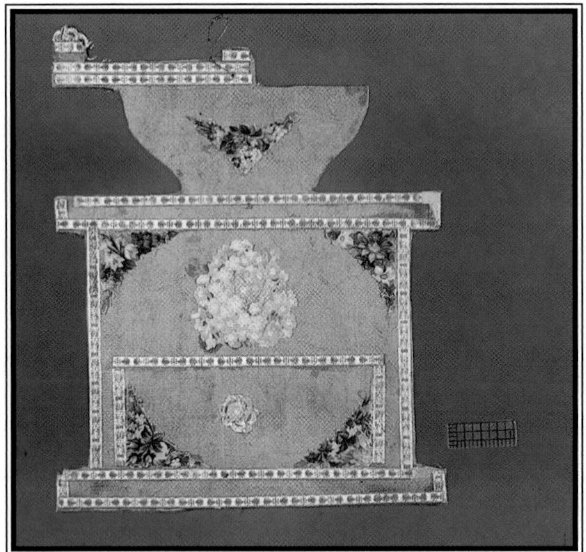

Pennsylvania Dutch Coffee Grinder, approx. 7"H. The cardboard is covered with material and scraps have been applied. Probably homemade circa 1890 [R2]. **$60.00–75.00.**

Pennsylvania Dutch Carriage, approx. 9"L. The cardboard frame is covered with pink material and scraps have been applied. Probably homemade circa 1890 [R2]. **$75.00–100.00.**

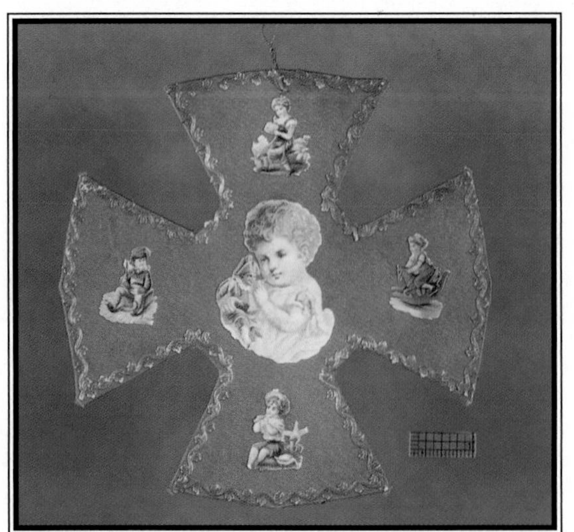

Pennsylvania Dutch Cross, approx. 6¾" dia. The cardboard cross is covered with red material and scraps have been applied. Probably homemade circa 1890 [R2]. **$60.00–75.00.**

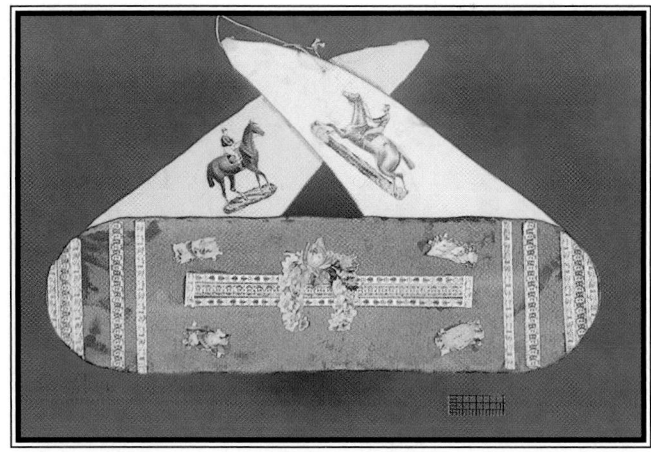

Pennsylvania Dutch Pocketknife, approx. 10½"L. The cardboard is covered with material. Scraps and Dresden trims have been applied. Probably homemade circa 1890 [R2]. **$75.00–100.00.**

Flat Cardboard Star with Tinsel Trim, medium, 7¼". **$35.00–45.00.**

Bell and Baby Jesus Flat Cardboard Ornament, medium, 2½" scrap, 7" overall [OP, R2-3]. **$35.00–45.00.**

Boy Angel Walking on a Cloud in Front of Cross, flat cardboard, medium, 6" scrap, 9¼" overall [OP, R2-3]. **$55.00–70.00.**

Crescent Moon and Star Flat Cardboard Ornament, medium, 7½". **$45.00–65.00.**

American Double-sided Paper Ornament, 2½" – 5", circa 1917 [OP, R2]. **$10.00–15.00** each.

Paper "Surprise Ball" with Face, 3⅛" dia. These were unwrapped to reveal small toys or trinkets inside [1950, R2]. **$20.00–25.00.**

Paper Surprise Ball Ornaments [NP (circa 1950), R2]: A. Santa, 5". **$20.00–25.00.** B. Snowman, 5". **$20.00–25.00.** C. Angel, 5". **$25.00–30.00.**

Box for Snow White and the Seven Dwarfs Cardboard Ornaments [OP-NP (1950s), R1]. Complete box and set, **$300.00–400.00.**

Snow White and the Seven Dwarfs Cardboard Ornaments/Candy Containers [OP-NP (1950s), Snow White R1-2, Dwarfs R3]: Snow White, 5¾". **$60.00–85.00.** Dwarfs, 5¼" – 5½". **$30.00–40.00.**

Fabric Ornaments

Homemade ornaments constructed from scraps of fabric, cotton, yarn, thread, or string were certainly among the earliest Christmas decorations. It was not until about the 1880s that fabric ornaments of several types, designed to be used for several years, were offered for sale commercially.

One fabric form that found little widespread use in the United States was crochet. Items such as miniature shoes, slippers, shopping baskets, birds, stars, etc. were crocheted with tight stitches of white or gold metallic thread. When finished, they were dipped into pots of hot white glue. As they cooled, the pieces were pulled back into their desired shapes and allowed to dry.

From the 1920s through the 1950s, some countries, most notably Japan, worked with long strings of a shredded material that had been closely compacted to give it a soft, velvety look and feel. High quality pieces of this chenille were made of shredded silk or rayon. Ropes of chenille for decorating the house were sold. In later years, chenille wrapped around wire, which resembles pipe cleaners, was used to make Santa figures with plaster or paper faces.

Fabric was also used in making Christmas stockings. Both Europe and America produced some beautifully lithographed and printed examples at the turn of the century. These came on sheets of material with instructions for cutting them out and sewing them together. Other Victorian stockings, cornucopias, and a wide range of similar decorations were made from tarlatan. This type of thin, stiff muslin with a net-like weave was used in the production of both homemade and commercial ornaments. Another form of popular fabric ornament was the mesh net candy bag filled with candy, nuts, or small gifts. These bags were generally used to make the body of a Santa with a celluloid face and small plaster arms and legs.

By far, the most popular of the fabric ornaments were those made from cotton. Cotton decorations for the tree can be divided into three general types: pressed cotton, also known as cotton batting; cotton wool, and spun cotton. Pressed cotton is smooth and found pressed together in thin layers. This could have been sprinkled with glitter and used as a tree skirt, but in another form was glued or sewn onto cardboard forms or frames in a seemingly endless variety of shapes. After fastening the cotton to the cardboard and trimming the piece, scraps and tinsel were added as decorations. Cotton batting or cotton wool was often used to portray figures in long hooded coats. These coats were cut from cotton layers and glued over a wire or cardboard frame. Scrap faces, feet, flowers, etc., were added, along with Dresden paper wings or star-shaped buttons. The most popular forms for pressed cotton figures were snow children, angels, and Santa Claus or Father Christmas. Cotton wool was often sold for creating snow scenes or placing on tree branches to give a snow-covered effect, and cotton wool ornaments appear rough and fluffy.

Spun cotton has a twisted texture to it and a slightly hardened outer shell. Spun cotton fruit seems to have been introduced about 1880. By the 1890s, cotton people and animals were being produced. The ornaments reached the height of their popularity around the turn of the century. Pieces from this time period had a lot of added detail. Fruits and vegetables had delicate painting and fabric leaves. People had scrap or composition faces, and clothes made from fabric or crepe paper. Originally, these pieces sold for as much as a fine Dresden ornament. People ornaments often had their arms, legs, head, and body twisted as separate pieces, usually with a wire armature inside. More deluxe models had porcelain, bisque, plaster, or composition faces that were provided by the toy industry. The earlier animals seem to have been more elaborate; late pieces have a spindly appearance, painted features, and little added detail. Although old, these later ornaments are considered less desirable by collectors.

Those spun cotton pieces in the shape of people or animals top the list in popularity of cotton or fabric ornaments. Japan as well as Germany produced spun cotton pieces, and ornaments from these two countries are sometimes hard to tell apart. It helps to keep in mind that Japanese pieces were less tightly wrapped and did not include the delicate details of the German ones. The Japanese also used clay or composition-like faces with a pinkish cast to them.

One recent type of cotton ornament drawing collectors' attention is the Russian cotton ornament. With the collapse of the Iron Curtain, many styles have come into the American market. These have a thicker, rougher texture than their German counterparts. They often have composition faces, are painted, and have Russian folklore and culture as main themes. These appear to have been made between 1900 and 1960.

No matter what the form, cotton or fabric decorations add a soft touch to an ornament collection. Antique pieces are cherished and eagerly sought after by many collectors.

Notes:

1. Although some icicle forms were produced into the 1950s, most cotton pieces are old, i.e., before 1939. Nevertheless, after being off the market for nearly fifty years, spun cotton decorations are once again being produced. The largest producer is D. Blumchen & Co. It has had many fruits and vegetables remade in Germany. It also designs and makes its own beautiful people figures. Cynthia Jones has also expertly reproduced some antique pieces.
2. Pink plaster-like and celluloid faces are generally later Japanese pieces.
3. Spun cotton animals are rarer than people and generally more collectible.
4. Cotton batting and pressed cotton pieces were constructed without set forms or patterns. Therefore, each piece is unique in its dress, decorations, and size. Most pieces have to be lumped into a general category. Prices and desirability will vary with the condition and quality of the construction of the piece, as well as any added decorations.
5. Some pieces, such as people and animals, use a combination of spun and pressed cotton. The arms and legs may be spun, with the clothing or torso made from cotton batting or pressed cotton. The forms are not always separate, and thus do not fit into neat individual categories.

Cotton Batting Santa, large, 9¾" [OP, R2-3]. **$200.00–250.00.**

Two Cotton Batting Santas, probably circa 1930s: A. Santa with Switches, 8¼" [R2-3]. **$200.00–250.00.** B. Santa with Scrap Tree, 8" [R2-3]. **$200.00–250.00.**

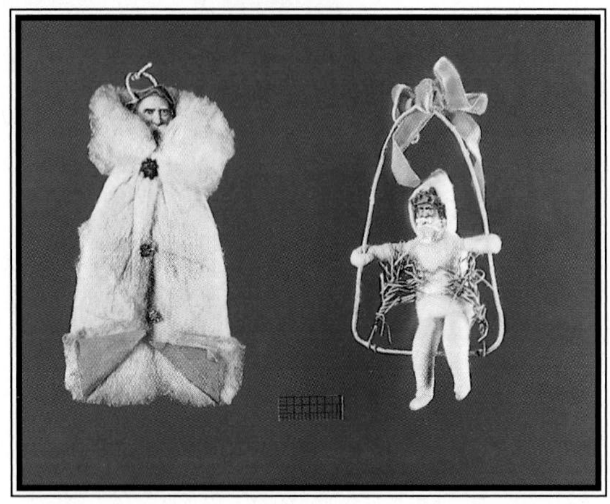

Cotton Ornaments: A. Pressed Cotton Santa with Scrap Face, 5" [OP, R3]. **$125.00–150.00.** B. Spun Cotton on a Swing (Type III), 4½" [OP, R1]. **$275.00–300.00.**

Pressed Cotton Over Cardboard Trolley Car, 14" [OP, R2]. **$225.00–275.00.** These were popular decorations with the Pennsylvania Dutch.

Pressed Cotton Over Cardboard Geometric Ornament, 11½" [OP, R2]. **$150.00–175.00.** It has an unusual tinted cotton.

Victorian "Gates of Heaven," cotton covering a cardboard frame, approx. 14½" [OP, R1-2]. **$175.00–200.00.**

A & D. Boats Made of Cotton Covering a Cardboard Frame, approx 6" L [OP, R2]. **$65.00–85.00.** B &E. Tarlatan Net-stockings [OP, R2-3]: B. 10½". **$75.00–100.00.** E. 4½". **$40.00–50.00.** C. Angel with a Cotton Dress, 6½" [OP, R2]. **$140.00–175.00.**

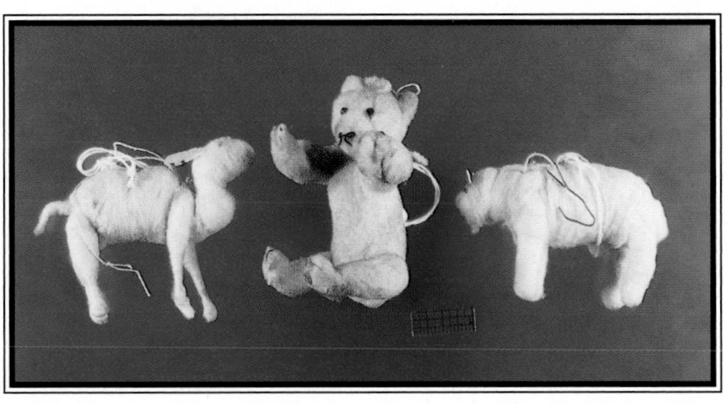

Cotton Animals: A. Camel with Two Humps, plain, 3½"L [OP, R2-3]. **$300.00–350.00.** B. Sitting Teddy Bear, 3½", movable arms and legs [OP, R1+]. **$450.00–500.00.** C. Polar Bear, plain, 3¼" [OP, R1]. **$350.00–400.00.**

Spun Cotton Animals: A & C. Songbirds with Painted Paper Wings, 2½" [OP, R3]. **$85.00–100.00.** B. Butterfly, 4¼", Dresden trim [OP, R1]. **$150.00–195.00.**

A. Early German Velour Butterfly, approx 5" [OP, R1]. **$50.00–75.00.** Early German Paper and Tinsel Flower, circa 1870, approx. 2¼" [OP, R1]. **$30.00–40.00.**

Spun Cotton Bear on a Swing. **$275.00–300.00.**

A. Squirrel with a Nut, 4" [OP, R1]. **$350.00–400.00.** B. Man with a Stick, 5" [OP, R2]. **$200.00–250.00.** C. Reindeer with a Rider, 3¾"L [OP, R1]. **$400.00–500.00.** D. Horse with a Saddle, 3¾"L. **$280.00–310.00.**

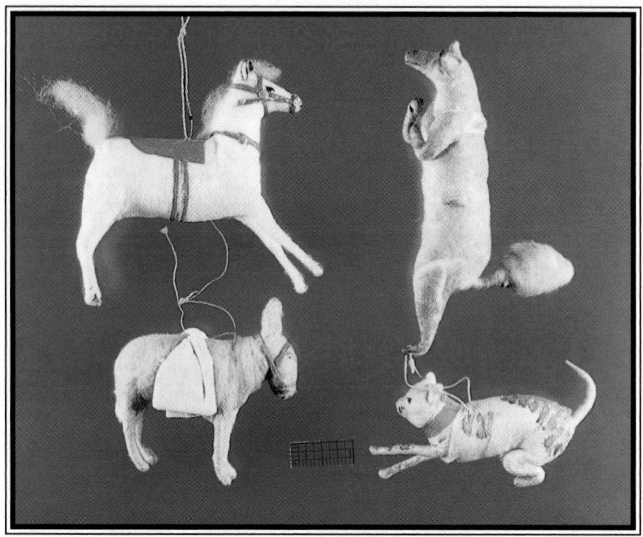

Spun Cotton Animals: A. Prancing Pony, 4"L [OP, R2]. **$295.00–325.00.** B. Fox, 4½" [OP, R1]. **$280.00–310.00.** C. Donkey with Bags, 3¾"L [OP, R2]. **$300.00–350.00.** D. Cat, 3¾" [OP, R2]. **$350.00–400.00.**

A. Sheep, 2¾" [OP, R2]. **$300.00–350.00.** B. Frog, 2½" [OP, R1-2]. **$200.00–225.00.** C. Dog, 3½" [OP, R2]. **$300.00–375.00.** D. Lion, 4½"L [OP, R1-2]. **$375.00–400.00.**

German Spun Cotton Animals: A. Cat Playing with a Ball, 3¾"L [OP-NP (Jones, 1990s) R1-2]. Old, **$350.00–425.00.** New, **$45.00–55.00.** B. Camel with Elaborate Saddle and Harness, 4"H [OP, R1]. **$450.00–550.00.**

Cotton Animals, both German: A. Donkey with Bags and Dresden Harness, 4" [OP, R2]. **$300.00–375.00.** B. Camel, plain, 2½" [OP, R2]. **$300.00–350.00.**

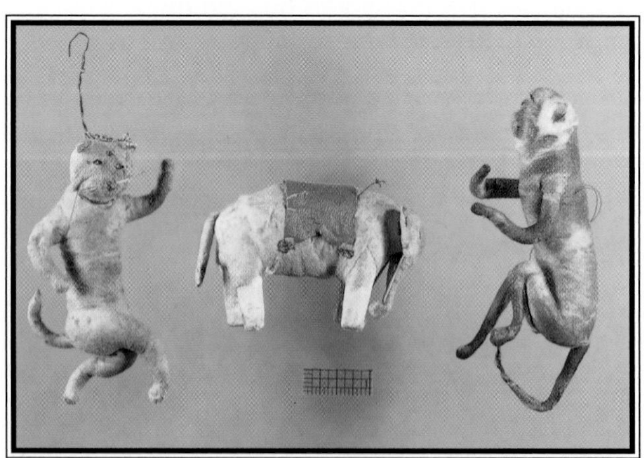

German Spun Cotton Animals: A. Dancing Cat, plain, 3¾" [OP, R1-2]. **$300.00–375.00.** B. Standing Elephant, small, 3½" [OP, R2]. **$280.00–310.00.** C. Climbing Monkey, 5" [OP, R2-3]. **$400.00–500.00.**

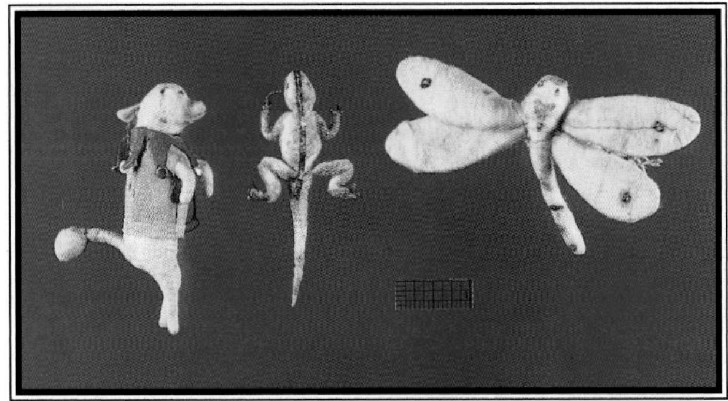

Unusual Spun Cotton Animals: A. Dog Clown, 3½" [OP, R1]. **$300.00–340.00.** B. Lizard, 3¼" [OP, R1]. **$295.00–325.00.** C. Dragonfly, 4¾" [OP, R1]. **$150.00–195.00.**

A. Monkey with a Ball in a Ring, scrap face, 3½" [OP, R1]. **$350.00–375.00.** B. Monkey, plain, 3½" [OP, R2]. **$300.00–350.00.** C. Stag, 4"H, antlers are paper over wire [OP, R1-2]. **$250.00–310.00.** D. Doe, 3"H, painted details [OP, R1-2]. **$275.00–300.00.**

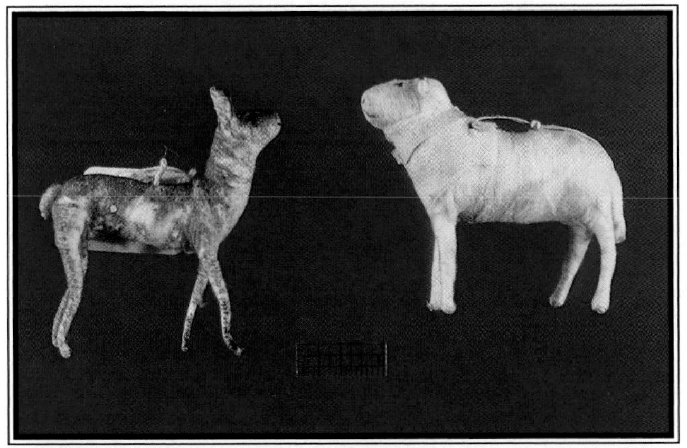

A. Fawn, 2½" [OP, R2-3]. **$275.00–325.00.** B. Sheep, 2¾" [OP, R2]. **$300.00–350.00.**

German Spun Cotton Animals: A. Llama, plain, 4"H x 3½"W [OP, R1]. **$310.00–340.00.** B. Fox, plain, 3"H x 4¾"L [OP, R2]. **$280.00–310.00.** C. Beagle with Painted Features, 2¾"H x 4½"L [OP, R1]. **$350.00–400.00.**

Cotton Animals: A. Elephant Woman Wearing a Dress and a Dresden necklace, 5" wooden tusks [OP, R1]. **$600.00–650.00.** B. Circus Elephant with Wooden Tusks, 2¼"H x 3½"L [OP, R2]. **$300.00–375.00.** C. Donkey with Bags, small, 3¾" [OP, R3]. **$300.00–350.00.**

Whimsical Cotton Ornaments: A. Party Pig, 4¼" [OP, R1]. **$500.00–600.00.** B. Elephant Maid, 5¼"; with apron, feather duster, and metal earrings [OP, R1]. **$600.00–650.00.** C. Pumpkin-headed Girl, 4¼" [OP, R1]. **$275.00–350.00.**

A. Horse, plain, 3½"L [OP, R2-3]. **$250.00–275.00.** B. Rabbit with Carrot, 4½" [OP, R1]. **$400.00–500.00.** C. Donkey, plain, 3½"L [OP, R2-3]. **$200.00–225.00.**

A. Monkey on Limb with Fruit, 4¼" [OP, R2-3]. **$400.00–500.00.** B. Tiger, 3¾" [OP, R1]. **$335.00–365.00.**

A. Ram, plain, 3½"H [OP, R1-2]. **$350.00–400.00.** B. Spider, 2½"H, with legs and mica covering [OP, R1]. **$115.00–125.00.** C. Prancing Pony, 3¾"H, paper saddle [OP, R1]. **$295.00–325.00.** D. Giraffe, 4¾"H, painted details [OP, R1]. **$650.00–750.00.**

Cotton Birds: A. Stork, 4½" [OP, R1-2]. **$85.00–95.00.** B. Swan, 3" [OP, R1]. **$135.00–165.00.** C. Stork with Paper Wings, 4½" [OP, R1-2]. **$135.00–165.00.**

A. Spun Cotton Dove with Paper Wings, 5½" [Japanese, OP, R3]. **$20.00–30.00.** B. Santa with Celluloid Face, net bag candy container, 5½" [Japanese, OP, R3-4]. **$75.00–90.00.** C. Two Spun Cotton Pears, small. **$20.00–25.00** each.

Spun Cotton Fruit. Grapes, 4" [OP, R1]. **$120.00–130.00.** Pears with Wire Wrapping and Fabric Leaves, 2" overall [OP, R2]. **$20.00–25.00.** Pear, small, 1¾" [OP, R2-3]. **$20.00–25.00.**

Spun Cotton Fruit: A. Carrot or Icicle, approx. 3½" [OP-NP, R3-4]. **$20.00–25.00.** B. Tomato, 2" [OP, R2-3]. **$50.00–75.00.** C. Turnip, 2½" [OP, R2-3]. **$45.00–65.00.** D. Pear, 3½" [OP, R3-4]. **$25.00–35.00.**

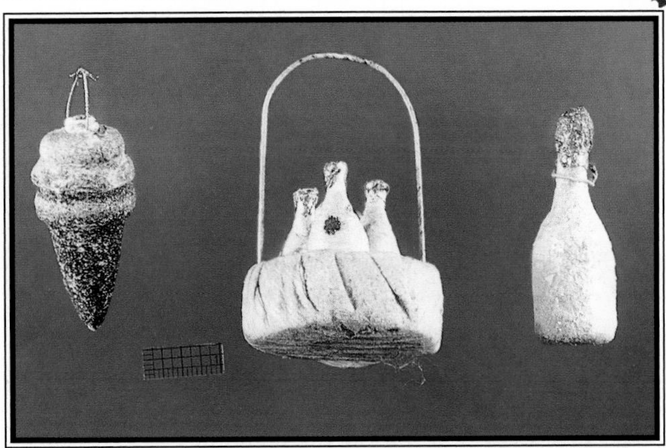

Unusual Spun Cotton Ornaments: A. Ice Cream Cone, 2½" [OP, R1-2]. **$25.00–35.00.** B. Bucket with Champagne Bottles, 3½" [OP, R1]. **$100.00–125.00.** C. Champagne Bottle, 3" [OP, R2]. **$50.00–75.00.**

Cotton Vegetables: A. Cucumber with Fabric Leaves, large, 4½" [OP-NP, R1-2]. Old, **$75.00–100.00.** B. Turnip or Radish with Tucksher Leaves, large, 3" [OP, R2-3]. **$45.00–65.00.** C. Carrot with Fabric Leaves, 4½", large [OP-NP, R1-2]. Old, **$60.00–75.00.**

Spun Cotton Ornaments: A. Snowman, 5" [OP, R3]. **$60.00–80.00.** B. Carrot, 4" [OP-NP, R1-2]. Old, **$35.00–50.00.** C. Turnip, 4" [OP, R3-4]. **$50.00–75.00.**

A. Snowball, large, 2¾", "Made in Germany"-tag [OP, R1-2]. **$30.00–45.00.** B. Icicle with Berry End, 3¾". **$30.00–40.00.** C. Cucumber, 4" [R2-3]. **$70.00–75.00.** D. Icicles, 3¼", "Made in Germany" tag [OP-NP, R4]. Small, **$20.00–25.00.**

German Fruits and Vegetables, marketed by D. Blumchen & Co. in 1992. The five vegetables were sold in a "crate." The orange was sold separately. All sizes are 2" – 4". **$20.00–30.00** each.

Blumchen's Cotton Fruit, made in Germany circa 1990: Plum, Cherries, Lemon, Apple, & Pear, 1¾" - 2¾" [R2-3]. **$15.00-20.00** each.

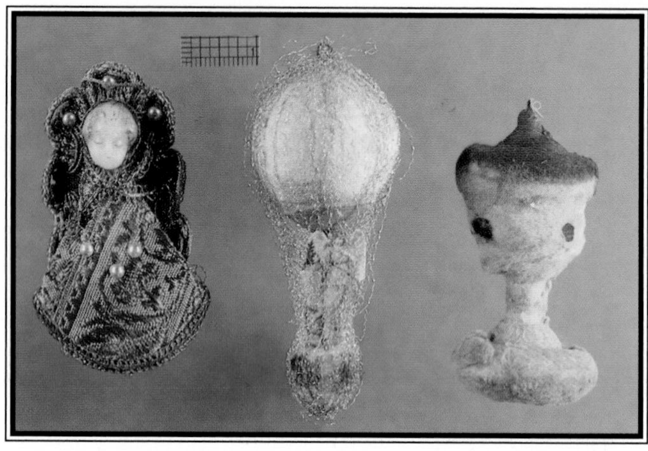

A. Jesus with Wax Face and Bunting, circa 1920 [German, OP, R1-2]. **$50.00–75.00.** B. Spun Cotton Hot Air Balloon, 5" [OP, R1-2]. **$125.00–150.00.** C. Spun Cotton Bird House, 3¾" [OP, R2]. **$100.00–125.00.**

Three German Cotton Figures, various applied faces of scrap, clay, and painted cotton: A. Girl in a Coat, 6" [OP, R1-2]. **$225.00–250.00.** B. Englishman, 4½" [OP, R1]. **$300.00–400.00.** C. Clown in Red Hat, 6" [OP, R2]. **$200.00–250.00.**

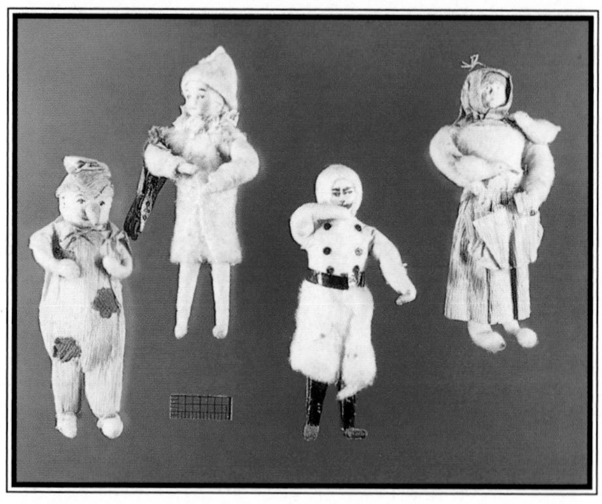

A Collection of Spun Cotton People, clothing includes cotton batting and crepe paper: A. Clown with a Carrot Nose, 4¾" [OP, R2]. **$350.00–400.00.** B. Ice Skater with Metal or Dresden Skates & Porcelain Face, 4¾" [OP, R1]. **$375.00–450.00.** C. Military Man, 4½" [OP, R1]. **$300.00–350.00.** D. Lady with Birds & Plaster Face, 5" [OP, R1]. **$275.00–325.00.**

A Collection of Spun Cotton People, most dressed in crepe paper: A. Man with a Top Hat, 5" [OP, R1]. **$450.00–550.00.** B. Peasant Lady, 4½" [OP, R1-2]. **$350.00–450.00.** C. Jester with a Porcelain Face, 5" [OP, R1-2]. **$300.00–350.00.** D. Snow Girl with a Scrap Face and a Muff, 4" [OP, R2-3]. **$190.00–210.00.**

A Collection of Four Spun Cotton Girls: A. Girl with Crepe Paper Clothes, 3¾" [OP, R2]. **$150.00–175.00.** B. Girl with a Crepe Paper Dress, 2¾" [OP, R2]. **$150.00–175.00.** C. Snow Girl with Cotton Clothes, 3¾" [OP, R1-2]. **$300.00–375.00.** D. Girl Jester with a Porcelain Face, 5½" [OP, R1]. **$300.00–375.00.**

Spun Cotton Ornaments: A. Boy with a Jacket and a Scrap Face, 4" [OP, R1-2]. **$200.00–225.00.** B. Snowman with a Painted Face Candy Container, approx. 4" [OP, R1-2]. **$275.00–350.00.** C. Girl with a Scrap Face and Pants, approx. 3¾" [OP, R1-2]. **$175.00–200.00.**

German Cotton People: A. Clown with a Dog, 4" [OP, R1]. **$275.00–325.00.** B. Pressed Cotton Angel, 4" [OP, R2]. Small, **$130.00–145.00.** C. Spun Cotton Rugby Player, 5" [OP, R1-2]. **$375.00–450.00.**

German Cotton People: A. Pressed Cotton Girl, 4" [OP, R2-3]. Small, **$150.00–200.00.** B. Boy on a Sled, 3¾"H x 6"L [OP, R1-2]. **$275.00–350.00.** C. Girl with a Muff, 4" [OP, R2-3]. **$190.00–200.00.**

German Spun Cotton People: A. John Bull with a Ball and a Cigar, 5" [OP, R1]. **$275.00–325.00.** B. Gibson Girl in Crepe Paper and Fabric Dress, 5¾" [OP, R1-2]. **$200.00–225.00.** C. Romeo, 4¾" [OP, R1]. **$275.00–325.00.**

A. Girl with an Umbrella, 4" [OP, R1-2]. **$225.00–250.00.** B. Girl, black (rare), 4¼" [OP, R1]. **$400.00–500.00.** C. Little Bo Peep with Crook, 5" [OP, R1]. **$300.00–375.00.**

Spun Cotton Girl on Glass Skis, 4½"H x 6"L [OP, R1]. **$400.00–500.00.**

Four German Spun Cotton Santas with Scrap Faces [all OP, R2-3]. A. 6". B. 5¼". C. 5". D. 5¾". **$225.00–250.00** each.

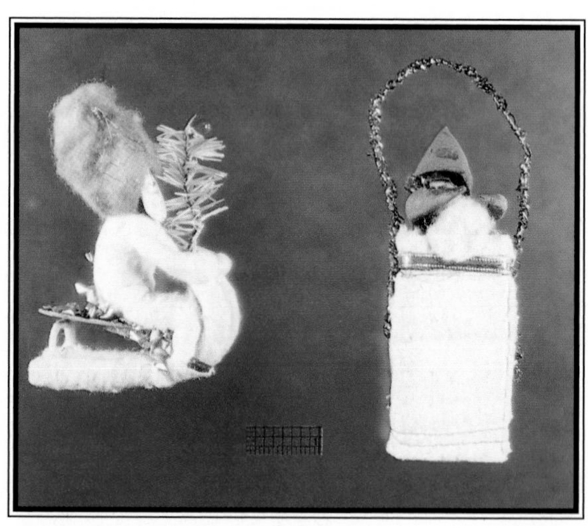

A. Spun Cotton Santa on a Sled, 3¾" [OP, R1]. **$350.00–375.00.** B. Santa in a Chimney, 4½" [OP, R1]. **$275.00–300.00.**

Cotton Santa on a Swing (Type II), 5½" [OP-NP, R2-3]. **$200.00–250.00.**

Cotton Ornaments with Plaster Faces, probably German: A. Boy on a Wood Sled, 4¼"L [OP, R1]. **$275.00–300.00.** B. Clown with a Crepe Paper Vest and a Dresden Sunface on His Bottom, 5½" [OP, R1]. **$300.00–350.00.**

Cotton Batting Santa with a Wax Face, approx. 5" [OP, R1]. **$250.00–275.00.**

A. Cotton Batting Santa, 7" [OP, R2]. **$175.00–200.00.** B. Santa, 5" [OP, R2]. **$250.00–300.00.**

A. Spun Cotton Girl with Pressed Cotton Clothes, approx. 3¾" [OP, R2]. **$275.00–325.00.** B. Pressed Cotton Girl with Doll, approx. 4½" [OP, R2]. **$125.00–135.00.** C. Pressed Cotton Santa, approx. 4" [OP, R2-3]. **$175.00–200.00.**

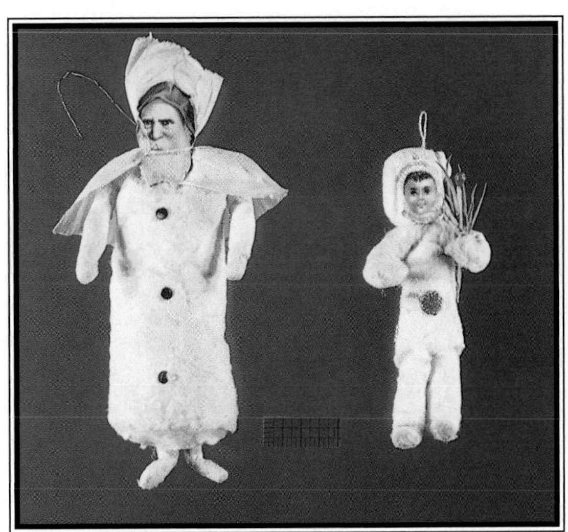

A. Cotton Batting Santa, approx. 5½" [German,OP, R2]. **$175.00–225.00.** B. Spun Cotton Girl with a Tree, approx. 4" [OP, R1-2]. **$175.00–225.00.**

A. Pressed Cotton Rabbit with Carrot, 5" [OP, R2]. **$60.00–75.00.** B. Japanese Spun Cotton Girl with Composition Face, no skis, 5" [OP, R3]. **$50.00–75.00.** C. German Spun Cotton Girl with Flowers, 5" [OP, R2]. **$200.00–250.00.**

Porcelain Face Cottons: A. Heubach Boy with an American Flag, 3½"H [OP, R1]. **$375.00–400.00.** B. Angel with a Porcelain Face & Dresden Wings, not Heubach, 2½" [OP, R1]. **$225.00–250.00.**

Heubach Ornaments: A. Girl with Metal Skates, 4½" [OP, R1]. **$400.00–450.00.** B. Boy on a Log with a Snowball, 3" [OP, R1]. **$350.00–400.00.** C. Boy on Skis, 4" [OP, R1]. **$350.00–400.00.**

Cotton Ornaments with Porcelain Faces, probably Heubach: A. Boy with a Pine Cone, 1¼" [OP, R2]. **$150.00–175.00.** B. Same Boy on a Candy Container, 2¼" [OP, R2]. **$225.00–275.00.** C. Girl with a Snowball, 3½" [OP, R1]. **$375.00–425.00.** D. Boy with Two Snowballs, 2½" [OP, R1]. **$350.00–375.00.**

Spun Cotton Figures by D. Blumchen & Co., 1987: A. Boy Throwing Snowballs, 5¼" [R2]. **$50.00–75.00.** B. Ice Skating Girl, 5" [R2]. **$50.00–75.00.**

Spun Cotton People, by D. Blumchen & Co.: A. Santa with Boughs, 5", porcelain face [NP (1989), R2]. **$50.00–75.00.** B. St. Nicholas, 6" [NP (1987), R2]. **$30.00–40.00.** C. Girl in Blue [NP (1986), R1-2]. **$35.00–50.00.**

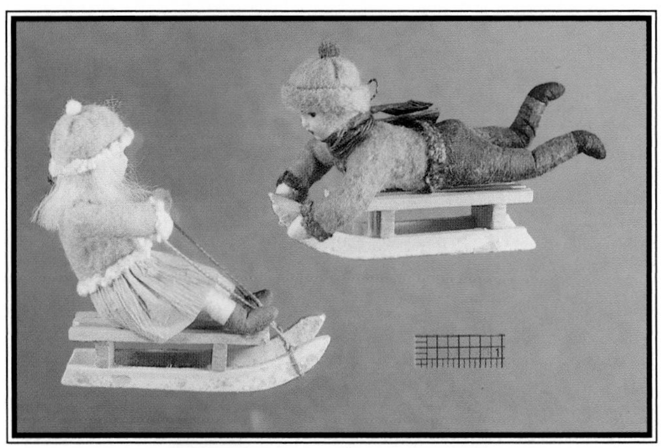

Cotton Ornaments with Porcelain Faces, by D. Blumchen & Co., 1990: A. Girl Riding a Wooden Sled, "Nicole", 3" [R2-3]. **$75.00–95.00.** B. Boy on a Wooden Sled, "Neil,"-3¾" [R2-3]. **$75.00–95.00.**

Cotton Ornaments, by D. Blumchen & Co.: A. & C. Snow Boy and Snow Girl Angels, 3½" [NP (1992), R2-3]. **$50.00–75.00.** B. Santa with Boughs, porcelain face, 5" [NP (1989), R2]. **$50.00–75.00.**

Cotton Ornaments, by D. Blumchen & Co., 1993: A. Gussie the Gardener, 5" [R2-3]. **$50.00–75.00.** B. Guss the Gardener, 5" [R2-3]. **$50.00–75.00.**

Cotton Ornaments, by D. Blumchen & Co., 1994: A. Baker, 4½" [R2-3]. **$50.00–75.00.** B. St. Nicholas with His Crook and a Cake, 6" [R2-3]. **$60.00–90.00.** C. Girl with a Candy Box, 4" [R2-3]. **$50.00–75.00.**

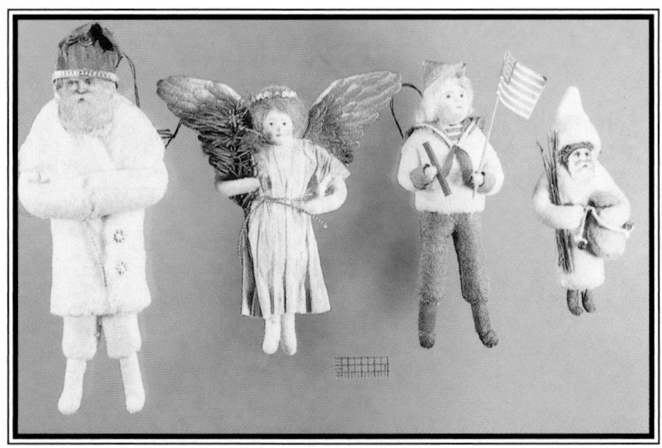

Cotton Ornaments, by Cynthia Jones: A. Santa, large, 6¾", made with antique scrap face [NP (circa 1991), R3]. **$50.00–60.00.** B. Angel with a Tree, 5¼" [NP, R3]. **$50.00–75.00.** C. Fourth of July Boy, 5¼" [NP, R3]. **$60.00–90.00.** D. Santa with a Bag, 4" [NP, R3]. **$40.00–50.00.**

Three Net Bag Candy Containers, all Japanese: A. Stocking with a Clay Face, 5½" [OP, R1]. **$50.00–65.00.** B. Santa in a Chenille Bucket, 7" [OP, R2]. **$150.00–175.00.** C. Standard Santa Body, 7" [OP, R3-4]. **$70.00–85.00.**

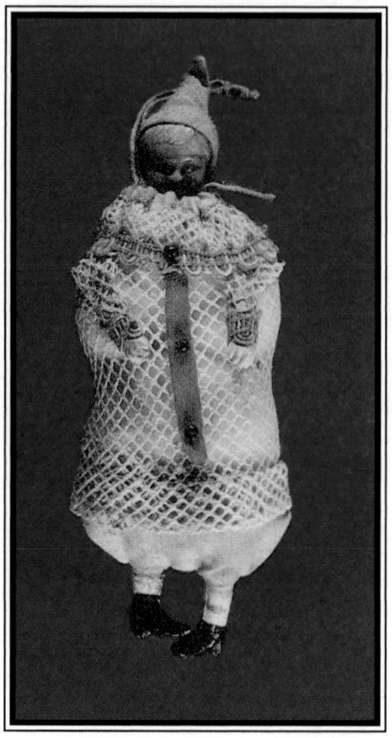

Girl with a Celluloid Face Net Bag Candy Container, approx. 7" [OP, R1]. **$150.00–175.00.**

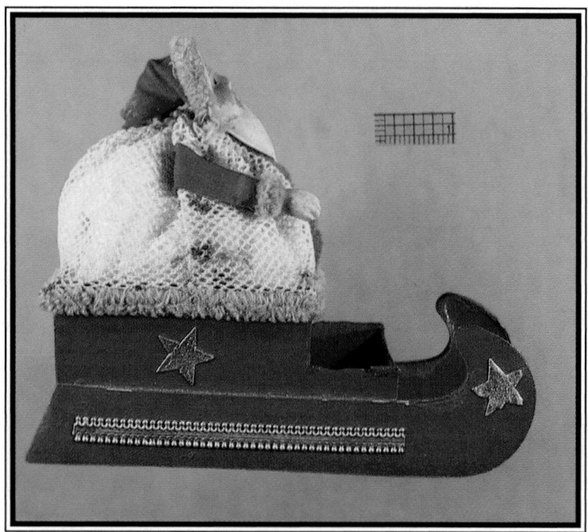

Santa on Celluloid Sleigh Net Candy Bag, Japanese, 4½"H x 5¾"W [OP, R1]. **$175.00–200.00.**

Boot Candy Containers with Plaster Santa Heads, both Japanese: A. Foil Covered, 6½" [OP, R2-3]. **$100.00–125.00.** B. Cotton Covered, 6½" [OP, R1]. **$100.00–125.00.**

A. Stocking, printed, 5" [NP, R3]. **$10.00–15.00.** B. Net Stocking, large [OP, R2-3]. **$40.00–50.00.**

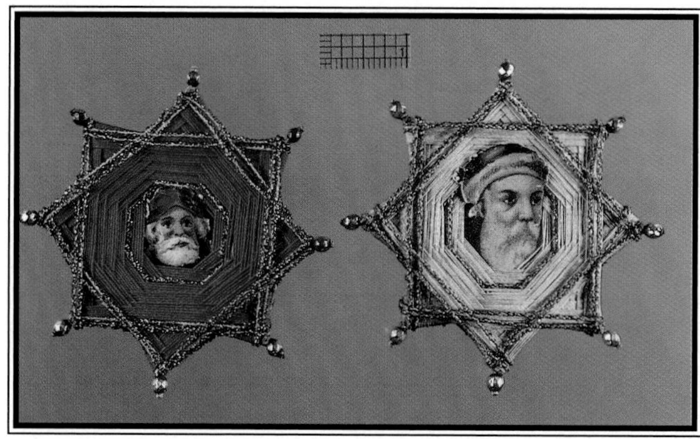

Stars Made of String and Scrap Santa Faces, 3¾" [OP, R1]. **$100.00–125.00** each.

Various Sizes of Japanese Cotton Batting Santas [all OP, R3-4]: A. 8". **$100.00–125.00.** B & C. 6½". **$60.00–75.00.**

A. American Pressed Cotton Santa, 5½" [American, OP, R3]. **$20.00–30.00.** B. Chenille Santa with a Paper Face, 5" [Japanese, NP (1950s), R4]. **$10.00–15.00.** C. Crocheted Slipper, 3½"; crocheted ornaments were popular at the turn of the century [German, OP-NP, R1]. **$20.00–30.00.** D & E. Japanese Chenille Santas with Plaster Faces, 3¼": D. **$10.00–15.00.** E. **$5.00–8.00.**

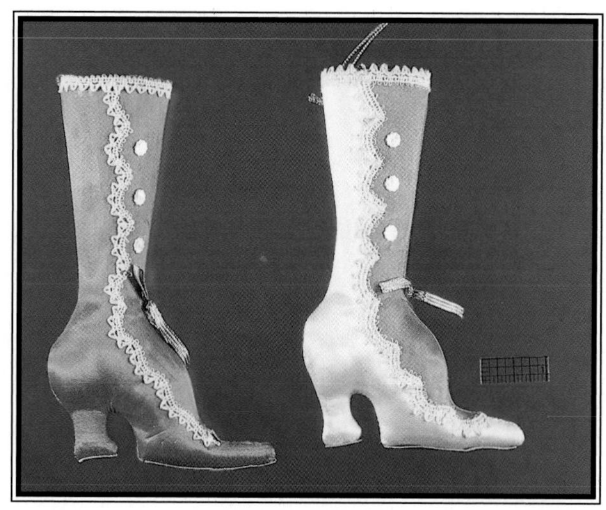

Two Lady's High Boot Candy Containers, approx. 5½". They are made of cardboard and covered with satin [NP (1950s only), R1-2]. **$25.00–35.00.**

Christmas Banners, approx. 7" x 5½". Stenciled on rayon fabric, these were possibly used as store decorations. American made, circa 1930s [R1-2]. **$15.00–20.00** each.

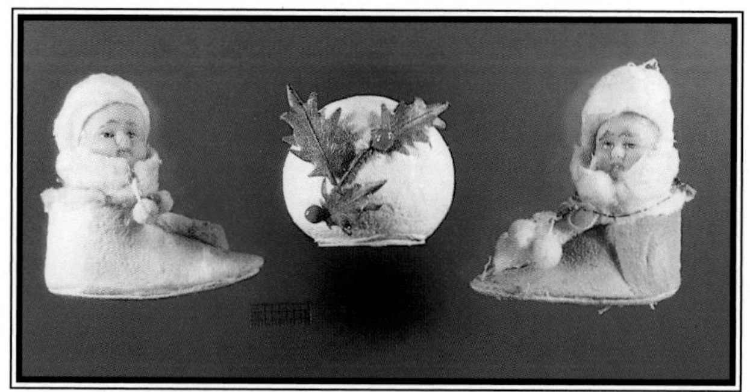

A & C. Wax Baby in a Shoe Candy Containers, approx. 3" [OP, R1-2]. **$225.00–250.00.** B. Snowball Candy Container, 2" [OP, R2]. **$100.00–125.00.**

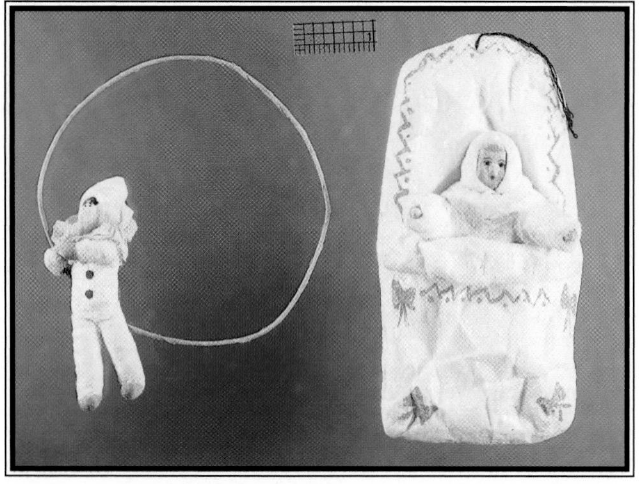

Russian Cotton People, circa 1950: A. Clown with a Hoop, 4" overall [R2-3]. **$100.00–125.00.** B. Baby in Bunting, 5" [R2-3]. **$100.00–125.00.**

Russian Cottons, circa 1930: A. Mushroom Man, 4" [OP, R2]. **$140.00–165.00.** B. Bear Sitting with a Ball, 2¾" [OP, R2]. **$150.00–175.00.** C. Bear Sitting with a Bandage, 4" [OP, R2]. **$200.00–225.00.**

Russian Cotton Ornaments, circa 1925, both with composition faces: A. Grandfather Frost, 5" [R2]. **$140.00–160.00.** B. Boy in a Coat and Blue Pants, 4½" [R2]. **$150.00–175.00.**

Russian Cottons, circa 1910; *A* and *C* have composition faces: A. Girl on a Stand with a Decorated Dress, 5¾" [R1-2]. **$150.00–175.00.** B. Puss 'N' Boots, 4" [R1-2]. **$175.00–200.00.** C. Newsboy on a Stand, 5" [R1-2]. **$150.00–175.00.**

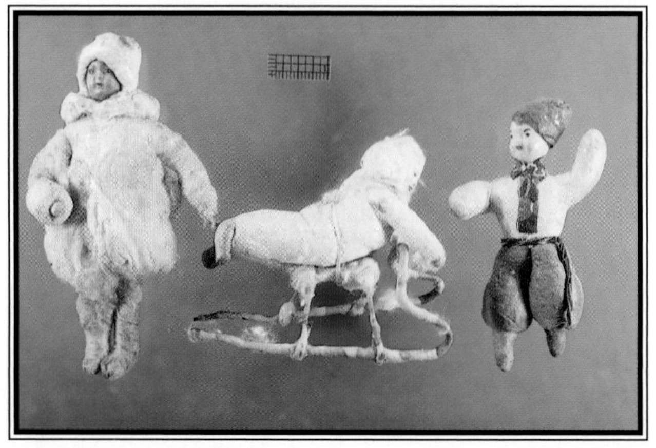

Russian Cottons, circa 1925: A. Girl in a Yellow Coat with a Muff, 5½" [R2]. **$125.00–150.00.** B. Boy on a Sled, 4½" [R2]. **$175.00–200.00.** C. Cossack Boy, 4¼" [R2]. **$125.00–150.00.**

Russian Cottons, circa 1910: A. Woman in a Scarf, 5" [R1-2]. **$160.00–180.00.** B. Girl's Head on Foil, 3" [R1-2]. **$130.00–150.00.** C. Girl with a Flower, 5" [R1-2]. **$250.00–275.00.**

Russian Cottons, circa 1950s: A. Rooster, 4" [R3]. **$40.00–50.00.** B. Girl in a Yellow Coat and Scarf, 3¾" [R3]. **$100.00–125.00.**

Russian Cotton Ornaments, circa 1935: A. Ivan and the Firebird, 6¼" [R2]. **$150.00–175.00.** B. Cat Woman, 5½", composition face [R2]. **$160.00–180.00.**

Russian Cottons, circa 1935: A. Rabbit Mother with Carriage, 5" [R2]. **$175.00–200.00.** B. Goat Mother, 6¼", painted face [R2]. **$175.00–200.00.**

Sebnitz Ornaments

These decorations were named after the German village of Sebnitz, located in the Erzgebirge Mountains near the Austrian border and around which the manufacture of these ornaments centered. The Sebnitz cottage industry specialized in wrapping cardboard forms in cotton, metallic foil, and plastic perforated with small holes. To this creation were added tiny glass tubes or beads and scrap or wax figures. The whole piece might then be wrapped in a web of fine crinkle wire.

These ornaments had interesting combinations of all the major ornament materials of glass, paper, fabric, metal, and wax, and incorporated the widest variety of materials used in any ornament. Most decorations of the day had only one or two types of garnishment, but Sebnitz makers used upwards of seven or eight materials in each piece. These included cardboard, cotton, crepe paper, perforated plastic, metal foil, heavy wire, crinkle wire, wax figures, fabric flowers, natural foliage, glass tubes, glass beads, chenille roping, and Dresden trims. The materials themselves were cheap, readily available, and often the by-product of other ornament-making materials. The charm of Sebnitz ornaments comes from the unique and creative way in which these materials were assembled.

One of the most characteristic materials, unique to the Sebnitz ornament, was the web of perforated plastic film that often covered the cardboard forms. Because of its shine and sparkle, this plastic has often been mistaken for metal. Pieces with the silvered backing worn away reveal a thin clear plastic. This perforated film was a by-product of the sequin business. The small round sequins — used in dresses, hats, and handbags — were stamped from long strips of plastic. What would normally have been considered scrap material was used for creating and decorating the Sebnitz ornaments. Gold and silver were the most common colors used, but red and purple were used also.

The Sebnitz ornaments that were made from about 1870 to 1914 are rare in this country. They seem to have been more popular in Europe than in America. Because they were labor intensive, they cost as much as Dresden ornaments. At the turn of the century, one could buy six figural or a dozen fancy glass ornaments for the same price as one Sebnitz piece. Sebnitz ornaments have become collector's items, especially the ones with wax figures, and have been reproduced.

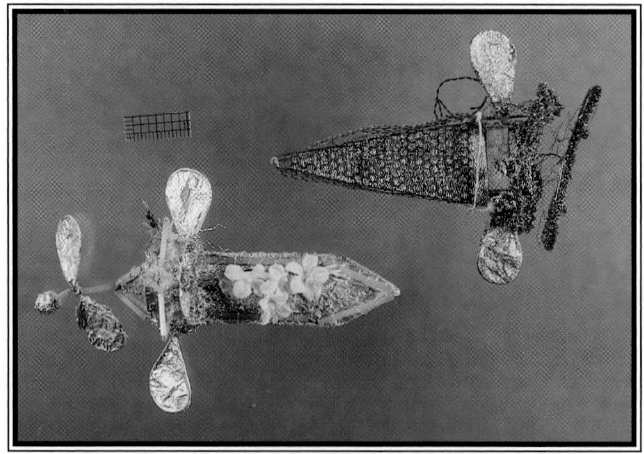

A. Airplane, "Flying Wedge," 5" [OP, R1]. **$300.00–350.00.** B. Flying Machine with Flowers, 5½" [OP, R1]. **$300.00–350.00.**

Mushroom Truck, 1¼"H x 3"L [OP, R1]. **$400.00–550.00.**

Baby Carriage, 2½"H x 2¾"L, cotton over cardboard with a wax baby inside [OP, R1]. **$400.00–500.00.**

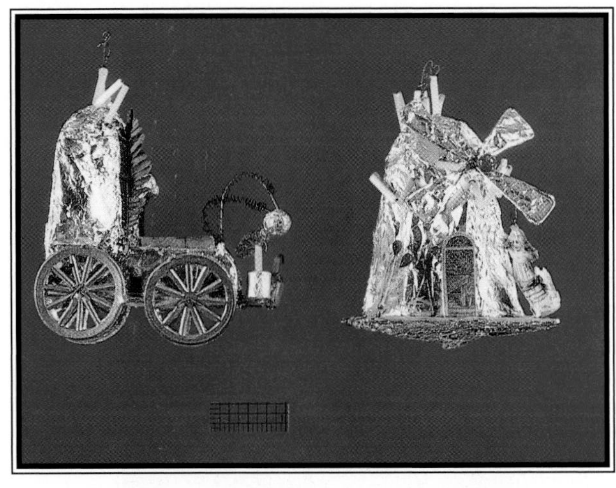

A. Baby Carriage with a Wax Baby, foil, 3" x 3" [German, OP, R1]. **$400.00–500.00.** B. Windmill, 3" [German, OP, R1]. **$200.00–250.00.**

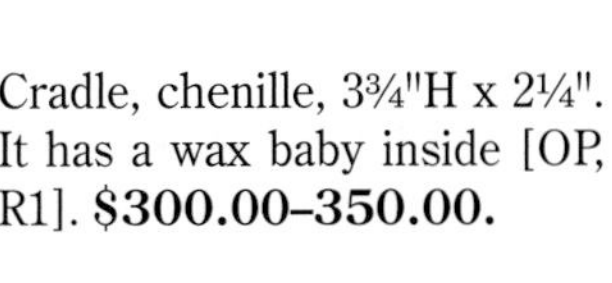

Cradle, chenille, 3¾"H x 2¼". It has a wax baby inside [OP, R1]. **$300.00–350.00.**

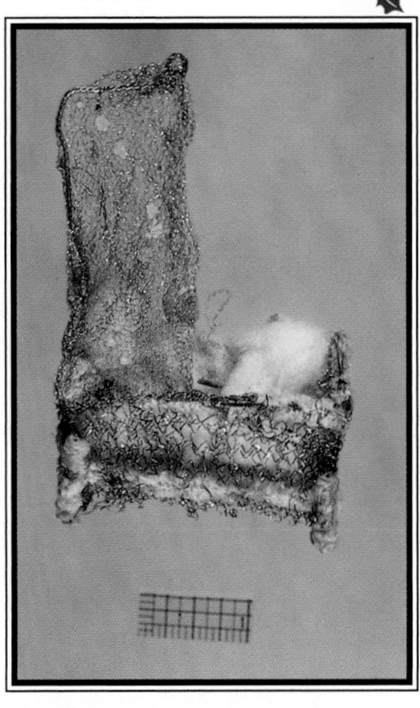

Cradle, 2½"L. It has a wax baby inside [OP, R1]. **$275.00–325.00.**

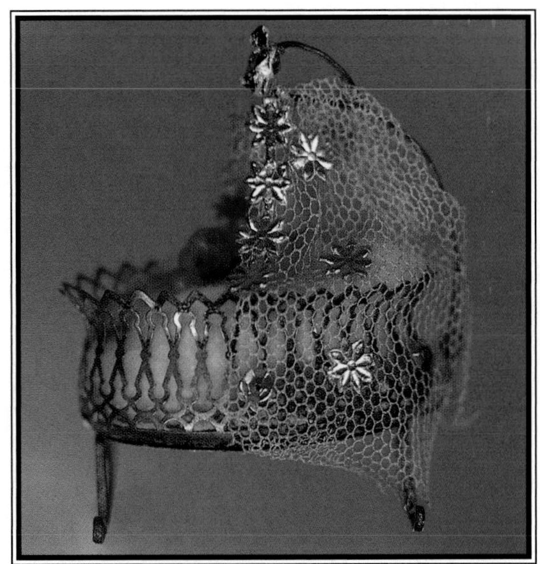

Crib with a Wax Baby, 3" [OP, R1]. **$300.00–375.00.**

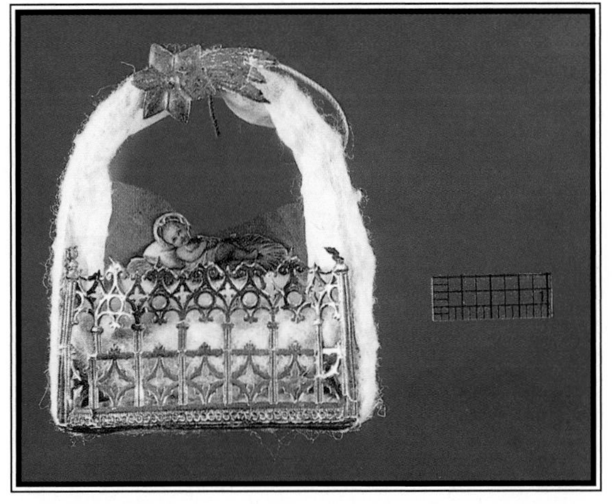

Bed with a Canopy and Baby Jesus, scrap, 3" [OP, R1]. **$275.00–350.00.**

Sebnitz Ornaments: A. Bucket, 3" [OP, R2]. **$60.00–75.00.** B. Butterfly, 3", 5¾" overall [OP, R1]. **$200.00–225.00.** C. Gazebo with Flowers, 2¾" [OP, R2]. **$70.00–80.00.**

Birdcage, domed, 4¾" [German, OP, R2]. **$150.00–175.00.**

A. House, 2¾"H x 1¾"W, has a metal chimney [German, OP, R1-2]. **$200.00–225.00.** B. Birdcage on a Pedestal, 3¾" [German, OP, R1]. **$225.00–250.00.**

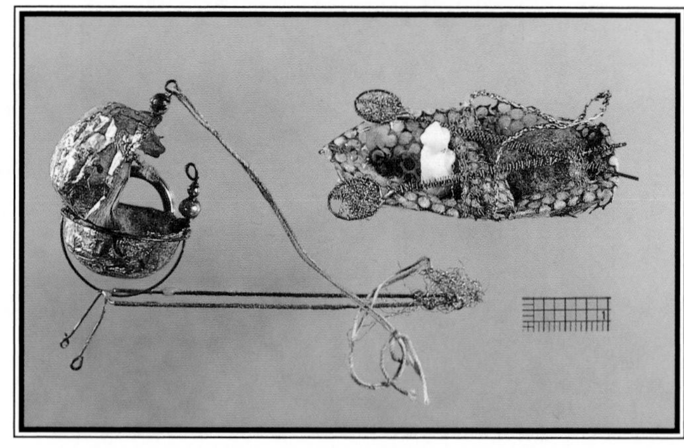

A. Chariot, walnut, 4½" [German, OP, R1]. **$125.00–150.00.** B. Rowboat, 3¼" [German, OP, R1]. **$350.00–400.00.**

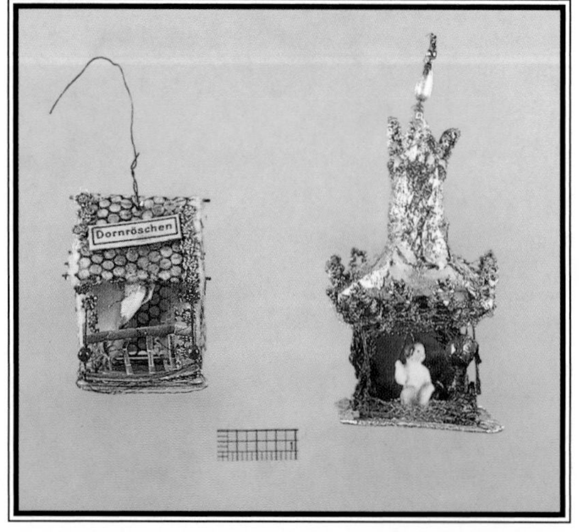

A. House, "Dornroschen," 2¼" [German, OP, R1-2]. **$175.00-200.00.** B. Pagoda with Wax Baby, 4¼" [German, OP, R1]. **$175.00-225.00.**

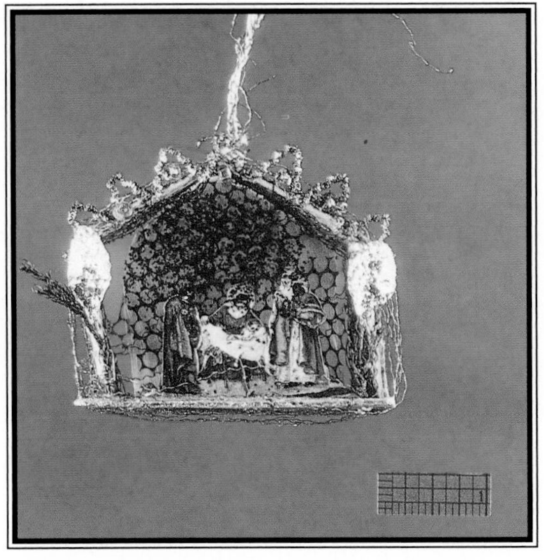

Manger/Nativity Scene, 2"H [German, OP, R2-3]. **$100.00–125.00.**

A. Crepe Paper Pocketbook, 2½" [OP, R1-2]. **$60.00–75.00.** B & C. Two Rectangular Baskets with Dried Flowers, 2" and 2½" [German, OP, R2-3]. **$50.00–60.00** each.

Four Sebnitz Ornaments: A. Flower Bowl, approx. 2½" [German, OP, R2]. **$60.00–75.00.** B. Angel Hair Boat, approx. 4½" [German, OP, R1-2]. **$150.00–175.00.** C. House/Stable with a Scrap of Baby Jesus, approx. 3¼"H [German, OP, R2-3]. **$110.00–135.00.** D. Wax Sheep in a Pen, approx. 2¾" [German, OP, R1]. **$150.00–175.00.**

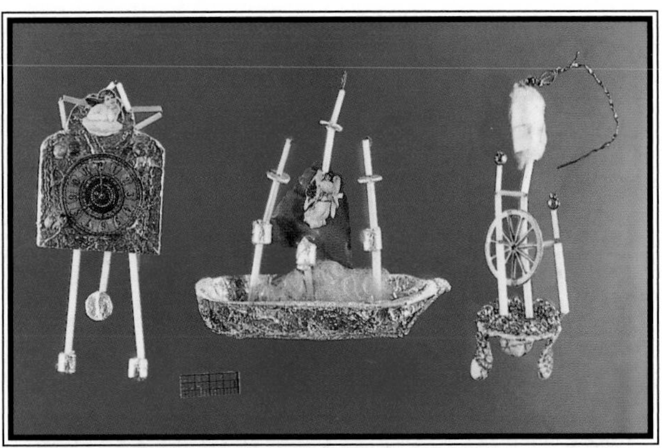

Three Sebnitz Ornaments: A. Wall Clock, 4½" [German, OP, R2]. **$150.00–175.00.** B. Foil Boat, approx. 4½" [German, OP, R1-2]. **$175.00–200.00.** C. Spinning Wheel, 5" [German, OP, R2]. **$225.00–250.00.**

Two Sebnitz Ornaments: A. Automobile, approx. 2¾"L [German, OP, R1-2]. **$350.00–400.00.** B. Wire Boat, approx. 3"L [OP, R1-2]. **$75.00–100.00.**

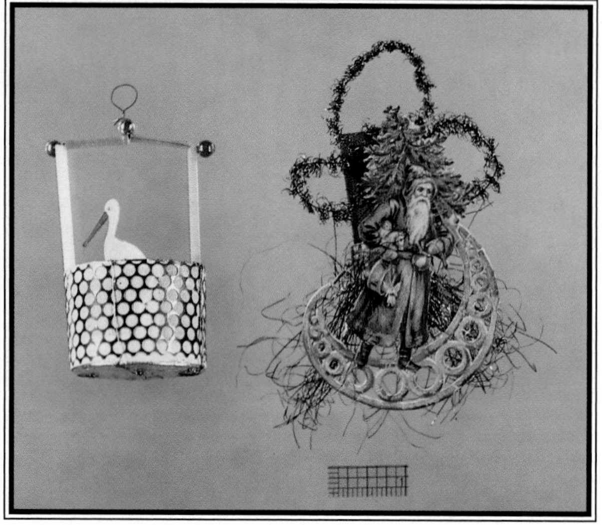

A. Stork in a Well, 3", the stork is a flat Dresden [German, OP, R2]. **$175.00–200.00.** B. Scrap Santa with a Tree and Toys (Type III), 3½" [OP, R1-2]. **$25.00–35.00.**

A. Stork in a Cage, 2¾" [OP, R2]. **$125.00–150.00.** B. Ball, 1¾" [OP, R1-2]. **$25.00–30.00.** C. Parachute with an Angel Rider, 3" [OP, R1]. **$150.00–175.00.**

Locomotive with a Cast Metal Engineer, 3¼" [German, OP, R1]. **$600.00–850.00.**

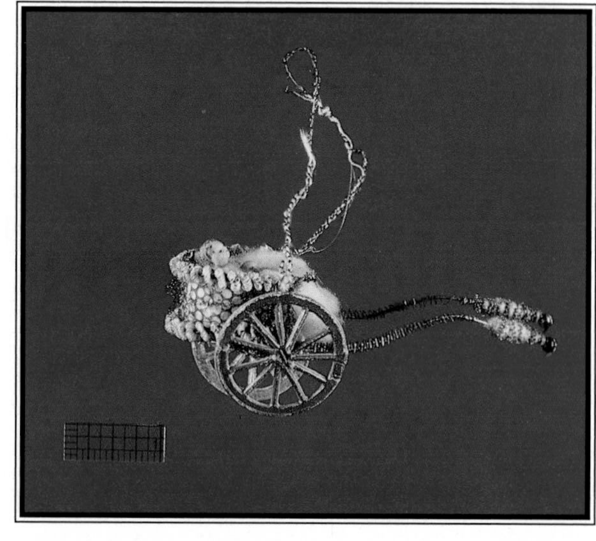

Rickshaw with a Wax Baby, 3¾"L [German, OP, R1]. **$450.00–550.00.**

A. Graf Zeppelin, 5¼"L [German, OP, R1]. **$750.00–850.00.** B. Sleigh with Wax Rider, 4¾" [German, OP, R1]. **$275.00–300.00.**

Wax Ornaments

Early wax ornaments are second only to metal in terms of age. Considered to be a more or less permanent decoration, they were offered for sale as early as 1800 by manufacturers in the German toy industry centered in and around Nuremberg and Sonneberg.

Wax ornaments can be divided into three major categories or styles: full-bodied, flat, and wax accessories. The most popular full-bodied form wax ornament was the angel. Angels came in a wide variety of molded styles; perhaps the most popular was the Nuremberg Angel, an angel in a wreath with outstretched arms, a high cap or crown, and a long stiff dress. She graced treetops from the 1700s to the 1950s. Her outstretched hands held candles or a wreath that arched overhead. Some smaller angels were made entirely from wax, and larger ones were made, like dolls of the period, from hollow cast wax. However, the most common angel forms were made from a composition material that was a combination of wood pulp, cellulose, glue, and plaster. They were then covered with layers of wax to give them a more delicate appearance. These pieces were much stronger than the all wax angels. Nevertheless, the composition pieces lacked the translucent glow of the cast wax angel. Some of the larger and more elaborate angels were molded in several separate pieces and assembled by local cottage workers.

The most popular hanging style for the flying wax angel was horizontal, suspended by a hook in her back. A slightly rarer form of the traditional angel is one that hangs from the head in a vertical or flying position with one hand raised in greeting or blessing. This design was popularly used as a treetop angel.

The wings for angels were made from spun glass, gilded cardboard, or wax that was molded onto the figure itself. A short dress, generally made of fabric and tinsel, was added for the sake of modesty. Some angels might also be found carrying trumpets made of lead or tin.

Besides the angel, another popular three-dimensional wax form was the baby, referred to as Baby Jesus when used as a Christmas ornament. These pieces might range in size from one to six inches and were used as toys, in Nativity Scenes, and in Victorian shadow boxes as well as other Christmas decorations. Other small wax figurines of people and animals were added to what are called Sebnitz ornaments.

The second major category of wax ornaments is that of those made in relief, or "flat" style. Extremely few of these have survived over the years, and they can be quite old. Makers of the wooden *lebkuchen* cookie forms that had been designed for shaping cookie dough first produced them. Instead of dough being pressed into the carvings, hot wax was poured into the mold. When cool, these wax reliefs were often painted with the same bright colors that were used to ice the cookies.

During the last half of the nineteenth century, these wax reliefs were widely sold on a commercial basis and were fairly popular in Europe. Old ornaments made from beeswax or paraffin had the singular disadvantage of being easily melted or distorted. This, coupled with the fact that the soft wax attracted dirt and dust, meant they were thrown out or replaced on a regular basis. Wax relief ornaments enjoyed a rebirth during the 1920s and were produced again, on a limited basis, during the 1980s and 1990s. Many of these wax ornaments were produced from antique molds.

A third major way in which wax was used can be found in wax accessories or decorations with wax heads, arms, or legs. These cast parts were often incorporated into angels, dolls, and Santas that were made of cotton, fabric, or foil-covered cardboard and sold commercially during the last half of the nineteenth century.

Because they were easily damaged by heat and dirt, wax ornaments did not survive well. The wax angel is without a doubt the most common form, but even these pieces are not commonly found. Wax ornaments make an excellent addition to a collection, but remember to keep them wrapped in order to protect them from dirt and mildew, and to keep them away from heat sources when you hang them on the tree.

Standard Form Wax Angel with Glass Eyes, large, 13½" [OP, R1]. Angels this large are rare. **$800.00–900.00.**

Standard Wax Angel with Horn and Fabric Flowers, 9", a wax over composition angel with an unusual mohair skirt [OP, R2]. **$500.00–650.00.**

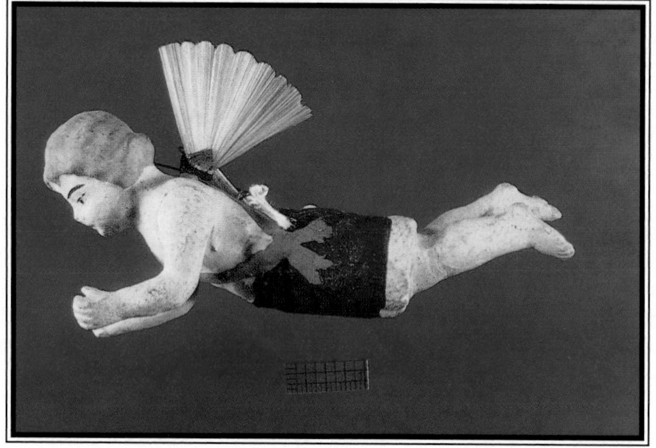

Standard Wax Angel with Molded Hair and Skirt, 7" [OP, R2]. **$225.00–275.00.**

Wax Angel with Glass Eyes, large, 14½" [OP, R1]. **$800.00–1,000.00.**

Angel with a Horn, approx. 6½" [OP, R2]. **$200.00–275.00.**

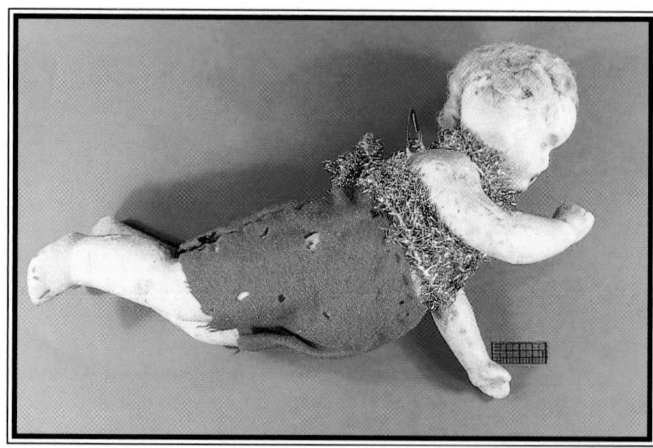

Standard Form Wax Angel, large, 14" [OP, R1]. **$650.00–750.00.**

A & B. Standard Form Wax Angels, approx. 3½", 4" (shown), 4¾" (shown), 5", 5¾", 6¼", 9", 9¾", 13½", 14", and 14½". Made of wax over composition [German, OP, Rarity varies with size]. Small (3" – 4", R3), **$90.00–125.00.** Medium (5" – 6", R2-3), **$150.00–200.00.** Large (7" – 10", R1-2), **$300.00–600.00.** X-Large (13" – 14", R1), **$800.00–1,000.00.** C. Coiled Wax Candle, used for lighting candles on the tree, 5" [OP, R1]. **$50.00–75.00.**

Angel with a Flower in Her Hair, approx. 5"; she has wax wings [German, OP, R1-2]. **$400.00–600.00.**

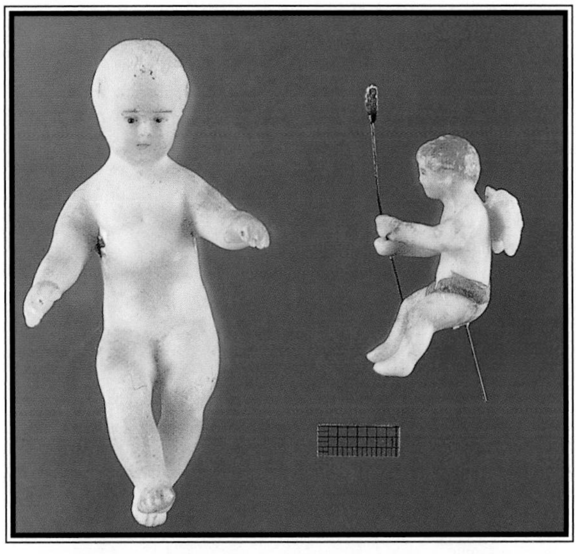

A. Large Wax Baby Jesus, approx. 1", 3", 3½", & 6" (shown) [German, OP-NP (1990s, 1" size), R2-3]. Small, **$15.00–25.00.** Medium, **$30.00–50.00.** Large, **$75.00–100.00.** B. Seated Angel, approx. 3", with a spike for holding it on the tree [German, OP, R1]. **$100.00–125.00.**

Flying Angel, large, 11", all wax with Dresden wings [OP, R1-2]. **$800.00–1,000.00.**

Flying Wax Angel, "Herald Angel," 7", 1988 version reissued by D. Blumchen & Co. [OP-NP, R1-2]. Old, **$350.00–450.00.** 1988 version, **$90.00–125.00.**

A. Standing Angel, 4¼", German made for D. Blumchen & Co., circa 1992 [R2-3]. **$50.00–75.00.** B. Small Boy Cherub (Type II), 2½" [OP, R1-2]. **$50.00–60.00.**

American Figural Wax Ornaments, original box [OP-NP, R3-4]: Angel, 3"; Sheep, 3"; Santa, 2¾"; Drummer, 3⅛". **$10.00–15.00** each. Original box of 12, **$150.00–175.00.**

American Wax Ornaments, approx. 2¼" – 2¾", circa 1950 [R3-4]. **$10.00–15.00.**

Wax Pear Candy Container, large, 4" [OP, R2]. **$100.00–125.00.**

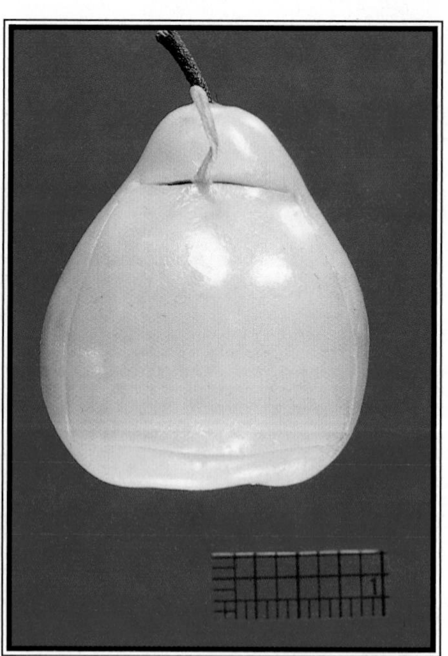

Wax Pear with Mary and Jesus Inside, 2", outside view [German, OP, R1]. **$150.00–175.00.**

Inside View of Wax Pear with Mary and Jesus Inside.

A. Wax Relief Ornament, circa 1980s [R3]. **$10.00–15.00.** B. Baby Jesus in a Hollow Wax Heart, 2" [German, OP-NP (1993), R1]. Old, **$100.00–125.00.** 1993 version, **$25.00–30.00.** C. Madonna Praying, 4¼" [OP, R1]. **$45.00–60.00.**

Wax Relief Ornaments: A. Standing Mary and Jesus, 4⅛" [OP, R1]. **$45.00–60.00.** B. Mary and Jesus in a Frame, 4" [OP, R1]. **$45.00–60.00.**

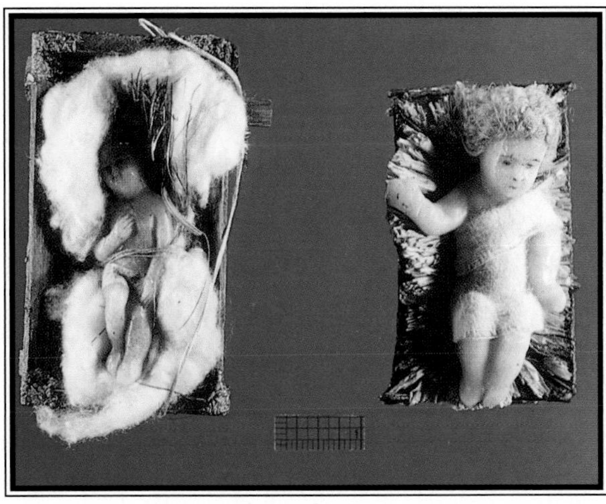

Two Forms of Wax Baby Jesus in a Manger. 3" & 3½" [OP,R2]. **$50.00–75.00** each.

Three Wax Relief Ornaments. These pieces are new, but made in antique cookie molds. Old, **$25.00–35.00** each. New, **$10.00–15.00** each.

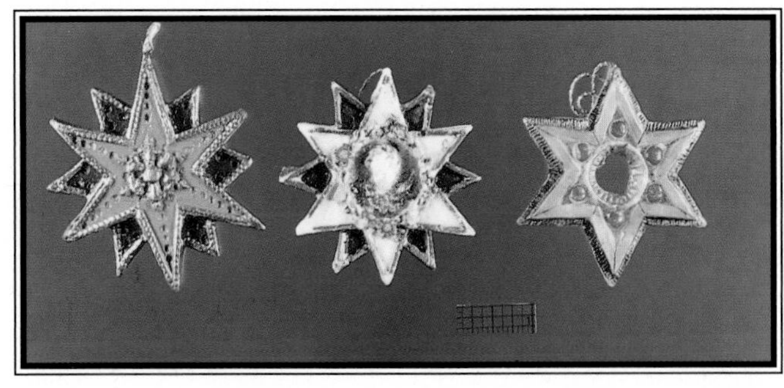

Metal Ornaments

Dating back to the late 1700s, metal ornaments are among the first permanent Christmas tree decorations ever made. Metal ornaments can be classified as cast tin, wire, tinsel, foil, stamped tin, and stamped brass.

Tin-lead alloy ornaments were the most popular of the metal ornaments and were originally called "sparkling tin brilliant ornaments." They were produced in a wide variety of styles, from geometric shapes and animals to three-dimensional birdcages, baskets, and cradles. These pieces were also designed to be hung by thread behind or near candles, so that they would twirl slowly and reflect the light. During the last part of the 1800s, tin ornaments, especially those in geometric or flower shapes, were applied as weights on pendulum candleholders. This provided a pleasing combination of both reflective ornament and candleholder.

While some tin decorations were cast as single pieces, others were cast in sections and assembled into more elaborate forms. They were usually bent into the desired position or shape and then soldered together. Examples of these include birdcages, baskets, boxes, and stars with filigree edges. Makers of such pieces indented many of them, to create small faceted reflectors that would add to their beauty. When painted with bright translucent lacquers, these indentations sparkled like gems.

The popularity of tin ornaments died out about the time of the First World War, and enjoyed a rebirth following World War II. Whether they are old or new, it must be remembered that tin decorations are soft and easily bent or melted if not handled with care. Their once brightly glistening surfaces are now most often seen in shades of dull gray.

Wire ornaments come in many forms and styles. The wire itself takes on a variety of forms: spiral wrapped, wavy, crinkled (leonic), and flat strips. The biggest use for wire of all types was to encase and decorate glass ornaments. Wire was also used by itself to form some interesting objects and designs. Some were twisted into spiraling icicles, while other wire was used to create spiraled wire decorations such as stars, comets, snowflakes, and hanging chandeliers. The Germans wove flat strips of gilded brass and silver nickel wire into small baskets designed to hold nuts or candies.

Tinsel is a separate but closely related form of wire and foil. First manufactured in the seventeenth century and used on military uniforms, by the 1870s tinsel was used in ornaments and roping for the Christmas tree. Tinsel made from flattened strips of wire or foil, known as lametta, was much like our modern foil icicles. Tinsel that was wrapped between string was soft and primarily used for tree and room garlands. Stiff tinsel, wrapped between wire, was used for outlining scraps or forming stars, snowflakes, hoops, or rosettes that might include glass beads or larger glass ornaments.

Tin foil wrapped over cardboard was popular for making both homemade and commercial decorations that flashed brightly in candlelight. Foil was also used for making the dresses of certain types of treetop angels, most notably the Nuremberg Angels. Some later pieces can be found constructed entirely out of copper, tin, or aluminum foil. Thin sheets of foil were fastened together in concentric circles, stars, or rosettes, forming foil ornaments that also served as light reflectors. Other foil was rolled, twisted, or bent into more three-dimensional shapes such as balls. Perhaps the most enduring use of foil is in the manufacture of icicles. Called lametta, they were first marketed in Germany in 1878. Sold in one-gram envelopes, they came in gold, silver, and a rarer purple. These early icicles had the major disadvantage of tarnishing easily.

During the 1870s–1890s, Germany also produced stamped tin decorations, some of which were painted or lithographed, in the shape of pipes, hearts, stars, globes, and eggs.

Cut tin ornaments saw limited use about 1910. They were painstakingly cut from sheets of tin, then twisted and formed into stars, snowflakes, and wreaths. The most unusual of these are tree-like shapes mounted in wire rings. Their branches were formed aerodynamically and they used heat from candles to spin on a pin-and-cup device.

Certain decorative pieces stamped out of sheet brass, such as angels, birds, roses, and reindeer, as well as geometrics like snowflakes and rosettes, found limited use as Christmas decorations. When gilded and trimmed with brilliantly colored lacquer, they made fine tree ornaments. Because they are nearly unbreakable, tarnish is the real enemy of these once-bright metal ornaments. Today, dull blacks and grays have replaced the once-gleaming golds and silvers that flashed and sparkled brightly amongst the dark branches of candlelit trees. Unfortunately, this tendency to tarnish has caused many of these wonderful decorations to be discarded over the years.

Whether tin, wire, tinsel, foil, or brass, these unique ornaments are a fascinating part of the colorful history of Christmas ornaments, and a worthwhile addition to any collection.

Tin-Lead Fancy Geometric Shape, large, 5½" [OP, R1]. Rare in this size. **$125.00–150.00.**

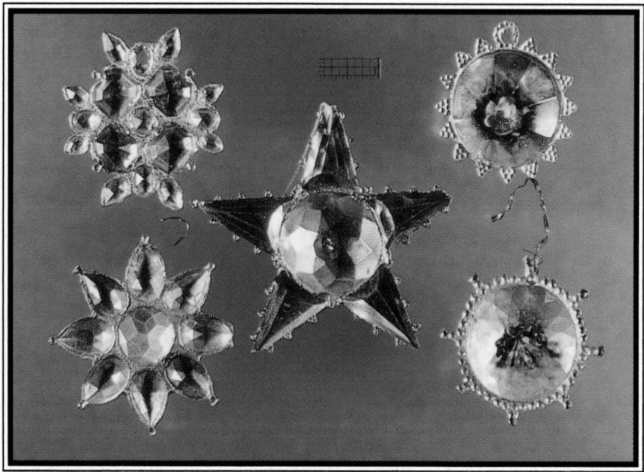

All Tin-Lead Ornaments: A. Standard Geometric Shape Medallion, medium, 2¾" [OP-NP, R3]. **$25.00–35.00.** B. Indented Round Reflector with Fabric Flower, 2¼" [OP, R3-4]. **$25.00–35.00.** C. Star with Five Points, 4¼" [OP-NP, R1]. **$40.00–60.00.** D. Standard Geometric Shape Flower, 3" [OP-NP, R3]. **$40.00–50.00.** E. Indented Reflector with Stamens, 2½" [OP, R3-4]. **$25.00–35.00.**

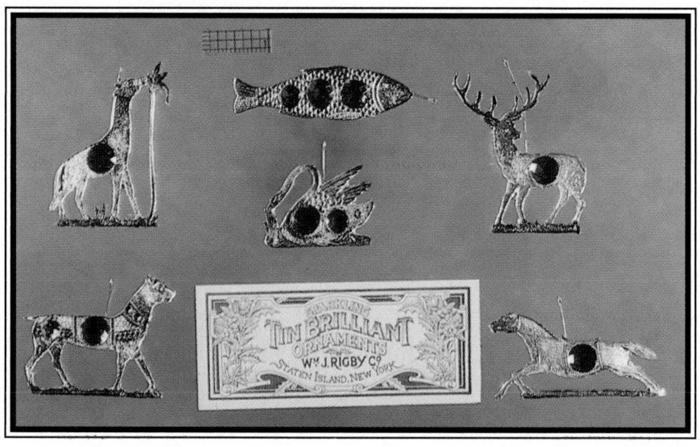

Tin-Lead Animals, recast by Wm. J. Rigby Co. of New York in original molds. Both old and new are American made: A. Giraffe, 2½" [OP-NP, R2]. New, **$12.00–15.00.** B. Fish, 2¾" [OP-NP, R2]. New, **$8.00–9.00.** C. Stag, 2⅜" [OP-NP, R2]. New, **$15.00–17.00.** D. Swan, 1¾" [OP-NP, R2]. New, **$9.00–10.00.** E. Dog, 2⅜" [OP-NP, R2]. New, **$12.00–13.00.** F. Horse, 2½" [OP-NP, R2]. New, **$12.00–15.00.**

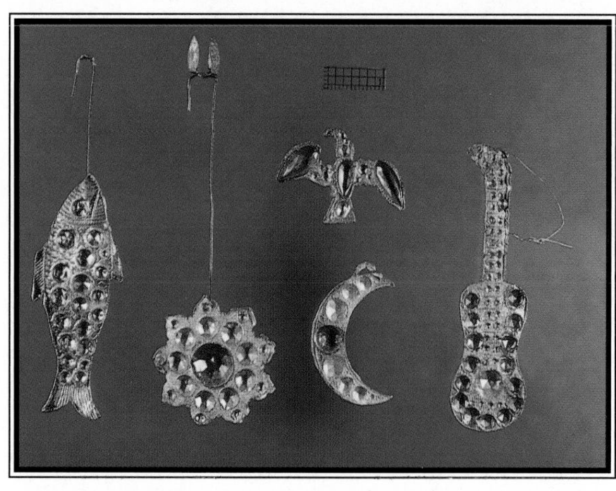

All-Tin Lead Sparkling Tin Brilliant Ornaments: A. Fish, large, 3¾" [OP, R2]. **$80.00–90.00.** B. Candle Holder with Geometric, 2" [OP, R3]. **$35.00–40.00.** C. Eagle, 2". **$50.00–60.00.** D. Crescent Moon, 2" [OP-NP, R2]. Old, **$30.00–35.00.** E. Guitar, 4½" [OP, R1]. **$90.00–100.00.**

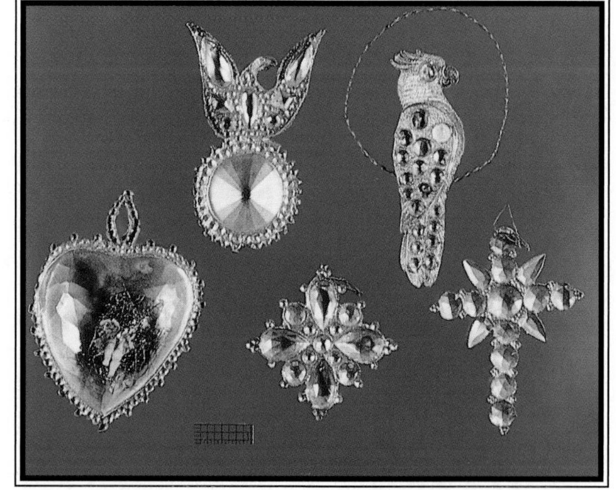

A Collection of Tin-Lead Alloy Ornaments Designed as Light Reflectors: A. Eagle on a Reflector, 4" [OP, R2]. **$125.00–150.00.** B. Parrot; 3½" (shown), 4", & 5¼" [OP-NP (1990s), R2]. **$40.00–50.00.** C. Heart, 4" [German, OP, R2]. **$75.00–100.00.** D. Fancy Geometric Shape, medium. **$25.00–30.00.** E. Cross with a Sunburst, 3¼" [German, OP, R2]. **$60.00–70.00.**

Three Fancy Geometric Shapes [all OP, R2-3]: A. Six-armed Star, 4". **$30.00–40.00.** B. Eight-armed Star, 4½". **$50.00–75.00.** C. Oval, 3¾". **$45.00–60.00.**

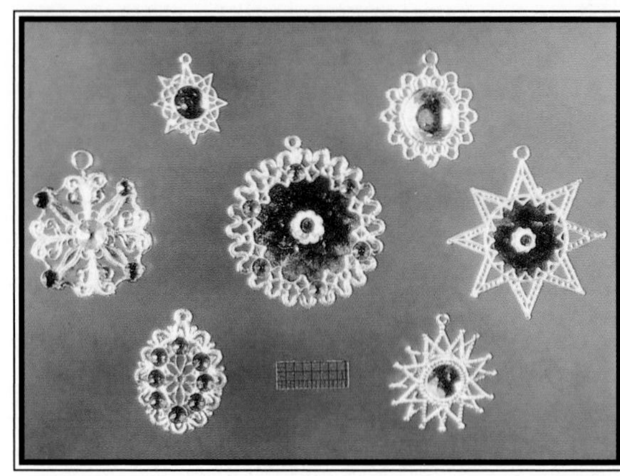

Seven Fancy Geometric Shapes, ranging in size from 1" to 2¼" [OP-NP, R1-2]: A. **$15.00–25.00.** B. **$20.00–25.00.** C. **$40.00–60.00.** D. **$50.00–75.00.** E. **$40.00–60.00.** F. **$25.00–35.00.** G. **$25.00–35.00.**

A. Cast Tin Baby Buggy, 3-D, 3" [OP, R1]. **$100.00–125.00.** B. Cast Tin Angel in a Wreath, 3½" [OP, R1]. **$35.00–45.00.** C. Stamped Tin Pipe Candy Container, 5⅜" [German, OP, R1]. **$80.00–100.00.**

A. Tin-Lead Basket, covered rectangular, large, 4" [OP, R1-2]. **$80.00–100.00.** B. Lithographed Tin Bucket. Not strictly ornaments, buckets like these could also serve as toy and candy containers when hung on the tree [OP, R3]. **$30.00–40.00.**

Tin-Lead Candelabrum, 8¼" x 4¾" [OP-NP, R1]. Made by Wm. J. Rigby Co. from original molds, **$45.00–60.00.** Original by G. Mayer, **$175.00–200.00.**

Five-sided Carriage Scene, 3" [OP, R1]. **$125.00–150.00.**

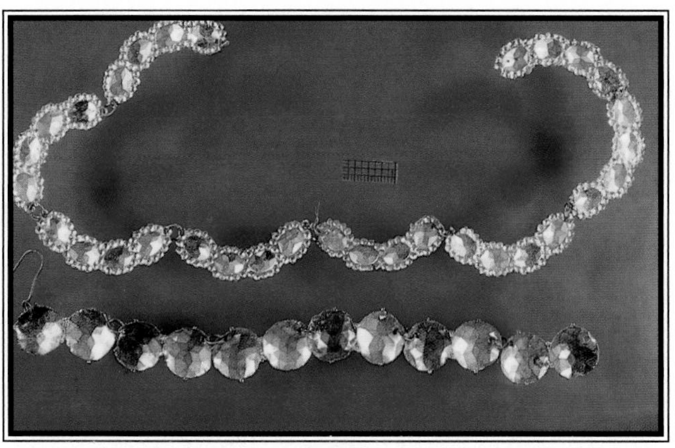

A. Chain of Crescent Jewels, 22", each of the eight crescents is 2¾" [OP, R1]. **$200.00–225.00.** B. Chain of Round Jewels, 12" long, each of the 12 jewels is 1" long [OP, R1]. **$100.00–125.00.**

Tin Lead Reflectors: A. Horseshoe with Dangle, 4" [OP, R1]. **$125.00–150.00.** B. Anchor, 3¼" [OP, R2]. Large, **$90.00–110.00.** C. Cross with Starburst, 3¼" [OP, R2]. **$60.00–70.00.**

Cross, large, 7", made by Wm. J. Rigby Co. as the 1995 ornament of the year, new design made from old molds [R3]. **$50.00–75.00.**

Tin-Lead Good Luck Charms. Each holds a fortune or motto [OP, R1]. **$20.00–30.00** each: A. Top Hat, "Prosit NewJahr," 1½". B. Stein, 1¼". C. Pine Cone, 1¼". D. Moneybag, "1,000," 1½".

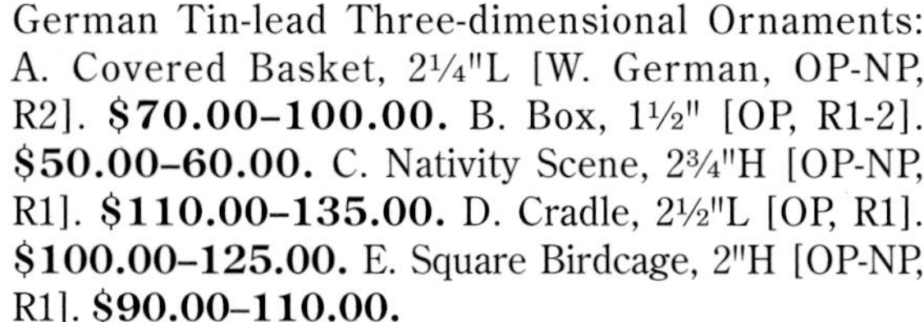

German Tin-lead Three-dimensional Ornaments: A. Covered Basket, 2¼"L [W. German, OP-NP, R2]. **$70.00–100.00.** B. Box, 1½" [OP, R1-2]. **$50.00–60.00.** C. Nativity Scene, 2¾"H [OP-NP, R1]. **$110.00–135.00.** D. Cradle, 2½"L [OP, R1]. **$100.00–125.00.** E. Square Birdcage, 2"H [OP-NP, R1]. **$90.00–110.00.**

A. Horseshoe with a Dangle, 4" [OP, R1]. **$125.00–150.00.** B. Standard Geometric Shape, oblong, 5¼" [OP-NP, R3]. **$75.00–100.00.**

All Tin Lead Reflectors: A. Small Standard Geometric Shape with Tinsel and Glass Bead, 1½" [OP-NP, R3]. **$20.00–25.00.** B. Six-armed Snowflake, 2½" [OP-NP, R2-3]. **$35.00–50.00.** C. Heart with a Cross, 2"H [OP, R2]. **$60.00–70.00.** D. Cross, small, 2"H [OP, R2]. **$45.00–55.00.** E. Unusual Five-armed Star, 2" [OP, R1-2]. **$30.00–35.00.** F. Small Five-armed Star, 2" [OP, R1-2]. **$25.00–35.00.**

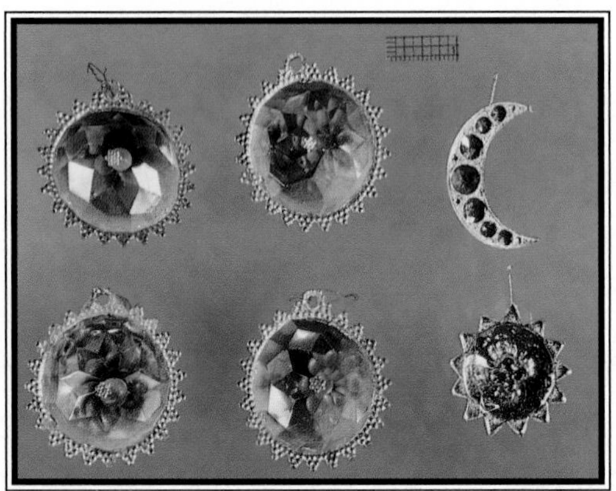

Tin-Lead Reflectors: A, B, D, E. Round Indented Reflectors, 2¼" – 2½" [OP, R3-4]. **$25.00–35.00.** C. Crescent Moon, flat, 2", new version by Rigby [OP-NP, R2]. New, **$10.00–15.00.** Old, **$30.00–35.00.** F. Sunburst by Rigby, 1¾" [OP-NP, R2]. New, **$15.00–20.00.** Old, **$25.00–30.00.**

Cast Tin Ornaments: A. Six-armed Snowflake with Dangle, 5¾" [OP, R1-2]. **$70.00–80.00.** B. Snowflake, 2½" [OP, R2-3]. **$35.00–40.00.** C. Snowflake, 2¾" [OP, R2-3]. **$35.00–40.00.** D. Cross in a Circle, 3¼" [OP, R2]. **$35.00–45.00.**

A. Five-point Dangling Star, 8½" [OP, R2]. **$60.00–75.00.** B. Eight-sided Snowflake, small, 3" [OP, R2-3]. **$35.00–50.00.** C. Six-sided Snowflake, small, 3½" [OP, R2-3]. **$35.00–50.00.**

Snowflake with Eight Arms and Double Layers, 4⅝" – 5" [OP, R1-2]. **$100.00–125.00.**

A. Round Tin-Lead Light Reflector, 2¾" [OP, R3-4]. **$25.00–35.00.** B. Six-sided Star of David, 3¼" [OP, R1-2]. **$60.00–70.00.** C. Eight-pointed Star, small, 3¼" [OP, R2-3]. **$50.00–75.00.** D. Eight-pointed Snowflake, 3¾" [OP, R2-3]. **$35.00–45.00.** F. Geometric Shape Gem, 3¼" [OP-NP, R3]. **$30.00–40.00.**

Five-pointed Tin-Lead Star, 6¾" [OP-NP, R1]. Recast in original molds by Wm. J. Rigby, **$55.00–75.00.** Original by Gustav Mayer, **$175.00–200.00.**

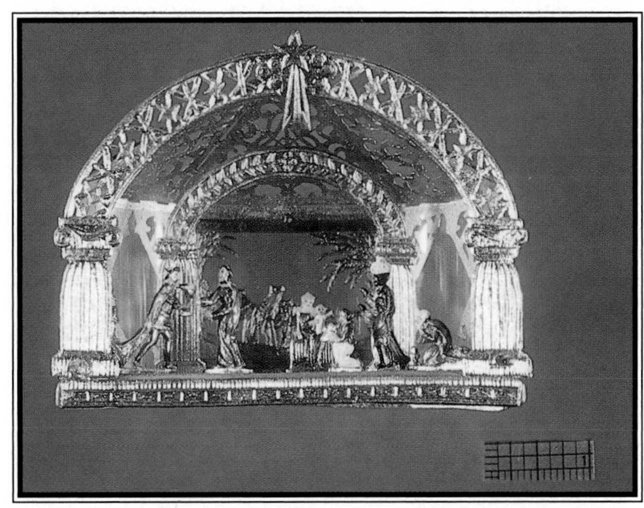

Cast Tin-Lead Nativity Scene, 3-D, approx. 4"L x 3"H; marked Germany, it has been recast in old forms, circa 2000 [OP-NP, R1]. Old, **$175.00–200.00.** New, **$40.00–50.00.**

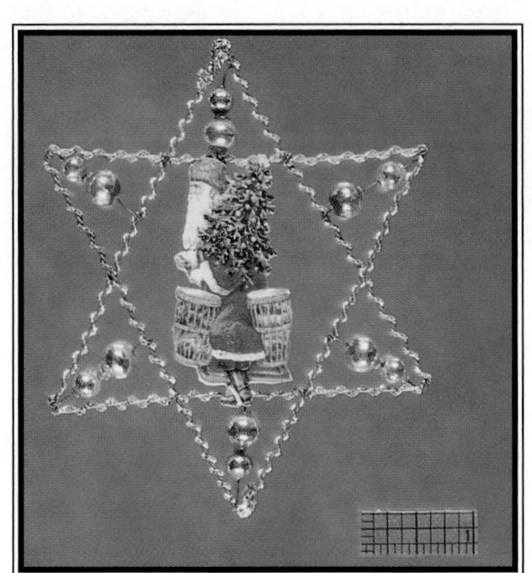

Wire Star with Scrap Santa, approx. 4". The star is made of twisted wire and embellished with silvered beads [possibly German, OP, R1-2]. **$35.00–45.00.**

Icicles of Twisted Metal, "Diamond Ray Jeweled Icicles," 5½", circa 1935 [R5]. **$.50–.75** each. Original box, **$10.00–15.00.**

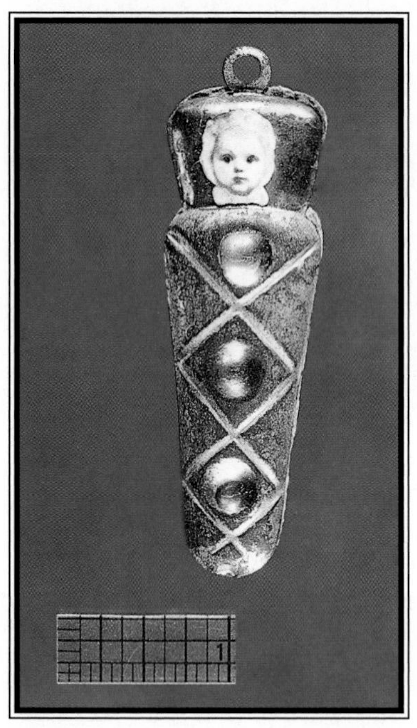

Stamped Tin Papoose, 3⅛" [OP, R1]. **$50.00–75.00.**

Cut Tin Ornaments: A. Wreath with Scrap Nativity Scene, 3½" dia. [OP, R1]. **$30.00–35.00.** B. Eight-armed Snowflake, 3½" [OP, R1]. **$30.00–35.00.**

A. Boat Basket of Woven Metal Strips and Wire, 4" [OP, R1]. **$70.00–90.00.** B. Rectangular Basket of Woven Metal Strips, 2½" x 1½" [OP (1920s – 1930s), R4]. **$20.00–25.00.** C. Filigree Basket, large, 3-D, with rose designs, 3¾" x 2¾" [OP, R1-2]. **$70.00–80.00.**

A. Square Woven Wire Basket, 1¾" [1920s – 1930s, R4]. **$15.00–20.00.** B. Cast Tin-Lead Basket, covered, rectangular, 3-D, 2" [OP, R1-2]. **$50.00–60.00.** C. Round Woven Wire Basket, 1½" [OP, (1920 – 1930), R4]. **$15.00–20.00.** D. Oval Woven Wire Basket, 2¼" [OP, (1920 – 1930), R4]. **$25.00–35.00.**

A & C. Foil Cornucopia Candy Containers, both circa 1950, 5½" [American, R4-5]. **$4.00–6.00.** B. Boot, 4½", circa 1950 [R3-4]. **$4.00–6.00.**

Foil Stars, circa 1950, 4" & 3" [American, R4]. **$3.00–5.00** each.

Embossed Foil Cornucopia, 9¼" [OP(1940s), R3]. **$10.00–12.00.**

Embossed Foil Figures, made from stamped aluminum: A. Angel, 4" [NP (1950s – 1960s), R3-4]. **$5.00–10.00.** B. Santa on Deer, 4" [NP (1950s – 1960s), R3-4]. **$5.00–10.00.** C. DoubleGlo Light Reflectors in Original Package [NP (circa 1955 – 1960), R3]. **$5.00–10.00.**

Two Tinsel Ornaments with Glass Beads, circa 1900: A. Comet Tail, 6" [R3]. **$10.00–15.00.** B. Horseshoe, 6" [R3]. **$15.00–20.00.**

German "Moss" or Icicles, circa 1910 [R2]. **$20.00–25.00.**

Early Package of Lametta or Icicles [R2]. **$20.00–25.00.**

Foil Icicles in Original Boxes, circa 1930 [R2]. **$15.00–18.00.**

A. Foil Icicles, circa 1935. Original box, **$20.00–25.00.** B. Foil Icicles, copyrighted 1925. Original box, **$15.00–20.00.**

A. DoubleGlo Icicles, circa 1930. **$10.00–15.00.** B. Ribbon Icicles, circa 1940. **$15.00–20.00.**

A. Foil Roping, 10', by DoubleGlo [NP (1950s), R4]. **$5.00–8.00.** In original packaging, **$10.00–15.00.** B. Cellophane Roping, 12', circa 1950 [R3-4]. **$4.00–6.00.** In original packaging, **$6.00–10.00.**

Stamped Brass Ornaments: A. Decorated Tree on a Stand, 2¼" [OP-NP, R1-2]. **$20.00–25.00.** B. Children Dancing Around a Tree, 2¼" [OP-NP, R1-2]. **$20.00–25.00.** C. Santa with a Tree, 2½" [OP-NP, R1-2]. **$25.00–30.00.** D. Angel Ringing Bells, 2" [OP, R1-2]. **$20.00–25.00.**

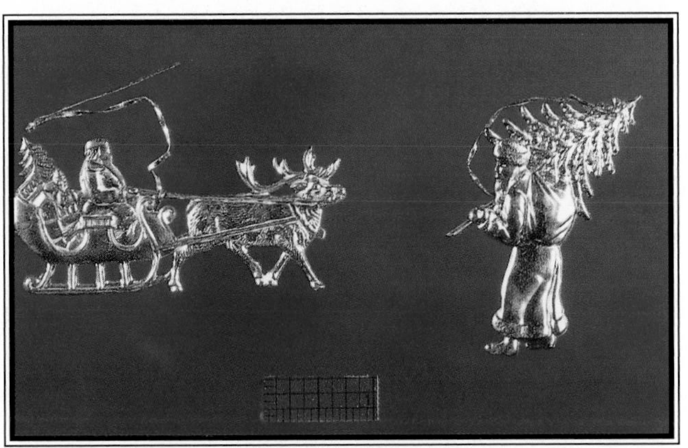

Stamped Brass Ornaments: A. Santa in Sleigh, 3" [OP, R1-2]. **$25.00–30.00.** B. Santa with Tree, 2½" [OP-NP, R1-2]. Old, **$25.00–30.00.**

Plastic Decorations

Plastic Christmas decorations have come into their own and are increasingly becoming more popular, and therefore, more valuable. Plastic items from the late 1940s and 1950s Baby Boomer era are now approaching or past the half-century mark.

From the 1880s to the 1920s, celluloid was used for making many Christmas and holiday-related toys. Celluloid ornaments were made in the United States, Japan, and Germany. Pieces designed for the tree usually had loops or rings in their tops. Early celluloid pieces were hand painted and used several different colors. Bakelite, in browns, greens, or marbleized, followed celluloid as the first entirely man-made plastic. Used for sockets and plugs on early electric lighting, it was a more cost-efficient alternative to porcelain sockets and connectors. In the 1920s and 1930s, acrylic plastics were used in icicles and balls, and light shades were created using lightweight and fireproof urea plastic.

Most of the hard plastic decorations from the 1940s and 1950s were made of polystyrene. A vast variety of Santas, sleighs, reindeer, angels, snowmen, snowflakes, bells, and geometric ornaments were created using this plastic. Red, white, blue, and green were common colors, and many ornaments were given a reflective silver undercoat that made them shine like glass ornaments. Although many plastic ornaments were flat, some consisted of two interlocking pieces that slid together to form three-dimensional snowflakes, trees, or stars. Most glow-in-the-dark ornaments were made of plastic. Usually pale white in color, with a slightly greenish tint (although blue and red fluorescent ornaments were also made), when charged in normal light they would fluoresce, or glow in the dark. They were a big hit with children from the late 1940s to the early 1960s.

Styrofoam ornaments were first manufactured in the 1950s. They were flat, stamped-out pieces in the shape of stars, snowflakes, reindeer, boots, bells, and other shapes and were a popular substitute for glass ornaments. Later, in the 1960s and 1970s, styrofoam balls were covered with fabrics like rayon satin. Popular homemade crafts of the period involved covering these balls with ribbons, sequins, and jewel-like plastic beads.

Vinyl began to become more widespread a short time later. Vinyl-faced elves, Santas, and angels with felt bodies or flock covering were imported from Japan in the 1970s as tree decorations.

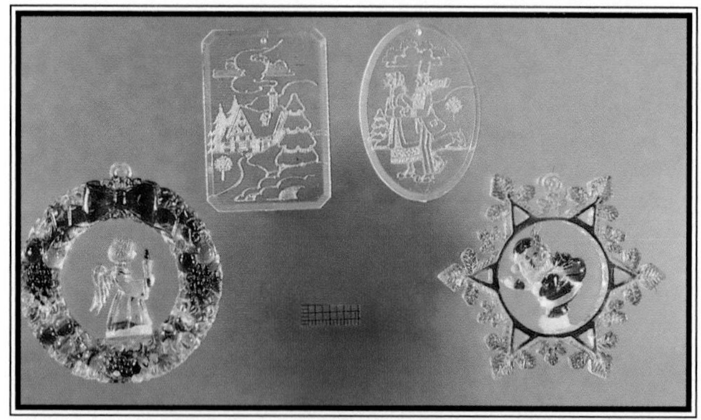

A & B. Acrylic Ornaments, flat and etched, 3" [NP (1970 – 1980), R4-5]. **$1.00–2.00.** C & D. Acrylic Wreath and Snowflake, 1980 [R5]. **$0.25–0.50.**

Celluloid Angel Dolls, 3¾" [OP, R2]. **$25.00–30.00.**

Celluloid Animals, small, circa 1915 – 1950 [Japanese, R4]. **$10.00–25.00.**

Celluloid Animals, medium, 3" – 4", circa 1915 – 1950. **$18.00–25.00.**

Celluloid Ornaments: A. Football Player, 4½" [Japanese, OP, R2]. **$15.00–20.00.** B. Ball, 2¾" [OP (circa 1930), R2]. **$5.00–6.00.** C. Ball, indented, 2¼", circa 1930 – 1940s [R3-4]. **$5.00–6.00.**

Two Celluloid Santas: A. Santa on Skis, 4" [OP (circa 1925 – 1930), R2]. **$55.00–65.00.** B. Santa with Pack and Switches, 4" [OP (1925 – 1930), R2]. **$35.00–45.00.**

Celluloid Santas: A. Santa with a Hand Behind His Back, 7" [OP, R2-3]. **$75.00–100.00.** B. "Square" Santa with a Wicker Basket on His Back, 7" [OP, R1]. **$135.00–150.00.** C. Santa with a Doll and a Zeppelin, 7¼", marked "SS" in a diamond [Japanese, OP, R1]. **$100.00–125.00.**

Celluloid Walking Santa, approx. 5½". There is a pack over the right shoulder. The maker's mark is a cross in a circle, which indicates Ando as the manufacturer [Japanese, OP, R1-2]. **$125.00–150.00.**

Celluloid Standing Santa with a Pack, approx. 5"H. The left hand holds a yellow bag and the belt buckle is unusually large. Made in Japan, by Irwin [OP, R2]. **$80.00–100.00.**

Three Celluloid Santas: A. Santa with Packages and a Green Pack, approx. 4"H. Made by the Viscaloid Company and marked by an intertwined *V, C, & O*, circa 1915 – 1927 [American, R2]. **$50.00–60.00.** B. Santa with Two Bags, large, approx. 4¼". He has green and tan bags. Marked "Made in Japan" [OP, R2-3]. **$35.00–45.00.** C. Santa with Two Bags, small, approx. 3¾", marked "Made in Japan" [OP, R2-3]. **$35.00–45.00.**

Three Celluloid Santas: A. Santa in a Round Chimney, approx. 3"H. Unmarked [OP, R1-2]. There are two small lines of bricks; the rest of the base is white. **$35.00–50.00.** B. Santa in a Chimney Rattle, approx. 3½"H, no maker's mark [OP, R2]. **$50.00–75.00.** C. Santa with a Horn and a Pack, approx. 4", marked "Japan" [OP, R2]. **$65.00–85.00.**

Two Celluloid Santas, both made by the Viscaloid Company and marked by an intertwined *V, C, & O*. Viscaloid was the forerunner of Irwin Plastics. These pieces were possibly designed by Paul Krammer, circa 1915 – 1927: A. Santa with a Pack and Flowers, approx. 5" [American, R2]. **$50.00–60.00.** B. Santa on a Ball, approx. 4¾"H [American, R2]. **$65.00–85.00.**

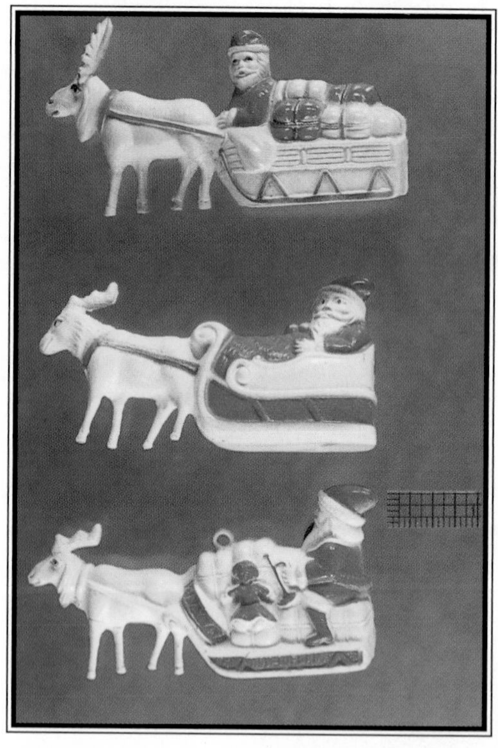

Three Celluloid Santas in Sleighs (small): A. Packages in the Rear of the Sleigh, approx. 3⅞"L x 2"H. Made by the Viscaloid Company and marked by an intertwined *V, C, & O*, circa 1915 – 1927 [American, R2]. **$100.00–125.00.** B. No Packages Show, approx. 3¾"L x 1¾"H, marked "Irwin" on the back of the sleigh [American, R2]. **$70.00–90.00.** C. Packages in the Front of the Sleigh, approx. 3¾"L x 1¾"H, marked "I USA" and "Non-Flam" on the runner [American, R2]. **$100.00–125.00.**

Celluloid Santa in a Sleigh, large, approx. 4½"L x 3"H [OP, R2]. **$100.00–125.00.**

Celluloid Santa in a Train, approx. 5¼"L x 2"H. Made by the Viscaloid Company and marked by an intertwined *V, C, & O*, circa 1915 – 1927 [American, R1]. **$175.00–200.00.**

Three Celluloid Santas, all by Irwin, all circa 1930. The actual material they are made from is called cellulose acetate: A. Roly-Poly Santa, approx. 2¾" [R2]. **$35.00–50.00.** B. Santa on an Egg Shape, approx. 3½" [R2]. **$60.00–80.00.** C. Roly-Poly Santa in a Chimney, approx. 2¾", stamped "Non Inflam" [R2]. **$35.00–50.00.**

A. Rubber Squeak Toy, 6½" [NP, R3]. **$10.00–15.00.** B & C. Small Celluloid Santas in Sleighs: B. 4" [Japanese, OP, R2-3]. **$35.00–45.00.** C. 4¼" [American, OP (circa 1920), R3]. **$100.00–125.00.** D. 4" [American, OP (circa 1920), R2]. **$100.00–125.00.**

A & D. Santa with a Pack, approx. 5". Made by the Viscaloid Company, circa 1915 – 1927 [American, R3]. **$45.00–60.00.** B. Waving Santa with a Lantern, approx. 4¾", marked "Made in Japan," circa 1920s – 1930s [OP, R3-4]. **$20.00–25.00.** C. Santa on a Dome with a Cane & Presents, approx. 3½", made of cellulose acetate [OP, R2]. **$30.00–40.00.**

Celluloid Santas by Irwin, approx. 5⅛"H. The front and back views are shown. The actual material used in these pieces is cellulose acetate, not celluloid [OP, R3]. **$45.00–60.00.**

Three Indented Celluloid Ornaments, approx. 2¼", 2½", and 3¼" dia. They have no maker's mark but are probably American, circa 1930s – 1940s [R2-3]. Small, **$5.00–6.00.** Medium, **$6.00–8.00.** Large, **$10.00–15.00.**

Boxed Set of Carnival Plastic Glow-in-the-Dark Animals, approx. 3¼" to 4¼" animals, 6¾" L box. The box contains eight animals. The original box is rare; the individual animals are not. Made by Carnival Toy MFG. Corp. of New York, circa 1950 [animals R3-4, box R1]. Individual animals, **$8.00–10.00.** Boxed set, **$125.00–150.00.**

American "Easy Set" Glo-in-the-Dark Animals by Carnival Plastic; they can also be found in yellow, red, orange, silver, and blue [all NP (1940s – 1950s)]: A. Elephant, 4¼" [R3-4]. **$8.00–10.00.** B. Vulture, 3¼" [R3-4]. **$8.00–10.00.** C. Donkey, 4¼" [R3]. **$8.00–10.00.** D. Sheep, 3¼" [R3]. **$18.00–20.00.** D. Lion, 3¼" [R4]. **$8.00–10.00.**

"Hard Set" Glo-in-the-Dark Animals by Carnival Plastic [all NP]: A. Sitting Dog, 4" [R1-2]. **$15.00–20.00.** B. Cat, 3¼" [R1-2]. **$15.00–20.00.** C. Penguin, 3½" [R2]. **$8.00–10.00.** D. Pig, 3¾" [R1-2]. **$15.00–20.00.** E. Duck, 3¾" [R1-2]. **$15.00–20.00.**

Carnival Plastic Animals, color variations. Six of the seven known color schemes are shown — yellow is missing: A &D. Donkey, 4¼". Green, **$20.00–25.00.** Silver, **$20.00–25.00.** B & E. Lion, 3¼". Blue, **$15.00–20.00.** Glow-in-the-Dark, **$6.00–10.00.** Penguin, 3½". Orange, **$20.00–25.00.** Red, **$20.00–25.00.**

Carnival Plastic Elephant, color variations, approx. 4¼": A. Green. **$20.00–25.00.** B. Glow-in-the-Dark. **$6.00–8.00.** C. Yellow. **$25.00–30.00.** D. Red. **$20.00–25.00.**

Candle in a Wreath, color variations, approx. 3¼". The pieces are double sided, and the white one is glow-in-the-dark. American made by Carnival Toy MFG. Corp. of New York, circa 1950. The colors are harder to find than the fluorescent [R3-4]. **$3.00–6.00.**

German Angel Children: A & B. Crescent Moons, 2½", marked "Germany" [OP-NP, R3]. **$9.00–12.00.** C. Angel on a Cloud and Star, celluloid, 2", marked "Germany West" [NP, R2]. **$5.00–6.00.** D & E. Stars, 4", marked "Germany" [OP-NP, R3]. **$9.00–12.00.**

A & B. German Angel Children, 2¾" [OP-NP, R3]. **$8.00–9.00.** C. Glass Point with Plastic Figure, 10" [NP (1950), R2]. **$25.00–30.00.** D & E. Nativity with Translucent Back, 3¼" [NP (Hong Kong, circa 1970), R2]. **$3.00–6.00.**

Five Crescent Moon and Angel Ornaments, approx. 2½" (small) and 3½" (large). Most of the moons are marked "Made in Germany," and all of the angel wings are marked "Germany." Circa 1930s – 1940s [R3]. **$4.00–6.00** each.

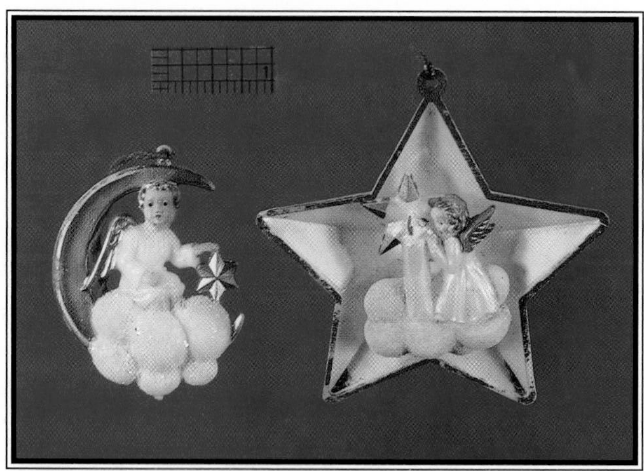

Two West German Plastic Ornaments, both made circa 1950 [R2-3]: A. Angel on a Cloud, approx. 2". **$3.00–5.00.** B. Star with Angel, approx. 3". **$5.00–8.00.**

Japanese Angel Children, 1¾" – 2¼" [OP (1930s – 1940s), R3]. **$4.00–5.00** each. Original Package, **$20.00–30.00.**

Angels with Widespread Wings, approx. 4¼". The picture shows the common white plastic and the very unusual pink plastic stamped with the original price of ten cents. Made by Bradford Novelty Co., circa late 1940s – 1950s [American, white angel R5, pink angel R1]. White, **$3.00–5.00.** Pink, **$20.00–25.00.**

A. Angel with Widespread Wings and Wreath, 6¾" [American, NP, R3]. **$20.00–25.00.** B. Angel with Widespread Wings, light [American, R2]. **$15.00–20.00.**

A. Angel with Widespread Wings on a Star, 5½" [American NP, R1-2]. **$20.00–25.00.** B. Four Indented Balls with Stenciling. Made by Bradford, 2¾" [American, NP, R4]. **$2.00–3.00.**

Standing Angels, variations, approx. 3¼". Variations include white plastic, silvered plastic, and two versions of fluorescent plastic, one outlined in blue and the other in silver. Made by Bradford Plastics, circa 1955 [R2-3]. **$10.00–12.00** each.

Angel in a Ring, color variations, approx. 3¼". American made, circa 1950 [R3]. **$4.00–5.00** each.

Nativity Scene in a Wreath, approx. 4" dia. The piece is made of fluorescent plastic and is backed by a disk of colored plastic. There is no maker's mark, but it is probably American, circa 1940 – 1950s [R2-3]. **$10.00–15.00.**

Hard Plastic and Celluloid Ornaments: A. Kneeling Angel, 3¼" [NP, R1-2]. **$15.00–18.00.** B. Celluloid Santa with Bag and Fruit, 4¾" [OP, R2]. **$40.00–45.00.** C. Wire-wrapped Plastic Tear Drop, 4¼" [NP, R1-2]. **$8.00–10.00.** D. Elf, 3¼" [NP, R2-3]. **$10.00–15.00.**

Two Christmas Elves: A. "Sinister" Elf, approx. 3¼" [NP, R3]. **$10.00–15.00.** B. Elf with a Toy Bear, approx. 3¼" [NP, R2]. **$15.00–20.00.**

Solid Balls, 2" & 3" [NP, R5]. **$1.00–1.50.** Faceted Balls, 2¼" & 2½" [NP, R5]. **$1.00–2.00.** Pieces *B, C, D,* and *E* were made by Bradford. All circa 1950.

Plastic Ornaments by Bradford: A & B. Balls with Filigree Holly Leaves, 3" [NP, R3]. **$1.50–2.50.** C. Indented Wedge Ball, 2¾" [NP, R4]. **$2.00–3.00.** D & E. Filigree Bells, 2¾" [NP, R4-5]. **$0.75–1.50.**

All Hard Plastic Ornaments: A. Faceted Ball in a Net [NP, R2-3]. **$4.00–5.00.** B. Filigree Ball with Snowflakes [NP, R2]. **$3.00–4.00.** C & D. Ball with Filigree Scenes, by Bradford [American, NP, R4]. **$2.00–3.00.**

A. Top, 3¾" [NP, R4]. **$2.00–3.00.** B. Ball with Frame Filled with Spun Glass, 3½" [NP, R4]. **$2.00–3.00.** C. Frame Bell, 3¾" [NP, R4]. **$1.00–2.00.**

"Kristles" Plastic Ornaments in Original Box, approx. 2" individual balls, made by Kusan Incorporated; Henderson, KY; circa 1930s. Individual ornaments, **$6.00–10.00** each. Ten ornaments in original box, **$80.00–100.00.**

Ball with Changing Pictures of Santa. Both views are shown [NP (Circa 1950), R1]. **$20.00–25.00.**

A & B. Tear Drop Shape, 4", one on the left is a candy container, [circa 1965 R5]. **$1.00–1.50.** C & D. Ball with Items Inside [NP (1960s), R5]. **$1.00–1.50.**

Plastic Bells: Three sizes of Solid Bells; 2", 2½", 3¼" [NP, R5]. **$0.50–1.00.** Two Filigree Bells, 2¾" & 3½" [NP, R4-5]. **$0.75–1.50.**

A. Geometric Prism, 5½" [NP, R4-5]. **$1.00–1.50.** B. Ball Candle Chandelier, 4¼" [NP, R3]. **$7.00–8.00.** C. Faceted Chandelier, 3½" [NP, R3]. **$2.00–3.00.**

Original Box of Shiny Brite Plastic Ornaments. Contents in next picture. Note that the lid says "glass ornaments" [NP, R3]. **$70.00–80.00.**

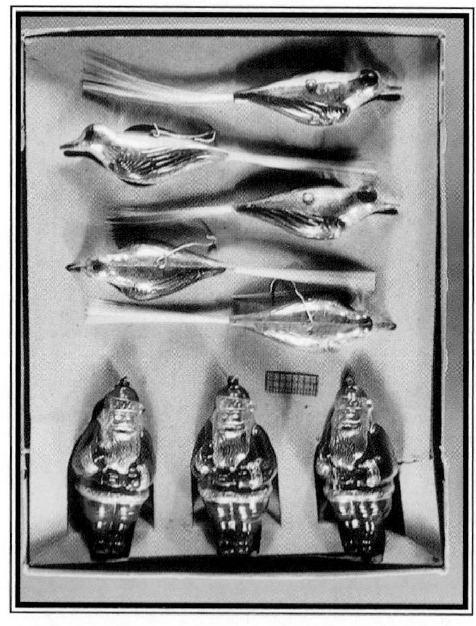

Plastic Ornaments by Shiny Brite: A. Silvered Birds with Spun Glass Tails, 3½" [NP, R3]. **$8.00–9.00.** B. Santas Standing with Packs (Type II), 3½" [NP, R3]. **$8.00–10.00.**

A. Birdcage Spinner/Twinkler, 3" [NP, R3-4]. **$10.00–15.00.** B. Spikey Star, 4¾" [NP, R4-5]. **$2.00–3.00.** C & D. Boots Candy Container, 2¾", by Rosbro Plastics [NP, R4]. Small, **$3.00–5.00.**

Original Box of Bradford Ornaments. Contents in next picture [NP, R3]. **$45.00–60.00.**

Bradford Ornaments: A. Choir Boy with a Candle, 3¼", version made with candle [American, NP, R4]. **$8.00–10.00.** B. Candle on a Dome of Holly, 2¾" [NP, R3]. **$4.00–5.00.** C. Angel with Widespread Wings, 4½" [NP, R3-4]. White plastic, **$3.00–5.00.** Silvered plastic, **$8.00–10.00.**

Choir Boy with a Candle, color variations, approx. 3¼". The silvered piece is reasonably common [R4], but the pink plastic version is rare [R1]. Made by Bradford Novelty Co., circa 1955 – 1960. Silvered, **$8.00–10.00.** Pink, **$20.00–25.00.**

A. Choir Boy with a Candle in a Wreath, 6¾" [NP, R2]. **$20.00–25.00.** B. Santa Head Light Cover, 5", resembles celluloid but is hard plastic, circa 1990 [R4]. **$1.00–2.00.**

Choir Boy with a Book, color variations, approx. 3¾". Red and silvertrimmed, glow-in-the-dark, and painted white plastic versions are shown. American made, circa 1950 [R4]. **$10.00–12.00** each.

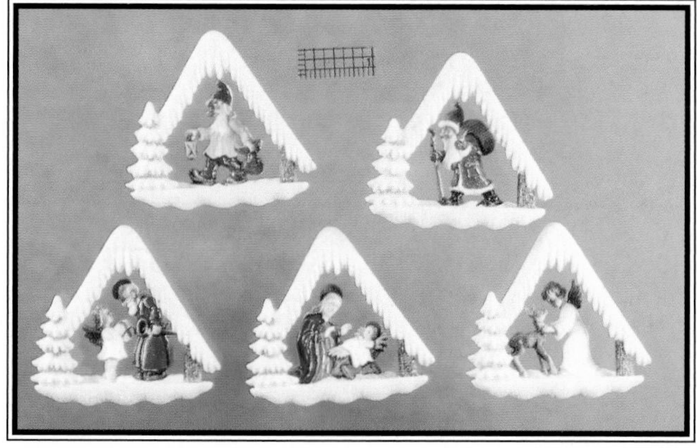

Chalet House with Figures, 2¼", marked "Western Germany" [NP, R3]. **$6.00–8.00** each.

A. "Rudolph," 3¾" [NP, R3-4]. **$5.00–6.00.** B. Running Deer, 3¾" [NP, R3]. White, **$4.00–5.00.** Colored, **$6.00–7.00.** C. Standing Deer, 3¾" [NP, R4]. White, **$4.00–5.00.** D. Silvered Standing Deer, 3½" [NP, R4]. **$6.00–7.00.**

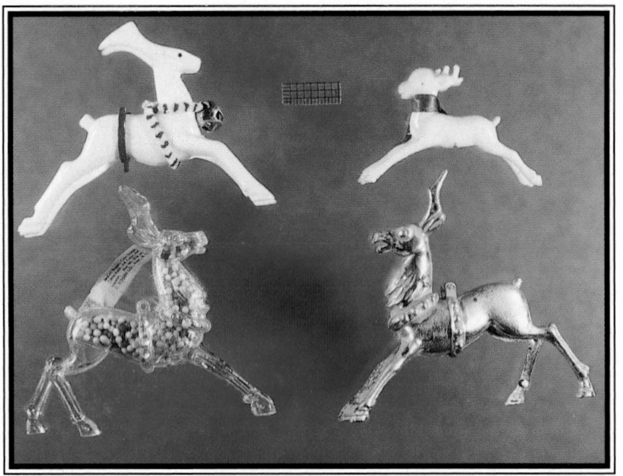

Hard Plastic Running Deer: A. 3¾" [American, NP, R3]. **$4.00–5.00.** B. 3¼" [American, NP, R3]. **$4.00–5.00.** C. Candy Container [American, NP, R3]. **$15.00–20.00.** D. Gold, made by E. Rosen Co. [American, NP, R3]. **$8.00–10.00.**

Celluloid and Plastic Deer: A & D. Celluloid Deer with Raised Legs, 4½" – 6½" [NP (1950s), R4-5]. **$4.00–5.00** and **$6.00–7.00.** B. Doe from Taiwan, circa 1985. **$0.50–1.00.** C & E. Standing Deer, silvered and large white [NP, R4]. **$6.00–7.00** and **$8.00–10.00.**

Hard Plastic Jeweled Geometric Shapes, shapes of various types, 3" – 3½", circa 1965 [R5]. **$1.00–1.50.**

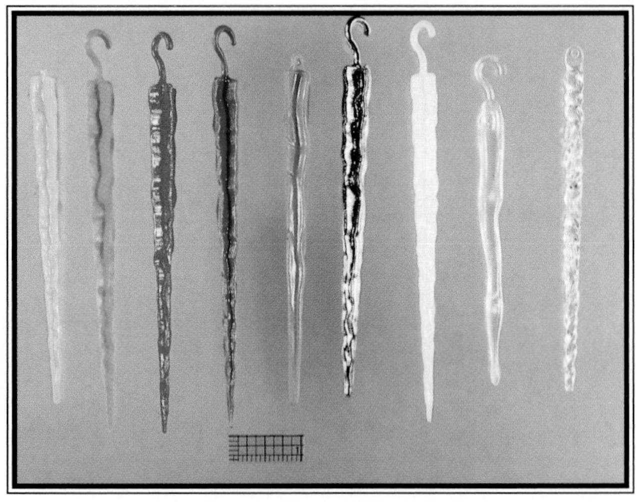

Icicles: A – G. Four-flanged, 4¾" – 5½" [NP, blue R3, white R5]. Hook, **$0.75–1.00.** Loop, **$1.50–2.00.** H. Round and Natural Icicle, 4½" [NP, R2-3]. **$0.50–1.00.** I. Twisted Icicle, 5" [NP, R4]. **$0.50–1.00.**

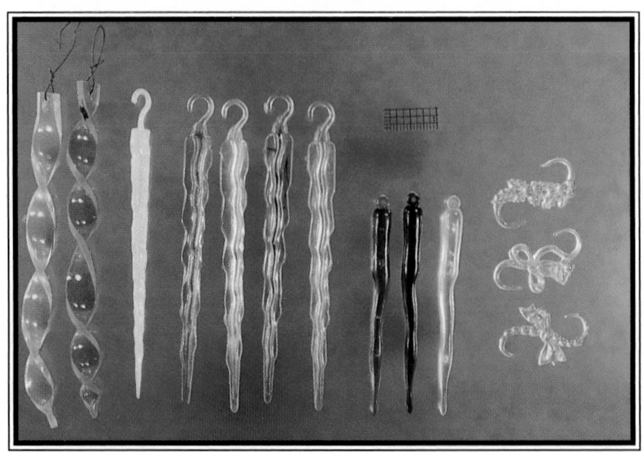

Icicles: A & B. Acrylic, 5¾", circa 1930 [R1]. **$4.00–5.00.** C. Glo-in-the-Dark [R5]. **$0.75–1.00.** D–G. Three-flanged, 5½" [R2-3]. **$0.25–0.50.** H–J. Round and Natural Icicles, 4" [R2-3]. **$0.50–1.00.** K. Plastic Ornament Hooks, circa 1965 – 1980s [R4]. **$0.05.**

A. Boot Candy Container, 2¾", Rosbro Plastics [NP, R4]. Small, **$3.00–4.00.** B. Teapot, 3", circa 1960 [R1-2]. **$8.00–9.00.** C. Musical Instrument, 4¾", circa 1950 [R3-4]. **$4.00–5.00.** D. Six-sided Lantern with Candle, 3¾", circa 1955 – 1960 [R4]. **$3.00–4.00.**

Hard Plastic Miniature Figures, 2", circa 1960 [R2]. **$1.00–2.00** each.

A. Santa Light Cover, 4¾", opening in back, circa 1950 [R3-4]. **$15.00–18.00.** B. Santa in Sled with Running Deer, 4", circa 1950 [R2]. **$10.00–15.00.** C. Santa in Sled with Leaping Deer, 5", circa 1950 [R2]. **$10.00–15.00.**

Santa in a Sled with a Running Deer, approx. 4"L, unusual sivered plastic and more common white plastic pieces are shown. Interestingly, the white piece is unmarked, but the silvered piece is marked "Irwin," American made, circa 1950 [R2 silver, R3 white]. Silver, **$15.00–20.00.** White, **$10.00–15.00.**

Santa on a Sleigh with Six Flying Reindeer, approx. 9½"L. Made in Canada by Reliable Plastics, circa 1955 [R1]. **$30.00–40.00.**

Jaunty Santas: A. Unusual Lavender Santa, 3¾" [American, NP, R3-4]. **$15.00–20.00.** B. Santa on Wheels, 4½", circa 1955 – 1960 [American, R3]. **$30.00–40.00.** C. Santa Behind a Sled, 5" [American, R3-4]. **$18.00–20.00.**

Jaunty Santa in a Sleigh, 5"L [American, NP, R3-4]. **$15.00–18.00.**

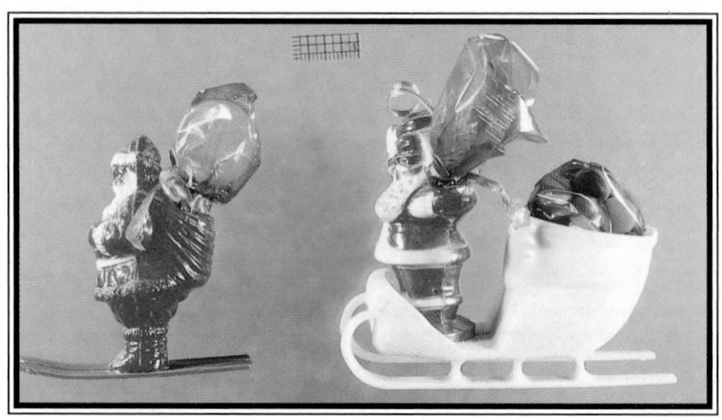

A. Santa on Skis Candy Container, 3½", circa 1955 [American, NP, R3]. **$12.00–15.00.** B. Waving Santa with a Bent Elbow, on a sled, 5", circa 1955 [American, R3]. **$15.00–18.00.**

A & C. Standing Santa Candy Container, two styles, both 4" [NP, R3]. **$18.00–20.00.** B. Standing Santa with a Pack, (Type I), 3¼" [NP, R3]. **$10.00–12.00.**

Surprize Santa, original packaging, 3½" Santa, approx. 7" blister card. The Santa opens around the seams and holds a small toy. Made by M. Pressner & Co. of New York, circa post-zip-code 1960s. The Santa is common [R5], the packaging is not [R1-2]. Santa in Blister card, **$12.00–15.00.**

A. Standing Santa, 3½" [American, NP, R2]. **$10.00–12.00.** B. Standing Santa with a Pack (Type I), 3¼" [American, NP, R3]. **$10.00–12.00.** C. Waving Santa with a Bent Elbow, 3¼" [American, NP, R4]. **$8.00–10.00.**

Plastic Santa with Suction Cup, approx. 5¼". This unusual piece was designed to stick onto windows or mirrors as a decoration. American made, circa 1960 [R2]. **$15.00–20.00.**

A & C. Two versions of Waving Santa Candy Container, 3½", circa 1960, made by the N. E. Plastic Factory [American, R3]. **$12.00–15.00.** B. Santa with a Pack Standing Inside a Wreath, 6¾" [American, NP, R2]. **$20.00–25.00.**

A. Waving Santa with a Large Pack, 4½" [American, NP, R1-2]. **$15.00–20.00.** B. Santa with Rabbit Fur Trim, pebbles inside make him a rattle, 4¾" [American, NP, R3-4]. **$15.00–18.00.**

A. Waving Santa with a Red Bag of Real Plastic Toys, 6" [American, R1]. **$35.00–45.00.** B. Vinyl Boot, 5½", circa 1950 [American, R2]. **$20.00–25.00.**

Three Snowmen: A & C. Snowman with a Top Hat, approx. 3¾", marked "Irwin" on the pack. *A* is glow-in-the-dark plastic, and *C* is white plastic [American, NP (circa 1950), R3]. **$12.00–15.00.** B. Snowman with a Peaked Cap Candy Container, approx. 3¾", open pack on his back holds candy, made by Irwin, circa 1950 [R3]. **$10.00–12.00.**

Five Snowmen Ornaments: A. Snowman Sucker Holder, approx. 3¼". A hole in the crook of the arm holds suckers. American made, circa 1955 [R3]. **$10.00–15.00.** B. Snowman with a Peaked Cap Candy Container, approx. 3¾", open pack on his back holds candy, made by Irwin, circa 1950 [R3]. **$10.00–12.00.** C. Waving Snowman with a Broom, approx. 3¾", probably American made, circa 1960 [R2]. **$10.00–12.00.** D. Snowman with a Broom, approx. 3¼", American made, circa 1955 [R3]. **$10.00–12.00.** E. Chubby Snowman with Earmuffs, approx. 3¼", probably American made, circa 1950 [R2]. **$10.00–15.00.**

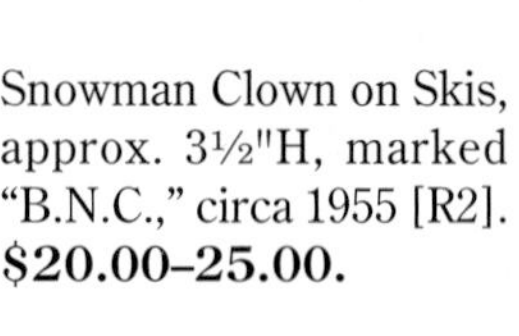

Snowman Clown on Skis, approx. 3½"H, marked "B.N.C.," circa 1955 [R2]. **$20.00–25.00.**

Jeweled Snowflakes, various colors, medium, size 4¼" [American, R2-4]. Clear, **$1.00–2.00.** Colored, **$4.00–6.00.**

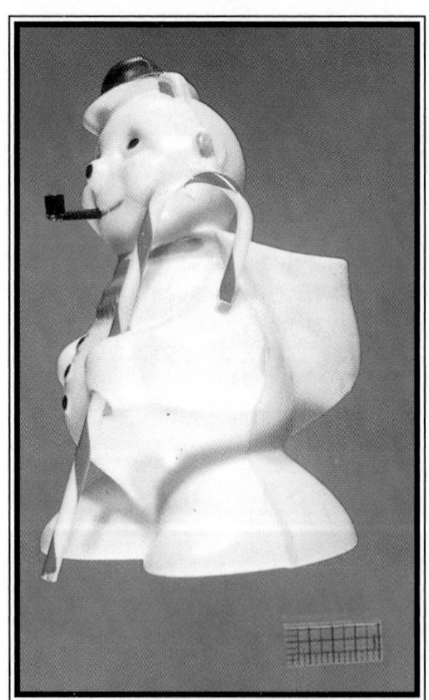

Snowman Candy Container, approx. 5". Made by Reliable Plastics in Canada, circa 1950 [R1]. **$35.00–45.00.**

Jeweled Snowflakes, all from same set, small ones are incorporated in large [American, R2-4]: A. 9". **$2.00–3.00.** B. 4⅝". **$1.00–2.00.** C. 2¾". **$0.50–1.00.**

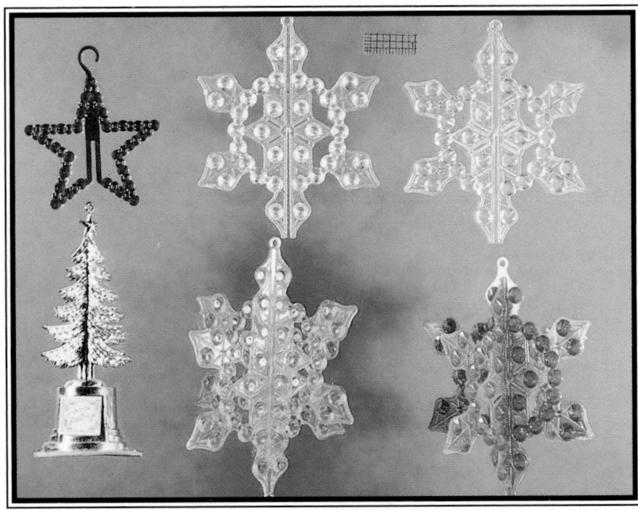

Interlocking 3-D Ornaments: A. Star, 3" [NP, R2]. **$2.00–3.00.** B, C, E, F. Snowflakes, 4¼" [NP, R2]. Clear, **$7.00–8.00.** Colored, **$8.00–10.00.** D. Tree, 4" – 5" [NP, R3]. **$8.00–10.00.**

Star Spinner or Twinkler, 3½" [NP, R3-4]. **$12.00–17.00** each. Original package, **$45.00–60.00.**

Wisemen, 4¼", circa 1955 [American, R4]. They were from the same mold, but painted differently. Solid-colored pieces were made later than pastel-painted ones. **$5.00–7.00** each.

Styrofoam Ornaments, 1970s – 1980s: A. Ball with Velvet [R5]. **$0.25–0.50.** B & C. Bell and Ball with Fabric and Beads, 2½" – 3½" [R5]. **$3.00–8.00.** D. Painted Ball, 2½" – 3½" [R4-5]. **$0.25–0.50.**

A & B. Vinyl Santa with Flocking, 4½" [NP, R5]. **$3.00–4.00.** C & D. Elves with Felt Clothing, 4" – 6" [Japanese, R4]. **$8.00–15.00.**

Pre-Electric Lighting for the Tree

For three hundred years prior to electric lights, a living flame lighted the tree. This took on two distinct forms: a candle or an oil burning light. By far, the most common and popular form of lighting at this time was the candle. The first recorded account of a lighted tree was in 1658, when the Countess of Orleans had a candlelit box tree in southern Germany. One of the earliest methods of candle attachment was to simply melt the candle directly onto the tree limb. At the turn of the eighteenth century, "hoops of fire" lit some German trees. These were graduated hoops or rings of wood with candles attached to them.

Among the first commercially made candleholders was one mounted on a long rod that was designed to screw into the trunk of the tree. By the mid-1800s, candleholders also had a small metal disk with turned up edges to catch dripping wax. In 1867, the "socket and pin" holder attempted to fasten the candleholder to the tree limb by using a tack or small nail. This nail was pushed through the branch to hold the candle in place. On Christmas Eve of 1867, Charles Kirchof of New Jersey patented the pendulum-weighted candleholder. This consisted of a candleholder with wax pan at the top; a long thin wire with a bent hook for hanging, hung from the drip pan; and a painted clay ball at the bottom that served as a weight. This bottom weight helped ensure that the candle remained upright on the branch. Later, the Germans took this basic idea of the counterweight and improved it by replacing the painted clay balls with molded lead weights in the form of pinecones, angels, birds, and stars. Tin-lead reflector ornaments were also used as pendulum weights. Another pendulum weight used was a blown glass ornament attached to the bottom of the clip so that the ornament hung below the candle as a type of counterweight. Most often these were unsilvered fruits or flowers that had been painted and covered with crushed glass to add to their reflective nature.

By 1878, German ornament makers were selling double counterweighted holders. Here, the socket was attached to an inverted *V* shape wire with weights on the two ends. The following year, a spring-operated clip-on candleholder was patented. It eliminated the weight problem and could be placed almost anywhere on the tree branch.

There were many variations of the clip-on candleholder. In one example, the part that held the candle in place was actually part of the wire spring. This type had no wax pan, but rather, caught the drips and funneled them onto the branch. As early as 1878, candleholders of stamped or embossed tin were produced in a variety of shapes including birds, butterflies, Santas, and angels. Around the turn of the century, beautifully colored and wonderfully detailed lithographed holders of angels, Santas, flowers, etc., were marketed. Right after World War I, the clip-on was significantly improved with the addition of a ball and socket joint under the holder and drip pan that allowed it to be rotated into an upright position regardless of the way it was placed on the tree branch.

The most beautiful and elaborate of the clip-on candleholders were those with free-blown or molded glass shades. The globes were fitted onto the candle clip by a row of metal flanges that held it firmly in place. These shaded candleholders seemed to enjoy their greatest popularity from about 1900 to 1920. About this same time, oilcloth tree skirts with printed Christmas designs were marketed. These were designed to spread out past the tree branches and catch the dripping wax, thus keeping it off floors and rugs.

Early lanterns for the tree were small squares with decorative windows cut out of brass or metal. Inserts of colored glass or cellophane were placed inside and added color to the tree. At the turn of the century, folding lanterns with colored celluloid panels were offered for sale, and about this same time, another interesting candle novelty was developed: the candle chime. A tree decorated with one of these provided not only light, but sound and movement as well.

The alternative to the various kinds of candle lighting was oil lights. These usually held water with a small amount of oil and a wick floating on top. In the 1700s, American Baron Stiegel created a free-blown glass container for floating wicks. Christmas lights, blown or molded out of glass, became more economical and popular when mold-blown versions became available in the mid-eighteen hundreds. These lights held small candles or a floating wick inside the colored glass tumblers. When a light of this type was used as a Christmas ornament, a piece of thin wire encircled the lip (opening); another wire formed the handle, or bail wire, used to hang the light on the tree. The lip of the lamp could be left rough (looking chipped or broken), tooled, or rolled over. These pieces came in several patterns and colors. The quilted pattern is by far the most common. These were produced in the U.S., Great Britain, France, and Austria until about 1920. During the early 1990s, reproductions of these lights were reproduced in India and Mexico, and they continue to be reproduced in these countries today. They are difficult to distinguish from the antique originals.

Starting in the 1870s, German glassmakers also blew paper thin ornament-style oil lamps. Most of these were beautifully painted and served not only as light holders, but also as ornaments. In 1887, John Barth of Louisville, Kentucky, patented a much safer oil lamp. Barth's lamp had a glass cylinder about two and a half inches long that hooked over the tree limb; it also had a small glass globe to protect the flame. Examples of the Barth lamp are quite rare today.

Horror stories of Christmas tree fires aside, the real reason for the disappearance of candles on the Christmas tree is the same reason candles and oil lamps stopped being used to light the home: convenience. By 1910, candleholders were already being replaced by the greatest advancement in tree lighting — the electric light blub, and by the 1920s, the use of electricity was sufficiently widespread and the cost of light bulbs low enough that there was a major switch to electric lights. Slowly, steadily, the light from the living flame dimmed and died, and the glow of the electric filament brightented the tree. Nevertheless, in recent days, many styles of pre-electric lighting have been reproduced.

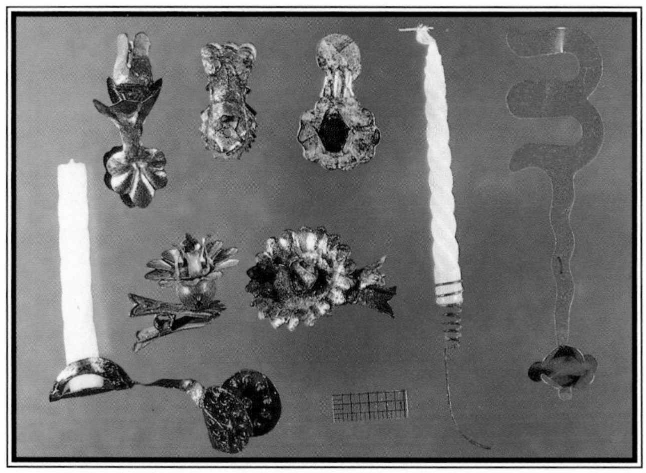

A, B, C, H. Generic Clip-on Candleholders, 1½" – 2" [OP-NP, R4-5]. **$1.00–2.00** each. D. Wire-on, 2" [OP, R1-2]. **$1.50–2.00.** E. Extension Candleholder by J. Stolze, 4", circa 1899 [R3]. **$2.00–3.00.** F. Extension Candleholder by L. Kregel, 4", circa 1896 [R3]. **$3.00–5.00.** G. Ball and Socket [OP-NP, R2-3]. **$2.00–3.00.**

A. Candleholder Embossed with Geometric Designs, circa 1890 [Europe, R3-4]. **$3.00–8.00.** B. Beehive Fairy Light, paper thin, 3", circa 1880. **$60.00–75.00.** C. Candleholder with a Glass Shade, cherries are embossed into the sides, 2¾" [OP, R2]. **$125.00–150.00.** D. Unusual Early Candleholder. **$2.00–3.00.** E. Candleholder with Embossed Geometric Designs, circa 1890. **$3.00–8.00.** F. Kregel Clamp-on Candleholder, circa 1896 [R3-4]. **$2.00–3.00.** G. Candleholder with Embossed Geometric Designs, circa 1890 [R4]. **$3.00–8.00.**

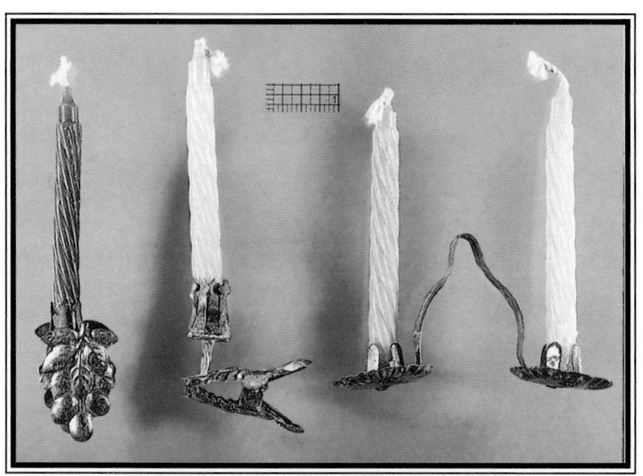

A. Candleholder Embossed with Cherries, 1½" [OP, R1]. **$55.00–65.00.** B. Pivoting Blade, Variation of Ball and Socket, 1½" [OP, R1]. **$10.00–15.00.** C. Double Balance, 3¾"L [OP, R1]. **$50.00–60.00.**

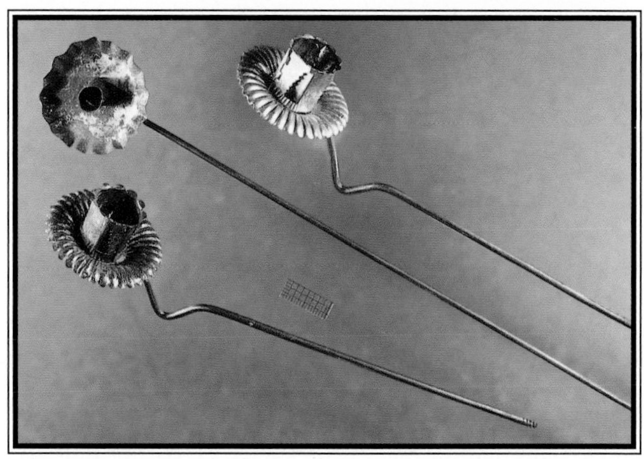

Three Screw-in Candleholders [OP, R1-2]: A. 10½". **$15.00–20.00.** B. 17". **$20.00–25.00.** C. 20". **$20.00–25.00.**

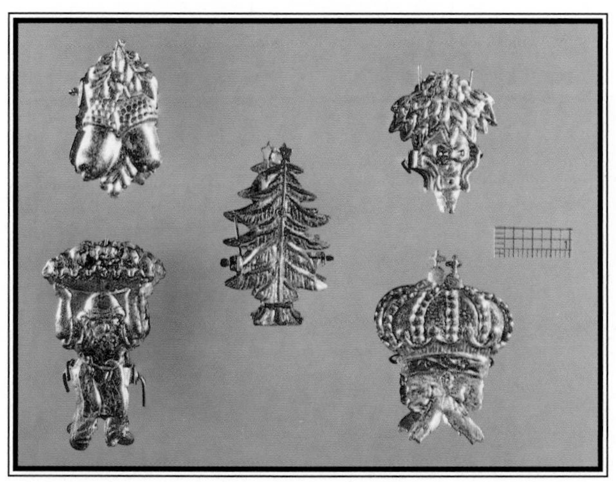

Embossed Candle Clips: A. Acorn, 2" [OP, R2-3]. **$40.00–45.00.** B. Poinsettia, 1¾" [OP, R2-3]. **$40.00–45.00.** C. Christmas Tree, 2¼" [OP, R2]. **$60.00–65.00.** D. Fruit Vendor, 2½" [OP, R1-2]. **$100.00–110.00.** E. Crown, 2¼" [OP, R1]. **$80.00–90.00.**

Embossed Candle Clips: A. Jockey on Rocking Horse, 2¼". **$80.00–90.00.** B. Santa with Tree, 3¼". **$110.00–125.00.** C. Bavarian Boy, bag over right shoulder, 2¾". **$80.00–90.00.** D. Angel Holding an Anchor, 2". **$80.00–90.00.** E. Boy with a Horn and a Dog, 3". **$80.00–90.00.** F. Flying Angel with a Cornucopia, large, 3½". **$110.00–120.00.**

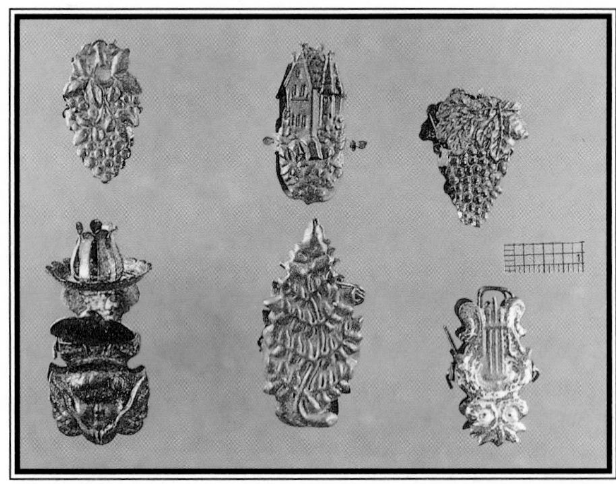

Embossed Candle Clips: A. Bunch of Grapes (Type I), 1½" [OP, R2]. **$35.00–40.00. B.** Castle/House, 2"H [OP, R1]. **$85.00–90.00.** C. Bunch of Grapes (Type II), 1½" [OP, R2]. **$35.00–40.00.** D. Angel/Putti Head, 2½" [OP, R2]. **$60.00–65.00.** E. Fern/Foliage, 2½" [OP, R1]. **$40.00–45.00.** F. Lyre, 1¾" [OP, R3]. **$25.00–30.00.**

Embossed Candle Clips: A. Flying Swallow, 2½" [OP, R1]. **$80.00–85.00.** B. Perched Songbird, 2" [OP, R2]. **$50.00–55.00.** C. Butterfly (Type I), 3"H [OP, R2]. **$60.00–70.00.** D. Butterfly in Profile, 2¾" [OP, R2]. **$75.00–85.00.** E. Bird Crested on a Branch, 2½" [OP, R1]. **$80.00–95.00.**

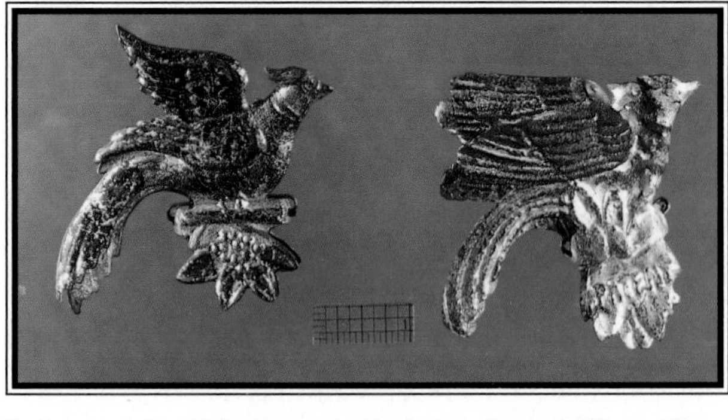

Embossed Candleholders: A. Bird with Raised Wings (Type II), 2¾" [OP, R2]. **$80.00–95.00.** B. Bird with Raised Wings (Type I), 3" [OP, R2]. "Patent" is embossed on the leaves. **$80.00–95.00.**

A. Lithographed Angel on a Cloud with Flowers, 1¾" [OP, R1-2]. **$100.00–110.00.** B. Bird with Raised Wings (Type II), 2¾" x 2¾" [OP, R2]. **$80.00–95.00.** C. Embossed Snowman, 2¼" [OP, R1]. **$90.00–110.00.**

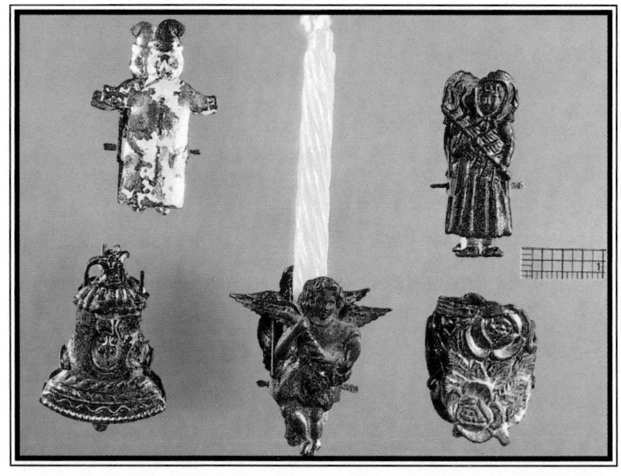

Embossed Candle Clips: A. Snowman, 2¼" [OP, R1]. **$90.00–100.00.** B. Girl with a Tree, 2" [OP, R1]. **$100.00–110.00.** C. Bell, 2" [OP, R1]. **$40.00–45.00.** D. Flying Angel with Cornucopia, small, 2" [OP, R1]. **$100.00–110.00.** E. Roses, 1¾" [OP, R1]. **$40.00–45.00.**

Reproduced Embossed Candleholders, all circa 1982. **$15.00–20.00** each: A. Children Dancing Around a Tree, 2¼". B. Bust of an Angel/Cherub with a Bow, 1¾". C. Santa in a Sleigh Pulled by a Reindeer, 3". D. Standing Santa with Pack and a Tree, 1¾". E. Two Angels with a Swag of Roses, 2½".

Reproduced Embossed Candleholders, all circa 1982. **$15.00–20.00** each: A. Star with Openwork Filigree, 1¾". B. Two Bells with a Holly Spray, 2". C. Stag, 1½". D. Putti Angel Head, 2".

Lithographed and Embossed Candle Clips: A & D. Butterfly (Type II), 1¾" [OP, R1-2]. **$90.00–100.00.** B. Church in an Eight-pointed Star, 2" [OP, R1-2]. **$80.00–90.00.** C. Embossed Poinsettia in a Pot, 1¾" [OP, R1-2]. **$25.00–30.00.** E. Angel on Cloud, 2" [OP, R1-2]. **$110.00–125.00.** F. Embossed Windmill, 2" [OP, R1]. **$55.00–65.00.**

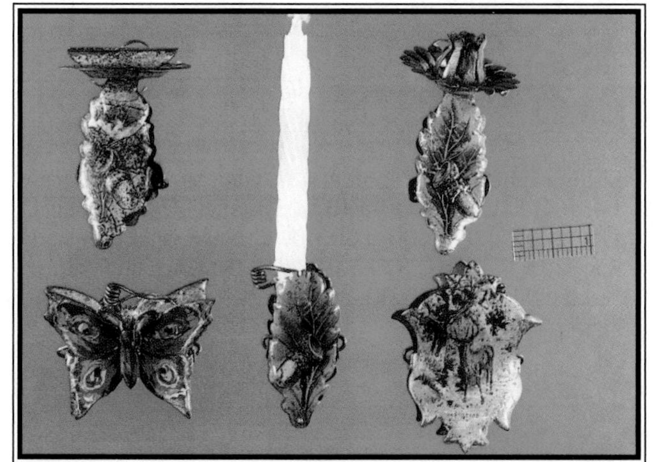

Lithographed Candleholders: A, B, D. Acorns on a Leaf; 2", 2¼", and 2½" [OP, R2]. **$60.00–65.00** each. C. Butterfly (Type I), 2" [OP, R1]. **$85.00–95.00.** E. Deer in Woodland Scene, 2¼" [OP, R1]. **$125.00–135.00.**

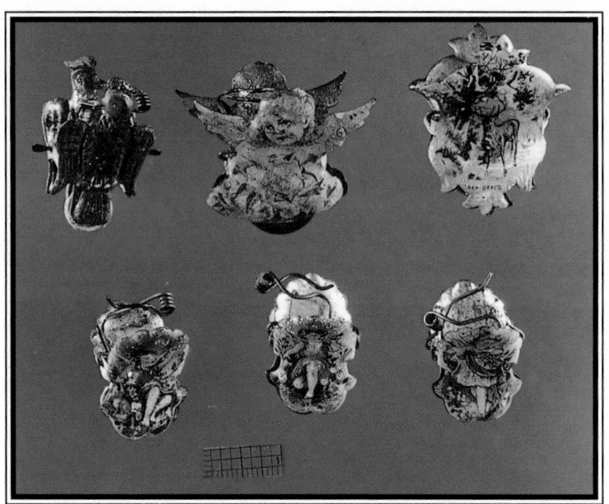

Embossed and Lithographed Candleholders, circa 1890: A. Embossed Parrot, 1¾" [OP, R2]. **$50.00–55.00.** B. Angel Bust with Spread Wings, 2" [OP, R2]. **$100.00–110.00.** C. Deer in a Woodland Scene, 2¼" [OP, R1]. **$125.00–135.00.** D. Angel with a Wreath, 2" [OP-NP, R2]. **$80.00–90.00.** E. Angel with a Rose, 2" [OP-NP, R2]. **$80.00–90.00.** F. Angel with a bundle of Flowers, 2" [OP-NP, R2]. **$80.00–90.00.**

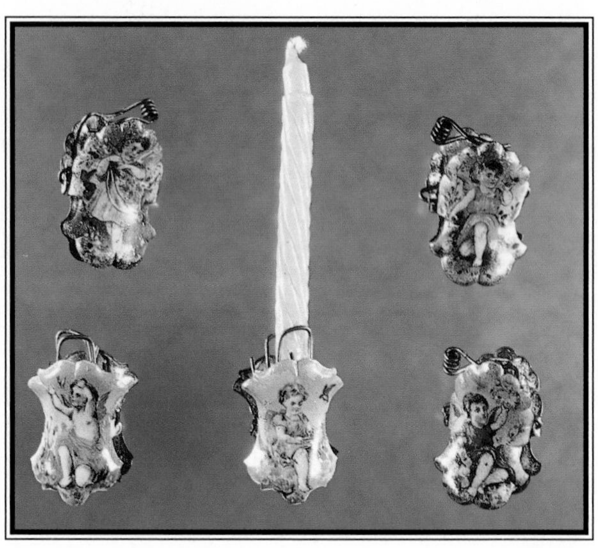

Lithographed Candle Clips, all five of these have been reproduced, the ones shown are old [All OP-NP (1980s), R2]. **$80.00–90.00** each: A. Angel/Cherub with a Bundle of Flowers, 2". B. Angel/Cherub with a Rose, 2". C. Angel/Cherub with a Butterfly, 2". D. Angel/Cherub with a Bird, 2". E. Angel/Cherub with a Wreath, 2". Close inspection shows the 1980s pieces are made up of larger dots of color.

Lithographed Candleholders: A. Raspberries, 2" [OP, R2]. **$80.00–85.00.** B. Pineapple with Orange and Lemon Slices, 2" [OP, R2]. **$80.00–85.00.** C. Blue Flowers in a Pot, 2" [OP, R2]. **$65.00–75.00.** D. Maple Leaf with Roses, 2¼" [OP, R1]. **$70.00–80.00.** E. Apple with Grapes and Plum, 2" [OP, R2]. **$80.00–85.00.**

Lithographed Candleholders: A. Gnome with a Horn, 1¾" [OP, R1]. **$125.00–145.00.** B. Angel Head in a Star, 1¾" [OP, R2]. **$90.00–100.00.** C. Santa with Tree and Bag, 2¼" [OP, R1]. **$175.00–200.00.** D. Santa with a Scroll [OP, R1]. **$175.00–200.00.**

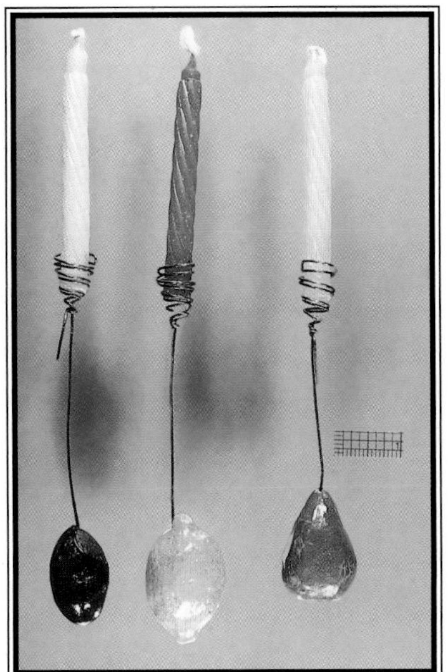

Pendulum Tin-Lead Weights: A. Sinker Style, 7" [OP, R2-3]. **$15.00–20.00.** B. Double-weighted Pomegranate, 5¾" [OP, R1]. **$90.00–100.00.** C. Ball, 5¾" [OP, R2-3]. **$10.00–15.00.**

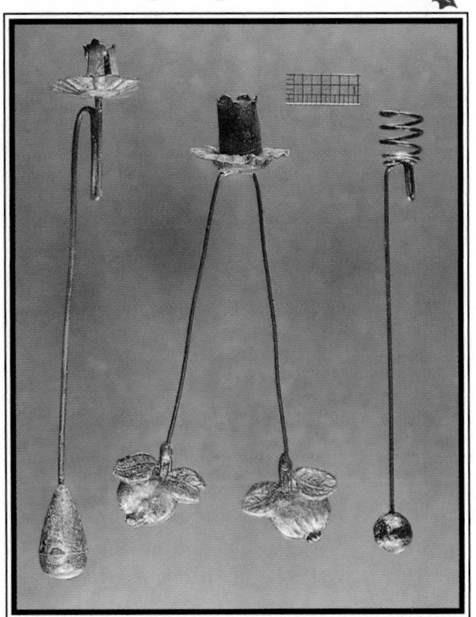

Pendulum-weighted Holders with Clay or Composition Weights: A. Plum, 5" [OP, R2]. **$40.00–50.00.** B. Lemon, 5½" [OP, R2]. **$40.00–50.00.** C. Pear, 5" [OP, R2]. **$40.00–50.00.**

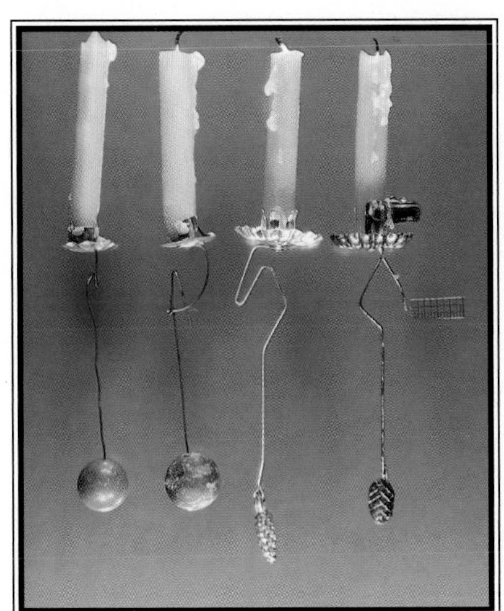

Four Pendulum-weighted Candle-holders: A. Kirchof Holder, marked "Kirchof, Pat. Dec. 24, 67." **$15.00–25.00.** B. Standard Holder with a Clay Ball Weight, American. **$10.00–20.00.** C & D. Later Versions with Cast Lead Pine Cones as Counterweights, German. **$30.00–40.00** each.

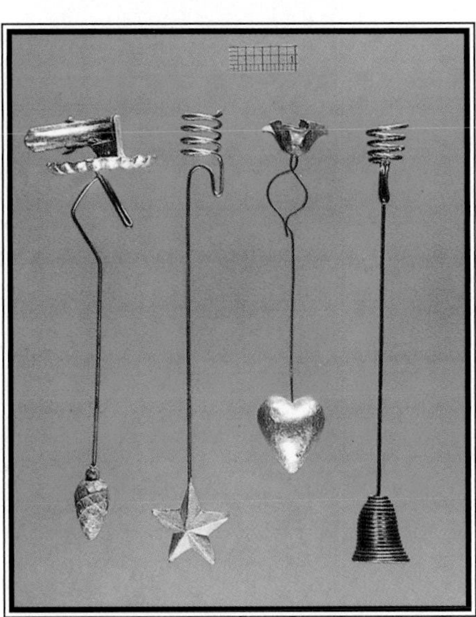

Counterweight Candleholders, *B & C* are composition, the rest are made from tin-lead: A. Pine Cone, 6" [OP-NP, R2-3]. **$30.00–40.00.** B. Five-pointed Star, 6½" [OP, R1]. **$65.00–75.00.** C. Heart, 5" [OP, R2]. **$40.00–50.00.** D. Bell, 6½" [OP, R2]. **$20.00–25.00.**

Two Double-weighted Candleholders, with Tin-Lead Angels [both OP, R1]. **$100.00–115.00** each: A. 6". B. 5½".

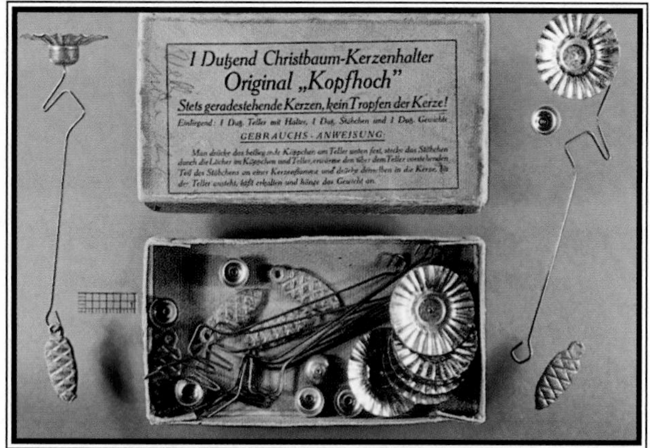

"Some Assembly Required" Box of Tin-Lead Pine Cone Counterweighted Candleholders, 6½" [OP, R1]. Complete box, **$200.00–250.00.**

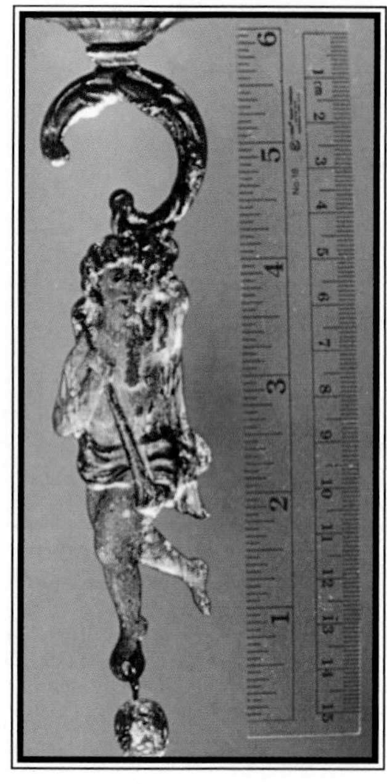

Angel Counterweight, 6" [OP, R1]. **$400.00–450.00.**

A. American Eagle, 5¼" [OP, R1]. **$100.00–125.00.** B. Composition Santa with Scrap Face, 4½" [OP, R1]. **$100.00–125.00.** C. Embossed Discs, 5¼" [OP, R1]. **$70.00–80.00.**

A. Composition Pine Cone, 2" cone, 6" overall [OP, R1-2]. **$40.00–50.00.** B. Tin/Lead Reflector, regular geometric shapes, oval, 2¾" [OP, R3-4]. **$40.00–50.00.** C. Tin-Lead Reflector, regular geometric shapes, flower, 2¾" [OP, R3-4]. **$40.00–50.00.**

Three Holders with Tin Reflectors, geometric patterns, 5" – 6" overall [OP, R3]. **$40.00–50.00.**

Three Tin-Lead Reflector Candle Weights: A & C. Regular Geometric Shapes, both 2¼" dia. [OP, R3-4]. **$35.00–40.00.** B. Cross in a Circle, 2½" dia. [OP, R2-3]. **$45.00–50.00.**

Tin-Lead Reflector Candle Weights: A & D. Regular Geometric Shapes, 2½" each [OP, R3-4]. **$35.00–40.00.** B. Snowflake, 2½" [OP, R2-3]. **$40.00–45.00.** C. Teardrop, 2¾" [OP, R3]. **$40.00–50.00.**

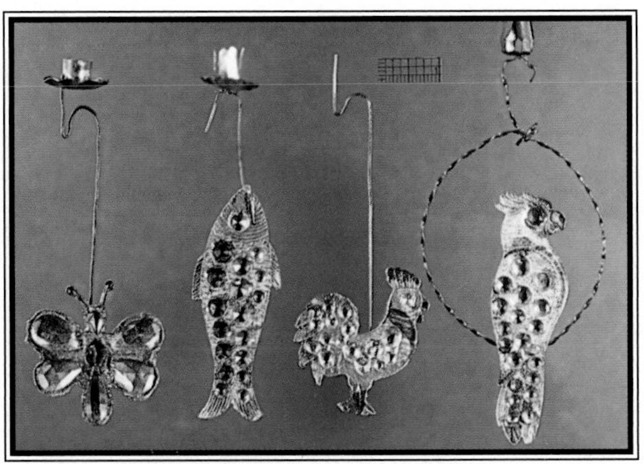

Tin-Lead Animal Weights: A. Butterfly, 2½" [OP, R2-3]. **$75.00–85.00.** B. Fish, 3¾" [OP, R1-2]. **$100.00–110.00.** C. Standing Rooster, 2½" [OP, R1-2]. **$90.00–100.00.** D. Parrot on a Wire Loop, 7" [OP, R1]. **$100.00–125.00.**

Double Pear Glass Ornament Weight, 2½" – 3" [OP, R2]. **$60.00–75.00.** The ornaments serves as a counter balance to the candle.

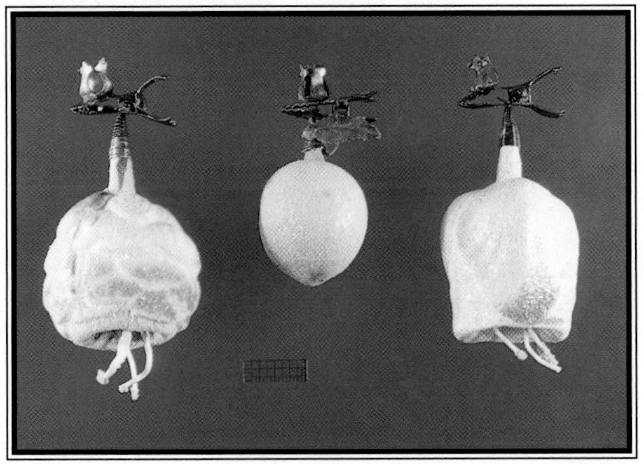

Three Glass Ornament Weights: A. Rose, 2½" – 3" [OP, R2]. **$60.00–75.00.** B. Lemon, 2½" – 3" [OP, R1-2]. **$40.00–45.00.** C. Tulip [OP, R2-3]. **$60.00–75.00.**

Three Glass Ornament Weights: A. Rose, round, 1½" [OP, R2-3]. **$30.00–40.00.** B. Double Plum, 1¾" [OP, R1-2]. **$50.00–60.00.** C. Pansy, 1¾" [OP, R1-2]. **$50.00–60.00.**

Candleholders with Glass Ornament Weights: A. Squash, 2", it has five lobed sections [OP, R1]. **$65.00–85.00.** B. Sour Grapes Face, 3½" [OP, R1-2]. **$250.00–300.00.** C. Strawberry, 2½" [OP, R1-2]. **$65.00–85.00.**

Clip-on Candleholders with Glass Ornament Weights, approx. 4" overall. A. Pear [OP, R3] **$40.00–60.00.** B. Apple [OP, R2]. **$55.00–75.00.** Tulip [OP, R2-3]. **$60.00–85.00.**

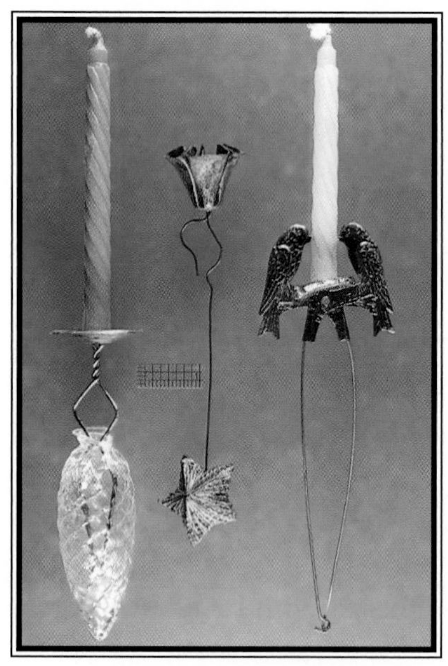

Three Miscellaneous Counter-weighted Candleholders: A. Pine Cone with Water, 3¼", cone 5"L, it could be filled with colored water [OP, R1]. **$135.00–150.00.** B. Five-pointed Composition Star, 6" [OP, R1]. **$65.00–75.00.** C. Pair of Birds, 6½", circa 1890 [R1-2]. **$90.00–100.00.**

Clip-on Candleholder with a Slender Rose Shade, molded, 3" [OP, R2-3]. **$100.00–125.00.**

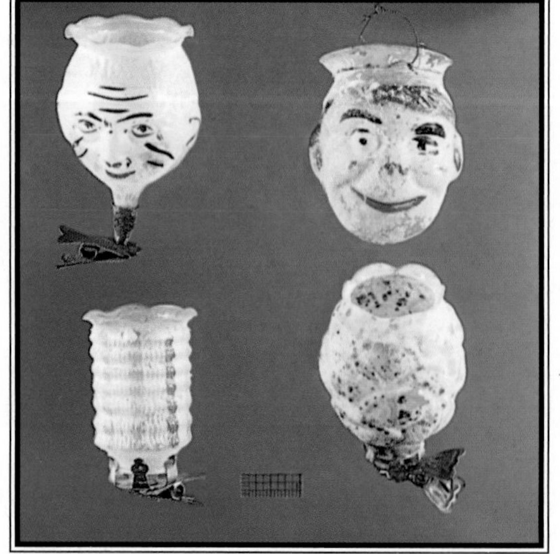

Candleholders with Glass Shades: A. Boy's Face, 2¾" [OP, R1]. **$325.00–375.00.** B. Smiling Boy's Head, 3¼" [OP, R1]. **$350.00–400.00.** C. Ribbed Cylinder, 2¾" & 3½" (shown) [OP, R1-2]. **$90.00–110.00.** D. Oval Rose, 3" [OP, R2]. **$100.00–125.00.**

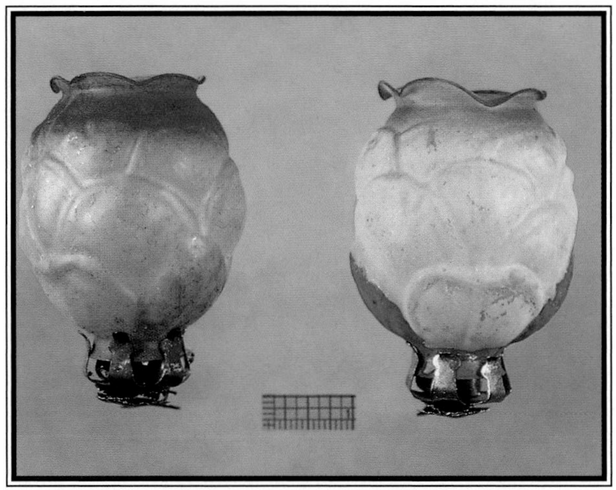

Candleholder with Rose Glass Shade, oval, 3¼". Shows two different painting patterns [OP, R2]. **$125.00–150.00.**

Calla Lily Candleholder with Glass Shade, 3½" [OP, R1]. **$150.00–200.00.**

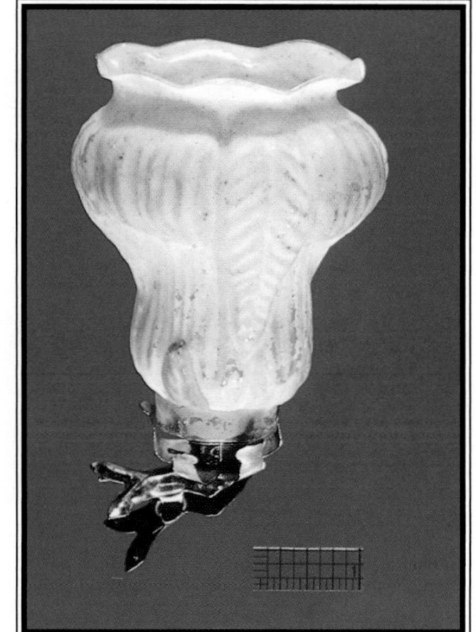

Clip-on Candleholders with Glass Shades: A & B. Japanese "Paper" Lantern, 3" [OP, R1-2]. **$80.00–100.00.** C. Paneled Lantern, 3" [OP, R2]. **$90.00–110.00.**

Candleholders with Unusual Glass Shades: A. Quilted Shade, 3¼" [OP, R1-2]. **$125.00–175.00.** B. Six-sided Shade with Circle Indents, 3" [OP, R1-2]. **$125.00–150.00.** C. Tulip (Type II), 2¾" [OP, R2]. **$100.00–125.00.**

Candleholders with Rare Glass Shades: A. Zigzag Pattern, 2¾" [OP, R1]. **$100.00–125.00.** B. Ear of Corn, 2¾" [OP, R1]. **$200.00–250.00.** C. Marigold, 2¼" [OP, R1-2]. **$100.00–125.00.**

A. Free-blown Oval Shade, 3½" [OP, R2-3]. **$75.00–100.00.** B. Rib and Dot Pattern, 3" [OP, R1-2]. **$100.00–125.00.** C. Honeycombed Shade, 2¾" [OP, R1-2]. **$100.00–125.00.**

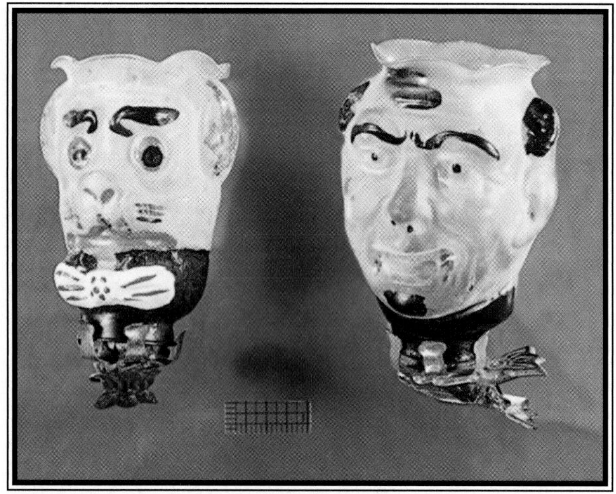

Candleholders with Rare Glass Shades: A. Spaniel Head, 3½" [OP, R1]. **$450.00–550.00.** B. Devil Head/Man with a Sour Face, 3¾" [OP, R1]. **$450.00–550.00.**

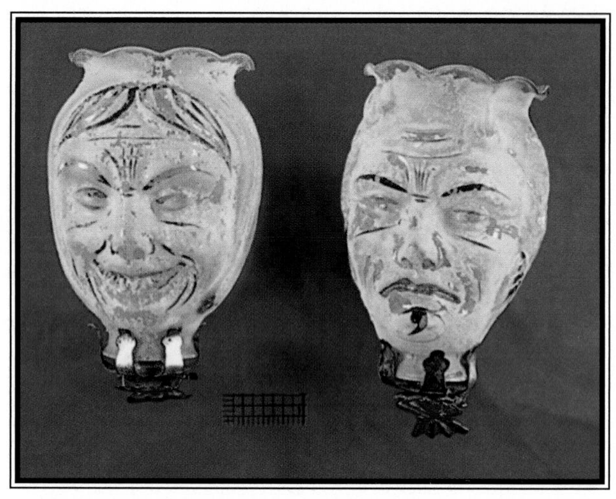

A. Witch's Face, large, 4" [OP, R1-2]. **$425.00–500.00.** B. Devil Head/Krampus Head, 4" [OP, R1]. **$450.00–500.00.**

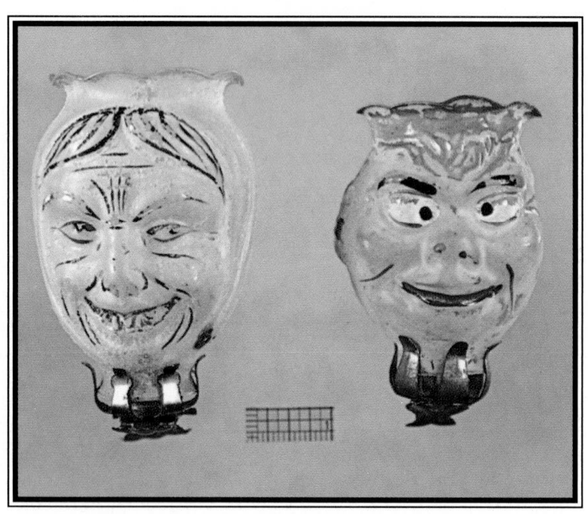

A. Witch's Face, small, 3½" [OP, R1-2]. **$400.00–450.00.** B. Chinese Man's Face (Type I), [OP, R1]. **$375.00–400.00.**

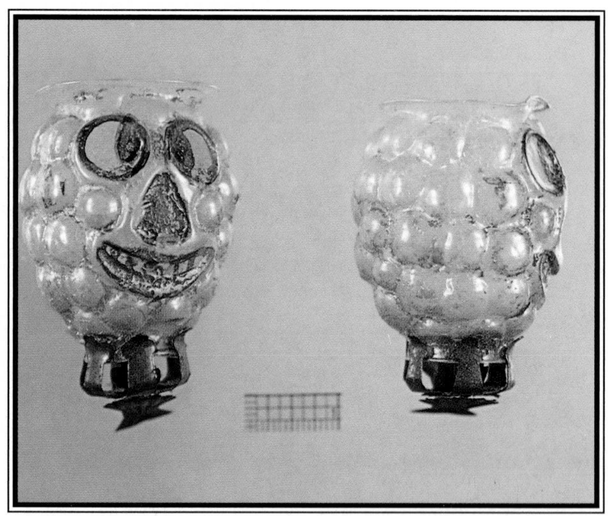

Two Views of the Popcorn Head Glass Shade on a Candleholder, 2½" [OP, R1]. **$375.00–425.00.**

Chinese Man's Head (Type II), flanges on the candle clip hold the shade securely in place [OP, R1]. **$375.00–400.00.**

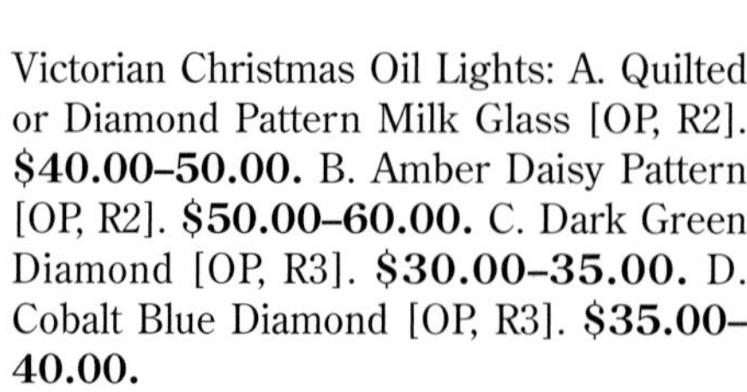

Victorian Christmas Oil Lights: A. Quilted or Diamond Pattern Milk Glass [OP, R2]. **$40.00–50.00.** B. Amber Daisy Pattern [OP, R2]. **$50.00–60.00.** C. Dark Green Diamond [OP, R3]. **$30.00–35.00.** D. Cobalt Blue Diamond [OP, R3]. **$35.00–40.00.**

Victorian Christmas Oil Lights, all with diamond quilted pattern, all 3¾": A. Light Blue [OP, R2]. **$40.00–45.00.** B. Cranberry [OP, R1]. **$110.00–120.00.** C. Amber [OP, R3-4]. **$30.00–35.00.** D. Teal Blue [OP, R2]. **$40.00–45.00.**

Oil Lights, Diamond Quilt and Variations: A. Diamond Quilt Variation, squat amber, 3¼" [OP, R2]. **$20.00–30.00.** B. Diamond Quilt Pattern, ruby [OP, R1-2]. **$100.00–110.00.** C. Diamond Quilt Variation, dark amethyst, straight sided with a rolled lip, 3¼" [OP, R1]. **$95.00–105.00.**

Diamond Quilt Pattern Variations: A. Ruby, embossed "Brocks Crystal Palace Lamp," 3¼" [OP, R1]. **$110.00–125.00.** B. Smooth, ruby, no pattern, 3¾" [OP, R1]. **$100.00–110.00.** C. Honeycomb Pattern, cranberry, 3¾". **$90.00–100.00.**

A. "Fat" Variation of Diamond Quilt Pattern, forest green, 3¾" [OP, R2]. **$30.00–35.00.** B. Diamond Quilt Pattern, forest green, 3¾" [R3]. **$30.00–35.00.** C. "Fat" with Rolled Edge Variation of Diamond Quilt Pattern, amber [R1-2]. **$55.00–65.00.** D. Punched Tin Shade, an oil lamp accessory, fits any of the Diamond Quilt Variations. **$25.00–35.00.**

Embossed Victorian Christmas Lights: A. Embossed Shield, Diamond Quilt Variation, 3½" [OP, R1]. **$130.00–140.00.** B. Cameo of Queen Victoria Figural Lamp, forest green, 3¾" [OP, R1]. **$280.00–300.00.** C. Shield with Embossed "VR" Diamond Quilt Variation, amethyst [OP, R1]. **$150.00–160.00.**

A & C are Variations of a Moonstone Pattern: A. Embossed "Chicago Lamp Candle Co.," 4", cobalt blue [OP, R1-2]. **$60.00–65.00.** B. Variation of Diamond Quilt Pattern, Lamp, screw-on metal base, amber, 3½" [OP, R1]. **$85.00–90.00.** C. Embossed "Acme Fairy Lamp Co.," cobalt blue [OP, R1]. **$60.00–65.00.**

A. Daisy Pattern, 3¾", bottom is embossed with a star and "G," light green [OP, R2]. **$60.00–65.00.** B. Moonstone Pattern, 3¼", dark green [OP, R1-2]. **$60.00–65.00.** C. Diamond Quilt Variation, "Saturn's Ring," blue milk glass [OP, R1]. **$90.00–100.00.**

Four Oil Lamps in the "Blown Squatties" Style, all 3¼": A. Clear with Bullseye [OP, R1-2]. **$75.00–80.00.** B. Amber with Ribbed Pattern [OP, R1-2]. **$75.00–80.00.** C. Light Green with Honeycomb Pattern [OP, R1-2]. **$75.00–80.00.** D. Amethyst with Honeycomb Pattern [OP, R1-2]. **$75.00–80.00.**

Three Figural Oil Lamps: A. Bunch of Grapes, 4", cobalt blue [OP, R1]. **$175.00–180.00.** B. Tulip, 3½", light aqua [OP, R1]. **$140.00–150.00.** C. Bunch of Grapes, 4", painted red, England, circa 1896 [R1]. **$150.00–160.00.**

Rare English Royalty Figural Lamps, all in cobalt blue: A. Head of George V, 4¼" [OP, R1]. **$300.00–350.00.** B. Head of Queen Victoria, 4" [OP, R1]. **$280.00–300.00.** C. Head of Prince Edward, 4", circa 1897 [R1]. **$280.00–300.00.**

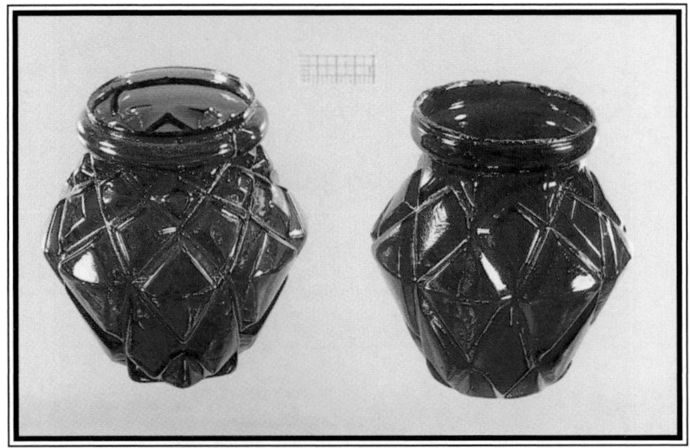

Two Harlequin Pattern Lamps, both 3½": A. Double Pattern [OP, R1]. **$80.00–90.00.** B. Single Pattern [OP, R1]. **$80.00–90.00.**

Four Hobnail Pattern Lamps: A & B. 2" Miniatures, amber and amethyst [OP, R1]. **$140.00–150.00** each. C. Dark Green, 3¾" [OP, R1]. **$85.00–90.00.** D. Pale Green Custard Glass, 4" [OP, R1]. **$140.00–150.00.**

A. Dot and Dash Pattern, 3¾" [OP, R1]. **$50.00–60.00.** B & C. Thousand Eye Pattern, both 3¾" [OP, R1]. **$80.00–85.00** each.

Stiegel Types [all OP, R1]. **$80.00–85.00** each: A. Light Green Fishnet, 3¼". B. Light Amethyst Swirl, 3¼". C. Dark Amethyst Diamond quilt, 3¼". D. Blue Fishnet, 3¾".

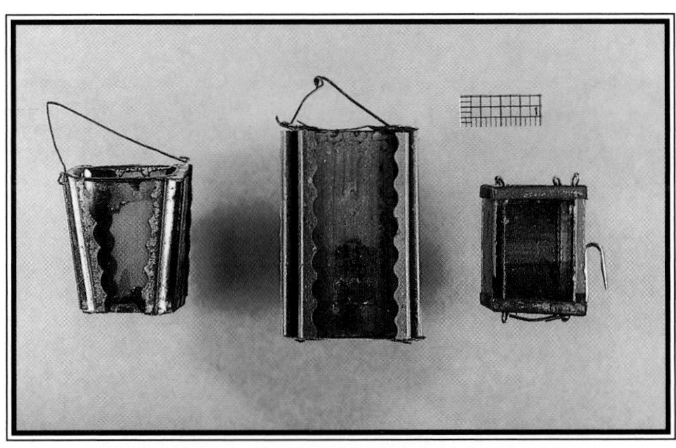

Three Stained Glass Lanterns: A. V-shape Miniature, 1⅝" [OP, R2]. **$40.00–50.00.** B. Four-sided, small, 2½" [OP, R2-3]. **$55.00–65.00.** C. Four-sided Miniature, 1½" [OP, R2]. **$60.00–70.00.**

A & C. Six-sided Pierced Metal Lantern (Type I), top and side views, 1½" [OP, R2]. **$45.00–55.00.** B. Fold-up Lantern, 3½"H [OP, R3]. **$15.00–25.00.**

Fold-up Lantern with Nazi Insignia [OP (1930s), R1]. **$175.00–200.00.**

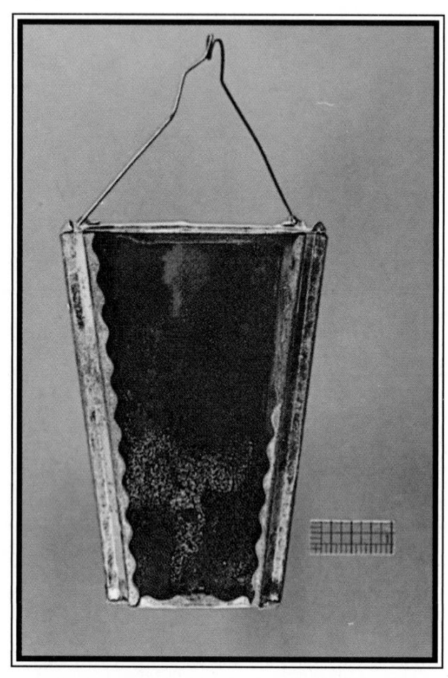

Small Four-sided Lantern, 2½" [OP, R3]. **$40.00–55.00.**

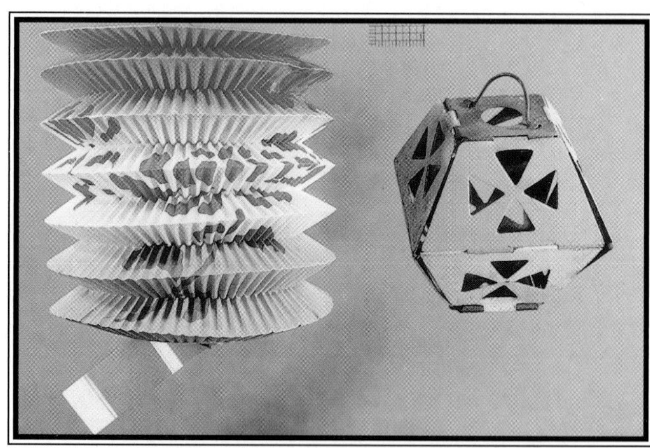

A. Japanese Paper Lantern, 5" [OP, R3]. **$3.00–5.00.** B. Fold-up Lantern, all metal, 3½" [OP, R1-2]. **$25.00–30.00.**

Rare Santa Head Lantern. (Type II), 3¼" [OP, R1+]. **$1,500.00–1,600.00.**

Santa Head Lantern (Type I), 12", this is a 1990s reissue made in Germany from original molds [OP-NP(1990s), R2]. **$75.00–100.00.** Original, **$1,600.00–2,200.00.**

Barth Oil Lamp, 3", circa 1887 [R1]. **$225.00–250.00.**

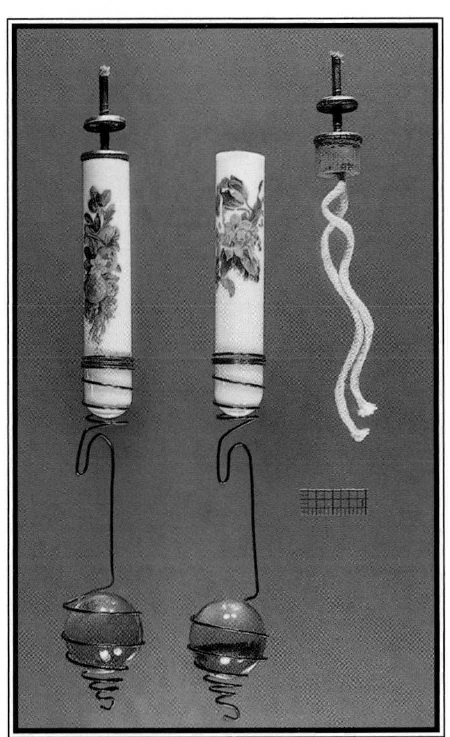

Milk Glass Oil Candle, 8½"L, an unusual pendulum weight oil candle made by Unicum Christmas [OP, R1+]. **$275.00–325.00.**

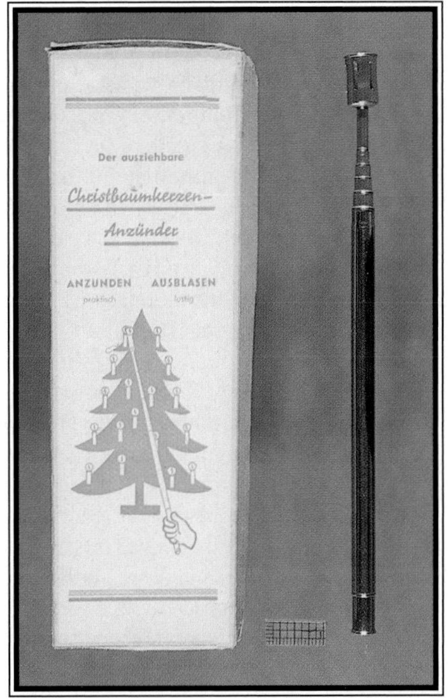

Candle Lighter and Snuffer, approx. 9½" closed & 36" extended. The wide end would hold a lit candle used for lighting candles on the tree. The tube was hollow, and was blown through to extinguish the candles. German, circa 1920 [R1]. **$75.00–100.00.**

Electric Lights for the Tree

In 1882, Edward H. Johnson, a vice-president in Edison's newly founded electric company, set up the first electrically-lighted Christmas tree. By the 1890s, electrically lit trees had become the rage among the wealthy. In the late 1890s, the first light set was marketed. Called a festoon lamp, this was a clear globe of glass with the filament running lengthwise.

However, it was not until 1903 that "strings", or true light sets, were marketed. Early light sets came in wooden boxes with printed advertising and graphics on paper labels glued to the sides. Mercerized cotton or silk covered the cords and the sockets were made of white or green porcelain. Porcelain sockets first changed to composition, then to Bakelite (a type of hard plastic), and then to the more familiar plastic used today.

Early Christmas lights themselves were pear shaped, with a sharp "exhaust tip" at the top, and are often called "Edison-type" light bulbs by collectors today. The exhaust tip was where the air was drawn out of the bulb to create the necessary vacuum inside. The first figural lights were marketed in 1909. These clear glass bulbs were hand blown, had exhaust tips, and were beautifully painted. Early shapes included Santa and St. Nicholas, dogs, canaries, songbirds, clowns, snowmen, flowers, and fruits. General Electric quickly responded in 1910 and marketed their own American-made figural lights in the shape of fruits and nuts. These early lights were wonderfully detailed, exquisitely painted, and rivaled the European ornaments of the time in beauty.

By the 1920s, the use of electricity was sufficiently widespread and the cost of Christmas light bulbs low enough that a major switch to electric lights began. People were attracted to them for three reasons. First, electric lights had the glamour of being new and modern. Second, many of the popular magazines of the day were encouraging the use of electric lights as tree decorations and decrying the horrible fires caused by candle lighting. Finally, the electric lights could be switched on and left relatively unattended for hours.

Two major changes took place in the light industry during the second decade of the twentieth century. Carbon filaments, which were heavy, hot, and burned out easily, were replaced by brighter, cooler, longer-lasting tungsten filaments. Collectors who wish to illuminate with carbon filament lights would do well to test and balance them before they go on the tree, and to keep them grouped the same way year after year. Do not mix carbon and tungsten filaments on the same string or the older lights will burn out quickly. The second major change occurring in the light industry was that World War I cut off imports of European figural lights. Within a year, Tokyo was the center for a new light bulb industry that had remarkable similarities to the European cottage industry. Early Japanese bulbs were hand blown from clear glass into metal molds. Yet the early Japanese lights had a major problem with flaking and peeling paint. In an attempt to improve the looks of the lights and help stop the cracking and peeling of the paint, lamp makers began to use white milk glass, which held the paint better.

There are probably as many different molded as there are figural ornaments. Fruits, flowers, birds, and Santas were, as always, popular subjects. But other popular themes were nursery rhymes, fairy tales, and popular comic strip characters of the 1920s and 1930s. Japan dominated the figural light business from the 1920s until World War II. After the war, the American desire for figural lights seems to have passed, and the lights were replaced by a new craze — the bubble light.

In 1936, an accountant for Montgomery Ward named Carl Otis invented the bubble light. It was destined to become one of the biggest selling Christmas products. A small 15 or 120 volt lamp was set inside a plastic base in this novel light that varied in design from globes to discs to rocket ships. Mounted atop this base was a long clear glass tube holding a clear or colored liquid that would send up a stream of small bubbles when heated by the lamp. As popular as they were, bubble lights were also replaced, as American tastes in lighted trees changed rapidly over the next 25 years.

The fluorescent light bulb appeared in 1945. Instead of using a filament and colored glass to produce color, it used different types of gas. One unique and totally nontraditional way of lighting the Christmas tree was a rotating color wheel. This system was used primarily with aluminum trees and consisted of a floodlight mounted behind a rotating wheel containing cellophane panels of red, blue, green, white, and yellow. This wheel covered the tree and its immediate background with color. This style was followed by a desire to have a tree full of flashing lights. This, of course, ushered in the age of the miniature, midget, or "twinkle" lights. In their variously modified forms, midget lights with their tiny star-like effect remain the most popular form of lighting today.

Another major form of lighting used the idea of a lamp cover. In these lights, a small plain lamp was the light source for a more elaborate outer cover usually formed of plastic. The advantage of using light covers was twofold. First, the designs could be more elaborate. Second, the light bulb could be replaced, at least in theory, thus allowing the cover to be used for many years. American figural light manufacturers experimented with this cover method from about 1919.

A new find to recently hit the collectors' market has been Russian figural lights. At this time, little is known about where, when, or how these lamps were manufactured. These figural light bulbs seem to have been manufactured in Moscow or St. Petersburg or both, circa 1920–1950. Many Russian pieces are crudely painted and have a wide metal collar where the glass joins the metal base. They have C6 bases and 14–16 volt bulbs.

There are many other styles and forms of lights. Silvered ornament lights were silvered on the inside and painted brightly on the outside to resemble ornaments on the tree when the lights were off. They are generally found as geometric styles, with the most common form being the indented oval, and they are hard to find in working order. The most common light forms have remained the cone or flame shapes that were designed to simulate candle flames.

Just as the collectors of glass ornaments prefer molded figurals, so too do the collectors of electric Christmas lights. They value bulbs that have no breaks or cracks in the glass, a base that is not loose or missing, and paint in good condition. To command the best price, the light should still work. A 9-volt battery may be used to safely check the light.

The lighted tree, whether lit with candles or bulbs, reflects the star-decked heavens and represents Christ as the "Light of the World." Having a lighted tree is a custom that goes back almost as far as the custom of having a Christmas tree.

Bird Lights: A. Songbird, clear glass with exhaust tip, 3½", C6 [German, OP, R2-3]. **$50.00–75.00.** B. Canary with Exhaust Tip Beak, 4¾", C6 [OP, R3]. **$35.00–50.00.** C. Mazda Songbird, 4½", C6 [OP, R2]. **$150.00–175.00.** D. Finch, made by Franco, 3½", C6 [OP, R2-3]. **$40.00–50.00.** E. Bird with a Crest, 3½", C6 [OP, R3-4]. **$25.00–35.00.**

A. Poulter Pigeon, 2½", C6 [OP, R4-5]. **$10.00–18.00.** B. Sitting Songbird, milk glass, 3", C6 [OP, R4]. **$15.00–20.00.** C. Songbird, common, milk glass, 4", C7 [OP, R5]. **$10.00–18.00.** D. Canary, common, 4", C6 [OP, R5]. **$15.00–20.00.** E. Songbird, common, clear glass, 4" [OP, R5]. **$15.00–20.00.** Note: C, D, & E. are all from the same mold.

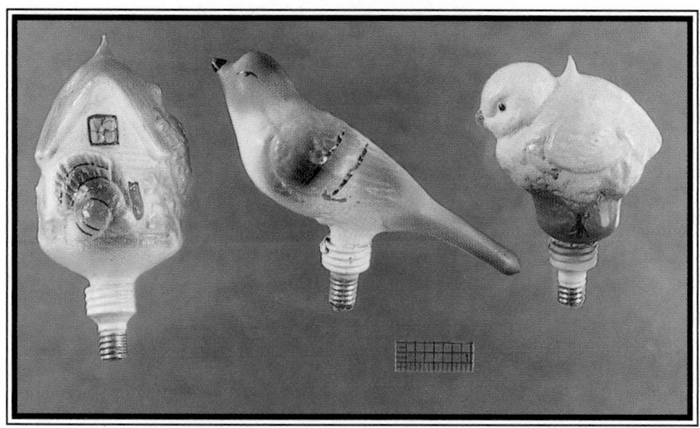

Rare German Lights: A. Turkey by a House, 3", C6 [OP, R1+]. **$350.00–450.00.** B. Songbird, large, exhaust tip, 5", C6 [OP, R1]. **$150.00–175.00.** C. Chick, large, exhaust tip, 2¼", C6 [OP, R1+]. **$350.00–450.00.**

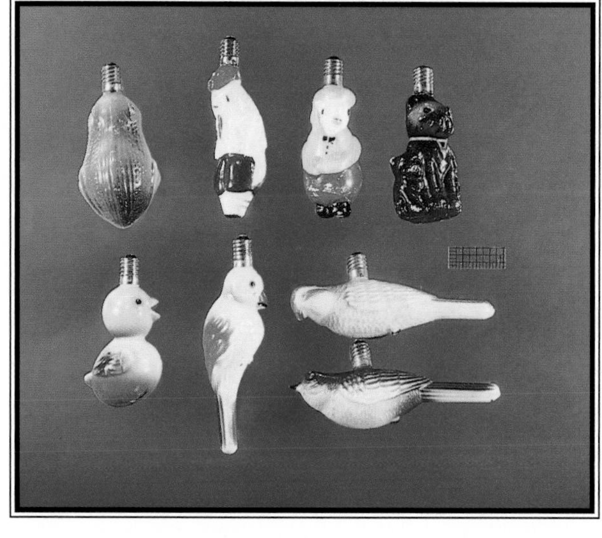

Japanese Milk Glass Animals, all have C6 base: A. Frog, 2¼", circa 1925 – 1955; one version, marked "Mazda," is American [R4]. Japanese version, **$15.00–20.00.** "Mazda" marked, **$30.00–35.00.** B. Rooster Playing Golf, 2¾", circa 1950 [R2-3]. **$25.00–30.00.** C. Dressed Duck, 2¼", circa 1920 – 1955 [R2]. **$25.00–35.00.** D. Mother & Pup Dogs, 2", circa 1950 [R1-2]. **$55.00–65.00.** E. Round Bird, 2", circa 1950 [R2-3]. **$25.00–35.00.** F. Parrot, 3", circa 1950 [R4]. **$10.00–15.00.** G & H. Common Songbirds, 3¼", circa 1920 – 1955 [R5]. **$10.00–18.00.**

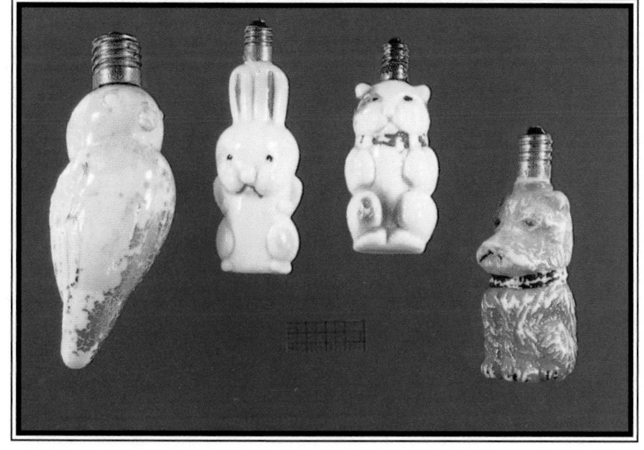

Animal Figural Lights: A. Robin, large, fat, 3½", C9 [OP, R2-3]. **$45.00–55.00.** B. Sitting Rabbit with Paws on Hips, 2½", C6 [OP, R3]. **$75.00–85.00.** C. Begging Cat (Type II), 2", C6, circa 1955 [R1]. **$165.00–180.00.** D. Sitting Scottie, 2½", C7 [OP, R3-4]. **$35.00–45.00.**

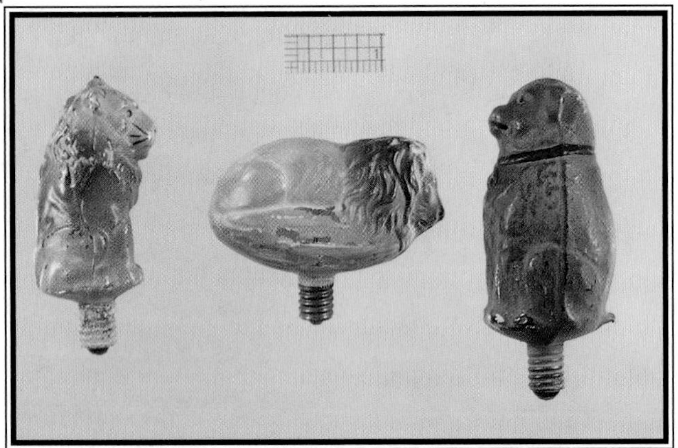

German Animal Lights: A. Sitting Lion, 2¼", C6 [OP, R1-2]. **$225.00–275.00.** B. Reclining Lion, 2¼", C6 [OP, R1]. **$275.00–325.00.** C. Sitting Dog with Exhaust Tip Tail, 2½", C6 [OP, R2]. **$125.00–150.00.**

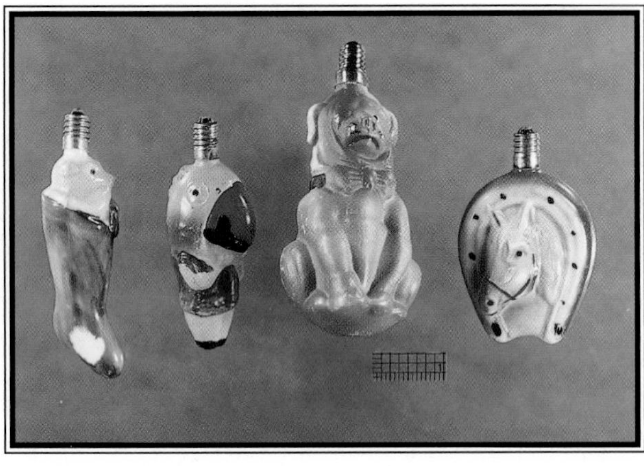

A. Dog in a Stocking (Type I), 3", C6 [OP, R2]. **$75.00–80.00.** B. Parrot-headed Girl, 2½", C6 [OP, R1-2]. **$90.00–100.00.** C. "Poor Poochie", 3½", C6 [OP, R1-2]. **$100.00–150.00.** D. Horse Head in a Horseshoe, double sided, 2¼", C6 [OP, R2]. **$55.00–65.00.**

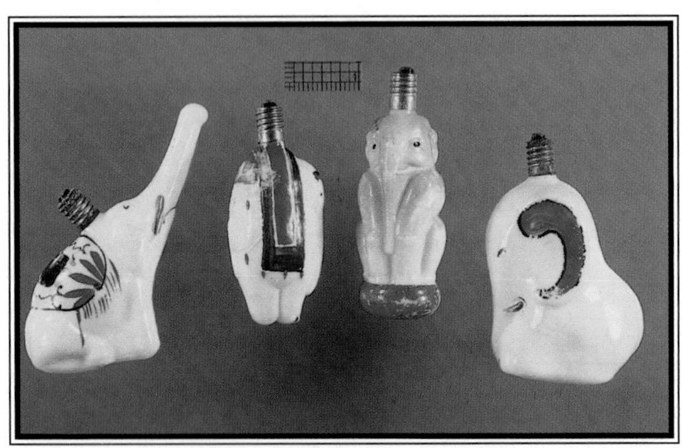

Four Milk Glass Elephants: A. Elephant with Trunk Up, 3", small, C6 [OP, R3-4]. **$20.00–30.00.** B. Egg-shaped Elephant, 2¼", C6 [OP, R1]. **$175.00–200.00.** C. Elephant Sitting on a Ball, 2¾", C6 [OP, R3-4]. **$30.00–40.00.** D. Elephant with Trunk Down, 2½", C6 [R3-4]. **$25.00–30.00.**

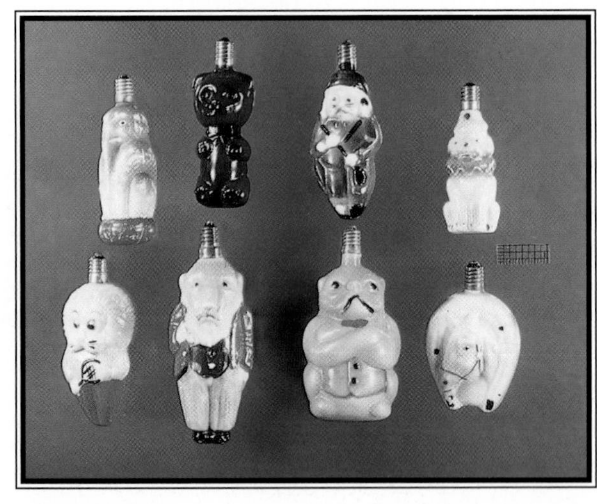

Japanese Milk Glass Animal Lights, all have C6 base: A. Elephant Sitting on a Ball, 2¾" [OP, R3-4]. **$30.00–40.00.** B. Sitting Teddy Bear, 2¾" [OP, R2]. **$25.00–35.00.** C. Dog in a Polo Outfit, 2¾", circa 1950 [R2-3]. **$25.00–35.00.** D. Dog in a Clown Outfit, 2¼", circa 1950 [R2]. **$25.00–35.00.** E. Lion with a Tennis Racket, 2¾", circa 1935 and 1955 [R3]. **$25.00–35.00.** F. Lion with a Suit & Pipe, 2½" & 3½" (shown), circa 1935 and 1955. Pieces marked "Buffalo" are Canadian [R3]. Small, **$25.00–35.00.** Large, **$55.00–65.00.** "Buffalo" marked, **$65.00–75.00.** G. Bulldog in a Vest, 2¾" [OP, R2]. **$90.00–110.00.** H. Horsehead in a Horseshoe, 2¼" [OP, R2]. **$55.00–65.00.**

Japanese Milk Glass Cats,-all have C6 bases: A. Cat with a Ball, 2¼" [OP, R2]. **$70.00–80.00.** B. Two Cats in a Basket, 2¼" [OP, R2]. **$55.00–65.00.** C. Sitting Cat with a Tag, 2", circa 1950 [R2]. **$30.00–40.00.** D. Begging Cat, 2½" [OP, R3]. **$35.00–45.00.** E. Goofy Cat, 3" [circa 1955, R2-3]. **$25.00–35.00.** F. Cat in an Evening Gown, 3", circa 1950 [R2]. **$150.00–175.00.** G. Cat with a Mandolin; 2½", 3¼" (shown), & 3½", circa 1925 – 1955 [R4]. Small, **$12.00–15.00.** Medium, **$15.00–20.00.** Large, **$20.00–25.00.** H. Double-sided Cat, 2¾" [OP, R2]. **$30.00–40.00.**

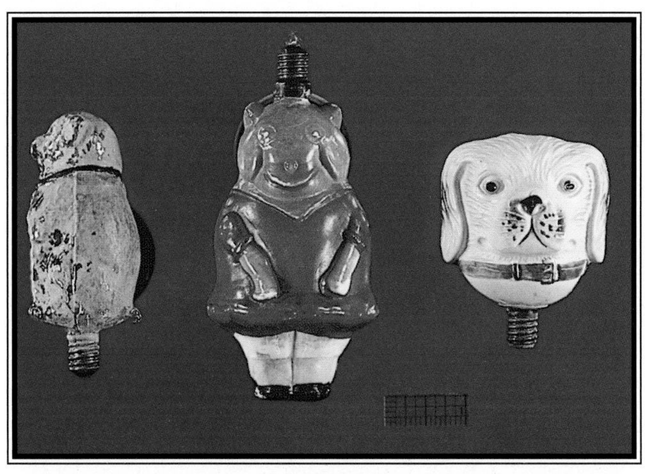

A. Sitting Dog with an Exhaust Tip Tail, 3" [European, OP (circa 1910), R2]. **$125.00–150.00.** B. Girl Hippo, 4½" [Japanese, OP, R1]. **$175.00–200.00.** C. Celluloid Spaniel Head, 2"; the head is a celluloid cover over the light bulb [OP, R1-2]. **$65.00–75.00.**

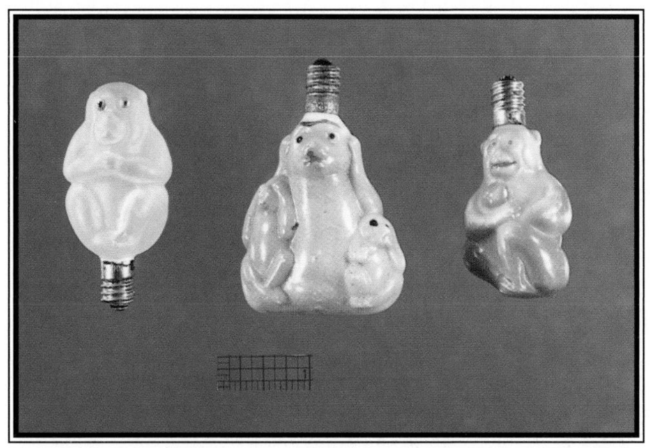

Monkey Lights: A. Sitting Monkey, 2", frosted glass, C6 [OP, R1-2]. **$100.00–125.00.** B. "See no evil," 2", C6 [OP, R1]. **$300.00–325.00.** C. Monkey Holding an Orange, 1¾", C6 [OP, R2]. **$125.00–150.00.**

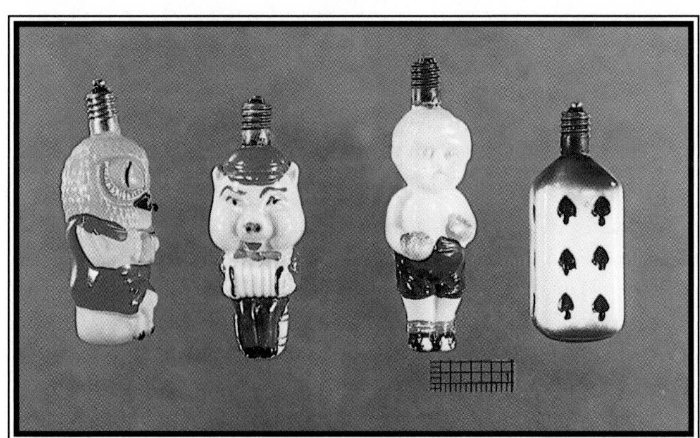

A. Owl-headed Girl, frosted glass, 2½", C6 [OP, R1-2]. **$75.00–90.00.** B. Pig Playing a Concertina, 2½", C6 [OP, R1-2]. **$80.00–90.00.** C. Boy Boxer, 3", C6 [OP, R1]. **$100.00–125.00.** D. Cards [OP, R1]. **$90.00–100.00.**

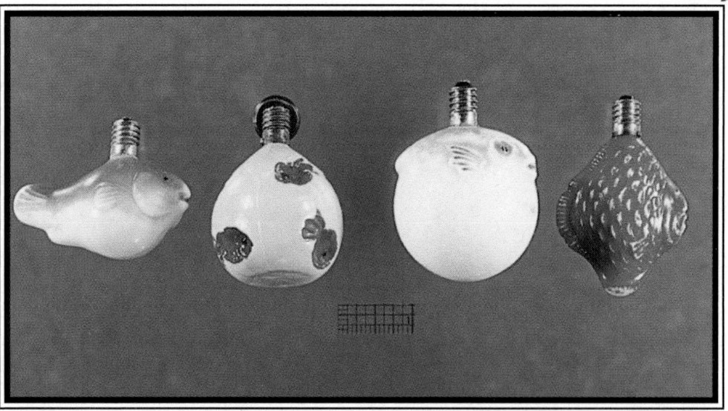

A. Guppy, 2½"L, C6 [OP, R3-4]. **$35.00–45.00.** B. Fish in a Bowl, 1¾"H, C6 [OP, R3-4]. **$30.00–35.00.** C. Large Puffer Fish, 2"H, C6 [OP, R2]. **$75.00–100.00.** D. Angel Fish, 2"H, C6 [OP, R2-3]. **$50.00–60.00.**

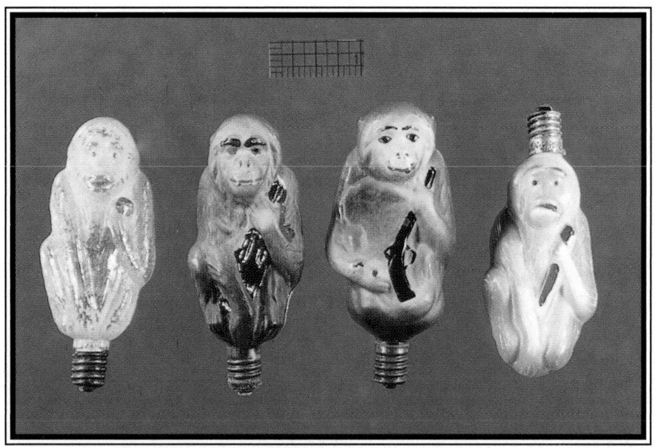

More Monkey Business: A. Monkey with a Vine, 2¼", C6 [German, OP, R2]. **$125.00–150.00.** B. Monkey with a Stick, clear glass, 2¼", C6 [OP, R2]. **$125.00–150.00.** C. Monkey Holding a Gun, 2½", C6 [OP, R2]. **$150.00–175.00.** D. Monkey with a Stick, milk glass, 2¼", C6 [OP, R2-3]. **$90.00–110.00.**

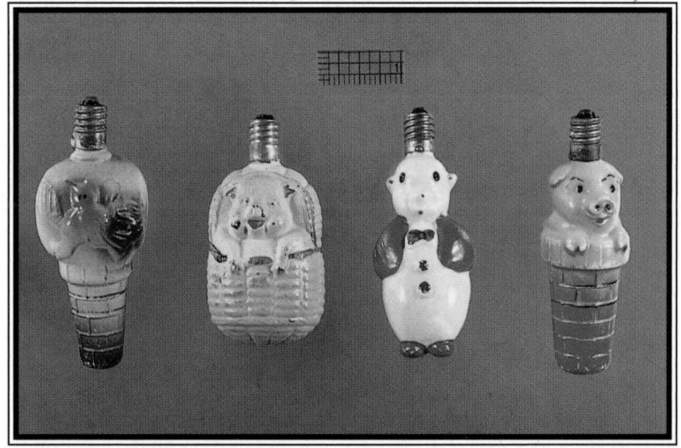

A. Birds in a Chimney, 2½", C6 [OP, R2]. **$90.00–100.00.** B. Pig in a Hooded Basket, 2", C6 [OP, R2]. **$100.00–125.00.** C. Pig in Jacket and Tie, 2¼", C6, circa 1950 [R2]. **$90.00–100.00.** D. Pig in Chimney, 2½", double face, C6 [OP, R2]. **$100.00–125.00.**

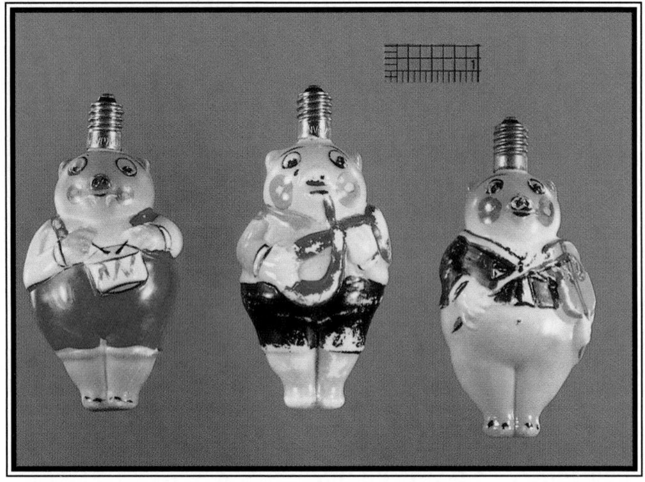

Three Little Pigs: A. Pig Playing a Drum, 2¾", C6 [OP, R2]. **$175.00–200.00.** B. Pig Playing a Tuba, 2¾", C6, circa 1950 [R2]. **$175.00–200.00.** C. Pig Playing a Fiddle, 2¾", C6, circa 1940 [R2]. **$175.00–200.00.** A & C are Japanese made with an *H* inside a diamond. Part of a set marketed by Peerless. Boxed Set, **$1,500.00.**

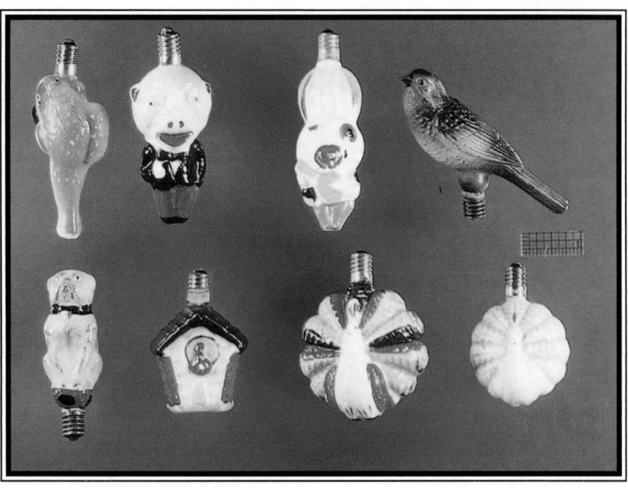

Animal Lights, all with C6 base: A. Tadpole, 2½" circa 1950 [Japanese, R2-3]. **$90.00–100.00.** B. Large-headed Pig in a Suit, 2¾" circa 1950 [Japanese, R2]. **$50.00–60.00.** C. Rabbit Playing a Banjo, 2¾" [Japanese, OP, R2]. **$20.00–25.00.** D. European Exhaust Tip Bird, 3½" [OP, R2-3]. **$60.00–85.00.** E. Bulldog Sitting on a Ball, 2¼", circa 1925 [Japanese, R3-4]. **$15.00–20.00.** F. Bird in a Bird House, 1½", circa 1935 – 1950 [Japanese, R2]. **$20.00–25.00.** G & H. Two Sizes of Full-feathered Peacocks, 1¾" (shown) & 2¼" (shown), circa 1950 [Japanese, R2-3]. Small, **$40.00–45.00.** Large, **$45.00–50.00.**

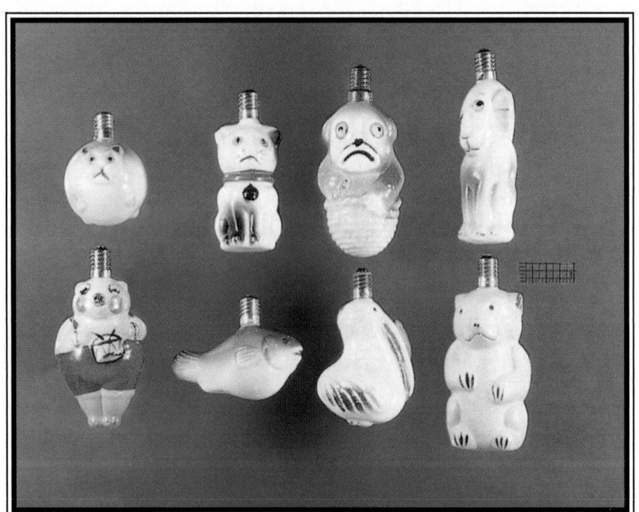

A Collection of Japanese Milk Glass Lights, all have C6 base: A. Puffed-up Cat, 1½", circa 1950 [R2-3]. **$55.00–65.00.** B. Sitting Cat with a Tag, 2", circa 1950 [R2]. **$30.00–40.00.** C. Frowning Dog in a Basket, 2¾" [OP, R2-3]. **$30.00–40.00.** D. Tall Hound Dog, 2¾", circa 1950 [R2]. **$30.00–40.00.** E. Pig Playing a Drum, 2¾", circa 1950 [R2]. **$175.00–200.00.** F. Guppy, 2¼", circa 1950 [R3]. **$35.00–45.00.** G. Pelican, 2¼", circa 1950 [R1-2]. **$30.00–40.00.** H. Sitting Bear, 2¾", circa 1950 [R2]. **$75.00–85.00.**

Early Clear Glass Lights, all have C6 base: A. Sitting Cat with a Bow, 2¼" [Japanese, OP, R3]. **$30.00–35.00.** B. Smiling Sitting Dog, 2½", circa 1925 [German, R3]. **$125.00–150.00.** C. Jack-o'-Lantern, 1½" [OP, R2]. **$30.00–40.00.** D. Joey Clown Head, 2" [Japanese, OP, R2]. **$30.00–40.00.** E & F. Two Versions of a Monkey Holding a Vine, 2¼" [Japanese, OP, R2-3]. **$60.00–90.00** each. G. Old King Cole, 2½" [OP, R2-3]. **$100.00–125.00.** H. Exhaust Tip Snowman with a Stick, 2½" [European, OP, R2]. **$65.00–90.00.**

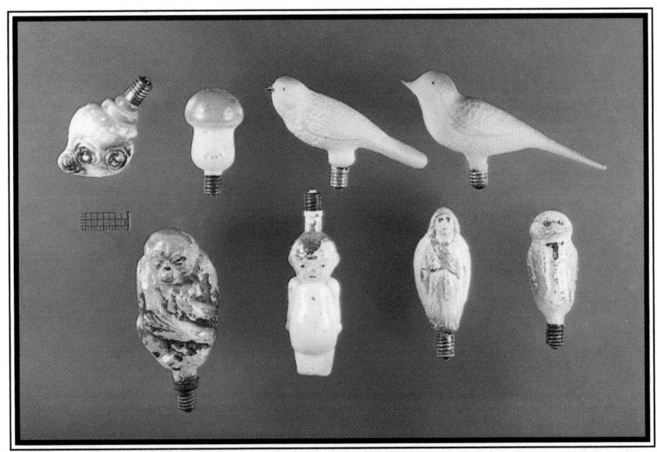

A. Milk Glass Seashell, 2" [Japanese, OP, R2]. **$40.00–50.00.** B. Mushroom, 2" [OP, R2-3]. **$20.00–25.00.** C & D. Two European Exhaust Tip Birds, 3" – 4" [OP, R2-3]. **$50.00–75.00.** E. "Mazda" Monkey, 3", circa 1920 [American, R1]. **$225.00–250.00.** F. Kewpie Doll with No Clothes, 3", circa 1925 [Japanese, OP, R2-3]. **$75.00–100.00.** G. Standing Angel, 2½", circa 1925 [Japanese, R2-3]. **$60.00–70.00.** H. Cat in a Suit with Glasses, 2¼", circa 1925 [Japanese, R2]. **$150.00–175.00.**

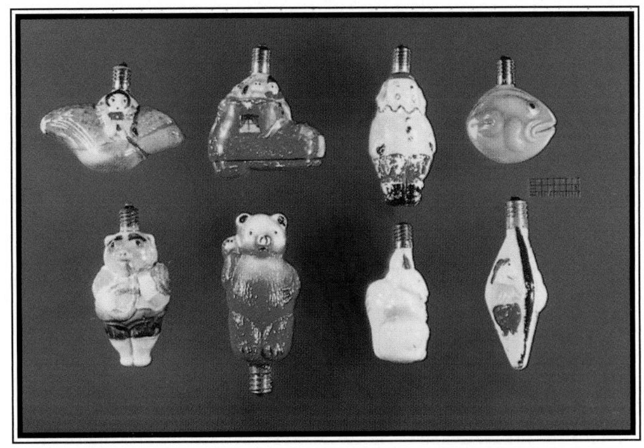

Japanese Figural Milk Glass Lights, all with C6 base: A. Mother Goose Riding a Goose, 3", from the Deluxe Nursery Rhyme Set, circa 1950 [R2]. **$50.00–65.00.** B. Children in a Shoe, 2¼"L, from the Deluxe Nursery Rhyme Set, 1953 [R3]. **$50.00–75.00.** C. Bozo the Clown, 2½", circa 1950, [R2-3]. **$30.00–35.00.** D. Egg-shaped Frog, 1½", circa 1950 [R1-2]. **$90.00–110.00.** E. Pig Playing a Tuba, 2½" [OP, R1-2]. **$175.00–200.00.** F. Waving Bear, 2¾", circa 1940 [R1-2]. **$55.00–65.00.** G. Squirrel, 2", circa 1950 [R2]. **$25.00–30.00.** H. Three-sided Light-of-Bunny, Chick, & Duck in a Bonnet, 2¾" [OP, R2-3]. **$135.00–150.00.**

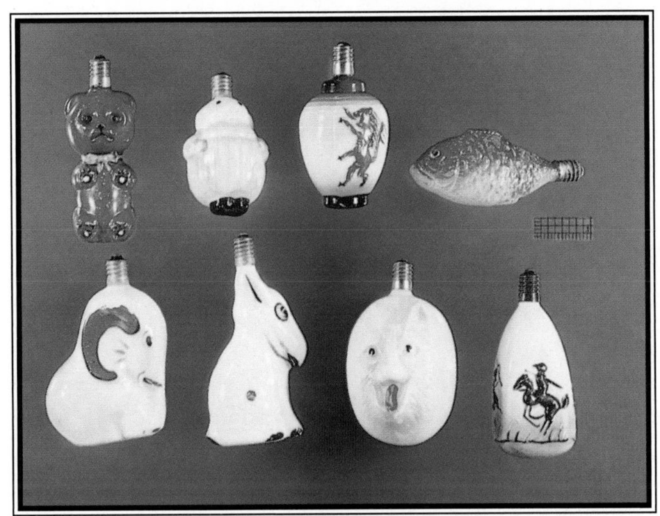

Japanese C6 Base Lights: A. Sitting Teddy Bear, 2¾" [OP, R2]. **$25.00–35.00.** B. Pig in a Dress, 2" [OP, R2]. **$60.00–75.00.** C. Dragon on a Lantern, 2¼" [OP, R3]. **$10.00–15.00.** D. Standard Form Fish, 2¼" to 2¾" (shown) [OP, R4]. Both sizes, **$10.00–15.00.** E. Elephant with Its Trunk Down, 2½", circa 1935 [R3-4]. **$25.00–30.00.** F. Pointyheaded Dog, 3" [OP, R2-3]. **$30.00–35.00.** G. Wolf Head, also called Rin Tin Tin, 2¾" [OP, R2-3]. **$55.00–65.00.** H. Indians on a Square, 2¾". Each side shows an Indian on horseback [OP, R3]. **$30.00–40.00.**

Japanese Figural Lights, all C6 base: A. Roly-Poly Boy, 2½" [OP, R2]. **$25.00–35.00.** B. Snowman Skier, 2¼" [OP, R2-3]. **$100.00–125.00.** C. Milk Glass Jack-o'-Lantern, 1¾", circa 1950 [R3]. **$50.00–75.00.** D. Owl in a Vest & Top Hat, 2¼", also made in clear glass [OP, R2]. **$100.00–120.00.** E. Cross on a Disc, 1¾" [OP, R3-4]. **$25.00–35.00.** F. Pineapple, 2", circa 1950 [R2]. **$70.00–80.00.** G. Celluloid Santa in a Cardboard Disc, 2¼" dia., marked "Nippon," circa 1930, an example of an early light cover [R1-2]. **$40.00–55.00.** H. Hippo with Raised Arms, 2" [OP, R2]. **$125.00–150.00.**

Japanese Milk Glass Lights, all C6 base: A. Olympic Torch, 2½" [OP, R2-3]. **$25.00–35.00.** B. Puppy on a Ball, 2¼" [OP, R2-3]. **$25.00–35.00.** C. Sitting Rabbit, 2", circa 1950 [R2]. **$25.00–35.00.** D. Small Girl in a Snowsuit, 2¼" [OP, R3]. **$25.00–35.00.** E. Large Spotted Clown, 3¼", circa 1950 [R2]. **$75.00–85.00.** F. Peacock with Wedge-shaped Tail Feathers, 2¼" [Japanese, OP, R2]. **$40.00–50.00.** G. Doc Head, 2" [OP, R2]. **$45.00–55.00.** H. Choir Girl (Type II), 3", circa 1950 [R3]. The base is marked with an "H" inside a diamond. **$25.00–35.00.**

A. Rooster in a Tub, 2¼", C6 [Japanese, OP, R2]. **$40.00–50.00.** B. Building on a Rock, "Alcatraz," 1½", C6, circa 1950 [Japanese, R2]. **$50.00–60.00.** C. Angel Fish, 2", C6 [Japanese, OP, R2-3]. **$50.00–60.00.** D. Flower in a Seashell, 2¼", C6 [Japanese, OP, R2]. **$100.00–125.00.** E. "The Aviator"; 2½", 2¾", & 3¼" (shown); C6 [Japanese, OP, R3]. Small, **$15.00–20.00.** Medium, **$20.00–25.00.** Large, **$25.00–30.00.** F. Marching Drummer, 2½", C6, circa 1950 [Japanese, R3]. **$35.00–45.00.** G. Canadian Mountie, 3", C6 [Japanese, R1-2]. **$175.00–225.00.** H. Banana with a Face, 2¾", C6, circa 1950 [Japanese, R2-3]. **$75.00–100.00.**

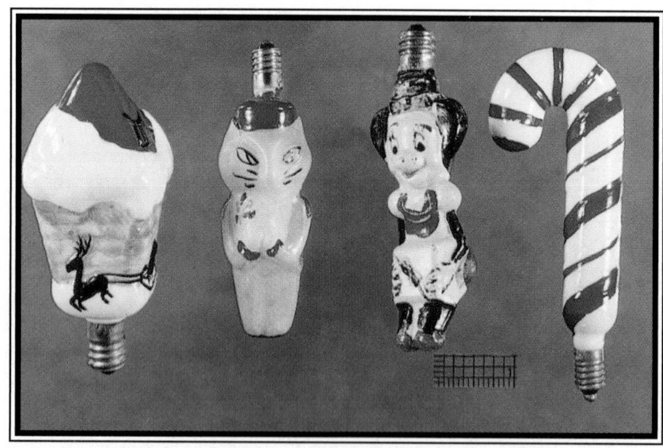

A. Lantern with Sleigh, 3", C7 [R1-2]. **$50.00–75.00.** B. Asian Cat Man, 2¾", C6 [OP, R1]. **$70.00–80.00.** C. Minnie Mouse, 3", C7 [R1-2]. **$200.00–225.00.** D. Candy Cane, 2¾" [OP, R2-3]. **$50.00–60.00.**

A. Snail on a Fat Toadstool House, 3¼", C6, circa 1935 [R2-3]. **$25.00–30.00.** B. Squash, long, 2¾", C6 [OP, R2]. **$20.00–25.00.** C. Angel Fish, 2", C6 [OP R2-3]. **$50.00–60.00.** D. Chrysanthemum, large, 2½", C6 [OP, R4]. **$30.00–40.00.** E. Mushroom, 1½", C6 [German, OP, R2]. **$25.00–30.00.**

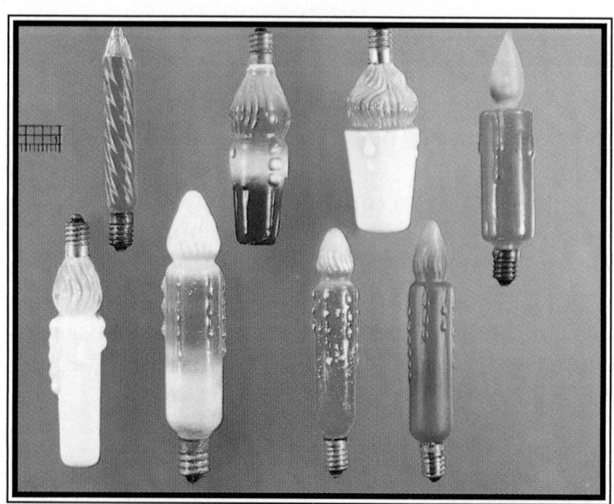

Top Row: A. Twisted Cable Candle, 2¾", C6 [OP, R4-5]. **$15.00–20.00.** B. Candle, short, 2½", C6 [OP, R2]. **$15.00–20.00.** C. Candle, squat, 2½", C6 [OP, R5]. **$10.00–15.00.** D. Exhaust Tip Flame, 3", C6. **$25.00–30.00.** Bottom Row: Four Variations of Candles with Dripping Wax; 3", 3¼", 3", and 3" respectively [OP, R4]. **$13.00–18.00** each.

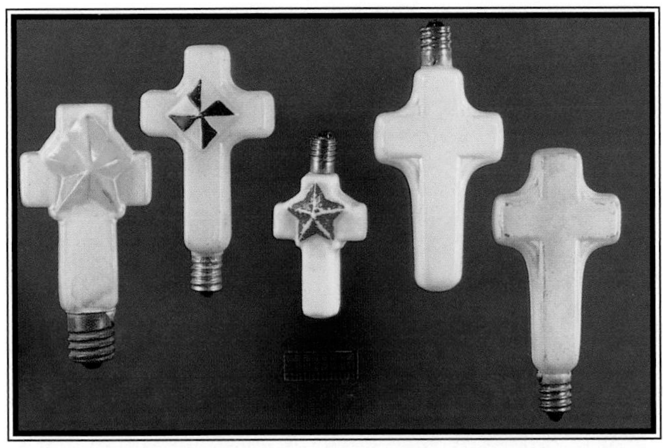

Crosses: A. Cross with a Star Center, large, 2¾", C9 [OP, R3-4]. **$30.00–35.00.** B. Cross with Windmill Arms center, 2¾", C7 [OP, R2-3]. **$60.00–75.00.** C. Cross with Star Center, small, 2", C6 [OP, R5]. **$15.00–20.00.** D & E. Crosses, molded, both 3", C7 [OP, R4]. **$20.00–25.00** each.

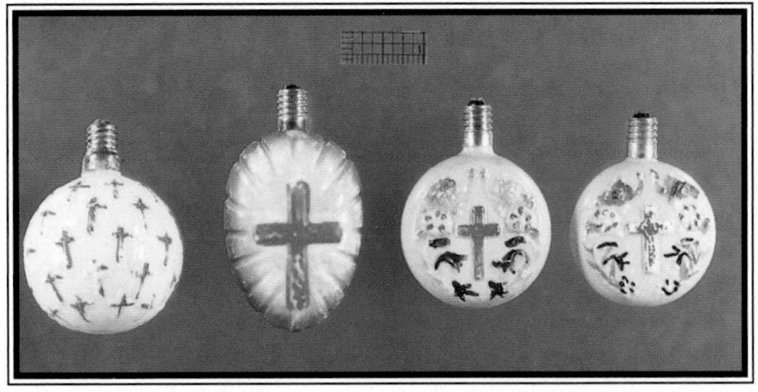

A. Crosses on a Ball, 1¾", C6 [OP, R4]. **$15.00–20.00.** B. Cross on an Egg Shape, 2¼", C6 [OP, R3]. **$35.00–40.00.** C. Cross on a Disk, marked "MHK," 1¾", C6, circa 1950 [R4]. **$25.00–35.00.** D. Cross on a Disk, thinner than C, 1¾" [OP, R4]. **$25.00–35.00.**

All Mazda Lamps: A. Trumpet Flower, 2¼" [OP, R3]. **$60.00–75.00.** B. Morning Glory, 2½" [OP, R3]. **$60.00–75.00.** C. Eggplant, 2½" [OP, R3]. **$50.00–60.00.** D. Lantern, 2¼" [OP, R3]. **$60.00–75.00.** E. Gifu Lantern, 2¼" [OP, R3]. **$60.00–75.00.** F. Faceted Bell, 2" [OP, R3]. **$60.00–75.00.**

A. Rosebud with Fabric Leaves, 2¼" [OP, R3]. **$30.00–35.00.** B. Trumpet Flower, detailed, 2½" [OP, R3]. **$40.00–50.00.** C. Flower Blossom, Mazda, 2" [OP, R2-3]. **$60.00–65.00.** D. Flower Basket, 2¼" [OP, R3]. **$30.00–35.00.** E. Chrysanthemum, 2" [OP, R4]. **$25.00–30.00.** F. Clover, 1¾", C6 [German, OP, R2]. **$30.00–35.00.**

A. Strawberry (Type I), 1½", C6 [OP, R3-4]. **$15.00–20.00.** B. Strawberry (Type II), 1⅝", C6 [OP, R4]. **$15.00–20.00.** C. Rosebud, marked "SK," large, 2½", C6 [NP, R4]. **$15.00–20.00.** D. Banana, clear glass, 2¾", C6 [OP, R2]. **$20.00–30.00.** E. Pear, "SK," small, 1¾", C6, clear glass [OP, R4]. **$10.00–15.00.** F. Pear, "SK," small, 1¾", C6,-milk glass [OP, R4]. **$10.00–15.00.**

Early Clear Glass Fruit, all C6: A. Exhaust Tip Walnut, 1½", circa 1915 [European, R2]. **$30.00–40.00.** B. Strawberry, 1½", circa 1920 [Japanese, R3-4]. **$15.00–20.00.** C. Plum, 1¾", circa 1920 [R2]. **$20.00–30.00.** D. Walnut, 1¾", circa 1920 [R2-3]. **$20.00–30.00.** E. Exhaust Tip Peach, 1¾", circa 1915 [European, R2]. **$30.00–40.00.** F. Orange, 1¾", circa 1930 [Japanese, R2-3]. **$12.00–18.00.** G. Peach, 2", circa 1920 [R2-3]. **$20.00–25.00.** H. Large Pear, 2¼", circa 1920 [R3]. **$20.00–25.00.**

A–F. Small and Common Flowers in Various Shapes, all C6, 1½", circa 1900–1950 [Japanese, R5]. **$8.00–12.00** each: G. Large Fruit Basket, 2¾" [Japanese, OP, R3]. **$25.00–35.00.** H. Apple, 2½" [Japanese, OP, R2]. **$15.00–20.00.** I. Large Open Rose, 2", circa 1950 [Japanese, R3]. **$15.00–20.00.** J. Ear of Corn, 4" [Japanese, OP, R2-3]. **$30.00–40.00.**

Early Clear Glass Lights: A. Watt Rose, 1½", circa 1920 "Watt" is marked on the base insulator [Austrian, R2-3]. **$25.00–35.00.** B. Watt Orange, 1½", circa 1930, "Watt" is marked on the base insulator [Austrian, R2-3]. **$15.00–20.00.** C. Exhaust Tip Raspberry, 1½" [OP, R2]. **$25.00–35.00.** D. Round Berry, 1¼" [OP, R2]. **$15.00–20.00.** E. Horn Player, 2¾" [OP, R2]. **$60.00–75.00.** F. Exhaust Tip Santa with His Hands in His Sleeves, 3" [OP, R2]. **$115.00–130.00.** G. Exhaust Tip Clown, 3" [Hungarian, OP, R2]. **$75.00–100.00.** H. Mazda Canary, 4½"L, circa 1920. There is a long light tube inside the body [American, R2]. **$150.00–175.00.**

A. Lemon, clear glass, 1¾", C6 [OP, R4]. **$12.00–15.00.** B. Clover Blossom, common, 1½", C6 [OP, R5]. **$10.00–12.00.** C. Orange, "SK," 1¾" [OP, R2]. **$12.00–18.00.** D. Lemon, milk glass. **$10.00–15.00.** E. Rosebud, small, 1½", C6 [OP, R4]. **$8.00–12.00.** F. Watt Orange, 1½", C6 [OP, R2-3]. **$15.00–20.00.**

A. Jack-o'-Lantern with Leaves, 1¾", C6, circa 1950 [R3]. **$45.00–55.00.** B. Mushroom Man, 2¾" [OP, R1]. **$100.00–125.00.** C. Jack-o'-Lantern (Type II), 1¼", C6 [OP, R3-4]. **$50.00–75.00.** D. Gourd Man, 2½", double sided, C6 [OP, R3]. **$35.00–55.00.** E. Banana Face, 2¾", C6 [NP (1950), R2-3]. **$75.00–100.00.**

A. Grapes, narrow, 2", C6 [OP, R5]. **$8.00–12.00.** B. Star with Crescent Moon, 2" [R4]. **$15.00–20.00.** C. Bell with Santa Face (Type II), milk glass, 2¼" [R5]. **$15.00–20.00.** D. Bell with Holly, 2" [R4]. **$10.00–15.00.** E. Wide Bunch of Grapes, 2½", C6 [OP, R5]. **$15.00–18.00.**

A. Acorn, 1½", C6 [OP, R3]. **$35.00–40.00.** B. Songbird, common, milk glass, 3¼" [OP, R5]. **$10.00–15.00.** C & D. Pine Cone, generic, 1¾", C6 [OP, R4]. **$5.00–10.00.** E. Flower, generic, 1½", C6 [OP, R5]. **$8.00–12.00.** F. Tomato, small, 1½", C6 [OP, R2]. **$30.00–35.00.** G. Rosette Lamp, glass light cover, 1½" dia., C6 [OP, R4]. **$10.00–15.00.** H & I. Pine Cones, exhaust tips, 2", C6 [OP, R4]. **$6.00–10.00.**

A. Star-covered Ball, small, 1¾", C6, circa 1950 [R4]. **$15.00–20.00.** B. Rosebud, large, 2½" [NP, R4]. **$15.00–20.00.** C. Ball with Holly Leaves, 1¾", C6, circa 1950 [R4]. **$15.00–18.00.**

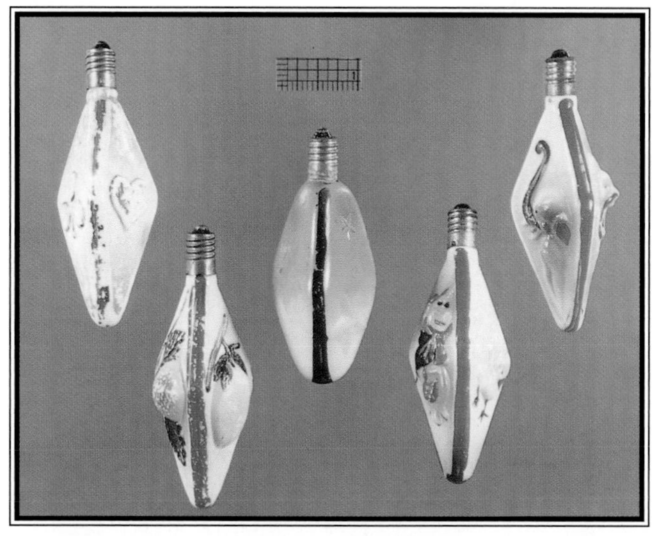

Geometric Diamond Shape Lights, all C6, all approx. 2½": A. Hearts, Spade, Clubs; circa 1950 [R1]. **$125.00–150.00.** B. Lemon, Grapes, Strawberries; circa 1950 [R1]. **$100.00–125.00.** C. Stars [OP, R3]. **$100.00–125.00.** D. Dressed Up Dog on a Diamond Shape, Rabbit and Chick are on the other two sides [OP, R2]. **$125.00–150.00.** E. Elephant on a Diamond Shape, Lion and Hippo are on the other two sides [OP, R2]. **$125.00–150.00.**

Silvered Ornament Lights, Japanese: A. Cube with Stars, 1½" [1935, OP, R3]. **$30.00–40.00.** B. Ball with Three Large Indents, 1½" [OP, R3]. **$20.00–25.00.** C. Four-petaled Flower on a Disk, 2" [OP, R1]. **$75.00–85.00.** D. Ribbed Egg with Bumpy Panels, 1¾" [OP, R3-4]. **$30.00–40.00.** E. Large Indented Ball, 2½" [OP, R3]. **$30.00–40.00.** F. Egg Shape with Embossed Stars, 2" [OP, R3]. **$30.00–40.00.** G. Ribbed Heart, 2" [OP, R1]. **$75.00–85.00.**

First Column Left: A. Lantern, round ribbed, 2", C6 [OP, R4]. **$15.00–20.00.** B. Acorn, 1½", C6 [OP, R3]. **$20.00–25.00.** C. Star with Base on Back, 1¼", C7 [OP, R4]. **$15.00–20.00.** D–G. Tops, generic, 2" – 2½", all C6 [OP, R4]. **$12.00–15.00.**

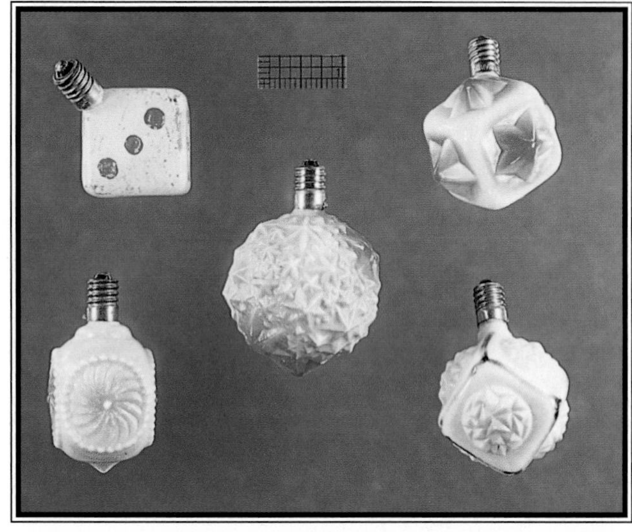

A. Die, 1¾", C6 [OP, R2]. **$90.00–100.00.** B. Cube with Stars, 1¾", C6 [NP(1950), R3]. **$30.00–35.00.** C. Daisy Covered Ball, 1¾", C6 [OP, R4]. **$20.00–25.00.** D. Railroad Lantern, 1½", C6 [OP, R3]. **$15.00–20.00.** E. Cube with Chrysanthemum, 2", C6 [NP(1950), R4]. **$20.00–25.00.**

A. Lighthouse, 2", C6 [OP, R3]. **$40.00–45.00.** B. Church with a Bell, 2½", C7 [OP, R3]. **$50.00–60.00.** C. Santa Beside a House, 2¼", C6 [OP, R3]. **$30.00–40.00.** D. Church with a Small Cross, 2¼", C6 [OP, R4]. **$25.00–30.00.** E. Church with a Large Cross, 2¼", C6 [OP, R3-4]. **$25.00–30.00.**

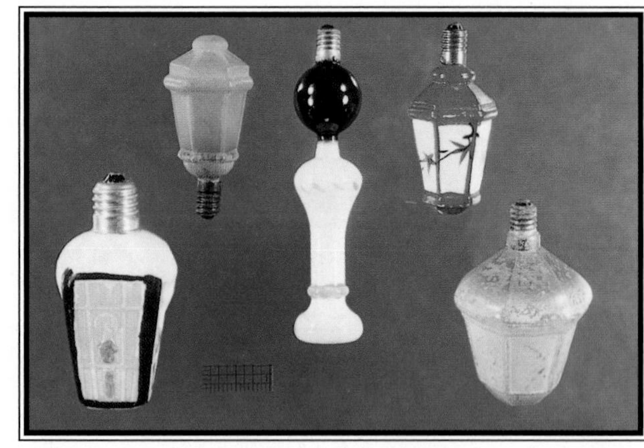

A. Street Lantern, 2", C6 [OP, R4]. **$15.00–20.00.** B. Banquet Light, 3¾", C6 [OP, R1]. **$160.00–190.00.** C. Lantern, six paneled, 2", C6 [NP(1950), R5]. **$5.00–8.00.** D. Lantern with Candle, 2¼", [NP, circa 1950, R4]. **$20.00–25.00.** E. Lantern, round top, 2¼", C6 [OP, R4-5]. **$10.00–12.00.**

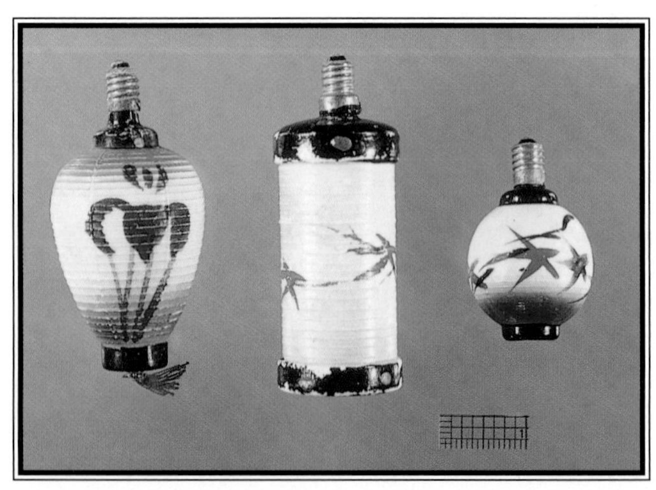

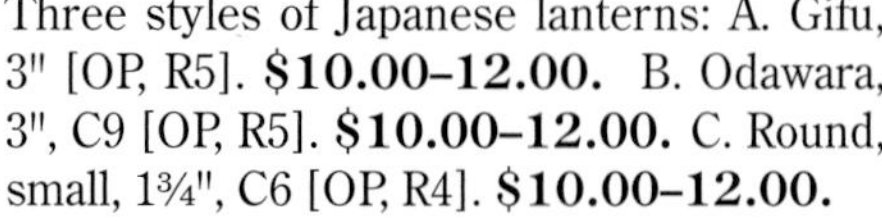

Three styles of Japanese lanterns: A. Gifu, 3" [OP, R5]. **$10.00–12.00.** B. Odawara, 3", C9 [OP, R5]. **$10.00–12.00.** C. Round, small, 1¾", C6 [OP, R4]. **$10.00–12.00.**

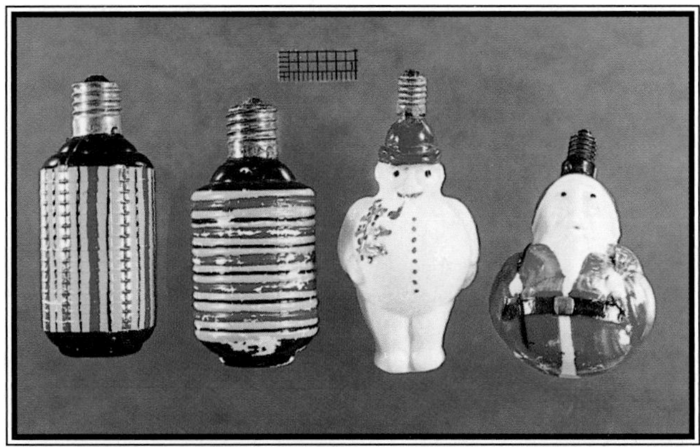

A. Cylinder-shaped Odawara Lantern, C9, 2¾" [OP, R5]. **$8.00–10.00.** B. Cylinder-shaped Odawara Lantern, C9, 2½" [OP, R5]. **$8.00–10.00.** C. Snowman with Holly, 3¼", C6 [OP, R2]. **$30.00–40.00.** D. Roly-Poly Santa, 2¾", C6 [OP, R2]. **$55.00–65.00.**

Various Japanese Lights: A, B, C. Three Sizes of Gifu Lanterns, 1¾"–3½", circa 1925 – 1950 [R5]. Large, **$10.00–12.00.** Medium, **$6.00–10.00.** Small, **$5.00–6.00.** D & E. Two Sizes of Round Lanterns, 1¾" & 2", circa 1950 [R4]. **$10.00–12.00.** F, G, & H. Miniature Lanterns, 1¾", circa 1925 [R4]. **$5.00–6.00.** I. Santa Face in a Bell (Type II), 2¼" [OP, R5]. **$12.00–18.00.** J. Santa Face in a Bell (Type I), 2", circa 1930 [R4]. **$12.00–18.00.** K. Cylinder Shape Odawara Lantern, 3¾" [OP, R4]. **$10.00–12.00.**

A. Log Cabin, 2", circa 1950 [Japanese, R3]. **$15.00–25.00.** B. Cottage in a Hillside, 2¼", circa 1950 [Japanese, R2]. **$30.00–40.00.** C. Snow-covered Lantern, 2" [Japanese, OP, R4-5]. **$8.00–12.00.** D. Small Square House, 1¾", circa 1925 [Japanese, R3-4]. **$25.00–35.00.** E. Kristolite Heavy Tin Light Reflector, by Noma, 3". **$1.00–1.50.** F. Snow-covered Cottage, large, 2¾" [Japanese, R4-5]. **$10.00–15.00.** G. Snow-covered Cottage, small, 2" [Japanese, R4-5]. **$10.00–15.00.** H. Double Row Matchless Star, C6 [OP, R2-3]. **$125.00–165.00.** I. Kristal Star, 2¾", circa 1935 [Japanese, R4]. **$5.00–8.00.** J. German Foil Light Reflector, 3½" [OP, R4]. **$2.00–3.00.**

All Lanterns: A. With Animals, 1¾", C6 [OP, R2]. **$50.00–75.00.** B. Twenty-four-sided, 1½", C6 [OP, R4]. **$15.00–20.00.** C. Six-paneled, 2", C6 [NP, (1950), R5]. **$10.00–12.00.** D. Cylinder with Wavy Lines, 3", C6 [OP, R3]. **$25.00–35.00.** E. Cone Shape, 2¼", C6 [English, OP, R3-4]. **$15.00–25.00.** F. Twelve-paneled, 2¼", C6 [OP, R4]. **$15.00–25.00.** G. Rectangular, 2¾", C6 [OP, R4]. **$15.00–20.00.**

Bells: A. "Christmas Greeting," 1¼", C6 [NP, (1950), R4-5]. **$10.00–15.00.** B. Bell with Trees, large, 3", C9 [OP, R5]. **$10.00–15.00.** C. Generic Bell, 1½" [OP, R5]. **$8.00–12.00.** D. Generic Bell, blue, 1¾" [OP, R5]. **$8.00–12.00.** E. Bell with Zigzag Pattern, 2¼", C7 [OP, R5]. **$12.00–14.00.**

A. Angel with a Violin, 2½", C6 [OP, R2]. **$60.00–80.00.** B. Kneeling Madonna, 2½", C6 [OP, R1]. **$100.00–135.00.** C. Angle with Trumpet, 2½", C6 [OP, R2]. **$60.00–80.00.**

Three Choir Girls/Angels: A. Short, 2½", C7 [OP, R4]. **$25.00–30.00.** B. Type I, 3", C6 [OP, R1]. With metal reflector wings, **$150.00–175.00.** Without wings, **$30.00–35.00.** C. Type II, 3", C6 [NP, (1950), R4]. **$25.00–30.00.**

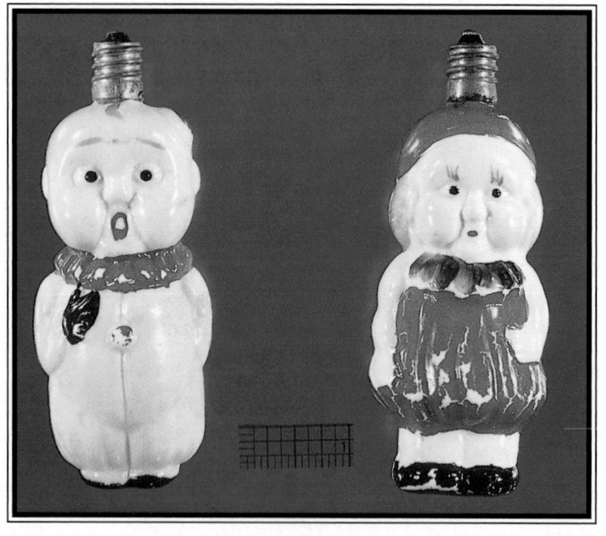

A. Baby in a Clown Suit, 3¼", C7 [OP, R2]. **$75.00–85.00.** B. Girl in a Sack Dress, large, 3¼", C7 [OP, R2]. **$50.00–75.00.**

A. Thumbelina, 3¼", C6 [OP, R3]. **$35.00–45.00.** B. Witch (Type II), 2¾", C6 [OP, R2]. **$100.00–115.00.** C. Baby in a Sock, large, 2¾", C6 [OP, R4]. **$20.00–25.00.** D. Clown Head with a Tall Hat, 2½", C6 [OP, R2-3]. **$35.00–45.00.**

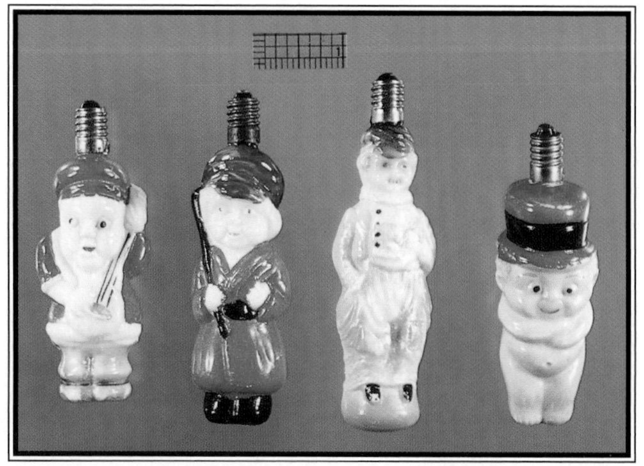

A. Dutch Boy with a Mandolin, 2½", C6 [OP, R2]. **$80.00–100.00.** B. Dutch Boy with a Stick, 3", C6 [OP, R2]. **$100.00–125.00.** C. Dutch Man with a Pipe, 3¼", C6 [OP-NP (1950), R2]. **$100.00–125.00.** D. New Year Baby, 2¼", C6 [NP (1950), R2]. **$125.00–150.00.**

A. Baseball Player, 2¼", C6 [NP(1950), R2]. **$65.00–75.00.** B. Baseball, 2" dia., C6 [NP(1950), R1]. **$100.00–125.00.** C. Soccer Player, 2½", C6 [NP(1950), R2]. **$75.00–85.00.**

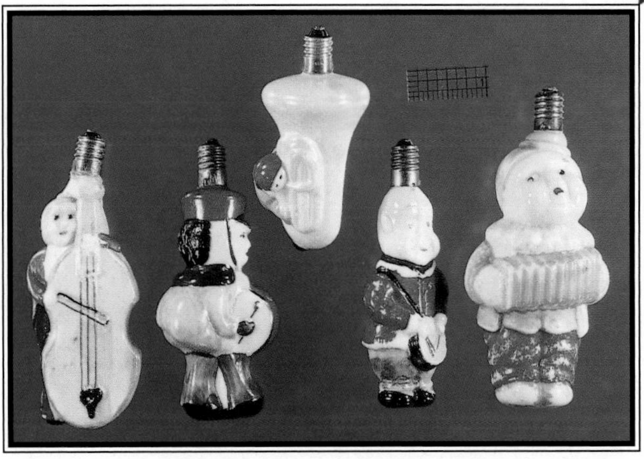

A. Man with a Bass Fiddle, 3", C6 [OP, R1]. **$275.00–300.00.** B. Marching Drum Player, 2¾", C6 [OP, R3]. **$35.00–45.00.** C. Man with a Large Tuba, 2¼", C6 [NP(1950), R1]. **$125.00–150.00.** D. Boy Playing a Drum, 2½", C6 [NP(1950), R3]. **$75.00–85.00.** E. Man/Clown Playing a Concertina, 3¼", C6 [OP, R3]. **$30.00–40.00.**

Four lamps from the "Canadian Mountie Set," all 3": A. Totem Pole (Type I), C7 [Japan, 1955, OP, R1-2]. **$150.00–175.00.** B. Indian Princess, C7 [OP, R1-2]. **$150.00–175.00.** C. Indian Chief, C7 [OP, R1]. **$150.00–175.00.** D. Canadian Mountie, C7 [OP, R1-2]. **$150.00–175.00.**

Paramount Diamond Brite Walt Disney Set, circa 1958, all can be found as either C6 or C7 pieces [R4]. **$15.00–20.00** each: A. Pluto. B. Pinocchio. C. Jiminy Cricket. D. Donald Duck. E. Minnie Mouse. F. Mickey Mouse. G. Fiddler Pig. H. Dwarf, Doc. Pieces in C6 set are 2¼". C7 lamps are 2¾". This set was *not* authorized by Disney. Set in the box, **$100.00–135.00.**

Disney's Snow White Set, all C7, circa 1940 [R2 Dwarfs, R1 Snow White]. Dwarfs are 2½" and **$100.00–125.00** each. Snow White is 2¾" and **$200.00–225.00.**

Original Box for Walt Disney Set, "Disneyland 'Santa Lites' " [OP, R1+]. Ten lights (eight different ones plus two duplicates) in original box, **$2,000.00–2,200.00.**

Walt Disney Set, "Disneyland 'Santa Lites,' " 3" – 3½", all C7, Mickey is missing [Japanese, OP, R1-2]: A. Minnie Mouse. **$200.00–225.00.** B. Donald Duck. **$200.00–225.00.** C. Pluto. **$150.00–175.00.** D. Goofy. **$150.00–175.00.** E. Jiminy Cricket. **$150.00–175.00.** F. Pinocchio. **$125.00–150.00.** G. Dopey. **$150.00–175.00.** Mickey is valued at **$200.00–225.00.** The pieces were made in both milk glass & clear glass.

A. Schmoo or Eggplant Man, 2", C6 [OP, R3-4]. **$30.00–45.00.** B. Charlie Chan, 2¾", C6, circa 1950 [R1]. **$400.00–450.00.** C. Two Friendly Men, 2" [OP, R1+]. **$400.00–450.00.** D. Roly-Poly Clown, 2¼", C6 [OP, R2]. **$80.00–90.00.**

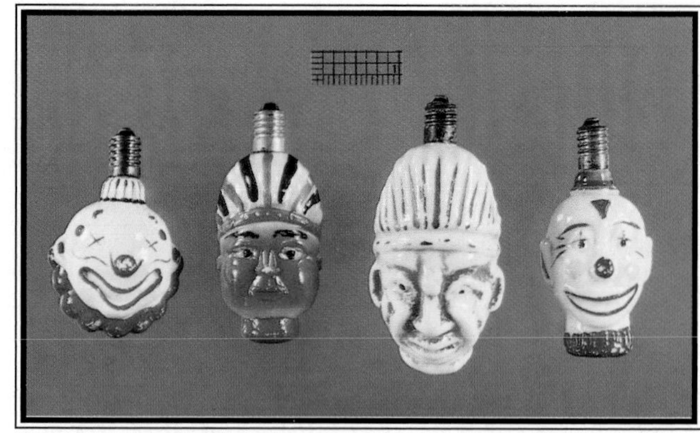

A. Clown Head, round, 1¾", C6, circa 1950 [R3]. **$50.00–60.00.** B. Indian Head, small, 2" [OP, R1]. **$175.00–200.00.** C. Indian Head, fierce, 2½", C6 [OP, R1]. **$125.00–150.00.** D. Clown Head with Neck, 2", C6 [OP, R3]. **$45.00–60.00.**

Early Clear Glass Figural Lights, all C6: A. Sitting Lion, 2¼" [OP, R1-2]. **$225.00–275.00.** B. European Sitting Cat with a Bow, 2½" [OP, R2]. **$80.00–100.00.** C & D. European Exhaust Tip Birds, 3" – 4", exhaust tip forms the beak [OP, R2-3]. **$45.00–75.00.** E. European Exhaust Tip Joey Clown Head, 2½" [OP, R1-2]. **$125.00–150.00.** F. Indian Chief, 3¼" [European, R1]. **$300.00–350.00.** G. Dwarf with a Shovel, 2½" [German, OP, R2]. **$150.00–175.00.** H. Judy Clown Head or Drama Face, double sided, 2½" [Japanese, OP, R2]. **$120.00–140.00.**

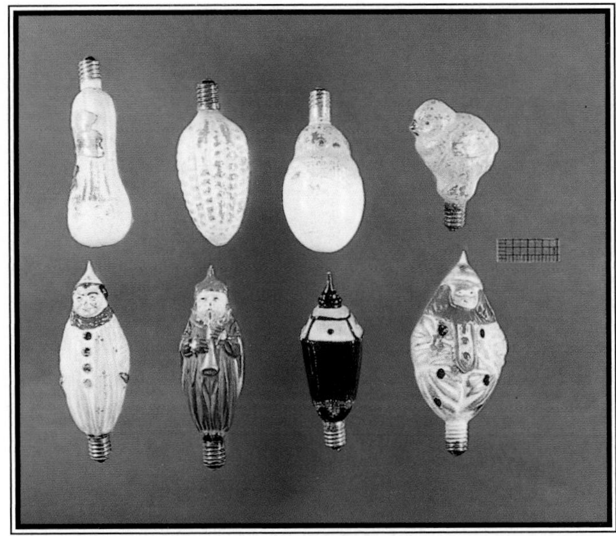

Early Clear Glass Lights, all C6: A. Long Squash, 2¾" [Japanese, OP, R2]. **$20.00–30.00.** B. Small Ear of Corn, 2¼", circa 1904 [European, R1-2]. **$225.00–250.00.** C. Chick in an Egg, 2¼", circa 1920 [Japanese, R1-2]. **$30.00–45.00.** D. Chick, 1½" [OP, R2]. **$25.00–35.00.** E. Exhaust Tip Clown, 3" [Hungarian, OP, R2]. **$65.00–80.00.** F. Exhaust Tip Horn Blower, 2¾" [European, OP, R2]. **$75.00–100.00.** G. Exhaust Tip Carriage Lantern, 2¼" [OP, R2-3]. **$50.00–75.00.** H. Exhaust Tip Fat Clown, 2¾", circa 1910 [European, R1-2]. **$100.00–125.00.**

Japanese Milk Glass Character Lights, all C6: A. Dutch Boy, 3" [NP(circa 1950), R2-3]. **$75.00–85.00.** B. Austrian Man with a Pipe, 2¾", also made in clear glass, circa 1925 – 1950 [R2]. **$15.00–20.00.** C. Doc from *Snow White*, 2¼", circa 1940 [R2]. **$100.00–125.00.** D. Kewpie with a Flapper Hat, 2¾", circa 1950 [R2-3]. **$50.00–65.00.** E. Tall Flapper Girl, 2¾", circa 1950 [Japanese, R2]. **$65.00–75.00.** F. Squatting Black Boy, 3¼", circa 1950 [R1-2]. **$65.00–75.00.** G. Clown Playing a Concertina, 3¼", circa 1935 – 1950 [R3]. **$30.00–40.00.** H. Large-headed Girl in a Snowsuit, 2¾" [OP, R2]. **$50.00–60.00.**

Early European Clear Glass Character Lights, all C6: A. Dwarf with a Shovel, 2½" [German, OP, R2]. **$150.00–175.00.** B. Putti Angel Head, 2¼" [German, OP, R1]. **$250.00–275.00.** C. Girl with a Trumpet, 2¾" [OP, R1]. **$175.00–200.00.**

Four Clear Glass Lamps, probably German: A. Putti Angel, 2¼" [OP, R1]. **$250.00–275.00.** B. Judy Drama Face, 2¼", C6, marked "German" [OP, R2]. **$120.00–140.00.** C & D. Two Versions of Comic Man in a Hat, 1¾", C6 [OP, R2]. **$160.00–175.00.**

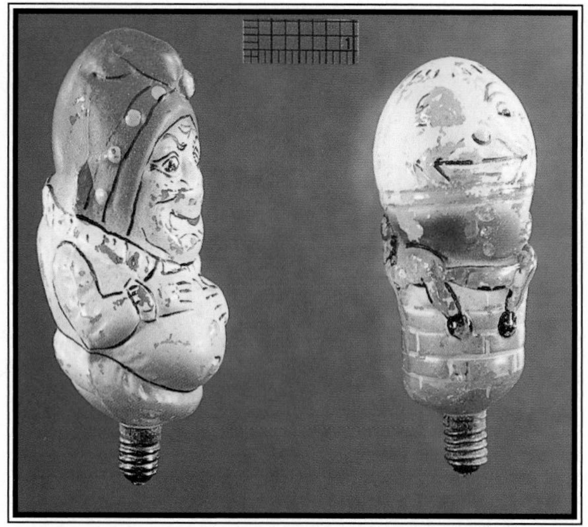

Two Early European Figural Lamps: A. Punch Clown, 3¼", C6 [OP, R2]. **$175.00–200.00.** B. Humpty Dumpty on a Wall, 3", C6 [European, OP, R2]. **$125.00–150.00.**

"Cartoon Character Christmas Tree Lights" Set, 2¼" – 2¾", all C6, circa 1955 [Japanese, R4]. **$30.00–35.00** each: A. Smitty. B. Moon Mullins. C. Andy Gump. D. Dick Tracy. E. Kayo. F. Little Orphan Annie. G. Sandy. H. Betty Boop.

A. Short Redheaded Woman, 2½", C6 [OP, R2]. **$50.00–60.00.** B. Wooden Doll, 2½", C6 [OP, R2]. **$70.00–90.00.** C. Wooden Soldier, 2½", C6 [OP, R2]. **$100.00–125.00.** D. Indian Chief, 2½", C6 [Japanese, OP, R1+]. **$125.00–150.00.**

Original box for "Cartoon Character Christmas Tree Lights." Complete boxed set, **$275.00–325.00.**

A. Smitty, 2¾" version, marked "@FAS," C6 [Japanese, NP (1955), R4]. **$30.00–35.00.** B. Clown with a Mask, 3", C6 [Japanese, NP(1950), R3-4]. **$20.00–25.00.** C. Kewpie with Large Head, large, 2½", milk glass, C6 [Japanese, NP(1950), R3-4]. **$25.00–35.00.**

A. Minstrel in Coat and Hat, 2¼", C6 [Japanese, OP, R3]. **$50.00–65.00.** B. Witch (Type II), milk glass, 2¾", C6 [OP, R2]. **$100.00–115.00.** C. Girl in a Pumpkin Dress, 2¾", C6 [NP(1950), R2]. **$75.00–100.00.** D. Girl with a Muff, 2¾", C6 [Japanese, NP(1950), R4-5]. **$15.00–20.00.**

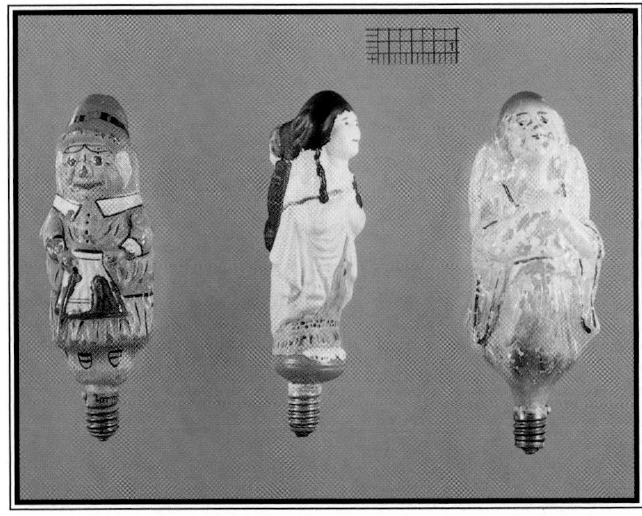

A. Witch, 3", C6 [German, OP, R1]. **$200.00–225.00.** B. Indian Woman with a Papoose, 3", C6 [German, OP, R1]. **$350.00–400.00.** C. Angel with Crossed Arms, 3¼", C6 [German, OP, R1]. **$200.00–250.00.**

This picture shows the reverse side of each head in the preceding picture. They are in the same order: A. Man in Glasses. B. Native. C. Worried Woman. D. Grotesque Face.

A. Statue of Liberty, 4½", C6 [OP, R1+]. **$750.00–850.00.** B. Miss Liberty, 3¼", C6 [OP, R1]. **$275.00–325.00.**

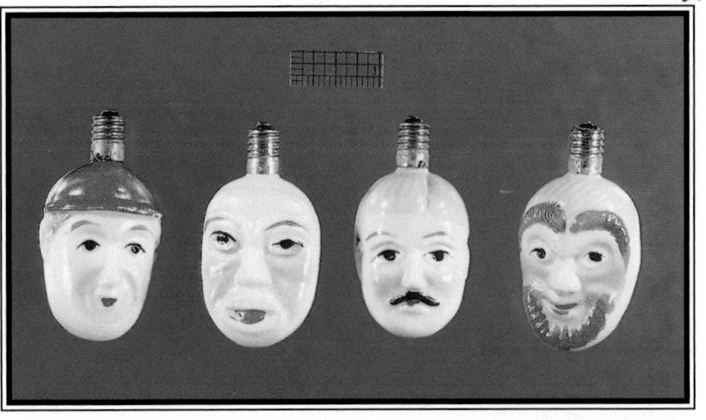

Double-faced Egg-shaped Heads, all circa 1950 [Japanese, R2]. **$150.00–175.00** each: A. Man in a Cap, 1¾". B. Droopy Face, 1¾". C. Mustached Gentleman, 1¾". D. Satyr Face, double sided, 1¾".

A. John Bull, 3", C6 [German, OP, R1]. **$200.00–225.00.** B. Martha Washington, 3", C6 [German, OP, R1]. **$250.00–275.00.**

Statue of Liberty, standard base, 10" overall [OP, R1+]. **$1,700.00–2,000.00.**

Soldier with an American Flag, 2¼", C6 [OP, R1+]. **$425.00–500.00.**

Howdy Doody Lights [Japan, NP(1955)]. **$200.00–250.00** each: A. Mr. Bluster, 2½", C7 [R2]. B. Princess Summerfall Winterspring, 2", C7 [R2]. C. Howdy Doody, 2", C7 [R2]. D. Dilly Dally, 2" [R2]. Claribell (missing), 2" [R1+]. **$300.00–350.00.** Boxed set, **$3,000.00.**

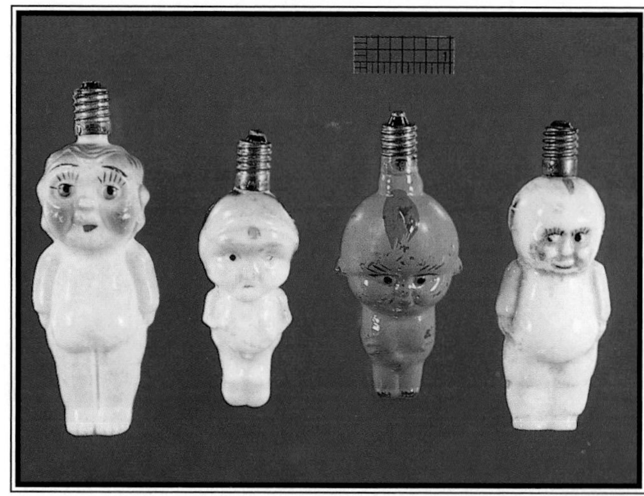

A. Kewpie with Wavy Hair, 3", C6 [OP, R4]. **$50.00–60.00.** B. Kewpie Boy with Cap (anatomically correct), 2", C6 [OP, R4]. **$25.00–35.00.** C large-headed Kewpie,, clear glass, 2¼", C6 [NP(1950), R3-4]. **$25.00–35.00.** D. Standard Kewpie, milk glass, 2½", C6 [OP, R4]. **$25.00–35.00.**

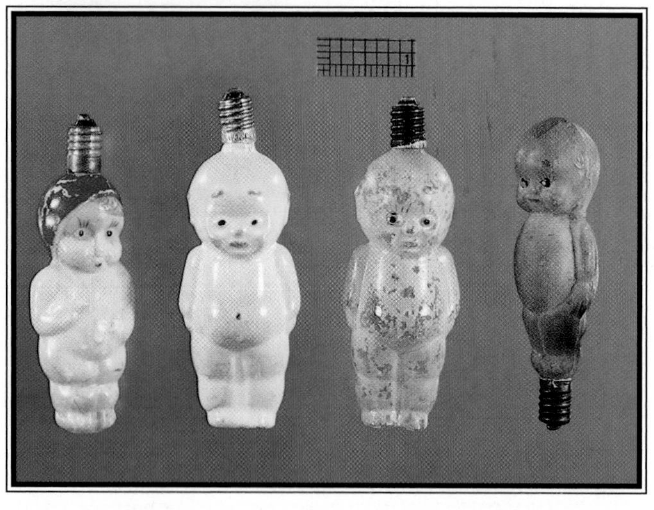

A. Kewpie Girl with Hat, 2½", C6 [OP, R4]. **$25.00–35.00.** B. Standard Kewpie, milk glass, 2¾", C6 [OP, R4]. **$25.00–35.00.** C. Standard Kewpie, clear glass, 2¾" [OP, R4]. **$30.00–50.00.** D. Standard Kewpie, clear glass, bottom base, 2½", C6 [OP, R4]. **$70.00–100.00.**

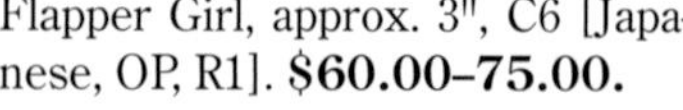

Flapper Girl, approx. 3", C6 [Japanese, OP, R1]. **$60.00–75.00.**

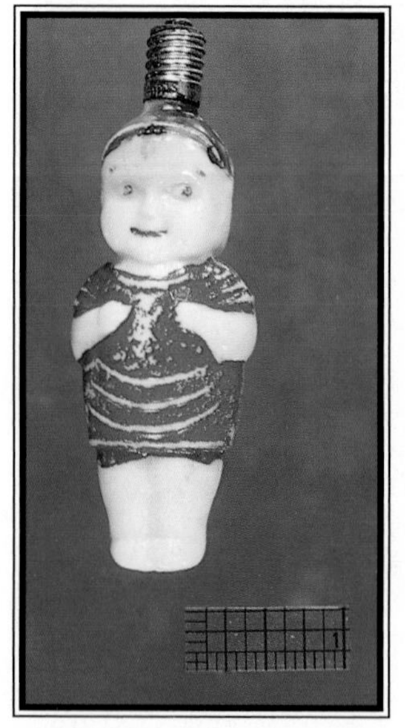

A. Zeppelin (Type II), 2¼", C6 [NP(1950), R2]. **$75.00–100.00.** B. Square Car, 2¼", C6 [NP(1950), R2]. **$100.00–125.00.** C. King's Head, comic, 2½", C6 [OP, R1]. **$275.00–300.00.** D. Clown on a Ball, 2¼", C6 [NP(1950), R2]. **$100.00–125.00.** E. Child Riding Swan, 2", C6 [NP(1950), R1]. **$150.00–175.00.**

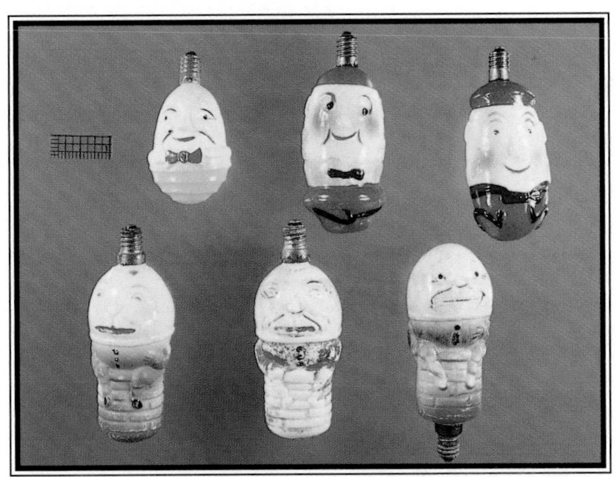

Five versions of Humpty Dumpty: A. Ribbed Bottom, 2", C6 [OP, R3]. **$100.00–125.00.** B. High Collar, 2¾", C6 [NP(1950), R4]. **$25.00–30.00.** C. Hat, 2¾", C6 [NP(1950), R4]. **$25.00–30.00.** D. Version on a Wall, 3", C6 [OP, R4]. **$25.00–30.00.** E & F. Version on a Wall, 3", C6 [OP, R4]. **$25.00–30.00.**

Paramount Nursery Rhyme Boxed Set, with light string [OP, R1]. **$225.00–250.00.**

Deluxe Nursery Rhyme Set, circa 1950, all approx. 2¾"H or 2¾"W, Japanese. The Metal Base is marked with an *H* in a diamond shape: A. Old Woman in a Shoe [R3]. **$50.00–75.00.** B. Tom, Tom the Piper's Son [R1]. **$175.00–200.00.** C. Mother Goose [R3]. **$50.00–60.00.** D. Humpty Dumpty [R1]. **$200.00–225.00.** E. Bo Peep [R1]. **$175.00–200.00.** F. Jack Horner [R1]. **$175.00–200.00.** G. Jack and Jill [R1]. **$175.00–200.00.** H. Old Mother Hubbard [R1]. **$175.00–200.00.**

Paramount Nursery Rhyme Set, 2¼" – 2¾", sold both individually and as sets, circa 1937 and 1955, all C6 [Japanese, OP]: A. Old Woman in a Shoe [R4]. **$15.00–25.00.** B. "Four and Twenty Blackbirds" King [R4]. **$15.00–20.00.** C. Three Men in a Tub [R3]. **$25.00–35.00.** D. Humpty Dumpty [R4]. **$15.00–25.00.** E. Little Boy Blue [R4]. **$15.00–25.00.** F. Red Riding Hood [R4]. **$15.00–25.00.** G. Mother Goose [R4]. **$15.00–25.00.** H. Queen of Hearts [R4]. **$15.00–25.00.**

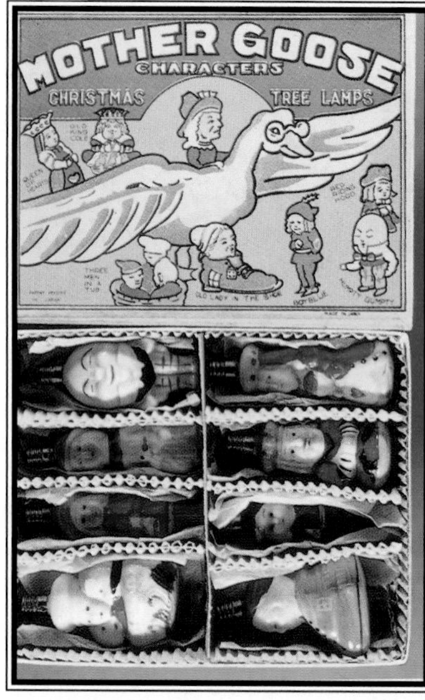

Paramount Set Generically Marketed, sold individually without light string, with lights [OP, R1]. **$175.00-200.00.**

Egg-shaped Nursery Rhyme Set, 2" – 2½", Japanese, circa 1955: A. Cat and the Fiddle [R2-3]. **$35.00-40.00.** B. Jack Horner [R2-3]. **$35.00-40.00.** C. Mother Goose [R2-3]. **$35.00-40.00.** D. Three Bears, 2½" [R2-3]. **$35.00-40.00.** E. Song of Six Pence [R2-3]. **$35.00-40.00.**

Egg-Shaped Nursery Rhyme Set (continued): A. Cow Jumping Over the Moon, 2¼" [R2-3]. **$35.00-40.00.** B. Little Boy Blue, 2¼" [R2-3]. **$35.00-40.00.** C. Little Red Riding Hood, 2¼" [R2-3]. **$35.00-40.00.** D. Humpty Dumpty, 2¼" [R2-3]. **$35.00-40.00.** E. King Cole, 2¼" [R2-3]. **$35.00-40.00.** Complete Set of 10 in original box [R1+], **$750.00-850.00.**

Alps Snow White Set, 2¼" – 2¾", C6 [Japanese, OP, R1+]. "Alps" is embossed on their backs; Dopey is missing. **$100.00-125.00** each. Complete Set in Original Box, **$1,000.00-1,200.00.**

Our Gang "Set." Each piece is **$100.00-125.00:** A. Darla, 2¾", C6 [Japanese, R2-3]. B. Alfalfa, 2¾", C6 [Japanese, R2-3]. C. Baby Patsy, 2½", C6 [Japanese, R2-3]. D. Jean Darling, 2½", C6 [Japanese, R2-3].

A. Santa Head in a Large Chimney (Type I), 2½", C6 [OP, R4]. **$15.00–20.00.** B. Santa with a Bag, Toys, and a Tree (Type I), marked with box and triangle, standard base [OP, R4]. **$50.00–75.00.** C. Santa Standing by Chimney, 2½", C6 [OP, R3-4]. **$15.00–20.00.** D. Common Santa, double sided, staff and bag, small, 2½", "MHK," C6 [OP-NP, R5]. **$10.00–15.00.** E. Santa Holding a Bag, double sided, 3"H, C6 [OP, R3]. **$15.00–20.00.**

A. Santa, double sided, common, 2½", C6 [OP-NP, R5]. **$10.00–15.00.** B. Santa Head, large, single sided, 2¾", C7½" [OP, R4]. **$20.00–25.00.** C. Santa with a Bag, small, 2¼", C6 [OP, R4]. **$10.00–15.00.** D & E. Snowman with a Bag, milk and clear glass, 2½" [OP, R5]. **$10.00–12.00.**

Mazda C9 Santas [all OP, R3]: A. 2½". **$35.00–45.00.** B. 3¼". **$50.00–75.00.** C. 2¼". **$30.00–35.00.**

Double-faced Lights: A. Girl's Head, 1¾", C6 [OP, R3]. **$20.00–25.00.** B. Santa Head, large, double sided, 2¾", C6 [OP, R4]. **$25.00–30.00.** C. Common Santa Head, double sided, 2"H, C6 [OP-NP, R4-5]. **$10.00–15.00.**

A. Santa on Top of a House, 2¼", C6 [OP, R3]. **$75.00–85.00.** B. Santa with a Satchel and a Tree, 4½", C6 [OP, R1-2]. **$100.00–125.00.** C. Santa Kneeling on a Disk, 2", C6 [NP (1950), R3]. **$75.00–85.00.** D. Santa Face on a Lantern, 2½", C6 [1950, R3-4]. **$50.00–60.00.** E. Santa Head in Small Chimney, 2½", C6 [OP, R2]. **$100.00–125.00.** All made in Japan.

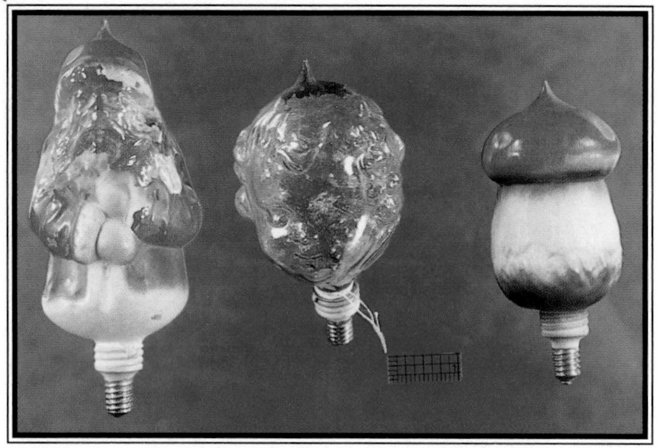

Rare German Lights: A. Santa with a Tree, large, exhaust tip, 4", C6 [OP, R1]. **$300.00–325.00.** B. Girl/Doll Head, exhaust tip, 2¾", C6 [OP, R1]. **$350.00–400.00.** C. Mushroom, large, exhaust tip, 2¾", C6 [OP, R1]. **$250.00–300.00.**

Milk Glass Santas, all C6, all Japanese: A. Santa Head in a Chimney (Type I), 2¼" [R4]. **$15.00–20.00.** B. Santa Face in a Pine Cone. C, E, F. Variations of Small Standing Santa with a Bag, all 3¾" [R4]. **$10.00–15.00.** D. Three-faced Santa Head. 2¼" [Japan, R2]. **$25.00–35.00.** G. Common Santa, 2½" (shown) & 3½", can be found as a double-sided piece, circa 1930 – 1950 [R4-5]. One sided, **$10.00–15.00.** Large, **$14.00–18.00.** Double sided, **$15.00–20.00.** H. Large Santa with a Bag, 3¾" [R4]. **$15.00–20.00.**

Early Clear Glass Santas, all have C6 base: A. Santa with Hands in His Sleeves, small, 2½", circa 1920 [R2]. **$75.00–100.00.** B. Exhaust Tip St. Nicholas (Type II), 3", circa 1915 [R2]. **$100.00–125.00.** C. Large Mazda Santa, 5½", circa 1920. There is a long tubular light bulb inside [American, R1]. **$275.00–300.00.** D. Green-coated Santa with Exhaust Tip, also called St. Patrick, 2¾", C6, circa 1920 [Austrian, R2]. **$125.00–150.00.** E. Exhaust Tip St. Nicholas (Type I fat), 2¾", circa 1915 [European, R2]. **$100.00–125.00.** F. Exhaust Tip St. Nicholas (Type I slender), 2¾" [Japan, circa 1920, R2]. **$100.00–125.00.** G. St. Nicholas without Exhaust Tip, 2¾", circa 1920 [Japanese, R2]. **$75.00–90.00.** H. Santa with His Hands in His Sleeves, large, 2¾", circa 1920 [R2]. **$100.00–125.00.** I. St. Nicholas in Robes, 3" [Japanese, circa 1920, R2]. **$35.00–45.00.**

A. Santa Emerging from a Round Chimney, 3¼", C6 [OP, R2]. **$50.00–75.00.** B. Santa Head in a Large Chimney (Type I), 2", C6 [OP, R4]. **$15.00–20.00.** C. Santa Head in a Large Chimney (Type II), 2", C6 [OP, R5]. **$15.00–20.00.** D. Santa Stepping from a Square Chimney, 3", C6 [R3]. **$55.00–65.00.**

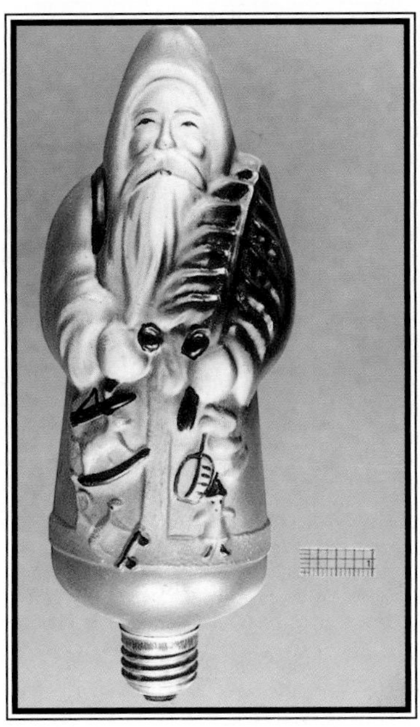

Large Hooded Santa with Tree and Toys, 7¼", standard base [R4]. **$125.00–150.00.**

Four Standard Base Santas, Japanese: A. Chunky Santa, 4¼" [R3]. **$75.00–100.00.** B. Santa with a Satchel and a Tree, 4" [R1]. **$125.00–150.00.** C. Santa with a Bag, Toys, and a Tree (Type I), 4½" [R4]. **$50.00–75.00.** D. Santa with a Bag, Toys, and a Tree (Type II), 4¼" [R4]. **$50.00–75.00.**

Six Stars: A. Spiked, C6 [OP, R3]. **$25.00–35.00.** B. Star with a Crescent Moon, 2", C6 [Japanese, NP(1950, R4]. **$15.00–20.00.** C. Mazda Star, 1¾", C6 [American, OP, R3]. **$20.00–25.00.** D. Star, common, 1¾", C6 [OP-NP, R5]. **$4.00–5.00.** E. Star with a Santa Face, 2", C6 [Japanese, NP(1950), R3]. **$55.00–65.00.** F. Star with a Smiling Face, 2", C6 [Japanese, NP(1950), R4]. **$25.00–30.00.**

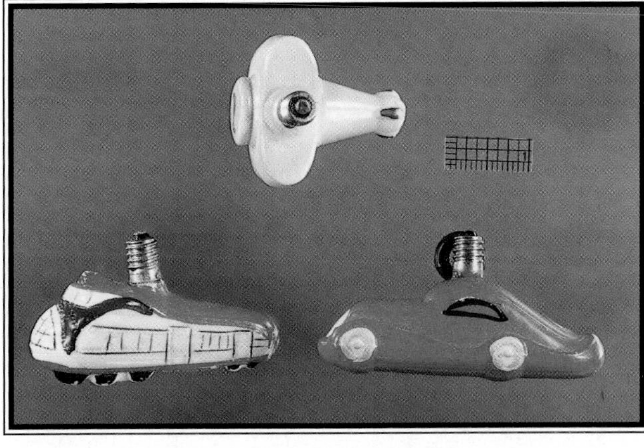

A. Airplane, 2", C6 [NP(1950), R1+]. **$400.00–450.00.** B. Train, 2¾", C6 [NP(1950), R1+]. **$350.00–375.00.** C. Sleek Roadster, 3¼"L, C6 [NP(1950), R1-2]. **$175.00–225.00.**

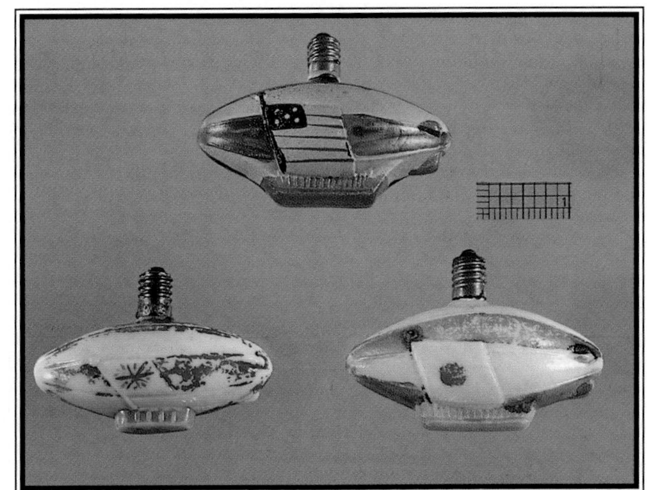

Zeppelins: A. American, clear glass, large, 2¾", C6 [OP, R4]. **$35.00–50.00.** B. British, 2", C6 [OP, R1]. **$200.00–225.00.** C. Japanese, 2¾", C6 [OP, R1]. **$200.00–225.00.** Note: All have different molding; this is the most noticeable in their gondolas.

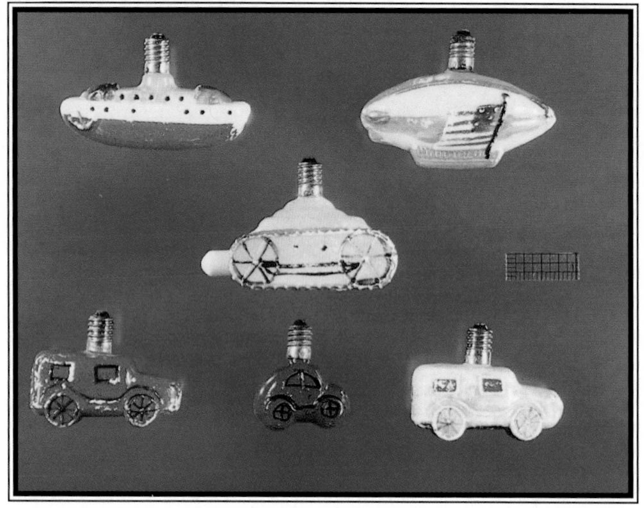

Transportation Lights: A. Ocean Liner, 2¾", C6, circa 1950 [Japanese, R1]. **$125.00–135.00.** B. Dirigible with the American Flag, large, 2¾", C6, circa 1925 – 1950 [Japanese, R3-4]. **$40.00–50.00.** C. World War I Tank, 2½", C6, circa 1950 [Japanese, R1]. **$175.00–200.00.** D & F. Square car, 2¼", C6, circa 1950 [Japanese, R1-2]. **$100.00–125.00.** E. Miniature Car, 1¼", C6, circa 1950 [Japanese, R3-4]. **$50.00–60.00.**

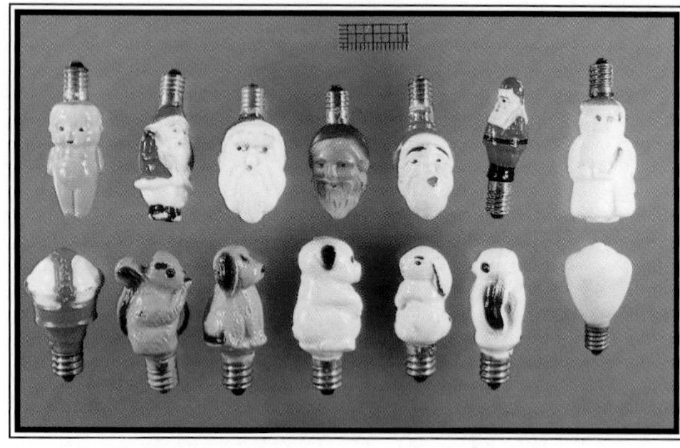

Miniature Lights I, all 1¼" – 1½": A. Kewpie Doll. **$20.00–25.00.** B. Santa with a Bag, double. **$20.00–25.00.** C. Common Santa Head. **$20.00–25.00.** D & E. Santa Head, double face. **$20.00–25.00.** F. Santa with a Pack. **$20.00–25.00.** G. Snowman with a Club. **$20.00–25.00.** H. Crown. **$65.00–75.00.** I. Squirrel Eating a Nut. **$50.00–75.00.** J. Sitting Spaniel. **$50.00–75.00.** K. Sitting Pig. **$50.00–75.00.** L. Begging Rabbit. **$50.00–75.00.** M. Penguin. **$50.00–75.00.** N. Street Light. **$20.00–25.00.**

Miniature Lights II: A. Drum. **$30.00–35.00.** B. Acorn. **$20.00–25.00.** C. Santa Face on Diamond. **$50.00–75.00.** D. Indian Head. **$65.00–75.00.** E. Snow-covered Lantern. **$20.00–25.00.** F. Snow-covered House. **$20.00–25.00.** G. Log Cabin. **$20.00–25.00.** H. Owl. **$20.00–30.00.** I. Sitting Bear. **$20.00–25.00.** J. Rabbit in a Suit. **$30.00–35.00.** K. Fish. **$45.00–55.00.** L. Sitting Dog, **$25.00–35.00.** M. Monkey Head, double. **$20.00–30.00.** N. Bird in a Cage. **$45.00–65.00.**

Miniature Lights III: A. Car. **$50.00–60.00.** B. Baby in a Stocking. **$25.00–30.00.** C. Santa with a Bag, double sided. **$20.00–25.00.** D. Santa Head. **$20.00–30.00.** E. Santa at a Chimney. **$20.00–30.00.** F. Geometric Shape. **$15.00–20.00.** G. Beach Ball. **$20.00–25.00.** H. Candle. **$15.00–20.00.** I. Parrot. **$15.00–20.00.** J. Begging Bulldog (Type II). **$25.00–30.00.** K. Cat Playing a Mandolin, **$25.00–35.00.** L. Hound Dog in Round Basket. **$20.00–30.00.** M. Polar Bear. **$20.00–25.00.** N. Candle. **$15.00–20.00.**

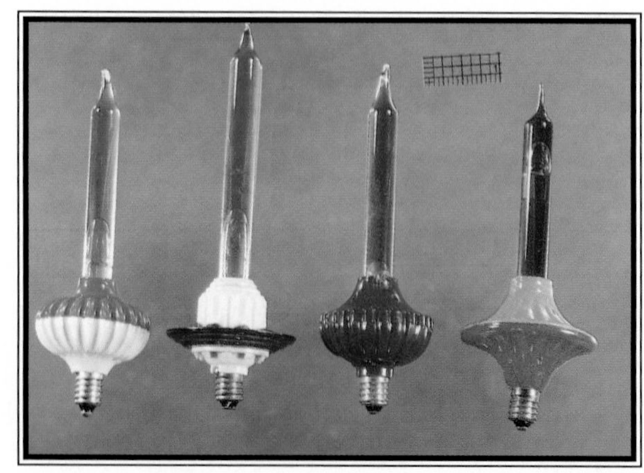

Bubble Lights: A. Noma Biscuit, C6, 1946–1960, also made by GloLite, Yule-Glo, and Amico [R5]. **$5.00–7.00.** B. Paramount Kristal Animated Snow (fluid is a thick oil that produces tiny bubbles), 1947 – 1948 [R2]. **$50.00–65.00.** C. Royal, C6, 1947 – 1954 [R5]. **$5.00–7.00.** D. Noma '48, flat, 1948 – 1949 [R4]. **$5.00–7.00.**

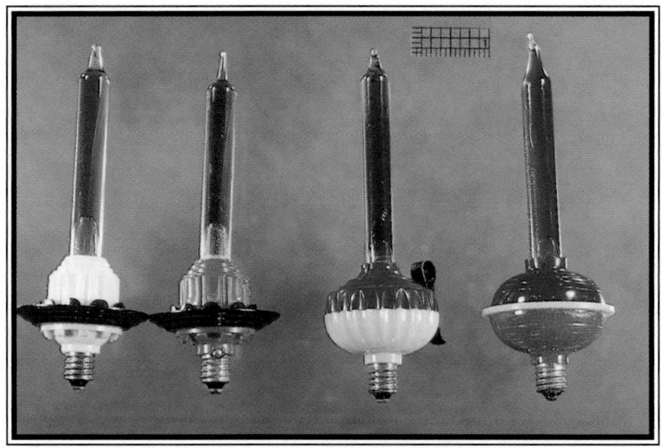

Bubble Lights: A. Made by Paramount and Sterling, oil [R2]. **$35.00–45.00.** B. Made by Paramount and Sterling, methelene chloride, 1948 – 1950 [R3-4]. **$9.00–12.00.** C. Peerless and Good-Lite Shooting Star, 1948 [R2]. **$80.00–100.00.** D. Made by Renown, Gem, and Everlite and Santa, 1948–1957 [R3]. Tricolor, **$15.00–25.00.**

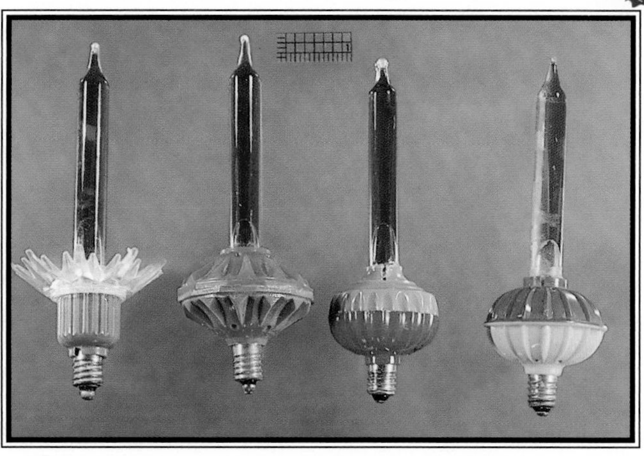

Bubble Lights, C6: A. Reliance Spark-L-Light, 1949 – 1951 [R4]. **$12.00–18.00.** B. USA Lite, 1949 – 1956; and ACLA, 1973 – 1978 [R3]. **$5.00–8.00.** C. Peerless, 1950 – 1955 [R3-4]. **$5.00–7.00.** D. Paramount Biscuit, 1951 – 1972 [R5]. **$4.00–7.00.**

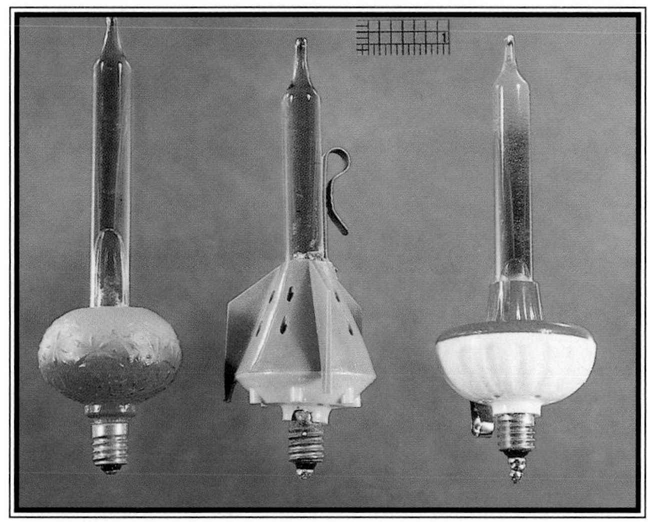

Bubble Lights, C6: A. Alps, glass base, 1954 [R1]. Working, **$60.00–80.00.** Not Working, **$4.00–5.00.** B. Noma Rocket, 1961 – 1962 [R2-3]. **$20.00–30.00.** C. Holly-Noma World Wide, 1957 – 1974 [R5]. **$4.00–6.00.**

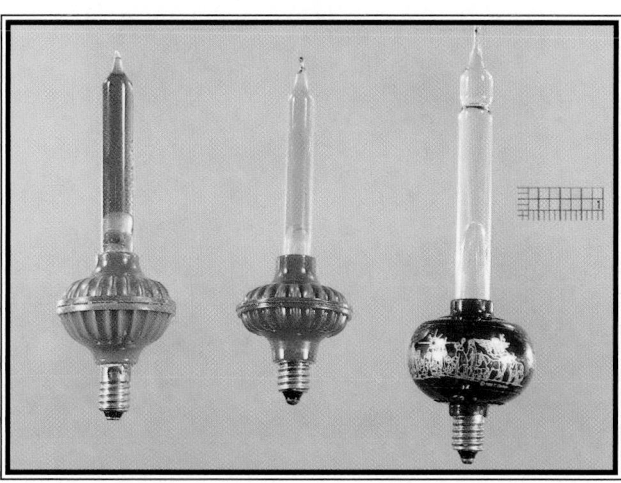

Bubble Lights, C6: A. World Wide, 1970 [R4]. **$4.00–6.00.** B. World Wide, 1973 – 1974 [R4]. **$3.00–5.00.** C. Carlisle, 1990 [R2-3]. **$8.00–10.00.**

Bubble Light Snap-ons for C6 or C7: A. Noma Snap-on, circa 1949–1950 [R3-4]. **$10.00–15.00.** B. Holly Berries and Leaves Snap-on, circa 1950; by Seda, Polly, and Spark-L-Light [R1]. **$70.00–80.00.** C. Clemco Snap-on, circa 1950 [R1-2]. **$70.00–85.00.**

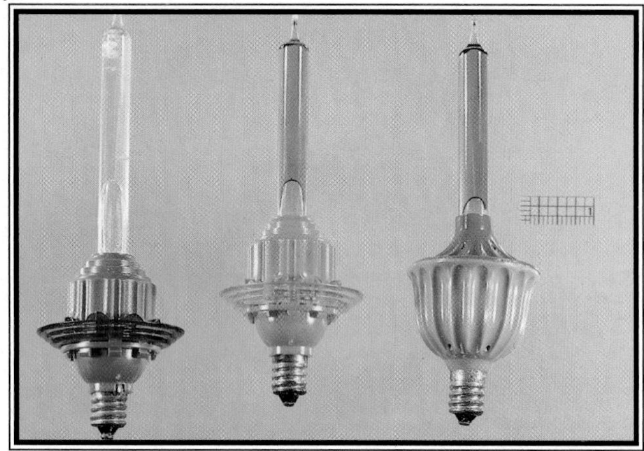

Bubble Lights: A. Paramount, C7, oil, circa 1947–1948 [R1-2]. **$40.00–50.00.** B. Paramount, methelene chloride, 1948–1950 [R3-4]. **$10.00–12.00.** C. Noma C7 Tulip, circa 1948–1960 [R5]. **$9.00–12.00.**

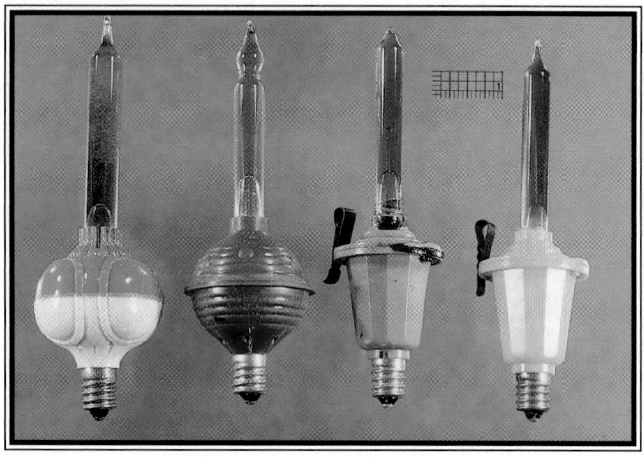

Bubble Lights: (*C & D* were made by Goodlite, Peerless, and Others): A. Royal, C7, circa 1948 – 1954 [R4-5]. **$14.00–18.00.** B. Renown and Gem, C7, 1948 – 1970 [R3-4]. **$5.00–7.00.** C. Shooting Star, 1948 [R1-2]. **$65.00–80.00.** D Methelene Chloride, Peerless, 1950–1955; made by others until 1963 [R3-4]. **$6.00–9.00.**

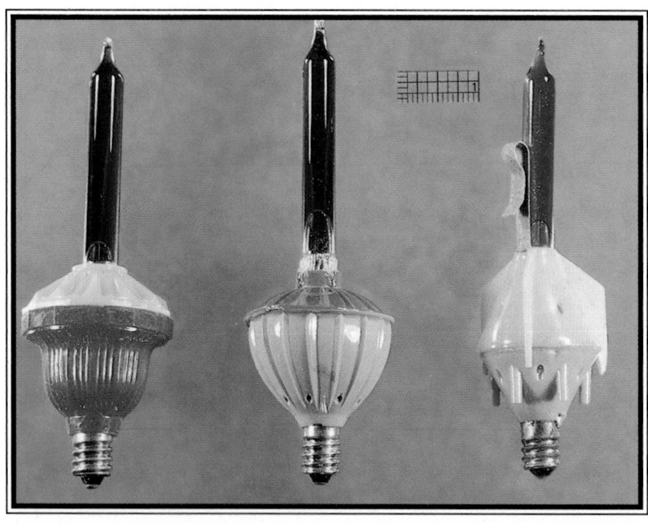

Bubble Lights: A. Made by USA Lite, 1949 – 1956 [R3]. **$6.00–8.00.** B. Paramount C7 Tulip, circa 1959 – 1972 [R5]. **$4.00–6.00.** C. Noma Rocket, C7, circa 1961 – 1962 [R2]. **$20.00–30.00.**

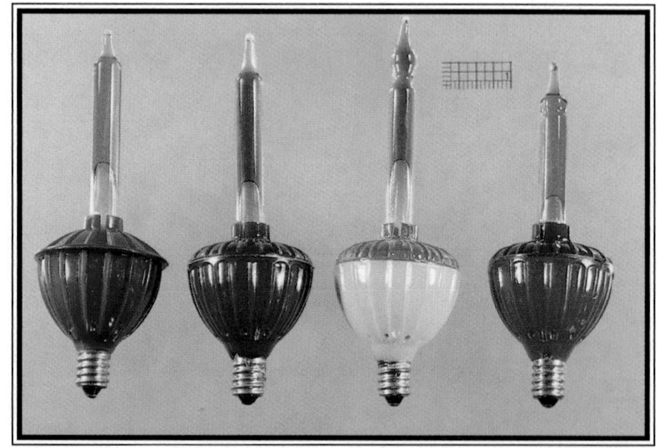

Bubble Lights: A & B. Noma, C7, circa 1976– 1977 [R5]. **$1.00–2.00.** C. Noma, C7, circa 1978 – 1988 [R5]. **$1.00–2.00.** D. Noma, C7, 1988 [R4]. **$1.00–2.00.**

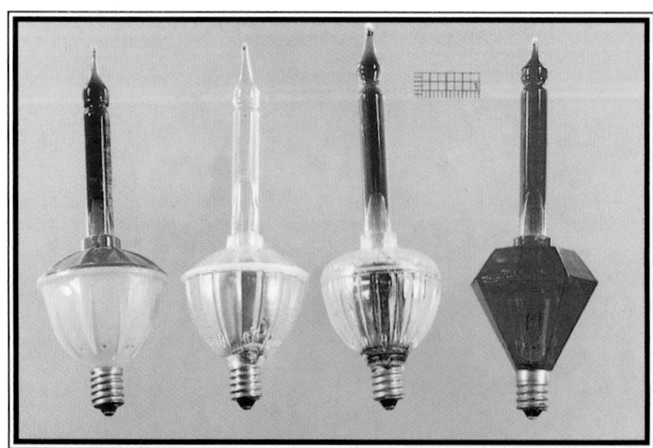

Bubble Lights [all R4]. **$1.50–2.50** each: A & B. Both Noma, 1988. C. GDK, 1988. D. Sterling, 1988.

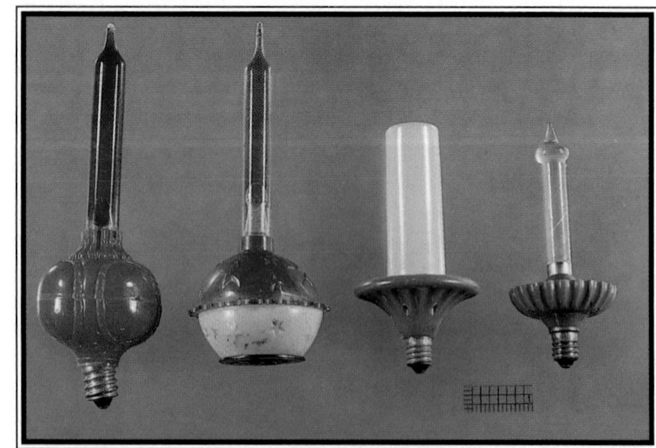

A. Royal, 1948 – 1954, C7 [R4-5]. **$14.00–18.00.** B. Noma Snap-on [R3-4]. **$10.00–15.00.** C. Noma Candle-lites, 3¾" [OP, R2-3]. **$8.00–9.00.** D. Glass Glolite Candle, 3" [OP, R3-4]. **$10.00–15.00.**

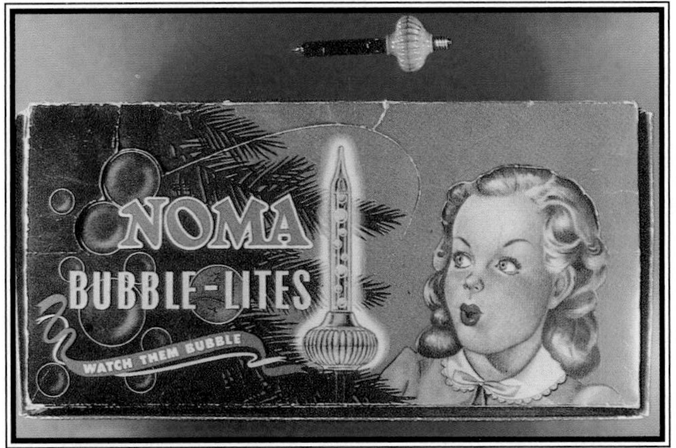

Noma Bubble-Lites Boxed Set. This is the classic Noma box with the girl on the lid. The set contains eight lights and the electric cord. American made, circa 1948 – 1949 [R3]. If all lights are working and in good condition, **$55.00–75.00.**

Noma Bubble-Lites Boxed Set. This is a later Noma box. The set contains eight lights and the electric cord. American made, circa 1950 [R3]. If all lights are working and in good condition, **$55.00–75.00.**

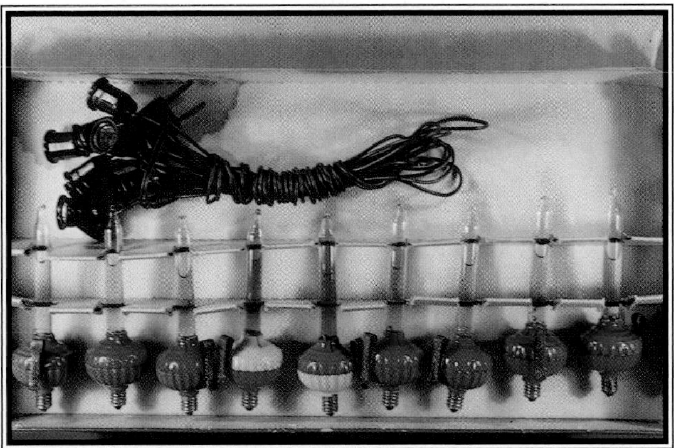

Goodlite Shooting Star Bubbling Lights Boxed Set. The set contains nine lights and the electric cord. Colored tubes are more valuable than the clear. This set contains seven colored tubes. American made, circa 1948 [R1]. Set of nine in original box, **$750.00–1,000.00.**

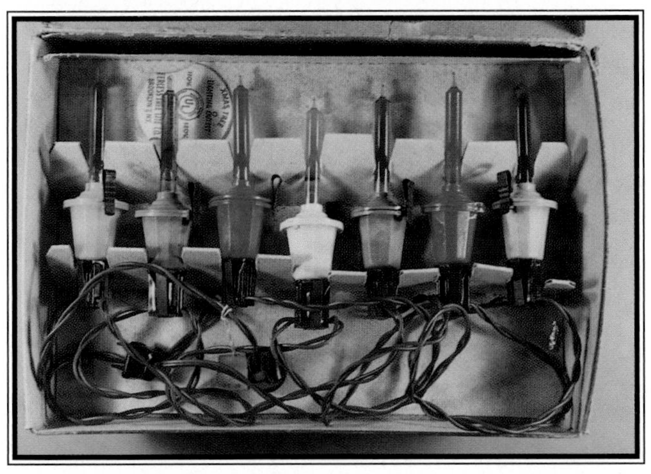

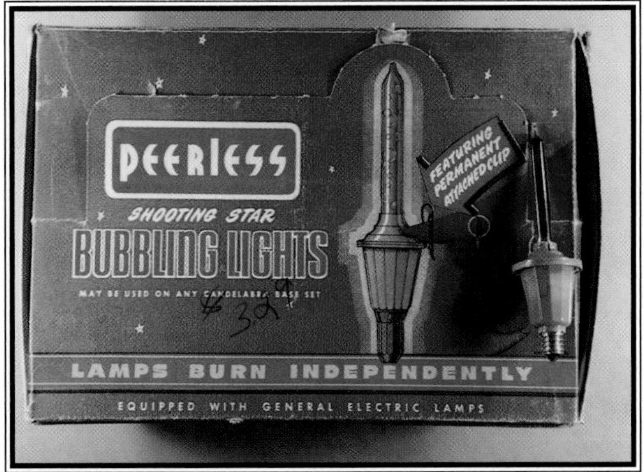

Peerless Shooting Star Bubbling Lights Boxed Set. This C7 set contains seven lights and the electric cord. Circa 1948. Boxed set of seven, all working [R1], **$500.00–600.00.** Individual lights, **$65.00–85.00** each.

Holly Bubbling Lights Boxed Set, contains eight lights and a cord. Holly was a branch of Noma. Circa 1957. Boxed set of eight in working order [R2], **$65.00–85.00.**

Boxed Set of World Wide Bubble Lites. Although these were C6 bulbs, they were produced in 1970. There were three lights in the box. World Wide was a subsidiary of Noma. Original boxes are harder to find than the lights [R3-4]. Individual light, **$3.00–5.00.** Boxed set, **$15.00–20.00.**

Celluloid Lights, C6: A. Bear in a Dress, 3¾" [OP, R2]. **$70.00–80.00.** B. Baby in a Bath Tub, 3" [OP, R1-2]. **$75.00–80.00.** C. Boy Clown, 5" [OP, R1]. **$80.00–85.00.** D. Sailor Boy Holding a Parrot, 4" [OP, R2-3]. **$45.00–50.00.** Caution: These have a lower voltage than most lights and usually operated on a battery system.

Celluloid Lights; these light covers are made of celluloid plastic. C6: A. Rooster, 2½" [OP, R2]. **$50.00–60.00.** B. Circus Elephant, 2½" [OP, R1]. **$75.00–85.00.** C. Fruit Basket, small, 2" [OP, R1-2]. **$50.00–60.00.** D. Walking Dog, 3¾" [OP, R1]. **$65.00–75.00.**

Early Celluloid Lights with Wooden Battery Connection: A. Kewpie Doll with a Pointed Hat, 3¾". **$60.00–70.00.** B. Large Swan, 3½". **$35.00–45.00.** C. Waving Santa with a Lantern, 4¼". **$35.00–45.00.** D. Santa with a Bag of Toys, 3". **$45.00–50.00.** E. Small Fish, 2½". **$35.00–45.00.** F. Large Parrot, 4½". **$50.00–60.00.** G. Goat, 3¾". **$40.00–50.00.**

Celluloid Lights, all C6 [OP, R2]: A. Apple, 1¾". **$25.00-35.00.** B. Pear, 2¼". **$25.00-35.00.** C. Standing Stork, 3". **$50.00-60.00.** D. Bunch of Grapes, 2". **$30.00-35.00.** E. Sailor Boy Holding a Parrot, 4". **$40.00-50.00.** F. Rabbit in Clothes Playing a Concertina, 4¾". **$50.00-75.00.** G. Small Swan, 2½". **$25.00-35.00.** H. Small Parrot, 3¾". **$30.00-35.00.**

Dresden Light Covers: A. Bunch of Grapes (Type II), 4" [OP, R1-2]. **$60.00-75.00.** B. Bunch of Grapes (Type I), 3½" [OP, R2]. **$55.00-65.00.** C. Ball of Yarn, 3" [OP, R1]. **$50.00-70.00.**

Dresden Light Covers: A. Cat, 4" [OP, R2]. **$90.00-110.00.** B. Face in a Pine Cone, 4¼" [OP, R2]. **$90.00-100.00.**

Dresden Light Covers: A. Sunburst, small, 2¾" [OP, R2]. **$50.00-60.00.** B. Basket of Fruit, 3" [OP, R2-3]. **$60.00-85.00.**

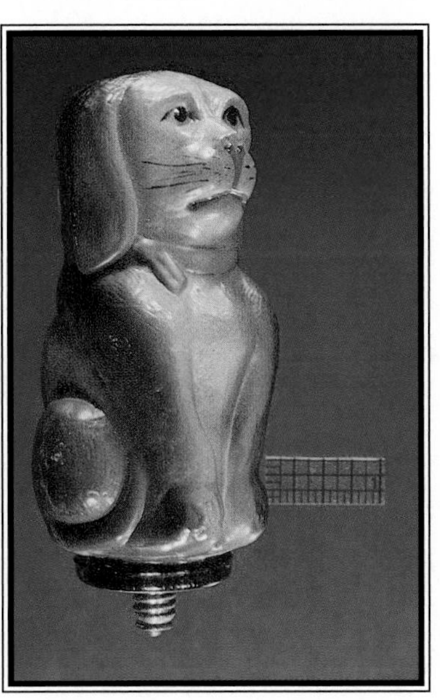

Dresden Dog Light Cover, 3¾" [OP, R2]. **$90.00-100.00.** Dresden light covers were marketed in 1927. The hollow glass covers were a product of Dresden, Germany, and assembled in the U.S. by Noma. The lights were sold indavidually and as a set of eight.

Dresden Light Covers: A. Rose, 2½" [OP, R2-3]. **$60.00–75.00.** B. Trumpet Flower, 3¼" [OP, R2-3]. **$60.00–75.00.**

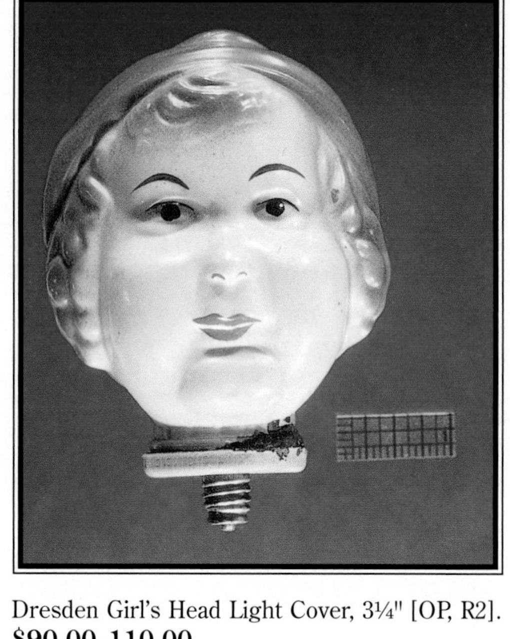

Dresden Girl's Head Light Cover, 3¼" [OP, R2]. **$90.00–110.00.**

Dresden Light Covers: A. Santa in a Long Coat (Type I), 6" [OP, R1]. **$150.00–200.00.** B. Santa in a Short Coat (Type I), 5½" [OP, R1+]. **$300.00–350.00.** C. Santa in a Long Coat (Type II), 6¼" [OP, R1]. **$200.00–250.00.**

Dresden Light Covers: A. Orange, 3½" [OP, R1]. **$175.00–200.00.** B. Snow-covered Lantern, 3½" [OP, R1]. **$175.00–200.00.**

Plastic and Metal Light Covers: A. Paramount Plastic Star, 2¾", C6, 1948 [R4-5]. **$4.00–5.00.** B. Kristal Star Tree Top, 4½", C6 [OP, R4]. **$15.00–20.00.** C. Paramount Metal Star, 3¼", C6 [OP, R3-4]. **$12.00–20.00.** D. Kristal Star, 2¾", C6 [OP, R4]. **$5.00–8.00.** E. Paramount Starlight, 2", C6, 1948 [R4]. **$4.00–6.00.**

Matchless Wonder Stars, C6: Top row, Single Row of Rays [OP-NP (2002), R3-4]. **$35.00–50.00.** Bottom row, Double Row of Rays [OP-NP(2002), R2-3]. **$125.00–165.00.**

A, C, D. Paramount Starlight, 2", C6, 1948 [R4]. **$4.00–6.00.** B. Star of Bethlehem Light, 4", C6 [NP, R2-3]. **$5.00–10.00.**

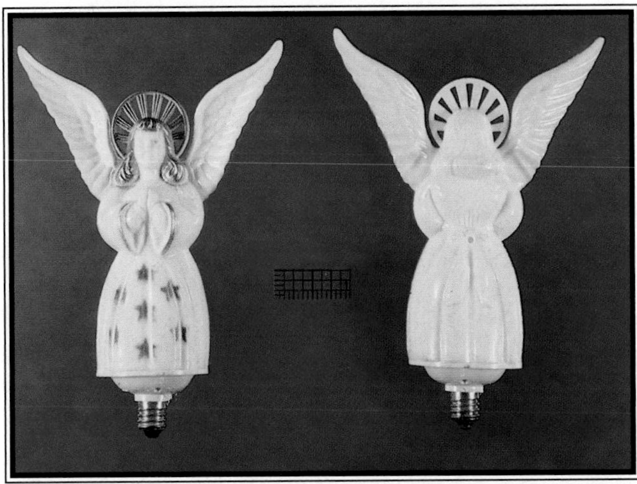

Angel Light with Widespread Wings, approx. 5½". Front and back views are shown. The plastic was made by Bradford Novelty; it is unknown who electrified the light. American, circa 1950 [R2-3]. **$12.00–18.00.**

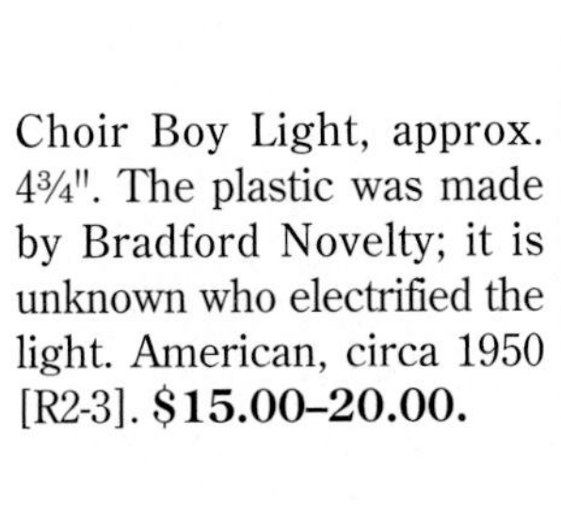

Choir Boy Light, approx. 4¾". The plastic was made by Bradford Novelty; it is unknown who electrified the light. American, circa 1950 [R2-3]. **$15.00–20.00.**

Illuminated Yule Birds Boxed Set, birds 3¾", box approx. 12½"L. The set contains 10 plastic birds of various colors, but no light cord. Made by Glolite, circa 1950. [American, R5 individual birds, R1-2 boxed set]. Birds, **$5.00–10.00** each. Boxed set, **$90.00–120.00.**

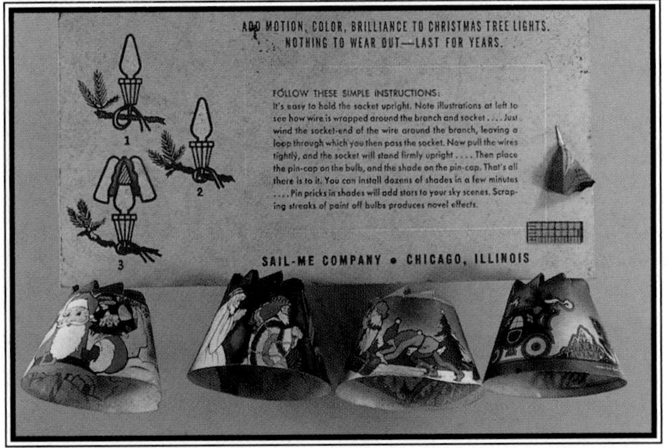

WhirlGlo Shades and Instruction Sheet, circa 1936 [R3-4]. Each shade, **$4.00–5.00.** Box of four, **$20.00–25.00.** Box of eight (must include spinner pins), **$40.00–50.00.**

Plastic Light Shades with Decals: A. Barney Google [R1]. **$6.00–8.00** each. B. Katzenjammer Kids [R1-2]. **$6.00–8.00** each. C. Scampy [R2]. **$10.00–12.00.** D & E. Flash Gordon [R1]. **$6.00–8.00.** F. Popeye [R1-2]. **$8.00–10.00.** These shades came in other colors besides blue.

Plastic Light Shades: A, B, D. Scampy Shades [R2]. **$10.00–12.00.** C & E. Plain Bell Shape Shade [R4]. **$1.00–2.00.**

Plastic Building Light Covers, American, circa 1950 [all R3-4]. A. Town Hall, 3⅛"L x 2⅞"H. **$5.00–10.00.** B. Theater, 2¼"L x 2"H. **$5.00–10.00.**

Plastic Building Light Covers: The buildings are open in the back and a metal insert holds the lights in place. American made, circa 1950, [all R3-4]. **$5.00–10.00** each: A. Cathedral with Double Spires, approx. 3"W x 3¼"H. B. "First National Bank," approx. 2½"W x 1¾"H. C. Victorian House, approx. 2½"W x 2¼"H.

Plastic Building Light Covers, American made, circa 1950 [all R3-4]. **$5.00–10.00** each: A. Single Spire Church, large, Approx. 3⅞"H x 2¾"W. B. Single Spire Church, small, approx. 3⅝"H x 2⅛"W. C. Colonial Town Hall, large, approx. 3¾"H x 2¾"W.

Reverse of Plastic Building Light Covers, showing metal light holders.

Plastic Building Light Covers, American made, circa 1950 [all R3-4]. **$5.00–10.00** each: A. Notre Dame Cathedral, approx. 4"H x 2½"W. B. Colonial Town Hall, small, approx. 2¾" x 2¾". C. Georgian House, approx. 2½"W x 2⅛"H.

Multilayer Foil Reflectors, all German, varying elaborateness, 3½" – 4¼" [OP, R4]. Simple forms, **$2.00–3.00.** Elaborate, **$4.00–5.00.**

A, D, E. Cardboard and Foil Reflectors, 3½" [OP, R3-4]. **$1.00–2.00** each. B. Cardboard and Foil Tree Top, 6¾" [OP, R2]. **$5.00–8.00.** C. Cardboard and Glitter, small, 3½" [OP, R2-3]. **$0.75–1.00.**

Plastic Building Light Covers, American made, circa 1950 [all R3-4]. **$5.00–10.00** each: A. US Post Office, large, approx. 3¾"W x 1⅞"H. B. "First National Bank," approx. 2½"W x 1¾"H. C. US Post Office, small, approx. 2⅞"W x 2"H.

A. Single Layer Foil Reflectors by National Tinsel Mfg. Co., 3" [OP-NP, R5]. **$0.10–0.25** each. Box of eight, **$2.00–3.00.** B. Multilayer by DoubleGlo [OP, R4]. **$1.00–1.50** each. Box of eight, **$15.00–20.00.**

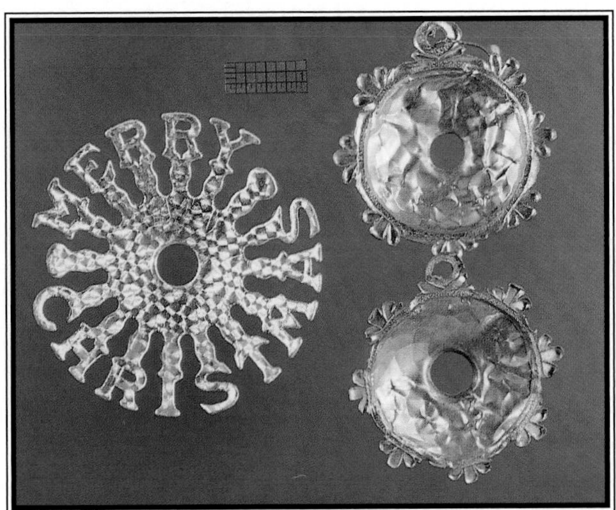

A. Cardboard and Foil Reflector, "Merry Christmas," 3½" [OP, R3]. **$4.00–6.00.** B & C. Tin-Lead Light Reflectors, 3", circa 1910 [R1-2]. **$25.00–35.00.**

Heavy Tin Reflectors, American made, 3". First four are Diamond Ray reflectors, circa 1927 [R4]. **$1.00–1.50.** Original boxed set, **$12.00–15.00.**

Kristolite Heavy Tin Reflectors by Noma, 3" [OP, R4]. **$1.00–1.50** each. Boxed set, **$12.00–15.00.**

A. Plastic and Glitter Reflector, 4" [R2]. **$1.00–1.50.** B. Plastic Jewel Reflector, 3", 1958 [R4]. **$0.75–1.00.** C & E. Noma Heavenly Star Reflectors, 3", 1958 [R4-5]. **$0.50–0.75.** D. Plastic Noma Light Star, 3" [OP, R4]. **$0.50–0.75.**

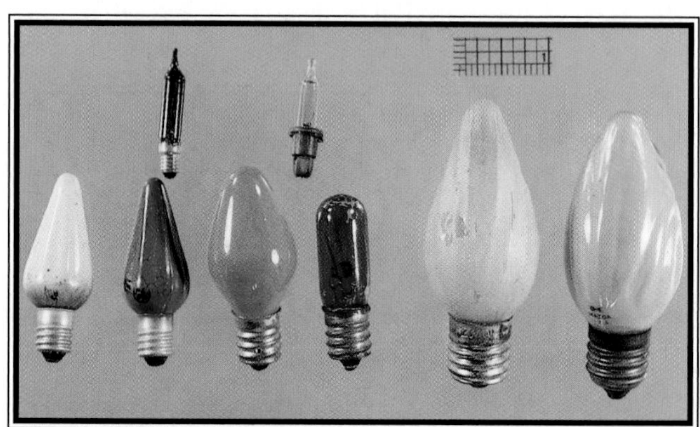

Various Sizes and Styles of the Common Cone-shaped Light; C6, C7, C9, and midget. C6, **$0.25–0.50.** C7, **$0.05–0.07.** C9, **$0.50–1.00.**

A. Edison–style Pear Shape, dated "Nov. 8. 1904" on base [OP, R2]. **$8.00–10.00.** B. Undated Edison–type Pear Shape [R2]. **$6.00–8.00.** C. Japanese Edison–type [R2]. **$6.00–8.00.** D. Globe Light, C7 [R2]. **$5.00–6.00.** E. Globe Light, probably GE, circa 1910 [R2]. **$4.00–5.00.**

A. Chinese Milk Glass Shape Candle [R1-2]. **$10.00–15.00.** B. Spiked Light (sometimes called Satellite or Sputnik Light) [R2]. **$2.00–3.00.** C. Egg with Embossed Stars Ornament Light, [OP, R3]. **$25.00–35.00.** D. Fluorescent Light [NP, R3]. All colors except blue, **$8.00–11.00.** Blue, **$25.00–35.00.**

Tree Tops and Tree Stands

Atop the Tree: Tree Tops

The crowning glory of the Christmas tree, whether it is full of antiques, crafts, memorabilia, or modern decorations, is the treetop, a special spot usually reserved for the most beautiful or significant of the family decorations. The earliest woodcuts and drawings of trees and tree tops show a single candle or nothing, but many items have been used as tree toppers down through the years. Paramount among them are stars and angels. The famous Nuremberg Angel may well be one of the earliest tree tops to be used year after year. We do know from period drawings that an angel in a wreath with outstretched arms, a high cap or crown, and a long stiff dress graced tree tops in the 1700s and early 1800s. Her outstretched hands held candles or a wreath.

In the early 1800s, such unusual tree tops as a golden apple, a springerle cookie horseman, or a rooster were reported in various regions of Germany. By the late 1800s, a wide variety of items were used as tops; flags, tinsel stars, cardboard stars, scrap angels, spun glass rosettes, wax angels, cotton batting dolls, and beaded crowns all found their way to the top of the tree.

Another popular style introduced at the end of the nineteenth century was the glass "point." Points were hand blown and had wide reinforced openings of thicker glass at the bottom end, which was placed over the top of the tree branch. The point almost always had a ball (more often than not, indented) under a long tapering point.

Tree tops, like the decorations clustered below them, were made of many different materials: glass, Dresden paper, cardboard, lithographed scraps, metal, tinsel, wax, plastic, cotton, porcelain, etc. Vintage photos of turn-of-the-century trees show that homemade cardboard stars covered with cotton were used as tree tops, as were scrap dolls with cotton clothes. Sometimes a papier-mâché Belsnickle was placed atop the tree. Other photos show wax angels or tinsel-embellished die cuts used as tree tops.

Candles around the tree's crown highlighted early tree tops. Some designs actually incorporated candles into the tree top itself. From about 1900 to about 1910, chimes with metal angels turned by the heat from candles were all the rage. These metal pieces were often beautifully lithographed. Later, as electricity came into private homes, so did electrified tree tops. Large tin-lead reflectors that once reflected candlelight were retrofit with an open ring in the center meant to hold a light bulb. Then, in the late 1940s through the 1960s, plastic tree tops became the rage. Various versions of hard plastic stars, angels, and Santas decorated the tree top. During the 1970s through the 1990s, tree tops incorporated many midget lights. Whatever the tree top, this piece is usually steeped in tradition and is often the most memorable of the family's Christmas tree decorations.

Under the Tree: Holders and Stands

Finding a way to hold cut trees upright and steady has been an annual problem for many centuries. One early solution, dating to the sixteenth century and continuing into the twentieth century, involved placing the trunk in a bucket and packing dirt and rocks or coal around it. Another early solution involved nailing the tree to a small stool, a wide board, or a cross-shaped stand. The tree could also be placed into a hole in a block of wood that was nailed to a Christmas garden — a larger, flat square of wood that often had a miniature fence around it encircling nativity scenes or miniature animals.

The first commercially made and patented tree stand was marketed in 1876, by Herman Albrecht and Abram Matt of Philadelphia. It resembled a flag stand with three legs. By 1880, an improved stand included a rotating ring that tightened internal cleats against the tree trunk. The following year, Johannes C. Eckardt of Germany invented and applied for an American patent for his revolving, musical tree stand. About the time of World War I, cups to hold water were added to tree stands. Electricity was also added to the tree stand and was used as early as 1900, but these stands were most prominent during the 1920s and 1930s. The lights that were added to the tree base supplemented the colors on the tree and lit up an otherwise dark area under it.

Cast iron tree stands, often elaborately embellished with Santas, angels, holly, and other holiday symbols, were popular from the late Victorian period through the 1930s. These were more popular in Europe than in the United States.

Although some early stands were made of wood, most have been made out of metal. Today, some are made of plastic. Whatever the material, keep in mind some simple precautions. Most antique stands were not designed to hold large live trees. They will, however, hold larger feather trees, because these are not as heavy and bulky. The width of the legs on the base is important, too. The wider the base, the sturdier the tree will stand, which is important when the tree is decorated with antique ornaments. If you are using a live tree, water it well; keeping it fresh is very important. If you are using an electrified tree holder, it is crucial that you remember that cracked insulation or bare wires, a metal tree stand, and liquid in the stand's water well make a dangerous combination. Whatever style you choose, the tree stand is the foundation of your tree's stability and safety.

Early Nuremberg Angel, approx. 11". Her head is made of plaster over composition, while the body is fabric filled with sawdust. The skirt is paper covered with brass foil, and the sunburst behind the upper torso is made of tinsel. Early engravings indicate that she may have once held an arch of pine or flowers in her outstretched hands. Early German engravings and woodcuts date this style of angel to the late 1700s to early 1800s [German, OP, R1+]. **$650.00–750.00.**

Nuremberg Angel, dressed in foil, circa 1870-1890. **$175.00–200.00.**

Noma Angel, non-electric, 8¼" x 11¼" [NP, R5]. **$10.00–15.00.** Original box, **$20.00–25.00.**

Composition Angel Tree Top, approx. 9". She has cardboard wings covered with foil. The torso, head, and arms are composition; the dress is fabric. A cardboard tube allows her to sit on the treetop. American made, circa 1930s – 1940s [R3]. **$15.00–25.00.**

Illuminated Halo Angel by Noma, 8¼" x 11¼" [NP (1940s – 1950s), R5]. **$20.00–25.00.** With original box, **$30.00–35.00.**

American Composition Angel, approx. 6". A large coiled spring in her back allows her to be attached to the treetop or suspended under a branch in the flying position. The arms are molded separately and are moveable. Copper foil covering the cardboard wings has oxidized to a green color. American made, circa 1925 [R1]. **$75.00–100.00.**

A. Composition & Plastic Standing Angel, 7½"H, 8" wing span [American, R2-3]. **$20.00–35.00.** B. Angel on a Ball or Globe, 6½" [American, R3-4]. **$20.00–35.00.**

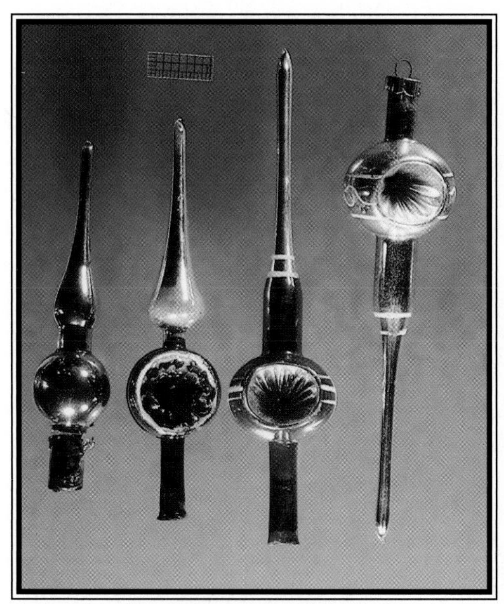

Glass Point Tree Tops: A. Single Ball [OP-NP, R4]. **$2.00–4.00.** B & C. Single with an Indent [OP-NP, R4]. Small/Medium, **$4.00–5.00.** D. Point Tree Top Used as a Hanging Ornament [OP-NP, R4]. **$4.00-5.00.**

Glass Point Tree Tops: A. Three-sided Indent with a Twisted Point, 11". **$12.00–18.00.** B. Three Balls with Tinsel Spray and Wire Wrap, 10"-12". **$30.00–40.00.** C. Point by Colby Glass, 11½". **$5.00–8.00.**

Indented Point Tree Tops: A. Single Ball with Triple Indent [OP, R4]. **$10.00–15.00.** B. Double Ball with Double Indent [OP-NP, R3]. **$18.00–25.00.** C. Triple Ball with Indent [OP-NP, R3]. **$25.00–35.00.**

Guardian Angel with Two Children, 6½" molded, 10¼" overall [OP, R1+]. **$800.00–1,000.00.**

Standing Angel Tree Top (Type II), 8½" [OP, R2]. **$250.00–300.00.**

Standing Angel Tree Top (Type II), 8½" [OP, R2]. **$250.00–300.00.**

A. Angel with a Flower, 10" [OP-NP, R1]. Old, **$250.00–275.00.** 1980s – 1990s, **$30.00–40.00.** B. Santa with a Standard Form Tree, 11" [OP-NP, R1]. Old, **$225.00–250.00.** 1980s – 1990s, **$30.00–40.00.**

Standard Form Owl Tree Top, 6½" [OP, R1]. **$175.00–200.00.**

Horned Owl Tree Top, 6½" [OP, R1]. **$175.00–200.00.**

Storks at a Fountain, 15¾" [OP, R1]. **$250.00–300.00.**

Santa with His Arms in His Sleeves Tree Top, 9" [OP, R1]. **$175.00–200.00.**

Spiked Star, free blown, 8" [OP, R2]. **$60.00–80.00.**

Sun Face Point, double sided, 7½" [OP, R1]. **$150.00–175.00.**

Czech Spike Tree Top, approx. 9". It is a blown glass spike that has been wrapped in glass beads and rods. Circa 1930s [R1]. **$40.00–60.00.**

Scrap/Lithograph Angel Tree Top, 14½" [OP-NP, R2-3]. Old, **$90.00–110.00.** New, **$8.00–10.00.**

Angel and Spun Glass Rosette Tree Top, 8" dia. [American, OP, R4-5]. Old, **$20.00–35.00.** 1970s – 1990s, **$5.00–10.00.**

Wax and Fabric Angel with Feather Wings, 10" [German, OP (circa 1930), R1]. **$175.00–200.00.**

Lithographed Metal Candle Chimes Tree Top, 13" [OP-R1]. **$150.00–175.00.**

Electric Metal Angel Chimes, 9", circa 1920 [R2]. **$60.00–75.00.** In original box, **$75.00–100.00.**

Foil Star, by National Tinsel, 6¼" star, 9" overall [NP, R3]. **$2.00–5.00.** With original box, **$6.00–8.00.**

Metal GloLite Illuminated Christmas Tree Star, 7½" [NP (1940s – 1950s)]. **$10.00–15.00.** With original box, **$15.00–20.00.**

Light-up Star of Bethlehem, 4¼" [OP, R4]. **$20.00–30.00.**

Noma Star, metal and plastic, 6¼" plastic star, 9½" overall, circa 1957 [R3]. **$18.00–20.00.**

Carrilon Spire Plastic Point Tree Top, 13½", circa 1960 by Bradford Plastics [R4-5]. **$4.00–8.00.** Electrified, **$6.00–10.00.**

Angel-Glo with a Magic Wand, 7", made by Noma, 1940s – 1950s [R4]. **$20.00–30.00.**

Angel-Glo with Sunburst, by Glolite, 9" [NP (1949), R3]. **$20.00–30.00.**

Paramount Illuminated Angel, 8¼" [NP (circa 1950s), R4-5]. Angel, **$15.00–25.00.** In original box, **$25.00–30.00.**

Royalite Illuminated Christmas Angel, 8½" [NP (1940s – 1950s), R3]. **$15.00–20.00.** Original box, **$20.00–25.00.**

A. Angel with Colored Wings, "Gem," 8" [NP, R3]. **$20.00–30.00.** B. Sterling Illuminated Angel, 8½" [NP (1940s – 1950s), R4]. **$20.00–25.00.**

"Heavenly Reflecting Light" Tree Top, approx. 10"H. A light behind the Angel reflects off of the faceted bowl. A plastic spinner (often missing) placed above the light causes motion to also be reflected in the bowl. Made by Bradford Novelty, circa 1955 – 1965 [R4]. **$20.00–25.00.**

A. "Brilliant Bethlehem Star" [NP (1958), R2]. **$12.00–16.00.** B. Star on a Disk, 8¾" [NP (1950s – 1960s), R2]. **$10.00–15.00.**

Color Point Star, by Noma, 9" [NP (1948 – 1950), R4]. **$12.00–18.00.** In original box, **$18.00–25.00.**

Cone-shaped Metal Tree Stand (Type I), by Noma, 13" [OP (circa 1928), R2]. **$150.00–175.00.**

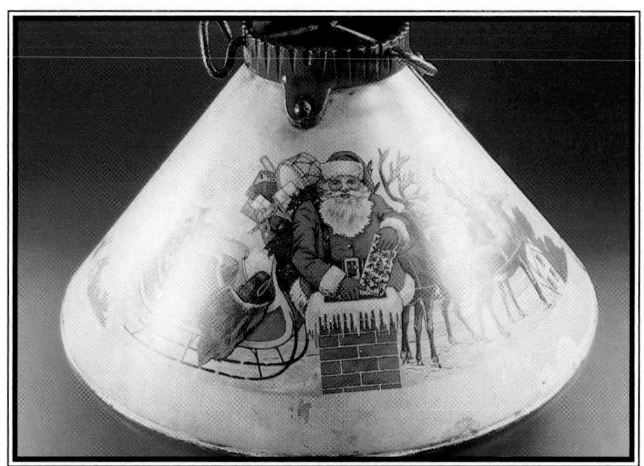

Cone-shaped Metal Tree Stand with Santa at Chimney (Type II), 13" [OP (1932), R2]. **$150.00–175.00.**

Metal Tree Stand with Lights and Four Legs, 14" [American, OP, R3]. **$60.00–75.00.** Note the Art Deco styling. Marked "North Bros. MFG. Co. Phila: PA. USA 'Yankee' No. 5A."

Electrified Metal Four-legged, 12", circa 1920s – 1930s [R2]. **$40.00–50.00.**

Metal Tree Stand with Four Legs, "Harras" embossed into one side, 11¾", marked "Germany" [OP, R1–2]. **$50.00–75.00.**

Albrecht Tree Stand, large, 10", made by North Bros. [OP (patented 1880), R1]. **$70.00–80.00.**

Albrecht Tree Stand, small, 7½", made by North Bros. [OP, R1]. **$45.00–55.00.**

Round Tree Stand with Christ Child, 10½" [OP, R1]. **$175.00–200.00.**

Square Tree Stand, "Frohliche Weihnachten," 9¾" [German, OP, R2]. **$175.00–200.00.**

Round Tree Stand, electric and musical, "Cameo," 13", circa 1960 [R3-4]. **$30.00–40.00.**

Round Tree Stand, musical, Eckardt, 14¼", plays two tunes [OP, R1]. **$550.00–700.00.**

Musical Tree Stand, 9"H, approx. 14" dia., marked "Ladoy Swiss," circa 1920 – 1930 [R2]. A hand crank winds the clockwork mechanism that turns the tree and plays chimes for the two songs. The wide collar under the cupped holder covers a brass electrical disk that rotates with the cup and allows a tree with electric lights to rotate without the cord wrapping around and entangling on the stand. **$550.00–700.00.**

Tree Stand, musical, rock-shaped, 12" dia. [OP, R1]. **$500.00–600.00.**

Miscellaneous Collectibles

Most of this book has dealt with those Christmas items that were designed to hang on the tree. However, many people who collect ornaments have also branched their interest out into Christmas decorations in general. This section is designed to cover some of those other collectibles of interest. Pieces in this area appeal not only to Christmas collectors, but to toy and doll collectors as well. This affects their prices accordingly.

German Belsnickle in Silver Mohair Coat Candy Container, 13½" [OP, R1]. **$2,300.00–3,000.00.**

Santa Doll Candy Container, has a basket with small doll inside, 11" [OP, R1]. **$1,300.00–1,500.00.**

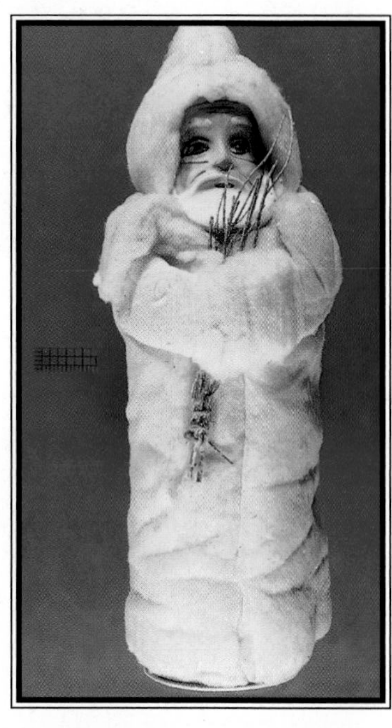

French Pere Noel Candy Container, 8" [OP, R1]. **$500.00–600.00.**

Clockwork Santa, approx. 24". A key-wound clockwork mechanism causes the head to move back and forth. Probably German, circa 1915 – 1930 [R1-2]. **$3,500.00–4,000.00.**

Santa Doll, approx. 10". Fabric arms and legs allow him to be posed. Probably German, circa 1920 – 1930s [R1]. **$650.00–750.00.**

Large Santa Candy Container, approx. 20". Candy container typically separates under the coat, at the waist. The size of this piece is unusual; most are smaller. Probably German, circa 1920 [R1]. **$3,000.00–3,500.00.**

Santa with a Pack Full of Toys Candy Container, approx. 12". The basket on his back is filled with period trinkets and miniatures representing toys [German, OP (circa 1920–1930), R1]. **$1,400.00–1,700.00.**

Post War Plaster Santa, 9¼", **$250.00–300.00.**

Large Straw-stuffed Santa Doll, 25½" [American, OP (circa 1920 – 1930s), R3]. **$200.00–275.00.**

West German Plaster Santa Doll. 9¼", **$250.00–275.00.**

German Santa Doll Candy Container, 12", pulls apart at waist [OP, R1-2]. **$900.00–1,100.00.**

Santa Candy Container with Composition Legs, approx. 5½". The torso is a cardboard tube that holds candy; the stomach and legs are composition painted blue [German, OP (circa 1930s), R2]. **$300.00–375.00.**

Santa Doll Candy Container, approx. 7". The body is a cardboard tube that slides out at the legs to hold candies or small presents. A paper stamp on the wooden base states, "Alexander Wiede Druck u. Papierhaus Chemnitz Theaterstr 5" [German, OP (circa 1920s - 1930s), R2-3]. **$450.00–550.00.**

Santa Doll Candy Containers, color variations, approx. 6½". The picture shows how candy containers of this type separate. Other color variations of this piece are mustard, white, and red. The bases are stamped "Germany" [OP (circa 1930), R2]. **$300.00–400.00.**

Santa Squeak Toy, 7½" [German, OP, R1]. **$400.00–500.00.**

Santa Candy Container with Heubach Head, 8". **$500.00–650.00.**

Santa Doll with Moveable Arms. He once held candy in his basket. Late 1930s or late 1940s [R2]. **$175.00–200.00.**

Christmas Gnome, approx. 8". Made of composition and cloth, he carries a basket for candy on his back. Marked "US Zone Germany" [NP (circa late 1940s – 1950s), R2-3]. **$150.00–175.00.**

Early Santa with Sleigh and Plaster Reindeer, 10" [OP, R1]. **$600.00–700.00.**

Santa on a Large Wooden Sleigh, 12". Sleigh used to contain candy [OP, R2-3]. **$700.00–800.00.**

Santa on a Bench, 3"H x 4"W, marked "Germany" on bottom [OP, R1]. **$200.00–250.00.**

Santa on a Sled, 3¼"H x 4½"W. The modern sled with candy shows how this Santa might have originally been marketed [OP, R2]. **$175.00–200.00.**

Santa in a Wooden Truck, 7"L x 3"W. The back of the truck once held candy. Marked "Germany" [OP, R1]. **$350.00–400.00.**

Santa with Sleigh and Reindeer, 11" x 6½", marked "Germany," circa 1930s. **$300.00–350.00.**

Santa Pulling a Sleigh, approx. 7"L. The sleigh originally held candy or small gifts [German, OP (circa 1920 – 1930), R2]. **$400.00–500.00.**

Santa on a Wooden Sled, approx. 6½"L x 5¼"H. The Santa is composition and cloth on a wire armature [German, OP, R2]. **$250.00–275.00.**

Rocking Santas, approx. 8½"L x 8"H. The wind-up, clockwork mechanism causes the two Santas to rock back and forth on the wooden base [German, OP (circa 1930), R1]. **$500.00–600.00.**

Santa on a Nodder Donkey, 8"H x 6½"L, [OP, R1]. **$1,200.00–1,500.00.**

Belsnickle with a High-collared Coat, 9¼" [OP, R1]. **$1,200.00–1,500.00.**

A. Belsnickle, 8½". **$800.00–950.00. B.** Belsnickle, 8" [probably German, OP (circa 1910 – 1920), R2]. **$700.00–800.00.**

Belsnickles, both 8½". White is a common color [OP, R3]: A. **$700.00–800.00.** B. **$800.00–950.00.**

A. Belsnickle, 7". **$300.00–400.00.** B. Candy Container, 6½". **$400.00–500.00.** C. Belsnickle, 7". **$500.00–650.00.**

Various Colors of Belsnickles; the purple, light blue, and dark blue are unusual: A. 6½". **$600.00–700.00.** B. 6½". **$700.00–800.00.** C. 6½". **$700.00–800.00.** D. 7½". **$1,000.00–1,200.00.**

A & C. Miniature Belsnickles for the Tree, 3", they once held small feather trees [OP, R1]. **$200.00–225.00.** B. Belsnickle Candy Container, 5". Note unusual left side placement of the tree [OP, R1]. **$400.00–500.00.**

Belsnickles by Nyla Murphy, circa 1987; pink, 10¼"; brown, 10". **$200.00–250.00.**

Belsnickle, pressed cardboard, 9" [German, OP, R2]. **$250.00–300.00.** Belsnickle, 7" [German, OP, R2]. **$450.00–550.00.**

Belsnickle, poorly detailed pressed cardboard, 8" [German, OP, R2-3]. **$175.00–200.00.**

Pressed Cardboard Santa Candy Container, approx. 8¾", circa 1930s – 1950s. Pieces such as this are made from two sheets of cardboard pressed by a mold and stapled at the seams. The candy container slides out of the feet [German, R1-2]. **$175.00–225.00.**

Pressed Cardboard Santa with a Flocked Coat, approx. 11". Santa's red suit is flocked and his fur trim is made from rough cotton. A pack shows on the back. Circa 1930s – 1950s [German, R1-2]. **$175.00–250.00.**

Pressed Cardboard Santa Candy Container, approx. 6½", circa 1930s – 1950s. The candy container slides out of the bottom. The "fur" trim is made of chenille [German, R1-2]. **$150.00–180.00.**

Krampus Doll, approx. 7½". This devilish figure accompanies St. Nicholas in Catholic Southern Germany and Austria, to punish bad children just as St. Nicholas rewards the good. A lever in his back makes his arms go up and down [German or Austrian, OP (circa 1920 – 1930), R1-2]. **$300.00–400.00.**

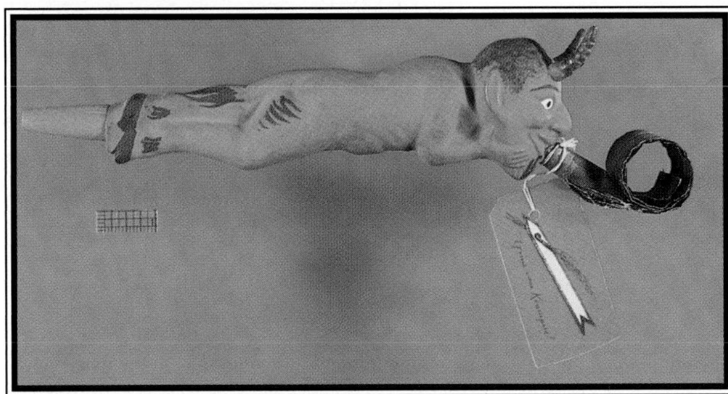

Krampus Noisemaker, approx. 11"L. This piece looks more like a Halloween noisemaker, but the attached tag proclaiming "Gruss von Krampus!" shows its Austrian or South German use as a Christmas toy [OP, R1-2]. **$325.00–400.00.**

Bisque Santa with a Tree and an Open Sack, 7½" [OP, R1]. **$600.00–700.00.**

Staffordshire China Santa, 6½", has spaces on the back to hold five small candles, circa 1870 [R1]. **$550.00–650.00.**

Santa Kerosene Lamp, 6" shade, 10"H overall [OP, R1]. The feet are the front of the lamp, and Santa's body, made of milk glass, is the shade. **$2,700.00–3,000.00.**

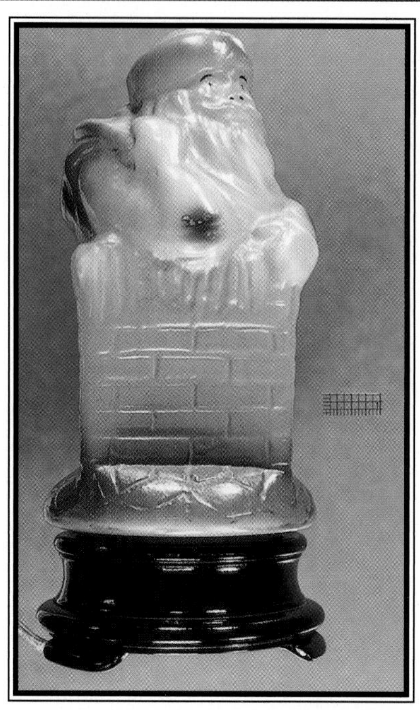

Santa in a Chimney Lamp, approx. 9¾". The black base holds a light bulb, and the molded glass Santa in the chimney is the shade. Made by U.S. Glass Co., circa 1920s – 1930s [R1]. **$1,200.00–1,500.00.**

Santa Lamp, approx. 8". The American-style Santa holding presents is the shade or cover for the light in the electrified base. The maker is unknown, but this is probably American [OP (circa 1930), R1]. **$300.00–400.00.**

A. Santa Lantern, 6½" [Japanese, NP (circa 1955)]. **$40.00–50.00.** B. Santa Head Lantern, 6", made by Amico. Santa is double faced [Japanese, NP (circa 1950), R3-4]. **$40.00–50.00.** C. Santa Light Lantern, 6½", made by Hilco in Hong Kong, circa 1960 [R3-4]. **$30.00–40.00.**

Santa Wind-up Drummer, celluloid face and hands, 10½" [Japanese, OP, R1]. **$310.00–350.00.**

Mechanical Santa, made in Japan, trademarked "Y," wind-up key is on the left side [NP, R2]. **$50.00–75.00.** In original box, **$90.00–125.00.**

Battery-operated Santa on a House, approx. 11"H. His eyes light up, he shakes his head, and both arms move up and down. Copyrighted 1960, by Noel Decorations, Inc. Made in Japan by HTC [R3]. **$60.00–80.00.**

Mechanical Santa, made by Chein. **$300.00–350.00.**

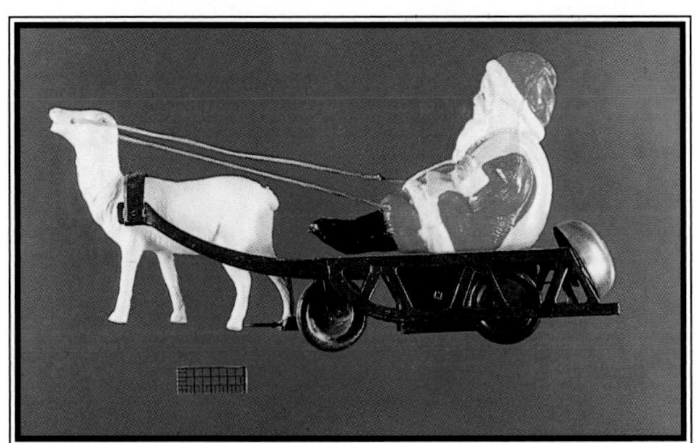

Windup Santa on a Sleigh, approx. 8", antlers are missing from reindeer [Japanese, OP, R3]. **$90.00–110.00.** Mint in box, **$175.00–225.00.**

Glass Santa Candy Containers, all have metal screw bases: A. Santa at the Chimney, 5", marked with a *V* over a *C* and "USA" [OP, R2]. **$150.00–180.00.** B. "Mean" Father Christmas, 5¼", circa 1910 [R1]. **$275.00–325.00.** C. Santa in Red, 4½", marked "AVOP LOS VC USA" [OP, R2]. **$135.00–150.00.**

Santa Glass Candy Container, 5½", metal lid screws onto bottom [OP, R1-2]. **$150.00–200.00.**

Glass Santa Candy Container, 7½". Santa's head is plastic [American, OP, R3]. **$50.00–75.00.**

Large Santa Head, 18", made of papier-mâché [American, NP (circa 1940s – 1950s), R4]. **$65.00–75.00.**

American Papier-mâché Waving Santa, 9", circa 1920 – 1930 [R3-4]. **$75.00–85.00.**

Papier-Mâché Santa with a Net Bag Candy Container, 9½". The net bag is what makes this piece unusual [American, OP (circa 1930) , R1-2]. **$100.00–125.00.**

Two American papier-mâché Santas: A. Santa with a Bag and at the Chimney, still has original cellophane covering, 9¾" [OP, R2-3]. **$90.00–110.00.** B. Santa with a Tilted Head, 9" [OP, R1]. **$170.00–190.00.**

German Roly-Poly Santa, 6" [OP, R1]. **$300.00–400.00.**

Bliss Wooden Sled with Lithographed Paper Over It, double sided, 12" [OP, R1]. **$1,750.00–2,300.00.**

Cast Iron Santa and Sleigh, 14½" [OP-NP, R1-2]. **$1,200.00–1,500.00.**

Santa Mechanical Bank, 7¾", 1884 [OP-NP, R1-2]. **$1,000.00–1,200.00.**

Two Santa Candy Containers: A. 9", Chenille strips form suit, crepe paper bag over shoulder is marked "Germany," circa 1935 [R3]. **$60.00–75.00.** B. Santa in a Night Cap, 7", marked "made in Western Germany," original box still marked "Germany, code #502," came in 7" and 10" [NP, R3]. **$45.00–55.00.**

Snowman Candy Container, 6", marked "Germany U.S. Zone," covered with Venetian dew [NP (late 1940s), R3]. **$50.00–75.00.**

Santa Plaque, approx. 10", made of stamped pulp cardboard [German, OP (circa 1930) R2-3]. **$100.00–125.00.**

Angel with Bell and Tree, 15", marked "Made in Germany" [OP, R1-2]. **$125.00–150.00.**

Angel with a Tree and Riding a Deer, 16", marked "Germany" [OP, R1-2]. **$125.00–150.00.**

Plaque of Santa at a Chimney, "A Merry Christmas," approx. 6¼"W x 9⅛"H. Marked "Made in Western Germany" [R2-3]. **$45.00–55.00.**

Plaque of Santa, Bag, and Gift, "A Merry Christmas," approx. 6"W x 9"H [West German, NP (circa 1955), R2-3]. **$50.00–65.00.**

Plaque of Santa with a Sleigh and Two Reindeer, "A Merry Christmas" Arch, approx. 12¾"W x 9¾"H [West German, (circa 1955) R2-3]. **$50.00–75.00.**

Plaque of Waving Santa with a Sleigh and Two Reindeer, "A Merry Christmas," approx. 9"W x 6"H. Marked "Made in Western Germany" [R2-3]. **$40.00–55.00.**

Plaque of Santa in a Sleigh (Type II), approx. 9". Made in Germany, circa 1930–1955 [R2-3]. **$75.00–100.00.**

Plaque of Snowman and Poodle, "A Merry Christmas," approx. 6"W x 9"H [West German, NP (circa 1955), R2-3]. **$30.00–45.00.**

Plaque of Two Candles with Holly, "A Merry Christmas," approx. 6"W x 9"H. Marked "Foreign" [West German, NP (circa 1955), R2-3]. **$25.00–35.00.**

Plaque of Candles and Bells, "A Merry Christmas," approx. 6"W x 9"H. Marked "Made in Western Germany" [R2-3]. **$25.00–35.00.**

Plaque of Three Candles with Halos, approx. 6½"W x 9"H. Made in Germany, circa 1930 – 1955 [R2-3]. **$25.00–35.00.**

Plaque of a Bird on a Lantern, "A Merry Christmas," approx. 6¼"W x 9"H. Marked "Foreign" [West German, NP (circa 1955), R2-3]. **$25.00–35.00.**

Plaque of a Cottage and Bells, "A Merry Christmas," approx. 6"W x 9"H. Marked "Foreign" [West German, NP (circa 1955), R2-3]. **$25.00–35.00.**

Plaque of House and People, "A Merry Christmas," approx. 12¾"W x 9¾"H. Marked "Foreign" [West German, NP (circa 1955), R2-3]. **$35.00–45.00.**

Plaque of Church, "Buone Feste," approx. 6¼"W x 9"H [West German, NP (circa 1955), R2-3]. **$25.00–35.00.**

Plaque of Steeple with Bells and Birds, "A Merry Christmas," approx. 6⅛" x 9"H [German, NP (circa 1955), R2-3]. **$25.00–35.00.**

Oval Plaque of Church, "A Merry Christmas," approx. 12½"H. Made in Germany, circa 1930–1955 [R2-3]. **$35.00–45.00.**

Heubach Candy Containers: A. Boy on a Snowball, 3" ball, 6½"H overall [OP, R1]. **$700.00–850.00.** B. Boy Pushing a Snowball, ball 3", 4½"H [OP, R1]. **$400.00–475.00.** C. Small Boy Pushing Cotton Snowball, ball 2¾", 3½" overall [OP, R1]. **$350.00–400.00.**

Heubach Boy Skier Candy Container, 9½" [OP, R1]. **$650.00–750.00.**

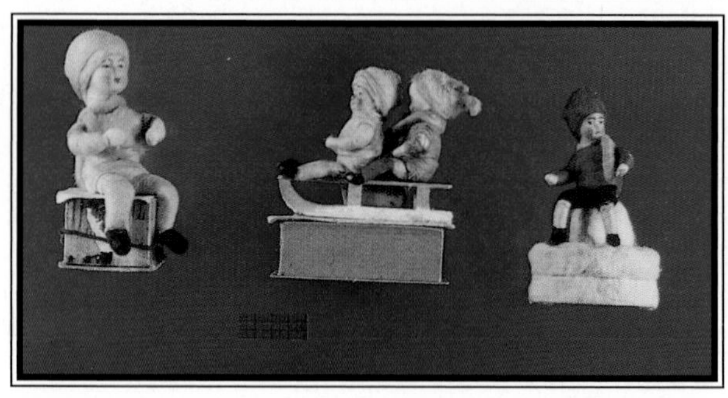

German Heubach Candy Containers: A. Boy on a Box, 3½" [German, OP, R2]. **$400.00–450.00.** B. Two Children on a Sled, 2¾"L [OP, R2]. **$425.00–500.00.** C. Boy on a Snowball, 3"H [OP, R2]. **$400.00–450.00.**

Two Heubach Children on a Sled, approx. 6½" [German, OP (circa 1930), R1]. The sled originally held candy or small gifts. **$650.00–800.00.**

Lithographed Tin Stable Candle Chimes, approx. 6"W x 12"H. Heat from candles held in the back of this piece turn the heat vane, causing the three Wisemen to move past the manger and the angels above to strike the chimes. The three-dimensional piece is composed of many small pieces that must be assembled [German, OP (circa 1900), R1+]. **$550.00–650.00.**

Chromolithograph Paper Nativity Scene, approx. 12"H x 11"W. This has five layers and is marked "Made in Germany" [OP (circa 1900), R2]. **$150.00–175.00.**

Nativity Figures, approx. sizes: Baby Jesus, 3¼"; Wisemen, 5½"; Camel, 6½". Made of composition and plaster, this 14-piece set was made in Germany, in the U.S. Zone [NP (circa late 1940s), R3-4]. Individual Pieces, **$8.00–12.00** each. Set in original box, **$150.00–175.00.**

Nativity Set of Wood and Wax, figures have wax heads [OP (circa 1820), R1]. **$275.00–325.00** per figure.

Close-up of Herald Angel from 1820 Nativity.

Various Composition Stags, all have cast lead antlers, most are stamped "Germany" in ink on stomachs [all OP, R3-4]: A. Approx. 3¼" H. **$25.00–35.00.** B. Approx. 2½" H. **$20.00–30.00.** C. Approx 4" H. **$40.00–50.00.** D. Approx. 3" H. **$25.00–35.00.** E. Approx. 2½" H. **$20.00–30.00.**

"King Santa" Plastic Light-up and Bank, 7", has a slot in the shoulder for coins or heat exhaust, marked "Harett-Gilmar, Inc NYC Pat Pend" [NP (circa 1955), R3]. **$30.00–40.00.**

Snowman "King Santa" Light-up, approx. 7", made of white plastic, adding a top hat and pipe turned this variation of King Santa into a Snowman. Made by Harett-Gilmar, circa 1955 [R3]. **$35.00–45.00.**

"King Santa" Behind a Fence Light-up, approx. 7" x 7". The front half of the Santa stands in the square plastic frame. This piece has a printed paper background. Made by Harett-Gilmar, circa 1955 [R2-3]. **$55.00–65.00.**

Royalite Santa with "Merry Christmas" Plaque Light-up, approx. 7½". This was one of several variations that kept this piece popular for many years [American, NP (circa 1955), R3-4]. **$35.00–50.00.**

Royalite Bubble Light Santa, approx. 7½". This was the most popular of the Royalite Jolly Character variations and remained popular for years. [American, NP (circa 1955), R3-4]. **$35.00–55.00.**

Royalite "Jolly Christmas Character" Santa with Bubble Light, 7½", hard plastic, circa 1955. **$35.00–55.00.** Original box, **$40.00–65.00.**

A. Santa with a Bag of Toys Light-up, 10", hard plastic [NP (1955), R2]. **$35.00–45.00.** B. Santa with Outstretched Arms Candy Container, 10½" [NP (1955), R3]. With original candy, **$40.00–50.00.**

Royalite Santa Light-ups, both 7½"; tree or wreath is often missing, which lowers the price; circa 1955 [R3-4]. **$30.00–40.00.**

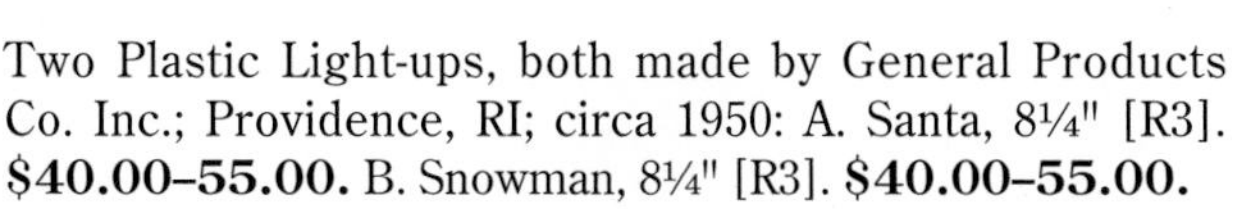

Two Plastic Light-ups, both made by General Products Co. Inc.; Providence, RI; circa 1950: A. Santa, 8¼" [R3]. **$40.00–55.00.** B. Snowman, 8¼" [R3]. **$40.00–55.00.**

Royalite Snowman with "Merry Christmas" Plaque Light-up, approx. 7½". The Snowman was made in the same variations as the Royalite Jolly Christmas Character Santas [American, NP (Circa 1955), R3-4]. **$35.00–50.00.**

Santas on Skis and Snowshoes, 4½"; light-up or candy container, it is the same Santa, made by Rosbro Plastics; Providence, RI; circa 1955 [R4]. **$14.00–18.00** each. **$20.00–30.00** as light up.

Santa on a Reindeer Light-up, 11"H, an open pack in the back holds a light or candy, no maker's mark, circa 1955 [R4]. **$25.00–35.00.**

A. Santa on a Reindeer, light-up or candy container, 9½", marked "Pat. No. 169,824," circa 1955 [R3-4]. **$25.00–30.00.** B. Santa on a Reindeer on Roof Top Light-up, hard plastic, circa 1955 [R2-3]. **$60.00–85.00.**

A. Snowman with a Lantern Light-up, hard plastic, 6½" [R3]. **$30.00–40.00.** B. West German Hard Plastic Santa, 10". **$20.00–25.00.** C. Santa on a Reindeer, small, non-lighting, 6¼"H. **$20.00–25.00.**

Hard Plastic Decorations: A. Santa Candy Container, 6"; made by Irwin, USA; circa 1950 [R2]. **$30.00–35.00.** B. Snowman Light-up; some were sold as candy containers, some as light-ups — the fiber board light holder shows its use, 1955 [R5]. **$20.00–25.00.**

"Illuminated Santa Face Plaque," by Noma, sold circa 1949, 15½", hard plastic and metal back [R2]. **$20.00–30.00.**

Angel, "Winter Scene," approx. 5¼". Made by Bradford Plastics, circa 1955 [R2-3]. **$20.00–25.00.**

A & B. "Winter Scenes," by Bradford Plastics, circa 1955 [R3]. **$25.00–30.00** each: A. Choir Boys, B. Snowman.

Snowman Wall Plaque Light-up, metal back, 9½", 1955 [R2]. **$35.00–50.00.** B. Royalite Snowman, 7½", hard plastic light, circa 1955 [R3-4]. **$30.00–40.00.**

Three Plastic Candy Containers, all made from the same snowman mold, by Rosbro Plastics; Providence, RI; all circa 1955, could also become light-ups: A. Standard Snowman, 5" [R4]. **$12.00–15.00.** B. Business Snowman [R1]. **$30.00–35.00.** C. Boy Skater [R3]. **$15.00–20.00.**

Two Hard Plastic Light-ups, circa 1955: A. Santa, 6¼", sits on a chimney, sold by Paramount [R2]. **$30.00–40.00.** Walking Snowman, 5", has a light in his open pack, also sold without a light as a candy container [R2]. **$15.00–20.00.** Without light, **$10.00–15.00.**

Santa Light-up, hard plastic, 1955 – 1960 [R4]. **$15.00–20.00.**

Jaunty Santa Music Box Light-up, approx. 6½". The snowball lights up, and twisting the Santa to the left winds the music box, which plays "I'm Dreaming of a White Christmas." Made by Rosbro Plastics, circa 1955 [R2]. **$125.00–150.00.**

"Santa's Candy Workshop" Original Boxed Set, approx. 15"L [NP (circa 1955), R1]. The box is constructed to look like a workshop, and Santa and his five helpers can be seen through "windows" in the box. Santa wears snowshoes; his jaunty helpers come in red, blue, lavender, yellow, and green. Each came with a candy sucker attached. Although not given credit on the box, Rosbro Plastics made the pieces. The box states, "Distributed by Sears, Roebuck and Company." Although individual pieces are fairly common, the boxed set is rare. Front and back views are shown. **$500.00–600.00.**

Figures from "Santa's Candy Workshop," Santa approx. 4¼", helpers approx. 3¾". Santa has an open backpack to hold candy. Each helper holds a plastic tool. Rosbro Plastic, circa 1955 [R3-4]. Red helper, **$8.00–10.00.** Santa and other colors, **$14.00–18.00** each.

Wheeled Candy Containers: A. Jaunty Santa on Wheels, approx. 4½" [R3]. **$30.00–35.00.** B. Waving Santa on Wheels, approx. 4¾" [R2]. **$30.00–40.00.** C. Boot on Wheels, approx. 4" [R3]. **$25.00–30.00.** All three were sold with candy attached and used as pull toys. All are American made by Rosbro Plastics, circa 1955.

Santas on a Toboggan, approx. 16"L, tallest Santa is 6¼". The sled contains three different Santas, all of which held candy suckers. Probably made by Rosbro Plastics, circa 1955 [R1-2]. **$100.00–135.00.**

Two Christmas Whirligigs made of celluloid, both are Japanese: A. Santa Pushing a Baby Buggy. **$250.00–275.00.** B. Santa on a Sled. **$250.00–275.00.**

Santa on a Motorcycle, approx. 3¾"L x 3½"H, possibly made by Rosbro, candy suckers were held in an opening between his arms [American, NP (circa 1955), R2]. **$35.00–50.00.**

Celluloid Santa Candy Container and Pull Toy, approx. 4½"L and 4½"H. The open basket at the front held candy. American made by Irwin, circa 1930 [R2]. **$45.00–60.00.**

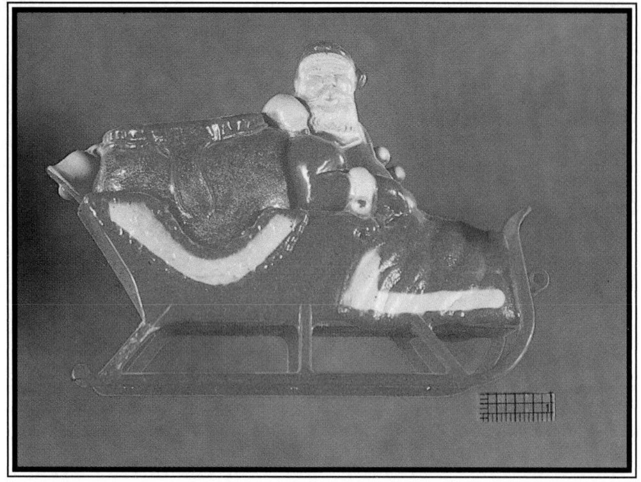

Santa in a Sleigh Candy Container, approx. 6"L. The pack in the back of the sleigh is hollow, in order to hold candy. Made in Canada by Cheerio, circa 1950 [R1]. **$50.00–75.00.**

Large Celluloid Santa and Sleigh, 13½" [Japanese, OP, R2-3]. **$75.00–90.00.**

Celluloid Santa and Reindeer with a Cardboard Sleigh, 12". **$65.00–75.00.**

"Rudolph Sled Set," by Bradford, 15", 1950s [R3]. **$25.00–30.00.** In original box, **$30.00–40.00.**

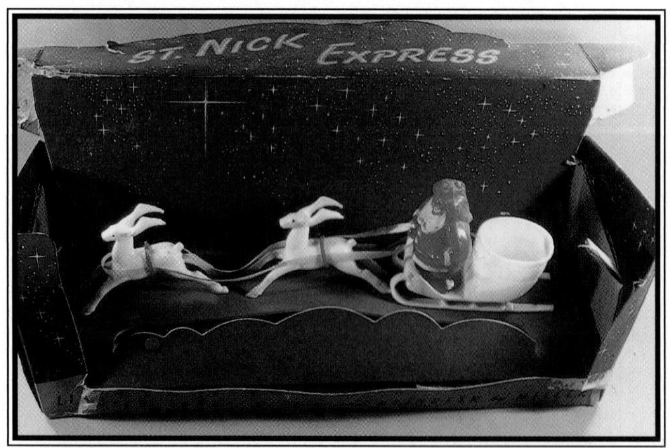

"St. Nick Express," by Miller Electric Co., bulb lights box up as a display piece, catalog #830, plastic by Rosbro Plastics; Providence, RI; circa 1955 [R2]. **$70.00–80.00.**

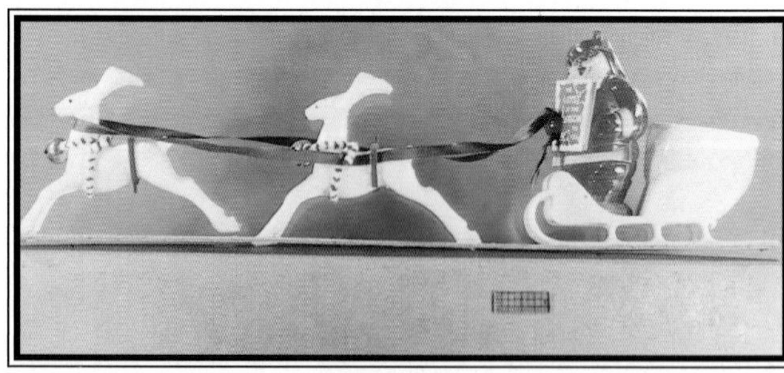

Santa and Reindeer with Sleigh, 15½", original box, both unmarked but probably Rosbro Plastics, circa 1955. **$20.00–25.00.**

"Santa's Candy Wagon," 8½"H x 9½"L, circa 1950 [R1]. **$125.00–150.00.**

Santa Claus Jack-in-the-Box, approx. 3¾"H. Made by Bradford Novelty, circa 1950. The original box indicates that a snowman, duck, and clown were also made [R1-2]. **$40.00–50.00.**

Santa in a Boot Jack-in-the-Box, approx. 7". Lifting the lid of the box allows the Santa, mounted on a spring, to leap up [American, NP (circa 1955), R2-3]. **$40.00–50.00.**

Snowman Jack-in-the-Box, approx. 3¾"H. Pushing the white button at the top releases the lid, and the figure pops up. Made by Bradford Novelty, circa 1950 [R1-2]. **$40.00–50.00.**

Three Fall-apart Santas: A. Santa in a Chimney, approx. 5". Made in Hong Kong, with a maker's mark of a *T* over an *M* inside a circle [R3-4]. **$15.00–20.00.** B. Santa with a Bell in a Chimney, approx. 5", "Fun World Inc. NY, NY #7015 Made in Hong Kong" [R3-4]. **$15.00–20.00.** C. Santa on a Green Base, approx. 3¾", "Made in Taiwan #3992 Kohner Bros. Inc. E. Paterson N.J." [R3-4]. **$15.00–20.00.**

Paramount Musical Angel, approx. 14½"H with an 18" wingspan. A light on the inside shines through the angel's bust and clear plastic wings. A windup music box in the back plays *Hark the Herald Angels Sing.* Marked "Manufactured by Raylite Electric Corp. New York, NY" [NP (circa 1950), R1]. **$450.00–550.00.**

Crysta-Lite Christmas Tree and Original Box, tree approx. 10". The plastic tree lights from the inside and light shines through the clear plastic edges. Made by Royal Electric, circa 1955. Colors other than green can be found [R2-3]. **$35.00–45.00.**

Two Plastic Pine Trees, approx. 6" & 4¾", marked "Rosbro Plastics Prov., R.I." [NP (Circa 1950), R2-3]. Tree, **$12.00–15.00.** Tree with pot, **$18.00–22.00.**

"Flat Back" Tree, approx. 14½". This light-up made of visca, shredded rayon, is flat on the back so that it can be placed on a wall. Seven light sockets are on the tree; an eighth is behind the plastic base. The tree is often used for bubble lights. American made, circa 1950 [R2]. **$135.00–165.00.**

Cast Tin Figures of an Ice Skating Scene, picture I, circa 1900. Small figures, **$9.00–12.00.** Large figures, **$15.00–22.00.**

Cast Tin Figures of an Ice Skating Scene, picture II. Old stock of these 1900 figures was sold by D. Blumchen & Co. in 1992. Complete set of pictures I and II, **$250.00–300.00.**

Composition and Plaster Table Decorations, all German, circa 1930 – 1950 [R2]: A. Santa in Front of a Fence, approx. 3". **$100.00–150.00.** B. Street Lamps, approx. 2¼". **$25.00–30.00.** C. Snowman, approx. 1½". **$50.00–75.00.** Tree with Birds, approx. 3½". **$45.00–55.00.**

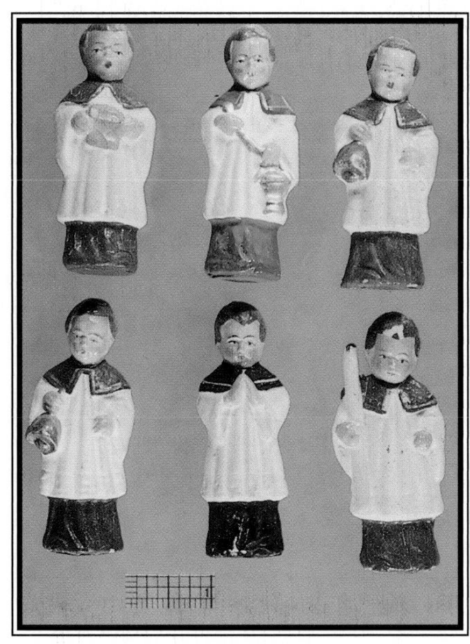

Set of Composition Choir Boys, approx. 3½" each, some are marked "Germany," some are marked "U.S. Zone," circa 1930 – 1940s [R2-3]. **$12.00–18.00** each. Boxed set of six, **$80.00–110.00.**

Box for Rudolph Game.

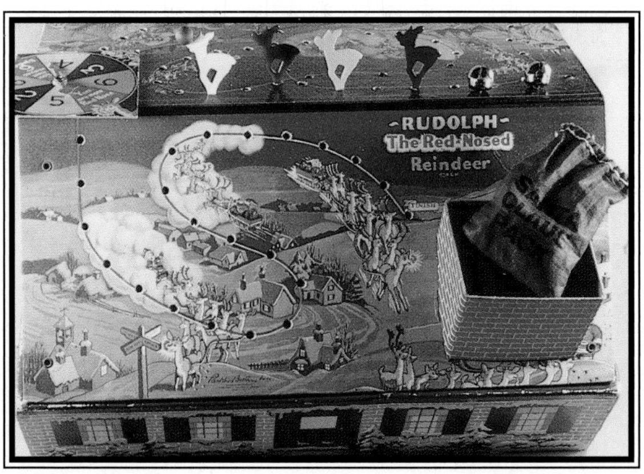

"Rudolph the Red-Nosed Reindeer" Game, made by Parker Brothers, copyright 1948 [R2]. **$75.00–90.00.**

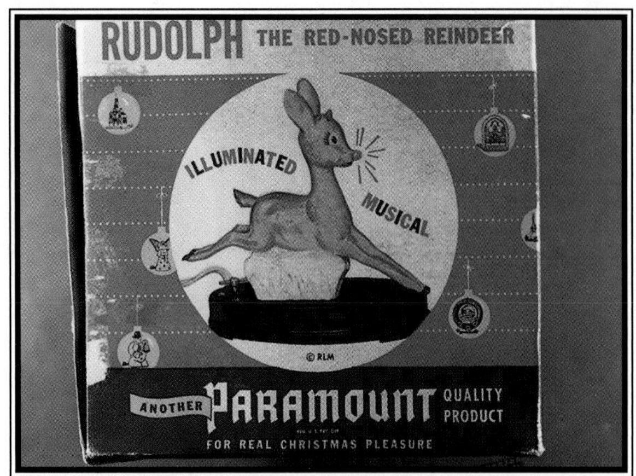

Paramount Illuminated Musical Rudolph, approx. 7¾" x 7¾". Rudolph's nose lights up and he plays *Rudolph the Red-Nosed Reindeer.* The base is marked "Raylite Electric Corp., New York," [NP (Circa 1950), R2]. **$100.00–125.00.** In original box, **$150.00–175.00.**

Rudolph Record and Record Topper. The golden record (33 ⅓ rpm) has a copyright of 1951. The plastic Rudolph, by Bradford Novelty, stands on a cardboard disc with a hole for mounting it on the spindle of the record player; it turns with the record. Record [R3], **$6.00–12.00.** Rudolph Topper [R2], **$20.00–25.00.**

Frosty the Snowman Record and Topper. The Peter Pan record (78 rpm) has a copyright of 1952. The plastic Frosty, by Bradford Novelty, stands on a cardboard disc that has a hole for mounting it on the spindle of the record player; it turns with the record. Record [R3], **$6.00–12.00.** Frosty Topper [R2], **$20.00–25.00.** Frosty sheet music, **$5.00–8.00.**

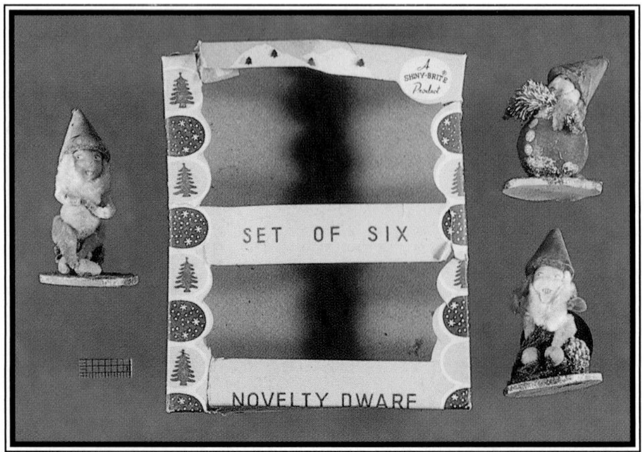

Pine Cone Dwarfs in Original Box, approx. 3" figures & 6½" box. Made in Japan by Shiny-Brite, circa 1950 [R4]. Dwarfs, **$10.00–15.00** each. Boxed set of six, **$50.00–75.00.**

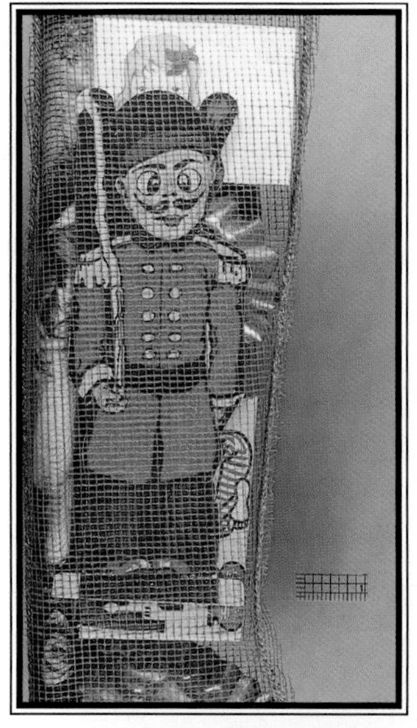

Net Stocking with Original Toys, 11', circa 1939. **$35.00–50.00.**

Feather Fence, approx. 12" per section. These came in sets or were purchased separately to create the desired size of fence around the tree [OP-NP, R2]. Gate section, **$75.00–100.00** each. Regular fence section, **$65.00–85.00** each.

Early Christmas Accessories in Original Packaging. These items are collected for their graphics and not the items inside. The earlier the packaging, the harder they are to find. All of these items are American and made circa 1915–1920 [R1]: A. Christmas Candles Box. **$25.00–35.00.** B. Santa Claus Snow. **$25.00–35.00. C.** Package of Tinsel Garland. **$25.00–35.00.** D. Artificial Snow Box. **$25.00–30.00.**

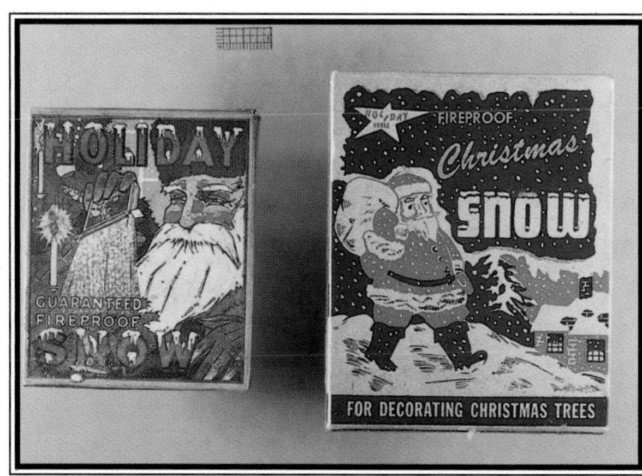

Two boxes of Christmas Snow. Boxes that are collected for their graphics should be clean, unopened, and in good condition to bring top dollar. These are American and made before WWII [R2]: A. Holiday Snow. **$30.00–40.00.** B. Christmas Snow, **$15.00–20.00.**

Three Boxes of Christmas Snow. These are bought by collectors for their graphics. Therefore, boxes should be clean, unopened, and in good condition. All are American and made before WWII [R2]: A. Christmas Snow. **$10.00–15.00.** B. Glo-Snow. **$20.00–30.00.** C. Christmas Mica Snow. **$10.00–15.00.**

Calendar Plate, 1901, shows Santa in a dirigible, 9½" dia., made by American China Co. of Toronto, Ohio; given away by Ware Robbins Co. [R1-2]. **$125.00–150.00.**

Schroeder's
ANTIQUES
Price Guide
OUR #1 BEST-SELLER!
FULL COLOR!
#1 BESTSELLING
ANTIQUES PRICE GUIDE
≈ More than 50,000 listings in over 500 categories
≈ Histories and background information
≈ Both common and rare antiques featured
Schroeder's ANTIQUES Price Guide
Twenty-sixth Edition
Identification & Values of Over 50,000 Antiques & Collectibl
only
$17.95
608 pages
COLLECTOR BOOKS
P.O. BOX 3009, Paducah KY, 42002-3009
1.800.626.5420
www.collectorbooks.com